D0331296

DISCARD

A History of Managing for Quality

A History of Managing for Quality

The Evolution, Trends, and Future Directions
of Managing for Quality

J. M. Juran, editor-in-chief

A research project sponsored by Juran Foundation, Inc.

ASQC Quality Press
Milwaukee, Wisconsin

A History of Managing for Quality: The Evolution, Trends, and Future Directions of Managing for Quality
J. M. Juran, editor-in-chief

Library of Congress Cataloging-in-Publication Data
A history of managing for quality: the evolution, trends, and future
   directions of managing for quality / J. M. Juran, editor-in-chief.
       p.   cm.
    Includes bibliographical references and index.
    ISBN 0-87389-341-7
    1. Total quality management—History. 2. Quality control—
History.   I. Juran, J. M. (Joseph M.), 1904–   .
HD62.15.H57   1995
658.5'62—dc20   95-17315
                                                                         CIP

© 1995 by Juran Foundation, Inc.

10 9 8 7 6 5 4 3 2 1

ISBN 0-87389-341-7

Acquisitions Editor: Susan Westergard
Project Editor: Jeanne W. Bohn

Printed in the United States of America

∞ Printed on acid-free paper

ASQC
Quality Press
611 East Wisconsin Avenue
Milwaukee, Wisconsin 53202

Contents

Chapter 11

Dr. Ludmila A. Konareva, Senior Researcher
Institute of the USA and Canada, Russian Academy of Sciences
Moscow, Russia

Chapter 12

Mr. Michel Deleforge, Naval Officer and Engineer (retired)
Member, French Movement for Quality
Saint Cloud, France

Chapter 13

Mr. Michel Dunaud, Ancien Chargé de Mission Qualité
Délégation Générale pour l'Armement Ministère de la
Défense France
Paris, France

Chapter 14

Mr. David Hutchins, Chairman
David Hutchins International Ltd.
Ascot, Berkshire, England

Chapter 15

Dr. Ludmila Cuřínová, Head of Sanitary Museum, Prague
Prague, Czech Republic

Dr. Frantisek Dudek, Private Scientist and Entrepreneur
Prague, Czech Republic

Chapter 16

Prof. Izumi Nonaka, Associate Professor, Faculty of Economics
Josai University
Tokorozawa, Saitama-pref., Japan

Preface

Study of history serves us in many ways. History enables us to retrace the past, to understand the significant events and the convergence of forces that stimulated those events. Study of history helps us to discover the trends and directions of past events and thereby to judge what may lie ahead. And, of course, well-written history makes fascinating reading.

Much of history deals with recurring cycles of events. A new force comes over the horizon—a military invasion, a flood, a birth or death in the family. The new force then generates streams of events that converge to respond to that new force. Those responses in turn contribute to creation of additional forces, which generate additional responses. So there emerges a continuing series of cycles of "challenge and response" as so eloquently described by Arnold J. Toynbee in his monumental *A Study of History* (Oxford University Press).

Why a History of Managing for Quality?

A history of managing for quality is timely because in recent decades the subject of managing for quality has moved to center stage. Achievement of quality has always been one of the goals of human effort, but seldom did it occupy the attention of the leadership. The events of the last few decades have changed all that. In addition, quality of product has become the focus of intense international competition. The emergence of Japan as an economic superpower is largely the result of its quality revolution. In addition, quality of product has emerged as the principal shield against damage to human safety and health, and to the environment.

A History of Managing for Quality is to my knowledge the first book devoted to the history of managing for quality. There is no lack of books dealing with the history of segments of the subject—metrology, statistical process control, and so on. Such books can and do contribute usefully to our subject. They can also be misleading if the authors assume that the entire history of managing for quality took place within their century or their specialty.

A widespread example of such misleading assumptions is the claim that certain twentieth-century individuals—Shewhart, Deming, Juran, Ishikawa, or others—"invented quality." Such simplistic hero worship has no basis in fact. Our archaeological sites, ancient cities, and modern museums provide convincing evidence that "invention" of managing for quality has been a continuing process over the millennia.

- The ancient Chinese, Greeks, Romans, and others built roads, bridges, temples, ships, and other masterpieces of design and construction, some of which endure to this day.

- For many centuries, trained craftsmen provided the skills needed to feed, clothe, and shelter growing populations, including equipping their armed forces.

- The Industrial Revolution opened the floodgates from which there poured out mechanical power, production machinery and processes, railroads, steamships, electrical power, automobiles, air travel, household appliances, and other marvels without end. Every one of these developments has demanded quality in the design and construction.

The history of managing for quality does include inventions. Today we take for granted such concepts as inspection or measurement, but somewhere in the dim past those concepts had to be invented. So it was with quality warranties, standardization, interchangeability, laws for consumer protection, and so on. We know that these inventions were of ancient origin, but we do not know with certainty who were the inventors. As to some twentieth-century inventions, we do know who were the inventors: the control chart (Shewhart), the Pareto principle (Juran), the cause-and-effect "fish bone" diagram (Ishikawa). What we tend to overlook are the contributions of the operating managers who successfully applied the inventions of the past and present.

The Origin of This Book

The July 1990 and August 1990 issues of *Quality Progress* included a serialized prepublication of the first chapter of *A History of Managing for Quality*. In the preface to that prepublication I wrote,

> *The history of managing for quality has long been a book waiting for an author. I have for years wanted to write that*

book, but other projects always managed to take precedence. During those same years it gradually became clear that the core content of such a book should consist of a series of chapters each of which would deal with how quality was managed in some specific civilization or country.

The first definitive step toward writing this book took place in 1982 during my visit to the People's Republic of China. I asked my Chinese hosts if they would be willing to prepare a chapter dealing with the history of managing for quality as it evolved in China. They agreed to do so, and I agreed to fund the project. They set up a team of experts for the purpose, and delivered the finished manuscript in 1989.

Meanwhile I created and funded Juran Foundation, Inc. The trustees have approved going ahead with completion of the book. Activity is under way to get chapters written about the history of managing for quality in certain other, selected civilizations. Once those chapters become available I will prepare a summary to generalize how managing for quality has evolved throughout the history of civilizations.

The concept of a series of stand-alone chapters, each focused on how quality was managed in earlier historical settings, appealed to the authors. They produced focused histories that enable us to clasp hands with our creative forebears, across the millennia and continents. Those same histories provide us with new perspectives of how managing for quality has evolved.

The book contains seventeen such chapters. They describe how quality was managed under widely different circumstances:

- Time spans—ancient, medieval, modern
- Geographical areas—Asia, the Middle East, Europe, and the United States
- Products—construction projects, capital equipment, consumer goods
- Political systems—monarchy, confederation, democracy

This wide assortment of situations provides a broad database from which to draw conclusions, identify trends, and suggest what lies ahead. That is what I have tried to do in the final summary chapter.

It is clear that during its long history, managing for quality has consisted of long periods of relative stability punctuated by short periods of turbulent change. One such period of turbulent change is of recent origin—it began with the Japanese quality revolution of the last several decades. This change has demanded that organizations undertake revolutionary rates of quality improvement in order to remain competitive. To date this response has become effective only in a relatively small proportion of the world's institutions.

There is an interesting parallel here. About a century ago there emerged the massive movement that came to be known as Scientific Management. Its major focus was on improving productivity, and its influence was felt throughout the twentieth century. We are similarly in the early stages of a massive movement, this time in managing for quality. It began in recent decades, but still has far to go before becoming widely effective among world economies. The likelihood is that it will require the entire twenty-first century to digest this change. As a result, the twenty-first century may well become known to historians as the Century of Quality.

About Juran Foundation, Inc.

Juran Foundation, Inc. was incorporated in 1986 as a nonprofit organization. Its mission includes support of research and learning in managing for quality.

A History of Managing for Quality is the first major research project undertaken by the foundation, which provided all the funding. J. M. Juran served as project director as well as editor-in-chief.

The board of trustees of the foundation consists of

J. M. Juran, chairman. Dr. Juran is chairman emeritus of Juran Institute, Inc.

J. Stuart Hunter, professor emeritus, Princeton University.

William W. Eggleston, retired corporate vice president, quality, IBM Corporation.

Acknowledgments

A History of Managing for Quality is the result of contributions from many sources.

The core contributions came from the authors. They are busy people, yet they took the time to contribute to a common cause which should benefit all who are active in the field of managing for quality.

While all authors were knowledgeable in the subject matter they chose for their themes, they nevertheless supplemented their knowledge by research in the literature and by enlisting the aid of specialists in universities, libraries, museums, archaeological sites, and so on. It was gratifying to discover that those specialists relished the opportunity to contribute to a scholarly book that could make use of their expertise.

Some authors faced the added complication of having their texts translated into English. In addition they were drawn into the process of supplying illustrations, and especially the associated complications of securing permissions from publishers whose interests ranged across the entire spectrum, from *pro bono publico* to the borders of greed.

A final chore for authors was to respond to the queries and suggestions offered by the editors. Here the spirit of collaboration prevailed, and problems were resolved amiably.

The authors are listed in the table of contents, along with their principal affiliations.

The second major contribution came from the editors. For this book the responsibilities of editors went beyond emending the authors' texts. Some editors became the means of recruiting the best qualified authors and helping them to select the themes for their chapters. Of course, the best qualified people are also the busiest, so the editors faced the problem of gently stimulating the authors to meet the schedules. The editors also shared the burden of finding translators, choosing illustrations, and securing permissions from publishers.

In two cases the untimely passing of editors broke the chains of communication with authors, and required the appointment of replacements. Dr. Valère Cantarelli had been the editor for the French chapters when he passed away. We were fortunate to secure the services of Mr. Bertrand Jouslin de Noray to complete Dr. Cantarelli's work. Similarly, Dr. F. H. Žalud had been the editor for the chapters prepared by authors from the Czech Republic. In this case Dr. A. H. Žaludová, who had been coeditor with her husband, capably assumed the entire burden.

The board of editors consists of the following:

Dr. Valère Cantarelli (deceased)
Former Quality Manager
Regie Nationale des Usines Renault
Paris, France

Dr. Ing. Tito Conti
Total Quality Management
Ing. Tito Conti & C., S.A.S.
Director Corporate Quality (retired)
Ing. C. Olivetti & C., S.p.A.
Ivrea, Italy

J. M. Juran, Editor-in-Chief
Chairman Emeritus
Juran Institute, Inc.
Wilton, CT, USA

Mr. Suresh Lulla
Managing Director
Qimpro Consultants Pvt., Ltd.
Bombay, India

Mr. Bertrand Jouslin de Noray
Technical Director
French Quality Movement
Nanterre Cedex, France

Prof. James F. Stoner
Professor of Management Systems
Fordham University Graduate School of Business Administration
New York, USA

Ir. Henk van der Weiden
Quality Manager, Philips (retired)
Eindhoven, The Netherlands

Dr. Ing. F. H. Žalud
Late Head of Engine and Reliability Research
Automobile Research Institute
Prague, Czech Republic

Dr. A. H. Žaludová
Honorary President
Czech Society for Quality
Prague, Czech Republic

I am grateful also to the supporting casts of the authors and editors—their assistants, secretaries, staff members (as well as family members)—whose dedication met the exacting task of preparing a scholarly manuscript. Another debt is owed to the translators who faced an equally exacting task of translating the manuscripts into the English language. Additional translation assistance was received from Mrs. Birgitta Hamann, as well as from Jacqueline Boissiere, Brian T. Eck, and Gabriel A. Pall of Juran Institute, Inc.

I owe special thanks to my assistant, Laura A. Sutherland, who has served this project in many ways. She presided over the schedule, formatted the manuscripts to be ready for production, provided the liaison with Quality Press, and in still other ways eased the burden of the editor-in-chief.

A note relative to gender-neutral language: Every effort has been made to use gender-neutral language in this book. However, we have retained terms such as *workmanship* and *craftsmanship* for which no generally agreed-upon gender-neutral equivalents exist; likewise in historical discussions we have not changed terms such as *master* and *journeyman* which had technical meanings within the guild systems of the medieval era; and we have not altered terminology used in direct quotations from other sources. In all those instances, the words should be taken in a purely generic sense, intended to apply to women as well as to men.

J. M. Juran

CHAPTER 1

Ancient China's History of Managing for Quality

Jin Qiupeng, Chen Meidong, and Lin Wenzhao

An Ancient Civilization

China is one of the earliest countries to have developed a civilization. A Chinese state had already been set up by the twenty-first century B.C. Despite the incessant changes of dynasties in China's history, its civilization has been developing without interruption. This continuing development has, in turn, determined the shape of China's civilization system.

Starting from the first dynasty—the Xia Dynasty, which was established in the twenty-first century B.C.—up to the destruction of the Qing Dynasty in 1911, a political system to rule the country by the imperial family was, basically, maintained in China. Under the domination of such an autocratic form of government, all spheres and departments of the state were strictly controlled by a bureaucracy. This was true not only in the political, military, and cultural spheres, but also in the economic sphere. The direct control over the economic sphere by the bureaucracy had influenced China's ancient productive activities and quality control.

Translated by Hu Longchang and others; and proofread by Yu Melfeng, Guo Gangwan, and Xiong Wei. The chapter was reviewed by the Appraisal and Examination Group, composed of eight experts of the China Quality Control Association. The experts include Song Jiwen, Song Ligang, Yue Zhigian, and Zhang Guihua.

The Ancient Handicraft Industry

China's handicraft industry historically reached a high state of development. The applicability, durability, and fine craftsmanship of Chinese products have long been the focus of world attention. Manufacturing industries for products such as woven silk, lacquer ware, porcelain, tea, paper, printing, gunpowder, and compasses were all pioneered and long monopolized by China. The quantity and quality of products of other Chinese industries such as metallurgy, shipbuilding, and architecture ranked at the world's forefront for a long time. This development of handicraft production and the attainment of large amounts of quality products could not be achieved without strict quality control.

The origin of handicraft industries and their quality control in China's history can be traced back from the sixteenth century B.C. to the eleventh century B.C. in the period of the Shang Dynasty. Handicraft industries at that time included trades in metallurgy, potterymaking, leather, textile, bamboo and woodworking, boats, vehicles, and architecture. Most of these industries were either officially operated or officially owned. The workshops were sizable and were organized and managed by government-dispatched officials who were responsible for production.

China's ancient handicraft industry can be divided into three broad sectors: the officially owned handicraft, including the palatial handicraft; the civilian handicraft; and the family handicraft.

The officially owned handicraft was the dominant sector. It was established specially for the living needs of the imperial family and the needs of the bureaucracy, military, a rewards system, and grants to foreign countries.

The workshops of the officially owned handicrafts were generally large. The smallest employed more than 100 craftsmen and the largest employed several thousand. The organizations and institutions of these workshops were complete and intact with minute division of labor internally. Various officials were set up for the management. Through political power, the materials selected were of the best quality, the craftsmen's techniques were excellent, and the management was strict. The resulting products reached the state's highest quality standards.

China's Ancient Quality Control System

China's ancient quality control system is closely related with China's ancient society. The centralized autocratic state included a centralized system of quality control over the whole process of handicraft production, from the beginning to the end. Starting from the Western Zhou Dynasty (eleventh century to eighth century B.C.), a system to control the production of handicraft had already been set up specially in the state administrative organizations. According to the *Records of Etiquette* of the Zhou Dynasty, such a system was composed of a number of specific organizations that were all managed by special officials. These organizations can be divided into the following five large departments according to their functions:

1. The department in charge of production, collection, storage, and distribution of raw and semifinished materials
2. The department of production and manufacturing
3. The department for storing and distributing completed products
4. The department for formulating and executing standards
5. The department of supervision and examination

The mutual relationships among these five large departments are shown in Figure 1.1. The first three departments are the basic links in the process of handicraft production. The fourth and fifth departments ensure the quality of the products. All are independent departments with their respective special functions; at the same time, they are coordinated to form a unified system of production.

The Organization of Industry

During the 3000-year period from the Western Zhou Dynasty to the Qing Dynasty, the basic organizational structure for control of industry changed little. A specific example is the organizational structure that prevailed during the Song Dynasty (960–1279 A.D.).

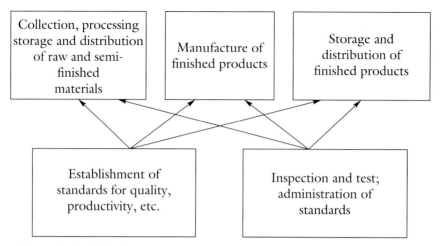

Figure 1.1. China's ancient organizations for handicraft production and their interrelations.

The highest industry organization in the central government of the Song Dynasty was called the Ministry of Works. It contained four bureaus:

- The Land Reclamation Bureau was in charge of the country's agricultural production.
- The Yubu Bureau was in charge of the mountain forests, lakes, and mines. One of the chief functions of this bureau (and also of the Land Reclamation Bureau) was to provide raw and semifinished materials for handicraft production.
- The Water Administration Bureau was in charge of water conservation, water communications, and transport.
- The Building and Repairing Bureau was in charge of handicraft production.

Three superintendents were set up under the Building and Repairing Bureau. The Jiang Zuo superintendent was in charge of manufacturing matters concerning palace rooms, temples, city walls, bridges, vessels, and carts. The Shau Fu superintendent was in charge of production matters concerning dyeing, weaving, embroidering, and articles of everyday use. The munitions superintendent was in charge of weapons manufacturing.

Special organizations like the Tai Fu Shi and the Wei Wei Shi were set up in the Song Dynasty to take charge of storing and distributing the products.

The Zhong Shu Sheng and the Shang Shu Sheng, the highest administrative organizations of the Song Dynasty, were jointly responsible for the formulation and promulgation of industry standards. Departments were set up under these two shengs to formulate government policies, decrees, standards, and production norms, while the officials of the Ministry of Works were responsible for meeting standards and decrees.[1]

The preceding organization was only the macroorganizational structure. Extensive supporting hierarchies were created to carry out detailed planning, supervision, and decision making over a wide variety of subject matter and numerous geographical areas. Yet despite the gigantic size of these hierarchies, they exhibited three all-pervasive features of central control:

- The central control extended over the entire progression of the processes through which end products were produced.

- The concept of special organization for quality control was an integral part of central control, as is seen in Figure 1.1.

- The special hierarchy for administration of quality control was linked to the overall control organization of the central government.

Laws and Decrees for Quality Control

Promulgation and enforcement of laws and decrees was an important means for the state to use its political power to carry out its control over handicraft production. According to the *Records of Etiquette,* the following were already specifically provided in the decrees of the Zhou Dynasty: "Utensils under standards are not allowed to be sold on the market; carts under standards are not allowed to be sold on the market; cottons and silks of which the quality and size are not up to the standards are not allowed to be sold on the market." These provisions not only reflect that there was already a certain quality standard for products like utensils, carts, cottons, and silks, but also that decrees had been promulgated to ban the sale of inferior products so as to consolidate the quality control over them.

During the period of the Warring State (475–221 B.C.), various ducal (regional) states inherited and developed these decrees of quality control of the Zhou Dynasty. In the tomb of the Qin Dynasty, excavated in December 1975 in Yunmeng County of Hubei Province, a batch of decrees before the unification of China by the Qin Dynasty (221 B.C.) was unearthed. They contain a number of provisions and demands for quality, reflecting the policies and laws of the Qin state's control over handicraft, commerce, and dimensions. For example, the law provided that, in the same category of utensils, shape, size, length, and breadth must be identical. For the mud tiles and tools made of iron and wood damaged when building the city wall, for the wheel hubs cracked while manufacturing the cars, for the products examined and found to be of inferior grade, the responsible officials and craftsmen were all to be penalized. The architecture of the city walls must have a guarantee period of one year. Should the architecture show damage within one year, the officials and workers who were responsible and participated in the construction were all to be punished and the work to be done over again without compensation.

These laws later became an important part of the laws of the dynasties in China's history. For example, the laws of the Tang Dynasty (618–907 A.D.) provided that "all bows and arrows, knives and lances are allowed to be sold only under the condition that they are manufactured according to the patterns stipulated by the feudal officials and inscribed with the full names of the workers. So is the case with other articles. The feudal officials will confiscate all false and indiscriminate goods in the trading. Those that fall short of specifications of the sizes and lengths are ordered to be returned."[2] Tang Dynasty laws also provided that should the quality of various categories of products be substandard, all craftsmen up to the responsible officials are to be flogged or otherwise punished. Laws of the Ming Dynasty (1368–1644 A.D.) stipulated that all those who have made articles and utensils that are not durable or who have woven cloths and silks short of specifications are guilty and shall be penalized.

Standardization and Metrology

Standardization of products is a major contributor to the national economy and the people's livelihood. A prerequisite to such standardization is standardization of metrology: the measurement of length, capacity, weight, and so on. For this reason, the past dynasties all paid close attention to standardization of measurement and gave the problem high priority in administrating the state.

The system of standards for length, capacity, and weight was formulated so as to carry on examination of the quality of products. It was said in China's ancient fairy tale, that the first ancestor of human beings (Fuxi) was the inventor of the rule and yardstick (Figure 1.2). According to *Zuozhuan, the First Year of Dinggong*, a historical book written in the third to fourth century B.C., there lived in the Xia Dynasty (twenty-first to seventeenth century B.C.) a man named Xi Zhong. He invented the vehicle. Therefore, the Xia government appointed him as the Che Zheng, an official to take charge of the manu-

Figure 1.2. This is a relief of the carved stone from the ancestral temple of Wulinang of Shandong province. It is about 2000 years old. The images are of the first ancestors of humans: Fuxi (right) and his spouse, Nuwa. Fuxi is holding the square, carpenter's square, and yardstick.

facture of vehicles. (This reflects that there was already an official to take charge of the manufacture of vehicles and an officially owned workshop in manufacturing vehicles at that time.)

According to what was recorded in *Guan Zi, an Explanation of the Situations,* tools such as the compass, square, carpenter's square, and yardstick had already been used at that time by Xi Zhong to examine the size, angle, soundness, and straightness of the parts and spares of various vehicles. Thanks to the use of such measurement, the parts and spares were all suitable to the quality demand, so the vehicles manufactured were sturdy, durable, and convenient.

From the utensils of round and square shapes that have survived from the Shang Dynasty (seventeenth to eleventh century B.C.), and from the geometric and triangular designs on these utensils, it is evident that the craftsmen at that time already made skillful use of the compasses, squares, carpenter's squares, and yardsticks. It can be said definitely that, more than 3000 years ago, the demand for quality and use of measurement as an aid to quality had already been in existence in China. This also is evidence that China had the budding of the idea of quality control at that time. Subsequently, through the long period of historical process, China's ancient quality control underwent continuing improvement until there emerged a quality control system with distinct features.

More Attention to Measurement

During China's period of the clan commune about 5000 years ago, people had begun to pay attention to measurement of length, capacity, and weight. Up to the period of the Shang Dynasty and the Zhou Dynasty, a system was set up for creating standard instruments for such measurement. The system included provision for state check of the accuracy of these instruments twice a year. A special organization was set up and special officials were assigned to carry out this control.

The control of measuring instruments continued during the Warring State period (403–221 B.C.). Even though the centralization had collapsed, the various separatist regimes still continued their own systems for the length, capacity, and weight. For example, the law of Qin state provided for an official check of measuring tools once a year. The scope of error allowed for measuring tools was also stipulated, and should the scope be outstripped, the responsible official would be fined.

After the Qin state unified the country in 221 B.C., the imperial edicts of the first emperor of the Qin Dynasty included an order to unify all systems of weights and measures. Meanwhile, large batches of standard measuring tools for length, capacity, and weight were manufactured by the state and inscribed with the imperial edicts of the first emperor of the Qin Dynasty to be dispatched to various localities for use as standards (Figure 1.3).

The decrees of the Qin Dynasty to standardize measurement significantly influenced later generations. For instance, the laws of the Tang Dynasty stipulated that measuring tools were to be checked every August and were to be used only after the seals were affixed. Penalties were provided for failing to make the checks or for use of privately made measuring tools.

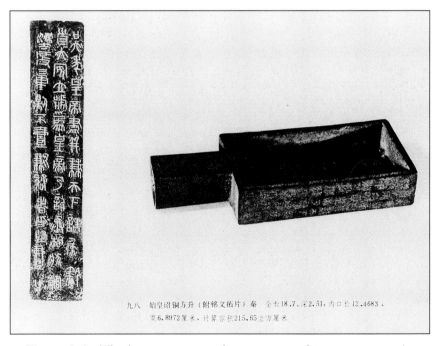

九八　始皇诏铜方升（附铭文拓片）秦　全长18.7、高2.51、内口长12.4683、
宽6.8972厘米、计算容积215.65立方厘米

Figure 1.3. The bronze square sheng was used to measure grain. The imperial edicts of the first emperor of the Qin Dynasty, concerning weights and measures, are inscribed on the side of the sheng. The other words describe its dimensions.

Standardization went beyond measuring tools; it extended to the industrial products themselves, especially those from the officially owned industrial departments. The best-known classics in existence concerning the standards and specifications for handicraft production are the *Records in Inspecting the Works* and the *Rules of Architecture.*

The *Records in Inspecting the Works* is a book written in about the fifth century B.C. It recorded the production standards of 30 special departments included in the officially owned industries of that time. The extensive contents relate to product designing, product specifications, quality requirements, manufacturing techniques, production tools, and methods of inspecting and testing vehicles, weapons, musical instruments, vessels, jade wares, leathers, and architecture. The book also expounds and proves the rationalization and the scientific nature of the related provisions. It is a book of overall standards concerning industrial production, being a systematic summary of the handicraft production during that time and the time preceding and playing a restrictive and guiding role for handicraft production. This is a rare classic work concerning quality control in the early period.

The *Rules of Architecture* was compiled and finished in 1100 A.D. The chief editor was Li Jie, the official in charge of the Jiang Zuo superintendent of the Northern Song Dynasty government. This classic work sets out production standards with laws and decrees applicable to the architectural trade of the official circles. This book includes details about the overall design of architecture; the specifications, structures, and decorations of various architectural components; and the different types of construction material, including mud, tiles, wood, brick, and stone.

Calculation of the sizes and the materials to be consumed was done through correlation with the consumption of a key component of ancient China's architecture: the *dou gong*. This is a system of brackets inserted between the top of a column and a cross beam. Each bracket is formed of a double bow-shaped arm, called *gong*, which supports a block of wood, called *dou*, on each side. The consumption of these brackets served as a standard yardstick for calculating the sizes and the materials required for the other architectural components. The *Rules of Architecture* further specified the calculation method to be used, this method being applicable regardless of the scale and size of the architecture. In this way, standardization of the

Figure 1.4 The standardized *dou gong* system of architecture was
used to build this pagoda in 1056 A.D.

different kinds of architecture was an aid to cost control as well as to
quality control (Figure 1.4).

Standardization of handicraft products in China's ancient times was
also embodied to a certain extent in various trades. For example, in the
case of textile products needed in people's daily living—especially the
specifications and standards for silk fabrics—there were always very explicit stipulations in China's ancient times. The Zhou Dynasty had
strict stipulations about the width and length of cloth and silk.[3] This
standard was followed in later generations and fixed in the form of law.
In order to ensure the density and quality of silk fabrics, the political
power of the later Zhou Dynasty of the Five Dynasties (951–960 A.D.)
further stipulated the weight of a bolt of officially made thin, tough silk
created in areas north of the Yellow River. This reflects that the quality
requirement had been established with due regard to the standards of
the silk fabrics in warp and weft. The different requirements in weight

for the north and south took into consideration different factors of weather and humidity. It is evident that much study had preceded the setting of the quality requirements.

Self-Inspection and Traceability

Ancient China attached much importance to the problem of examination for quality, and it formulated systems for this purpose. Such examining systems ran through the process, from the collection of raw and semifinished materials to production, storage, and distribution. Of course, the production activities in ancient times were mainly accomplished by relying upon the craftsmen's techniques and simple machinery. Consequently, self-inspection at various work stages by the producers themselves became an important means for establishing responsibility for quality. For this reason, the important measure called Articles to Be Inscribed with the Craftsmen's Name was formulated and carried out by the management organizations of ancient times.

The measure required that the names of the craftsmen who made the products be carved or inscribed on the products. In some cases, this requirement extended to the names of the industrial officials or the industrial officials' organizations (Figure 1.5). This measure began during the Zhou Dynasty, according to the *Records of Etiquette,* Yue Ling. The resulting traceability became a powerful aid for ensuring the quality of the products. If the quality was inferior, the responsible craftsman was to be penalized and the causes were to be determined. When the measure was enacted into law, the authority of the political power added to its effectiveness. The measure was considered to be so important that it was continued by the governments of later generations.

An example of the strictness in adopting the measure can be seen in the inscriptions on the Warring States' arms and on the lacquer wares of the Han Dynasty. The inscriptions include not only the names of the technical craftsmen and the workers involved in production, but also the names of the supplementary slaves. In addition, the names of the handicrafts officials or the industrial official's organization were inscribed, reflecting the strictness of the system of responsibility.

The measure went beyond officially owned handicrafts to civilian handicrafts. The decrees of the Jin Dynasty (281–420 A.D.) especially stipulated that all those who made lacquer wares for sale must obtain the approval of the government's related department. Often,

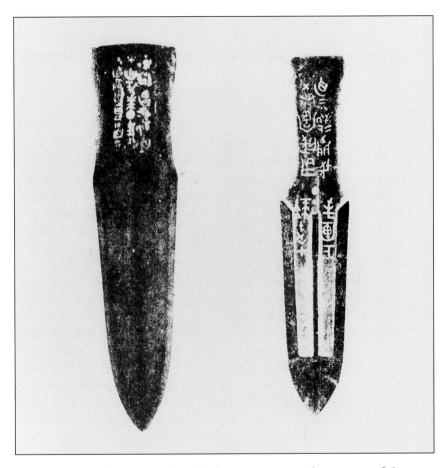

Figure 1.5. During the third century B.C., the names of the craftsmen and officials responsible for making bronze weapons were inscribed directly on the arms.

the finishing of the lacquer wares, which were made of superior raw materials and in accordance with a certain specification, were to be identified using paint mixed with cinnabar to show the date, month, and year when the lacquer wares were made and the names of the makers.[4]

Another form of The Article to be Inscribed with the Craftsmen's Name was that only the names of the manufacturing plants or the examining officials who were in charge were recorded. There were the

Handan dagger-axe, Shangdang Weapons Warehouse's dagger-axe and lance, and sword smelted by the Weapons Warehouse in the period of the Warring States when the names of the producing plants were inscribed.

In the period of the Western Han Dynasty, the names of the examining officials were inscribed in various brass products. The inscribing forms of later generations were simplified somewhat so that the names of the manufacturing plants were inscribed. The porcelain pillows of the Cizhou Kiln in the Song Dynasty carried inscriptions such as "made by the Zhong family," "made by the Zhao family," and "made by the Wang family."

Broad Planning for Production

In China's ancient times, state planning permeated all industries. These plans included the volume of goods to be produced, schedules for construction projects, and which activities were to be carried out during which season of the year. A system of reports enabled officials to keep informed of performance according to these plans. Provisions for enforcement included a severe system of penalties for failure to meet the plans. Penalties could also be applied to the planners if their estimates were inaccurate.[5]

Product and process designs attained high levels of proficiency in China's ancient times. Bronze wares from that era have been the focus of world attention. Pig iron smelting and casting reached sophisticated levels, including multilevel "stack" casting (Figures 1.6 and 1.7). Pig iron could be smelted and tapped directly from iron ores, and the pig iron could then be smelted into wrought iron, reflecting the organized quality control in effect at that time. Silks, satins, and porcelains attained world renown.

Sophisticated design also extended to architectural projects like the metropolis, palaces, and bridges. Superior design theory and technique is evident in the large-scale stone arch Anji bridge (Figure 1.8) in Zhao County of Hebei Province and in means of communication such as vessels and carts.

The design capabilities of China's ancient handicraft production can be judged from surviving objects and documents. The set of bells made in 433 B.C., unearthed in recent years in Hubei's Sui County, is a

Figure 1.6. The Chinese became adept at pig iron smelting and casting using molds such as this one. It was possible to stack the molds.

model of bronze ware casting and musical instrument design in China's ancient times. As much as 10 tons of bronze was used to make the bell bodies, the bronze pillars on either side of them, and the bronze hoods on the crossbeam (Figure 1.9). There are 65 bells in the set. Each bell

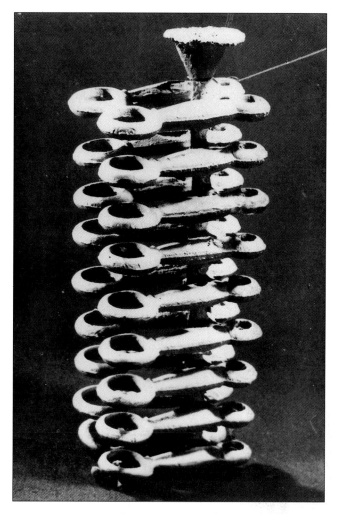

Figure 1.7. Stack molding provided a significant
improvement in productivity.

can sound two tones, and is marked with the musical alphabet and temperament. The set has a range of $5\frac{1}{2}$ octaves. The bells, though buried deep in the earth for more than 2000 years, still can be used to perform Chinese and foreign melodies new or old. They fully illustrate the prevailing level of music theory and product design capability.

Figure 1.8. The large-scale stone arch bridge is in its second millennium. Located in Zhao County of Hebei Province, it was built from 590 to 608 A.D.

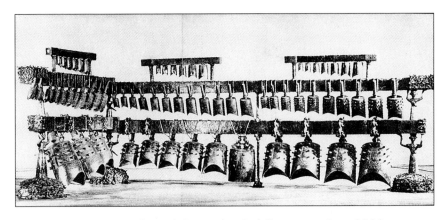

Figure 1.9. Even though it was buried for more than 2000 years, this set of bronze bells can still be used to perform Chinese and foreign melodies.

Application to Architecture

Ancient Chinese architecture similarly exhibits examples of high capability in planning and product design. According to the famous commentary by Zuo Qiuming in *The Spring and Autumn Annals*, in the sixth century to fifth century B.C., the Chu State adopted methods of planning and organization prior to construction of the city walls. The responsible officials and engineers had to explore and survey the foundation of the site and calculate the volume of the earthwork, the distance that supplies needed to be transported, and the required labor force. Then the tools and instruments had to be prepared, the grain supply raised and collected, and the civilian laborers organized. Following this planning, the construction was completed within three months.

The construction of Chang-an City during the Sui Dynasty (581–618 A.D.) was an architectural miracle. Figure 1.10 is a picture of the city plan. It was a great metropolis built in a vast piece of wilderness under careful planning and design. The area of the whole city reached 84 square kilometers in neat formation and orderly distribution and was divided into three parts to include the palace city, the imperial city, and the extensive city.

Each city required high protective walls. In the palace city were palaces, imperial halls, and buildings where the emperor lived and ex-

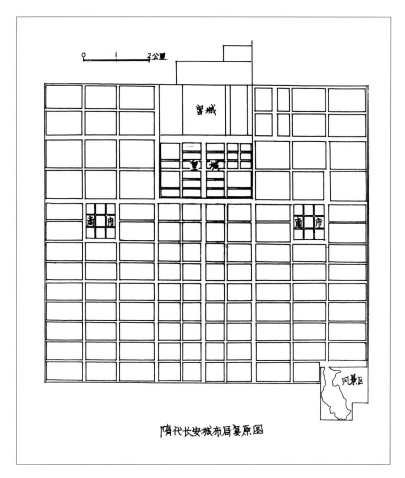

Figure 1.10. The city plan for Chang-an City shows carefully designed streets over an 84-square-kilometer area. Between 1 million and 2 million civilian workers were involved in the city's construction.

ercised his rule. The imperial city contained the central government's office buildings. There were 11 big streets leading from south to north and 14 big streets leading from east to west. These were further divided into 108 lanes and alleys to include the official residences, people's living quarters, and the commercial markets. There were also rivers and channels providing the city with water and drainage as well as a means for transporting goods and materials necessary for living.

There were recreation sites as well. In the course of the city's construction, 1 million to 2 million civilian workers were mobilized.

Construction of this large-scale metropolis was started in June 582 and finished nine months later. This was possible only through superb planning, design, construction, and high-level management. The architects in the Sui Dynasty had already used the 1:100 ratio in designing the drawings and making the wood models. The key measurements like the area and width of the houses, the height of the pillars and platforms, and the length of the outstretching of the eaves were all marked in ratios that were clear at a glance. This shows that the technology of designing had advanced to a quantitative stage.

Division of Labor in the Workshops

To improve product quality, there was division of labor among the craftsmen in the production process of handicrafts, both the officially owned and the private. Such division of labor was already carefully drawn, to a certain extent of detail, more than 2000 years ago. *The Records in Inspecting the Works* identifies 30 kinds of techniques: seven woodworking techniques for making things like bows, arrow shafts, and the wheels and compartments of carts; six metalworking techniques for making items such as swords and sabers, arrowheads, clocks, and measuring tools; five leatherworking techniques; five techniques for painting and dyeing; five techniques for making jade wares; and two techniques for making pottery. Every one of these techniques could involve several work procedures.

An example of division of labor is seen in the field of bronze casting, which in ancient times had already reached a fair degree of maturity. Roughly, the technological process included mould making, design engraving, clay pottery preparing, clay pith scraping, pattern pith assembling, bronze liquid pouring, pattern tapping, pith tapping, processing by repairing and maintaining, and finally polishing into a finished article. This set of technological processes could be used to cast not only large-sized bronze vessels, but also exquisite articles with fine designs.

The biggest bronze vessel of remote ages still in existence is the square cooking vessel of Simu Wu, which is 133 cm high, 116 cm long, 79 cm wide, and weighs 875 kg. It was cast in about the twelfth century B.C. (Figure 1.11). The casting mold of the entire vessel body

Figure 1.11. The square bronze cooking vessel of Simu Wu is the largest such object still in existence from the twelfth century B.C. About 200 to 300 workers made it.

is composed of the belly pattern (the vessel belly together with the vessel legs; each side is a block of whole pattern that contains six blocks of branch patterns in flower designs), clay pith, bottom pattern, top pattern, and the pouring-mouth pattern of the vessel belly. After the vessel body was cast, the molds were assembled at the loop handles with the pattern everted so as to cast and connect the loop handles. Then a series of repairing, maintaining, and processing steps is carried out so a magnificent cooking vessel unrivaled in history comes into being.

The entire technological process embodies the superb delicacy of designing, smelting, casting, and processing. Close coordination of about 200 to 300 workers was needed to make such a gigantic vessel. Most of all, it could not have been made if there were no relatively strict quality control. In addition, according to the study and analysis of documentary records and unearthed artifacts, it is evident that compasses, squares, and yardsticks had been used in examining the vessel's levelness and straightness.

The division of labor became more and more minute with the gradual growth of volume production. Examples can be seen in the lacquer ware, textile, architecture, and porcelain trades.

• The inscription on a lacquer cup made in the first year of the Eastern Han Dynasty (the first half of the first century) recorded the division of labor at that time: the responsible officials, the plain worker making the inner tube of the lacquer ware, the painter to administer the lacquer, the goldsmith to do the goldplating work on the ornaments of the copper-made accessories, a second painter to touch and depict the veined ornaments, the engraver doing the engraving work, the cleanup worker doing the final repairing and polishing work, the worker in charge of supplying materials, and the manufacturing worker (somewhat similar to today's engineer), who was responsible for the whole working procedure.

• In the officially owned textile trade of the Tan Dynasty, the Textile Bureau, subordinated to the Shao Fu superintendent, was the biggest in scale. Under this bureau were 25 workshops, each of which had its respective function in producing goods of different qualities and specifications. There was again minute and careful division of labor among various working procedures in each workshop.

• In eleventh-century architecture, there were 13 types of work in the processing of various materials. By the seventeenth century, there were more than 30.

• Jingdezhen in the Qing Dynasty was the center of porcelain-making trades, and its division of labor was very minute, whether in the official kiln or in the civilian kiln. In making the porcelains, there were special craftsmen from earth making, base preparing, and on to glaze administering. Every link in the process included a minute division of labor. For example, making the bases included inlaying, engraving, printing, shaping, wheel turning, color dyeing, drilling, engraving, and inscribing. There was an even more minute division of labor among the craftsmen, who all had their respective areas of expertise though they were subordinated to the broader specialties. It was just such minute division of labor and in-depth specialization that made possible Jingdezhen's production of such artistic and exquisite porcelain articles, which won popular acclaim.

Recruiting and Training Craftsmen

In China's ancient times, craftsmen were subordinated to the feudal officials and under the jurisdiction of the officials in charge of the industries. Craftsmen were required to offer their productive techniques. Production of the officially owned handicrafts relied on conscription and transfer of craftsmen and on the utilization of a number of slaves and criminals.

Such recruitment of craftsmen was practiced by various generations after the Qin Dynasty. Because the officially owned handicrafts could use the force of political power, the craftsmen conscripted and transferred were mostly men of relatively high technical capability. Records in volume seven of the *Six Laws of the Tang Dynasty* state that "Craftsmen [of officially owned handicrafts] who are to be distributed to various prefectures must be hale and hearty as well as technologically dexterous." That is why craftsmen of superior skills tended to be centralized in the officially owned handicrafts. In turn, such centralization of skills tended to make the resulting products superior in quality.

In ancient times, the techniques mastered by the craftsmen were generally heritable and inherited. This concept of inherited crafts was further stimulated by requiring workers of the same craft to live in the same geographical area, rather than being scattered according to their clans.[6] "Hundreds of workers have to live in the shops so as to ensure the works being done accordingly."[7]

This policy of craftsmen living collectively was convenient not only for management, but also for technical cultivation, training, and teaching. Collective living could make the sons and younger brothers of the craftsmen feel at ease to learn the techniques from their fathers and elder brothers. "The workers are ordered to live collectively so as to have them examined the year round, to differentiate their merits and hard labor, to regulate their uses, to comment and compare their talents—and to make their sons and younger brothers' minds at rest so they will not change their minds the moment they see something new. Thus their fathers and elder brothers' teaching will be fulfilled without strict rules and their sons and younger brothers' learning will be accomplished with much more ease."[8] This key channel in the technical teaching and vocational training of the craftsmen, as a tradition, was already formed in the time of the Warring States (475–221 B.C.) and was carried on with little change.

The scale of the officially owned handicraft was ordinarily very large, and involved minute division of labor. Training of craftsmen was essential, and the system of technical and vocational training was mapped out for this. The law of the Qin State stipulated that new workers were to do part-time work for the first year and that, after the second year, they would do work similar to that done by the formal workers. Many techniques were strictly taught and guided by worker-teachers. The new workers could complete their course of study within two years while the old workers could finish the course in one year. Those who failed to finish their course in time would be reported to the controlling officials of the upper level to be put on file.[9]

The Tang Dynasty had this to say about the learning hours of the new workers: "The amount and difficulty of the workload are to be calculated first, then to be calculated in average." The techniques of boring, carving, jagging, and forging metals like gold, silver, copper, and iron required four years of training. The making of carts and musical instruments required three years. The making of bamboo wares, lacquer wares, and wickers required two years. For still others, the training might be as short as 40 or 50 days. Such a system of training and teaching the craftsmen was an important measure in the management of the officially owned handicrafts, enabling large amounts of quality products to be made for the rulers' enjoyment. Such systematized measures for training craftsmen also stimulated a major dedication to quality control.

Control of Costs

Management coordination of work included control over product costs. These costs were chiefly composed of two factors: labor and materials consumed. China's officially owned handicrafts had rather strict control over both.

With respect to cost of labor, the governments of various generations all made use of clear and definite standards. These standards took seasonal differences into consideration. Summer days are long, while winter days are short, with resulting differences in the time available for work. Therefore, stipulations of different seasons with different calculations of labor had long existed in China's history. The Qin State of the third century B.C. stipulated that three labor-days in winter are tantamount to two labor-days in summer.[10] The Han Dynasty followed such a system, while other dynasties introduced variations and refinements.[11]

The calculation of labor-days of craftsmen and other supplementary laborers was also differentiated to a certain extent according to the types of work, sex, and age. The law of the Qin Dynasty of the third century B.C. stipulated that miscellaneous work done by two maid servants corresponds to that done by one worker and that five juvenile maid servants capable of doing corvee work are equal to one worker. It was provided at the same time that one labor-day of work done by a woman worker with special technique can be equal to that done by one man worker; one woman worker doing embroidery work with a needle should be equal to one man. The Tang Dynasty had similar stipulations.

There was also a certain quota stipulated for the quantity of the products to be made every year by the various officially owned handicrafts' departments. For instance, volume six of the *Jinling New Records* noted that the Eastern Weaving and Dyeing Bureau of the Yuan Dynasty (1279–1368) "controls 3,600 households of craftsmen and 154 looms, and must produce 4,527 bolts of satins and raw silk of 11,502 jin and 8 liang." (One jin equals a half kilogram, and one liang equals 50 grams.)

There was also a strict system for controlling use of materials. The production department had stipulations with regard to how much material was to be drawn and how many products were to be manufactured. For example, there were detailed stipulations as to the specifications and quantities of the materials to be used on various kinds of wood structures in architecture. Specifications and standards on the use of materials for various kinds of ships of different sizes were recorded in the *Records of the Longjiang Shipyard*, written in the middle of the sixteenth century. In textile production, there was also a system for specifying how much silk to use in order to weave a certain number of bolts of finished material. These stipulations were formulated, in general, according to the practical conditions prevailing during use of materials in actual production.

Some cost controls extended to calculating the overall costs of resources such as material, labor, and energy. An example is a record in the iron provision in volume five of the *Wu Bian the Former Chapter* by Tang Shunzhi of the Ming Dynasty: "Ten jin of ore can smelt iron for 3 qian [1 qian equals 5 grams of silver], five labor-days are to be used with the labor meal costing 2.5 qian, and the charcoal to be consumed costs 1.6 qian. Calculated as a whole, every jin of iron smelted will cost 1.666 qian of silver. This is only a rough account of smelting. If swords or gun are to be made, then still more labor is to be added and the iron needed is to be converted in the calculation. This must be produced one by one, first under supervision, so as to fix their respective prices." It is seen here how minutely and carefully the Ming Dynasty established its control over the cost of iron smelting and how the cost quota was fixed only after practical production or experimentation.

Examination and Custody

In addition to the implementation of The Articles Inscribed with the Craftmen's Name (a practice discussed in the first part of this chapter), other forms and methods of quality control evolved in China's ancient times. These methods included systems of mutual, patrol, and final examination to be carried out on products.

Under mutual examination, the officials of different localities carried out a mutual examination of products. During Emperor Yuan Feng's period of the Song Dynasty (1018–85), the government had issued the order "By the end of every season, the officials of different levels are entrusted to mutually inspect the quality and quantity of the arms manufactured by various localities."

Patrol examination was the routine examination of production units, with persons dispatched to patrol and inspect every month or once every season. In the meantime, patrol and inspection by the highest administrative authority was to be directed against any problems that cropped up in the course of production.

Final examination of products took two forms: extensive and selective. Extensive examination of products was adopted early and widely in China's ancient times. However, the volume of some products grew to colossal proportions. An outstanding example was the volume of arms produced during the Song Dynasty. The bow-manufacturing yard alone "has to manufacture a total of more than 16.5 million bows with handles made of horn every year."[12] It would take a lot of labor and time to examine these products one by one, and this was also unnecessary. Thus the method of selective examination (sampling) was invented. This method was rather mature in the Song Dynasty.

There were two imperial edicts concerning arms production during the 30th year of the Shaoxing emperor of southern Song Dynasty (1160) saying,

• "The related arms must be meticulously made that are to be examined by the departments, level by level. When the volume ordered to be made is fulfilled, samples of them should be packaged by the departments and section, level by level, and submitted for examination."[13]

• "Take the names and the units of arms manufactured in every 10 days and ask the supervising official to look and examine them over in person and have them counted, recorded, and sealed up for safekeeping. . . . Then have the names and units of the ordered arms counted, fixed, and sealed up every 10 days and go to the department to have them looked and examined over."[14]

The former required that, after the products reached a specified volume, random sampling would be done to carry on the examination; the latter required the random sampling to be done from the products manufactured in a certain period of time (10 days) to carry on the examination. In this way, the examination was done based either on sampling from the batches of products of a specified volume or sampling according to certain intervals of time. This examination method of systematic random sampling was rather a scientific and reasonable method of examination. The second method, sampling from the products manufactured in a certain interval of time, seems to have been applied extensively in the Song Dynasty.

As to the further development and the specific details of the sampling examination method, we can catch a glimpse from volume seven of the *Guide to the Industrial Department's Plants and Warehouse of the Ming Dynasty.*

In order to examine the quality of copper produced by various localities, random samples were taken from hundreds of thousands of packages of copper. This was the first level of sampling. A composite was then prepared by taking two packages from each sample of 100. This was the second level of sampling. Finally, these packages were broken up, and pieces weighing 100 jin (50 kilograms) were selected to become the third level of sampling. These were then halved, and the halves were smelted in two different stoves to calculate the general rate of consumption of copper ores and to judge whether the ores conformed to the specified quality standard. This sampling method was rather effective and reasonable as far as large batches of copper and iron ores were concerned. This method was described in the *Guide to the Industrial Department's Plants and Warehouse* as the "traditional regulation." It could be seen that this method was already adopted in the Ming Dynasty at the latest.

When He Shijin and others compiled the *Guide to the Industrial Department's Plants and Warehouses*, they again had the previously mentioned method improved. They thought the traditional regulation "It takes 1 million jin of copper to fix the consumption with 200 jin" still seemed improper, so they proposed, "From now on, another two stoves shall be added correspondingly while the copper is to be smelted. Temporarily eight packages of copper are to be selected and 50 jin of copper are to be taken out of each package totaling 400 jin that are weighted and put into the stoves. That means half of the volume of the eight packages are smelted. Take the average of the four stoves to calculate how much is the consumption; then the result will be the accurate average." Of course this was still the method of three-level sampling. However, this technique represents an improvement in the sampling of the latter two levels. The increase of the sampling volume and the increase of the volume of copper directly used in chemical examination all tended to make the observed rate of consumption still closer to the actual rate of consumption. Thus the whole process was done still more effectively and reasonably.

Once products in the officially owned handicrafts had been qualified through examination, they entered a strict system of storage. Detailed accounts were to be kept as to the categories of the products and as to when the products entered or left the warehouse. Products in custody in the warehouse were to be guarded against any damage and going bad. Any violation of the accounts registration or damage of products because of careless custody was to be punished severely. The difference in practice was that the examination and custody of the products of the civilian handicrafts were directly connected with industrial and commercial interests. Hence, unlike that of the officially owned handicrafts, this system was not based on imperial decrees.

The Mainstream

During the long years of China's history, a system of quality control was formed based on use of state authority. The mainstream of quality control was carried out through the state's administrative departments. Regardless of the standards of quality, the control of the overall production process, or the examination and appraisal of the quality of the products, the influence of the state's political power was all-pervasive. The depth and extent of such influence had rarely been seen in world history. These were the characteristics of this system of quality control.

1. The evolution of China's civilization has been continuous since ancient times. In contrast to some other ancient civilizations, the evolution in China has never been suspended. Similarly, the system of quality control that evolved in China's ancient times has also followed an uninterrupted evolution. Once established, the system remained in effect and was readjusted and consolidated as centuries passed.

2. The level of quality control in China's ancient times reached an outstanding height. It was formed and developed from an extensive accumulation of quality control experiences. Some of these experiences went beyond qualitative control—they possessed the feature of quantitative control. Such was the case in the instances of specifying the length, capacity, and weight of products, and of quantitative requirements for the designs and raw materials used. This reflects the fairly brilliant accomplishments of quality control in China's ancient times—accomplishments that have been acknowledged around the world and which serve as valuable references even up to the present.

3. The historical continuity has also resulted in historical conservatism. China's quality control originated from the period of Shang and Zhou Dynasties (seventeenth century to eighth century B.C.).

The various management systems had already been set up in about the times of the Spring and Autumn and the Warring States (770–221 B.C.) and were readjusted and consolidated through the period of the Qin and Han Dynasties (third century B.C. to the second century A.D.), thus forming a relatively complete system. Thanks to the tradition of respecting the classics and worshipping the ancient in China's history, the system set up by the Chinese took deep root and could hardly be changed. Consequently, the basic quality control system and its corresponding laws and decrees were followed generation after generation. The basic setup remained almost intact. The only changes consisted of minor readjustment of the specific laws, decrees, systems, and measures so as to make them still more well-organized. Such historical inheritance and the associated conservatism contributed to the backward status of China's modern industrial production and quality control even after the abrupt rise of modern industry and commerce. Thus modern quality control could hardly break through China's traditional state of inertia.

4. The priority given to quality control in China's ancient society was closely related with the monarchic power and served the bureaucratic policies of the monarchic autocracy. Because the imperial family and bureaucrats desired many luxurious daily articles so they could enjoy life, political power was used to design the system of quality control to meet these goals. This stimulated the development of quality control systems on the one hand, but also gave rise to big drawbacks: there was little done to satisfy the demands of the common people.

Because of the demand for luxurious, high-quality goods, there was often a total neglect of the cost of production, which resulted in enormous waste of labor and materials. In addition, the highly centralized system covering a wide range of excessively rigid controls seriously hampered the enthusiasm of the craftsmen and restricted the development of a commodity economy.

The evolution of China's quality control system is closely related to the development of its people. Its quality control methods have slowed China's pace and contributed to the country's backwardness in modern times.

Notes

1. *The History of the Song Dynasty*, General Records of Government Posts, Vol. IV.

2. *The Six Laws of the Tang Dynasty*, Vol. 20.

3. *Etiquette of the Zhou Dynasty.*

4. *The Decrees of the Dynasty*, Vol. 756, *Introduction of the Taiping for the Emperor's Reading.*

5. *Bamboo Records of the Qin Tomb in Shuihudi, Law of Corvee;* and *Bamboo Documents of the Qin Tomb in Shidhudi.*

6. *Yi Zhou Book*, the chapter on laws and regulations.

7. *The Analects of Confucius*, the chapter on Zi Zhang.

8. Guo Yu, Qi Yu.

9. *The Six Laws of the Tang Dynasty*, Shau Fu Superintendent.

10. *Bamboo Records of the Qin Tomb in Shuidihu*, p. 73, Law of the Qin Dynasty, The Worker's Regulations.

11. *The Six Laws of the Tang Dynasty*, the chapter on work.

12. *The History of the Song Dynasty*, Records of Weapons, II.

13. *Hui Yao of the Song Dynasty*, Zhi Guan.

14. *Hui Yao of the Song Dynasty*, Zhi Guan.

CHAPTER 2

Managing for Quality in Ancient Israel

Dr. Ron S. Kenett, Senior Partner
Kenett–Preminger Associates
Management Consulting Services, Israel

Introduction

The Holy Land is a historic region on the east coast of the Mediterranean. It was the site of the ancient kingdoms of Israel and Judea and comprises areas of the modern states of Israel and Jordan. The borders of this region have fluctuated throughout history but have generally included the territory lying between the southeastern Mediterranean coast to the west, the Dead Sea Valley to the east, the Negev Desert to the south, and the Litani River to the north—an area of only about 280 km (175 mi.) long by 128 km (80 mi.) wide.

Four thousand years ago the Holy Land was inhabited by a hodge-podge society of agricultural villagers, sheep- and goatherding nomads, and urban artisans. These populations evolved under the influence of cultural currents flowing from Egypt, Hittite Anatolia, the Semite-populated deserts to the east, and the Minoan island of Crete. In the year 1250 before the common era (B.C.E.) Moses led the Exodus of the ancient Hebrews from slavery in Egypt to freedom and sovereignty in the Holy Land, in Canaan. The Hebrews saw periods of extraordinary achievement, such as the building of Solomon's

Temple, and periods of downfall such as the annihilation of their independent nation and the Babylonian exile. Throughout these years, oral and written laws were intensively studied and applied in jurisprudence and work regulations. Jewish laws set forth in the Old Testament, precedents, innovations, and traditions were codified in the year 200 of the current era (C.E.) in a text entitled the Mishnah. Later commentaries on the Mishnah were compiled around 500 C.E. in another unique literary document—the Talmud.

The objective of this study is to provide, through a selective analysis of relevant texts, a perspective on the role of managing for quality in what has been labeled the Cradle of Civilization. Three aspects of quality management have been emphasized: quality improvement, quality planning, and quality control. Quality improvement is the organized creation of beneficial changes in process performance levels. Quality planning, on the other hand, is the activity of determining customer needs and the development of products and processes required to meet those needs. Quality control is typically defined as the managerial process during which actual process performance is evaluated and actions are taken on unusual performance. A major feature of quality control is the establishment of self-control where a party producing a product has the means and knowledge to determine compliance with specifications and, furthermore, is empowered to initiate corrective actions when needed. (For more details on topics of quality management, see Juran, 1989.) In particular, this chapter provides examples designed to demonstrate

- Self-control
- Organization of work
- Specifications and work standards
- Applications of measures
- Procedures and regulations
- Warranties and consumer rights

The period covered begins with the description of the act of Creation in the book of Genesis and ends with the Omayyad caliphs' Arab conquest in 637 C.E. The material used consists of written texts, such as the Old Testament, the Mishnah, and the Talmud, as well as archaeological findings. The contextual background of the quotations is succinctly presented. Readers interested in more details are referred to the bibliographical list. The chapter is structured according to different facets of daily life, major projects, and various industries. Material availability mostly determined the selected topics which include early examples from the Old Testament, laws and regulations, measures and weights, buildings and dwellings, roads and tunnels, and textiles and pottery. A final section reviews the examples in light of general quality management principles. The appendix consists of an annotated chronological list of events designed to put the chapter in a historical context.

Early Examples from the Old Testament

The Act of Creation, Inspection, and Self-Control

Verses from the Old Testament, written over 2500 years ago, are surprisingly modern in their content. In fact, many of today's organizations are rediscovering concepts and methods described in these old scriptures. A key concept in the quest for improved competitiveness is self-control: allowing individuals performing the work to conduct the inspection of their products. Implementing self-control implies a comparison of actual results to specifications. Such a process is evinced by God's daily inspection of his creation. When there was more than one creation, as on the third day, there were two acts of inspection for the earth and vegetation respectively. On the sixth day the Creator completed his work and used self-control to determine if further action was needed. The 31st verse of Genesis reads,

> *And God saw every thing that he had made, and, behold, it was very good.* (Gen. I:31)

Noah's Ark, Rework, Quality Planning, Quality Improvement, and Warranty

The concept of product quality is present in the Old Testament in many forms. God periodically reassessed his creation and, after initially finding it satisfactory, determined that it required rework. The decay of society's moral fabric led him to destroy all living creatures. Noah, a worthy example of God's creation, survives the impending destruction. Exact specifications for the ark that is to protect him from the deluge, along with a list of representatives of other species, can be found as close as five chapters after the act of Creation.

> *And this is the fashion which thou shalt make it of: The length of the ark shall be three hundred cubits, the breath of it fifty cubits, and the height of it thirty cubits.* (Gen. VI:15)
>
> *A window shalt thou make to the ark, and in a cubit shalt thou finish it above; and the door of the ark shalt thou set in the side thereof; with lower, second and third stories shalt thou make it.* (Gen. VI:16)

Modern scholars assume that one cubit = 20.6 inches = 52 centimeters so that the dimensions of Noah's ark were 156 meters in length, 26 meters in width, and 15.6 meters in height—an impressive construction project. Noah's story is a prime example of embarking on a new beginning after several unsuccessful improvement attempts were made. It also demonstrates that such an effort requires extensive planning and preparation.

After the deluge, the Lord first makes a promise to himself and then to Noah whereby total destruction of earth, God's creation, will not reoccur. A contract is established in very clear terms including a spectacular symbol of the expressed warranty—the rainbow.

> *. . . and the Lord said in his heart, I will not again curse the ground any more for man's sake . . . neither will I again smite any more every thing living, as I have done.* (Gen. VIII:21)
>
> *And God said, This is the token of the covenant which I make between me and you and every living creature that is with you, for perpetual generations. . . .* (Gen. IX:12)
>
> *I do set my bow in the cloud, and it shall be for a token of a covenant between me and the earth.* (Gen. IX:13)
>
> *And it shall come to pass, when I bring a cloud over the earth, that the bow shall be seen in the cloud. . . .* (Gen. IX:14)

Sodom and Gomorrah and Product Standards

The concept of *product* is omnipresent in the Old Testament. It applies to the total creation, to Noah's ark, and also to cities such as Sodom and Gomorrah. As God has promised that he will never again destroy his creation, Abraham allows himself to bargain with God about the destruction of Sodom and Gomorrah. Once a standard is established, whether or not the standard of excellence has been met can be assessed in order to determine if the cities are to be spared. In this instance, the criterion is the existence of "a few good men" in sufficient numbers to compensate, in their virtue, for the sins of their fellow citizens.

> *And Abraham drew near, and said, Wilt thou also destroy the righteous with the wicked? . . . and not spare the place for the fifty righteous that are therein?* (Gen. XVIII:23, 24)
>
> *. . . Peradventure ten shall be found there. And he said, I will not destroy it for ten's sake.* (Gen. XVIII:32)

The Ark of the Covenant and Product Specifications

Another product that received much attention and detail is the Ark of the Covenant containing the stone Tables of the Law. The specifications for this holy place are given in much greater detail than Noah's ark. Its unique role warrants the extensive details on size and type of materials to be used. Minute details such as outer dimensions, material for the Ark itself, the number and color of the veils and surrounding curtains are all described in the biblical verses.

> *And they shall make an ark of shittim wood: two cubits and a half shall be the length thereof, and a cubit and a half the breath thereof, and a cubit and a half the height thereof.* (Exod. XXV:10)
>
> *And thou shall make curtains of goats' hair to be covering upon the tabernacle: eleven curtains thou shall make.* (Exod. XXVI:7)
>
> *And thou shalt make a veil of blue, and purple, and scarlet, and fine twined linen with cherubims shall it be made of cunning work.* (Exod. XXVI:31)

Moses, Organizing for Quality and the Pareto Principle

During the Exodus from Egypt, the progress of the Israelites toward the Promised Land was hindered by the lack of effective social organization for teaching God's laws and for governing their society during and after the journey. Jethro, Moses' father-in-law, recognized that the entire enterprise was put at risk by the heavy burdens shouldered by Moses.

> . . . *Moses sat to judge the people: and the people stood by Moses from the morning unto the evening.* (Exod. XVIII:13)

> *And Moses' father in law said unto him, The thing that thou doest is not good.* (Exod. XVIII:17)

> *Thou wilt surely wear away, both thou, and this people that is with thee; for this thing is too heavy for thee; thou art not able to perform it thyself alone.* (Exod. XVIII:18)

To build a well-functioning society and to improve the quality of life, it was necessary for the Israelites to invent new ways of working together. Jethro advised Moses to begin with an emphasis on training.

> *And thou shalt teach them ordinances and laws, and shalt shew them the way wherein they must walk, and the work that they must do.* (Exod. XVIII:20)

He next suggested a form of organization that would empower others to relieve much of Moses' burden and gave specifications for selecting qualified individuals to fill the roles he was describing.

> *Moreover thou shalt provide out of all the people able men, such as fear God, men of truth, hating covetousness; and place such over them, to be rulers of thousands, and rulers of hundreds, rulers of fifties, and rulers of tens.* (Exod. XVIII:21)

Finally, Jethro proposed an approach that hints strongly at the Pareto principle to guide the work he had recommended.

> *And let them judge the people at all seasons; and it shall be, that every great matter they shall bring unto thee, but every small matter they shall judge: so shall it be easier for thyself, and they shall bear the burden with thee.* (Exod. XVIII:22)

Maintenance Work

However, complying with specifications does not guarantee a product free from deficiencies or wear and tear. Defects, maintenance work, and repairs are extensively documented in the Old Testament. In the second book of Kings, one finds a dialogue between King Jehoash, Jehoiada, and other priests on the method of payment for maintenance work at the Temple.

> *Then king Jehoash called for Jehoiada the priest, and the other priests, and said unto them, Why repair ye not the breaches of the house? Now therefore receive no more money of your acquaintance, but deliver it for the breaches of the house.* (II Kings XII:7)

In the second book of Chronicles one can learn how this maintenance work was eventually conducted.

> *And the king and Jehoiada . . . hired masons and carpenters to repair the house of the Lord, and also such as wrought iron and brass to mend the house of the Lord.* (II Chron. XXIV:12)
>
> *So the workmen wrought, and the work was perfected by them, and they set the house of God in his state, and strengthened it.* (II Chron. XXIV:13)

In some cases the damage was beyond repair and there is not even a mention of attempts to make repairs.

> *And the ships were broken, that they were not able to go to Tarshish.* (II Chron. XXI:37)

Workforce Qualifications, Training, and Rewards

Workforce needs and expectations is another issue dealt with in several parts of the Old Testament. In particular the concept of qualifying and training the workforce is delineated.

Worker qualifications for priesthood jobs were partly determined by age and lineage.

> *These were the sons of Levi . . . that did the work for the service of the house of the Lord, from the age of twenty years and upward.* (I Chron. XXIII:24)

Supervisors had to come from the Levite clan.

> *And the men did the work faithfully: and the overseers of them were Jahath and Obadiah, the Levites. . . .* (II Chron. XXXIV:12)

In addition to Jethro's recommendations to Moses already cited from Exodus XVIII:20, educational and training needs of the workforce are also addressed elsewhere.

> *And I have filled him with the spirit of God, in wisdom, and in understanding, and in knowledge, and in all manner of workmanship.* (Exod. XX:3)

Many Old Testament passages consist of descriptions of rewards and recognition for work well done.

> *The joints of thy thighs are like jewels, the work of the hands of a cunning workman.* (Song of Sol. VII:1)
>
> *. . . and let not your hands be weak: for your work shall be rewarded.* (II Chron. XV:7)
>
> *As a servant earnestly desireth the shadow, and as an hireling looketh for the reward of his work.* (Job VII:2)
>
> *. . . recompense her according to her work. . . .* (Jer. L:29)
>
> *The precious sons of Zion, comparable to fine gold, how are they esteemed as earthen pitchers, the work of the hands of the potter!* (Lam. IV:2)

Another form of reward is to establish pride of workmanship.

> *There is nothing better for a man than that he . . . should make his soul enjoy good in his labor.* (Eccles. II:24)

Knowledge and Vision

Finally, the Old Testament is very explicit on the need for knowledge and vision in organizations.

> *My people are destroyed for lack of knowledge. . . .* (Hos. IV:6)
>
> *Who is this that darkeneth counsel by words without knowledge?* (Job XXXVIII:2)
>
> *Where there is no vision, the people perish.* (Prov. XXIX:18)

The vision of perfection—the goal of many modern organizations—has a very early origin.

> *He is the Rock, his work is perfect. . . .* (Deut. XXXII:4)

This section considered examples of inspection; self-control; rework; quality planning and improvement; warranty; specifications; standards; workforce qualifications, training, and reward; and the visionary goal of perfection. Perfection is the ultimate goal of a six-sigma company whose defect levels are measured in parts per million. We are now ready to expand on specific topics supported by more elaborate examples. The next section deals with written standards and regulations.

Standards and Regulations

Information on how people lived and worked 2000 years ago is difficult to collect. However the written text provides us with surprisingly detailed clues on the standards and regulations they used to conduct their lives and work.

Material Durability

A procedure for testing the durability of materials is implicitly described in the following verses:

Take the girdle that thou hast got, which is upon thy loins, and arise, go to the Euphrates, and hide it there in a hole of the rock. (Jer. XIII:4)

And it came to pass after many days, that the Lord said unto me, Arise, go to Euphrates, and take the girdle from thence, which I commanded thee to hide there. (Jer. XIII:6)

Then I went to the Euphrates, and digged, and took the girdle from the place where I had hid it: and, behold, the girdle was marred, it was profitable for nothing. (Jer. XIII:7)

Food and Drink

Another product for which explicit standards were set was wine. To have wine turn to vinegar was a problem of economic and ritualistic consequences as the benediction of wine could not be performed with vinegar. Thus, the Talmud offers a procedure for determining the stage at which wine becomes vinegar.

If one tested a [wine] jug for the purpose of taking from it, . . . and, subsequently, it was found to contain vinegar. . . . During the first three days [after the test, it is regarded as] certain wine; after that, [as] doubtful. What is the reason?—[Because] wine [begins to] deteriorate from above, and this [man] had tested it [and ascertained that] it had not deteriorated; [and] if it be assumed that it had deteriorated [immediately] after it had been tasted, [even then during the first three days], it had the odour of vinegar and the taste of wine, and whenever the odour is of vinegar and the taste is of wine, it is regarded as wine. (Baba Bathra, VI:96a)

Health

Consumer goods were not the only aspect of life for which standards were established. The procedure for diagnosing leprosy delineates both the steps to be taken and the criteria to be used by a priest to determine if an individual is free of disease or must be quarantined.

When a man shall have in the skin of his flesh a rising, a scab, or bright spot, and it be in the skin of his flesh like the plague of lep-

rosy; then he shall be brought unto Aaron the priest. . . . (Lev. XIII:2)

And the priest shall look on the plague in the skin of the flesh: and when the hair in the plague is turned white, and the plague in sight be deeper than the skin of his flesh, it is a plague of leprosy: and the priest shall look on him, and pronounce him unclean. (Lev. XIII:3)

If the bright spot be white in the skin of his flesh, and in sight be not deeper than the skin, and the hair thereof be not turned white; then the priest shall shut up him that hath the plague seven days. . . . (Lev. XIII:4)

And the priest shall look on him the seventh day: and behold, if the plague in his sight be at a stay, and the plague spread not in the skin; then the priest shall shut him up seven days more. . . . (Lev. XIII:5)

And the priest shall look on him again the seventh day: and behold, if the plague be somewhat dark, and the plague spread not in the skin, the priest shall pronounce him clean: it is but a scab: and he shall wash his clothes and be clean. (Lev. XIII:6)

The Red Heifer and Sigma Levels

An example of quality levels in parts per million from 200 C.E. is provided by the requirements for the red heifer (red cow) used in sacrifices. The requirement is that animals with only red hair are to be sacrificed. The Mishnah indicates very clearly the standards to be applied and even provides a method of rework in case some black or white hair is found.

If it had two black or white hairs [growing] from within a single hole it is invalid. R. Judah says: Or even from within a single hollow. If they grew from within two hollows that were adjacent, it is invalid. R. Akiba says: Even though there were four or even five but they were dispersed, they may be plucked out. R. Eliezer says: Or even fifty. R. Joshua b. Bathyra says: Even though it has but one on its head and one on its tail, it is invalid. If there were two hairs with their roots black but their tips red, or their roots red but tips black, all is according to what is the more manifest.

So R. Meir. But the Sages say: According to the root. (Mishnah, Tehoroth, Parah, 5)

Municipal Regulations and Quality of Life

As society became more urbanized, municipal regulations were formulated to address relevant concerns and to improve quality of life.

> *If a tree overhangs a public thoroughfare the branches should be cut away to a height sufficient to allow a camel to pass underneath with its rider.* (Baba Bathra, II:27b)

> *He who owns a cistern within another man's house, goes in when it is usual for people to go in, and goes out when it is usual for people to go out. . . . One of them may make for himself a lock, and the other may [also] make for himself a lock. Where [is] the lock [to be attached]?—R. Jonathan said: Both to the cistern. This is right [in the case of] the owner of the cistern, [for] he has to protect the water of his cistern; but for what purpose does the owner of the house [require a lock]?—R. Eleazar said: In order [to avert] suspicion from his wife. (By affixing a lock to the cistern he prevents the other from using the water in his absence and, consequently, deprives him of the excuse of entering his house while his wife is alone.)* (Baba Bathra, VI:99a)

Consumers' Rights

A similar level of detail is given to regulating customer and suppliers' rights in commercial transactions.

> *And if thou sell ought unto thy neighbor, or buyest ought of thy neighbor's hand, ye shall not defraud one another. . . .* (Lev. XXV:14)

> *And if a man sell a dwelling house in a walled city, then he may redeem it within a whole year after it is sold; within a full year may he redeem it.* (Lev. XXV:29)

> *Four [different] laws [are applicable] to sales. [If] one has sold wheat as good, and it turns out to be bad, the buyer may withdraw [from the sale]. [If sold as] bad, and it turns out to be good, the seller may withdraw. [If as] bad, and it was found to*

be bad; [or as] good, and it was found to be good, neither may withdraw. (Baba Bathra, V:83b)

These regulations define service levels to be expected. They look much like modern warranty statements.

Measures and Weights

Many business transactions described in the Old Testament relied on barter where the exchange of goods or services did not require measurements. However, tracking how measurements were used provides another perspective on the period.

Abraham purchased the cave of the Machpelah with silver.

. . . and Abraham weighed to Ephron the silver, . . . four hundred shekels of silver, current money with the merchant. (Gen. XXIII:16)

The shekel was the basic unit of weight and the term means to weigh in all Semitic languages. Researchers have established that one shekel = 0.4 ounce = 11.4 grams so that the famous cave in Hebron cost Abraham about 4.5 kg of silver.

Other examples of measures of distance, angles, and volume used in the Old Testament include

And he set three days' journey betwixt himself and Jacob. . . . (Gen. XXX:36)

. . . the shadow go forward ten degrees. . . . (II Kings XX:9)

Yea, ten acres of vineyard shall yield one bath, and the seed of an homer shall yield an ephah. (Isa. V:10)

where one bath = 5 liquid gallons and one ephah = 5 dry gallons.

The practical need to have several units of measurement has led to a standardization of the pound, half pound, and quarter pound.

Our Rabbis taught: If one asked him for a pound, a pound must be weighted. [If] half a pound, half a pound must be weighted. A quarter of a pound, a quarter of a pound must be weighted.

What does this teach us?—That weights must be provided in these [three] denominations. (Baba Bathra, V:89a)

The Talmud also provides clear regulations on how length, volume, and weight measurements should be carried out.

Our Rabbis taught: . . . In meteyard *relates to the measuring of ground; one should not measure out for one person in the hot season (when the measuring rope is dry and unyielding) and for another in the rainy season (when the rope is moist and capable of extension).* In weight, *[means] that one shall not keep one's weights in salt (salt reduces the weight),* In measure, *that one shall not cause [liquids] to froth (by pouring rapidly from a certain height, foam is generated and, consequently, less liquid enters the measure).* (Baba Bathra, V:89b)

Rab Solomon said in the name of Rab: A person is forbidden to keep in his house a measure [which is either] smaller or larger [than the nominal capacity] even if [it is used as a] urine tub (even if not intended to be used for measuring purposes; since others may use it as a measure, by mistake). (Baba Bathra, V:89b)

The Talmud is even alert to the danger of tolerance stack-up and provides a procedure for avoiding it.

Our Rabbis taught: If he ordered from him ten pounds, he shall not say, "Weigh out for me each [pound] separately and allow overweight [for each]." But all are weighted together and one overweight is allowed for all of them. (Baba Bathra, V:89a)

The Old Testament is very explicit in requiring honest measurement.

Ye shall do no unrighteousness in judgement, in meteyard, in weight, or in measure. (Lev. XIX:35)

Just balances, just weights, a just ephah, and a just hin, shall ye have. (Lev. XIX:36)

The corruption at the end of the First Temple era, as described by Amos, is also apparent in the use of measurements.

. . . making the ephah small, and the shekel great, and falsifying the balances by deceit? (Amos VIII:5)

Measuring devices need maintenance and calibration. The proper maintenance procedure for scales is widely debated in the Talmud. The following quotation sounds like a dialogue between two contemporary engineers.

A wholesale dealer must clean his measures once in thirty days, and a producer once in twelve month. R. Someon b. Gamliel says: The statement is to be reversed. A shopkeeper must clean his measures twice a week, wipe his weights once a week and cleanse the scales after every weighing. (Baba Bathra, V:88a)

The use of measures also requires an organizational structure for traceability to assure that measures are comparable. The Levites were assigned this responsibility and it is written that, as part of their duties as priests, they will oversee measurements.

. . . their office was to wait on the sons of Aaron for the service of the house of the Lord, in the courts, and in the chambers, and in the purifying of all holy things, and the work of the service of the house of God. . . . (I Chron. XXIII:28)
. . . and for all manner of measure and size. . . . (I Chron. XXIII:29)

Buildings and Dwellings

Specifications for the Temple of Solomon

The most renowned temple at the time was the Temple of Solomon in Jerusalem. It was completed around 950 B.C.E., with the aid of Phoenician artisans, and was destroyed in 586 B.C.E. Most present-day knowledge about this temple comes from the Old Testament and from evidence supplied by other contemporary temples. Apparently the Temple faced east and had three main rooms disposed axially with the entrance. The anteroom, or *Ulam*, was a rectangular space entered through one of the short sides; flanking the Ulam were square rooms that led to the small storage rooms, or *Yasiya*, that surrounded the Temple on the other three sides. Beyond the Ulam was the main sanctuary, or *Hekal*, and beyond that, a flight of stairs that led to the Holy of Holies, or *Debir*, where the Ark of the Covenant was kept. The Temple was built out of stone and had a flat wooden roof made from imported cypresses and cedar. Bronze pillars known as *Yakhin* and *Boaz*, which may have symbolized the relationship between the monarchy and the Temple, stood in front of the edifice.

Specifications for the Temple of Solomon are given in such details that modern scientists are able to prepare reconstructed models of a temple erected almost three millennia ago.

> *And the house which king Solomon built for the Lord, the length thereof was threescore cubits, and the breath thereof twenty cubits, and the height thereof thirty cubits.* (I Kings VI:2)

> *And the porch before the temple of the house, twenty cubits was the length thereof, according to the breath of the house; and ten cubits was the breath thereof before the house.* (I Kings VI:3)

Planning for Quality

The careful preparation of the stones before they were brought to the construction site indicate thorough planning and quality control that enabled the actual construction to proceed more effectively.

> *And the house, when it was in building, was built of stone made ready before it was brought thither: so that there was neither hammer nor axe nor any tool of iron heard in the house, while it was in building.* (I Kings VI:7)

The Customer–Supplier Relationship Between King Solomon and Hiram of Lebanon

A major supplier to the Temple builders was Hiram of Lebanon who provided cedar trees. These trees are still world-famous for their quality and strength. The customer–supplier relationship between King Solomon and Hiram of Lebanon is described in an almost journalistic style. It appears that they were able to establish a win–win relationship.

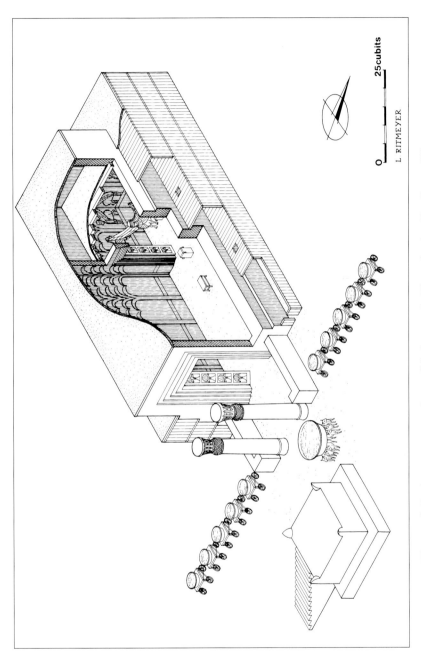

Figure 2.1 A reconstruction of Solomon's Temple, by Dr. Leen Ritmeyer.

Now therefore command thou that they hew me cedar trees out of Lebanon; . . . for thou knowest that there is not among us any that can skill to hew timber like unto the Sidonians. (I Kings V:6)

And Hiram sent to Solomon, saying, I have considered the things which thou sentest to me for: and I will do all thy desire concerning timber of cedar, and concerning timber of fir. (I Kings V:8)

My servants shall bring them down from Lebanon unto the sea: and I will convey them by sea in floats unto the place that thou shalt appoint me, and will cause them to be discharged there, and thou shalt receive them: and thou shalt accomplish my desire, in giving food for my household. (I Kings V:9)

So Hiram gave Solomon cedar trees and fir trees according to all his desire. (I Kings V:10)

And Solomon gave Hiram twenty thousand measures of wheat for food to his household, and twenty measures of pure oil: thus gave Solomon to Hiram year by year. (I Kings V:11)

Organization of Solomon's Workforce

Organizing the workforce needed to build the Temple of Solomon was no trivial task. Most workers were drafted by royal decree. The book of Kings describes the hierarchical structure of the workforce as well as employment conditions.

And king Solomon raised a levy out of all Israel; and the levy was thirty thousand men. (I Kings V:13)

And he sent them to Lebanon, ten thousand a month by courses: a month they were in Lebanon, and two months at home: and Adoniram was over the levy. (I Kings V:14)

And Solomon had threescore and ten thousand that bare burdens, and fourscore thousand hewers in the mountains. . . . (I Kings V:15)

Beside the chief of Solomon's officers which were over the work, three thousand and three hundred, which ruled over the people that wrought in the work. (I Kings V:16)

And the king commanded, and they brought great stones, costly stones, and hewed stones, to lay the foundation of the house. (I Kings V:17)

And Solomon's builders and Hiram's builders did hew them, and the stone squarers: so they prepared timber and stones to build the house. (I Kings V:18)

Quality Planning and Control for the Temple of Herod

Solomon's Temple was destroyed by Nebuchadnessar II, 340 years after King Solomon's death. Five hundred and fifty years later, Herod rebuilt the Temple on a grandiose scale. Not satisfied with the size of the Temple Mount that Solomon had built, Herod doubled its span by lengthening the eastern wall and by building a new wall on the other three sides.

Herodian masonry has a characteristic fine finish with a flat, slightly raised, center boss and typical flat margins around the edges. As in the construction of Solomon's Temple, the stones were cut with such precision that mortar was not used to get a good fit between the stones. The stonecutters first straightened the face of the stone by chiseling the rock in such a way as to produce a flat vertical surface and a flat surface on the top. Quarrymen than inserted dry wooden beams into grooves cut at right angles. They would hammer them tightly into place and pour water over them. The water would cause the wood to swell, and under the consequent pressure the stones separated from the lower rock layer.

Some of these stones weigh over 50 tons and required special transportation techniques. The quarries were located uphill, about one mile from the Temple. Using the force of gravity, cranes, and ropes, the stones were positioned according to the architects' plans.

All these activities required proper quality planning and quality control. The precision of the stones implies strict compliance with specifications. In the heart of modern Jerusalem there still are 50-foot-long columns attached to the bedrock. These are the scrap from the stone cutting process. The workmen simply stopped work and left the damaged columns in place.

Specifications for a Partition Wall

On a more mundane level, the Talmud provides specifications of raw materials to be used in a partition wall put together by ordinary citizens.

If joint owners agree to make a Mehizah (a partition or divi-
sion) in a courtyard, they should build the wall in the middle. In
districts where it is usual to build of Gebil, Gazith, Kefisin or
Lebenim (names of various bricks), they must use such materials,
all according to the custom of the district. If Gebil is used, each
gives three handbreaths (because a wall of Gebil usually was six
handbreaths thick).... (Baba Bathra, I:2a)

Traditional Dwellings

Hirschfeld extensively studied Roman and Byzantine dwellings in the area and also interviewed Arab house builders that are still using traditional methods. These master builders have carried their trade for generations using preindustrial technologies that can be traced to the first century of the common era. Stone houses built hundreds of years ago are securely holding heavy cement constructions which were added in modern times to accommodate larger families.

Building a traditional stone house typically involves only one paid master builder. All other construction workers are members of the family for whom the house is built. The master builder is in charge of building the house from start to finish. He prepares the house plans, marks the plot of land under construction, and supervises the construction itself. The master builders rely on experience and good construction practices for meeting their customers' requirements. This expertise is passed on from fathers to sons, as a family secret.

Even though houses have kept a common external appearance, their interiors are designed to meet specific customer needs. The house plans themselves are rarely put on paper. A one-meter stick is used to measure lengths, especially of openings in the walls. Standardization of the size of doors and windows is needed in order to meet the carpenter's requirements. Once the walls are completed the most crucial step in the house building process begins. It involves putting the roof on the top of the house. One method of constructing a roof is to lay wooden beams across the side walls and cover them with leaves and mud. The drawbacks of this method are that such a roof requires yearly maintenance and that the beams' lengths pose a restriction on the size of the rooms. Stone arcs and cross vaults are a major improvement to the roofing method. They eliminate the need for maintenance and allow for bigger rooms to be constructed.

Hirschfeld concludes his study by stating that a big improvement in Byzantine construction standards was achieved by recognizing the master builders as professionals who are in charge of a turnkey construction project. Traditional stone houses are therefore examples of quality planning, quality control, and quality improvement.

Roads and Tunnels

This section focuses on examples of civil engineering projects. The first example is a famous tunnel constructed 27 centuries ago. The other examples are derived from an exhaustive study of Roman roads in Israel.

The Tunnel of Siloam

In the city of Jerusalem, at the entrance of the Siloam tunnel, there is an inscription by an unknown author who lived in 700 B.C.E., during the reign of Hezekiah, king of Judea. It states,

> *This is the boring through. This is the story of the boring through: whilst the miners lifted the pick each towards his fellow and whilst three cubits yet remained to be bored through, there was heard the voice of a man calling his fellow, for there was a split in the rock on the right hand and on the left hand. And on the day of the boring through the miners struck, each in the direction of his fellow, pick against pick. And the water started flowing from the source to the pool twelve hundred cubits. A hundred cubits was the height of the rock above the head of the miners.*

One can only admire the skills of these workers who began digging a tunnel from two opposing ends and achieved incredible accuracy without modern technology.

The books of Kings and Chronicles mention many other hydraulic engineering projects accomplished by King Hezekiah.

> *And the rest of the acts of Hezekiah, and all his might, and how he made a pool, and a conduit, and brought water into the city, are they not written in the book of the chronicles of the kings of Judah?* (II Kings XX:20)

*This same Hezekiah also stopped the upper watercourse of Gihon,
and brought it straight down to the west side of the city of David.*
(II Chron. XXXII:30)

Roman Roads

An impressive indication of the high level of cultural and commercial
activity in Roman times is provided by the Roman road network
throughout the provinces of Judea. About 1000 Roman miles (1500
km) of major roads were gradually built with accompanying bridges,
supporting terraces, and land leveling operations, as well as many an-
cillary constructions such as caravanserai, reservoirs, guard stations,
milestones, and other official structures. The earliest milestone found
in Israel is from 69 C.E. It was discovered in the outskirts of the city of
Afula near Mount Tabor. The milestone inscription testifies to roadlaying work undertaken by soldiers of the tenth legion on the Cae-
sarea—Scythopolis Road, under the care of its commander, Marcus
Ulpius Traianus (Emperor Trajan's father). During wartime, the
roads were under the responsibility of the military authorities. However, in times of peace, the roads were under the jurisdiction of the
provincial administration. An example of roadbuilding in Judea during a military campaign can be found on Trajan's column in Rome.

What were the Roman techniques of roadlaying, and how did
they choose and plan the proposed routes? In the valleys and flatlands,
the Romans chose as straight a route as possible. However, Roman
engineers did not hesitate to circumvent areas that would make roadlaying difficult. Roll and Ayalon (1986) studied construction methods
of Roman roads in western Samaria and found adherence to standards
enforced throughout the Roman Empire. In particular the builders
first cleared the future roadway down to bedrock to provide a firm
base for the fill. They then proceeded to lay a filler consisting of larger
stones which was eventually covered with a layer of smaller stones and
earth. This roadlaying process gives some elasticity to the road and
prevents damage from earth movements and traffic vibrations. Finally,
a pavement consisting of large rough stones was laid closely, with the
flat sides up, so as to make a reasonably smooth surface for traffic. In
later periods, roads were paved with fairly small stones. The roads
were completed with either a single row of large curbstones or a supporting wall. Planning and execution of such a network of roads required extensive knowledge of quality planning and quality control.

Some of the Roman roads in Judea and Samaria are still in use today, an impressive tribute to Roman quality achievements.

Pottery

Pottery is easy to break but difficult to destroy. There is therefore more evidence of the potter's craft than of any other trade in Old Testament times. Archaeologists have traditionally used pieces of jars and jugs to date the various strata of excavated sites. Indeed, excavations in the Holy Land have revealed pottery as old as any known in the world.

The clay used was usually a red variety taken from just below the surface of the soil. Before it was ready to be placed on the wheel chemical impurities had to be removed and it had to be broken up into an homogeneous dough of clay. Leaving the clay in the sun, rain, and frost, before it was kneaded by treading, was adequate preparation for most items. If a clay of better quality was required, an additional filtering was performed using large vats. This is reminiscent of modern attempts at improving quality by additional testing and inspection. For example, higher-quality components for military systems undergo additional testing steps over and beyond their civilian counterparts. Special applications required certain additives to be mixed with the clay. For example, crushed limestone was added to prepare clay for heat-resistant cooking pots.

The potters of the Old Testament produced articles for everyday life such as storage jars, house lamps, cooking pots, pitchers, and children's toys. They used mass-production methods using the fast-spinning potter's wheel. The wheel was fixed to the top of a spindle which ran through the center of another wheel below. The lower wheel was heavier to give momentum as the potter spun it by hand. Evidence of foot-operated mechanisms dates from 200 B.C.E. In order to satisfy demand, various mass-production methods were applied. For example, a great cone of clay would be worked on the wheel and articles would be shaped and pinched off from the top until it was all used up. Using a similar concept, modern machines for automatic placement of electronic components on printed circuit boards carry cartridges of individual components.

Standardized shapes and sizes were developed so that the various manufacturing stages could be divided among different workers. Young apprentices were responsible for making handles of jars. Indeed, their inexpert fingers have left traces which are still visible. Apprentices would also rough out articles which were then handed to skilled craftsmen to finish. There is evidence from stamps and trademarks that potters worked together in cooperative enterprises consisting of families or guilds.

After the clay was turned into a vessel that was shaped on the wheel it was left to dry and harden. The vessel was then returned to the wheel for finishing operations using cutting tools. The final step consisted of baking in a furnace. Quality deficiencies of amphoras used for storage have been amply reported and studied in the Mishnah and Talmud. See, for example, Brand (1953) for an investigation into the causes of poor quality in pottery and the methods for repairing these deficiencies using tar.

Discussion

This last section reviews and discusses the overall picture drawn in the previous seven sections. The first lesson learned is that inspection is a natural complement to creation. The book of Genesis also demonstrates, with Noah's story, that improvement efforts do not always succeed and sometimes there is a need for planning a new beginning. The warranty—embodied by the rainbow—that God will not destroy civilization again led Abraham to bargain for the survival of Sodom and Gomorrah. Standards and warranties often lead to such discussions.

The Old Testament also demonstrates that important projects, such as the Ark of the Covenant and Solomon's Temple, require detailed specifications. The references to the Temple bring out the point that maintenance work has to be budgeted and that there is a need to develop trustworthy suppliers and organize the workforce.

The Talmud and Mishnah provide detailed examples of procedures in economic, medical, and religious applications. Such detailed descriptions of procedures have made these ancient processes accessible to our modern days. The chapter provides several examples on the need for standardization, such as in buildings and pottery. Finally it is worth noting that the concept of special orders has a long history. An example of this is the requirements for red cows to be used in sacrifices.

Godfrey (1988) lists seven milestones that delineate a road map for the top management of organizations planning their journey toward continuous quality improvement. These milestones provide, with some modifications, an excellent frame of reference for discussing some of the examples presented in this chapter. The milestones are

1. *Awareness* of the competitive challenges and current competitive position: Competitive challenges were practically nonexistent in ancient times. Hiram of Lebanon had a monopoly on the supply of cedar trees. The quality of his products was essential to uphold his reputation as a supplier, but no efforts had to be invested in "beating the competition."

2. *Understanding* of the definition of quality and of the role of quality in the success of the organization: Major projects require detailed planning and quality of execution. The Siloam tunnel is one such example. Other examples are provided by the Temples of Solomon and Herod. However, defects in ancient storage vessels seemed to be the norm, and fixing these defects appears to have been an acceptable practice.

3. *Vision* of how good the organization can really be: The Old Testament is very explicit on the need for a vision and the Ten Commandments provided such a vision for the Israelites. Clearly King Solomon had a vision for his kingdom and so did Bar-Kokhba who rebelled against the Romans in order to let his people practice their religion. A far-reaching example of the power of a vision is provided by the Jewish people in exile, who, for over 2000 years, kept alive the vision of their return to their homeland.

4. *Planning* for action with clearly defined steps needed in order to achieve the vision: Very few examples of large-scale planning exist in written form, but some clearly defined steps have been recorded. Jethro's advice to Moses contained detailed steps for teaching, guiding, and governing the Israelites during their journey to the Promised Land. The Arab master builders plan the construction of the traditional house in detail but do not put anything in writing. The Old Testament provides very elaborate details on specifications of various construction projects—completing these projects required quality planning and control, but, again, there are no records of such plans.

5. *Training* of the people so as to provide the knowledge, skills and tools needed to make the plan happen: The need for training of workers is clearly recognized in the Old Testament. Training is also necessary for individuals to comply properly with religious laws and regulations.

6. *Support* actions taken to ensure that changes are made, problem causes are eliminated, and gains are held: Records of actual improvements are scarce. However, indirectly, one can observe improvements such as in the construction of traditional houses.

7. *Rewards and recognition* of achievements to make sure that quality improvements spread throughout the organization and become part of the business plan: Master craftsmen are a major way quality standards are maintained and quality improvements are spread from generation to generation, and they are recognized in several verses of the Old Testament. Roman milestones, carrying the names of the troops' commanders, recognized their achievements and have made them famous throughout human history.

In sum, the history of ancient Israel provides examples that demonstrate many of the basic principles of quality management. Quoting again from Juran: "For most companies and managers, annual quality improvement is not only a new responsibility; it is also a radical change in style of management—a change in culture. . . ." This chapter demonstrates that the concepts of managing for quality are deeply rooted in the Cradle of Civilization. Managers interested in creating such a "radical change in style of management" might get inspired by going back to these sources.

Acknowledgments

In gathering material for this chapter I was generously helped by Ms. Ziva Patir and Mr. Rafael Levy, LL.B. of the Standards Institution of Israel and Dr. Etan Ayalon, Curator of the Man and his Work Center, Haarez Museum, Tel-Aviv, Israel. Ms. Lisa Sherwin's comments greatly improved the first draft and provided insights which were critical for the completion of this work.

Bibliography

Baras, Z., Safrai, S., Stern, M., and Tsafrir, Y., editors, *Erez Israel: From the destruction of the second Temple to the Muslim Conquest* (in Hebrew), Yad Yzhak ben-Zvi, Jerusalem, 1982.

Brand, Y., *Klei Haheres Besifrut Hatalmud* (Ceramics in Talmudic Literature, in Hebrew), Mossad Harav Kook, Jerusalem, 1953.

Danby, H., *The Mishna* (translated from the Hebrew with introduction and brief explanatory notes), Oxford University Press, London, 1933.

The Electronic Encyclopedia™, Grolier Electronic Publishing, Inc., 1988.

Epstein, I., editor, *The Babylonian Talmud: Tractate Baba Bathra,* Hebrew-English edition, The Soncino Press, London, Jerusalem, New York, 1976.

Godfrey, A. B., "Buried Treasures and Other Benefits of Quality," *The Juran Report,* 9, Summer 1988.

Heaton, E. W., *Everyday Life in Old Testament Times,* C. Scribner's Sons, New York, 1956.

Hirschfeld, Y., *Dwelling Houses in Roman and Byzantine Palestine* (in Hebrew), Yad Yzhak ben-Zvi, Jerusalem, 1987.

The Holy Scriptures: A Jewish Bible According to the Masoretic Text (Hebrew and English), Sinai Publishing House, Tel Aviv, 1972.

Juran, J. M., *Juran on Leadership for Quality: an Executive Handbook,* the Free Press, 1989.

Kotlar, D., *Human Ecology in the Ancient World (Eretz Israel, Greece and Rome)* (in Hebrew), M. Newman Publishing Co. Ltd, Jerusalem and Tel Aviv, 1976.

Levy, R., "Standards and Quality in Ancient Times, part I" (in Hebrew), *MATI: The Bulletin of the Standards Institution of Israel,* 18–19, June 1973.

———, "Standards and Quality in Ancient Times, part II" (in Hebrew), *MATI: The Bulletin of the Standards Institution of Israel,* 20–21, December 1973.

———, "Standards from Ancient Times to Modern Days" (in Hebrew), *MATI: The Bulletin of the Standards Institution of Israel,* 23, July 1974.

———, "Safety problems known to our ancestors" (in Hebrew), *MATI: The Bulletin of the Standards Institution of Israel,* 62, June 1987.

Ritmeyer, L., "Quarrying and Transporting Stones for Herod's Temple Mount," *Biblical Archaeological Review,* 6, pp. 46–48, November/December 1989.

Ritmeyer, K., and Ritmeyer, L., "Reconstructing Herod's Temple Mount in Jerusalem," *Biblical Archaeological Review,* 6, pp. 23–42, November/December 1989.

Roll, I., "The Roman Road System in Judea," in *The Jerusalem Cathedra: studies in the History, Archeology, Geography and Ethnography of the Land of Israel,* vol. 3. edited by L. I. Levine, Yad Izhak ben-Zvi Institute, Jerusalem; Wayne State University Press, Detroit, 1983.

Roll, I, and Ayalon, E., "Roman Roads in Western Samaria," *Palestine Exploration Quarterly,* 113–34, July–December 1986.

Sperber, D., *Roman Palestine: 200–400 the Land,* Bar-Ilan University, Ramat Gan, 1978.

Steinsaltz, A., *The Essential Talmud,* Basic Books, Inc., New York, 1976.

Tuchman, B. W., *Bible and Sword: England and Palestine from the Bronze Age to Balfour,* Ballantine Books, New York, 1956.

Appendix

Chronology of Main Events

• 2000 B.C.E. Abraham enters the Holy Land after migrating from Ur on the Persian Gulf to Haran in Mesopotamia and from there to the land of Canaan. Eventually the Hebrews migrate to Egypt and settle in the fertile eastern part of the Nile called the land of Goshen.

• 1250 B.C.E. Moses leads the Exodus of Hebrews to the Holy Land from Egypt.

• 1020 B.C.E.–926 B.C.E. Kingdoms of Saul, David, and Solomon, divided into 12 administrative districts, undergo rapid development. The period is characterized by heavy taxation and grandiose projects. King Solomon indubitably puts Israel on the international map.

• 950 B.C.E.–586 B.C.E. First Temple era. Solomon's glorious 40 years are followed by chaos. After his death in 926 B.C.E. the kingdom is split into two: Israel (in the north) and Judea (in the south). The prophets Amos, Hosea, Isaiah, and Micah provide firsthand evidence of the corruption, collapse of justice, and greed of the period.

• 721 B.C.E. Sargon II of Assyria conquers and liquidates northern Israel, deporting 27,000 prisoners.

• 586 B.C.E. Fall of Jerusalem to Nebuchadnessar II, followed by a second deportation of thousands of Judeans to Babylon.

- 586 B.C.E.–536 B.C.E. Babylonian captivity.
- 539 B.C.E. Cyrus of Persia topples Babylonian Empire and frees Jerusalem.
  - 539 B.C.E.–332 B.C.E. Persian rule.
  - 520 B.C.E. Zerubbabel begins rebuilding the Temple.
  - 515 B.C.E. Rebuilt Temple inaugurated.
  - 332 B.C.E.–140 B.C.E. Greek rule.
  - 167 B.C.E.–162 B.C.E. Maccabean revolt.
  - 140 B.C.E.–63 B.C.E. Hasmonean dynasty.
  - 63 B.C.E. Pompey conquers Jerusalem.
- 37 B.C.E.–4 B.C.E. Herod is crowned by the Romans as King of the Jews.
  - 20 B.C.E. Herod begins reconstructing the Temple.
  - 4 B.C.E. Death of Herod.
  - 30 C.E. Crucifixion of Jesus Christ.
  - 66 C.E.–70 C.E. First Jewish Rebellion repressed by Gesius Florus.
  - 70 C.E. Destruction of Herod's Temple by Titus.
  - 73 C.E. Fall of Massada.
  - 132 C.E.–135 C.E. Bar-Kokhba's rebellion repressed by Hadrian.
- 200 C.E. Codification of the Mishnah by Rabbi (R.) Judah Ha-Nassi who succeeded in classifying and organizing oral laws into a fundamental document of great importance and sanctity to the Jewish people.
  - 200 C.E.–500 C.E. The Amoraim interpret the Mishnah.
- 499 C.E. Codification of the Babylonian Talmud (R. Ashi) and the Palestinian Jerusalem Talmud (R. Yohanan). The Talmud is an uncompleted summary of discussion and elucidation of the Mishnah that evolved through centuries of scholarly efforts by sages who lived in Palestine and Babylonia.
  - 324 C.E.–640 C.E. The Byzantine era.
  - 632 C.E. Death of the prophet Muhammad
  - 637 C.E. Arab conquest by the Omayyad caliphs.

CHAPTER 3

Quality Management in the Construction of Ancient Greek Temples and Theaters

Dr. A. S. Frontistis, Chairman
Effective Management International, Ltd.
Athens, Greece

Introduction

Greece, or in the term the Greeks themselves have always employed, Hellas, is a member country of the European Community, located on the southern end of the Balkan peninsula. In antiquity, Greek communities were scattered from Phasis, at the eastern end of the Black Sea, all the way to the Pillars of Gibraltar and to the Atlantic Ocean. With a current population of ten million people in the country, and at least another ten million spread all over the world, Hellas's contributions to Western civilization have been much greater than its size. There is wide consensus that Hellas has been the cradle of European civilization and democracy and the base of the European culture.

The legacy of Greece and its contributions to the Western world cover a wide area of human endeavor, activities, and achievements. Indeed, the Greeks invented politics in the sense that they located the source of authority in the *polis* (city-state) and decided on policy in open discussion. Homer's *Iliad* and *Odyssey* are by general consent the beginning of European literature. Greek poetry includes every kind and has been written more or less continuously from the sixth century B.C. to the present day; indeed, two Greek poets have been awarded the Nobel Prize for poetry since the Second World War. There is no disagreement on the fact that European drama is descended from ancient Greek tragedy and comedy. *History* is a Greek word (*historia*), and the Greek historian Herodotus is accepted as the Father of History. Science, technology, and mathematics were founded by ancient Greeks—Aristotle, Archimedes, Euclid, Democrates, Pythagoras, Hippocrates, just to mention a few. The Greeks initiated and developed all the major fields of philosophy; Greece is the home country of Socrates and Plato. In the fields of economy, ship construction, agriculture, metal working, and others, the Greeks made important, almost unique contributions.

Last, but not least, architecture and the figural arts were developed almost to perfection by ancient Greeks, as evidenced by the many buildings and art pieces uncovered by excavations during the last hundred years.

This chapter is an account of the quality management system the ancient Greeks practiced in the building of temples and theaters.

Figure 3.1 The Parthenon and the Erechtheion on the Acropolis of Athens. Source: "Hannibal," Athens, used by permission.

The Quality of Greek Architecture As Evidenced in Ancient Temples and Theaters

In the general calamities of mankind the death of an individual, however exalted, the ruin of an edifice, however famous, are passed over with careless inattention. Yet, we cannot forget that the temple of Diana at Ephesus, after having risen with increasing splendor from seven repeated misfortunes, was finally burnt by the Goths in their third naval invasion. The arts of Greece and the wealth of Asia had conspired to erect that sacred and magnificent structure. It was supported by a hundred and twenty-seven marble columns of the Ionic order; they were the gifts of devout monarchs, and each was sixty feet high. The altar was adorned with the masterly sculptures of Praxiteles, who had, perhaps, selected from the favorite legends of the place of the birth of the divine children of Latona, the concealment of Apollo after the slaughter of the Cyclops, and the clemency of Bacchus to the vanquished Amazons. . . . The temple of Diana was . . . admired as one of the wonders of the world. Successive empires, the Persian, the Macedonian, and the Roman had revered its sanctity, and enriched its splendor.

—Edward Gibbon

Thus does Gibbon deliver a eulogy upon one of the foremost glories of the ancient world in his inimitable manner. In so doing, he calls to mind the excellence that was the mark of ancient Greek temples. As shown by the example of the temple of Artemis at Ephesus, aesthetic sensibility was the quality that elevated Greek architecture.

Although there has been agreement down the ages on the excellence of ancient Greek architecture and its aesthetic effect, questions remain to be explored concerning its causes. For example, how did the ancient Greeks organize their scarce resources so as to produce such lasting memorials? How did they work the raw materials? What was the rationale behind their unified approach to architecture?

The following examination of the various ways quality was built into the progress of construction and was managed suggest some of the answers to such questions. This examination is followed by a review of some of the most famous sites to clarify the interpretations offered.

Quality Management

Architects played a decisive role in the building of temples in classical Greece, and were, in the final analysis, responsible for the high standard of quality attained. More than just another craftsman or merely an overseer, the architect was the person who designed a temple and saw it through to completion. Skopas of Paros provides clear-cut evidence that such was the case: archaeological remains and literary evidence show that this architect of the fourth century B.C. conceived the design, oversaw the operations, and took part in the work to establish the temple of Athena Alea at Tegea.[1] The architect entered into a contract with the overseers of a sanctuary to provide models for the construction of a temple. In one of the earliest epigraphical notices regarding these models (*paradeigmata*), it is stated in a law of 449 B.C. at Athens that the temple of Athena Nike will be built according to Kallikrates' description.[2]

The models used in describing a temple seem to have consisted of full-scale replicas of architectural components (such as capitals for columns), and perhaps measurement for others.[3] Using the models provided, craftsmen would quarry the stones and finish cutting them on the site for final incorporation into the temple. Measurements were important for acquiring materials that would be consistent within a building, and the architect was responsible for these. The architect was also on-site to see that the parts of the temple were correctly assembled.

Epigraphical and literary evidence demonstrate that, from very early on, architects took responsibility for construction of temples. At Syracuse, Klemenes and Epikles constructed the sixth-century B.C. temple of Apollo and their names were consequently inscribed in the stylobate; the architects Trophonios and Agamedes were immortalized in epic poetry for their foundation at Delphi.[4] From conception through completion, the architect was the craftsman present to see that all went according to a plan agreed upon in the contract.

The fact that architects were considered craftsmen of a sort by the ancient Greeks raises the question of training. Indeed, how did architects become adept at their profession so that they might provide models, oversee the general construction, and deal with technical difficulties encountered? Very little remains of the once vast corpus of literature by ancient architects. Mathematicians from Alexandria in the late fourth and early third centuries B.C. make occasional comments on architecture that sometimes throw light on the question, but the building of temples lies at the periphery of their interests.[5] The main importance of their writings for our interests derives from the way in which they serve as means for verifying the reliability of later Roman authors who are directly concerned with Hellenic art and architecture. Vitruvius' work in Latin dates from the late first century B.C. and is more authoritative for practices in his own day, but materials pertinent to Hellenic usage do survive.[6] Pliny the Elder wrote a natural history in the first century A.D. and included much material gleaned from earlier accounts, but the same limitations apply.[7] Writing in the mid–second century A.D., Pausanias mentions architects associated with specific buildings, but does not mention the corpus.[8] Study of these surviving references indicates that architects wrote down accounts of their systematic approach to construction.[9] Thus did they pass on the wisdom that they had gained in dealing with practical matters. To a certain extent, then, architects learned their craft through study of their predecessors.

Evidence does exist to support the pragmatic view that the development of Greek architecture involved considerable trial and error by the architects. Philon's comment upon the systematic changes that occurred in temple building seems illustrative of the way in which advances took place.

> *For it was not possible to create the [proper] forms of buildings from the start, without first engaging in experiment, as is clear indeed from ancient buildings, which are extremely unskillful not only in construction, but also in the design of forms for the individual parts. The change to what was required was not the result of a single or random experiment; some of the individual parts of a building, although they were in fact of equal thickness and straight, seemed to be neither of equal thickness nor straight, because our sight is misled in such matters by differences in distance. So by trial and error, by adding to and subtracting from the sizes, by tapering, and by all sorts of experiment, they made them [the parts] in accordance with vision and, apparently, well-shaped; for this was the goal in that art.*[10]

Some have disputed this interpretation by claiming that it is too pragmatic, but one may well ask if the architect was not pragmatic who exchanged the use of whole columns—such as those found in the first Argive Heraion—for that of column drums—as were used in all Doric temples subsequent to the sixth century B.C.[11] It has been argued that the Greeks took the conception of a temple's various architectural parts from the Egyptians,[12] but, even if they did so, they broke with centuries of tradition by converting those parts into objects easily handled and not requiring the effort of multitudes of slaves or earthen ramps.[13]

Another matter of importance in considering the role of architects, is that of their social status. As a rule, architects seem to have come from families of substance. But their pay and relationship to the other craftsmen working upon the building still leave some doubt about their social position.[14]

Regulations

There are a few surviving examples of laws regulating the business of construction in ancient Greece. Two epigraphical pieces of evidence indicate the legal status quo at Tegea and Eretria.[15] They indicate a highly developed litigation system and a need to state in clear terms the liabilities accruing to the various parties.

A law governing the execution of contracts survives from fourth century B.C. Among its many concerns is the welfare of the workers.

> *And let the one injured dismiss the one doing the injury within three days from that on which the injury occurs, but not later, and whatever the officials letting the contract may decide shall be authoritative.*[16]

The law goes on to treat matters, such as war, that impede the progress of work.

> *If war shall prevent any of the jobs let out for contract or destroy any of those worked out, let the Three Hundred determine what must be done; let the generals make available the funds even if they think war is preventing or damaging the jobs, from the officer in charge of the booty which is in the city. If a person taking a contract does not take in hand the job, and war stops it, let him return the cash which he may have taken, and give up the job if the officials letting the contract bid.*[17]

War and shoddy workmanship were not the only practical problems requiring rectification. There was evident concern over the fair apportionment of work.

> *And if anyone resist the letting of contracts for the jobs or be abusive in any way that might be destructive, let the officials letting the contract assess such damages as they think proper and call them up to judgment and summon them into the court in session for the amount of the fine.*[18]

Care to ensure fair working practices extended itself as well to the specification of how contracts were to be undertaken. On occasion the law would specify a limit to the number of contractors and thereby reduce the possibility of losses on the sanctuary's part.[19]

Finally, the law covered actions taken at the site of work and dealt with issues ranging from abusive manners to damage incurred in the course of work.

> *And if any one of the contractors or those contracting seems to be insolent on the job or to disobey those supervising, or to be contemptuous of the penalties arranged, let the officials letting out the contracts have power to evict the worker from the job and assess damages on the contractor in adjudication, just as has been written shall be done to those resisting the letting of contracts.*[20]

The Letting of Contracts and Their Enforcement

A main reason for the high quality achieved in the ancient Greek temples was the efficient manner in which contracts were let out and their execution enforced. Personal initiative seems to have been encouraged and flourished accordingly; however, the penalties for failure and the mechanisms for smooth functioning of the process kept a close, practical rein upon the system. An example of personal initiative is found within the accounts for the building of the Prostoon of the Telesterion at Eleusis. The desire to earn the bonus offered by moving material as quickly and inexpensively as possible drove down the price of the job until someone made a mess of the job which led to legal complications.[21]

Fines for unsatisfactory workmanship and for delays provided another incentive to contractors to finish the work on time.[22] The judicious utilization of bonuses and fines helped to bring ancient Greek temples to fruition.

The initial step of letting out a contract for work was itself designed to minimize the financial losses that could possibly accrue to the undertaking. As noted in the previous section, a law at Tegea stated,

> *Let it not be possible that there be in common more than two contractors for any of the jobs. Otherwise let each one owe fifty drachmae. . . .*[23]

This piece of legislation seems to have had, for its immediate aim, a reduction of conflicts of opinion on the work site. Of course, accomplishment of the immediate goal meant that the operation would also be more financially sound. Avoidance of dissension among the workers saved time, and saving of time meant saving of money—which was always a precious commodity for such projects.[24] An inscription for work upon Delos reveals another way in which financial risk in the letting of contracts was reduced. It states that a guarantor is to be appointed for every 1000 drachmae of the contract price.[25] This provision spread the financial risk of default more widely and thereby reduced its probability.

Quality Planning

The Periclean program of construction—as described by Plutarch—shows the heights that ancient quality planning could reach.[26] Construction was undertaken with a comprehensive view of its diverse aspects. From the obsessive search for the best marble available on Pentelikon (a mountain near Athens) to the calculation of political gains deriving from urban beautification, quality was at a premium. What the state could achieve thereby is seen in buildings such as the Parthenon, the Propylaea of Mnesicles, and the Erechtheion.

The Arsenal of Philon, albeit on a smaller scale, serves as another admirable example of quality planning. Surviving specifications for this building show what Philon contracted to do.[27] The people (that is, the *demos* or government) were concerned with the building's having adequate space for passage and displaying the tackle of the

Figure 3.2 Mnesicles' Propylaea of the Acropolis of Athens. Source: Editions "Hannibal," Athens, used by permission.

Athenian fleet. These are the requirements that were inscribed for public display, and they are apparent within the surviving structure as well.

For a final example of quality planning, there is the case afforded by the Tholos at Epidauros. Work there dragged on for a number of years under an inefficient administration. Then, as the records show, a new management took over the affair, and construction was completed in timely fashion.[28]

Quality Specifications and Controls

A glance at any Greek temple will immediately reveal the fact that different types of stone were utilized in the construction. Likewise, a comparison of temples at differing sites will indicate a wide range in the quality and type of stone used. The basis for the first observation is both structural and aesthetic. On the second point, economy and geography were the determining factors.

As a general rule, for monumental structures such as temples, porous and conglomerate stones were deemed worthy only for the foundation courses.[29] These types of stone were able to bear the weight, but did not weather well; hence their position within the building. Aesthetic sensibility also demanded that these coarse stones give way to the refined appearance of limestone and marble. The alteration in use of limestones and different varieties of marble was also due to the aesthetic effect achieved. Thus, the gray Eleusinian limestone and a pink marble are combined within the facade of the Propylaea on the Acropolis to shape the viewer's understanding of space.

Yet, the different types of marble to be found in Greek temples is itself due to the fact that transportation was costly and fraught with uncertainty. The end result was that the builders of temples sought their marble from as geographically convenient a source as possible. Therefore, while situated within Attica and theoretically having access to the marble of Hymmetos and Pentelikon, the temple of Rhamnous derived its marble from a much nearer source.[30]

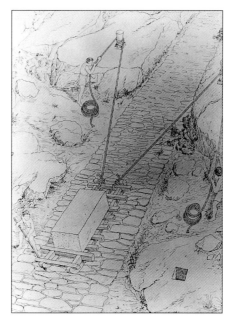

Figure 3.3 Marble being bought from Mount Pentelikon near Athens. Source: Orlandos, 1966–68. Used by permission of The Athens Archaeological Society.

The materials constituting the finished temple also included wood and metal. During the fifth century B.C., cypress wood was used for the *empolia* that connected column drums. For example, cypress wood was used in the *empolia* in the Erechtheion, as shown by tests conducted on wood uncovered in the course of restoration.[31] On the connecting sides of the two drums—lower and upper—were carved two square depressions, and in these were set the *empolia* to be joined by a centering pin of wood. Sometimes, as at Eleusis for instance, the *empolia* would instead consist of bronze.[32] Dowels were used to connect two courses of blocks, and, depending upon the circumstances, consisted of wood, lead, iron, or bronze.[33] Iron clamps were also widely used in construction for the purpose of securing joints within a particular course of blocks. The iron is quite suitable for this purpose because it possesses enough flexibility so that, with the change of seasons it does not fracture the expanding and contracting stone. The ancients ensured against damage from the iron by surrounding it with lead.[34] Finally, it should be noted that the use of *empolia* allowed for the better employment of column drums in place of monolithic columns. The reduction in accidents and expense must have been sizable.

Inspection of Products

An inscription from Lebadeia, in Boeotia, describes a process that seems to have been commonplace for the examination of products in the course of temple construction. The inscription provides a detailed account of the procedure for checking to see that the joints of blocks have been cut back smoothly.[35] Vermilion, a bright red pigment, was applied to a block termed a *kanon*. The kanon was a large block that was perfectly smooth and regular. Covered with the vermilion, it would be applied to the surface of a joint. If the coloration of the joint should prove uneven, it was clear that the joint was not yet physically even. In such a case, the temple overseers would demand, in accordance with the contract, that the worker cut away the uneven portions. Such a process would continue until satisfaction was achieved.

Quality Controls

To achieve the high quality of the ancient Greek temples, the builders had at hand a number of tools suited to special tasks. The inscriptions give information on most of these. For instance, a "half-sharp chisel" is specified within a Delian inscription, and the *anathyrosis* done at Lebadeia requires a "sharpened" chisel.[36]

To achieve the high quality of molding for their temple super-structure, the Greek architects employed templates, which were called *anagrapeis* or *paradeignata* by the ancients. Heron of Alexandria pro-vides a description of what these looked like.

> For there being three surfaces on the anagrapheus (which some also call emboleus) the two outer ones concave and the middle one convex, the revolution of these three generates the type of base (or toroid) which is set beneath columns.[37]

In recent times, such a template came to light in excavations at Kerkyra. Made of a thin sheet of lead, which was 0.117 m by 0.142 m and just over 1 mm thick, this *anagrapheus* has incised upon it the profile of a *cyma reversa* followed by a half-round. This example dates from the fifth century B.C. Confirmation of this find is provided by an unfinished block cut for a column base. The faint beginnings on this block preserve an outline like that of the template.[38]

Process Controls

In addition to the quality controls on the final product, controls were used during the building process. For example, the inscription relat-ing to the construction of the temple of Zeus the King at Lebadeia displays considerable care in the oversight of workmanship.[39] Lines 47–58 treat a common phenomenon in Greek temple building and yet, perhaps, also give an insight into why there is a tone of paranoia in the working of this particular inscription. The lines in question state that the worker will be paid in sections as the work progresses and that the remainder will be given upon completion of the job. Many inscriptions preserve evidence of a similar arrangement between the workers and the temple overseers in charge of the funds.[40] This ar-rangement existed so that people would not abscond with the money without having done the job. It seems that skilled craftsmen able to do the work required for completing a temple were in demand. If that was so, then Lebadeia would have had a hard time in obtaining and retaining workers by virtue of the locale's geographical isolation within the countryside of Boeotia. Unlike Athens or Epidauros, Lebadeia was not blessed with a location near a major commercial route.

Quality Improvement

Improvements in the quality of buildings occurred by increments and in various ways. Inventions facilitated the progress and ease of construction. Cranes allowed for the lifting of stone that otherwise would have required much more human effort.[41] At Didyma, the architect devised a special crane in order to lift the lintel block.[42] At Ephesus, as Vitruvius records, the architect made the ingenious decision to use blocks of marble, which were to be transported, as the axles for large wooden wheels.[43] Supposedly, the device made for an easy passage.

As noted by Philon of Alexandria, refinements were a way of improving the building aesthetically without need for any structural change in plan.[44] These refinements are small but unmistakably present. For example, the height of an exterior facet of the bottom drum of a corner column of the Parthenon is 4 cm greater than that of an interior facet of the same drum.[45] Other examples are the *entasis* (tapering) of the columns and the curvature of the stylobate of the Parthenon.

Tools and Techniques

Building inscriptions, occasional literary references, and Roman funeral monuments attest to a vast array of tools used in the construction of ancient Greek temples. These tools included hammers, points, chisels, and others. Each was suited for a particular task in the process of construction. For instance, as stipulated within the inscriptions from Lebadeia, one would use a toothed chisel (otherwise known as the clawed chisel) for rough work and a flat chisel for a finer texture.[46]

Other tools available to Greek temple builders include such things as the level (*diabetis*) and the *kanon*, both of which served, in different ways, to determine the finished state of a stone. The level consisted of pieces of wood put together to look like the letter *A* (*alpha*), whence the modern Greek name *alphadi*.[47] From the apex of the level, there hung a cord with a stone. If this cord inclined too far to one side or the other, it was an indication that the stone being

Figure 3.4 Relief showing cranes. From Orlandos, 1966–68.
Used by permission of The Athens Archaeological Society.

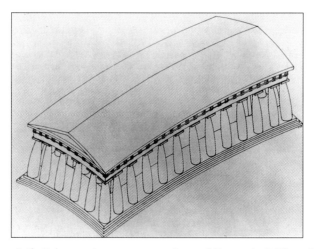

Figure 3.5 Schematic representation of "entasis." The sketch
deliberately exaggerates the effect. Source: Coulton, 1977.
Used by permission of Elek Books, Ltd.

checked was not level. As described earlier, the *kanon* was a large, even stone used to establish the even surface of the stones being incorporated into the building.[48]

Market Realities

In the ancient world, prices tended to be stable. Labor skilled for temple building seems to have been relatively scarce, and yet, as far as can be told, wages did not fluctuate greatly, nor were they high. Architects did not make large sums, if the Epidauran pay of one drachma per day is accepted as standard in the Greek world.[49] The cost of materials could vary somewhat as a result of bidding, but the force of circumstances caused this too to stabilize in a world where things were done in the traditional manner. An inscription relating to the Telesterion at Eleusis shows that bidding could drive prices lower in a competitive market.[50] But, as indicated in the description of that example, there was a limit, and this limit was quickly reached.

Training

The precise manner in which architects and craftsmen received their training is unknown. A corpus of architectural literature did exist in antiquity, but it most likely played a minor role in the making of architects. When architects wrote, it would seem that they described their solutions to specific problems encountered in the course of construction.[51] Far more pervasive and of greater import was tradition. As is the case in modern Greece, stonemasons learned their craft through an apprenticeship. This traditional approach reveals itself in things

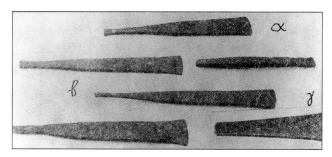

Figure 3.6 Stone-working tools. Source: Orlandos, 1966–68. Used by permission of The Athens Archaeological Society.

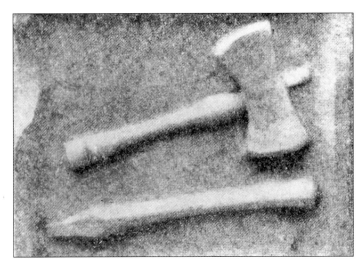

Figure 3.7 Stone-working tools. Source: Orlandos, 1966–68.
Used by permission of The Athens Archaeological Society.

such as the coinage of the term *anathyrosis* for the dressing of stones
to be joined. *Anathyrosis* means that a block's side that is to be joined
is to look like a door. Taken from the language of carpentry, this im-
agery suggests the fundamental conservatism of Greek craftsmen.[52]

The archaeological remains themselves give witness to a tradition
that was highly conservative. So slowly did the minutiae of the Doric
order evolve in mainland Greece that these details provide the basis
for the precise dating of temples. Only insofar as they were interested
in applying refinements for aesthetic reasons were architects progressive; otherwise, conservatism was their hallmark.

Characteristic Cases

Athens: The Acropolis

More than two millennia after their foundation, the Parthenon and its
associated buildings on the Acropolis continue to elicit viewers' admiration for the Athenian democracy that built them. Ancient sources
such as Thucydides and Pausanias also reveal the widespread admiration for "the foundations of Pericles," as Plutarch described them.[53]

Constructed in that Golden Age in which Pericles governed democratic Athens, these buildings give witness to the heights to which Greek labor and intellect could soar when given financial support. Just as rapidly as the Periclean Era—with its awe-inspiring building program—began, so did it close with the advent of the Peloponnesian War.[54] There would follow other examples of Greek excellence in the field of architecture, but none would be accomplished with such care in as short a span of time.

This short burst of architectural activity in Periclean Athens was a direct result of Athens fighting the Persian Empire in the first half of the fifth century B.C.[55] By the opening of that century, Athens had become a leading city of Greece by dint of her locale and maritime policies. When Persia took military action against Greece, Athens was first among those to oppose the invader, and consequently the city itself was ransacked and destroyed in two consecutive years.

Domestic quarters were rebuilt, but the temples remained in their ruinous condition in accordance with the Plataean Oath of 479 B.C. Affairs would remain thus for the next three decades while Athens led the Delian League in the fight against Persian influence in the eastern Mediterranean. Finally, in 451 B.C., after losses at Cyprus, the Persians decided to treat with the Athenians for a peace that recognized the status quo. In late 450 B.C., the Peace of Kallias formally ended hostilities between Athens and Persia. Then Pericles, a leading Athenian statesman, played an important role in the transformation of the League and the development of Athenian imperialism to the benefit of Athenian democracy. The treasury of the league was transferred from Delos to Athens, and Pericles himself effected the allotment of five talents to the building program.

Plutarch describes the implementation of Pericles' plan, which had quality as its concern.

He boldly laid before the people proposals for immense public works and plans for buildings, which would involve many different arts and industries and require long periods to complete, his object being that those who stayed at home, no less than those serving in the fleet or the army or on garrison duty, should be enabled to enjoy a share of the national wealth. The materials to be used were stone, bronze, ivory, gold, ebony, and cypress-wood, while the arts or trades which wrought or fashioned them were those of carpenter, modeller, copper-smith, stone-mason, dyer, worker in gold and ivory, painter, embroiderer, and engraver, and besides these the carriers and suppliers of the materials, such as merchants, sailors, and pilots for the sea-borne traffic, and wagon-makers, trainers of draught animals, and drivers for everything that came by land. There were also rope-makers, weavers, leather-workers, road-builders and miners.[56]

With such a workforce, the construction of the buildings upon the Acropolis proceeded apace.

Refinements, modification of Doric principles in temple architecture, and dealings of the state directly with the laborers were just a few of the ways in which quality came to be embedded in the Parthenon. The state contracted with the laborers and avoided the problems of middlemen. The Doric canon itself was changed for the purposes of the Parthenon. Far from canonical is this best-known example of Doric architecture. The number of columns in the *peripteros* was not according to standard formulae. The interior of the temple had one more room than is standard. The use of frieze on a Doric temple was perhaps the most outstanding aberration. Yet the Parthenon would be unimaginable without that element which imitates the Persian reliefs of Persepolis and celebrates the Greek victory over the Persian Empire.

Athens: Theater of Dionysos

Immediately south of the Acropolis, the Theater of Dionysos today presents a mysterious spectacle with its various layers of alterations visible to tourists and scholars. The most influential theater ever built within the Greek world is also the most debated of all.[57] Ever since the building's conclusive identification and excavation in the nineteenth century, fierce controversy has raged over the dating of the different architectural stages. Insufficient archaeological evidence and the difficulty of reconciling literary evidence with the remains mean that a definitive conclusion is far from possible. What follows has been culled from the interpretations that seem most tenable in the light of present knowledge.

Originally Athenians held dramatic festivals within the open space of the Athenian agora. These festivals were held in honor of the god Dionysos Elefthereus.[58] However, their beginnings are shrouded in legend, and uncertainty even attaches to the introduction of the cult of Dionysos Elefthereus to Athens. In the middle of the fifth century B.C., the *ikria*—the wooden scaffolding for spectators—collapsed.[59] Following the collapse, a decision was made to build the first permanent theater in Athens and, in so doing, to place it where the Theater of Dionysos still stands today. The Athenians took advantage of the natural slope of the south side of the Acropolis to construct their theatron (viewing place). Some benches of wood and stone were placed upon the slope, and this was the aspect that the theater presented at the time of the great plays of Sophocles and Euripides.[60] Not until the latter half of the fourth century B.C. did the theater receive a permanent stage.

Delphi: Temple of Apollo

The sanctuary at Delphi was the seat of the most important oracle of Apollo within mainland Greece and received visitors from the whole of the Greek world.[61] In the seventh and sixth centuries B.C., the oracle became more renowned as first the western Greek colonies, and

Figure 3.8 The Temple of Apollo at Delphi. Source: Editions "Hannibal," Athens, used by permission.

then the rulers of Asia Minor, began sending deputations. In 582 B.C., the Pythian Games were instituted on a quadrennial basis with competitions like those of the Olympics. Because of its close connection to Sparta and an inept handling of the Persian advance against Greece, the sanctuary did not prosper as it might have. Yet throughout antiquity, it remained the object of veneration and amassed great wealth.

In the course of the sanctuary's history, three temples of Apollo were built. In the middle of the seventh century B.C., the architects Trophonios and Agamedes constructed the first.[62] Although very little survives of this structure, the evidence indicates that it was a well-built temple. In 548 B.C., a fire destroyed this temple. The Amphictyonic League, which was a board responsible for the upkeep of the sanctuary, undertook to finance a new temple. But problems with money caused the project to take 40 years to execute. Delphi's location made the transportation of stone for the temple extremely expensive.[63] The Alkmaionidai, a wealthy aristocratic family from Athens, stepped in and provided the funds for completion.[64] On their own volition, they paid for the substitution of Parian marble for porous stone in the eastern end of the temple. The final result was a Doric temple of large proportions with a *peripteros* of six by 15 columns. An earthquake destroyed this temple in 373 B.C. The third temple followed the plan of the former and reused what blocks it could for the sake of economy. For example, the old column drums were restored and their damaged sections covered over with stucco.[65] Although the temple builders were chary with money as the previous example indicates, the money still ran short. War broke out in the middle of the fourth century B.C. and funds for reconstruction were seized for other purposes. Eventually work resumed, and the temple was finished by approximately 330 B.C.

Delphi: Theater

Although technically located outside the sanctuary of Apollo at Delphi, the theater at Delphi is a part of the whole complex made up by the sanctuary with its dedications and the stadium. Pausanias, that second-century A.D. traveler and frugal bestower of compliments, noted that the theater was worth seeing.[66]

This theater is an example of a building whose construction dragged on for a long time because of a dearth of funds. Work on the

Figure 3.9 Theater at Delphi. Source: Editions "Hannibal," Athens, used by permission.

theater started in the late third century B.C., but it did not come to completion until the middle of the second century B.C. The Attalid ruler of Asia Minor, Eumenes II, provided the money needed for finishing the work.[67]

Epidauros: Temple of Asklepios

The cult of Apollo, which was associated with healing, existed first at Epidauros. Then, in the fifth century B.C., the cult of Asklepios came to share the sanctuary. In the fourth century B.C., the cult of Asklepios at Epidauros took on an international character. Pilgrims from the Greek world attended to receive healing, and a busy building program was started.

While the sanctuary's popularity was ephemeral, as the evidence of votive finds shows, the buildings remained.[68] Numerous buildings and building inscriptions survive to document the history of Epidauros as a sanctuary, but three buildings—the Asklepieion, the Tholos, and the theater—best illuminate the achievement of quality in ancient Greek architecture.

Figure 3.10 Section of the internal colonnade of the Tholos of Epidauros. Source: Editions "Hannibal," Athens, used by permission.

The temple of Asklepios was the first of the fourth-century building projects. Probably begun around 375–370 B.C., this temple was completed within four years and eight months.[69] Doric in style, it had a peripteros of six by 11 columns. In scale, its area was only one-ninth that of Parthenon.[70]

Epidauros: The Theater

The theater was built around 350 B.C. by the architect Polykleitos the Younger, who also built the Tholos at Epidauros. Pausanias notes that the theater surpasses all others in harmony and beauty.[71] Apparently

Figure 3.11 Epidauros: Apella's inscription describing his cure.
Source: Editions "Hannibal," Athens, used by permission.

based upon geometric principles—enunciated in Vitruvius 5.7—this theater presents an excellent example of the ancient Greek ability to build a theater in an area in which acoustics are clear and the view unimpeded. In its final form, the theater accommodated 14,000 spectators.[72] Seats were designed to provide a comfortable space for seating and allowed people to pull their feet out of the way of traffic. Overall, the symmetrical aspect of the theater and its wonderful acoustics make it an unrivalled accomplishment. Ancient drama performances are given in this theater to this day.

Lebadeia: Temple of Zeus Basileus (The King)

Lebadeia was a small town in the countryside of ancient Boeotia. It was best known for its oracle of Trophonios. But it did have another, important monument. This was the temple of Zeus Basileus, which was an unfinished edifice of the Hellenistic Age. This temple was probably begun with funds provided by the Seleucid king Antiochos

Figure 3.12 The Theater at Epidauros. Source: Editions "Hannibal," Athens, used by permission.

IV Epiphanes, who was a devotee of the cult of Zeus the King.[73] Started toward the middle of the second century B.C., the temple was never completed "because of the storms and eddies of war, or simply [its] size."[74]

As we have seen, the inscriptions on the contracts for the temple provide many examples of the various ways in which the overseers of the sanctuary sought to achieve quality.

Didyma: Temple of Apollo

In ancient times an important oracle of Apollo existed at Didyma, near the flourishing commercial center Miletos. From time immemorial, people flocked to the temple of Apollo at Didyma to receive answers from the oracle. The archaeological record indicates that three successive foundations existed in antiquity. The one for which the most evidence survives, and which was the most grandiose of all, was the last, begun in Hellenistic times and finished in the Roman imperial period.[75]

This Hellenistic temple of Apollo was monumental in proportions and lavish in its ornamentation. Work began in the last third of the fourth century B.C., and it was built upon the foundations of the earlier temple that the Persians destroyed in 494 B.C. when they quelled the Ionian Revolt. The Seleucids provided a sizeable endowment for the construction with the gains won in the Hellenistic conquest of the Persian Empire. Indeed, this dynasty procured the return of the cult statue that had been stolen in 494 B.C. The new edifice sat upon a foundation of seven tiers, and access was provided by a stairway with the dimensions of 51.13 m by 109.34 m. The cella was surrounded by a *dipteros* of Ionic capitals, whose inner ring consisted of eight by 19 columns and the outer ring of 10 by 21 columns. The columns stood far apart with a standard distance of 5.3 m in between, and the colonnade was not covered by a roof because the sacred grove grew within it. At the temple's center stood a smaller, roofed sanctuary, which housed the oracle itself. A span of five centuries—the result of intermittent work due in part to limited funds for construction—was required for the completion of this gargantuan building.[76]

Due to its very size, this temple's problems of construction furnish material relevant to quality control. Unfinished column drums, uncovered in the course of excavations, provide rare evidence for the accomplishment of entasis.[77] Entasis, which was the tapering of a column's width for aesthetic reasons, was a refinement developed by Greek architects adhering to a tradition that stressed the visual enhancement of a building's architectural parts. Numbers on the drums indicate how much stone is to be cut and where it is to be cut so as to produce entasis in the final product. Another aspect of the building pertaining to the search for greater quality is that of the engineering involved in placing the architectural members. An inscription, noteworthy because of the rarity of its type, records the construction of special winches for the lifting of blocks.[78] Unfortunately, the inscription does no more than to describe them as "four-legged" and "two-legged" machines employed in the lifting and placing of the lintel. But comparison of this scant evidence with what else remains shows that the architect was doing something extraordinary to deal with an unusual problem.

Olympia: Temple of Zeus

Tradition records the establishment of the Olympic Games in the year 776 B.C., starting a quadrennial panhellenic festival. In the following centuries, Olympia became an important center for Greeks to come together from all over the Mediterranean.[79] Situated near the city-state Elis in the extreme western Peloponnese, Olympia possessed a location that made it a natural and attractive site for a panhellenic gathering. Being in the western Peloponnese, it was the focus of attention by the west Greeks of Magna Graecia and Sicily. Its political neutrality gave it a special status in mainland Greece. As the site's prestige increased, so did the attention paid to the cult of Zeus Olympios.

Construction of the temple to Zeus at Olympia occurred between 470 and 456 B.C.[80] Built within an important sanctuary, the temple was the largest of its kind within the Peloponnese and was executed in what is called the "Severe style."[81] The building was *peripteral* (surrounded by a single row of columns) with six by 13 Doric columns. Nothing is known of the architect, save that he was named Libon and was a native of Elis.[82]

Both the construction of the temple and the cult statue within it illustrate aspects of the search for quality. The area surrounding Olympia is deficient in marble, but does have an abundance of shell-limestone.[83] This material is not particularly suitable for monumental construction because it eventually disintegrates through contact with water and by no means has marble's aesthetic appeal. Since it was economically desirable to utilize the local stone, Libon solved the problem by plastering the stone with a stucco containing marble dust. As is shown by the state of preservation of the temple's remains, the solution was satisfactory.

Pheidias worked upon the cult statue of Zeus at Olympia after having completed work upon the chryselephantine statue of Athena Parthenos for the Acropolis of Athens. His accomplishment at Olympia came to be considered one of the Seven Wonders of the ancient world. Made of gold and ivory and richly decorated, the cult statue of Zeus caused a sensation.[84] It was itself the result of the sanctuary's emulation of the Athenian accomplishment. The Eleans specially brought in Pheidias for this commission because they knew the excellence of his work. Centuries later, Pausanias used the statue as an example of the lengths to which the ancient Greeks were willing to go in supporting the quest for quality in their temples.[85]

Segesta: The Temple

The shell of the temple at Segesta is an excellent example of how the Greeks took their cultural legacy with them as they moved across the Mediterranean. No records deal directly with the subject of this temple's construction, but the archaeological record is of great interest.[86] First of all, the care of construction apparent within the surviving ruins shows that this is a Hellenic temple. Secondly, examination of the shell reveals how Doric temples usually went up in the course of construction. In discussing how the architects controlled the quality of temples, it is useful to have in mind an actual, instead of an idealized, version of the order of construction. Finally, the good state of preservation of this particular monument makes it the ideal choice in explicating various refinements in Hellenic architecture.

The Golden Section

An important decision for architects is the choice of proportion in structures. A frequent example of the need for such choice occurs in designing a rectangular structure. What should be the dimensional ratio of length to width? Historically the preferred ratio has been the "golden section."[87] It was known to the ancient Greeks and was referred to in Euclid.[88]

Numerically the golden section proportion is about 1.6 to 1. More precisely, the number is 1.61803. . . . If a straight line of length *a* is divided into two parts, of lengths *x* and 1, respectively, such that the ratio of *a* to *x* is equal to the ratio of *x* to 1, then *x* will equal 1.61803. . . . The proportion is derived from the formula

$$x = \frac{1}{2}(\sqrt{5} + 1).$$

The importance of the golden section lies in the fact that people tend to prefer it over other ratios. "Statistical experiments are said to have shown that people involuntarily give preference to proportions that approximate to the golden section."[89] If people are shown a number of rectangles with ratios of base to side varying from 10:1 to 1:1 (a square), their preference will center around the ratio 1.6:1 (experience of the editor-in-chief).

Some of the proportions of the human body exhibit ratios equal to the golden section: the height of the human figure when divided at the navel, the hands, and so on. The ancient Greek world had profound respect for the human body and its proportions. The contemporary Greek sculptor Mrs. Aspasia Papadoperaki gives some insight into this matter by stressing the dimensions of measure and time as basic pillars of the harmony characterizing some of the wonderful buildings of Greek antiquity.

According to Papadoperaki, the value of measure in Greek antiquity—both archaic and classic—is found in its basis in the relations among the proportions of the human body and in its use for the needs of man generally—practical needs and those of mental expression. These measures were called *feet* and were used in the construction of objects, houses, temples, and sculpture.[90]

Conclusions

The ancient Greeks are to this day widely acclaimed as major contributors to numerous fields of human endeavor, including philosophy, politics and democracy, literature, the performing arts, mathematics, science, and technology. The enduring nature of these contributions is traceable in large part to the ancient Greek urge for excellence—for quality. Nowhere is this urge as obvious as in the architecture and construction of their temples and theaters.

To attain such high levels of quality, the Greeks employed a broad array of managerial and technological processes. The former included an efficient system of letting contracts, circumscribed by laws and guarantees, and enforced by fines, penalties, and bonuses.

The central role was played by the architect. Knowledge of this craft was acquired from predecessors, supplemented by quality improvement through trial and error. The architect's role included preparing the conceptual design, making the scale model and overseeing the contractors at the construction site. Supporting the architect were the various building trades, each based on apprenticeship and employing the skills, tools and measuring instruments acquired during generations of practice.

The system worked despite interruptions due to wars and delays due to shortages of financing. It produced visible and enduring symbols of a society which many regard as the cradle of European civilization and democracy.

Acknowledgments

I am most grateful to Dr. J. M. Juran who challenged me into what has been the most interesting and most demanding work of my career. This chapter would not have been possible, however, without the invaluable assistance of Mr. Richard Westall a late-antiquity classicist, graduate student of the American School of Classical Studies in Athens, Greece, who conducted the research and edited the text. I am most indebted for his great contribution. Many thanks are owed to Professor Robin Ward of Nottingham Polytechnic of the United Kingdom, a classicist, who offered suggestions to approaching the subject and structuring the research. Many thanks are also owed to contemporary Greek painter Mr. Stavros Katsireas, Athens, Greece, who made comments on the subject of column extension of the Parthenon and actually took two difficult photos indicating the extension and the curvature of the stylobate of the Parthenon. Contemporary Greek sculptor Mrs. Aspasia Papadoreraki offered insights into the subject of golden section, which concludes the chapter. I am grateful for her contribution. Last, but not least, I must acknowledge with gratitude the great assistance offered to me by my wife Helen, a philologist-archaeologist, throughout the planning and the execution of this work.

Notes

1. Pausanias 8.45.5. On the sculptures, see Gruben, 1986: 132.

2. IG I^3 35.7.13. For the date of the decree, see Meiggs, 1966.

3. Heron in Coulton, 1976: 302–4, and Travlos, 1982: 172 + pl. 22.

4. As regards the Syracusan temple of Apollo, see IG XIV 1, and interpretation with commentary at Jeffrey 1961: 265, 275. For Delphi, see Hymn to Apollo 294–99.

5. Philon and Heron were interested in military architecture and technique. On their dates, see Marsden, 1971: 9 ff.

6. Vitruvius, 1990: Introduction.

7. Rouvert, 1981: Introduction.

8. Pausanias *passim*. For example, Polykleitos with the theater of Epidauros, 2.27.5

9. Coulton, 1977: 24 ff.

10. Philon in Coulton, 1977: 97.

11. Coulton, 1977: 144 ff.

12. For the most recent discussion, see Howe, 1985: chapter 7.

13. Coulton, 1977: 144 ff.

14. Coulton, 1977: 25 f.

15. IG V 2:6; IG XII 9.

16. IG V.2.6.3–6.

17. IG V.2.6.6–15.

18. IG V.2.6.15–21.

19. See the following section.

20. IG V.2.6.45–51.

21. IG II^2 1673; Clinton, 1971: 83 ff., 11.64 ff.

22. IG II^2 1.

23. IG V 2.6.21 ff.

24. Note in the sections on Delphi, Epidauros, Lebadeia, and Segesta the important role that money played in the pace of construction.

25. IG II^2 1678.17 f.

26. Plutarch, *Pericles* 12.

27. IG II^2 1668, with 11.85–94 in particular.

28. IG IV^2 1.103.

29. Orlandos, 1966–68: 2.2 ff., 9.

30. Dinsmoor, 1951: (2)182.

31. Paton, 1927: 226 f.

32. Dinsmoor, 1951: 171 n.3.

33. Dinsmoor, 1951: 390.

34. Casanaki and Mallouchou, 1983: 58. Unfortunately this fact was learned after the major restorations by Balanos in the first half of the century.

35. IG VII 3073.115 ff.

36. ID 507.6–13; IG VII 3073.104.

37. Coulton, 1976: 302–4.

38. Travlos, 1952: 172 + pl. 22.

39. IG VII 3073.

40. For example, IG II^2 1678.21 ff.

41. Coulton, 1977: 144 f.

42. Rehm, 1958: no. 32.9–17.

43. Vitruvius 7 pr. 12.

44. Coulton, 1977: 97.

45. This fact was most helpfully demonstrated by Dr. Judith Binder in a talk on the site itself. For a full discussion of refinements in Greek architecture, see Penrose, 1555: (2) 3.

46. IG 7.3073.104. *Entasis* (extension) is observed mainly in the columns of ancient temples of Doric order. It is a tapering that starts developing gradually after the base drum, which is located at one-third of the height of a column. Entasis constitutes an optical correction of the column which otherwise would look concave and thus weak. See also Figure 3.5. These two refinements help optical corrections which influence the viewers' perception of reality.

47. Orlandos, 1966–68: 2.62 ff.

48. IG 7.3073.115 ff.

49. IG IV^2 1.102.9, 32, 54, 104 f., 110 f.

50. IG II(2) 1673; Clinton, 1973:83 ff., 11.64 ff.

51. Coulton, 1977:24 f.

52. This idea is owed to a lecture at the American School of Classical Studies at Athens by Dr. T. Leslie Shear, Jr.

53. Thucydides 1.10; Pausanias I *passim*; Plutarch *Pericles* 13.4.

54. This is not to say that all construction within Athens ceased for the duration of the Peloponnesian War. Rather, the munificence of public buildings was toned down.

55. For the fortunes of Athens in the fifth century B.C., see Meiggs, 1972.

56. Lykourgus, Leocrates 80 f.; Pausanias 10.35.2; Diodorus Siculus 11.29.2 f. A great deal of controversy has existed over the historicity of this event. For an introduction to the modern debate, see Meiggs, 1972: 504–7.

57. For an introduction to the voluminous bibliography, see Townsend, 1982.

58. Pausanias 1.2.5; schol. Aristophanes Acharnseis 242. For a modern view of the question, see Pickard-Cambridge, 1946: 3 f.

59. For a comprehensive treatment of the testimonia, see Pickard-Cambridge, 1946: 10 ff.

60. Dinsmoor, 1951:1.310–14. Townsend, 1982: 127 ff., convincingly dates part of the theater later than Dinsmoor would.

61. For a concise review of the sanctuary's history and an introduction to the subject, see Walker, 1977: 15 ff.

62. Pausanias 10.5.13; Hymn to Apollo 294–99.

63. Stanier, 1953: 73 f.

64. Herodotos 5.62.2 f.

65. Walker, 1977: 86.

66. Pausanias 10.32.1.

67. Walker, 1977: 72.

68. For history of the site and of the cult of Asklepios, see Burford, 1969: 45–52.

69. IG IV^2 1.102.9, 32, 54, 104 f., 110 f. The date of inception depends upon argumentation dealing with the economy of Greece after the Peloponnesian War and the availability of skilled labor; see Burford, 1969: 32 ff., 54.

70. Burford, 1969: 51.

71. Pausanias 2.27.5. This attribution has been heavily contested.

72. Gruben, 1986: 144.

73. Fabricius, 1881: 95.

74. Pausanias 9.39.3.

75. For a recent and thorough study of Didyma, see Fontenrose, 1988.

76. *Princeton Dictionary of Classical Sites* 1976 under *Didyma.*

77. Rehm, 1958: 68, no. 48.

78. Rehm, 1958: no. 32.9–17.

79. For a brief history of the site and its influence, see Mallwitz, 1972: 77–119.

80. For 470 B.C. as the *terminus post quem,* see Pausanias 5.10.2; for 456 B.C. as the *terminus ante quem,* see Pausanias 5.10.4.

81. Gruben, 1986: 55.

82. Pausanias 5.10.3.

83. Pausanias 5.10.3; Mallwitz, 1972: 212.

84. *Greek Anthology,* 16.81: "Pheidias, either the god came down to earth from heaven to reveal his image, or you in fact went to see the god."

85. Pausanias, 5.12.

86. Burford, 1961: 87–93.

87. Oxford, 1989: 656–57.

88. Oxford, 1989: 656.

89. Oxford, 1989: 656.

90. For a more extensive treatment of the subject of the golden section, see Kidson, 376.

Bibliography

Bundgaard, J. *Mnesicles, an Architect at Work.* Copenhagen, 1957.

Bundgaard, J. "The Building Contract from Lebadeia," *Classica et Medievalia* 8 (1964): 1–43.

Burford, A. "Temple Building at Segesta," *Classical Quarterly* 11 (1961): 87–93.

Burford, A. *The Greek Temple Builders at Epidauros.* Liverpool, 1969.

Casanaki, M., and F. Mallouchou. *The Acropolis at Athens: Conservation, Restoration, and Research 1975–1983.* Trans. J. Binder. Athens, 1983.

Clinton, *Archeologikes Ephemerides* (1971) pp. 11, 53 ff., 64 ff.

Coulton, J. J. "Towards Understanding Greek Temple Design: General Considerations," *British School at Athens (BSA)* 70 (1975): 59–99.

Coulton, J. J. "The meaning of Anagrapheus," *American Journal of Archaeology* 80 (1976): 302–4.

Coulton, J. J. *Ancient Greek Architects at Work. Problems of Structure and Design.* Cornell: Ithaca, 1977.

Dinsmoor, W. B. *The Architecture of Ancient Greece.* New York, 1950.

Dinsmoor, W. B. "The Athenian Theater of the Fifth Century," *Studies Presented to David M. Robinson on his Seventieth Birthday.* Ed. G. E. Mylonas. St. Louis, Mo., 1951.

Dittenberger, W., and Purgold, K. *Olympia V: Die Inschriften.* Berlin, 1896.

Fabricius, E. *De Architecture Graece.* Berlin, 1881.

Fontenrose, J. *Didyma. Apollo's Oracle, Cult, and Companions.* Berkeley, 1988.

Gibbon, E. *The History of the Decline and Fall of the Roman Empire.* Ed. J. B. Bury. London, 1906. 1.267.

Gruben, G. *Die Tempel der Griechen.* Munich, 1986.

Heron, Metrica 2, p. 126.22 (ed. H. Stone, Leipzig, 1903). Translated in Coulton, J. J. "The meaning of Anagrapheus," *American Journal of Archaeology* 80 (1976): 302–4.

Hill, B. H. "The Older Parthenon," *American Journal of Archaeology* 16 (1912): 535–58.

Howe, T. N. *The Invention of the Doric Order.* Ph.D. diss. Harvard University, 1985.

Hymn to Apollo, in *Homeric Hymns.* Ed. A. N. Athanassakis. Baltimore/London: The John Hopkins University Press, 1976. 294–99.

Inscriptiones Deliae (abbreviated ID).

Inscriptiones Graecae (abbreviated IG). To be read as follows: IG I^3 35.7, 13 = Inscriptiones Graecae, third edition of volume one, inscription no. 35, and lines 7 and 13.

Jeffery, L. H. *The Local Scripts of Archaic Greece: A Study of the Origin of the Greek Alphabet and Its Development from the Eighth to the Fifth Centuries B.C.* rev. by Λ. W. Johnston. Oxford, 1990.

Jeppesen, K. *Paradeigmata.* Aarhus, 1958.

Kidson, P. "Architecture and City Planning," in *The Legacy of Greece*. Ed. M. I. Finley. Princeton: Oxford University Press.

Mallwitz, A. *Olympia und seine Bauten*. Munich, 1972.

Marsden, E. W. "Greek and the Roman artillery," *Technical Treatises*. Oxford, 1971.

Meiggs, R. "The Dating of Fifth-Century Attic Inscriptions," *Journal of Hellenic Studies* 86 (1966): 86–98.

Meiggs, R. *The Athenian Empire*. Oxford, 1972.

Orlandos, A. K. *Les matériaux de construction et la technique architecturale des anciens Grecs*. 2 vols. Trans. V. Hadjimichali and L. Laumonier. Paris, 1966–68.

Oxford English Dictionary, 2nd ed., volume VI. Oxford: Clarendon Press, 1989.

Paton, J. M., ed. *The Erechtheum*. Cambridge, Mass., 1927.

Pausanias. Citations to be read as follows: 8.45.5: 8 = Book, 45 = Chapter, 5 = Section.

Penrose, F. C. *An Investigation of the Principles of Athenian Architecture*. London, 1888.

Philon of Byzantium, ed. E. W. Marsden, *Greek and Roman Artillery: Technical Treatises*. Oxford, 1971.

Pickard-Cambridge, A. W. *The Theater of Dionysos in Athens*. Oxford, 1946.

Randall, R. H., Jr. "The Erechtheum Workmen," *American Journal of Archaeology* 57 (1953): 68–76.

Rehm, A. *Didyma II: Die Inschriften*. Berlin, 1958.

Rouvert, A. "Introduction" in the Budé edition *Virtruve: De Architecture, Livre I*, Paris, 1990.

Rouvert, A. "Introduction" in the Budé edition *Pline l'ancien: Histoire naturelle*. Livre XXXVI. Ed. J. André. Paris, 1981.

Roux, G. *L'architecture de l'Argolide aux IV- et III-siecles avant J-C* Paris, 1961.

Stanier, R. S. "The Cost of the Parthenon," *Journal of Hellenistic Studies* 73 (1953): 68–76.

Townsend, R. F. *Aspects of Athenian Architectural Activity in the Second Half of the Fourth Century* B.C. Doc. diss. at U. of North Carolina, Chapel Hill, 1982.

Travlos, J. "Paradeigma," *Hesperia Suppl.* 19 (1982) 172 + pl. 22.

Travlos, J. *Pictorial Dictionary of Ancient Athens.* New York, 1971.

Vitruvius, Budé Edition *Vitruve: De Architecture, Livre I.* Introduction by A. Rouvert. Paris, 1990.

Walker, A. *Delphi.* Athens, 1977.

CHAPTER 4

Quality in Early India
Different Levels of Understanding; Different Concerns

Dr. B. N. Goswamy, Professor of Fine Arts
Panjab University

Yogah karmasu kaushalam
(Dexterity in action is yoga*)*
— Bhagavadgita

If any producer of a play will
perform the Preliminaries according
to the rules laid down, nothing
inauspicious will happen to him, and
(after his death) he will reach the
heavenly regions.
(On the contrary) whoever produces a
play in wilful violation of the rules
(in this matter) shall be re-born as a
creature of lower order.
— *Bharata's* Natyashastra

Introduction

The concept of quality and the pursuit of quality in daily life and work is deeply embedded in Indian culture as reflected in early Indian languages and writing. However, it is not treated in a systematic manner

Figure 4.1 Work in an Imperial atelier, under the vigilant supervision of a masterpainter. Folio from an *Akhlaq-i-Nasiri* manuscript, Mughal, ca. 1590. From the collection of Prince Sadruddin Aga Khan, Geneva.

in either language or writing, and many references are indirect rather than direct. This chapter discusses the concept of quality, the difficulties of piecing together a history of quality in India's early years, the emergence of measurement standards, penalties for quality failures, and the improvement of quality in precious metalwork and in the arts.

The chapter draws upon five major treatises on Indian life spanning the two millennia from the fourth century B.C. to the sixteenth century A.D. One of the richest documents is the fourth-century-B.C. *Arthashastra* of Kautilya, which includes detailed descriptions of standards for working that very important item in Indian life, gold, penalties for improper actions in such work; and many detailed standards for performing a variety of measurements. It also defines extensive sets of units, and the relationships among them, for measuring weight, length, and time. The fourth-century *Manasara* indicates some of the progress made in improving measurement standards over the next five to eight centuries, and addresses evolving standards for materials. It also provides very detailed specifications for the ideal measurements to be used in constructing sacred idols. Passages in the *Vishnudharmottaram,* from the sixth to seventh century, provide guidelines for maintaining high levels of uniformity in the representation of images of the deities and in paintings. Al-Biruni's celebrated eleventh-century treatise provides extensive observations on conditions as they existed, but adds surprisingly little to the literature on quality. However, the sixteenth-century classic, the *Ain-i-Akbari* of Abul Fazl, continues to add to ideas and standards relating to gold, measurement, and painting.

The Concept of Quality in Early Indian Life

If one were to translate the word *quality,* as seems initially appropriate, simply as *guna,* one would find oneself entering the world of early Indian thought and life at several levels at once. For the concept is many-sided, and concern with it in India is of an enduring character. When the three pervasive *gunas: sattva, rajas,* and *tamas,* are spoken of, they refer to *purity, passion,* and *darkness,* or *clarity, cloudiness,* and *impurity.* Evidently levels are being established, alike in the areas of abstractions like thoughts and ideas, and of materials like food and clothing.

The word *guna,* per se, figures in intense philosophical debates. Treatises on grammar refer to it as "that which qualifies or differentiates a thing from others of the same class, that (through which) . . . degree in a thing can be expressed." Authoritative works on poetry ceaselessly elaborate upon *gunas* and *doshas,* merits and blemishes, counting sweetness, energy, and perspicuity among the former, and unmelodiousness, improper signification, and obscurity among the latter. The idea of *guna* seems never to be far from anyone's thoughts.

At another level, the concept of understanding quality as excellence and of striving toward excellence is a recurring, even dominant, concern. The very purpose of life is defined in its terms, and texts speak again and again of the need to raise the level of one's being to an ever higher plane. Perfection, completeness, and enlightenment are defined as goals, and both body and mind are sought to be disciplined and propelled toward attaining them. Various paths leading to a goal are delineated and ideals are worked out, all with great subtlety of thought and refinement of language.

The domain of the spirit apart, even at the practical level of making and doing things, excellence is something perceived as always worthy of being sought. When philosophers and codifiers set themselves the task of stating things in *sutra* form, the most compact and terse manner possible, the abbreviating of statements becomes a challenge in itself. We hear of the delight, the merit, to be gained from saving a page, a sentence, a verse, a word, even a syllable. *Laghava,* reduction or condensation, becomes an end excellent in itself. When a poet composes verses that can be read in five different ways to yield five different meanings, like Shriharsha did in the *Naishadhacharita* in the fourteenth century, his composition gains celebrity as being "the touchstone of poetic excellence." When a sixth-century text, like the *Brihatsamhita* of *Varahamihira,* lays down the method of preparing *vajralepa,* a plaster to be used on the walls of temples and as a surface to be painted on, with "unripe fruit of *tinduka* and flowers of silk-cotton, bark of *dhanvana* and seeds of *shallaki,*" and so on, or "buffalo-hide and wood apple and myrrh and *neem* fruits," all boiled together, it says that it is for this *lepa,* this "adamantine glue," to last "tens of thousands of years."

In the area of the arts and related skills, in particular, tales abound that tell of a heightened awareness of quality. Today's traditional painters speak, for example, of "an ancestor" who, when commissioned by a patron-king to paint the walls of a palace, did no apparent work for several months and caused comments to be made against his inactivity by detractors. However, when the king went to check on the painter, he found him sitting on the floor of his simple village home, absorbed in grinding pigments. Questioned about his not having started work, the painter said, with quiet disdain, that he was not yet ready, and would begin to paint only when his pigments were ground fine enough for them to penetrate by a single application the whole depth of a lump of earth even if a line were to be drawn around it very lightly. In a similar vein, the great connoisseur, the seventeenth-century Mughal emperor, Jahangir, is said to have ordered an attendant to apply a drop of perfume, newly-presented to him by a grandee, to the tail of his horse, "in appreciation." For, while the perfume was excellent, the imperial nose had detected in it a lingering trace of the margosa tree under which it seemed to have been prepared. As such, the chagrined grandee noted, it was apparently not fine enough to be used by the emperor on his person!

Of the same order are accounts such as those of the muslins of Dacca woven so fine that an entire bolt could be made to pass through a finger-ring; of a woollen shawl of Kashmir resting over the shoulder so weightlessly that the wearer would forget its presence; of a whole scene of a polo game with riders in the field, a pavilion in the background, and a couplet inscribed at the bottom, all being painted on a single grain of rice. Each of these accounts is a reminder of the awareness of quality, of standards that the craftsmen often set for themselves.

Difficulties in Piecing Together a History of Quality

From accounts like these, and considering some of these sharply defined attitudes, it would seem as if it might be relatively simple to piece together a history of quality in India. And yet, when it comes to writing something approaching this history, at least as it would be understood in conventional terms, one runs into a series of difficulties. Some of these need to be noted.

The Private Nature of Quality

For one thing, it is clear that in a large number of areas, including some of those mentioned above, the effort was purely individual, private. It is as if all attempts at maintaining levels of quality, or striving toward them, were seen as part of an intensely personal domain. Here, as in the case of raising the level of the quality of one's conduct or thought or life, ideals can be spoken of, but the processes, individual approaches, would be seen as subject to no control from the outside: all discipline, all effort, was to come from within. Thinkers and poets and grammarians apart, even the makers of objects, would often work, each in his individual capacity, according to his own wont, to privately held or evolved ideals. *Pramana,* an inwardly known criterion, was the guide, not some law or universally applied standard to which everyone was subject.

The judgments upon an individual work, when such work was subject to judgment at all, came, of course, from the outside; but it is difficult to conceive of many situations in which any firm control could be exercised from without. In the case of the crafts, at best two mechanisms of control can be thought of. One, that the production of goods, artifacts, was often within a workshop situation in which the *guru-shishya* or *ustad-shagird* (master–disciple) system prevailed. In such a situation, it is not difficult to visualize the exercise of stern controls by the master, and one is aware of the almost absolute powers he commanded over his pupils in this respect: strict tests, encouragement and appreciation as much as censure and reprimand, calling to order, and rejection were all built into this system. But parables and tales that are still repeated in hushed tones within *guru-shishya* circles (as in the case of dancers and musicians) apart, little seems to have been reduced to writing, or systematically recorded.

The Lack of Emphasis on Formal, External Controls on Quality

Secondly, in the few surviving texts that deal with the making of things, for example the *shilpa-shastras* which deal with the making of things by craftsmen, there occur meaningful passages listing *gunas* and *doshas,* merits and blemishes, at some length. They are held up and repeated from generation to generation, but their status is recommendatory or exhortatory, rather than prescriptive or mandatory. No controls are spoken of, except, interestingly, in the oblique, indirect form often of formulations that tie the matter up with belief in ritual and omen, prognostication and sin: these seem to have weighed heavily as considerations in early India. Thus, a text like the sixth-to-seventh-century *Vishnudharmottaram* would lay down with marked clarity the ideal proportions of an image to be made, and then follow the section up by what consequences would befall the craftsman who departs from this ideal. An elaborate schemata would be worked out, relating the making of images *against* the prescription of the *shastra* to sins of various kinds, alerting the craftsman to the ill effects that would follow. One sees much the same situation in texts on architecture where, for example, clear statements would be made initially about which wood would be suited to a particular kind of construction. And then these would be followed by passages which mention at some length what misfortunes would befall the craftsman who uses other woods, each of which is then listed in detail, along with the specific sin or consequence that would issue from its unfortunate use.

It is difficult to guess how all this worked in life, but the mere presence of these intimidatory passages in works of this category suggests that outside controls either did not exist in these matters, or were ineffective: reliance was placed upon the craftsman either following his instinct for craftsmanship—which was often the case—or staying within limits on account of these ritualistic or religious considerations.

Unevenness in Documentation

The informal, private level at which quality or excellence was a consistent concern, even if it remained—somewhat expectedly—largely undocumented, is one matter; but there are other, more "public," areas in which one legitimately looks for evidence of the society or state's clear formulations on quality, and mechanisms of control. Even here, however, one runs into problems, for the whole character and quantum of information on the past of India is very uneven. There are long and silent gaps in our information; documents especially from the early period are few and often laconic; historical accounts are all too often mixed with myth and hearsay and shot with the colors of ambiguity. The whole concept of history in India is, in fact, in material ways, different from that generally taken for granted elsewhere.

The paucity of information and the difficulty of interpreting it are further compounded by the fact that the sources become still thinner when it comes to documenting the history of material objects or processes, what could in fact be broadly described as "worldly activity." It still remains virtually impossible to pick up the thread of quality in any given field and pursue it uninterruptedly over a period of time. The possibility left to one, then, is to pick up such insights from various works or accounts spread over almost 2000 years as one can, and regard them as some kinds of markers in this silent field. It needs to be emphasized yet again that it is not as if quality were of no concern to India: the problem simply is our inability to reach documents in which this concern is formally articulated. Like elsewhere, here too there were regulations, superintendence, guilds, an apparatus of rewards and punishments, attempts at standardization, and the like; but one has to pick up the whispers and read the silences of the past with a measure of care.

The *Arthashastra* of Kautilya

For gaining some of the insights of which we speak one could usefully go back to one of the key documents of early India, the *Arthashastra* of Kautilya, which is dated in the fourth century B.C. Nothing from later periods comes close to the range and texture of this celebrated treatise on statecraft, politics, and government. A wide range of regulations are incorporated in the early sections of the work, the whole text extending to "fifteen books, one hundred and fifty chapters, one hundred and eighty sections and six thousand *shlokas.*"

The writer of this remarkable text opens by stating that it brings together the teachings of "as many treatises on the science of politics as have been composed by ancient teachers for the acquisition and protection of the earth," and perceives it himself as being "easy to learn and understand, precise in doctrine, sense and word, free from prolixity of text. . . ."

The treatment of the themes in the work is very methodical, the author proceeding from the enumeration of the sciences which are headed by philosophy and the study of *Vedas,* to the establishment of (the necessity of) economics and the science of politics—with agriculture, cattle-rearing and trade brought prominently into the former topic. The means of ensuring that all goes well in these fields, the text says, is the "Wielding of the Rod" by the king: strict regulation, control, is obviously what the writer has in mind. After discussing the king's person, his duties, his powers, along with those of princes and envoys and counsellors, the text proceeds to the need to establish different departments, each under its own head. A host of these is treated, from the offices of record and audit, to the superintendents of mines and factories, customs and yarns, agriculture and spiritous liquors, shipping, and various wings of the army. At each step, tests are prescribed and the means of judging qualities of persons, like those of an envoy, scribe, or writer of edicts, are put down. Some matters are dealt with in specific, dense detail, like the evaluation of gems and pearls, or textiles and yarns, according to their qualities—which are gone into at amazing length. The chapter on gems and pearls ends with this authoritative, uncompromising statement on what is to be expected from a superintendent of these departments.

> *Of precious articles other than these, he should be conversant with the amount, price, characteristics, class and appearance, their storing, manufacture of new ones and repair of old ones, secret treatment, tools, their use according to place and time, and remedies against things destructive [to them].*

Standards for Supervising the Working of Gold

Of greater value, in the context of quality, are sections of the work that lay down standards and detail a carefully worked out system of fines and punishments wherever departures from the norms established come to light. In keeping with India's great fascination for, and preoccupation with, gold, and of course with the highly specialized nature of the subject, the two chapters dealing with the work of the "Superintendent of Gold in the Workshop" come in for unusually detailed treatment. Of interest are passages like these that deal with specifications for constructing gold workshops, standards for judging the quality of gold, procedures for testing gold samples, proper testing materials, methods for avoiding theft, and specifications of work methods.

> *The Superintendent of Gold should cause to be built a workshop with a court-yard having four work-halls without intercommunication [and] with a single door, for the manufacture of gold and silver. In the middle of the market highway he should establish the Goldsmith, skilled in his profession, of noble birth and trustworthy.*

That from the Jambu river, that from [Mt.] Shatakumbha, that from Hataka, that from Venu, that produced in Shringa-shukti, that found in a natural condition, that transmuted by means of liquids and that produced from mines—these are [types of] gold. [Gold] of the color of the lotus-filament, soft, smooth, not producing a sound and lustrous is best, reddish-yellow is of a middling quality, red of the lowest quality.

One suvarna *of pure, turmeric-colored [gold] is the standard. Thence by the substitution of one* kakani *copper onwards [in a* suvarna *of gold] up to the limit of four* [mashakas], *sixteen standards [are obtained].*

After first rubbing the gold [to be tested] on the touchstone, he should afterwards rub the standard gold [on it]. That with a streak of the same color [as the standard] on places [on the stone] that are neither depressed nor elevated, he should know as properly tested; what is over-rubbed or lightly rubbed or powdered over with red chalk from underneath the finger-nail, he should know as deception. Gold, touched with the forepart of the hand smeared with jati-*vermilion or sulphate of iron dissolved in cow's urine, becomes white. The streak [of the gold] on the touchstone, that has filaments, is smooth, soft and lustrous is best.*

Stone from the Kalingas or from the Tapi, which is of the color of the mudga-*bean, is the best touchstone. That which shows the exact color is advantageous for either sale or purchase. That which has the color of an elephant, with a green tinge, is oversensitive to color [and] is advantageous for sale. That which is firm hard and of uneven color, is not sensitive to color [and] is advantageous for purchase.*

The cut [of gold] that is sticky, of even color, smooth, soft and lustrous is best. The heating that is uniform outside and inside, [and] has the color of the lotus-filament or the color of kuran-daka-*flower, is best. That which is dark or blue shows impurity.*

An unauthorized person shall not approach the workshop. One approaching is to be extirpated. Even an officer, if carrying gold and silver [inside], shall be deprived of the same.

Artisans doing the work of setting in gold, bead-making, plating and gilding and ornamental gold, [and] blowers, servants and dust-washers, shall enter and leave after their garments, hands and private parts are searched. And all their tools and uncompleted works shall remain just there. He should hand over the gold received and the work being carried out into the office. In the evening and in the morning, he should deposit [the gold and the articles], marked with the seals of the maker and the overseer.

Setting, stringing and minor work, these are ways of working [in gold]. . . . In the work of setting, he should use one-fifth part as fastening at base and tenth part as side-fastening. Silver with a quarter-part copper, or gold with a quarter-part silver is artificial; against that he should guard. In the work of fixing of beads, [there should be] three parts enclosing at the sides and two parts base, or four parts base and three parts enclosing at the sides.

Penalties for Improper Actions

The work of the "Superintendent of Gold in the Workshop" is separated from that of the "Goldsmith in the Market Highway," evidently also a senior official, technically equipped, exercising control and supervision, but not engaged in manufacture himself. This latter official is invested, in the *Arthashastra*, with considerable powers in the matter of levying fines and inflicting punishments. Thus, after stating that this official should cause the work of the citizens to be carried out by workshop artisans, the author of the *Arthashastra* proceeds to state that,

> *They should do the work with the time and the [nature of the] work stipulated, without stipulation as to time where there is the requirement of the nature of the work. In case the work is done otherwise [than as ordered] [there shall be] loss of wage and a fine double that [amount]. In case the time limit is exceeded, [he shall receive] a wage reduced by one-quarter and a fine double that [amount].*
>
> *The [artisans] shall deliver in the same condition as to quality as they receive the entrusted metal. And even after a lapse of time, [customers] shall receive it in the same condition, except what is lost [in manufacture] and worn away [by time].*
>
> *The [Goldsmith] should be conversant with every detail in connection with the characteristics and the manufacture of gold and its articles by workshop artisans.*

In the case of gold and silver [used in the manufacture of articles], a loss of one kakani *in a* suvarna *may be allowed.*

In case of diminution of quality to the extent of one masa *at least, the lowest fine for violence [shall be imposed]; in case of diminution of quantity [to that extent], the middle [fine]; in case of deceit in scales and weights, the highest [fine], also in case of fraud in an article manufactured.*

For [a person] causing the manufacture [of an article] unseen by the Goldsmith or in some other place, the fine shall be twelve panas. *For the artisan, [the fine shall be] double, if there is a valid excuse. If there is no excuse, [the person] shall be taken to the magisterial court. And for the artisan, [the punishments shall be] a fine of two hundred* panas *or the cutting off of the fingers of his hand.*

They shall purchase the scales and weights from the Superintendent of Standardization. Otherwise, [there shall be] a fine of twelve panas.

After this follows a fascinating subsection that treats of the kinds of faults that can be committed in the treatment and trade of gold and the methods through which these can be detected.

Making solid objects, making hollow objects, plating, coating, fixing and gilding constitute an artisan's work.

Fraud in the balance, removal, tapping, boxing and embedding are the means of pilfering [by artisans].

[Easily] bending, carved out, with split top, with a subsidiary [false] neck, with bad strings, with defective scales, given to swinging, and magnetic,—these are false balances.

A dummy crucible, foul dross, the "crane's beak," the blowpipe, the pair of tongs, the water-vessel, borax, and the same gold, these are the ways of removal. Or, sand made into lumps and placed [there] beforehand, is taken out of the fire-place on the breaking of the crucible.

At the time of fixing together afterwards or at the time of testing the laid-on plating leaf, interchange [of a gold article] by a silver article is tapping, or [the interchange] of sand lumps [containing gold] by sand lumps containing iron.

He should find these two out by heating and testing on the touchstone or by failure of [right] sound and by scratching. The

removable [enclosing] they set down in the acid of the badara-
fruit or in salt-water. Thus the "enclosing."

*In the course of testing articles that are made or in the course
of repairs to old articles, four ways of stealing [are practiced]:
knocking off, cutting out, scratching out, or rubbing off. When
under the pretext of [discovering] an "enclosing," they cut out a
bead or a string or a casing, that is knocking off. Or, when in an
article with a double-base, they insert an object of lead and cut
the interior out, that is cutting out. When from solid objects they
scratch out with a sharp tool, that is scratching out. When after
coating a piece of cloth with the powder of one of the following,
[viz.] yellow orpiment, red arsenic or vermilion, or with powder
of kuruvinda[-stone], they rub the article with it, that is rubbing
off. By that articles of gold and silver lose in weight and yet no
part of these [articles] gets bruised.*

*Of plated articles that are broken or cut or rubbed off, he
should form an inference [as to loss] with the help of a similar
article. Of coated articles he should form an estimate by cutting
out as much as has been cut out [by the artisan]. Or, of those that
have changed their appearance, he should do heating and rubbing in [acid] water a number of times.*

*Sudden movement of the hand, the weights, the fire, the
wooden anvil, the tool-box, the receptacle, the peacock's feather,
the thread, garment, talk, the head, the lap, the fly, attention to
one's person, the bellows-skin, the water-platter, and the fire-
pan—these he should know as the means of pilfering.*

*Of silver articles he should know that as fraudulent which
smells like raw flesh, easily catches dirt, is rough, very hard or
changed in color.*

*In this manner he should test the new and the old as well as
the article that has changed its appearance, and should impose
penalties on the [guilty artisans] as prescribed.*

Measurement Standards

Chapters 19 and 20 of Book 2 of the *Arthashastra* deal with the important matters of weights and measures, and of units of space and
time. An official designated as the "Superintendent of Standardization" is enjoined, at the outset, in the first of these two chapters, to
"cause factories to be established for the manufacture of standard

weights and measures." Then follow details of the different kinds of weights, procedures, and materials to be used in constructing scales to measure weight.

> *Ten* masa-*beans make one* masaka *of gold, or five* gunja-*berries. Sixteen of these make one* suvarna *or* karsha. *A* pala *is equivalent to four* karshas. *Eighty-eight white mustard-seeds make one* mashaka *of silver. Sixteen of these make one* dharana, *or twenty* shimba-*beans.*
>
> *A* dharana *of diamonds weighs twenty rice-grains.*
>
> *A half-*mashaka, *a* mashaka, *two, four, eight* mashakas, *a* suvarna, *two, four, eight,* suvarnas, *also ten, twenty, thirty, forty [and] one hundred* [suvarnas], *[are denominations of weights]. By that are explained [denominations of]* dharanas.
>
> *Weights should be made of iron [or] of stone from the Maga-dhas or the Mekala hills or such as would not increase in weight by water and smearing or decrease in weight by heat.*
>
> *Beginning with six* angulas *[in length] and rising succes-sively by eight* angulas, *he should cause ten balance-beams to be made, one* pala *of metal onwards [in weight] increased succes-sively by one* pala, *with scale-pans on the two sides of the fulcrum or a pan [on one side only].*
>
> *He should cause the* samavritta *[balance] to be made of metal thirty-five* palas *[in weight] and seventy two* angulas *in length. Fixing a ball [of metal] five* palas *in weight [at one end], he should cause the level to be secured [for marking zero]. From that [point] onwards, he should cause markings to be made for one* karsha, *increased by a* karsha *up to one* pala, *then increased by a* pala *up to ten* palas, *then for twelve, fifteen and twenty* palas. *Thereafter, he should cause markings to be made increased by ten up to one hundred* palas. *In the "fives" he should cause it to be covered with* nandi *[the* svastika *mark].*
>
> *He should cause a balance [called]* parimani *to be made with double this amount of metal and ninety-six* angulas *in length. On that he should cause markings to be made beyond one hundred for twenty, fifty and [two] hundred* [palas].
>
> *The balance made of wood [should be] eight* hastas *[long], provided with markings [or] with weights [and] supported by "peacock's feet."*

A "Superintendent of Measurements" is mentioned in the next chapter, and here an absorbing account of units of space and time is first given. Remarkable refinements are to be seen on a theme that surfaces again and again in the centuries that follow. Measurements are unexpectedly detailed and there are surprises at both ends of the scale, singularly minute units at one end, and remarkably extended ones at the other. In treatises on crafts like image-making and architecture, concern with units like these was directly relevant; so is it in the case of other important areas like medicine and astronomy, for instance, in which impressive advances had been made in early India, and precision was a vital concern. The *Arthashastra* goes into the subject in this manner.

> *The Superintendent of Measurements should be conversant with the measurements of space and time.*
>
> *Eight atoms make one* rathachakraviprush *[chariot-wheel particle]. Eight of them make one* liksha *[nit]. Eight of them make one* yuka *[louse]. Eight of them make one* yavamadhya *[barley-grain middle]. Eight* yavamadhyas *make one* angula *[finger]. Or, the maximum width of the middle [part] of the middle finger of a middling man is an* angula.
>
> *Four* angulas *make a* dhanurgraha. *Eight* angulas *make a* dhanurmushti. *Twelve* angulas *make a* vitasti *[span] and the height of the shadow-gnomon. Fourteen* angulas *make a* shama, *a* shala, *a* pariraya *and a* pada *[foot].*
>
> *Eighty-four* angulas *make a* vyama, *a measure for ropes and a* paurusha *[man's height] for [measuring] moats [or diggings].*
>
> *Four* aratnis *make a* danda, *a* dhanus, *a* nalika, *and a* paurusha *for the householder.*
>
> *Ten* dandas *make a* rajju. *Two* rajjus *make a* paridesha. *Three* rajjus *make a* nivartana *on one side. A* bahu *has two dandas more.*
>
> *Two thousand* dhanuses *make a* goruta. *Four* gorutas *make a* yojana. *Thus measurements of space [have been explained].*
>
> *Hereafter [are explained] measurements of time.*
>
> Tuta, lava, nimesha, kashtha, kala, nalika, muhurta, *forenoon and afternoon, day, night, fortnight, month, season, ayana, year and cycle [of years] are divisions of time. Two* tutas *make a* lava.

Two lavas *make a* nimesha. *Five* nimeshas *make a* kashtha. *Thirty* kashthas *make a* kala. *Forty* kalas *make a* nalika. *Or, a hole in a jar [with a dimension] of four* maskas *of gold made four* angula *in length, [with] an* adhaka *of water [running through it] measures one* nalika. *Two* nalikas *make a* muhurta.

A day of fifteen muhurtas *and a night [of the same length] occur in the months of Chaitra and Ashvayuja. After that, one of them [first] increases and [then] decreases by three* muhurtas *during a period of six months [and vice versa the other].*

The *Manasara* and Progress in Improving Measurement Standards

The range of subjects with which the *Arthashastra* deals is by no means exhausted with this. But it is useful to take into account later developments in the field and speak of other evidence from other texts that take up the same theme. For example, progress in measuring and standardizing units of time and space, a prerequisite of precision and maintenance of quality, can be spoken of. That seminal work on Indian architecture, the *Manasara*, datable to anywhere between the first and the fourth century A.D., gives the lineal measurements in familiar terms, and then goes on to speak at length of the controls necessary to ensure proper measurements with wood and rope scales.

Sami [acacia suma], shaka *[ocimum* sanctum*]*, chapa *[bow-tree]*, khadira [acacia catechu], tamalaka [xanthochymus pictorius], kshirini *[milk-tree] and* tindini *[tamarind tree] are known as the kinds of wood for the yard-stick.*

After selecting the wood [for the yard-stick] it should be soaked in water for three months. After having been washed it should be taken out [of water] and be split by the carpenter. The sapped part of that hewn timber should be shaped into a [solid] four-sided [piece].

It should be one cubit long, one angula *[three-fourths inch] broad, and its thickness is stated to be a half* angula. *The yard-stick [lit. cubit measure] should be accurately marked.*

Either kramuka *[betel-nut tree] or* venu *[bamboo] is stated to be [fit as] the timber for the [measuring] rod [which should be] neither bent, nor broken, nor porous, but smooth.*

Vishnu is stated to be the tutelary god [of the wood for] both the yard-stick and the [measuring] rod.

The rope-maker should make the rope [rajju] *with the split husk of coconut, with the kusha-grass* [poa cynosuroides], *the bark of the banyan tree, silk-cotton, and* kimshuka [butea frondosa] *fibers, bark of the palm tree, and* ketaka [pandanus odoratissimus], *or with any other suitable bark.*

Measuring sidewise, the width of the measuring should be one angula.

The rope should be made free from knots and three-fold for [measuring the architectural objects of] the Gods, Brahmins [earthly gods] and kings [Kshatriyas]; *two-fold for [those of] the* Vaishyas; *and single-fold for [those of] the* Shudras. *[Within the fourfold caste division of society,* Vaishyas *are the trading caste or group, while* Shudras *are the menial or serving caste or group.]*

Vasuki [the divine serpent] is the presiding deity of the [measuring] rope, and Brahma is known as the presiding deity of measurement.

The chapter ends with the familiar exhortations and warnings.

Thus ascertaining the yard-stick, the rope and, similarly, the measuring rod, and remembering those presiding deities, the vardhaki *[carpenter, worker and designer in wood] should carry out the measurement of objects.*

Thus measured, the architectural objects are attended with success.

One who does what is not prescribed becomes the reaper of scanty results.

The architect should, therefore, avoid [the unprescribed things], but he should thoroughly do that [which has been prescribed].

Ideal measurement is a concern that emerges again and again in the *shilpa-shastras*, especially when it comes to the fashioning of a *pratima*, a sacred idol. Here, very detailed prescriptions are given. Even a text like the *Brihatsamhita* of Varahamihira, the celebrated sixth-century astronomer, goes into the precise measurements and proportions involved in idol-making, prefacing his treatment with the units of measures involved.

The smallest particle of dust that comes to sight, when the sun passes through the interstice of a window, is to be understood as a paramanu [atom].

An atom, a dust particle, a tip of the hair, a nit, a louse, a barley corn and a digit are in order eight times bigger than the preceding measure. One digit becomes an integer.

The height of the pedestal [of an idol] is a third of the height of the temple-door diminished by an eighth part. The idol will be twice as high as the pedestal.

The face of the image should be 12 digits long and broad, in terms of its own digit. According to sage Nagnajit, however, its face should be 14 digits long and 12 digits broad, which is the measure prevalent in the Dravida country.

The nose, forehead, chin and neck are four digits long; so are the ears. The jaw and the chin are two digits broad.

The forehead is eight digits in breadth. Two digits further off on both sides are the temples, being of four digits. The ears are two digits in breadth.

The tip of the ear should be $4\frac{1}{2}$ digits off the corner of the eye on a level with the brows. The ear-holes and the raised margin near it should lie at the same level as the corner of the eye and measure one digit.

The long passages proceed like this, giving precise measurements for every conceivable part of the body down to each toenail, and end with this:

An image should be made in such a way that its ornaments, dress, decorations and form conform to the traditions and practices of the country. If such an image, possessed of all good features, be installed in a place, it would bestow prosperity on the people that live in its presence.

Standards for Materials

When the text speaks of materials, like wood that would be appropriate for the making of an idol, a familiar mixture of ritualistic considerations and omens and sound practical sense marks the treatment of the subject. Thus,

The maker of the image should enter a forest on an auspicious day that is presided over by a planet conducing to prosperity and which has an unhurt asterism, when good auguries are discovered by the astrologer and when there are auspicious omens prescribed for a journey.

The following trees are to be rejected: those that grow in cemeteries, roads, temples, ant-hills, penance-groves, sacred spots, near the confluences of rivers . . . those that are stunted, those that are joined with others, those that are infested with creepers, that have been struck down by lightning and storm, those that have fallen by themselves, that have been broken by elephants, that have withered, are burnt by fire and that contain bee-hives. Those trees which have glossy leaves, flowers and fruits will be beneficial. One should go to the desired [selected] tree and offer worship to it with food and flowers.

The *Vishnudharmottaram* and Standards in Art

Much the same mixture of considerations is to found in the *Vishnudharmottaram*, a sixth-to-seventh-century text, when it treats images of deities and paintings. Thus,

Their [the gods'] look should be free from a tilt upwards or downwards or lateral, nor should it be too pronounced a gaze, or feeble, plaintive, angry or fierce. An upward look forebodes death, the same downward brings sorrow, the lateral destroys wealth, the feeble brings on death. The pronounced or plaintive look creates sorrow, the fierce look depletes wealth, the angered promotes fear. . . . The figure should neither be executed with sunken stomach nor bloated, nor should any disfigurement be presented. The figure should be neither excessive or diminutive in proportion, or lurid in color, with mouth agape or bent down. . . . The pronouncedly west-gazing destroys the offspring, the north-gazing enhances fear. The disproportionate one is generally destructive, the over-sized devastates the country. . . . The figure that conforms to prescription is considered to assure prosperity to the creative craftsman as well as the ruler of the realm. Hence it should be fashioned according to rules, with a special effort made to follow its own definitive characteristics.

One may be led to conclude from all this that the craftsman of early India, as indeed other workers, would have found it extremely hard to work within such rigid bounds, with so many constricting rules and prescriptions. But it is more than likely that he found his own solutions to the situation, and succeeded, as evidenced by the great works of art that have survived in all their splendor and variety, in using his own finely honed instincts while observing—in spirit alone, not in letter—the prescriptive formulae. Once again, however, firm evidence of the situation as it really prevailed, is not easy to locate.

The *Ta'Rikh al-Hind* and *Ain-i-Akbari*

With time, much changes in India. The medieval period, the establishment of Islamic power, the turmoils of the mind, the expansions of physical limits, all come in. But, with respect to documentation concerning quality, the tenor of our evidence changes but little. As perspicacious an observer and inquirer as the Arabic scholar al-Biruni, who wrote his celebrated account of India, *Ta'Rikh al-Hind (A History of India),* in the early eleventh century, does not add much to our information concerning quality, as commonly understood, or controls on quality. He describes things as he saw them, or attempts to reconcile, on occasion, different systems or views, even scales that he found in use. To take an example from an area to which some attention has been drawn earlier, that of metrology, al-Biruni starts his chapter promisingly, by providing definitions or general statements like, "Counting is innate to man. The measure of a thing becomes known by its being compared with another thing which belongs to the same species and is assumed as a unit by general consent. Thereby the difference between the object and this standard becomes known." Or, "Since the unit of measure is not a natural unit, but a conventional one assumed by general consent, it admits of both practical and imaginary division." But soon he settles down to noting things as they existed, giving units or scales laid down by Varahamihira or Brahmagupta or Charaka, and the like.

One of the greatest, and most detailed, documents from medieval India is the sixteenth-century classic, the *Ain-i-Akbari* of Abul Fazl, the third volume of that gigantic work, the *Akbar Nama*. This volume, as Blochmann says in his preface to the translation, contains "that information regarding Akbar's reign which, though not strictly historical, is yet essential to a correct understanding of the times, and embodies, therefore, that for which in modern times we would turn to Administrative Reports, Statistical compilations, or Gazetteers. It contains the *ain* [that is, mode of governing] of Akbar and is, in fact, the Administrative Report and Statistical Return of his government, as it was in about 1590 A.D."

The treatment of the subjects that are dealt with in the *Ain-i-Akbari* is remarkably detailed: The first of the five books treats of Akbar's household and, of course, of the emperor himself. The books that follow address the "servants of the throne, the military and civil services, and the attendants at court"; regulations for the judicial and executive departments; "the establishment of a new and practical era, the survey of the land"; the Hindus' social conditions and literary activity, especially in philosophy and law; and, finally, the moral teachings and epigrammatical sayings of the emperor whom Abul Fazl so admired and eulogized. The work is truly remarkable, for in it, as Blochmann remarks, "men live and move before us, and the great questions of the time, axioms they believed in and principles they followed, phantoms then chased after, ideas then prevailing, and successes then obtained, are placed before our eyes in truthful and, therefore, vivid colors."

In a work such as this, it would be legitimate to expect information of the kind that one seeks respecting the history of quality in India, for Abul Fazl was interested in simply *everything*. But, once again, little comes our way in the manner that one might have liked. There are very elaborate descriptions of the countless departments set up under Akbar, chapters on the Imperial Treasury, the Mint, Encampments and Illuminations, Fruitery and Perfumes, Shawls and other stuffs, the Imperial stables of Elephants and Horses and Camels, and the like. There is dense, textured information, and one learns a great deal about organization, order, the passion for excellence, and so on. The emphasis, however, is on description, on classification, not on the mechanisms of control, or standards as evolved: these are treated rarely, being taken for granted, and requiring us to read the materials presented in a different manner.

There was obvious regard for and emphasis on quality in Mughal India, especially under the emperor Akbar, but one has to search with great care to glean relevant facts from the accounts of the times.

Controlling the Quality of Minted Gold

Abul Fazl's chapter on the Imperial Mint is reminiscent in some ways of the *Arthashastra*, but is still of great interest.

> *The Workmen of the Mint: Ain 5*
> *1. The* Daroghah *[Superintendent]. He must be a circum-spect and intelligent man, of broad principles, who takes the cumbrous burden of his colleagues upon the shoulder of despatch. He must keep every one to his work, and show zeal and integrity.*
> *2. The* Sairafi *[Department of banking and money-chang-ing]. The success of this important department depends upon his experience, as he determines the degrees of purity of the coins. On account of the prosperity of the present age, there are now num-bers of skilful* sarrafs; *and by the attention of his Majesty, gold and silver are refined to the highest degree of purity. The highest degree of purity is called in Persian* dahdahi, *but they do not know above ten degrees of fineness; whilst in India it is called* barahbani, *as they have twelve degrees. Formerly the old* hun, *which is a gold coin current in the Deccan, was thought to be pure, and reckoned at ten degrees; but his Majesty has now fixed it at 8 1/2: and the round, small gold* dinar *of Alauddin, which was considered to be 12 degrees, now turns out to be 10 1/2.*
>
> *Those who are experienced in this business have related won-derful stories of the purity of gold at the present time, and re-ferred it to witchcraft and alchemy; for they maintain, that gold ore does not come up to this fineness. But by the attention of his Majesty, it has come up to this degree; hence the astonishment of people acquainted with this branch. It is, however, certain that gold cannot be made finer, and of a higher degree.*
> *Banwari: Ain 6*
> *Although in this country clever* Sairafis *[bankers, money changers] are able from experience to tell the degree of fineness by the color and the brightness of the metal, the following admirable rule has been introduced, for the satisfaction of others.*
> *To the ends of a few long needles, made of brass or such like metal, small pieces of gold are affixed, having their degree of fineness written on them. When the workmen wish to assay a new piece of gold, they first draw with it a few lines on a touchstone, and some other lines with the needles. By comparing both sets of lines, they discover the degree of fineness of the gold. It is, however,*

necessary that lines be drawn in the same manner, and with the same force, so as to avoid deception.

 To apply this rule, it is necessary to have gold of various degrees of fineness. This is obtained as follows. . . .

Progress in Improving Measurement Standards

Standardization was a serious concern to the emperor, and Abul Fazl discusses the *Ilahi gaz,* "a measure for length and a standard gauge," at some length, after stating that "His Majesty in his wise statesmanship and benevolence of rule carefully examined the subject of all arbitrary taxation, disapproving that these oppressions should become established by custom. He first defined the *gaz,* the *tanab,* and the *bighah* and laid down their bases of measurement: after which he classed the lands. . . ." Noting that different systems of measurement prevailed in India, and giving some details of these, Abul Fazl records, "His Majesty in his wisdom, seeing that the variety of measures was a source of inconvenience to his subjects, and regarding it as subservient only to the dishonest, abolished them all and brought a medium *gaz* of 41 digits into general use. He named it the *Ilahi gaz* and it is employed by the public for all purposes." Also that,

> *His Majesty fixed for the* jarib *the former reckoning in yards and chose the measurement of sixty square, but adopted the* Ilahi gaz. *The* tanab *[rope] was in Hindustan a measure of hempen rope twisted which became shorter or longer according to the dryness or moisture of the atmosphere. It would be left in the dew and thus fraudfully moistened. Oftentimes it would be employed in the early morning when it had got damp and had shrunk, and by the end of the day it had become dry and had lengthened. In the former case, the husbandmen suffered loss, in the latter the royal revenues were diminished. In the 19th year of the Divine era, the* jarib *was made of bamboos joined by iron rings. Thus it is subject to no variation, and the relief to the public was felt everywhere while the hand of dishonest greed was shortened.*

Supporting Quality in Painting

There is much in this strain in the work, and one gains much understanding of the way things worked in sixteenth-century India, even if one is not able to write, with its help, a conventional history of quality in any one given industry or craft. But then this is the way things seem to have been, and been viewed, in India. One sometimes even understands things at a deeper level through this manner of indirect recording, as one does from Abul Fazl's celebrated and oft-quoted chapter on the "Art of Painting."

> *Drawing the likeness of anything is called* taswir. *His Majesty, from his earliest youth, has shown a great predilection for this art, and gives it every encouragement, as he looks upon it as a means, both of study and amusement. Hence the art flourishes, and many painters have obtained great reputation. The works of all painters are weekly laid before His Majesty by the* Daroghas *and the clerks; he then confers rewards according to excellence of workmanship, or increases the monthly salaries. Much progress was made in the commodities required by painters, and the correct prices of such articles were carefully ascertained. The mixture of colors has especially been improved. The pictures thus received a hitherto unknown finish. Most excellent painters are now to be found, and masterpieces, worthy of a* Bihzad, *may be placed at the side of the wonderful works of the European painters who have attained world-wide fame. [Bihzad was the name of a famous painter in Iran who has become a byword for excellence and refinement.] The minuteness in detail, the general finish, the boldness of execution, etc., now observed in pictures, are incomparable; even inanimate objects look as if they had life. More than a hundred painters have become famous masters of the art, whilst the number of those who approach perfection, or of those who are middling, is very large. This is especially true of the Hindus: their pictures surpass our conception of things. Few, indeed, in the whole world are found equal to them.*

Summary

This, then, was what early India was like, in the broadest outline, in respect of its awareness of quality and of its pursuit of excellence. The earliest writings date back to an era in which achievements of quality depended heavily on the workmanship of the individual—the training, experience, and conscientiousness of the craftsman. (Industrialization, which relies heavily on technology and elaborate systematic processes, had not yet come over the horizon). Under such conditions it is understandable that those earliest writings are rich in philosophical and spiritual motivations for pursuing quality in life, art, and work. The appeal to achieving quality is inner directed, with few if any indications of how officials, customers, suppliers, or others can direct and control the achievement or improvement of quality. Success or failure to achieve quality in workmanship or in the living of one's life may be rewarded or punished by the consequences of that success or failure.

As the centuries pass, there is a shift in the writings from the broadly philosophical and spiritual to very concrete, elaborate, and perhaps mundane details that support the achievement of quality. These include specifications of materials, processes, finished products, and tests; standards for measures and measuring tools; codes of conduct; definitions of wrongdoing; and punishments according to the severity of the misdeeds. Some of these evolving aspects of managing for quality are articulated; others are taken for granted; for still others one has to read into the silences.

With the coming of the British, the tenor of things changes and one enters, as concerns quality, a relatively familiar world—familiar from the European ways of recording and regarding things. One finds oneself in a period of carefully worked out regulations and manuals of standards, and the like. Enormous undertakings are embarked upon, but understanding them takes no special effort. Unless, of course, even during the British period, one retreats into the world of princely India where, for the most part, things continued to be what they were before the coming of the British; what they had been for more than 2000 years before that, in fact.

Bibliography

Abul Fazl Allami. *Ain-i-Akbari.* 3 vols. Translated by H. Blochmann and H. S. Jarrett. First published 1868–94. Reprint, Osnabruck, 1983.

Acharya, P. K. *Architecture of Manasara.* Oxford, 1934.

Bhat, M. Ramakrishna (ed. and trans.). *Varahamihira's Brhatsamhita.* 2 vols. Delhi, 1981.

Iyer, K. A. Subramanian. *Bhartrihari: A Study of the* Vakyapadiya *in the Light of the Ancient Commentaries.* Poona, 1969.

Kangle, R. P. (ed. and trans.) *The Kautiliya Arthashastra.* 2 parts. Bombay, 1969.

Sachau, Edward C. *Alberuni's India.* 2 vols. Reprint, Lahore, 1962.

Sivaramamurti, C. *Chitrasutra of the Vishnudharmottara.* Delhi, 1978.

Visvanatha Kaviraja. *The Sahitya Darpana, or, Mirror of Composition: A Treatise on Literary Criticism.* Translated by James R. Ballantyne and Pramada-Dasa Mitra. Osnabruck: Biblio Verlag, 1980.

CHAPTER 5

Quality in Early Scandinavian Shipbuilding

Ir. Carl A. Kofoed, former Chief Engineer, Quality
Danfoss A/S, Denmark

Coauthor: Mrs. Grete Kofoed

Introduction

Discovery and study of ancient Scandinavian ships provides an opportunity to identify the evolution of quality management practices over the four-thousand-year period from the beginning of the third millennium B.C. to the end of the first millennium A.D. The building of progressively more sophisticated ships during this period was made possible by improvements in design, tools, materials, and production processes. These improvements can be interpreted as increases in the ability of the peoples involved to develop and use elements of quality planning, control, and improvement. The success of these improvements led, at the end of the first millennium A.D., to Scandinavian ships of a sufficiently high quality to enable the Vikings to spread their name and elements of their culture across much of northern Europe and even to North America.

Over the years, the high quality of early Scandinavian and the later Viking ships were made possible by a combination of situations and achievements in design, materials, and tools. Ten of these elements were

1. An ample supply of straight trunks of oak and other woods
2. Development of a technique for splitting the trunks

3. The development of tightening material, woolen strings impregnated with resin and oil

4. Production of high-quality iron based on bog iron ore

5. Production of iron tools especially for shipbuilding

6. Production of iron rivets in great numbers

7. Rust prevention surface treatment of rivets and discs

8. Steady improvements in hull design and construction, based upon new materials, tools, and concepts

9. Training of sufficient numbers of specially qualified craftsmen

10. The ability to organize and coordinate complex productive processes

Advances in materials and tools were foundation stones for the progress of Scandinavian shipbuilding. Scandinavia benefited from the availability of local and imported materials, sometimes of very high quality, and from the development and production of tools useful for shipbuilding and many other purposes. Early shipbuilding depended on tools made from high-quality local flint and abundant local timber, including oak, pine, and lime trees, initially for the body of the ships and later for masts. Imported copper and tin allowed bronze tools to be developed although the low cost and high quality of local flint combined with the skills of flint knappers enabled some stone tools to remain in use until eventually they were replaced by tools of iron and steel based upon very-high-quality local bog iron and charcoal. The high-quality iron made possible not only superior tools but also rivets and other fasteners for shipbuilding. These fasteners in turn allowed for lighter and more effective ship designs to be developed and produced.

Advances in ship design occurred in three major areas. The improvements in the design of ship hulls occurred steadily, including the emergence of the keel and the clinker-built hull. Masts and sails represented a major step forward. Effective tightening and fastening materials were also developed. These included woolen strings impregnated with resin and oil, and rivets and other fasteners based on iron.

Advances in methods of production included progressively greater skill in working with wood, including the development of a variety of ways of splitting tree trunks. The usefulness of iron rivets and other fasteners was enhanced by the development of surface-coating techniques that protected them.

Finally, the success of Scandinavian shipbuilding suggests that effective means of organizing and leading the construction work and methods of training craftsmen to conduct it evolved over time.

Raw Materials and Tools

Scandinavia, which was once joined with Great Britain when the Baltic Sea was still a freshwater lake, had rich deposits of high-quality flint, good straight trees for lumber and ship masts, bog iron ore and charcoal suitable for making high-quality iron. Each of these materials played important roles in enabling a high-quality shipbuilding industry to emerge. These materials were used to make shipbuilding tools, in the production of ships, or both.

The flint deposits were used to make axes and other tools. The archeological records of tool manufacturing show that, even in 3000 B.C., quality control was an essential part of each stage of tool manufacture. The quality of the tools to be used in constructing ships can be considered a factor in the subsequent development of leading shipbuilding, maritime commerce, fishing, and exploring industries in Scandinavia.

Construction of tools from flint was a highly skilled, multistaged process. Refinements in tools have been traced by archaeologists over hundreds of years. Archaeologists can tell by examination the origin of a particular flint instrument. They can, therefore, trace the geographic patterns of trade in flint instruments.

The raw material for flint axes, which was the prime tool when building a boat in the Stone Age and early Bronze Age, was found in chalk deposits. Denmark and southern Sweden had flint in abundance. This flint was of very high quality, just right for making such tools as axes and adzes. With the growing demand for high-quality flint, men in Denmark as well as in other regions, began to mine the substance from pits and tunnels. Most of the Scandinavian flint mines were concentrated in northern Jutland and in the southeastern part of the Danish island, Zealand and Mon (Moen).

The best flint was mined in places where the Senonian outcrops at the surface. The photograph in Figure 5.1 shows a mine gallery,

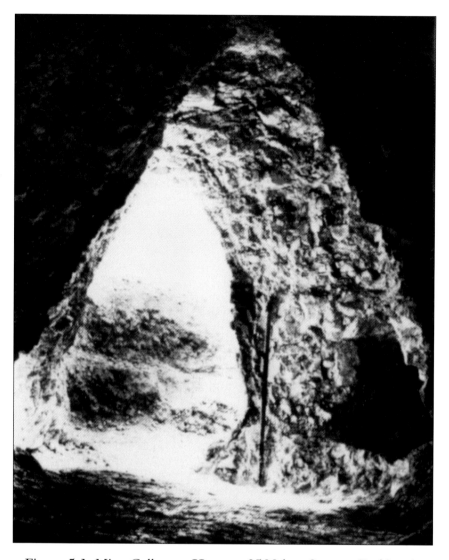

Figure 5.1 Mine Gallery at Hov, ca. 3500 b.c. Source: *Prehistoric Denmark*, The National Museum Copenhagen 1978.

active about 3500 B.C., that was excavated at Hov in northern Jutland.

When archaeologists began to investigate these mines they discovered some interesting facts. First, they found the flint was rough-shaped at the mine site and made into "blanks" or semifinished products to be refined by toolmakers elsewhere. They also came upon quantities of flint flakes and half-completed tools discarded because they were flawed. Thus, the traders in effect were carrying only saleable goods— flint that had been pretested and released for sale. To us, quality control had been applied in the form of standardization of the blanks and quality inspection and selection of only useable blanks for export.

Figure 5.2 shows several stages in the manufacture of flint axes. First, roughly worked natural flint modules were produced at the mine. Samples are shown in Figure 5.2a. The next stage in the process involved preparation of semifinished tool heads. Deposits of axes from this stage of the process have been found far away from the flint mines. Nearby scrap heaps indicate quality control, and that the semiworked products were a commodity being exported. Semiworked products from Denmark have been found as far away as northern Sweden (near the Gulf of Bothnia). Figure 5.2b shows some semievolved modules.

Figure 5.2c displays some of the finished products, at the stage before grinding and polishing. Deposits of finished blanks like the ones in Figure 5.2c are often found where large-scale boatbuilding was likely to have taken place.

In addition to these tool blanks, flat arrowheads of Danish manufacture have been found north of the Arctic Circle. In these northern areas, most locally produced tools were of slate, which is softer than

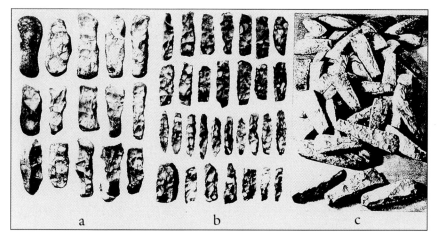

Figure 5.2 Flint blanks used for tool-making.
Source: Therkel Mathiassen. *Flinthandel i Danmark,*
Nationalmuseets Arbejdsmark 1934.

glass-hard flint. Thus, high-quality tools were produced in what today is Denmark, and the tools were traded and used throughout Europe. The high quality of the tools enabled shipbuilding to develop and created a widespread reputation for Danish craftsmen.

Although subsequent use of bronze and iron replaced flint as a material for tools and weapons, mining and working Danish flint had a very late renaissance when the flintlock rifle was developed in France. Military forces used these weapons from the end of 1600 until about 1850. At first Denmark imported ready-made flintlocks from France and Italy, but detailed military accounts in Denmark reveal that 40,000 flintlocks were ordered to be delivered from Stevns, Moen (Danish island) in 1738, and that another flint knapper from the same region in 1757 delivered 96,000 on time and up to standard. The dimensions of these tiny bits of flint had to be accurate and not vary many millimeters.

Before they were replaced by bronze and then iron tools, tools of flint played an important role in the building of Stone Age ships.

Ships As History

The rise of shipbuilding techniques can be traced by examining archeological finds. Early ships were dugout canoes produced in the Era of Stone Age Farmers (4200 to 1800 B.C.). They were followed by slowly modified models from the Bronze Age (1800 to 500 B.C.) to the Iron Age (500 B.C. to 1050 A.D.), including the Viking Age (800 to 1050 A.D.). These archaeological eras are shown in Figure 5.3.

There can be little doubt that for the greater part of our prehistoric period, as well as the medieval period, wood was the predominant material used for tools and vehicles of all kinds, as well as for construction work. In those rare cases where organic materials have survived to be excavated from prehistoric sites, the wealth of types and shapes of wooden objects, as well as the quality of craftsmanship, is striking. Such finds call attention to the importance of expanding the generally neglected study of the wood technology of the past.

Ship finds have a great potential for expanding our knowledge of the evolution of wood technology and other aspects of cultural history. Ships are built as complex structures to serve specific needs. They offer us the opportunity to study a wide field of human activities, ranging from technology and economics to social organization and politics.

ARCHAEOLOGICAL TIME TABLE

		1050
	Viking Age	
		800
	Germanic Iron Age	
		400 A.D.
IRON AGE	Roman Iron Age	
		0
	Pre-Roman Age	
		500 B.C.
	Late Bronze Age	
BRONZE AGE		1000
	Early Bronze Age	
		1800
	Dagger Period	
		2400
	Single Grave Culture	
		2800
STONE AGE FARMERS	Middle Neolithic Funnel Beaker Culture	
		3200
	Early Neolithic Funnel Beaker Culture	
		4200
	Ertebelle Culture	
		5200
	Kongemose Culture	
		6000(?)
STONE AGE HUNTERS	Maglemose Culture	
		7400(?)
	Bromme Culture	
		10000(?)

Figure 5.3 Archaeological Eras.
Source: The National Museum Copenhagen.

Full advantage of the evidence thus offered can only be taken, however, if the ship can be securely anchored in time and space. It is necessary to know when and where the ship was built, even if it is wrecked or buried far from the building site and after a long time span. In this respect, the construction details as well as selection of timber give us some useful guidelines, though we will have to keep in mind that timber for shipbuilding may have been imported, or reused from scrapped ships. It thus requires detailed studies in the technology of shipbuilding and in the use of wood to establish a firm base on which to draw conclusions about the origin and date of a ship. A series of ship finds is also needed to provide a sufficiently broad base to develop and test hypotheses.

The Dugout Canoe (3500–1500 B.C.)

Early specimens of dugout canoes come from the Era of Stone Age Farmers and have been dated circa 3400–3300 B.C. Archaeologists have also found several canoes from the period 3000–1500 B.C. Despite the fact that Danish Mesolithic settlement sites generally have fine preservation conditions for organic materials, especially wood, boats or fragments of such are rare. However, some farily well-preserved canoes have been found in recent years in cultural layers dated to 5200–5000 B.C. Prehistoric dugout canoes are numerous in Scandinavia, but most of them are dated to a much later period: Bronze, Iron, and even Viking Age.

The boats are often found inland from present-day coasts. Coastlines have changed greatly since the glaciation periods due to various movements of the Earth's crust. As a result, today the prehistoric coastlines are exposed and lying far inland in northern Denmark while the opposite is the case in central and south/southwest Denmark. Here the glacial and Mesolitic coastal sites are now submerged, and are either completely eroded away or very difficult to discover.

Two early canoes were found at Tybrind Vig on West Funen. This site was the first and largest excavation of a submerged Mesolitic settlement in Northern Europe. Among the many finds were the two dugouts, on the sea floor 250 feet offshore of present-day coastlines. The site had, at the time of use, been on the coast.

The canoes were well preserved, as they had always lain in a wet and oxygen-free environment.

The canoes were made of almost knot-free lime tree. Tybrind 1 was about 10 meters long, and 65 centimeters in width at the stern, and the greatest thickness of the bottom was 3–5 cm. Tybrind 1, shown in Figure 5.4, was found in 1979 and is the more complete of the two. Tybrind 2, excavated in 1984, consists only of fragments, but was probably larger. Tybrind 1 was apparently designed to have a separate removable bulkhead at the stern (Figure 5.5), secured with eight oval holes located within 3 cm of the stern. The holes are arranged in a radial way; an arrangement which gives an extremely tight position of the bulkhead when it is in position and expanding a little due to the absorption of water.

By having a loose bulkhead instead of keeping a section of the trunk as stern, several advantages were obtained. First, the boat is not heavy in the rear end. Second, it is much easier to manufacture. Finally, risks of radial splitting are removed.

From the midsection of the boat and forward to the bow is a 10 cm wide and 2 m long thickness along the bottom. This is positioned 15 cm to the port of the central axis and runs asymmetrically through the boat. As the boats clearly bear testimony to a highly developed technology in wood, in which shape and manufacturing are nicely adapted to each other, this longitudinal thickness is not accidental. Because it is running lengthwise in the bottom where the only two large knots are found, it may be interpreted as a result of difficulty in the removal of wood around these. Additionally, it may have improved the stability of the boat in water, taken the burden of wear during landing, and strengthened the boat in a longitudinal direction.

The preserved side (port side) is very thin (1–2 cm thickness) and terminates in a smoothly rounded gunwale, which is thicker due to a list. The list is 105 cm long and gradually diminishes along the gunwale. The gunwale ends in a rounded tenon which protrudes to the rear of the boat side. The preserved part of the gunwale is completely straight in longitudinal section. On its upper side, behind the bulkhead, is a 1–1.5 cm wide transverse depression which must have been caused by wear or pressure of a transverse lashing positioned as a sort of lock behind the bulkhead and at the same time preventing the boat from opening up. There are no holes in the gunwale, and there are no traces of arrangements for fastening an outrigger.

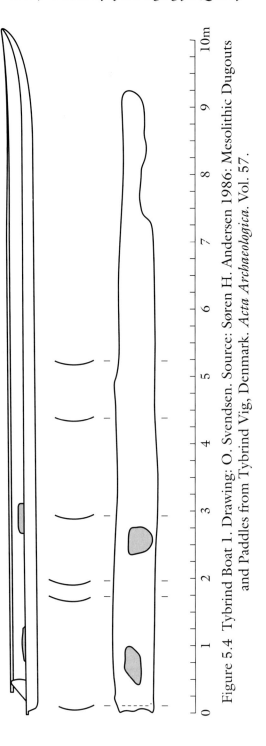

Figure 5.4 Tybrind Boat 1. Drawing: O. Svendsen. Source: Søren H. Andersen 1986: Mesolithic Dugouts and Paddles from Tybrind Vig, Denmark. *Acta Archaeologica*. Vol. 57.

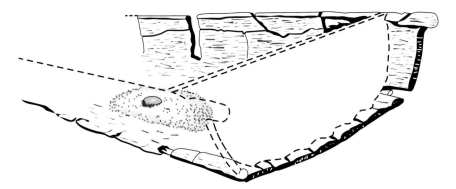

Figure 5.5 Reconstruction of the stern of Tybrind Boat 1.
Source: Søren H. Andersen 1986: Mesolithic Dugouts and Paddles
from Tybrind Vig, Denmark. *Acta Archaeologica*. Vol. 57.

Function

The Tybrind boats were essential as a means of transportation for the Mesolithic people—both as tools for extensive fishing activities and sea hunting and also for communication along the coastline, lake shores, and streams. In combination with fishing, the fireplace, a large flat-sided stone, may also have had an essential function—perhaps for eel flaring. In all probability it also served as a stabilizer, to assure smooth nagivation, and as a weight to keep the boat under water when it was not in use (to hinder drying out). Canoes such as these may have been capable of carrying a considerable cargo or a family of six to eight persons.[1]

Manufacture

Manufacturing methods for the Tybrind canoes were estimated by modern efforts to construct such vessels using tools available at the time of original production. Such experiments yield an estimated weight of 250–500 kg for the dugouts. The same experiment also shows that two persons are able to manufacture such a canoe in one week by means of stone adzes and wedges. In the analysis of the Tybrind canoes, two different types of manufacturing techniques were observed: (1) chopping with adzes and (2) cleaving in a longitudinal direction. The first technique appears to have been the one most frequently used.

Traces of chopping from adzes were found throughout the inside of both canoes, especially on the sides where wear by use was not as intense. The chopping marks suggest the use of core or diabase adze of the Ertebolle culture. New experimental investigations with the manufacture of dugout canoes have clearly demonstrated that the typical Ertebolle flat flaked flakeadze is much more effective for such work than the coreadze. Besides, flakeadzes with a worn edge give the same type of chopping marks as are seen on the two Tybrind canoes. No indication of the use of fire in the production of these boats has been recorded.

Bronze Age Boats
(Circa 1800–500 B.C.)

At about 2000 B.C., the country farmers were becoming acquainted with such new materials as copper, tin, and gold, which were acquired by barter from distant regions. Not long afterward bronze, an alloy of copper and tin, had completely displaced flint as the most important material for tools. The period from 1800 to 500 B.C. is therefore described as the Bronze Age.

The only Bronze Age boat excavated in Denmark so far was found at Varpelev near Stevns, Zealand (Figure 5.6). It is dated to 1030 B.C. Its original length was 14 m and breadth 85 cm. The thickness of the sides were 2–3 cm, with the bottom almost 10 cm thick. The stern is nearly intact, so it has been possible to make a reconstruction of its original form though some of the stern is missing. The boat was made of oak, of a perfectly straight, nearly knot-free trunk. At the root-end it has measured at least 1.1 m in diameter. Evenly cut out in the boat three "frames" are left proud on the inside, about 20 cm broad and 2–3 cm high. Such strengthening frames are not known from Stone Age dugouts, and they represent an advance in quality of construction since the Tybrind dugout era.

These strengthening frames are also seen in the dugout exhibited at the Archaeologisches Landesmuseum in Gothorp (Figure 5.7). This construction of dugouts with transverse frames to balance the boat improved stability and maneuverability, representing the next stage of boat development.

Figure 5.6 Denmark's only Bronze Age boat found at Varpelev,
Stevns, Zealand. Source: Photo and Information—Helge Nielsen,
Køge Museum, 1973.

Figure 5.7 Dugout with transverse frames exhibited at the
Archaeologisches Landesmuseum, Gothorp, Schleswig.
Photo: Carl A. Kofoed. Source: Harald Aakerlund 1963,
Tidig skandinavisk skeppsnadskonst.

Bronze Age Tools

Bronze opened a new world of possibilities within the field of tools and weapons. The foreign wares that had most interest for the local peasants were tools and weapons, as they were tougher and lasted longer than those they had used before.

New founding techniques were developed, methods which have been used until our time. Every gram of the new material had to be brought from outside the country. A fine network of trade connections seems to have existed over the whole continent of Europe. Through this network, not only bronze was exchanged, but also products such as wax (used in the casting process), honey, hides, amber, and many other things.

Founding by means of cores and lost-wax casting were the dominant techniques. These techniques led to the first standardization program in history. The spearhead shown in Figure 5.8 is an example of such standards. Thousands of spearheads like the one shown have been found in places of sacrifice where people offered booty acquired in battle in gratitude for their victory.

The bronze axe came into use for boatbuilding and other purposes considerably slower than other bronze articles. The stone axe was excellent; it served its purpose well, and it was much cheaper than the bronze one.

The making of other tools was more substantially influenced by the availability of bronze, coming from the south. Flint toolmakers, the flint knappers, had the competitive advantage of cost because the material they used was very cheap compared with bronze. The "bronzellsmiths," on the other hand, had much more freedom when forming and processing their products. Long swords and daggers, for instance, were impossible to make in flint. The flint-makers' efforts to reach far also in this direction deserve our respect, but it is clear that it does not work. Figure 5.9 shows Bronze Age spearheads still made of flint before such items were replaced with ones made from bronze. The axe, on the contrary, survived as a useful product made of flint well throughout the Bronze Age, until iron took over and became the prime material for utensils and weapons.

Most of the foreign bronzes were melted down by local founders. These freed themselves remarkably quickly from the influence of foreign models and developed a north European style of bronze work, characterized in particular by spiral ornament, which was quite as good as the work of the regions the metal came from.

Figure 5.8 Bronze spearhead. Source: Johannes Brøndsted, 1958, *Danmarks Oldtid*, Vol 2.

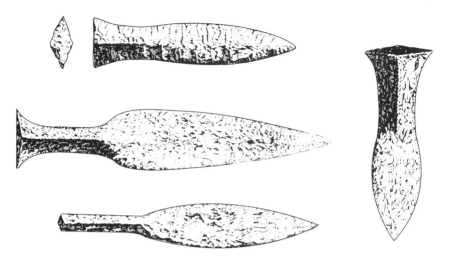

Figure 5.9 Flint daggers based on bronze prototypes.
Source: Johannes Brøndsted, 1958, *Danmarks Oldtid*, Vol 2.

Early Iron Age Boats (500 B.C.–300 A.D.)

The Hjortspring boat, shown in Figure 5.10, is dated at 350 B.C., during the Celtic Iron Age. It was probably an offering to gods. In the early 1920s, it was unearthed by peat diggers in a bog close to the Hjortspring farm on the island of Als in the southern part of Denmark.

Design

It is quite clear that the Hjortspring boat evolved from the much older hide boats in which a hide cover is lashed to a wooden framework or skeleton. We only know about these boats from rock carvings, stylized drawings carved into rocks in many places in the Scandinavian countries 5000–6000 years ago.

In every detail, the Hjortspring boat was dimensioned to be as light as possible. In addition, it was elegantly structured, so the slender-lined vessel was easy to paddle through the waters. It has been estimated that, unequipped, the weight of the boat was approximately 530 kg, which is extremely light for a boat of its size.

The boat is an agile war canoe more than 19 meters long. It consists of a bottom-plank and two wide boards on each side, whose ends are held together by two wooden fitting-blocks, yielding a keelless,

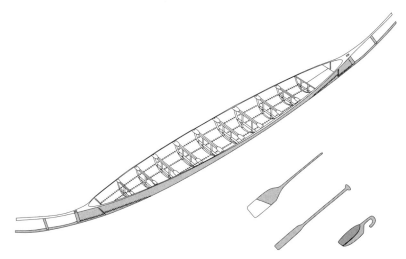

Figure 5.10 The Hjortspring Boat: Drawing: Chr. Thomsen, 1990.
Source: Model built by Morten Grønbeck in 1988
for the Hedeby Museum.

round-bottomed vessel. At each end the boat is given two upward bent extensions or beaks, the lower ones an extension of the bottom plank, the upper ones an extension of the top of the fitting-blocks.

The boat's inner dimensions are about 13 m long, 2 m wide. It would have held a complement of at least 20 men, in addition to a helmsman, whose place would be at the broad steering oar. A good deal of the steering oar is preserved. It is wide-bladed with a short shaft about 90 cm long. This oar was found at the boat's north end. A small piece of a similar oar was found at the south end, suggesting that one was fitted there too, so that the vessel, equipped to travel in either direction, could quickly change its course.

The slim vessel gives evidence of a long tradition of handicraft. With its five-plank thoroughly planned construction, it is light and slender with no risk to its stability. All details are refined to the thinnest and lightest possible, while the big well-finished planks are worked to fine dimensions. This speedy vessel, together with its oars, weighed about 530 kg. A crew of presumably 24 men, each weighing 72 kg, gives a further weight of 1730 kg, while a weight of weapons and equipment at 16 kg per man yields another 380 kg. All in all then, the boat, when fully loaded, would have weighed about 2640 kg.

Since the ends of the boat were not fully preserved, the possibility cannot be excluded that the upper beak may have continued upward to form majestic figurehead-like structures, such as we see in the representation of ships among Bronze Age carvings illustrated in Figure 5.11. It is certainly possible that many Bronze Age boats were built in the same way as the Hjortspring boat.

Manufacture

With the tools at hand when the Hjortspring boat was built, an enormous step forward had been reached. The techniques used in its construction must have employed many of the helping tools still in use today; for instance distance indicators, jigs, and calibration. The techniques also called for a trained workforce of shipwrights and carpenters.

For the construction of this boat, the Iron Age boatbuilder used more than five planks over 15 m long and 70 cm wide of nearly knot-free lime wood. Such wood came from lime trees with very straight trunks 15–16 m tall and about 1 m in diameter. Such trees are rarely

Figure 5.11 Bronze Age Carvings. Hammeren, Bornholm.
Source: *356 oldtidsminder på Øerne*. Henning Dehn-Nielsen.

found in Danish forests today. The trunks were split to form planks, of which one constituted the bottom plank. If this plank was all of a piece, as is strongly suggested, it must have been about 15 m long and a little more than half a meter wide at the middle, narrowing toward the end.

At intervals of exactly 1 m along the board's inner side, there were cleats to be used for the fastening on the boat's "timber," though these are better described as a kind of fixed ribs. Each single rib arrangement consists of a bent hazel branch which was lashed to the cleat, together with a system of ribs athwart the boat. The upper ribs were broad and flat and served not only to hold the gunwale in place, but also as seats for the rowers.

There were 10 such fixed ribs with seats and, as we may suppose two men to each seat, this means 20 men, to whom may be added one or two helmsmen and perhaps a leader who took part in the rowing. All fixings (fastenings) in the boat were made with rope of lime tree bast and not a single piece of metal was used in its construction. As will be seen later on our journey up through the ages, the use of metal facilitates a number of construction details. We must assume that iron at that time was not sufficiently known to be used in structural details, but was used for weapons.

Organizing for Quality

The building of boats like the Hjortspring boat required an organization with a strong leader who coordinated a range of specialties. A leader was needed to coordinate the different specialties like choosing trees for felling, working the trees into planks according to specified dimensions, and making material for lashing or sewing. Most importantly, the leader had to have the overall idea—the design of the boat.

Scandinavia, like most of northern Europe, was at that time divided into a number of small tribal regions or pocket states ruled by petty kings or headsmen. The beginning of these petty states had begun when a leader emerged for a tribe. The leader was usually the best among the members in terms of leading the fight against adversaries, so that the tribe could keep intact. As we know from the history of man, there are always persons who will try to extend their domain and power. So it was in Scandinavia in 350 B.C. Often the strong leader of the tribe was not only a strong warrior but also the man of the highest intelligence. The stability arising from strong leadership over generations opened the possibility of establishing an organization with specialties within a range of fields.

Later Iron Age Boats (300 A.D.–1050 A.D.)

The Nydam boat (310–320 A.D.) (Figures 5.12 and 5.13) shows that the speed of technological progress is increasing. For the first time we see iron used as construction material in Scandinavian boatbuilding. Where the Hjortspring boat was stitched or lashed together, all joints of the Nydam boat were riveted together with iron rivets. Iron had come to Scandinavia some centuries before. On the whole, bronze was only used in connection with boatbuilding as tool material, not as construction material; but iron was soon accepted as superior to bronze for tools and weapons and as extremely suitable for the construction as well as for tools. The building of furnaces for iron smelting started in Scandinavia in the beginning of the Christian era. As a result, iron was available at a much lower cost than bronze.

Discovery of iron and its utility for joining wooden parts was a necessity for the development of ever larger ships. The Nydam boat,

Figure 5.12 The Nydam Boat exhibited since 1948 at the
Archaeologishes Landesmuseum, Gothorp, Schleswig.
Photo: Landesmuseum.

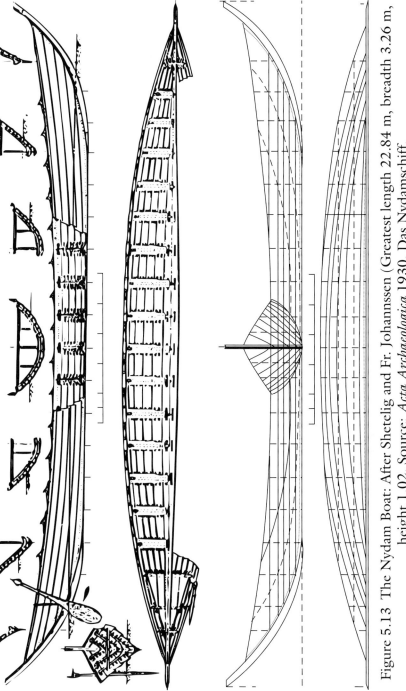

Figure 5.13 The Nydam Boat: After Shetelig and Fr. Johannssen (Greatest length 22.84 m, breadth 3.26 m, height 1.02. Source: *Acta Archaeologica* 1930, Das Nydamschiff.

however, retained the best features of the Hjortspring boat. It was constructed of eleven well-dimensioned, large, whole planks.

The boat was built to be manned by 30 rowers. The weight of the boat and the oars has been estimated to be 3300 kg. Fully equipped with men, weapons, supplies, and ballast, the total weight would be approximately 8800 kg. With this weight amidship, the gunwales would be about 60 cm above sea level. The slender boat might have been rather unstable, but the Nydam boat represents, with its good and bad sides, advantages and disadvantages, an interesting step in the development from paddle to sailing ship.

The Development of Keels, Masts, and Sails

About the time of the Nydam boat, a true keel was emerging on Scandinavian ships. As Figure 5.14 shows, there was no identifiable keel on early boats. A dorsal plank emerged in the period 500 B.C. to 400 A.D., and the beginning of a true keel, a skid keel, began to be used in the period 300–500 A.D. Following the emergence of the keel, the

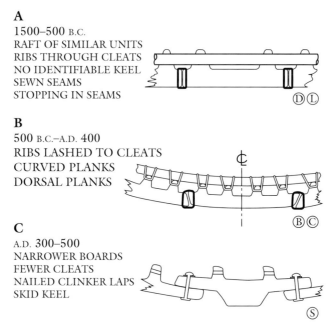

A
1500–500 B.C.
RAFT OF SIMILAR UNITS
RIBS THROUGH CLEATS
NO IDENTIFIABLE KEEL
SEWN SEAMS
STOPPING IN SEAMS

B
500 B.C.–A.D. 400
RIBS LASHED TO CLEATS
CURVED PLANKS
DORSAL PLANKS

C
A.D. 300–500
NARROWER BOARDS
FEWER CLEATS
NAILED CLINKER LAPS
SKID KEEL

Figure 5.14 Emergence of the keel. Source: Eric McKee, Timbers from Old Ships. *Nautical Archaeology* 5.1.

most important developments in this period were the mast and sails. Skillful working of the sails gave great maneuverability of the slender and flexible boats and optimal speed.

This evolution of ship design and construction reached its peak in the Viking Age (800–1050) with the Nordic Vikings dominating much of northern and western Europe. The Vikings sailed to such far-away destinations as the Mediterranean, Iceland, Greenland, and North America. We may safely assume that in the Viking days of glory, there were about half a million ships of different sizes in northern Europe. William the Conqueror alone used about 1000 ships for the invasion of England.

The Norwegian Viking Ships

In the past 50 years, we have gained much new knowledge about shipbuilding techniques in the Viking Ages. The discovery of ship burials, especially in Fladby in Denmark and Gokstad (Figure 5.15) and Oseberg (Figure 5.16) in Norway, aroused great interest in the general public in the 1930s and onward.

These burial finds were graves of high-born leaders/chiefs buried together with ship and grave goods.

The Gokstad ship dates to about 895–900 A.D. It was found in 1880 in a grave mound in Gokstad, in southern Norway, near Oslofjord. It is 23.3 m long, 5.24 m broad and is about 60 to 70 percent preserved. In the grave was the skeleton of a man along with a rich assortment of household goods, sleighs, boats, and domestic animals.

The Oseberg ship dates to 820 A.D. It was found in a grave mound in Slagen Sogn, Vestfold, in southern Norway, near Oslofjord. The ship is 21.5 m long and 5.1 m broad, and is in a state of about 90 percent preservation. The grave included the skeletons of two women along with household equipment, a carriage, sleighs, looms, textiles, domestic animals, and so on. Many of the grave contents were beautifully ornamented.

The two Norwegian Viking ships are impressive masterpieces of ship design and construction, and they testify to the high technical capabilities as well as the artistic sense of the builders.

The elaborate grave goods and the magnificence of these ships suggests that the deceased were either persons of great wealth or were high-born leaders/chiefs who were thus honored at their departure.

Figure 5.15 The Gokstad ship. Length 23.3 m, breadth 5.24 m.
Source: Vikingeskipsfunnene, negative number 8612.
Copyright, Universitets Oldsaksamling, Oslo, 1969.

The Ships in the Fjord

At the close of the Viking Age—presumably some time between 1000 and 1050 A.D.—the navigable passages of Roskilde Fjord were blocked by a series of barriers to protect the important trading town of Roskilde from enemy fleets. The blockage manifested itself as a ridge of stones. It had always been known to fishermen in the fjord, and local tradition claimed that it held a ship sunken at the command of Queen Margrethe (1412). Not until underwater excavations, carried out between 1957 and 1959 by the Danish National Museum, was it

Figure 5.16 The Oseberg ship. Length 21.5 m, breadth 5 m.
Source: Vikingeskipsfunnene, negative number 1098.
Copyright, Universitets Oldsaksamling, Oslo, 1969.

established that the blockage dated from the Viking period and contained not one but several ships, which the underwater archaeologists examined and charted.

What was originally believed to be five Viking ships were excavated from the blockage in the Peberrenden channel at Skuldelev, 20 km north of Roskilde (Figure 5.17). Three ships were sunk across the channel and heaped with boulders. Shortly afterwards, the barrier was strengthened by sinking a further two ships at the spot. The barrier was erected at the time when Norwegian Vikings ravaged Denmark, but no definite historical event has been linked with the blockage.

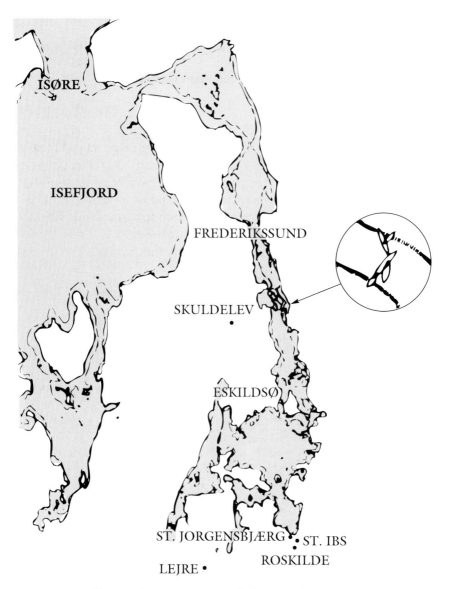

Figure 5.17 Location of Ships in the Fjord.
Source: The Viking Ship Museum in Roskilde.

In June 1969, the Viking Museum at Roskilde, a specially designed museum for the ships of the fjord, was opened. It was opened
to the public before the first ship was completely reassembled, in order
to give visitors an opportunity to follow how the ships were gradually

pieced together, one by one, from thousands of pieces of wreckage both large and small. A full-scale "skeleton" model is shown of the ship not yet reassembled, built entirely of new wood, to give visitors an impression of the dimensions, lines, and shapes of the ships.

The Deep-Sea Trader (Wreck 1). The deep-sea trader in Figure 5.18 is a broad solid vessel with high sides. It is currently the only example yet found of a type known as a knarr, a seagoing cargo ship that sailed to England, Iceland, and Greenland. On the site of a Viking-period Norse settlement in Greenland, a few planks have been found from a knarr. It had either carried settlers from Iceland or a cargo of European goods for the little community of Norsemen in Greenland. This ship was built of pine, oak, and lime, most likely in south Norway. It had a half-deck fore and aft separated by a hold amidships, but there was

Figure 5.18 A Deep-Sea Trader of the Viking Period.
Source: Vikingeskibshallen, Roskilde.

nowhere for people in the boat to take shelter. Its primary means of propulsion was provided by a broad square sail with a tacking spar that could be secured in three different positions to a forward cleat. Between 60 percent and 70 percent of the ships's timber is preserved. This ship was 16.5 m long with a breadth of 4.5 m and a height of 1.9 m.

The Longship (Wrecks 2 and 4). One of the ships in the blockage was so long that it was first assumed to be two different vessels. The wreckage proved to be a single ship (Figure 5.19), the only known example of the dreaded Viking man-of-war used for long-range raiding. It was fitted with a mast and sail, and the crew of 40–50 oarsmen gave it speed and maneuverability in battle. It was a light resilient craft of oak that was both seaworthy and easy to pull ashore.

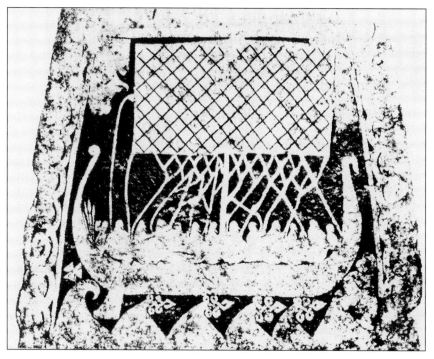

Figure 5.19 Longship carved on an 8th century picture stone from Gotland. Source: The Viking Ship Museum in Roskilde.

The Merchant Ship (Wreck 3).   A third ship was identified as a merchant ship, a trim oak-built craft. The prow was fashioned from one piece of wood and preserved intact. It is a typical small merchant ship of the Viking period, used for carrying cargo across the Baltic (possibly also across the North Sea and up large rivers). Its freight was stowed amidships under some hides, while the crew of not more than 4–6 men kept to the half-deck fore and aft. If necessary, the crew could use oars thrust through oarholes in the gunwale strake at the half-deck, but generally they traveled under sail. The mast was amidships, fitted into a mast step in the keelson and braced by a mast beam. Shrouds led from the mast-top to sides and to stays at the forward end of the ship. The shrouds were tied to the outside of the gunwale strake with osier rings. The ship was 13.3 meters long.

The Warship (Wreck 5).   The Danish Viking warship (Figures 5.20 and 5.21) is long (18 m), low (1.1 m high amidship), and narrow (2.6 m in breadth) like the Ladby burial ship in Funen (excavated in 1935) and the ships portrayed in the Bayeux Tapestry (embroidered in Normandy shortly after William the Conqueror's invasion of England in 1066). This type of ship is also represented in the Skuldelev find. It was normally propelled by sail, but when becalmed it could be rowed by 24 oarsmen, their oars passing through oarholes in the gunwale strake.

The three upper strakes are of ash, and had earlier been used in another ship. New oarholes had to be made and several of the old ones blocked before the uppermost plank could be fitted into the new ship. On the outside of the next plank below this is a simple Viking decoration.

Development of Riveting Technology

The Hjortspring boat planks were sewn together, whereas the Nydam boatbuilders replaced the stitching with iron rivets. In the period between the Nydam boat (310–320 A.D.) and the Vikings, a number of new construction details emerged. Apart from mast and sails, one was the riveting of the frames to the planks. This, of course, made possible a much more effective utilization of the wood and, combined with the refined splitting technique for tree trunks, provided the opportunity for light and elegant hulls.

Figure 5.20 Viking Warship. Source: Vikingeskibshallen, Roskilde.

Figure 5.21 "Sebbe Als" Replica of Wreck 5.
Source: The Viking Ship Museum in Roskilde.

Riveting was accomplished using iron. The iron came to Europe with the Celts before the birth of Christ, but the boats found so far indicate that iron was introduced in boatbuilding about 300 A.D. The Nydam boat is an example of this introduction of iron.

At first, archaeologists were surprised that many iron rivets were intact after having been in salt water for many hundreds of years. The explanation came recently (in 1990). The iron used was of very high quality won from ores in Jutland (the Danish peninsula) and from northern Germany. Figure 5.22 shows rivets and work-ups of iron from about 300 A.D.

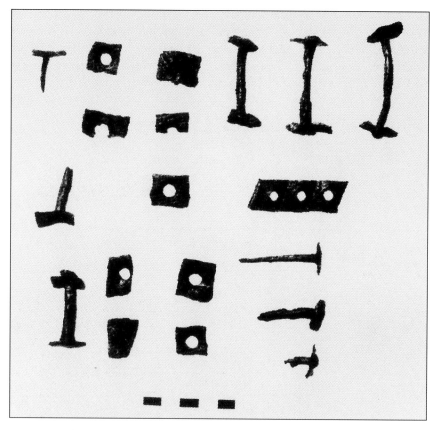

Figure 5.22 Rivets and "Work ups" of iron from about 300 A.D.
Source: Thomsen, Per O. 1987. Svendborg Museum.

Continuing Changes in Technology

The rapid pace of technological change in ship styling, design, size, means of propulsion, and construction technologies is evidence of a culture where changes were an ongoing part of the production process. This industry, shipbuilding, can be thought of as the essential transportation industry of coastal communities. The Scandinavians, in comparison to the other world-class coastal cultures, such as the Greeks and Romans, developed their iron-based construction later than did southern Europe and the Middle East, but they did not blindly follow or copy the construction techniques of those Mediterranean countries.

Scandinavia had a high-quality iron derived from bog iron ore (limonite). It also had the charcoal necessary for processing the iron into hard steel. This steel was ideal for making, among other items, tools used to construct ships. The most important of these are shown in Figure 5.23 and are also illustrated in the Bayeux tapestry.

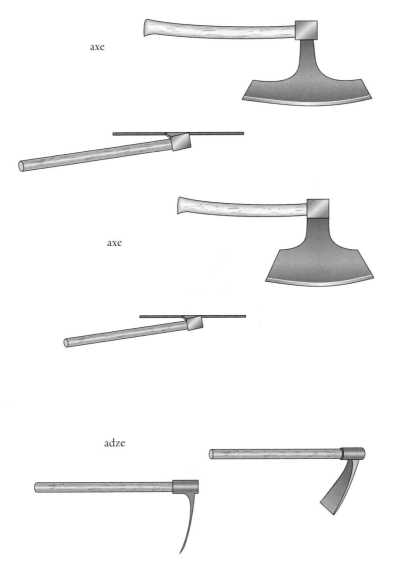

axe

axe

adze

Figure 5.23 Iron woodworking tools. Drawings.
Source: Architect Christian Thomsen, Nordborg.

In addition to the favorable raw materials for iron, the soil and climatic conditions prevailing in the Scandinavian countries from 3000 B.C. to 1000 A.D. were very favorable for tree growth.

The shipbuilders capitalized on the particular characteristics of local raw materials—hard steel and plentiful lumber to create their designs and manufacturing processes. They created a way of forming planks, for example, which can only be described as extravagant of material. However, the material was plentiful (and, therefore, presumably inexpensive) and the ship planks, gunwales, keels, and so on that were derived from these woodworking materials were highly exact: their dimensions did not vary greatly from one component to the next nor between each component and the standard.

The techniques used to split wood are depicted in Figure 5.24. In Viking Age shipbuilding the elements of the ship were worked out of the tree trunk in one of four ways; A, Cut directly from the trunk (for keel, stems, frames); B, Trunk split in two, each half then worked down to one tangentially oriented plank (for long and wide planks and stringers); C, Trunk split in four, each quarter worked down to one element (for beams and stringers); D, Radial splitting of the trunk into "cloveboards" by repeated halving ($1/2$, $1/4$, $1/8$, $1/16$) for radially oriented planks. In some cases the direction of the final split was shifted slightly away from the radius in order to give half the planks extra width.

Splitting in this manner required greater accuracy than had been required when splitting with a wedge. A splitting wedge could go

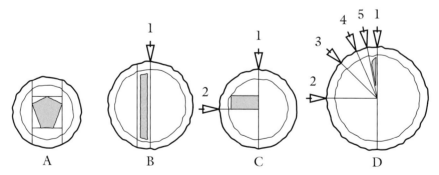

Figure 5.24 Four techniques to split wood.
Source: Ole Crumlin-Pedersen, Aspects of Wood Technology
in Medieval Shipbuilding. Sailing into the Past. The Viking
Ship Museum, Roskilde.

completely astray (rendering the product unusable) if it were placed only a few millimeters out of position. The new techniques enabled far fewer rejects and more output meeting production specifications.

The Viking ships were significantly different from those of at least one other successful maritime culture—the Greeks. The Greeks, of course, navigated in the enclosed Mediterranean, not the open northern Atlantic. The Scandinavians, in contrast to the Greeks, developed a keel construction method that produces a more flexible hull, one better able to withstand the heavy sea without leaking. It did not only withstand, it absorbed the heavy sea and transformed it into speed. The Scandinavian ships were light, could easily be pulled or run ashore, and needed no harbor.

The Greek keel construction, exemplified in a Greek warship from 500–600 B.C., is caravel-built with planks joined edge to edge, as shown in Figure 5.25. Ship hulls were constructed in the ancient Mediterranean by joining planks edge to edge with tenons inserted into individual mortices cut into the edges of the planks. Each tenon

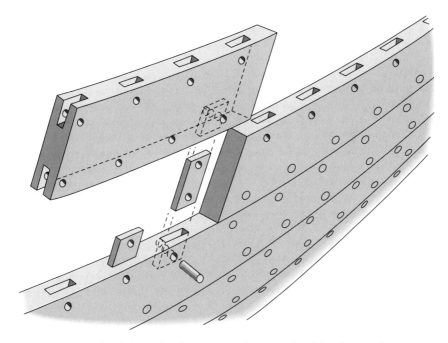

Figure 5.25 Ship hull construction method in the ancient Mediterranean. Source: John F. Coates, *Scientific American,* April 1989.

was built from the keel up. Frame timbers were added as the hull was completed far enough to receive them.

The Scandinavians, as early as the Hjortspring boat (350 B.C.), had adopted another method of keel construction, the clinker-built keel illustrated in Figure 5.26. In this method, which was perfected during the Viking period, planks on the hull overlap and were lashed to cleats left proud on the inside of the plank. The overlapped portions of the hull planks were riveted together with high-quality bog iron which had been treated in a rust-preventive manner (the rivets have survived underwater for about 800 years). The construction technique capitalized on the available raw materials. It used a lavish amount of lumber because it meant cutting away about half of the original thickness of the planks so as to get strong and accessible cleats. The cleats were attached to the ribs via a specially developed tightening material, woolen strips impregnated with resin and oil. The resulting flexible ship hull was well suited to the requirements of the harsh North Atlantic environment.

Shipbuilding Quality and Scandinavian Power

Shipbuilding in Scandinavia from 3000 B.C. to 1100 A.D. highlights an industry improving over thousands of years. Technology is constantly modified to create products more suited to customer require-

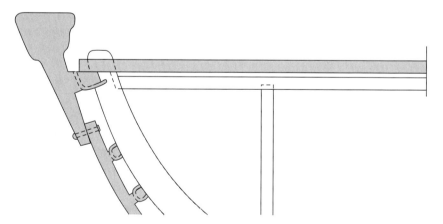

Figure 5.26 Clinker-build hull. Northwest European tradition. Drawing made by architect Christian Thomsen, Nordborg.

ments. Naturally occurring raw materials are considered, in their relative abundance, in developing engineering designs. Craftsmen are carefully trained, and production techniques are developed to minimize deviations from product specifications.

These improvements were especially important for the Scandinavians because the expansion of shipbuilding as an industry was essential to the spread of Scandinavian culture and power. Ships provided for transport in open and sheltered waters for peaceful trade and communication, conquest, and colonization. The Scandinavians built ships to high quality standards, able to withstand the often brutal seas of the North Sea and northern Atlantic, as well as the inland fjords of the Scandinavian countries. This may have reached its peak with the Vikings who dominated shipbuilding in the northern Atlantic. They had the transportation, tools, and equipment during the period to enable them to invade and colonize Ireland, England, France, and Friesland, among other countries.

Notes

1. Andersen, Søren H., 1986: Mesolithic Dug-outs and Paddles from Tybrind Vig, Denmark. *Acta Archaeologica*, Vol. 57.

Bibliography

Aakerlund, Harald, 1963: *Nydamskeppen. En studie i tidig skandinavisk skeppsbygnadskonst.* Gøteborg.

Beck, Jens, 1968: *Skalk 1968,* Vol. 1.

Brøndsted, Johannes, 1957: *Danmarks Oldtid,* bd.1. Stenalderen, Køvenhavn.

Brøndsted, Johannes, 1958: *Danmarks Oldtid,* bd.2. Bronzealderen, Køvenhavn.

Brøndsted, Johannes, 1960: *Danmarks Oldtid,* bd.3. Jernalderen, Køvenhavn.

Coates, John F., 1989: *Scientific American,* April.

Crumlin-Pedersen, Ole, 1986: Aspects of Wood Technology in Medieval Shipbuilding; Ole Crumlin-Pedersen and Max Vinner: *Sailing into the Past.*

Dehn-Nielson, Henning. *356 Oldtidsminder på Øerne*. (356 stories from the islands), 1977.

Hagen, Anders, 1969: *Vikingeskipsfunnene*. Universitetes Oldsaksamling. Oslo.

Kaul, Flemming, 1988: *Da våbnene tav (When the Weapons Were Stilled)*. København.

McKee, Eric: Timbers from Old Ships. *Nautical Archaeology 5.1*.

Nielsen, Helge, 1973: Baaden ved vejene. *Skalk 1973,* Vol. 6.

Rieck, Flemming, and Ole Crumlin-Pedersen, 1988: *Baade fra Danmarks Oldtid, Vikingeskibsmuseet*. Roskilde.

Rosenberg, Georg, 1937: Hjortspringfundet. *Nordiske Fortidsminder*. Bd. 3, hefte 1. København.

Sheteling, Haakon, 1930: Das Nydamschiff. *Acta Archaeologica,* Vol. 1, København.

Thomsen, P.O. Thomas, 1986: Annual Publication, Svendborg Museum.

Mathiassen, Therkel, 1934: Flinthandel i Danmark. *Fra Nationalmusets arbejdsmark 1934*. (Annual Publication).

CHAPTER 6

Managing for Quality in Ancient Rome

Dr. Marco Bigliazzi (Author)
History of Arts Department, University of Pisa

Prof. Roberto Mirandola (Scientific Supervisor)
Mechanical and Nuclear Department, University of Pisa

Introduction

A brief description of quality management in ancient Rome must begin with a look at the organization of Roman society. Power was highly centralized. To maintain their prestige the ruling classes had to offer acceptable living conditions (a sort of minimum standard) to obtain the consent of the populations and thus legitimize their own position. In this regard, there was a great deal of truth in the saying *panem et circenses* (bread and circuses)—satisfy the people's basic needs and organize displays of urban opulence and mass entertainments.

This hierarchical social system was constantly obliged to subjugate new populations for two reasons: first, to fuel an economy whose principal source of labor was slaves and freedmen and whose material resources were depleted by the huge growth of the central system itself; and second, to satisfy the market demand—particularly evident during the imperial period—for precious materials and exotic goods. Examples of the search for prestige that required the acquisition of exotic goods include the fashion of collecting items from the Greek civilization in vogue among the upper middle classes, and the tendency to face the "noble" parts of brick buildings with rare marbles. The former built the personal *gloria* of private individuals; the latter, with the beautification of public works such as the city forums, contributed to the prestige of the state and its representatives.

The Roman civilization was consequently aggressive and expansionist. The Romans' objective, from the beginning, was to conquer and maintain control over extensive territories inhabited by other populations. To extend the *Pax Romana* over these conquered lands, the Romans required up-to-date information on conditions in even the farthest flung corners of the empire. The history of the great Roman roads, which became increasingly direct, rapid, and durable, and were furnished with numerous reference points, is the history of the information network created for that purpose by the central power in Rome. The function of these roads was to act as an information communication channel rather than as a general transport system.

Road construction is only one of the areas in which the ancient Romans' skills as builders supported the expansion and maintenance of the empire. These building skills relied heavily on the development and use of many of the basic tools and concepts of managing for quality. These are particularly apparent in three activities: the mastery of territory, the production and use of building materials, and the administration of cities and living conditions. We will begin this chapter with a short description of the importance of building skills in the expansion of the Roman Empire and the key role of standardization. Then we will discuss in greater detail how the evolution of quality management concepts, practices, and tools influenced and was influenced by those three activities related to territory, building materials, and cities.

An Empire of Builders

The Romans developed highly sophisticated techniques, such as territorial surveying, division, and mapping. They used these to master the rural and urban lands incorporated into the empire. They developed quality standards, measurement methods, and tools. They employed sophisticated customer–supplier relationships to increase production.

The execution of large construction projects required effective working relationships among the various parties as well as effective processes for producing the individual buildings and other structures (Figure 6.1). The administration of urban life and living conditions

Figure 6.1 Trajan's Column: legionary soldiers building a
fortification, possibly with unbaked bricks; masons and a painter
using scaffolding to apply a layer of plaster.
Source: Adam, p. 85, fig. 177.

involved the balancing of needs for urban administration with requirements of the social hierarchy. In doing so, political considerations often dominated juridical considerations. Thus, aims common to the individual building yards or to the development of a particular technique were influenced by the wider context.

The Important Role of Standardization

The definition of various types of standards played a key role in expanding and maintaining the empire as well as serving as the foundation for many of the Romans' achievements in managing for quality. These standards differed somewhat from the types of standards that later emerged in modern industrial processes. However, the Romans came very close to matching those modern standards in their work in territorial planning and in various aspects of construction.

Standardization was achieved in many fields. The first was units of measurement. A uniform measurement system was adopted throughout the empire. Its importance can be seen in land surveying, in construction work, and in stone quarrying. This achievement led to the development of high-precision instruments, the acquisition of technical skills and the emergence of measurement as a specific component of the production process. A second example was size normalization for mass production of bricks and lead pipes to meet the growing demand for reliable and inexpensive building materials. The quality of bricks reached such a high level that they were considered more reliable than stone. A morphological normalization also developed to facilitate the use of certain architectural structures and construction techniques. Finally, a sort of housing standard existed with the building regulations that we know were in force at least from the time of Augustus.

The Augustan period, during which the last republican political structures disappeared as imperial power achieved official status, is in fact a very important point in the history of Rome. It was after Augustus, for example, that mass brick production spread and the gradual move toward the imperial monopoly of the third century began. It was during the Julian–Claudian age, too, that masonry bridges began to replace boat bridges, and it became the rule rather than the exception to pave the major roads. Work on the majority of the monumental buildings, whose impressive ruins became centers of attraction for artists and tourists from the Renaissance to the present, also began at this time.

Mastery of the Territory

The distinctive layout of Roman cities and the way in which rural lands were organized can still be seen today. This layout arose from the military encampments, the Roman *castra*, on which many cities were founded, in the historic centers of many Italian cities, and in the layout of rural lands. The distinctive form of the *castrum*, with its regular grid of orthogonal roads, is also recognizable in cities outside Italy, like Timgad in Algeria (Figure 6.2a), which were part of the

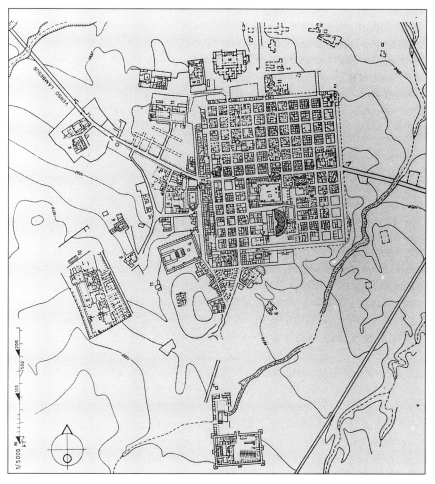

Figure 6.2a Map of Timgad, Algeria. Example of the subdivision of a city into *insulae quadratae*. Source: Adam, p. 10, fig. 2.

progressive expansion of the colonial empire. Many regions, such as the region of Imola (Figure 6.2b), show clear signs of the work of the military *mensores* (land surveyors) who divided the land into square *centuriae* (an area equivalent to 0.622 acres).

Centuriation

Posts found in Mediterranean Africa and in Italy illustrate the land organization procedure adopted by the Romans. In the process of subdividing the land into centuriae (centuriation), stone posts were located

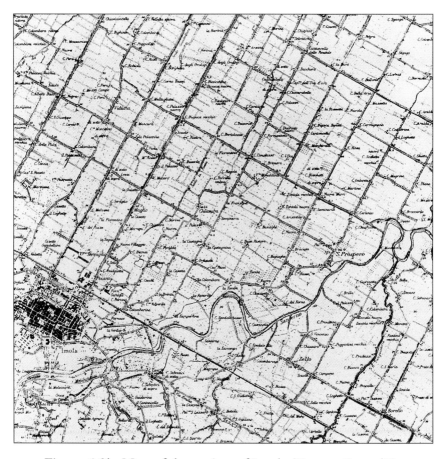

Figure 6.2b Map of the region of Imola (Forum Cornelii).
Source: Adam, p. 13, fig. 9.

at the intersection of the two main roads and at all the intersections of the secondary axes that constituted the centuriae. A *decussis* (diagram cut into the stone) at the top of the post showed the orthogonal directions, while the position of the stone in relation to the intersection of the two main roads was marked horizontally—thus providing the reference coordinate (Figure 6.3). These posts facilitated land surveying and subsequent construction work, and also provided precise points of reference for land jurisdiction.

This division of the land into regular and, in many cases, square blocks, was dictated by the requirements of Roman social organization. First of all, this system permitted a rapid overall view and therefore control by a hierarchical organization, even when the various offices were held on a rotational basis by people from different places. The system also facilitated apportionment of land by a central power into private lots and public urban areas, with a view to the subsequent infrastructure construction and property census operations. To support those census operations, accurate surveying enabled the monetary value of the lots to be easily calculated in terms of a uniform unit adopted throughout the empire.

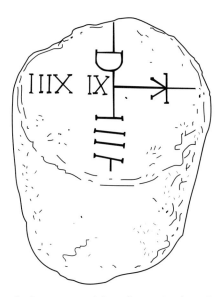

Figure 6.3 Centuriation post with a decussis showing the orthogonal directions of the Cardo (K) and the Decumanus (D) and distances. Source: Adam, p. 12, fig. 6.

In this way, the Romans managed to institute centralized control both on a local level and in relation to the capital. They also met the related need for units of measurement of the value of land lots. In surveying the territory in preparation for infrastructure projects and to guide optimal exploitation of the land and natural resources, the Romans assessed each area separately, mainly on the basis of military strategy and provision requirements. We know, in fact, that the orthogonal grid was not planned in strict accordance with the cardinal points. Instead, the planning was an eminently practical arrangement based on the characteristics of each portion of land. Religious prescriptions regarding land division were adopted only in the case of sanctuaries. Operational planning was handled by the military, whose main concern in achieving an orderly and parceled land structure was the collection of physical data (geological configuration, type of soil, location of springs, wind exposure) for insertion in a standardized measurement system. The use of precision instruments played a major role in this work.

Pompeii provides a particularly clear example of the way urban growth was regulated. The irregularity of the ancient Greek-Oscan city, built on a sloping lava bed for defense purposes, is immediately obvious. During the fifth century, the town was systematically extended northeastward on a lava slope with a 34-meter height difference between Porta Vesuvio and Porta Stabia (Figure 6.4). The Romans developed this extension in the form of an isotropic small-square grid, with a system of roads marking off the lots and designed to accommodate the curving slope of the land. Despite the changes that took place over the centuries until 79 A.D., the year of the famous eruption of Mt. Vesuvius, at least half of the urban fabric consisted of *insulae quadratae* (rectangular blocks).

The reorganization of Pompeii's civil forum during the second century B.C. provides clear evidence of urban planning. The outline of the great square was deliberately, though not precisely, aligned with the surrounding insulae. The addition of retaining walls and overlaps to the tuff colonnade gave a uniform appearance to the square. This operation indicates a conception of urban space as an ordered space, which hides the city's historical stratification: the slow process by which a city is formed. The quality specifications for a space of this type are regularity and symmetry, studied and presented for scenic effect. Historical stratification is not considered relevant.

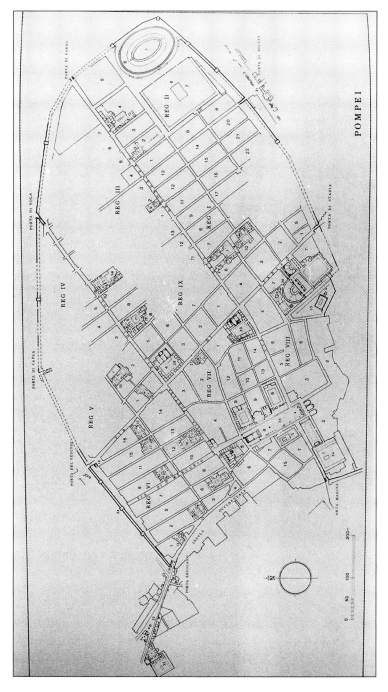

Figure 6.4 Map of Pompeii, drawn by J. P. Adam from a general survey by H. Eshenbach.
Source: Adam, p. 318, fig. 666.

Another early illustration of the ways in which cities were planned is provided by the *Forma Urbis* (Figure 6.5), a plan of imperial Rome carved in marble in about 200 A.D., which was exhibited in the library of the Forum of Peace in Rome. Although only fragments remain today, verification with the archeological remains of the city proves how accurate the plan must have been, especially in view of the fact that, at that time, Rome must have had a population of more than one and a half million inhabitants. This accuracy was possible thanks to the high precision of various instruments used to conduct surveying operations (Adam 1988; Almeida 1981)

Measuring Instruments and Methods

Two valuable and sophisticated instruments used for these measurements were the *groma* and the *chorobates,* shown in Figures 6.6 and 6.7. These two instruments were basic tools in the construction of a building or an aqueduct and above all in the territorial planning operations

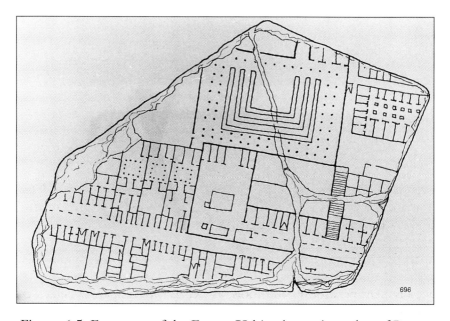

Figure 6.5 Fragment of the Forma Urbis, the ancient plan of Rome carved in marble dating from about 200 A.D.
Source: Adam, p. 330, fig. 696.

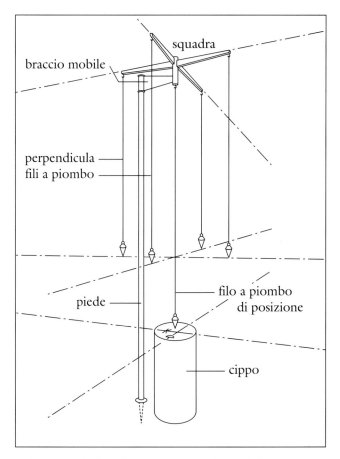

Figure 6.6 Graphic reconstruction of the groma.
Source: Adam, p. 11, fig. 5.

performed when founding, restructuring, or expanding a city. The groma was used to divide up and measure the territory, the chorobate to level the ground and terrace hillsides. These two instruments and others are described in the *Gromatici Veteres,* such as Frontino's *Agrimensura,* a collection of texts on land surveying written during the final period of the Roman Empire. These texts are full of descriptions of measurement procedures and tools, as well as the complex calculations that were performed. Archeological findings and stone iconography (such as the gravestone of a surveyor) have enabled scholars to reconstruct precise replicas of the groma and to confirm its efficiency, so that the Roman surveyor can be likened to his modern-day counterpart.

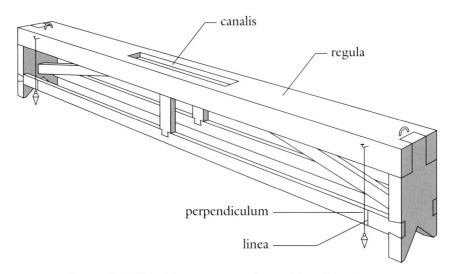

Figure 6.7 Graphic reconstruction of the chorobates.
Canalis = water-level; Regula = graduated rule;
Perpendiculum = plumb line: Linea = reference mark for the
plumb line. Source: Adam, p. 18, fig. 16.

In surveying and mapping land that was not flat, horizontal and vertical measurement procedures were adopted. Horizontal distances were measured by means of ropes and wooden sticks which were divided according to the linear units of the measurement system. To guarantee the accuracy of measurement the groma was also employed. The accuracy of the groma was due to the precision of the Greek cross–shaped arms placed on its tip, as the plumb wires hanging from the ends of the arms were subject to the influence of winds. The accuracy of the *centuriatio* (square subdivisions of land) was tested by measuring to assure that the two diagonals linking opposite corners were equal.

The chorobate was a stand with a water level, plumb wires, and references to ensure that a perfectly horizontal position was achieved. It was placed in a level position—possibly using wedges—and the surveyor was then able to use it to obtain a projection of the differences in heights by sighting pickets or leveling rods of a known height.

Cultellation (Figure 6.8), from the Latin verb *cultello*, is a surveying term meaning "to level with a ploughshare." It is a method of calculating length when the distance to be measured lies in flat but not

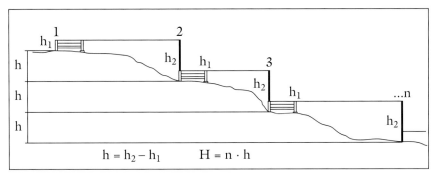

Figure 6.8 Illustration of constant-height cultellation.
Source: Adam, p. 19, fig. 18.

entirely level land. The surveyor proceeds with two measuring rods fixed to each other so as to form a right-angled triangle. The sloping land forms the hypotenuse and the rods form the other two sides. The sum of the rods gives a horizontal projection of the distance to be measured.

These surveying techniques were adopted in the construction of a number of subterranean canals, where tunnels had to be dug out according to a precise route. When working from both ends of the tunnel at the same time, the surveyor had to avoid the risk of the two teams failing to meet. Instead of plotting a straight-line course above the differences in height, he would plot a goniometrically constant course, a progression of orthogonal ranges and sights, using the chorobate to calculate the vertical distances. The most spectacular example of this technique was the drainage of Lake Fucino, planned by Caesar and completed in 52 A.D. This was a tunnel measuring 5679 meters, which took 50,000 workers 11 years to build, and required 42 air and evacuation shafts.

Land Surveyors in the Military

Many of the mensores were military technicians and engineers, who worked with the Roman legions. These surveyors were specialized army personnel, who acquired their skills in special training sections and whose accountability with regard to the central power was through the commanding officers, who were responsible for monitoring their work. It should be stressed that in this instance *military* means not only a corps trained in logistics and combat, but also an organization that reported to the central authorities and provided a range of public services. Thus, urban development and infrastructures always had a strategic military component. And, as Bodei-Giglioni notes (1974, 82–83), "The army itself frequently intervene[d] in the construction of roads, particularly consular roads, bridges, shipping canals and defence works." The construction of the great Roman road system, which was the empire's information communication infrastructure, was of paramount importance.

The Roman Roads

The great Roman roads were never just beaten tracks. The first-century surveyor Siculus Flaccus lists the various types of road: *viae publicae*, built at the expense of the state and bearing the name of the builder; *viae militares*, built by the army at its own expense, which became public roads; *actus*, minor roads built and maintained by the local villages and hamlets (like the roads built by today's local authorities); and *viae privatae*, built by private individuals entirely at their own expense. The only difference between the public and the military roads, however, lay in the fact that the military roads served an immediately strategic purpose in wartime. In practice, each major road was of political importance as a channel for circulating the up-to-date information that was vital to preserving the stability of the empire as a whole. Directness, rapidity, durability, and the maintenance of all the stretches were the main requirements for the great Roman roads.

From the construction point of view, the roads were composed of a series of more- or less-compressed layers of earth, flanked by drainage channels and covered by the *summum dorsum* (top layer). The roads were composed of three layers and had a total thickness varying from one to one and a half meters. For the first layer, cobbles were laid on a flat or flattened surface to render the earth compact and to provide drainage. The second layer consisted of a thick layer of sand, gravel and sand, or sometimes gravel and sand mixed with clay. The third layer was composed of a curved surface of cobbles or sometimes stone slabs. Beginning in the Julian–Claudian age, the top layer was systematically paved.

The winding course of the first roads, such as the Tiberina and the Salaria, marks the stages of the Romans' occupation of Latium. However, as early as 312 B.C., the Appian Way (Figure 6.9), a straighter

Figure 6.9 View of the via Appia near Rome.
Source: Adam, p. 301, fig. 645.

road already paved in 296 B.C., became the prototype of the great Roman road. It displayed the specific technical and political features already described, and was a direct link between Rome and Campania and, further toward the southeast, between Rome and Apulia and Greece.

Figure 6.10 shows the special construction techniques used for the via Mensuerisca, built in Belgian marshlands. Two parallel posts, about two meters apart, were laid on crosspieces and fixed to the ground with struts. Layers of stakes, limestone slabs and tightly packed cobblestones were laid on top.

After the early period, Roman roads cut a direct path across flat areas with the aid of escarpments or embankments (unlike the routes followed by medieval roads, which fulfilled other needs), and were

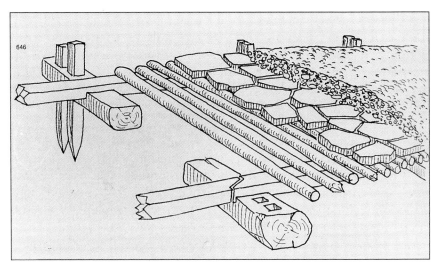

Figure 6.10 Structure of the via Mensuerisca, built in Belgian marshland. Two parallel poles, about two meters apart, are laid on crosspieces and fixed to the ground with struts; layers of stakes, limestone slabs and tightly packed cobblestones are laid on top. From Maertens, *Industrie,* October 1955, p. 39. Source: Adam, p. 302, fig. 646.

marked with milestones and *tabellarii* (stones marking smaller distances than the milestones marked), showing not only that the road belonged to the Roman people, but also the distances from the major centers (Bodei-Giglioni 1974, 79). In this way, each route was provided with a normalized system of reference and signposting, which was extremely useful, for example, for the upkeep of the roads. As we know from Cicero, the administration of the roads and the great public works in general was at first the responsibility of the censores, and subsequently passed directly to the emperor. Travelers—who lodged along the routes in the *stationes* and *mansiones* shown on special maps—were, in the main, state officials (couriers, messengers, excise officers with armed escorts). They provided the administration with immediate information on the condition of the communication network, including precise points of reference. Because roads constituted public land, their upkeep was also guaranteed by legislation against incursion by private property or removal of paving for building construction.

The quality management features that led to the high quality and long useful lives of the renowned Roman roads included planning and building by skilled engineers, the use of accurate measurement and standardized signposting (milestones and tabellarii) along the route; and a continuous flow of data on the condition of the roads (as well as the flow of information on conditions throughout the empire, which was the main purpose for the extensive road system). The information was provided by travelers, most of whom were state officials and therefore in contact with the road administration.

Of course, these roads also carried information out to the empire's hinterlands. They carried the Roman urban planning and construction techniques used to remodel the newly conquered lands and cities. These techniques became increasingly specialized and refined, in terms of materials, engineering procedures, and juridical procedures. Over time, the roads served the needs of the constantly expanding empire spawned by the metropolis for which they had originally been developed.

Production and Use of Building Materials

Important aspects of the production and use of building materials include the contractual and personal relationships enabling contractors and architects to accomplish large and small construction projects; the production methods used to produce important materials, such as bricks; and the standardization techniques used in design and construction. Each of these contributed to the Romans' ability to complete extensive construction projects throughout the empire and to maintain excellent standards of quality in those projects.

Contractors and Architects

Roman contractors were similar to today's managers, who often begin their careers on the shop floor, where skills are passed on not through hereditary channels but through the relationship between superior and subordinate. Relations between building contractors and clients were regulated very early on. An epigraph preserved in the National Museum in Pozzuoli reproduces a decree of 105 B.C., which specifies contractual terms of delivery, payment, and assessment of structural integrity. These terms obviously applied to works let out on contract by both the state and by private clients. Other major projects, such as infrastructure and engineering projects, developed at least initially for strategic purposes, were built directly by the army, which had its own engineers and the necessary funds.

It was practically impossible for any craftsman or engineer to earn a living without a rich and influential *patronus*. The celebrated Roman architect Vitruvius, whose treatise *De Architectura* is dedicated to Augustus, points out that the expertise of certain craftsmen was sometimes unrecognized because they lacked the type of patronage on which the entire Roman society was based and which, at the time, offended no one.

Many architects and craftsmen were slaves or freedmen. One of Cicero's slaves was an architect, for example. Because slaves were a market commodity, it was not in the owner's interest to "ruin" his investment. This meant that slaves with a store of skills acquired in their homeland or through experience in building or production work (who were therefore worth more), became socially mobile and could attain their freedom as their earnings increased. As freedmen, they could subsequently set up their own business, obviously with the support of a patronus.

Major public works were often financed—if not commissioned—by wealthy property owners, who were not necessarily politically active. The motive lay not in a kind of general *beneficentia,* but in the fact that the construction of public works was one of the few ways of investing capital that were not only possible but also socially acceptable. Such investments boosted the gloria of the financier. The quality requirements for such projects included grandeur and opulence, even at the expense of the functionality of the construction. For public works, the state stipulated an agreement with a building contractor, who would hire workers and craftsmen. An official architect was appointed to plan and organize the project. The architect was also responsible for supervising work in progress, and payment of the agreed price to the contractor was conditional on his approval. The contract could stipulate the number of men to be employed and hours to be worked, as well as the tools and materials to be used and the penalties for delays.

Responsibility was organized hierarchically: each person was accountable to his immediate superior and any penalties imposed by the state were applied only to the contractors (Burford 1972, 147). In short, management for quality in this case was based on a distribution of responsibility established by contractual regulations and on the planning and supervisory functions performed by the architect. As general coordinator, the architect had to be an eclectic figure and familiar with the workings of the building yard. It has been noted that architects, as well as other craftsmen involved in the various areas of the building sector, must have acquired most of their training on the work site, and not just in the carpentry shops and forges (Burford 1972, 102).

Vitruvius' description of the role of architects, the wishes of clients and the continuous interactions in the building yard suggests an early echo of what was later called "the voice of the customer."

> *It is not the job of the architect to decide on the type of material to be used . . . it is also up to the owner to decide whether the building is to be constructed in brick, in rubblestone or in squared stone. In fact, each yard can be considered worthy of merit at three levels: for construction technique, for magnificence, for architectural design. If a building has a magnificent aspect its costs will be approved by all the controlling bodies; if it is technically perfect the craftsmen will be praised; if, on the other hand, it possesses that elegance that is achieved through the symmetry of the proportions, the glory will go to the architect. All this will be possible if the architect is willing to accept the advice of the craftsmen and of the private citizens. (VI, VIII, 9–10)*

Vitruvius lists some of the professional requirements of the architect in his *De Architectura*, a handbook for architectural composition and technology: "He should be competent in the field of letters and above all of history, skilled in drawing and a good mathematician; he should cultivate his knowledge of philosophy and music; he should not neglect medicine, he should know jurisprudence and the laws that regulate the movement of the stars."

Though it may not be immediately apparent, all these points served a practical purpose. Knowledge of astronomy was useful for the construction of clocks. Medicine was useful for housing hygiene or for the use of certain materials. The importance of medicine can be seen from the use of terracotta rather than lead for water pipes. Vitruvius notes that "Daily experience shows that water supplied in terracotta pipes tastes better; everyone uses clay dishes to preserve the natural taste of food, even if they possess silver tableware." But it was not just a question of taste. Vitruvius, who had studied medicine as had every quality architect, knew that lead was harmful.

The architect's need for musical knowledge, to take another example, was not just a cultural element related to the creation of formal abstract harmonies. The study of music would enable the architect to "set ballista, catapults, and scorpions precisely." Because architects were also military engineers, the effective use of those war machines were also their responsibility and those machines used gut traction cords. The pitch of the sound made when these cords were vibrated enabled the expert to set the machine. The study of music also enabled the architect to calculate the exact positions of the *èkheia* (Greek ηχεια), a set of bronze resonator vases, whose dimensions were calculated on an octave scale and which were placed beneath the steps of the theater *cavea*, the semicircular area where the audience sits, to amplify the actors' voices.

Broad knowledge was necessary because the architect was expected to be able to design any type of building in accordance with the particular priorities of each client. When building civic works for the state or opulent works for wealthy patroni, *magnificenza* was at the top of the list of requirements. The symbolic value of the building would be conveyed through its forms and the use of valuable materials. For other types of building, particularly major infrastructure projects, the aim was to achieve a morphological-construction standard to optimize the production process, enabling works to be built rapidly throughout the empire.

Production of Building Materials

Metric normalization and mass-production processes were adopted in the manufacture of lead pipes, but most notably in the manufacture of bricks. Bricks became the key components of Roman architecture. Because of their assembly versatility, stability, and transportability, their use was widespread, particularly after Augustus's reign.

As early as the first century A.D., potteries that produced a variety of items (tiles, clay statues, vases, and so on) were just a memory. Although skilled potters still produced architectural ceramics such as antefixes and sarcophagi, whose prices and costs were obviously higher, production of material used in large quantities became standardized. To remain competitive and cut costs, production had been geared toward a limited number of standard bricks. Tile production also became standardized although every region had its own particular form of tile. In the Rome area, for example, all tile manufacturers adopted the same basic form and the same system of overlaying for plain and bent roofing tiles.

Types of Bricks

Use of the brick began to spread under Augustus (until then it had been mainly restricted to particularly damp environments such as burial chambers or the cavea of theaters). Systematic use of brick walls (*opus testaceum* from the arrangement of the *teste* of the bricks) began under Tiberius. The *Castra Praetoria* of 23 A.D. were built with the classic triangular bricks.

The main standardized sizes are shown in Figure 6.11. The *bessales* was two-thirds of a Roman foot (19.7 × 19.7 cm). The *semilateres* or *sesquipedales* were one and a half Roman feet (44.4 × 44.4 cm). The *bipedales* were two Roman feet (59.2 × 59.2 cm.)

Thickness of the bricks varied from 4.5 cm to 2.8 cm from the Flavian to the Severan emperors. The facing brick from the best period was 3.5 to 4.5 cm thick.

Triangular bricks (*lateres trigones*) were obtained from these basic units by cutting the square bricks along one or both diagonals, which had already been scored in line with regulations. They were used to face and restrain concrete walls. When the bricks were cut, an operation that never produced an even edge, the corners sometimes broke off and were reused in mixing cement. A more precise but slower cutting method used water and sand. Under Domitian, the Romans began to use courses of bipedal bricks to improve the laying surface and the stability of the structure.

Special bricks included pipes used for heating, which had a rectangular cross section, and pipes for sewage, which had a circular cross section. There were also other-shaped bricks and small rectangular flooring bricks, which were laid in a herringbone pattern (*opus spicatum*).

Manufacturing Bricks

Figure 6.12 shows a reconstruction of a brick kiln by J. P. Adam (1988). *A* is the combustion chamber; *B,* the door for introducing fuel; *C,* the roof of the combustion chamber which was perforated for

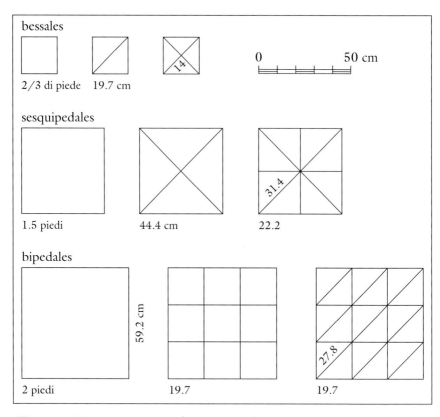

Figure 6.11 Dimensions of square bricks according to current units of measure. Source: Adam, p. 159, fig. 347.

heat emission; *D,* a pile of bricks ready for baking; *E,* the entrance for placing bricks in the oven which is walled up during the baking; *F,* fuel store; and *G,* mounds of bricks, stone, and clay to provide insulation.

The potteries were located on the estates of large landowners, generally close to waterways for ease of transportation, which would have been extremely arduous by road. Production was regulated by a *locatio-condutio,* a contract under which the owner supplied the raw material and the equipment, and the contractor undertook to produce a certain number of bricks and to supply the necessary manpower. Many shop foremen were slaves and freedmen, whose pecuniary obligations toward the landowner made them suitable candidates for running the potteries on a subcontract basis. This created a process of social mobility: with his earnings the slave acquired his freedom, after which he could stipulate other contracts.

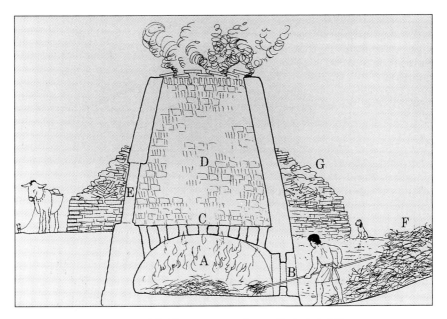

Figure 6.12 Reconstruction of a brick kiln.
Source: Adam, p. 64, fig. 140.

The pottery owners, many of whom were women, were often great landowners from one of the powerful families, who took no direct part in overseeing the production process (a function generally assigned to agents, proxies, administrators, and so on), but whose social position was of the utmost importance when selling the bricks. Toward the end of the second century, the names of the emperor or his family appeared increasingly frequently among the names of pottery owners. The imperial monopoly was actually achieved in the third century, through confiscations and bequests, making the control of brick production one of the elements of the increasing wealth of the emperors.

The quality of a brick was specified in terms of its durability and the precision of its dimensions, and—depending on its composition and baking—could be assessed by an expert eye from its weathering and the color acquired over the years. Vitruvius notes,

Unfortunately it is impossible to assess the quality of baked bricks beforehand. They have to be laid: if they are of good quality they

will withstand storms and the heat of the summer; but if they have been made from unsuitable clay or if they have been insufficiently baked, then they will reveal their defects. Therefore it is best to build roofs from old tiles; then the walls too will certainly be solid. (II, IX, 19)

This quality assessment, where the craftsman depended on the experience of his eye, was of prime importance in the process of quality management. In fact, old bricks were often called *tegulae* (tiles), because their greater exposure to atmospheric agents meant they had weathered better and were more reliable.

Brick Stamps and Contracts

We can reconstruct the organization of brick production thanks to more than 5000 known brick *bolli* or stamps (Figure 6.13). These stamps show, separately or together, the date, the name of the workshop manager, the names of the brick shop foreman and owner, and the location of the shop (Pisano Sartorio and Steinby, 1989). These stamps were not quality marks or trademarks, but a summary of the contract. The owner gave the foreman an order for a certain number of bricks. Because the owner could have several shops on his land and each shop could have several foremen, the name of the workshop had to appear on the brick, as well as that of the foreman. If different foremen in the same shop each handled a variety of orders, the stamps still had to distinguish each specific production order from each pottery (Lugli 1957; Bloch 1947).

Arches and Vaults

Another normalization process, in this case a morphological normalization of construction elements, occurred with the adoption and development of the Romans' characteristic system of arches and vaults. The Romans used arches and vaults at least from the second century B.C. These construction principles first spread gradually through the Italian peninsula thanks to the Greeks and the Etruscans, but the Romans perfected the techniques and, with the introduction of *opus caementitium* (the equivalent of modern-day concrete), generalized their use in every type of architectural form. Their expertise also extended to large-block constructions: in 62 B.C. Lucius Fabrizius linked the

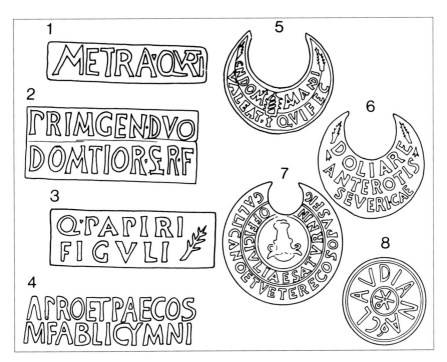

Figure 6.13 Brick stamps. Source: Adam, p. 67, fig. 146.

left bank of the Tiber and the Tiber Island with a tuff and travertine bridge, whose arches gave 24.50 meters of light.

The standardization process that enabled the Romans to develop and spread their expertise in arch and vault construction evolved through the operations of the building yard. The expansion of the empire called for extensive public projects for roads, aqueducts, bridges, and public buildings. Low cost and speed in completing these projects were important problems facing the Roman leaders. The Romans moved to solve this problem by establishing a number of basic topologies that could be replicated with reusable tools and machines. This standardization allowed them to rationalize the use of the materials and labor, such as engineers and workers. These steps enabled them to accelerate the completion of major projects throughout the empire.

Just as limiting the number of mass-produced items made it easier to find personnel and contain labor costs, developing a technical-construction standard offered similar advantages. The Romans adopted the round arch. Unlike the catenary arch, this arch did not offer the theoretically optimum form of load distribution. However, it was very easy to design and to build, and its stability could be optimized through a series of extremely practical devices. Those devices, in turn, could be rapidly produced in the building yard. They included chains, architraves, relieving arches, variations in the mass of the piers or the imposts. A graphic procedure that provided satisfactory estimates for the sizes of the various parts of the arch was in use at least as early as the Renaissance. Adam (1988, 82), has hypothesized that the technique may have been handed down from the Roman age.

Three additional achievements contributed to the Romans' expertise in building arches and great vaults. These involved rationalizing the processes by which the stone or brick blocks were prepared and laid, developing the opus caementitium technique (in which the equivalent of modern-day concrete was cast in the cavity between two walls of brick which acted like a form), and, at the most fundamental level, learning to construct centerings as part of the building process.

The Romans rationalized the dressing and laying of stone blocks in arch construction by squaring the connections between the voussoirs with the vertical and horizontal planes of the wall (Figure 6.14). This facilitated the calculation and dressing of the blocks, because only a single curved surface was required, and curved surfaces were more difficult to achieve. Connection with the rest of the wall was also easier because there was no need for other special pieces. In the case of temporary carpentry work, scaffolding could be totally independent of the structure. More frequently, however, the use of wood was rationalized by resting the beams on grooves on the wall face and using rope struts and joints.

The centerings (Figure 6.15) were wooden frameworks that provided support during construction and sections on which the voussoirs were arranged and cement cast. The centerings were the result of advances in carpentry and in the construction of building equipment and scaffolding. They became necessary with the increased use of small blocks (that is, bricks) as opposed to large blocks (cut stone). Because it was not possible to work on the top of very high small-block masonry, the construction of scaffolding gradually became a standard technique in the production process, a necessary activity in the majority of building yards. Figure 6.16 illustrates scaffolding used to build a brick wall. In the figure, 1 is the foundation trench; 2 shows a worker preparing mortar; 3 is rabbeted scaffolding; and 4, cantilevered, rabbeted scaffolding.

Figure 6.14 Arch of the "Pantani" in the Forum of Augustus: the voussoirs of the arch provide an example of rationalized stone cutting. Source: Adam, p. 186, fig. 408.

Vaults were often assembled from parallel rows of voussoirs with the joints left open, so that each section was independent. A single centering could then be slid along the axis of the vault until the construction was completed with the arches laid in parallel, one against the other. This meant that only one centering with a reduced thickness needed to be built for a much thicker vault, with obvious savings in terms of time, materials, and transport weight. The Romans even managed to resolve the problem of finding wood for centerings in areas like Tunisia where wood was scarce, by using permanent ceramic centerings. These were composed of preshaped ceramic parts, which could be fitted together easily and rapidly, and became an integral decorative part of the construction (Olivier and Storz 1982).

Arch and vault construction reached its greatest potential with the use of concrete. The stability of concrete vaults depends on their degree of monolithicity and therefore on the strength of the mortar. To minimize the stresses caused by imperfections in the binder, the concrete

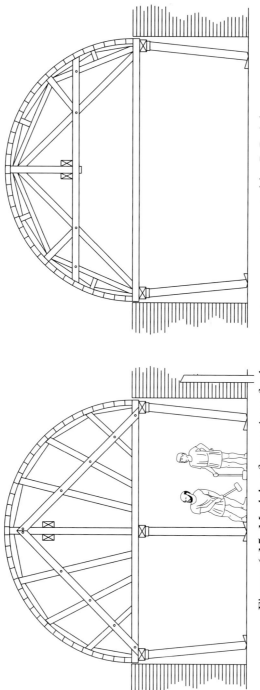

Figure 6.15 Models of centerings for large structures, reconstructed by J. P. Adam.
Source: Adam, p. 190, fig. 418.

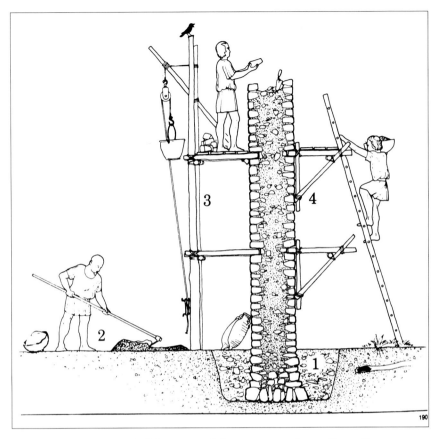

Figure 6.16 Diagram of the construction of a wall.
Source: Adam, p. 90, fig. 190.

was often cast not directly on the centering but on a series of radial brick or stone wedges. This was a way to correct the quality of the mortar: the appearance of the binder would be inspected and strike resistance tests would probably also be conducted. If there were any doubts about the quality of the binder, the cast could be integrated with suitable statically optimized materials.

Arches and vaults were used in an enormous variety of situations. They were used in any architectural volume to contain earth masses in foundations and embankments. The great Roman domes merit special mention. Besides demonstrating Roman efficiency in the construction of scaffolding and enormous centerings, these domes demonstrate an extremely rational use of materials in relation to the stability of the construction. The Romans built great ribbed domes, an extremely refined type of spatial element, which adopts a special system to lighten the load of the masonry mass. Examples of this type of dome include the dome in the central hall of the Baths of Pompeii and, most notably, the dome of the Pantheon (Figure 6.17), which can be dated accurately between 118 and 125 A.D., thanks to the stamps on the bricks. (This great spherical dome, a masterpiece of Roman architecture, is still virtually intact and its 43.50 meter diameter was surpassed only in 1958, when the CNIT vault was built in Paris.)

The Building Yard

One of the most important elements of quality management in the general organization of building was the coordination of the production functions (temporary works/structural normalization/evaluation of materials/stress optimization) performed on the work site by the various categories of craftsmen under the supervision of the architect. Thus the building yard became a center for exchanging and comparing ideas and for continuous training.

The building yard was the place where the Romans' achievements in design, materials, process, and standardization came together. There were many worker categories in the building yards. The foreman (*magister structor*) supervised the masons (*structores*). Wooden structures—ranging from frameworks and scaffolding to roofing—were built by the *carpentarii*. Walls were built by the *parietarii* and whitewashed by the *dealbatores*.

This first layer of workers was followed by the plasterers (*tectores* for ceilings and *gypsiarii* for the walls), *lapidarii* for marble decorations, *tassellarii* for floor laying, and *musivarii* for mosaic laying. An important role was played in the building yard by the *mensores aedificiorum*, mentioned earlier, the *mechanici,* and the *geometrae,* who were skilled in surveying operations. But the outstanding figures, particularly for public works or major urban works, were the *machinatores* and *architecti*—the engineers and architects.

Stone was handled by stonecutters and chiselers (*lapicidinarii*) and, for more refined works, by sculptors (*marmorarii*) and inlayers (*sectores serrarii*). Because the quarried blocks had to be dressed with the utmost precision, we know that measuring instruments were

Figure 6.17 View of the interior of the dome of the Pantheon in Rome. Source: Adam, p. 202, fig. 445.

constantly used in quarrying work. The setsman used a *regula*, a one-foot-long ruler marked off with all its submultiples, which were generalized under the empire. Setsmen also used bronze squares, bevel rules (T-bevels) and the plumb rule (*libella cum perpendiculo*), an instrument used to check that a surface was perfectly horizontal.

The organization of the building yard system can be summarized as follows.

* *General objectives:* opulence for public and private monumental works; speed of execution and reliability in other types of building.

* *Specific objectives:* exploitation of the most easily found materials and their construction features; possibility of monitoring work in progress by regulating the contractual obligations of the parties.

* *Socioeconomic conditions:* building materials and workshops owned by important landowners; craftsmen, architects, foremen, and engineers from various economic and social situations, but all dependent on their patroni; slaves, working in a variety of roles, were a market commodity.

* *Production preferences:* wide use of standardized bricks produced with standardized production organization; diffusion of opus caementitium because of its low cost and flexibility; orders let out on contract to workshops and building yards.

* *Technological preferences:* development of carpentry and scaffolding for small-block buildings; morphological normalization of construction elements (arches and vaults).

* *Organization:* many types of specialized workers; layers of variously skilled personnel, interlinked hierarchically; hierarchical distribution of contractual obligations; checking and approval organs (the architects themselves as well as other representatives of the clients); building yard experience fundamental to the training of the individual.

* *Management priorities:* importance of standard measurements both in materials and in structural topologies; skills in assessment of materials and construction preferences acquired mainly in the yards; regulation through the distribution of contractual obligations; planning, production coordination, and assessment of work in progress performed on the job (by the architects).

Cities and Urban Quality

We said earlier that the population of imperial Rome must have been more than one and a half million, and other cities in the empire were certainly more than villages, too. The composition of the urban social classes reflects deep divisions in terms of well-being and prosperity (and therefore of power). Under Constantine, the ratio of the two main classes must have been one to a hundred. On one hand were the wealthy classes, on the other, a varied collection of urban proletariat, small tradesmen and so on. Now we will look at how this society was organized in relation to the themes of surveying and mapping discussed in terms of mastery of the territory.

The Forma Urbis (town plan) and the technical skills needed for its realization were used by the central authorities as some of the tools to control this vast urban system. The authorities were organized into various state departments, who managed the city on the basis of building laws and regulations. Their main objectives were to keep private property in the hands of the ruling class, to restructure urban areas that were becoming crowded and therefore losing their economic and representative value, to safeguard the public interest with respect to general services, to build intensively in order to provide housing for rental to the lower classes, and simultaneously to maintain a minimum housing standard in terms of hygiene and urban life. These latter considerations—together with public works and spectacles—were means of ensuring popular consensus.

The great fire of Rome in 64 A.D., traditionally attributed to Nero, provided the opportunity—if not the means—for a radical restructuring of the rapidly expanding city, with its overcrowded center. In order to prevent similar catastrophes, the Romans passed a number of laws laying down safety standards in terms of the maximum size and materials for various types of building. Under Augustus, the height of buildings had already been limited to 70 feet, about 21 meters, for a total of six or seven stories. This decree is in itself an indication of the skill of Roman builders as such a restriction means that it was possible to build well above 70 feet. However, its main purpose was to regulate the use of urban space in relation to the quality of urban life. It was a solution dictated by considerations of hygiene and stability, designed to prevent overcrowding (Figure 6.18), to facilitate

Figure 6.18 The via Biberatica in Rome, flanked by shops and pavements in the Trajan Markets. Source: Adam, p. 303, fig. 648.

the distribution of services and maintenance, and, perhaps, an attempt to limit building speculation with regard to the lower classes.

The buildings directly affected by this type of decree were the *insulae*, multistory residential condominiums. The insulae, such as the ones shown in Figure 6.19), were upward extensions of the *tabernae* built during the republic, when the population began to increase. Subsequently, the Romans constructed multistory buildings designed specifically as such and used for the restructuring of many Roman cities between the third and fourth centuries A.D. Maintenance of private property was regulated by the law of *ab imo usque ad coelum* (from the ground up to the sky). This stopped the inhabitants of the insulae from acquiring individual ownership of the apartments in which they lived, since it stipulated that ownership over any surface area had to extend from the ground to the sky, in other words, through all the stories of the building (Pierotti 1972). Clearly, none of the families of the lower classes could afford such an expense, so

Figure 6.19 Remains of multistory insulae at Ostia.
Source: Adam, p. 157, fig. 344.

the insulae height restriction may also have been intended as a means of curbing speculation and thus regulating popular consent by providing minimum housing standard in terms of construction stability, density, and so on.

In addition to these measures conserving private property and creating a minimum housing standard, there must have been decrees regulating the property market for those who had access to property, the distribution of urban public services, and the collection of taxes, one of the state's principal sources of revenue.

We saw earlier that territorial division was a way of monetizing land; other procedures, conducted by special personnel, were adopted in property market management to assess the value of buildings. As Vitruvius notes (II, VIII, 8–9),

> . . . when arbiters are asked to assess the value of walls on common property, they consider not only the production cost, but, after consulting the building contract to establish the price, they decrease it by one eightieth for every year since the date of construction. Thus, in pronouncing their verdict . . . the implication is that the walls cannot last for more than eighty years. None of this applies to brick walls, which, as long as they are plumb, never lose value but are always considered as new.

Aqueducts and Water Quality

Starting with the Aqua Appia (312 B.C.), Rome was equipped with eleven aqueducts. The first elevated aqueduct, with the classic appearance of an endless flight of arches, was the Aqua Marcia of 144 B.C. Although the cost of these constructions was certainly enormous, due to their length, it was sustained by the ruling classes, partly out of considerations of prestige (and perhaps with little concern for the countryside). The technology of the aqueducts was studied in the greatest detail to ensure maximum efficiency in transporting the water. The degree of slope was carefully studied and the length of the aqueducts was partly due to the fact that the incline could not exceed a certain gradient (Figure 6.20). High-pressure piping and siphons were used. Vitruvius considered them the most reliable method of overcoming height differences. Filters were used to remove impurities and improve the taste and salubrity of the water supply.

Figure 6.20 The arches of the Aqua Claudia in Rome, an aqueduct built between 38 and 52 A.D.; 68 km long, including 15 km in superelevation. Source: Adam, p. 262, fig. 555.

Vitruvius gives us an insight into the way the structure of the social system and related regulations could influence the configuration of an urban space with regard to fiscal obligations, when he talks about another technique in which the Romans excelled, the canalization and transport of water from the main *castellum aquae* (Figure 6.21) to secondary *receptacula*.

> *Pipes take the water from the central reservoir to all the public fountains; of the secondary reservoirs, one provides water for the baths, for which the people pay an annual tax, and the other provides water for private homes, but is regulated to ensure that*

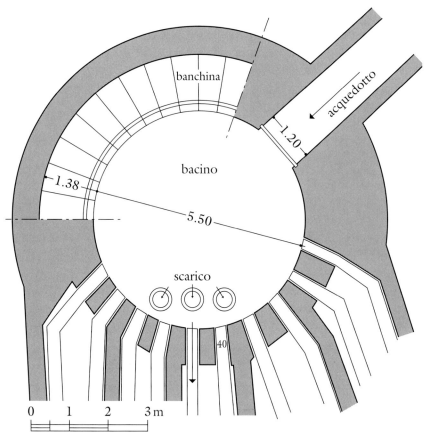

Figure 6.21 Plan of the Castellum Acquae in Nimes.
Source: Adam, p. 275, fig. 581.

there is never a shortage of water for public needs. Private citizens with their own water system will not be able to use the public water supply for their own requirements. The reason for the creation of these three separate systems is therefore due to the fact that private citizens have to contribute to the maintenance of the aqueducts for the water supplied to their homes. (VII, VI, 2)

Just as with the roads, up-to-date information on the condition of the water network was important for monitoring the system. As in the case of other services, special officials were appointed, such as Frontino, *curator aquae* under Nerva in 97 A.D. Frontino described the urban water supply system in a treatise titled *De aquaeductibus Urbis Romae.*

It is difficult today to establish how effective regulations and rules were, and how closely they were enforced: archeological excavations show only part of the picture, and written documentation is generally the one-sided view of a member of the ruling class. We can be certain that, as relations among the state, economic power, and citizens were based on the system of patronage described earlier, the hierarchical Roman society was regulated internally by interpersonal relationships. These relationships moved through channels that were clearly defined, if not specified in any law. This system also included the application of building regulations.

Summary

The development of standards in a variety of areas provided an important foundation for many of the Romans' achievements in managing for quality. Among the areas of standardization are units of measurement, sizes and shapes of building materials, structures and techniques used in construction, and building regulations that provided a form of housing standards.

Examples of these standards include the uniform measurement system for urban and rural land adopted throughout the empire; standard sizes and shapes of bricks and pipes; the adoption of the round arch as a standard architectural form; standardized construction techniques such as the use of scaffolding for complex structures like the vault of the Pantheon; and the regulations that controlled the height of buildings in Rome.

The existence of these standards supported the development and use of measuring instruments such as the groma and chorobate and techniques such as cultellation. The ancient Romans were also successful in developing efficient and effective methods of organizing the production of high-quality materials, in using standardized architectural shapes and methods of design and construction, and in developing processes for governing and controlling large urban areas as well as rural settlements. Together these achievements enabled the Romans to found cities and to construct roads, aqueducts, and buildings of great beauty and durability, some of which have endured for our admiration for two millennia.

The organization of management for quality in Roman architecture and urban planning described here was valid as long as the political and socioeconomic system was capable of performing all these tasks organically. That is, as long as everyone shared the same basic objectives. It is no coincidence, for example, that brick standards disappeared as the empire declined. During the Middle Ages, brick standards reemerged only with the communes, but they were local regulations, which applied to a specific area. Brick size was established by the local authorities, and as units of measurement, always based on parts of the human body, varied from one place to another, it was not uncommon to find stone tablets near the marketplace giving the sizes of the various types of "legal" brick in that commune. With the loss of the power of the Roman Empire, the organization of managing for quality had changed.

Bibliography

Adam, J. P. *L'arte di Costruire Presso i Romani*. Milan: Longanesi, 1988.

Almeida, E. Rodriguez. "Forma Urbis marmorea." *Aggiornamento Generale 1980*. Rome, 1981.

Bloch, H. "I bolli laterizi e la storia edilizia romana." *Studi e materiali del Museo della Civilt Romana*, no. 4. Rome, 1947.

Bodei-Giglioni, G. *Lavori pubblici e occupazione nell'Antichità Classica*. Bologna, Pàtron, 1974.

Burford, Alison. *Craftsmen in Greek and Roman Society*. London: Thames & Hudson, 1972.

"Curiosum Urbis Romae Regionum XIII." In P. M. Lugli, ed. *Storia e cultura della città Italiana*. Bari, Laterza, 1967.

Frontinus, Sextus Iulius. "Agrimensura," and "De aquaeductibus urbis Romae," in Gromatici Veteres, ed. *Die Schriften der römischen Feldmesser*. Berlin: Ed. Blume, Lachmann, Rudorff, 1948.

Lugli, Giuseppe. *La tecnica edilizia romana, con particolare riguardo a Roma e Lazio*. Rome, 1957.

Olivier, A., and S. Storz. "Analyse et restitution d'un proced de construction antique: ralisation d'une vote d'arte sur coffrage perdu en tubes de terre cuite." *Recherches Archologiques franco-tunisiennes Bulla Regia, Miscellanea*, 1. Coll. de l'Ecole Franaise de Rome, 1982.

Pierotti, P. "La cultura delle città." In Pierotti, P., ed. *Urbanistica: storia e prassi*. Firenze, Marchi & Bertolli, 1972.

Pisani Sartorio, Giuseppina, and Steinby, Eva Margareta. "Costruire L'impero." *Archeo,* no. 56. Oct. 1989.

Veteres, Gromatici. *Die Schriften dermischen Feldmesser*. Berlin: Ed. Blume, Lachmann, Rudorff, 1948.

Vitruvius, Marcus Pollio. *De Architectura*. Pordenone, Studio Tesi, 1990.

Glossary

Note: Latin terms being defined are shown in **boldface italics**. English terms being defined are shown in **boldface Roman**. Within the definitions, terms shown in **boldface italics** are themselves defined elsewhere in the glossary; terms shown in *italics* indicate technical terminology or the equivalent Latin expression.

***Actus** (actus, -us)*. In land surveying, a unit of area: *actus minimu*s, 120 meters wide by 4 meters long; *actus quadratus,* 120 square feet. In the hierarchical subdivision of roads, a minor road built by a village or hamlet.

***Agrimensor** (agrimensor, agrimensoris)*. Land surveyor.

Alidad. A surveying instrument equipped with sights for determining direction.

Antefix. An architectural element in stone or terracotta placed at the eaves to hold the tiles of the roof, also used as an ornament on tombs.

***Aribiter** (arbiter, arbitri)*. Arbiter, judge.

Arch. A structural architectural element in the system of arches and vaults.

The arch stands on *piers* or directly on the load-bearing walls in two points called the *imposts.*

Architrave. An architectural element which together with the *piers* forms a *trilith.*

Beneficentia (beneficentia, -ae). In Roman society, an operation for the public good.

Brick courses. Horizontal layers of bricks laid at various heights in stone masonry for stabilization purposes.

Cardo (cardo, cardinis). The first main line, together with the *decumanus,* in territorial mapping, and the main road in Roman military camps and cities.

Carpentarius (carpentarius, -i). Carpenter in the building yard whose job was to build temporary wooden structures such as platforms and scaffolding.

Castellum acquae. Cistern.

Castrum. Castle, fortress, fortified encampment.

Catenary. A curve assumed by a rope or chain of uniform density hanging freely from two fixed points. *Catenary* arches, whose curve reproduces the form of a catenary, are not found in Roman architecture.

Cavea (cavea, -ae). In theatres, the semicircular area where the audience sits.

Censor (censor, censoris). Censor, a public official. There were two censors, whose roles were to keep account of the names and property of Roman citizens, monitor contracts and keep a watch over public morals.

Centering. Temporary framework, usually in wood, for the construction of arches and vaults.

Centuria (centuria, -ae). In land surveying, a unit of area equal to 200 jugers (*iugerum,* a land area unit equivalent to 240×120 feet or 0.622 acre).

Centuriatio (centuriatio, centuriationis). Subdivision of the land into *centuriae.*

Chain. Flexible metal traction device. In architecture, chains may be stretched between the imposts of arches to eliminate thrust.

Chorobates (chorobates, -ae). An instrument of Greek origin for measuring differences in elevation.

Cliens (cliens, clientis). A person protected by but also subjected to *a patronus,* under the widespread patronage system of Roman society.

Cultellation. A method of calculating length when the distance to be measured lies in flat but not entirely level land.

Curator (curator, curatoris). Curator, administrator, superintendent. A public official. There were different *curatores* in different public areas (*curator viae*, a road superintendent; *curator aquae*, acqueducts superintendent; and so on).

Dealbator (dealbator, dealbatoris). A housepainter.

Decumanus (decumanus, a, um). The noun is derived from the adjective and indicates the second main line, together with the **cardo;** in territorial mapping, the main road in Roman military camps and cities.

Decussis (decussis, decussis). Diagram carved on the top of stone posts placed at the intersections of the **centuriae;** it showed the orthogonal directions of the location and, vertically, the position of the post in relation to the intersection of the **cardo** with the **decumanus.**

Eques (eques, equitis). Belonging to the *equestrian order* (the class of *equites* or cavalry).

Forma urbis. Street plan of a city, street plan of Rome (since *Urbs* means Rome as an antonomasia for city).

Forum (forum, -i). Square, market, but above all *forum*, the center of public life.

Geometres (geometres, -ae). Land surveyor.

Gloria (gloria, -ae). Glory, good name, renown.

Groma (groma, -ae) / Gruma (gruma, -ae). Alidad, surveyer's measuring instrument. Central point of an encampment, the intersection of the **cardo** and the **decumanus.**

Gromaticus (gromaticus, -i). Land surveyor.

Gypsiarius (gypsiarius, -i). A plasterer.

Imbrex (imbrex, imbricis). Flat tile.

Insula (insula, -ae). Block of houses. The *insulae quadratae* were rectangular blocks with right-angled corners. The insulae were multistory buildings of rented apartments.

Lapicidinarius (lapicidinarius, -i) / Lapidarius (lapidarius, -i). A stonemason who worked in the stone quarries *(lapicidinae, -arum)*, or stone dresser who worked on marble decorations in the building yard.

Later (later, -is). Brick. There were various types of *lateres* according to their shape and size.

Levelling rod. A graduated rod used to measure vertical distances.

Libertus (libertus, -i). A freedman or freed slave, who had obtained his freedom but had pecuniary obligations toward his **patronus.**

Locatio-conductio. A contract between the owner of workshops and/or materials and the work manager.

Machinator (machinator, machinatoris). Machine manufacturer, engineer.

Magister (magister, magistris). Head, master; *magister structor,* foreman of the building yard workers.

Magnificentia (magnificentia, -ae). Magnificence, opulence. A quality required for public and private monumental buildings.

Mansio (mansio, mansionis). Stretch, stop, wayside inn.

Marmorarius (marmorarius, -i). A stonemason in the quarries skilled in the sculpture of particularly refined pieces.

Mechanicus (mechanicus, -i). An expert in mechanical constructions who worked with the *geometrae* and the *mensores aedificiorum* during surveying and planning operations for the construction of a building.

Mensor (mensor, -is). A land surveyor; *mensor aedificiorum,* a surveyor skilled in measuring operations for the construction of a building.

Miliarium (miliarium, -ii). A milestone.

Musivarius (musivarius, -i). A mosaic worker.

Opus (opus, operis). In architecture, a construction built with a particular technique.

Opus incertum. Masonry consisting of stone and earthenware fragments of various sizes, arranged in an irregular fashion.

Opus quadratum. Masonry of square blocks arranged in horizontal courses, usually in stone.

Opus reticulatum. Brick masonry of small rectangular bricks arranged in a diagonal pattern.

Opus spicatum. Usually brick masonry with the blocks arranged in a herringbone pattern. Mainly used for floors.

Opus testaceum. Brick masonry where the bricks (headers) are laid with their ends toward the face of the wall.

Pagus (pagus, -i). A village or hamlet.

Parcellation. Subdivision of land into lots.

Parietarius (parietarius, -i). A worker skilled in the construction of walls.

Patronus (patronus, -i). An influential person, the patron of the **libertus** or the protector of the **cliens.**

Pax romana. "Roman peace," peace imposed by the Romans in conquered territories.

Pier. Vertical structural element, part of the ***trilith.***

Plumb rule *(lat. libella cum perpendiculo).* A measuring tool consisting of a board with plumb line and bob.

Pottery. A place where earthenware is made and fired.

Receptaculum *(receptaculum, -i).* A cistern.

Regula *(regula, -ae).* A graduated rule for measuring.

Scandula *(scandula, -ae).* Small wooden planks for roofs.

Senator *(senator, -oris).* Senator, member of the Roman senate.

Statio *(statio, -onis).* A wayside stopping place.

Structor *(structor, -oris).* A mason.

Summum dorsum. The top layer of a road, with gravel or paving.

Tabellarius *(tabellarius, -i).* A messenger or letter bearer. *Tabellarii* were also stones showing distances, at more frequent intervals than the milestones ***(miliaria).***

Taberna *(taberna, -ae).* A shop or workshop. Architecturally, the *tabernae* were one- or two-story houses built under the republic, where the lower floor was occupied by the shop. The ***insulae*** were upwards extensions of the *tabernae.*

Tabula *(tabula, -ae).* Painted and/or written board, map.

Tassellarius *(tassellarius, -i).* A worker skilled in laying floors.

Tector *(tector, tectoris).* A worker skilled in plastering ceilings.

Tegula *(tegula, -ae).* Tile, element used for roofing. Masonry bricks were often known as *tegulae.*

Trilith. An architectural structure consisting of two upright elements **(piers)** surmounted by a horizontal element **(architrave).**

Via *(via, -ae).* A road. There were various types of *viae*, ranked according to their importance.

Vicus *(vicus, -i).* A quarter or district (in a city); a village or hamlet.

CHAPTER 7

History of Quality Assurance in Germany

Franz Lerner

Craftsmanship and the Mark

The urge to achieve quality has been observed in all cultures, and is probably instinctive in the human spirit. In the German-speaking areas this urge is not documented prior to the Christian era. Family crests are no doubt older, but their connection with trade was limited. It is however certain that the use of identifying marks stems from this old tradition. Such marks could be understood even by people who lack literacy.[1]

The oldest evidence on German soil dates back to the Roman occupation. The Romans built garrisons in the occupied territories. Their buildings included the use of standard-size kiln-dried shingles, each of which was clearly marked with a stamp displaying the number and honorary title of the legion that produced it. Centuries later those Roman garrison structures became sources of building materials for Christian buildings. Recent excavations in the Frankfurt Cathedral brought to light shingles of the 22nd Legion, which the architects of the first Carolinian church had found at the former site of a Roman watchtower and were able to reuse after six centuries. Many more such examples can be found in the area of West Germany, which was once enclosed by the Roman border.[2]

Figure 7.1 Imprint on brick of the 22nd Roman legion from the frontier base camp Nida in Frankfurt-Heddernheim. Foto Museum für Vor-und Frühgeschichter, Frankfurt am Main.

A famous example of the use of identifying marks is the weapons owned by the great figures of the time. These gentlemen were especially proud of their swords, which displayed the individual mark of the honorable and famous blacksmiths who created them. Sometimes swords even had names; for example, Excalibur in the King Arthur legend. The scanty and partly corroded remains of those weapons no longer show any recognizable marks by the craftsmen. But the memory of these famous blacksmiths and their highly regarded products is preserved in legends. Some modern thinking is to the effect that those marks were merely the artists' signatures and were not intended to guarantee the products. This ignores the then-prevailing ideology influenced by Christianity, that the artist would modestly take second place to his work, leave all the glory to the Creator and be grateful for the recognition his human work had received from his fellow humans.

In this way, the marks of the early period must be regarded as the manufacturer's guarantee of quality, and as establishing responsibility for the craftsman's work.[3]

Such marks had no application to goods not intended for sale. Everyday essentials such as clothes, tools of all sorts, buildings, and furniture that were typically homemade by a family, a clan, or the employees of a gentleman or convent, were not intended for sale but were only to meet their own requirements.

A further source of products came from traveling merchants—peddlers. Here, appearance was the first priority, especially where rare, valuable, and mostly foreign products were concerned. These had to be paid for with the less-used and carefully saved coins. The products offered by the peddlers, who had traveled extensively and were knowledgeable and financially strong tradesmen, needed neither proof of origin nor a guarantee of their quality. These products, which included corals, amber, metal tools, especially jewelry, incense and foreign spices, maybe even fine textiles, were not essential to daily life but were rather luxury goods, purchased by those who could afford them to make life easier and to treasure as custom-made objects. The quality of the product was therefore the reason for the purchase. These were traded solely on the basis of trust between the buyer and the seller. The seller had purchased his goods on markets far away with the help of personal relations and his expertise.

During the High Middle Ages, a period of 250 years following the successors of Charlemagne, craftsmanship developed toward specialization with craftsmen working in their individual shops. There is very little reliable information about the manufacturers, the artists, or their form of organization during those "dark ages." Yet there was a degree of progress. Some good and even outstanding quality was produced, though the products were neither affordable for everyone nor designed for daily use. Not only the great gentlemen, princes, counts, and noblemen of the time but also a great number of their entourage, employees, squires, and trusted friends as well as the ministers and the high clergy, desired an increasing number of luxury goods for their personal use. These desires could no longer be satisfied by in-home production. Independent craftsmen, who either were of free descent or had earned their freedom, settled under the protection of these gentlemen. They produced weapons; leather collars and other such equipment for horses; magnificent clothes for both ladies and gentlemen;

furs and jewelry; wood, stone, and metal altar decorations; and other skillfully crafted luxury items such as chessmen made from stag-horn or pictures made from colored glass to match the small windows found in Romanic architecture.

The master craftsmen and their apprentices no longer had the time to be self-sufficient for daily subsistence, particularly as they needed the daylight hours to do a job that was more critical regarding quality. On the other hand the gentlemen under whose protection they lived could not be considered the sole consumers of their goods. In order to obtain the supplies they needed for daily subsistence, and to do their work, and in order to sell their products the craftsmen had to rely on the market.

In those days the market was closely related to church activities and festive gatherings of the upper class. On Sundays the whole parish would come together in the church to hold services. Sunday mass was also an excellent opportunity to meet with friends and neighbors, to relax together and talk about the news over a drink, to play and dance together, and also to admire the beautiful things displayed in the craftsmen's booths. Especially during the warm season parishes held fairs and people came from all over the county. On those days the concluding words of every service, *ite missa est*—go, it is done— meant the beginning of secular togetherness rather than an invitation to go home. After all, the German word for large, regularly repeated fairs, *Messe,* is derived from this concluding salutation.

The members of the upper class usually held their services in private chapels. For their social life they often gave lavish parties. At occasions like family reunions, weddings, baptisms, and rites of passage, people from all over the county came together; the festivities lasted for days, and craftsmen were essential to their preparation. At such occasions guests and hosts competed with each other, not only in sports, dancing, and small talk but also in clothes, jewelry, weapons, gifts, in short, in their whole appearance. There was therefore ample opportunity for the craftsmen to sell their products even before the festivities began. They could also set up their booths during tournaments and attract buyers, especially the ladies. The custom of periodically held markets slowly developed aside from the still-popular trade with the peddlers.

As with any economy, the German areas evolved specialization of labor according to demand and talent. First, small workshops, such as potteries and mills, developed locally and expanded later on in order to serve the markets. The development of professions and skilled trade progressed steadily because technical discoveries, innovations, and invention were inevitable and often spread quickly. Local political and financial leaders were also involved in this, as they intervened early on in the development of economic life. They imposed taxes, duties, and customs. The clergy claimed 10 percent of every item sold.

From the beginning the administration worked to control the work of the specialists (the tradesmen), by setting rules that were enforced by the police in the interest of the public. These were rules concerning fire hazards and using open flames; they regulated the use of local raw materials and the protection of local taxpayers from foreign competitors. Both spiritual and secular leaders focused especially on military aspects, such as weapons and equipment for the soldiers, their board and lodging, their support, and the building and maintenance of the fortifications and war machinery. Just the protection of a village with a hedge of thornbushes and a moat and the maintenance thereof was a task that required the organization of community efforts. This defense task was even bigger where it involved settlements of several thousand people, surrounded by one wall, such as castles and their surrounding villages, big convents, or the seat of the bishopric.

The Crusades of the eleventh through thirteenth centuries exposed many western Europeans to the Byzantine practices of the East. The Byzantine practice included a slightly changed version of the old Roman system of marks, information about the origin on most products, and the strict organization of the trades in the cities. The intensive contact with the East also brought an abundance of new goods and thus evoked a need for things unknown before. Goods that were brought home by some crusaders as gifts or souvenirs soon became desirable to others. The already flourishing trade with the East boomed.

In addition the growth of population in western Europe stimulated a migration of hordes of settlers across the Oder and Weichsel Rivers into eastern Europe. Hundreds of new cities were founded, and unemployed villagers flocked to them. The new cities thrived and offered employment to the newcomers, including opportunities to become craftsmen, provided their products could stand up to the growing competition. Quality was the decisive factor from the beginning.

As was natural, craftsmen associated with people of the same trade, with the same interests and talents, who were maybe even acquaintances from the past. Their devoutness and the fact that they felt helpless when facing the uncertainty of an existence subject to diseases, starvation, and wars, made them search for a safe harbor. They found it in their patron saint, who functioned as a communicator between them and God, the Almighty, whom they didn't dare face without the help of an advocate. They thus put their trust in a saint who, according to the legend, carried out their trade or was in some way connected to it. In this way like-minded people came together in church fraternities. They worshiped their patron saint and dedicated to him a wayside shrine, sometimes even an altar in their church or a chapel; they lit candles and celebrated his anniversary.

These fraternities were not restricted to holding service together. They also offered the opportunity to come together and talk about problems in everyday life and try and solve them together after the service. In those days, as in all times, there were enough problems to be solved. Some of them were the purchase of raw materials, the training of new recruits, or the guarantee of the goods produced by them. These matters of existence and survival, and the family, wives, and children, were included in these unions from the start. Family celebrations, such as baptisms, weddings, but also funerals, were celebrated together. The reputation of the trade and of every one of its representatives soon became the main concern. This good reputation was based on the quality of the product.

The fraternities had to be able to stand up to the competition with their products. There have always been outsiders, loners, and failures, whose competition was much more dangerous during the hard times of the High Middle Ages than in newer times. In the German-speaking area cooperative thought was one of the earliest traditions, probably a Germanic heritage, and was always cultivated. Equity, honor, and community spirit were values that many generations held on to and that were passed on through many centuries. Mutual control, conscientious training of the young generation, and limited competition were the results of this attitude. Every craftsman was to have a livelihood. This is the reason that many traditions survived for centuries.

In every trade there are knowledge, skills, and techniques that have to be learned with difficulty and must be concealed from strangers, in order to prevent imitators or competitors from copying. For many centuries such secrets were not recorded; the apprentices had to learn certain rules by heart and the journeymen had to swear that they would maintain silence. Later, this was extended to rituals that were known only to the "honest" craftsman, which assured all of them that no unauthorized person could enter into competition with them. The best examples for such professional secrecy come from old cookbooks. Cooking for those with discerning taste is a highly regarded profession, then and today. In the German-speaking area the indications of quantity are missing from all the recipes in the records from the Middle Ages, and then in the printed cookbooks until the end of the sixteenth century. Anyone who hadn't learned the trade of cooking could find in a cookbook the ingredients for a recipe but not the amounts or the instructions. The trained craftsman might be illiterate but could prepare the dish. In the view of the fraternities, the trade secrets were of no concern to outsiders. This was especially true for the means of quality assurance for the products of the individual trades. Quality assurance was and remained for a long time a personal matter that was concealed from outsiders, in order to prevent provoking claims and creating information in forms that could be examined from the outside. Quality was indispensable but its protection was the duty of every individual trade, was part of its honor and integrity, and wasn't discussed with outsiders. This was handled in that way by many generations.

Hidden Beginnings of the Mark

The origins and purposes of craftsmen's marks are still somewhat ambiguous because of lack of complete documentation. Some of the marks that stonemasons put on their building stones are still visible today, even though they are usually hidden. However the fact that generally the individual phases of construction were documented in chronicles and records, presents us with the rare possibility of a chronological classification. Observations indicate that in the High Middle Ages this marking of the building stones was done for reasons of payment. Research adduces the relative rarity and the simple nature of the marks. The list of registered marks of stonemasons on German soil so far is incomplete but absolutely can be extended if attention is paid to new finds.

The architects of the High Middle Ages had to be very concerned with the cost of their buildings. The material was not available everywhere, it had to be transported over long distances, and it was generally not paid for in goods. It had to be paid for in money, coins made

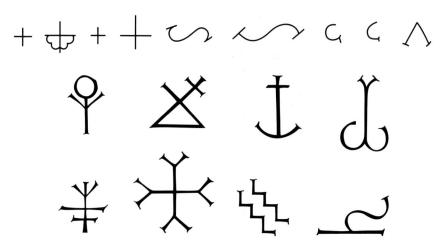

Figure 7.2 Stonemasons' marks and place marks in Romanesque
churches and buildings in South West Germany.
Source: *Scripta Naturae*.

from precious metal, which were much less available in those days
than in later centuries. Some architects encountered financial problems, so their accountants paid close attention to the number of delivered stones, and controlled the delivery men and the construction
workers. Written bills were unknown to the High Middle Ages, probably because of widespread illiteracy. But everyone knew how to
count. Thus the accountants ordered the workmen to record the
number of stones or bricks used in the construction.

The oldest marks by stonemasons in the German-speaking area
were found in the Cathedral of Speyer, which was erected 1080–1106.
In the latest chronology a gap of nearly half a century follows. Only in
the Cathedral of Worms (erected 1150–1165) did more such marks
appear and they were discovered in greater numbers. During the time
of the Hohenstaufen dynasty these individual marks were found in as
many as 15 secular buildings, such as the residences of emperors and
ministers, and in 10 convents and monasteries. These finds were well
recorded and are, especially in modern times, well published.[4] The
perfect examples are the palace of Gelnhausen, built 1155–1170,[5] and
the Wildenburg castle.[6] Some of the convents and monasteries in
question are Disibodenberg (1088–1143), the earliest example,
Maulbronn (1155–1178), Schonau (1167–1220), Enkenbach (1220–
1272), and Eusserthal (1200–1262).[7]

For the quality control of the cloth manufacturers, we have an indisputable document from the second half of the thirteenth century. In this document the older, but still small royal capital Berlin gave to the city of Frankfurt on the Oder the right to control cloth manufacturers. One of the powers described in the document was the nomination of experts who were to be sworn in and who, along with representatives of the city, controlled the quality of the woolen cloth that was produced by the cloth manufacturers of this and other cities and was offered for sale in Frankfurt on the Oder, for which they charged the weavers a fee. It was particularly emphasized that only impeccable and controlled goods could be sold.[8] This document is also an unambiguous example of the emerging fiscal and administrative interests of the town officials. It originated in the newly colonized territory between the Elbe and Oder Rivers, but did not develop in the center of the empire until exactly a century later.

The fact that city officials and landowners gradually turned this means of quality assurance into a means of control and constantly imposed taxes on it, seemingly became matter of course for everybody. It lasted for more than half a millennium—until the beginning of the nineteenth century—when it was invalidated by the Industrial Revolution.

The mark was an advantage to everyone. It usually consisted of a lead seal bearing the coat of arms of the city where the item was produced, as well as other important information. It saved merchants, tailors, or users the time and effort of inspecting and measuring the cloth themselves—they could rely on the information supplied by the mark. By the end of the fourteenth century it became therefore customary to purchase "sealed" cloth, sometimes in bales, without inspecting it, and to sell it "as is."

Of course, the tradesmen had to learn the meanings of the marks, such as the name of the manufacturer, the lengths and widths of cloth, and so on, as part of their apprenticeship. The seal was cut off only by the tailor, when he unfurled the cloth and spread it out. The buyers of the textiles trusted the seal, and they were rarely disappointed. The high quality was not solely the result of the controls and the inspections, though these were essential. The high quality resulted mainly from the effect of the control process on the craftsman and his reputation, as well as the city and corporation he belonged to. Every abuse of the professional code of ethics or the rules was a threat to their existence and to the personal well-being of the craftsmen.

The weavers' union rightfully saw the implementation of the quality inspections of their products as an important institution that would secure their community. The board of inspectors was therefore filled equally with representatives of the weavers and city officials. These individuals had to solemnly accept the regulations and duties of the commission, and they generally had a share in the fees charged of the weavers at every inspection. This institution, which operated for a long time without written records, in general proved useful, and survived for centuries while changing only its exterior form due to the process of bureaucracy. In addition, what worked for the weavers was also applied in due course to other trades.

Quality Assurance and the Professional Ethics of Master Craftsmen

Beyond providing for the well-being of capable, honest craftsmen, the fraternities also faced the need to protect themselves and the public against deception by unscrupulous workers such as are found in all societies. In part, this need was met by the use of apprenticeship, examinations, marks, trade secrecy, and inspections. In addition, other means were employed, including punishments.

There are many examples of how the market and the consumers reacted to deceitful practices. One such example is saffron. It was a much appreciated spice and was also known as an aphrodisiac. The tiny pollen of the *Crocus sativus* was often mixed with sand and dust and was contaminated in other ways before it was sold on the market. In the big trading cities, like Frankfurt am Main and Nürnberg, inspectors were appointed to control the saffron and to punish all violators severely, even to the extent of handing them over to the authorities.[9] Bakers who reduced the weight of bread, cakes, and pastry were punished by being locked up in a basket and lowered into the river in front of the whole town. Such punishments had a deterrent effect on outsiders as well as everyone involved. The feeling of mutual closeness for better or worse, a feeling that in the late Middle Ages was nourished by authorities and the church and enforced by experience, was accepted by everyone, and was part of this deterrence.

Undoubtedly, many master craftsmen were rightfully proud of their knowledge and their success. Superior knowledge, which in many trades distinguished individual members and set them apart from the rest, was dangerous for those less distinguished and was therefore not welcomed by them. Trade corporations always attempted to guarantee the same conditions of existence to all their members. For this reason admittance to the corporation was connected to certain conditions, such as the limitation of the number of assistants a master craftsman could have, usually two journeymen and one apprentice; the obligation to purchase raw materials together and divide them evenly; and the regulation of the supply by limiting sales to certain shops.

In old German cities the members of one trade lived in the same streets, and offered their products in neighboring booths of the same size. The butchers, for instance, stood chopping block next to chopping block to sell their meat. Shoemakers and tailors had their workshops in the first floor of their neighboring houses. (In some cities the street names remind us of such former practices.) Other trades, like the dyers, tanners, and coopers, were forced to live and work along the rivers for reasons of fire hazards, noise, and air pollution. The enforcement was carried out by the trade police (*Gewerbepolizei*), the forerunners of the later Occupational Safety and Health Administration (OSHA) of the United States.

None of these measures had anything to do with the recognition of the individual master craftsman. He didn't find his recognition in outstanding personal success but rather in a product that was of average quality, of almost interchangeable uniformity, and manufactured according to the rules of the individual trade. In order to achieve this "perfection" the craftsmen submitted to controls and inspections, and to the marks that proved them.

The Quality Inspection of the Guilds

From the end of the thirteenth century to the fall of the Holy Roman Empire in 1806, with the resignation of Franz II, organized unions of all professions, especially trades but also services, medicine, and music, developed in the free cities of the empire and later on also in the new territorial states. These corporations, often called *guilds,* were generally coercive. Whoever wanted to carry on an organized trade had to become part of the institution. He was then under their protection. The corporations protected all their members from competition by nonmembers—it was forbidden by law to practice a trade if you didn't belong to its union. At the same time membership guaranteed the livelihood of every craftsman. Moreover, the right to belong and work for a corporation could be inherited. Strict rules, which in the course of time became more and more detailed, regulated the working conditions and even some aspects of the social life of the workers.

The rules concerning the quality of the products and services were strictly enforced. Inspection committees identified flawless goods with visible marks, which guaranteed their quality. Such committees were called *Schau* (show) in large parts of the country. These quality inspections were done everywhere, from Flensburg to Zurich and from Aachen to Königsberg (Kaliningrad), as well as in the Habsburg territory in the southeast. The inspections evolved at first in the cities. They then spread into the territories across the nation, so that even workers in the villages were registered in these corporations (but they were generally allowed to sell their products only on the local markets and thus didn't need marks for their goods). There were of course regional differences due to language barriers and political developments, but the conceptual approach was alike. The inspections in the large cities of the empire became the models and were accepted everywhere, especially by the trades and fairs.

The available documentation suggests that at first the corporations of the trades established their own inspection institutions. Soon after, public authorities, such as the Gewerbepolizei intervened. Such interventions resulted in political debates between the tradesmen and the civic authorities (the *patriciate*). Sometimes there were compromises such as the equal appointment of knowledgeable representatives of the trades and of the city to the inspection committees.

In all cities the tradesmen resisted the authorities, but in the end they were the losers and had to tolerate further restrictions of their authority, especially concerning the quality inspections. In the Modern Age, especially after the Thirty Years' War (1618–1648), the members of the inspection committees often came exclusively from the patriciate in the city and from the landlords. These could of course not do without the help of some knowledgeable craftsmen. The corporations though had lost the privilege to propose members of their own.

Early in the evolution of quality control, there developed the marking of the products with the mark of the craftsman, the so-called "master craftsmen's marks." The corporations demanded them in order to be able to apprehend the responsible craftsman should there be a complaint about the product. Only through the course of time did there emerge the idea that this mark represented the good reputation of its owner, the craftsman. The same is true for the members of the Lukas guild (*Lukasgilde*) of painters in the late Middle Ages. Its rules dictated that each member had to sign his works with an individual mark. The great masters among them elevated this duty to the status of an artist's signature, which didn't need a confirmation by third parties.

It is not known with certainty which trade first introduced master craftsmen's marks. Most likely it was the blacksmiths, following the tradition of the swordsmiths. Some early dates can be derived from the chronicles of the respective trades: the weavers of Schweidnitz (1335); the coopers of Lübeck (1354); the boilermakers of Lübeck (1354); the goldsmiths of Strassburg (1363). In general one may assume that by the fourteenth century the master craftsmen's marks were customary in all trades possible.[10]

It was different for producers of foodstuffs. Bakers, butchers, fishermen, gardeners, and winegrowers could not readily mark individual items of product. However, the fact that they were forced to sell their products next to one another gave the consumers a chance to compare products. This created a very different form of quality inspection—inspection by consumers. This approach helped German cities to provide their inhabitants with sufficient, affordable, and high-quality food products.[11]

The marks of the master coin manufacturers were an exception. They can be found on many coins in the late Middle Ages. Because the coin manufacturers often had more than one employer and sometimes worked on their own, their marks, which were naturally very small and almost hidden, do not represent a means of local control. They rather belong in the category of artists' signatures. In any case they were a guarantee for the quality of the product, in this case for the product's correspondence with the rules of the mint in question, such as the content of precious metals and the weight of the coins.[12]

Figure 7.3 Master craftsmen's marks of the goldsmiths' guild of Ulm in the late Middle Ages. Source: *Scripta Naturae*.

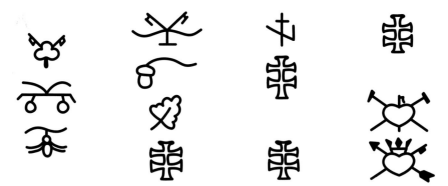

Figure 7.4 Master craftsmen's marks of the mint in Goslear in the
sixteenth century. Source: *Scripta Naturae*.

For some trades, notably those concerned with luxury products,
the tradesmen could not earn their living solely through local sales.
Their market was the whole region. Such products demanded intense
attention to the reputation for quality and hence to the assurance provided by the mark. An obvious example is the goldsmith and silver-
smith trades. The chief clientele of goldsmiths and silversmiths were
the clergy and the noblemen. Lacking knowledge and experience with
the products, these buyers had to rely on the tradesmen and the merchants. Hence they set great store by the master craftsman's mark and
the stamp of the city where he worked, the coat of arms of which was
widely known. If in doubt, especially in cases where the tradesman
had passed on, the consumer could verify that the tradesman was indeed a member of the corporation, as very early the corporations had
started to keep record of their members and their individual marks.

The statutes of these corporations regulated the use of the master
craftsmen's marks. Generally the craftsmen used the same mark during their whole lives without changes. The corporation of the goldsmiths and silversmiths in Frankfurt on the Main kept a magnificent
record of its members between 1624–1863, in which two pages are
dedicated to each member. This wasn't the first book of its kind; its
predecessors from 1229 on had been confiscated during the suppres-
sion of the uprising of the tradesmen in 1614 and are unfortunately
still missing today.[13] Of course books like these were kept in all cities
where members of that trade were joined together in corporations.
Historians have collected the master craftsmen's marks and the coats
of arms for all cities involved in the trade of the gold- and silversmiths
and have published them in several volumes.[14]

Figure 7.5 Magnificent cover of the second master craftsmen's book of the goldsmiths' guild in Frankfurt used between 1618 and 1864. Historisches Museum, Frankfurt am Main.

This is equally valid for the trade of the pewterers. The master pewterers, like the goldsmiths, sold their products nationally and were widely recognized for their art. The pewterers of Lüneburg are just one example. They mainly produced dinnerware for the upper class, who could afford to use pewter plates instead of plates made from clay or wood. This was an extravagance compared to the humble traditions of the common man. The rich didn't drink their wine from common cups either, but rather from magnificent tankards made from pewter. The pewterers thus manufactured bowls, cans, cups and plates, even dessert plates and dishes for the doll houses of the children of rich families, and sold them at the large international and smaller local fairs. All of these products bore the craftsman's mark and the stamp of the city. The corporations of the pewterers also kept registers. The marks of the pewterers have been collected by historians, and today enable those who are interested to determine the place and time of origin of each individual object made from pewter.[15]

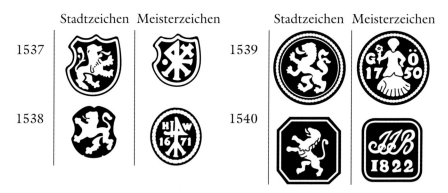

Figure 7.6 Quality guaranty on pewterer's products from Lüneburg; city marks and master craftsman's marks. Source: *Scripta Naturae*.

The same is valid for the so-called "fire trades" (*Feuerhandwerk*) which used an open flame to melt their metals. They included coppersmiths, as well as boilermakers and iron casters, who manufactured the heavy cauldrons, pans, and pots, which were used until the nineteenth century to prepare the foods in the kitchens of the poor as well as the rich. The craftsmen's marks of these trades have been registered by area historians. One example is the stamp of the needle smiths from Berlin and Cologne in 1560. These marks were found on the packages as early as the beginning of the eighteenth century.[16] The master craftsman's mark was always accompanied by the stamp of the city in which the craftsman was living, such as the falcon of the coat of arms of Aachen.

Other trades followed similar practices. Saddles were widely used until the nineteenth century in cities as well as in the country. The trade

Figure 7.7 Marks of the needle makers of Aachen on the packages of their sewing needles. Source: *Scripta Naturae.*

of the saddler was therefore booming, and corporations were organized everywhere. A register of such a saddler corporation with the marks of its members used to be kept in the Museum of the Berlin Castle (*Schlossmuseum*), perhaps to inform clients of their names and the fact that they were members.[17]

Stonemasons' marks can be found on structures such as castles, churches, bridges, gates, and homes of patricians. Yet, the interpretation of those marks remains difficult because there is no record as to which mark belonged to which craftsman. This was a secret of the fraternity that was kept through the centuries. Though the preserved documents shed no light on this secrecy, they do stress that each member was obliged to satisfy his customers with good work and thus to enhance the good reputation of his trade through his products. In 1498 a letter was drafted by the stonemasons of the cities of Strassburg, Frankfurt on the Main, Ensisheim, Schlettstadt, Heidelberg, Basel, and Zürich that put all legal members from Constance to Koblenz and in Franken, Swabia, and the Moselle area, under the main corporation in Strassburg. This arrangement was approved by Emperor Ferdinand I in a 1563 document, but the craftsmen's marks were not mentioned.

Figure 7.8a Master craftsmen's marks on tombstones at the Marienkirche (church of St. Mary) in Greifswald. Source: *Scripta Naturae.*

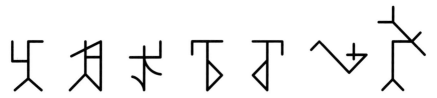

Figure 7.8b Stonemason's marks from the 2nd story of the Kaiserdom (cathedral) in Frankfurt am Main (built between 1423 and 1439). Source: *Scripta Naturae.*

At the release ceremonies for every journeyman, and when a new master craftsman was admitted into the corporation of stonemasons, an assembly of stonemasons in his town would decide on a personal mark for him and swear to keep it secret. The main corporation in Strassburg kept records of all such matters and functioned as an arbitrator in case of disagreements between craftsmen. All this is prescribed in the letters from 1498/1563.[18] There is no information about what was recorded in the book or where it is.

In contrast, the regulations for quality assurance in the trade of textile manufacturing are well preserved and are very detailed. They also date back to the fourteenth century. At that time the wool weavers' corporations had more members than any other trade in many cities and towns of the Rhine area from Basel to Cologne. The noise of the looms could be heard everywhere in those cities, which is brought back to memory by the name of one of Frankfurt on the Main's largest streets, *Schnurgasse* (string lane). German wool cloth was sold on the international fairs in large quantities. As early as 1321 a document about trade traditions in the city of Budapest mentions cloth from Hesse, a gray, very tough and durable material called the lansquenet's cloth [in the sixteenth century a lansquenct (*Landknecht*) was a foot soldier] from Frankfurt.[19]

There was also international competition. The large textile manu-facturing areas of Great Britain, Northern France, and Flanders even then produced high-quality cloth that was accordingly more expen-sive, while the German weavers manufactured simpler products, which satisfied the needs of a wide range of consumers in the late Middle Ages. At the end of the fifteenth century this division of the markets changed within a few decades. The good products from northwestern European textile manufacturers completely replaced the German goods on the international market. The German weavers lost their important role in the cities, and their number diminished in such a way that they could barely fill the needs of the local market. Their corporations in the smaller cities had to content themselves with the regional fairs. After three centuries of wealth, they soon became so poor that they had to go back to wage-labor. Everywhere merchants took over the trade of textile manufacturing. They purchased the raw wool, paid for the dyeing and gave the weavers, who were now inde-pendent only on paper, a piece rate to finish it. This type of division of labor, in which the merchant alone took the financial risk and made the profit, while the weavers disappeared more and more from the market of the small cities, was called *verlegen* (to move, to change).

The remaining corporations of weavers in the larger cities were under great pressure and facing tough competition, because of this relatively sudden development in the early modern times. This is why they had to be especially sure of the flawless quality of their products. A system once voluntarily established by their predecessors to pre-serve the good reputation of the trade, now became a strict law that was imposed on them during the early modern times by the town council and the patriciate, after they had fought for participation of the trades in the administration of the cities and lost. This regulation was called *Tuchschau* (showing of cloth) for which sworn quality in-spectors were put in office. Still, the help of experts was needed and the city councils let the corporations of weavers propose master crafts-men for the job, from which the council elected those that were agreeable to them. These craftsmen were sworn in and were compen-sated for their work with the fees that they imposed on others. They observed the whole manufacturing process together with an equal number of city council members. No piece of cloth could be sold by any member of the corporation, unless it had been produced under such supervision. This supervision started at the loom, where warps

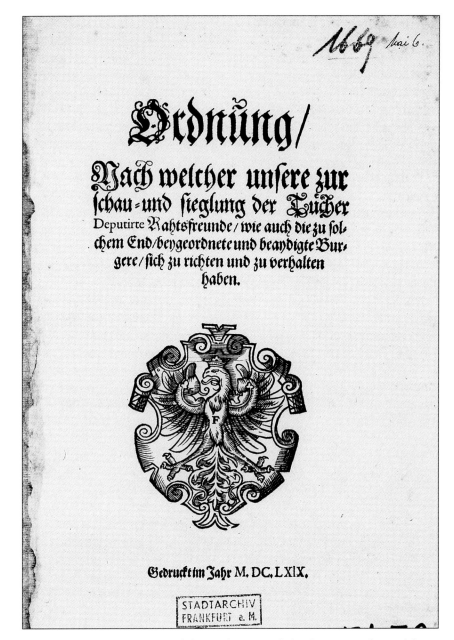

Figure 7.9 Cover page of the ordnance of the free city of Frankfurt am Main for the Tuchschau (official inspection of woolen cloth) of 1669. Source: *Scripta Naturae*.

were inspected. After the cloth was taken off the loom, it was sheared and fulled. Now the products were inspected again, to see whether they met the standard measurements for length and width. All flaws in the weave were marked with a linen hook. Only flawless products were considered perfect. According to the number of linen hooks, the imperfect cloth was divided into several groups. Faulty products were cut up and could only be sold in pieces, not as a whole, on the local market. The cloth then had to be moistened and after the drying it had to be pulled back into shape and folded according to the norm.

Throughout this whole working process the craftsman had to cover his own mark so that it was invisible to the inspectors. These inspected the folded cloth one last time and attached a lead seal, which bore the coat of arms of the city on one side and the coat of arms of the weaver's corporation on the other side. Depending on the quality of the cloth, it was marked with one to four such seals, four being the highest and representing flawless quality. These lead seals, which are about the size of a penny, are now very rare because they were cut off by the tailor, collected, and sold as used lead. From many cities only the document, which regulated the use of the seals, is preserved, but no seals. Steel pliers, which had the coats of arms of the city and trade on the inner sides, were used to press the seals into a small plate of lead previously attached to the cloth. The inspectors were therefore often called *Stahlmeister* (steel masters); those from Amsterdam were

Figure 7.10 Stamp on the seal of the bales of linen inspected by the Königlich Preussischen Leinenlegge (Royal Prussian Linenleague) in Bielefeld, used after 1823. Source: *Scripta Naturae*.

depicted by Rembrandt van Rijn (1662) in his famous art work *Dutch Masters,* which is today exhibited in the Rijksmuseum in Amsterdam.

For this detailed inspection the weavers had to pay a fee, which varied based on the number of flaws. The merchants on the other hand trusted the inspectors and their seals. At the large trade fairs it was customary that the wholesaler abstained from inspecting and measuring the bundles of cloth before buying them. The cloth was unfolded only by the retailer, who cut it; but often consumers bought whole cloth and used it to dress all their servants or children in the same way. In J. W. Goethe's childhood memories *Dichtung und Wahrheit* (*Fiction and Truth*) we learn that his economical father did exactly that, much to the annoyance of his family. But trust in the dependability of the quality inspection by the local authorities is very important. In the German-speaking area this was generally valid for all other trades and remained so for at least 500 years, from the late Middle Ages to the end of the eighteenth century. In some cities it continued even until the middle of the nineteenth century, as for instance Frankfurt on the Main, which renounced the trade corporations and their regulations only in 1864.[20]

In the textile trade quality inspections at first were customary only for woolen cloth. In more recent times cotton and silk were similarly controlled. Linen on the other hand, was for a long time not subject to any official inspections because until the nineteenth century it was produced by farming families for their own personal use during winter and was only occasionally sold on local markets. It was only in the nineteenth century that the number of linen manufacturers working for the market had increased so much that the landowners, for financial reasons, became interested. They initiated official inspections for linen and soon forced all subjects trading in linen to sell only goods inspected by their institutions and marked for flawless quality. They imposed taxes in order to pay for these actions and through political measures and customs regulations they assured that only inspected linen could be sold.

The Manufacturers' Marks Guarantee Quality

Assurance of product quality by commercial corporations under the supervision and with the help of city and county officials served as an advertisement, while promoting sales. In turn, such assurance stimulated or even forced independent trades that had no corporations and were at least of free origin to take similar measures. There are several examples of measures that were taken voluntarily by those involved, later becoming institutions guaranteed by organization.

The watermark on paper is an obvious example. The first paper mill built in Germany was in 1389, by Ulrich Stomer, a merchant from Nürnberg. He soon began making his paper with an indelible mark which was worked into the sieve, as was general practice in Europe. The watermark enables historians today to determine the place of origin and sometimes even the time of production and thus provides a good clue for the chronological classification of undated documents on such paper. The science of watermarks is therefore indispensable for today's historical research, especially as paper manufacturers frequently

Figure 7.11 Papermaker's mark before 1400, flowered head of an ox as watermark on every sheet, from the archives of the Deutscher Orden (German Order) in Vienna. Source: *Scripta Naturae*.

changed the marks they used in order to distinguish different working periods and, later, different sorts of paper.[21]

The subsequent processors also provided their work with individual marks. The molders, who engraved texts and illustrations into the wood-blocks gave their forms personal marks, which were intended as a guarantee for quality but were also a form of advertisement.[22] The printers followed their example as early as the fifteenth century. The printer's mark, consisting of personal illustrations or coats of arms, can already be found in the earliest prints, the incunabula. In early history they decorated the last page of their prints with such marks. Later the printer's personal mark and the publisher's imprint were also printed on the front page. A regulation of the imprints was achieved only at the time of the joining together of all printers in corporations.[23]

Figure 7.12 Two printer's marks of the Early Modern Age, like those usually found on the last page of a printed work.
Source: *Scripta Naturae.*

The clocks (an invention of the fourteenth century) on church towers, courthouses, gates, and private buildings of the rich, had the mark or name of the manufacturers engraved on the back. The same is valid for the expensive table clocks that they made for their clients. In contrast to the paper manufacturers and paper processors, clockmakers generally were members of some corporation, usually the corporation of smiths or fire trades, and thus were familiar with the regulations concerning quality control that were laid down for other members of their corporation. Their number was so small and their art so unique that they had to guarantee their products themselves and be liable for them.[24]

Things were similar for the glass refiners. While the glassworks abstained from marking their products for technical reasons, the glass cutters and the glass engravers marked their artful work with their individual sign and sometimes with their full name. This too has to be viewed as a guarantee for quality and maybe as an advertisement.[25] From this tradition, researchers in glass derive reliable clues for the classification of the art works and the identification of the craftsmen.

The factory system of division of labor within a trade started in Germany only after the Thirty Years' War (1618–1648). The mercantilists following the example of Louis XIV's minister Jean-Baptiste Colbert, developed large factories where semiskilled workers each performed a part of a work process. One result was that the mark on the product was the mark of the factory rather than the mark of an individual tradesman.

One area of factory growth was in ceramics production. While potters kept on producing pottery with their wheels and continued selling it on the local markets, factories were set up by the British, Portuguese, and Dutch to produce imitations of the porcelain imported from China. These products found enthusiastic customers among the upper class, especially after the factories started decorating

Figure 7.13 The marks of the most important German porcelain manufacturers of the eighteenth century, left to right: Meissen, Hoechst, Vienna, and Nymphenburg. Source: *Scripta Naturae*.

the dishes with colorful flowers, which accommodated the taste of the Baroque.[26]

Joh. Friedrich Böttger's imitation of porcelain in 1708 in Meissen and elsewhere met with even more approval. The fragile and pretty porcelain remained affordable only by the rich. Only gradually could the middle class afford complete sets of dinnerware. The conservative pewter disappeared from the tables of the upper class only when the British earthenware came to the market at the end of the eighteenth century. The majority of the population stuck with the simple pottery, which needed no special recommendation, until the beginning of the twentieth century. Those who purchased porcelain though, paid great attention to the manufacturer's mark.[27]

With the help of manufacturers, luxury items from overseas were brought to the market. Cocoa from the West Indies, coffee from Arabia, and tea from the East Indies were imported and packaged for retail. They were marked with the name of the wholesaler and sometimes with imaginary names for advertisement and competition. The packaging usually consisted of tin cans or paper with colorful decorations. During the Baroque period, tobacco manufacturers used tastefully decorated packaging to sell their goods retail. On the other hand a wide variety of pipes and snuff boxes, some very valuable, made from fine metals and decorated with diamonds, soon became available.

The ladies and gentlemen of the Baroque and Rococo also appreciated perfumes and used them in large quantities, provided they could afford them. Glasswork and ceramics manufacturers produced charming bottles to serve as containers. The guarantee of quality through the marks was equally fundamental for these products. This was also true for example, for eau de cologne, which was always sold under the name of the producer and with the packaging that he designed.[28]

The tradition of labels for wine bottles also started back in the eighteenth century. The differences in wine-growing areas, location of the vines, and vintage had been known for a long time, but for many centuries wine could only be sold in large wooden barrels. The coopers marked their barrels, especially the most magnificent ones, with their individual sign. Those marks were a guarantee only for the barrel and not for its contents. The decisive factors in the wine trade were for a long time taste and the reputation of the winegrower or the merchant.

Figure 7.14 Business mark and at the same time quality guaranty of
the Zacharias Krämer trading company in Nürnberg,
eighteenth century. Source: *Scripta Naturae.*

Mass Production and Liberalism

With the fall of the Holy Roman Empire in 1806, a period of one
thousand years ended and the already loose system of quality assurance collapsed. On German soil only relics survived until the middle
of the nineteenth century. At the same time the Industrial Revolution,
based on technological progress, advanced from Great Britain, northern France, and the south of The Netherlands (later Belgium) into
Germany, mainly through coal mining and the associated iron industry. Along the Lower Rhine, in the Ruhr district and in Upper Silesia
there emerged factories, powered by steam engines, to mass produce

homogeneous goods. With these advantages came disadvantages, such as the exploitation of workers and the pollution, which were already evident in England. Meanwhile, through the spread of potato and sugar beet cultivation, which represent inexpensive basic foods for the majority of the population, and through the tremendous innovations in medicine, the conditions of life for the masses were changed fundamentally for the better. In addition, the ideas of the French Revolution (1789) were being spread by the Enlightenment.

A leading concept of the Enlightenment was *Liberalism*. In those times Liberalism included the idea of putting an end to antiquated customs, and liberating individuals and the economy from old chains, "cutting off old tails" (*Abschneiden der alten Zöpfe*).

The climate for Liberalism had become favorable. Those who accepted Liberalism included journalistic propagandists and intellectuals who were aroused by the slogans of the Paris revolutionaries. They also included those young entrepreneurs and merchants who had experienced Liberalism during their training in Great Britain and France (international internships and study trips had long been a custom in the German upper class). For the followers of these new ideas there was no longer any room for imposed systems of quality control. They demanded freedom, and were understood and supported by progressive ministers and leading government employees.

But Great Britain flooded the German market with inexpensive factory products, textiles, hardware, sheet metal and brass, instruments, and earthenware, which were the most important import articles of the early nineteenth century. Many trades suffered from this and some, for instance the nail smiths and potters, were wiped out within only a few years. The young German factories had to sacrifice the quality of their products in order to be able to compete. Liberalism had provided the necessary liberty, but soon complaints about defects, lack of taste, and unattractiveness of these factory products could be heard everywhere.

Only gradually did individual producers fight back during this early phase of German industrialization. For this purpose they used their marks, most of which had been conferred in the eighteenth century and were guaranteed by the control institutions. The best known example for this is the twin sign (*Zwillingszeichen*) of the knife smiths in Solingen, which now became the trademark of a company.[29]

Where luxury articles were concerned, the marks remained the decisive factor because even the foreign competitors had to hold on to

Figure 7.15 Quality mark of the Henckel's Zwilling factory in Solingen for their products of iron, steel, and brass (knives, scissors, and related products), nineteenth century. Source: *Scripta Naturae.*

them. This system of individual marks was preserved through decades in the German Union (1815–1866) without legal protection.

At the same time, during the early phase of industrialization, a change in the transportation system took place. At first the roads and thus the paths for the carriages were improved. Then, with the appearance of the railroads and steamboats in the 1830s, the way of trading was fundamentally changed. The fairs lost their importance. As soon as a schedule for the mail coach was established, the *commis voyageur,* the commercial traveler, started to visit his clients regularly with his case of samples, in order to present the collection personally. The sending of packages became matter of course. Roads and the restaurants along them became more lively. It was a very active, mobile period, during which the merchants and factory owners had to convince their clients personally of the superior quality of their products over foreign imports. (During those times, advertising was rare and very simple.)

With the broadening of markets, the age-old problem of measurement became more and more an obstacle to trade. Weights and measures differed from city to city in Germany. Even though the differences were only minimal this could become quite a nuisance when large quantities were concerned. Complicated conversions were inevitable for the international trade. Only the territorial states, which developed as a result of the political reorganization during the time of Napoleon, tried to establish standardized measurements at least for their territory. But part of the difficulty was the old measurements in themselves. Many arable crops, especially the grains, were measured in capacities. Depending on the quality of the crop the content of these measurements differed by up to ±5 percent. There were also differences in weight according to the condition of the crop, dry or wet, but those were much less obvious.

A major aid toward solving these problems was the metric system. It became the basis for a worldwide standardization of measurements. It met cultural resistance, and not only in Germany. However, the German-speaking nations did adopt the metric system during the second half of the nineteenth century. Another hundred years then passed until the west European and the North American cultures accepted the metric system. Meanwhile, complicated handbooks were used in Germany for the conversion of common measurements and weights.[30]

Progress-oriented people did of course try to master problems of standardization through international agreements, regulations, and mergers, against the constant objection of the conservative powers. The most successful in this matter was the German Customs Union (*Deutscher Zollverein*), which was founded in 1827 by Prussia. Within two decades most German states—with important exceptions, such as the Hanseatic cities (Hansestädte)—had become members of this union because the fiscal advantages were evident to their finance ministers.

A by-product of the Customs Union was the statistical data it collected, analyzed, and published. The science of statistics proved to be a useful aid for the analyzing of such data. The bureaucrats recognized the importance of such data early on, and supported them. Statisticians soon observed the ups and downs of seasonal and economic cycles, and derived certain natural laws. During their research they came upon the problem of random variation and undertook the first steps to define it. Such issues were regarded as useless intellectual games by the few contemporaries that were even interested. Only decades later did science go back to their proposals.[31]

The statistics of the Customs Union, and even more those of individual German states, provided quantified data on population growth and mobility. People migrated to areas that offered job opportunities and affordable cost of living. But the flow of job seekers often exceeded the needs of the factories. This surplus of workers often decided to emigrate overseas. Hundreds of thousands of Germans left for the United States. Some headed for the southern half of the new world and founded for example the large settlement called *Blumenau* close to Sao Paulo in Brazil. The princes of the German Union watched this steady drain of people with mixed feelings. On the one hand, it relieved them of the obligation to provide for unemployed subjects; on the other hand, they were losing potential taxpayers and recruits for their armies.

It should be understood that the growth of Liberalism created problems for those with vested interests in the established order. Liberals supported the right of the individual to carry on a business and to develop economically. Liberals opposed every attempt to limit such development, whether through laws or otherwise. Yet the authorities were forced to take such measures. Merchants and industrialists repeatedly asked the authorities for help against those who misused their personal marks and those who attempted to deceive the consumer by using someone else's marks for products of lower quality. At first the ministries dealing with these cases referred them to the civil courts. But the judges, based on the number of complaints, pushed for a prosecution of such abuse.

During the period of 1815–1848, this forced the authorities of Prussia, Bavaria, and Hesse to provide measures to protect, for instance, the knife industry of Solingen, related industries in Nürnberg and Schwabach, and the businesses of Schmalkalden. During the conference of the Customs Union in Munich in 1836, the government of Baden took the first steps to introduce a standard criminal law against such abuse. But the German Union did not get past these initial stages until 1866.[32] The establishment of the second German Reich on January 18, 1871, and the agreement of the German princes after the Franco-Prussian war (1870–1871) then created the basis for new solutions to legal as well as administrative problems.

Trademarks and Consumer Protection

Despite the attractions of Liberalism, the fluctuations of economic forces resulted in booms, crises, and business failure of economically weak companies. Such events forced the authorities of the empire to take the first steps to revoke laws that, under the influence of the liberal ideology granted personal freedom, and to reinstate principles of order in the communities.

The pending changes in Germany then received an unexpected stimulus from the competition on the world market. During those years there were world exhibitions which enabled buyers to compare the technology and quality of competitive products. The rise of Germany became evident, and challenged the previous British domination of the European market. A fierce competition developed in quality, price, and prompt delivery. This competition then attracted the attention of the government ministries. In 1887 the British government passed the Merchandise Marks Act, according to which all merchandise not produced in Britain was to be marked to show the country of origin when imported to Great Britain or its colonies. The mark "Made in Germany" under which German products were now offered on the world market, soon proved to be an excellent advertisement. With this short-sighted measure the politicians had achieved the opposite of what they had in mind. The consumers were now able to make comparisons, and the enterprises had to produce merchandise that could withstand those comparisons.

This open competition led to a demand, on the part of those involved in the economics of the German nation, for federal measures to aid the economy. This hurt the liberal movement and brought back to life regulations long believed outdated. The trades, for instance, reestablished apprenticeship and examinations for the master craftsman's certificate. The organization of the corporations and the title of master craftsman were reinstated and protected. But the legislators and the minister of justice as well as the parliament, gave priority to the individual right of the owner of a mark for protection against abuse. The rejection of unfair competition was included in both the German and the British regulations.

Neither the political authorities nor the bureaucracy had been much concerned about the consumer. During the second half of the nineteenth century, public opinion did not give this aspect much thought either. Nevertheless, there already existed strict regulations, based on age-old experience and traditions, to protect consumer health and safety. An example was the measures enforced by the veterinary police, to assure that meat was free from diseases.

On November 30, 1874, the Statute to Protect Marks (*Marken-schutzgesetz*) was passed by the German Reichstag (government). It became effective May 1, 1875. It preserved the system of registering and keeping of marks, which so far had been supervised by the states themselves. The imperial authorities however lacked the means for enforcement, and had to establish them at the courts.[33] The protection of the owners of these marks, which could be inherited or sold with the business as a part of it, was however essential. The main purpose of the law was to protect the interest and rights of third parties. The law did not mention the quality or value of the product, nor the effectiveness of advertisement. As long as the mark did not violate the sovereignty or national emblem of the empire and its states and didn't otherwise cause offense it could be registered.

Soon technical problems developed with the implementation of the law. Complaints from businesses affected by the law flooded the authorities. The producers of steel items in Solingen and Remscheid were dissatisfied with the law because it did not include the connection of a mark with a specific industry, but allowed similar marks to be used for very different products, which confused the public. The tobacco industry demanded that its long customary vignettes, which decorated the cigarette packages, be accepted as marks. Similar requests were voiced over the course of years by the producers of rice starch and noodles, and by the chemical industry. After two decades, the government of the empire was compelled to change the 1874 statute. By that time the economy of the empire and even more so the imperial government had clearly distanced themselves from the liberal movement. The demand for free trade had been abandoned and protective tariffs were strictly enforced. The landowners in east Prussia insisted on protection by the empire for the sale of their grain, and secured limits on imports from overseas. The sympathy of the emperor and the bureaucracy for the interests of members of their class played a large role.

The Statute to Protect Trade Marks (*Gesetz zum Schutz der Warenbezeichnung*) was passed by the German Reichstag on May 12, 1894. The name of the statute indicates the change that took place. The procedure of examining and registering the trademarks—not *marks* anymore—was now in the hands of the Patent Office of the Empire. The regulations proved to be so effective that they have continued essentially unchanged for over a century up to the present. So far as the owners of trademarks were concerned, the fundamentals were in place by the end of the nineteenth century. But as far as quality assurance was concerned, the needs of consumer protection required further development.

Standardization and Interchangeability

The advent of mass production intensified greatly the problems of standardization and interchangeability. Clients and especially retailers increasingly complained about the number of competing products that differed in size by minimal amounts. Such small differences were nevertheless an obstacle to interchangeability. Bolts from one producer were interchangeable with nuts from that producer, but not with nuts from other producers. Similar problems existed in other products—textiles, stationery, and so on. Retailers were forced to maintain large inventories of almost identical competing items. The producers resisted standardization for fear of losing market share. The problem was international in scope, and was worsened by the Anglo-American resistance to adoption of the metric system.

In Germany the experience of World War I forced industry to change its negative attitude. The military services mandated standardization for the products they purchased—uniforms, accessories, and so on. Experience in producing for the military then convinced suppliers of the merits of standardization and reduced objections to it, even in the civilian sector. In 1917 the Committee for Norms for Mechanical Engineering (*Normalienausschuss für Maschinenbau*), was founded in Berlin. It began to establish standardization for its products. After the fall of the empire this volunteer work expanded into all sorts of mass production and continued despite the postwar political turmoil. The benefit to society was obvious, and the climate for change was favorable, so the interest in norms spread to more and more areas of goods and services. All sectors of the economy benefitted.

In 1926 the work of standardization was brought together in the German Standards Committee (*Deutscher Normenausschuss*), which, under the abbreviation DNA, became an indispensable helper for many branches of the economy. This committee publishes continuously numbered lists of standard specifications under the abbreviation DIN—German Industrial Standard (*Deutsche Industrienorm*). DIN is a registered trademark of today's German Institute for Standards (*Deutsches Institut für Normung*) (registered since 1975). It can be used by all tradesmen whose products meet all the requirements that can legitimately be expected and that are quoted in the individual lists of standard specifications (DIN 31). It has long been customary for manufacturers to cite the applicable DIN number in their correspondence, in advertisements, and often in the packaging or on the product itself. Similarly, when buyers put orders out to tender, they specify the applicable DIN numbers.

Standardization is carried out by volunteers. They are organized into committees according to work branches. Their results are published by the DNA (today the DIN) and are registered under DIN numbers in the German Standards Book (*Deutsches Normenwerk*).

The number of standards has meanwhile reached 20,000. They include a wide range of subject matter: definitions of terms, units of measure, methods of measurement, formulas, and so on. They extend to input materials, processes and products, construction and building codes, grades of quality, product labeling, terms of delivery, human safety, and so on. Further developments have led to DIN standards for services, under rules prepared by trade associations in the respective industries. The principles, channels of business, and designing of standards are generally regulated in DIN standard 820. For apprenticeship and practice the different trades have handbooks, in which the applicable standards are listed.

One example of the useful work of standardization is the DIN standards for paper sizes, which were introduced in Germany decades ago. Herein one square meter is the basic standard DIN A2. By dividing this surface, the smaller sizes are created. The normal size paper (DIN A4) measures 210 x 297 mm. Half a page is A5 and a postcard is DIN A6. These are matched by the respective sizes of DIN B and DIN C for the envelopes.

Standardization has contributed greatly to the assurance of quality. Beyond the advantage to manufacturers, it has aided consumers by defining what to expect when the product carries a given DIN number and by providing assurance that the expectation will be met.[34]

A further aid to rationalization has been the creation of a coordinating board for all economic organizations that work in the field of rationalization. All unions, scientific institutes of business management and technology, as well as departments and companies, employers, and anyone interested in this field, are part of this nonprofit organization. The latest name for this board is Board for Rationalization of the German Economy [Rationalisierungs-Kuratorium der Deutschen Wirtschaft (RKW)]. An unusual amount of painstaking and detailed work has been done in this field over the course of decades.[35]

The VDE-inspection sticker (*VDE-Prüfzeichen*) is a good example of such work. The association of German Electronics Engineers [*Verband Deutscher Elektrotechniker* (VDE)] had been founded in 1893. In 1920 it established a facility for testing the products of its members. At first fuses and plugs were tested. This concept was then expanded, and coordination was established with the test laboratories of industrial companies. In 1971 it became the VDE Institute for Inspection and Certification (*Prüf- und Zertifizierungsinstitut des VDE*) in Offenbach am Main. Of the almost 4000 DIN standards for electronic products, nearly 1200 have become VDE regulations; most of those now have become European Standards [*Europäische Norm* (EN)]. VDE also ensures the observance of the DIN standards at other national and international inspection facilities, and gives permission for the accepted products to bear the triangular VDE mark. About 200,000 electronic items currently bear that mark. VDE inspection has been extended to cover about 60 percent of household appliances and even motorized tools if electrically powered. The Institute at Offenbach serves over 2000 German companies and over 2000 international companies. The VDE mark has become a symbol of high quality and safety for the consumer.[36]

Quality As a Legal Problem

Once voluntary standards are incorporated into a contract they have legal consequences. This is true at all stages of product progression through manufacturing and sale. In Germany these legal consequences were recognized at the time of introduction of standardization. This was achieved on a voluntary basis and without pressure from the authorities. In contrast, public invitations to tender insisted on express guarantees.

In 1925 the Imperial Committee for Terms of Delivery [*Reichs-Ausschuss für Lieferbedingungen* (RAL)] was founded in Berlin by numerous organizations of industry and representatives of the imperial government. Under the abbreviation RAL it was added to the RKW (Imperial Board for Economic Viability). It was intended, on a voluntary basis, to establish means to regulate problems of a technical nature, especially those concerning quality assurance, and thus to save the legislature, the government, and its departments from the need to enact appropriate rules. For reasons of rationalization the regulations were to be established for all tradesmen of the particular industry. The main concern was consumer protection. With this goal in mind, regulations were created for quality, for the control thereof, and for the system of marking products in different industries. They were each worked out by experts of the involved industries under the supervision of the RAL, and then established as quality marks, as proof for a quality continuously assured by a neutral institution. In the organization of the RKW the RAL was under supervision of the Imperial Minister of Economy (*Reichswirtschaftsministerium*), but always remained an independent and responsible institution of the economy.

The regulations worked out by the RAL in cooperation with the different industries, summarize generally known rules of techniques, explain them, and set compulsory regulations for quality and safety. Being a registered organization, the RAL soon earned legal status and consequently had the abbreviation of its organization registered nationally and internationally as a trademark. Since then this trademark has served as proof of compliance with the regulations of the RAL. It also was established as additional proof for the quality of the product.

With the transition to a market economy after World War II, there arose a need to reestablish an institution to regulate business dealings and for use of a mark to prove quality of products. For this purpose, the RAL was affiliated with the German Committee for Standardization [*Deutscher Normenausschuss* (DNA)] in 1952. This provided a legal basis for the RAL activities. Nevertheless the RAL operated independently. Later the responsibilities of the RAL were increased, and it became necessary to reinstate a legal capacity to the RAL. In 1972 the registered RAL was reactivated and remained on good terms with the DNA.

The leadership of this reestablished institution was now composed of a board of trustees instead of the old advisory committee. The board composition includes membership from a broad spectrum of society: industries, agriculture, trade unions, government ministries, DIN, RKW, the Patent Office, and so on—a total of 24 institutions. It identifies the RAL as a nonprofit organ of self-government of the economy by supporting its work financially and in a nonmaterial way. The federal government grants the RAL a state subsidy but essentially the work is funded by those industries that use its fiduciary function to keep order. The unions, organizations, and companies linked with the RAL raise the necessary funds to support the work of the RAL by contributing according to a voluntary agreement.

The work of the RAL is spread across all of Germany. On an international level it acts as a representative of the German interest in different industries. The responsibilities of the RAL include RAL regulations, RAL registrations, RAL certifications, seals to guarantee the geographical origin of a product, and the seal for environmental protection. The main task in all these fields of activity is the assurance of quality of products and services, as well as the labeling with the appropriate quality seals.

When problems arise because of improper labeling, those involved may contact the RAL on a voluntary basis. It is then the responsibility of the RAL to research the demands and opinions of the involved institutions. Then a regulation is drafted to the satisfaction of all, which is binding for everyone that signs the draft, which will be published by the RAL as a pamphlet.

A similar process is followed in cases where regulations are drafted internally within an industry. In such cases the RAL also seeks the approval of the involved parties and expert institutions, and then publishes the findings with the approval of those involved, in the form of a RAL publication.

The RAL has a deciding role in the process of creating and accepting quality marks. These marks are in principle given only to entities created especially for this purpose, and not to individuals or companies. The entity, which is then called a Community of Property (*Gütegemeinschaft*), has to be organized as a registered association and may give its quality mark to each applicant only according to the published regulations for quality and inspection. Only one quality mark is established for each sector. After it has been accepted, this mark is registered in the RAL List of Quality Marks, published by the Federal Minister of Economy in the Federal Gazette, and registered as a trademark with the German Patent Office. The RAL constantly supervises the use of the term *quality mark* and takes action against misuse.

In the interest of consumers the RAL gives out information to enable them to evaluate the suitability of a certain product for the intended use. The RAL for this reason inspects for the properties that are marked on the product label, the composition of textiles, and whether appliances operate according to the instructions. Only the information about technical use is explicitly noted as approved. This information is thus clearly distinguished from the RAL quality mark, which guarantees the quality of the product. The information on the label of the product is thus intended to contain the essential information for the consumer and the dealers to be able to judge the suitability for use of the product.

Finally, the RAL has the task of supervising the use of the environmental mark, which was created by the Federal Minister of the Interior. This mark is intended to provide consumers with a dependable and neutral confirmation of the environment-friendly property of a product thusly marked. This responsibility of the RAL is not directly associated with the assurance of quality but that aspect of course is not forgotten.[37]

The Emerging Revolutions in Quality

The nineteenth century witnessed a broad movement to mass produce the goods needed to serve a growing affluence among consumers and the associated growing middle class. Technological innovation flourished and achieved acceptance among all industrial nations. As this movement progressed, the problem of quality assurance in mass production emerged as a major difficulty. Even small percents of defects resulted in numerous complaints, with associated increases in costs and damage to quality reputations.

The revolutionary nature of mass production required adoption of methodologies beyond those employed by craftsmen. These new methodologies in effect consisted of three revolutions—revolutions in technology, in business management, and in statistics.

Technology and Quality

The contributions of technology included the machines, tools, and measuring instruments needed for precision manufacture and quality control. In addition, technology provided new forms of organizing the workplace to enable semiskilled and unskilled workers to carry out the production process. The system of Frederick W. Taylor (1856–1915) known as *scientific management* (*Wissenschaftliche Betriebsführung*) included the concept of separating planning from execution, and was widely adopted. The automobile assembly line of Henry Ford (1863–1947) was an important application of this concept. The productivity of such manufacturing processes was far greater than that of craftsmen, and contributed to the decline in the numbers of trained craftsmen.

A further contribution of technology was a revolutionary growth of application of the ancient concept of automation. Even in classical antiquity, contemporaries were astonished at the genius of the manufacturers of machines. In the Middle Ages Leonardo da Vinci invented many machines that were built and able to work only many generations later. Clockmakers and mechanics in the Baroque period invented truly magnificent marvels of automatic figurines, which enriched the collections of their princes. Some of these artistic works eventually ended up at the fairs, were marveled at by many, but were for a long time considered useless by more serious people. Finally, they were considered outdated, and gathered dust in museums.

With the advent of electricity, inventors revived their interest in automated machines. Some of this was directed at robots, as human looking as possible. These were sensationalized in the media and in the movie industry in the form of monsters.[38]

Other inventors directed their attention to the problems of mass production. Their ideas resulted in integrated manufacturing systems, electronic data processing, and real-time control systems which made the measurements, analyzed the resulting data, and energized actuators to close the feedback loop.

These developments completely changed the work environment. The early factories had employed few machines and many unskilled workers. The revolution in technology made it possible for factories to employ many automated machines and controls, but only a few unskilled workers. There was less and less demand for unskilled or semiskilled workers but the demand for technologically skilled workers grew.

The technology of measurement and control engineering (*Mess- und Regeltechnik*) is essential to the assurance of quality. It has experienced an important theoretical as well as practical widening due to the introduction of cybernetics. In this doctrine, discoveries in technology, biology, sociology, and psychology were summarized and were used by the American mathematician Norbert Wiener (1894–1964) to explain terminology and methods. Researchers in all parts of the world, including Germany, have contributed to this wide field.

Business Management and Quality

The chief decisions leading to the growth of mass production were made by the entrepreneurs and business managers. They began with the premise that mass production would lower prices dramatically. In turn this would create mass markets by making the products affordable to the growing middle class. Acting on this premise, they raised the capital needed to design products and manufacturing processes, build factories, produce the products, and sell them through new marketing channels with the aid of advertising. There were many brilliant successes along with the high mortality rate of new ventures.

A major by-product of technological changes such as the assembly line was a decline in quality of work life. Most workers resented the monotony of performing short-cycle tasks over and over again. The managers deplored this but accepted it as a necessary evil. Nevertheless, as education levels rose during the twentieth century, the workers in such jobs became a major underemployed asset. The companies were employing the physical bodies of the workers, but not their education or creativity.

In due course progressive companies responded by changing the organization of the workplace and the allocation of responsibilities. These changes took multiple forms. Some workers were assigned multiple production tasks to minimize monotony. Other workers were assigned multiple functions relating to the same production task, which required them to carry out planning and coordination. Some workers were organized into teams which became largely self-directing through being given responsibility for many functions previously assigned to supervisors and technical specialists. These and other efforts to improve quality of work life will no doubt continue into the next century.

The Japanese Quality Revolution.   At the end of World War II Japanese industry faced a severe quality crisis. The major companies had lost their chief customer—the armed forces, so they converted to making civilian products. They then discovered that foreign importers were reluctant to buy these products due to Japan's reputation as a producer of poor quality.

To deal with this crisis, the Japanese managers made some revolutionary changes in their approach to managing for quality. They focused on perfecting the production processes to avoid making defects in the first place. Their measure of defectiveness changed from percent defective to defective parts per million (ppm).

The Japanese also adopted the concept of improving quality at a revolutionary rate, year after year. Major quality problems were solved by teams of managers and engineers. The much greater number of minor problems were solved by teams of workers—the *QC circles*. In addition, as the universities began to graduate large numbers of engineers, the companies shifted away from copying the designs of competitors and undertook product innovation.

To make these and other changes required unprecedented actions. Japanese senior managers personally became the leaders of the quality revolution. Managers at all levels received training in managing for quality. Company business plans were enlarged to include goals for quality.

The Japanese quality revolution was remarkably successful. Japan became the world quality leader in many product lines. The huge numbers of improvements greatly reduced costs in business processes as well as in manufacturing processes. The need for product inspection was greatly reduced. Japan became an economic superpower, and the major reason was its quality revolution. The mark "Made in Japan" became a symbol of world-class quality.

The growth in export of Japanese goods forced other countries to take defensive action. The most heavily impacted was the United States, which lost large shares of market and thereby "exported" huge numbers of jobs to Japan. Gradually the impacted countries began to close the quality gap, but not before all quality levels had been raised as a result of the Japanese quality revolution.

Statistics and Quality

The cost advantage of mass production came in part from use of low-priced, semiskilled or unskilled workers in lieu of skilled craftsmen. However, this change eliminated a major source of product quality—the training and expertise of craftsmen. It became necessary to find a new concept to prevent defects from being made in the first place.

What emerged was the concept of designing and maintaining the production processes in ways that avoided making defective product. This concept then evolved from the empiricism of master mechanics into the use of inspection data for evaluating and controlling the performance of production processes. Such use of inspection data required use of the methods of statistics—the science of collecting and analyzing data.

The roots of statistics go back to the nineteenth century and are based on methods of applied mathematics. An early application of statistical analysis was to interpret data generated by national census. A national census provides only a snapshot-like body of information. If such a census is taken at regular intervals, statistical analysis will disclose any trends taking place with respect to the population. Such results become more interesting and politically valuable.

The first president of the Imperial Department for Statistics (*Kaiserliches Statistisches Amt*), founded in 1872 in Berlin, was Karl Becker (1823–96). He was formerly the head of the Office for Statistics (*Statistisches Bureau*) in Oldenburg, and made great contributions to the organization and analysis of such surveys by introducing checklists to the national census. He especially made a lasting contribution with his records of deaths that were published in Prussia in 1869 and later in the German Empire. These were of great importance to medicine.[39] During the 1920s, two German scientists engaged in the solving of the problem of the analysis of large numbers (*Grosszahlen*) and based their work on methods of mathematical statistics. Karl Daeves (1893–1955) was an expert engineer and head of the research department of the Phönix AG of the United Steel Manufacturers (*Vereinigte Stahlwerke AG*) in Düsseldorf from 1923 until 1945. August Beckel (1876–1970), a food chemist at the University of Marburg was another important contributor in the field. These two men collaborated, and called their related researches *large number research* (*Grosszahl-Forschung*). They published their results and methods first in 1933, and as a summary in 1942. They were specifically concerned with the assurance of the homogeneity of large production series and with the prevention of rejects by discovering small, but not accidental abnormalities in industrial production as well as in chemical processes in biology. They also contributed to the problem of randomness and to calculation of averages and deviations in the field of demography.[40]

Of the applications of statistics to quality control, one of the most useful was to employ inspection data to understand the performance of the manufacturing process. Inspection of a single unit of product not only discloses the condition of that unit of product; it also discloses the conditions prevailing in the manufacturing process at the time it produced that unit of product. Inspection of multiple units of products produced in sequence can disclose the inherent variability of the process and its ability to meet the specifications. Inspection of such groups at regular intervals can disclose the trends taking place in the process.

A tool that has achieved wide application is the control chart (*Kontrol Karte*), invented in 1924 by Dr. Walter A. Shewhart of the Bell Telephone Laboratories. This chart is used to distinguish real process changes from false alarms. It features two lines drawn to represent the limits of random variation, based on some selected value of probability such as 95 percent. Product variations that fall within these limit lines are assumed to be caused by random variations within the processes. Product variations that extend outside of the limit lines are assumed to have been caused by real changes in the process, because the odds against this happening due to randomness are greater than 20 to 1.

Additional uses of statistical methods included the use of sampling (*Stichproben*) to evaluate the quality of batches of product without resorting to 100 percent inspection. Here again it was necessary to apply the laws of probability in order to quantify the effect of random variations. Research in this field then led to the publication of sampling tables, notably those by H. F. Dodge and H. G. Romig.[41]

German research participated in these efforts. For instance, the term *control charts*, as well as the supporting technology, go back to the experiences in demography, as they were developed by A. Becker. Following World War II, the adoption of decision theory (*Entscheidungstheorie*), developed by A. Wald in 1950 in Great Britain, essentially influenced the German work in this field.[42] There were also German contributions to sampling plans, with special emphasis on plans that could be carried out at minimal cost.[43] Implementation of the European Community will likely bring added needs for uniform regulation for quality assurance of products and services.[44]

Summary

Throughout many centuries a central feature of German quality assurance has been the mark. A mark, whether stamped into the product or attached as a seal, could serve multiple purposes: to provide information about the product; to identify the producer, whether a craftsman, a factory, or a merchant; to identify the town of origin; and so on. It could also provide assurance that the product was of high quality.

In the German lands the evolution of towns led to a division of work among the inhabitants and to emergence of recognized trades and tradesmen. These tradesmen competed in the market but they also formed guilds (fraternities, corporations, and so on) to deal with common problems. The guilds then established rules to assure a livelihood for each member and to protect the reputation of the guild. The chief basis of a guild's reputation was the quality of its members' products. To protect this quality the guilds increasingly imposed independent inspections to assure that defective products did not reach the market.

With the growth of commerce, export of local products became essential to the economy of the towns. The town governments took steps to stimulate such exports. They granted monopolies to the guilds but also imposed taxes and regulations. In due course these regulations included mandated independent inspections of products to protect the quality reputations of the towns.

The system of quality controls based on trades, craftsmen, guilds, marks, and independent inspections endured for centuries. It was then weakened by the liberalism of the Age of Enlightenment, which opposed all forms of government mandates.

In addition, the rise of the factory system introduced a division of labor within many established trades, and destroyed the then-prevailing systems of quality control. Many trades disappeared, and individual marks lost their meaning—now the marks showed the factory of origin.

The factory system stimulated higher productivity, lower prices, and growth in the volume of trade. New ways were adopted to deal with the resulting quality problems. A system of national standards was evolved to rationalize undue variety and to provide interchangeability. New laws emerged to protect consumers; other laws were enacted to protect trademarks.

The twentieth century then brought changes of a revolutionary nature. Some were technological, such as automation and the electronic computer. Others were changes in business management, such as the spectacular Japanese revolution in quality. Still others related to adoption of statistical methods for controlling quality through data collection and analysis. Collectively these revolutions are leading producers to unprecedented achievements in quality of products.

Notes

1. Gustav Homeyer, *Die Haus und Hofmarken,* 1870, rev. (Aachen: 1967). In the following: Homeyer.

2. Cf. Dietwulf Baatz, Fritz Rud. Hermann, *Die Römer in Hessen* (Stuttgart: 1982), p. 303 ff.; also: Heinz Cüppers, *Trierer Ausgrabungen und Forschungen: Trierer Römerbrücken,* vol. 4 (Mainz: 1969).

3. Jungwirth, "Schmied," [H. Bächthold-Stäuble, ed.], *Handwörterbuch des Deutschen Aberglaubens,* vol. 9, 1941, (Berlin, New York: 1987), p. 257 ff.

4. Michael Werling, *Die Baugeschichte der ehemaligen Abteikirche Ottersberg unter besonderer Berücksichtigung ihrer Steinmetzzeichen* (Kaiserslautern: 1986), p. 37 ff. and pictures 12–13. In the following: Werling.

5. Walter Niess, *Romanische Steinmetzzeichen der Stauferburgen Büdingen und Gelnhausen* (Büdingen: 1988).

6. Walter Hotz, *Burg Wildenberg in Odenwald* (Armorbach: 1963), p. 85 f.

7. Werling, p. 41, picture 14.

8. Riedel, *Codex diplomaticus Brandenburgensis,* vol. A 23, 1862, p. 3 f. The original of the document depicted here was, according to a letter by the archives of the City of Frankfurt (Oder) from January 14, 1992, located there until reported missing in 1945. Cf.: Ernst Walter Huth, *Die Entstehung der Stadt Frankfurt (Oder)* (Berlin: 1975), p. 54.

9. Alexander Dietz, *Frankfurter Handelsgeschichte,* vol. 1 (Frankfurt am Main: 1910), p. 367 ff. Cf.: P. Schneider, "Nürbergisch gerecht geschaut Gut: Nürnberger Schauanstalten im Spätmittelalter," *Nürnberger Beiträge zu den Wirtschafts- und Sozialwissenschaften,* 77 (Nürnberg: 1940).

10. Otto Lauffer, "Meisterzeichen und Beschau," *Karl Koetschau von seinen Freunden zum 60. Geburtstag* (Düsseldorf: 1928), pp. 37 and 44. In the following: Lauffer.

11. A. Jegel, "Ernährungsfürsorge des Altnürnberger Rates," *Miteilungen des Vereins für Geschichte der Stadt Nürnberg* (1940), p. 119 ff.

12. Homeyer, pp. 171 ff. and 213. Cf.: Wilhelm Jesse, "Probleme und Aufgaben der Münzmeisterforschung," *Hamburger Beiträge zur Numismatik,* 9/10 (Hamburg: 1956), p. 31 ff. Since 1872 all German coins, first

in the Empire, then in the Weimar Republic and later in the Federal Republic of Germany, bear the first letter of the city in which they were minted: A = Berlin, B = Hannover (only until 1878), C = Frankfurt am Main (only until 1878), D = München, E = Dresden (only until 1887), F = Stuttgart, G = Karlsruhe, H = Darmstadt (only until 1882) and I = Hamburg (only since 1875). Only in Muldenhütten (1887–1953) and in Wien (1938–1944) were coins minted without letters.

13. Patricia Stahl, ed., *Brücke zwischen den Völkern: Zur Geschichte der Frankfurter Messe,* vol. 3 (Frankfurt am Main: 1991), pp. 75–81. In the following: Stahl.

14. Marc Rosenberg, *Der Goldschmiede Markenzeichen,* 4 vols. (Frankfurt am Main: 1922–28); Hubert Sterling, *Golschmiedezeichen von Altona bis Tondern* (Neumünster: 1955); Wolfgang Scheffler, *Die Goldschmiede Niedersachsens,* 2 vols. (Berlin, New York: 1965); Scheffler, *Berliner Goldschmiede* (1968); Scheffler, *Die Golschmiede am Main und Neckar* (1972); Scheffler, *Die Goldschmiede im Rheinlande und Westfalens,* 2 vols. (1973); Scheffler, *Die Goldschmiede Hessens* (1976); Scheffler, *Die Goldschmiede Mittel- und Norddeutschlands* (1980); Scheffler, *Die Goldschmiede Ostpreussens* (1983); Heinrich Kohlhausen, *Nürnberger Goldschmiedekunst 1240–1540,* III (Berlin: 1968); Helmut Selig, *Die Kunst der Augsburger Goldschmiede* (München: 1980); Istvan Dombe, Bernd Höfer, Ingrid Loschek, *Bruckmanns Silber-Lexikon* (München: 1982).

15. Erwin Hintze, *Deutsche Zinngiesser und ihre Marken,* 7 vols. (Leipzig: 1921–31); Ludwig Mory, Eleonore Pichelkampf, Bernd Höfler, *Bruckmanns Zinn-Lexikon* (München: 1977); Stahl, p. 108 ff.

16. Stahl, pp. 118 and 121; Franz Lerner, "Aachener Nadlermarken," *Scripta Mercaturae* (1978), p. 149 ff. The marks of these manufacturers were included on the packaging.

17. Lauffer, p. 44. The plate with pewterers' marks described herein can't be found at the Museum for Art and Trades in Hamburg (letter from October 18, 1991); also the Museum for History of Hamburg sent a negative answer (November 13, 1991). Unfortunately the other mentioned pewter plate from the museum of the castle (Schlossmuseum) in Berlin, has as well been reported missing as the Museum of Art in Berlin (Kunstgewerbemuseum der Staatliche Museen Preussischer Kulturbesitz zu Berlin) informed me in a letter on December 5, 1991.

18. Karl Bücher, Benno Schmidt, ed., *Frankfurter Amts- und Zunfturkunden,* III (Frankfurt am Main: 1914), p. 271 ff.

19. Franz Lerner, "Qualitätsüberwachung in den vorindustriellen Epochen," *Rundschau* (1968), 452; cf.: Andras Kubinyi, "Die Auswirkungen

der Türkenkriege auf die zentralen Städte Ungarns bis 1541," Othmar Pickle, ed., *Die wirtschaftlichen Auswirkungen der Türkenkriege: Grazer Forschungen zur Wirtschafts- und Sozialgeschichte,* I (Graz: 1971), p. 201 ff.

20. Cf. Friedrich Bothe, *Goethe und seine Vaterstadt Frankfurt* (Frankfurt am Main: 1948), p. 88; Friedrich Bothe, "Wirtschaft und Kultur in Goethes Vaterhaus," *Archiv für Frankfurts Geschichte und Kunst,* 4th ed., III, 1 (1932), pp. 1–31 and 132. Goethe's father records in his diary a 1 fl 15 kr salary for the tailor who made a suit for his son. Cf. J. W. Goethe, *Dichtung und Wahrheit,* II (concerning clothes for dolls).

21. Karl Theodor Weiss, *Handbuch der Wasserzeichenkunde* (Leipzig: 1962), pp. 254 and 308 ff. (concerning the numbers mentioned there: the collection of the main archives of the city of Stuttgart today includes 79,000); Alfred Schulte, "Papiermühlen und Wasserzeichenforschung," *Gutenberg-Jahrbuch 1934,* p. 9 ff. According to Schulte there were 218 paper mills in Germany before 1600, which used around 25,000 watermarks.

22. Imre Reimer, *Das Buch der Werkzeichen* (St. Gallen: 1945), p. 17–114. This is a selection of only 288 marks, of which only some are of German origin. They include marks of stonemasons, gold- and silversmiths, book printers, and potters. In the following: Reimer.

23. Reimer, ibid.

24. Ernst von Bassermann-Jordan, *Uhren,* 5th ed. (Braunschweig: 1969); cf. Jürgen Abeler, *Meister der Uhrmacherkunst* (Wuppertal: 1977), p. 413 ff. (concerning signatures and marks).

25. Harold, *Illustrated Dictionary of Glass* (London: 1977), p. 135.; cf. Gustav Weiss, *Ullstein Gläserbuch,* 4th ed. (Berlin, Frankfurt am Main, Wien: 1966), p. 155 ff.

26. Konrad Hüseler, *Deutsche Fayencen,* III (Stuttgart: 1958), p. 479.

27. J. P. Cushon, W. B. Honey, *Handbook of Pottery and Porcelain Marks,* 4th ed. (London, Boston: 1980), p. 8 ff. (Austria), and p. 56 ff. (Germany and related areas).

28. Franz Lerner, *Diener der Schönheit: Gedenkblätter zum 150jährigen Bestehen des Hauses J.G. Mouson & Co. Frankfurt am Main 1798–1948* (Frankfurt am Main: 1948), p. 119 ff.

29. Wulf-Henning Roth, "Warenzeichenrecht," *Luchterhands Ergänzbares Lexicon des Rechts,* 17/1710, p. 1 ff. In the following: Roth.

30. For example: J. C. Nelkenbrecher, *Allgemeines Taschenbuch der Münz, Mass- und Gewichtskunde für Bankiers und Kaufleute . . .* (Berlin: 1828). Other important works are compiled in: Moritz J. Elsas, *Umriss einer Geschichte der Preise und Löhne in Deutschland,* II A (Leiden: 1940), p. 19.

31. Franz Lerner, "Geschichte der Qualitätssicherung," *Handbuch der Qualitätssicherung,* Walter Masing, ed. (München: 1980), p. 13 ff. In the following: Masing.

32. Elmar Wadle, *Fabrikzeichen und Markenrecht: Entfaltung,* I (Berlin: 1977); Frauke Henning-Bodewig, Annette Kur, *Marke und Verbraucher,* I (Weinheim: 1989), p. 211 f. In the following: Bodewig.

33. Bodewig, p. 249 ff. Very detailed descriptions and portrayal of the developments.

34. Hinterhuber, "Normung, Typisierung und Standardisierung," Grochla, Wittmann, ed., *Handwörterbuch der Betriebswirtschaft: Encyklopädie der Betriebswirtschaftslehre,* II, 1 (Stuttgart: 1975), 2776 ff. In the following: Grochla; cf. H. Halberstädter, "Typung-Sonderung-Normung," H. Nicklisch, ed., *Handwörterbuch der Betriebswirtschaft,* IV (Stuttgart: 1928), 449 ff.; DNA, ed., *Deutsche Normen DIN 69910* (Berlin: 1973).

35. Hans Rühe von Lilienstern, "Rationalisierungs-Kuratorium der Deutschen Wirtschaft," *Grochla,* 3311 ff.; M. Schweitzer, U. Kipper, "Rationalisierung," *Grochla,* 3303 ff.; Anon., *Das Handbuch der Rationalisierung* (Bonn: 1977).

36. Alfred Warnr, "Mit dem Testen von Sicherungen fing es an," *Stromthemen,* 9, Nr. 3 (1992), p. 6 f.

37. *RAL Grunsätze für Gütezeichen* (1988); *RAL Gütezeichen übersicht* (1991); *RAL Fakten zum Gütezeichenwesen* (1984); *RAL, Fakten zu RAL Farben* (1985); *RAL Fakten zum Umweltzeichen* (1988); *RAL Druckschriften-Verzeichniss* (1989).

38. Heron von Alexandria, *Pneumatica.* Heron von Alexandria, who is thought to have lived during the first century A.D., described in his book *Pneumatica* how the doors of the temples were opened and closed with the help of steam- and coin-operated stoups.

39. Ernst Meier, "Becker, Karl Martin Ludwig," *Neue Deutsche Biographie,* I (1953), p. 720.

40. Dr. Ing. Karl Daeves was also director of the Association of Coal and Iron Research in Düsseldorf and received high decorations for his work. Cf. Anon., *Kürschners Deutscher Gelehrten Kalender,* I (1940), p. 275. In the following: Kürschner; Dr. phil. August Beckel, *Kürschner* (1961), p. 294; Daeves, Beckel, "Auswertung durch Grosszahl-Forschung," *Kürschner* (Berlin: 1942), 1954 ff.; Daeves, Beckel, *Die Entwicklung des Verkehrs in der Bundesrepublik auf Schiene und Strasse: Versuch einer Prognose* (1965).

41. H. F. Dodge and H. G. Romig, *Sampling Inspection Tables,* 2nd ed. (New York: John Wiley & Sons, 1959).

42. Cf. M. Henke, "Stichprobentheorie," *Grochla,* 794 ff.; Werner Uhlmann, *Statistische Qualitätskontrolle,* 2nd ed. (Stuttgart: 1982), p. 52 ff. and 103 ff.

43. D. Hochstädter, "Qualitätskontrolle, Statistische," *Handbuch der Wirtschaftswissenschaften,* VI (Stuttgart, New York: 1981), p. 382 ff.; Karl Stange, *Stichprobenpläne für messende Prüfung: Aufstellung und Handhabung mit Hilfe des doppelten Wahrscheinlichkeitsgesetzes* (Frankfurt am Main: 1974); Wolfgang Dutschke, *Deutsche Prüfplanung in der Fertigung* (Mainz: 1975).

44. Detailed descriptions can be found in: Masing, Roth, p. 9. Roth notes that the German trademark law, which was passed on January 29, 1979, and revised on March 7, 1990, is facing another revision. This is to be expected according to the first regulation of the European Council that is intended to bring in line the different trademark laws. The goal is to create a trademark that is protected in all the membership nations of the European Council.

CHAPTER 8

Development of Quality Control in Mining, Metallurgy, and Coinage in the Czech Lands (Up to the Nineteenth Century)

Jiří Majer, Ph.D., C.Sc.
Scientific Chief, Geology and Mining,
National Technical Museum, Prague (Retired)

Introduction

Mining precious metal ores and converting them into media of exchange played a major role in the development of the Czech lands from the beginning of their settlement until the middle of the Eighteenth century. Successive waves of discovery and then depletion of rich deposits of silver- and gold-bearing ores provided stimulants for the economy and infusions of wealth for its peoples and the emerging Czech state. For a thousand years, locally minted precious metal coins were the predominant means of exchange in those lands and, many times, in a number of neighboring states. The need to assure the supply of silver and gold for minting, the need to convert ores of different qualities and quantities efficiently and with minimal loss of precious metal, the need to protect a very valuable commodity from

259

theft, and the need to maintain a consistent and predictably high-quality product provided a series of challenges that called forth, over the centuries, a wide variety of quality management techniques.

In the multiple-stage process of converting ore into coins—mining, smelting, refining, and minting or coining—emphasis and means of improvement shifted from one stage to another over the centuries. Four major vehicles for improving the quality of productive processes and the quality of the finished product were employed: a series of mining codes and laws, a series of formal administrative and supervisory roles, a series of monetary reforms, and advances in the production technologies and measurement methods and instruments associated with each stage of production.

The series of mining codes and laws—most notably those of 1249, 1305, and 1548—provided successively more detailed administrative procedures and systems of inspections to assure efficient and honest production processes. These codes and laws established detailed procedures and created specific administrative roles to see that the procedures were followed. Over the years, successive layers of inspectors and inspectors of inspectors were created to assure that operations were conducted according to those procedures. Although the stage or stages of the production process receiving the most emphasis differed from one code or law to the next, three themes were reasonably consistent for all of the codes and laws: a consistent objective of maintaining uninterrupted operation of the production process, particularly the uninterrupted extraction of ore from the mines and delivery of it to smelters; the primacy of the monarch's rights and prerogatives with respect to the mining and coining of precious metals; and the progression toward greater and greater centralization of administrative and supervisory control—subordinate to the monarch—over all aspects of the conversion of precious metal ores into coins.

These laws and codes were the vehicle for creating, elaborating, and recognizing a sophisticated set of formal roles in mining, smelting, refining, and minting. Over the centuries, this elaborate set of official positions evolved into progressively more specialized and detailed organizational roles to perform the ever more sophisticated production work and multiple inspections used to assure that officials performed their duties honorably and conformed to the prescribed procedures for their posts.

These laws and codes had one other special aspect which contributed to their special place in the history of the Czech lands and

Europe as a whole. In part because of the economic importance of precious metal mining and coining, various aspects of the industry became technologically and organizationally sophisticated before many other industries. As a result, laws attempting to guide, control, and regulate it frequently broke fresh ground in developing new administrative approaches for internal management of operations as well as new social approaches for protecting workers and regulating working conditions.

A series of monetary reforms sought to establish coins that would hold a true and predictable value. These reforms provided standards for new coins to replace previous ones that had loss their acceptability because of gradual erosion of their original precious metal content and purity. In these reforms, the denar, bracteate, groschen, and thaler followed one after the other, but each served as a well-accepted currency of exchange for a major period of time. Each was a victim of periodic shortages of minting material as mines were depleted and the more frequent temptation to increase the profitability of the coining process by reducing the precious metal contained in each coin.

The importance of mining and minting precious metals also encouraged the development of many types of mechanical and chemical technologies as well as new methods of measurement and instrumentation. Creative uses of water power were, for example, called forth by the need to move large quantities of very heavy materials from great depths. Polymetallic ores encouraged the development of chemical methods of treatment when mechanical approaches were ineffective. The complexity and variety of the production processes also provided a wide variety of challenges in measurement and standardization.

Use of Precious Metals in the Early Historic Era (Fourth Century B.C. Through the Tenth Century A.D.)

The Importance of Precious Metals and Coins

From the very beginning of the settlement of the Czech lands (Bohemia and Moravia), extensive ore deposits containing various metals and their subsequent utilization were an important factor in forming the economic macrostructure of the region. Precious metals—particularly gold processed into coins in the earliest period—became the main barter and currency media. The beginnings of this process date back to the Celtic period in Bohemia (from the fourth century B.C. to the beginning of Christianity). The end of the Celtic presence in this region of Central Europe was a period of systematic exploitation of gold-bearing minerals and their alluvia in the basins of water streams (Filip 1956).

Coins and Coining Processes

Processing precious metals from their ores and converting them into minting metal showed good knowledge of the properties of these metals, their melting and refining requirements, and the techniques of metal casting. This knowledge made it possible to achieve high purity of the metal and good quality coins. It also yielded masterpieces of the casting art, as witnessed by the great variety of decorations and jewelry of that period (Filip 1959).

Relations between the suppliers of the gold metal and the coin producers were simple and direct. The metal was gained by gold panning, washing gold-bearing sands in a water stream in simple washing pans or wooden troughs. Gold found in natural surroundings was of high purity. The process of actual minting was precisely defined. The gold was first accurately weighed on scales. Small sheets were used as weights to ensure accuracy in weighing. The metal was then melted in a flat crucible with a spout or in a small pear-shaped enclosed melting pot made of celled clay and kaolinite, similar to that used in melting other nonferrous metals, such as copper and tin. Admixed into the clay of the melting vessels was charcoal powder which helped to create the necessary thermal balance. The molten gold was cast into clay plates with shallow depressions in the shape of the future coin. The gold disks thus obtained were coined by the blow of a hammer on a coining die into which was engraved the coin design. The coining die was made of steel obtained by carburizing puddled iron, followed by quenching (Nemeškalová-Jiroudkova 1980).

Celtic coins minted in the Czech lands between 125 and 50 B.C. were shell shaped. Their minters copied the shape of the Macedonian Hellenic coins of the fourth and third centuries B.C., called *staters* (Greek *stateros*). However, the Celtic coins differed from the Macedonian ones, being lighter in weight but having a higher gold content. Whereas the Greek staters were coined from an alloy of gold and silver of a gross weight of 14.1 grams, the oldest Celtic coins minted in the

Czech lands—bearing the figure of a warrior with a shield—weighed 8 grams and were of a purity of up to 98.6 percent, with a small tolerance. Proof of the minter's ability to weigh the gold precisely is the fact that fractions of these coins were also cast and coined in units of thirds, eighths, and even twenty-fourths (Nemeškalová-Jiroudkova 1980).

In addition to the gold coins, the Celts also minted silver coins of like shape and similar mass, as well as their fractions. They obtained the minting metal from veins of silver, which were strongly oxidized at the outcrop, but frequently also in pure form. The production process was the same as that used for making the gold coins.

Decline and Recovery in Use of Coins

At the beginning of the first century B.C., the Celtic period of processing this type of natural resource was interrupted by an invasion of Teutonic tribes. Many Celts moved westward, some assimilated with the new population. With the ensuing drop in economic activity—caused by the lower culture of the arriving population—coins lost their function and there was a return to simple barter of produce and products. During the course of the fifth and sixth centuries A.D., that is during the so-called "migration of peoples," the Teutonic tribes succumbed to the influx of a Slav population coming from the East. The Slavs founded the Great Moravian Empire which comprised the Czech lands, part of Hungary, Poland, and the western part of Austria. During the second half of the ninth century A.D., the economic and social development of the Great Moravian Empire—particularly the development of specialized production—led to the need for a means of exchange more sophisticated than barter which, in turn, led to the reintroduction of coins (Turek 1963).

Gold once again became the minting metal. As in the earlier period, the metal was gained by panning, generally in the basins and streams previously exploited by the Celts, and was highly pure. The Slavs adopted the Celtic method of preparing the metal for processing into coins as well as the coining technique. The tools continued to be the coining die and hammer, the blow of the latter coining the mint design. The weight units did change, however. The Great Moravian Empire reorganized its currency system on the basis of the Byzantine monetary system, the basic unit of which was a pound of gold weighing 327 grams which, in turn, equalled 72 gold Byzantine *solids* (Latin *solidus*).

In addition to this type of currency, use was also made of un-minted metal. In trade, its value was determined by means of small scales and weights of various shapes and kind. The weights were mostly made of copper and its alloys (particularly bronze and brass). Special weights were also made for comparing the prescribed amount of precious metal in a given number of coins (Skalský 1937).

During the existence of the Great Moravian Empire, coins played an important role in setting the mass of currencies. In the ninth century the terms *mass* and *coin* were frequently interchangeable because each represented a given amount of precious metal. This relationship was particularly clear for the pound which, together with the mark, metrologically dominated the entire Middle Ages and modern times in all of Europe. Both of these mass units were used for coining a number of coins equal to the mass of a pound or a mark. In the Great Moravian Empire of the ninth century, the minted coins (solids) played more the role of counting units because preminting forms of payment—such as objects in the form of small iron hatchets of diverse shape and mass—predominated as an exchange medium. Unminted metal in the form of gold rubble and pieces of gold sheet were also used as currency. Their mass and purity were determined on scales which formed an inseparable part of a trader's equipment (Nohejlová-Prátová 1986).

The Great Moravian Empire fell apart at the very beginning of the tenth century. However, its influence lingered on in a number of countries which originally were a part of the empire and affected the form of their currencies. This was particularly true of the new Czech state where—from the middle of the tenth century—a different type of coin began to be minted, called a *denar* (Greek *denarios*). Availability of this coin initiated the so-called "denar period" which lasted for three centuries.

Precious Metals in the Denar and Bracteate Era (Tenth Through Thirteenth Centuries)

The Czech Denar and Mark

The denar was the first truly Czech minting and currency unit, coined late in the reign of the legendary Prince Wenceslaus (921 to 935 A.D.).

It was a relatively large, highly pure coin, roughly 20 mm in diameter and weighing more than 1 gram. Its name and weight came from the pound used during the era of the west Frankish Empire of Charles the Great (771 to 814 A.D.). Initially, the Czech coins simulated the design of the Charles denars. Roughly 400 denars were coined from this 408-gram pound. Silver rather than gold became the main minted metal. Although there are no written documents on the mining of silver in the tenth century, it appears that silver was in sufficient supply in Bohemia (part of the Czech lands) both for minting coins and for export. Chroniclers from the second half of the tenth century wrote of the rich reserves of this metal in Bohemia and of its export to eastern and southeastern Europe (Majer 1991).

The Czech denar—varying in weight in the tenth century from 1.27 grams to 1.33 grams—was a highly valued coin of a nominal value expressed by its silver content and was an important European exchange currency. According to archaeological finds, the Czech denar penetrated the flourishing settlements established by Norman and Slav seafarers on the Baltic Sea coast. The route connecting the Black and Caspian Seas with the Baltic Sea passed through Prague and was lively in both directions. Of particular importance was the route emanating in Byzantium and connecting Kiev, Cracow, Prague, and Regensburg, continuing on to Verdun, to Spain, and then to North Africa. The Czech denar squeezed out other means of payment even in smaller trade relations. In the first years of the eleventh century alone, Czech mints produced some 400,000 of these coins (Skalský 1937).

Changes in Weight and Purity

At the turn of the tenth and eleventh centuries, during the struggle for political power in the Czech lands, the purity of the silver coins diminished because of a shortage of minting metal. Following the Scandinavian and Anglo-Saxon pattern, a mark weighing approximately 210 grams was introduced in 1050. The introduction of the mark represented the first Czech monetary reform. The number of coins minted from the mark was probably set at 200 denars. Their size diminished to 16 mm and the weight was kept to approximately 1 gram. The purity of the silver was reduced to about 83 percent. In the following decades, similar reductions in silver content occurred many times because such a change meant a considerable income for the royal treasury (Skalský 1937).

The weight and purity of the denar declined to such a degree that at the end of the twelfth century it weighed only 0.6 grams and contained 0.1 to 0.2 grams of silver and up to 90 percent of a copper alloying addition. This deterioration of currency was not only a Czech phenomenon but could be traced all over Europe at that time (Cach 1970–74).

The silver content of the Czech denar also fell at the turn of the twelfth and thirteenth centuries and the outflow of silver from the country in the form of unminted metal motivated King Premysl the First (1197–1230) to carry out another currency reform around

Figure 8.1 Front of silver denar of Bohemian King Vladislaus I, coined 1109–17, Prague mint. Numismatic collections of National Museum, Prague.

1210. Minting of the practically worthless denars was halted and a uniform coin—the bracteate—was introduced. These coins were 38 to 42 mm in diameter and had a somewhat smaller silver content than the denars. They were based on a mark with a mass of 253 grams. From this mark, which was almost pure silver, 240 bracteates were coined with an average mass of 1 gram and bearing the portrait of the Czech ruler seated on the throne (Skalský 1937).

It is a paradox that during this period of great minting deterioration the Czech and Moravian denar coins ranked among the most beautiful in Europe. Their detailed and rich design normally presented in symbolic form the ideas and principles of the Christian faith and the legal character of the Czech state by illustrations of the ruler and patrons of the Czech lands. They are depicted on the small area of the coin in a masterly manner. Symbolic illustrations on Czech denars of the tenth and eleventh centuries were based on coins from western and southern France, northern Italy, and Byzantium. The illustrations are eloquent proof of the cultural environment and spiritual life in the Czech state of that time and an expression of its statehood, which was raised to the status of a hereditary kingdom in 1198 (Nohejlová-Prátová 1986).

The Manufacturing Process

The technique of coining denars was divided into several operations. First, silver metal of a specified purity was hammered into sheets of a prescribed thickness for a given type of coin. Minters then cut the sheets into strips from which—using iron shears—they cut off pieces the size of the future coins. These were then filed into a round shape which other workers coined by a hammer blow on a coin die, thereby imparting a design on the coin. Originally, each coin was coined separately. In the thirteenth century, when two-sided denars were replaced by the one-sided bracteates (a bract being a thin sheet), the production process was speeded up by placing five to 10 thin sheets on top of each other and marking them with the design by a single hammer blow on the coining die (Nohejlová-Prátová 1986).

Organization of Coining

As in many other European countries, there is a scarcity of information on how the coining of denars was organized in Bohemia in the tenth to twelfth centuries. Metrological analysis of coins from that period indicates that the organization of minting was intensively developed and required considerable organizational skills. It is presumed that minting work was directed by minters, generally rich persons who most probably came from the ranks of patricians active in trade. They would rent the royal mint for a fee, either as individuals or in cooperatives. An exchange office, for the purchase of the minting metal, was connected with the mint and the two were rented simultaneously.

Thus, the lessees of the mint were entrepreneurs engaged in the manufacture of coins because it was a lucrative business. They changed the locality of their activity, and so even in Bohemia we find the names of persons who were engaged in this field in England, France, the Rhineland, and elsewhere. The business character of minting in Bohemia and the value and importance of the product suggest strong supervision and control over minting by the central power. There are no documents describing the supervisory process in Bohemia at this time. However, in view of the practices used in European minting and the migration of the minters, it is likely that supervisory and control bodies in Bohemia were similar to those elsewhere in Europe, particularly those existing in British mints. The influence of Anglo-Saxon minting on the beginning of Czech coining was strong. Concrete indications of this influence are Czech denars coined in the tenth century bearing the names of mint masters originally engaged in England. Thus, we may assume that—in addition to mint masters responsible for the manufacture of coins—there very likely were also control bodies made up of monetary clerks (*custodes cambii* or *custodes monetae*—curators of the exchange or curators of coins) who were accountable to the monarch (Nohejlová-Prátová 1986).

Jus Civium et Montanorum.   Discovery of a rich and easily accessible silver-ore deposit in Jihlava, south Bohemia, in the 1230s provided the impetus for a major step in the organization of coining. This discovery encouraged extensive mining activity which led to the discovery of further Czech silver-ore deposits and their extraction. The average annual yield of silver from these deposits between 1240 and 1260 is estimated at 4000 to 5000 kg and enabled the coining of bracteates with high silver content.

To ensure a continuous supply of this minting metal, King Wenceslaus the First (1230–53) granted the Jihlava mining community a special statute, the so-called *Jus civium et montanorum* (Communal and Mining Laws of 1249). This statute combined local customs with the legal practice of the Alpine countries, and the Roman, Flemish, and Lower Saxon laws. As the first legal regulation of its kind in Europe to combine various laws and customs so effectively, it influenced the legal development of European mining for a full three centuries. It became known as the Magna Carta of mining legislation with Bohemia as its cradle.

The law contained precise regulations for performing mining operations and gave significant administrative and inspection responsibilities to a land registrar (Latin *urburarius*). The land registrar was the king's highest officer and the representative of the mining office in the mine region. At first, he exercised his authority over a number of mining districts, but in the fourteenth century a separate land registrar was appointed for each new mining area. It was in his power as the agent of the king—the owner of all the land in the kingdom—to grant mining rights and to stipulate the area where mining operations were to be performed. A mining field covered an area of 98×64 meters (Kořan 1955).

The duties of the land registrar included supervising the proper performance of mining operations, so that the king's interests were not impaired, and collecting fees from the mine operators for the king's treasury. The fees were one-eighth of the silver mined. The land registrar swore in the head operating clerks (minting masters) of the individual mines. He had the right to dismiss them if they did not perform their duties and to punish them in the event of a serious offense in accordance with a ruling of a mining court. The land registrars kept accurate records, which today serve as a guide in computing the extent of mine extraction in given historic periods. They were assisted by two aides (Latin *iurati*) who were experienced miners employed by the mine operators but were sworn in by the land registrar. They performed the function of mine surveyors but also handled operating problems, performed certain inspection duties to ensure smooth operation of the mine, and were associate judges at the court of mines (Jangl and Bílek 1976–79).

A second element of the increased organization of coining operations was a king's mint for minting silver denars established concurrently with the opening of mines in Jihlava and its surroundings. The practice of leasing the mint to individuals or cooperatives was continued. The mint master continued to be the head officer, responsible for proper minting. The Jihlava code of 1249 gave the mint master additional duties. These included strict supervision to preclude mint workers from misusing coining dies for coining false coins. Such falsification was a crime subject to capital punishment (Nohejlová-Prátová 1986).

Decline in Minting and Reorganization.   Toward the end of the thirteenth century, the Czech state was in danger of being relegated to a mere exporter of silver. Discovery of many silver-bearing deposits in a number of other countries eventually caused a collapse of the denar system throughout Europe. In spite of another minting reform in 1260, minting of bracteates did not keep pace with intense production and trading activities and the availability of unminted silver. Bracteate coins were almost completely eliminated from domestic and foreign markets. Silver, valued according to weight and purity, dominated 90 percent of the market in Bohemia and in much of Europe (Skalský 1937).

The role of the Czech state in European coinage was revived by a rich silver discovery in eastern Bohemia and actions taken in the name of the king. In 1290 a rich silver deposit was discovered in Kutna Hora, eastern Bohemia. Within a single decade, a new town was founded and the entire region was rapidly populated by several thousand immigrants, mostly experienced prospectors and miners from other European mining regions. Even before 1300, the yield of the Kutna Hora mines reached 25,000 to 30,000 kilograms of silver annually. The quantity and stability of silver extraction elevated the Kutna Hora mining region to one of the most important mining centers in Europe. According to approximate estimates, local extraction accounted for about 41 percent of total European silver production. It was thus the most important factor in creating Europe's silver reserves at the turn of the thirteenth and fourteenth centuries (Majer 1991).

In 1292 the king moved to take into his hands the inspection and control of mine activities and to centralize minting operations under his royal power. Management of Czech mining and minting operations was joined in the hands of the royal mint master, who thus became one of the king's highest officers. His official title was *magister urburae et monetaeper Bohemian* (master of mining and minting for Bohemia). He was entrusted not only with supervising the proper payment of fees (Latin *urburs*) for mining activities but also with supervising the proper minting of coins of the prescribed type, size, weight, and metal purity. King's superintendents, the so-called *Notarii monetae* (money notaries), were appointed to ensure strict supervision of the quality of the minted coins. Their duty was to check the quality of the minting metal prior to beginning the coining operation.

To support those measures, it was also necessary to introduce a new monetary system and suitable legal measures. The groschen system, introduced in Venice in 1202 and later spreading to France, became the model for the monetary unit. A minting reform in 1300 and the mining law of 1305 established the conditions to support the introduction of a payment medium based on a hard coin of high-purity silver. These measures launched a new era in the economic development of the Czech lands (Skalský 1937).

The Groschen Coining Era
(Fourteenth and Fifteenth Centuries)

The Groschen System

The minting reform proclaimed in the Czech lands in 1300 and carried out by a consortium of Italian bankers was based on the complete abolition of the bracteate coins and the launching of a heavy, permanent currency made of silver, the so-called "Prague groschen" (Latin *grossi pragenses*). Its nominal value corresponded approximately to the price of the silver metal contained in it. At the same time, the free circulation of silver was prohibited and it became compulsory to exchange all silver for minted coins. In this way, the foundations were laid for a monetary economy based on a coin of a constant, full value. Bohemia thus followed Italy and France, becoming the third country to employ the groschen system (Nohejlová-Prátová 1973).

The basis of the reform rested on minting groschen and its twelve parts—parvi or hellers. Sixty-four groschen—27 mm in diameter and weighing 3.98 grams, with a high silver content and a high purity of 93.7 percent—were minted from each Prague mark of 253.14 grams. Because the hellers were more expensive to mint, they were of somewhat lesser purity than the groschen. A heller weighed 0.51 grams and had a silver content of 0.277 grams (Nohejlová-Prátová 1986).

The Prague groschen preserved its exterior appearance throughout the whole first minting period—from 1300 to 1547. Combining the French groschen (Latin *grossus turonensis*—Tours groschen) with Italian influences yielded a perfect work of art. On the obverse of the coin were two circles bearing the name and titles of the monarch and an illustration of the royal crown. The reverse side bore the Czech lion with a circular inscription "Grossi Pragenses." Thanks to their quality—determined mainly by their weight and purity—they very soon became an international European unit of payment. The position of the Prague groschen in the economic and business world was also strengthened by the increasing political power of the Czech kings. Until the end of the fourteenth century, groschen became the currency used in a number of central and east European countries.

Figure 8.2 Reverse of silver grossus of Bohemian King Wenceslaus II, coined 1300–05, Kutna Hora mint. Numismatic collections of National Museum, Prague.

However, the foreign military adventures of King John of Luxembourg (1310–46), the ambitious policies of the Czech king and emperor of the Roman Empire Charles the Fourth (1346–78), and the worsening political and economic situation in the Czech lands during the reign of his successors contributed to a decline in the quality of the groschen. During the reign of Charles the Fourth, 70 groschen instead of the previous 64 were minted from each mark and, during the reign of Wenceslaus the Fourth (1378–1419), the figure reached $95\frac{1}{2}$ groschen, weighing only between 2.90 grams and 2.70 grams, with a purity of 61 percent. At the beginning of the fifteenth century, the weight of the groschen dropped down to 2 grams and the purity to 42.2 percent (Skalský 1937).

Launching a New Era—The 1305 Mining Law

The mining law of 1305 declared by King Wenceslaus the Second (1278–1305) bore the name *Constitutiones iuris metallici* (Provisions of Mining Laws). It declared the inalienable right of the monarch to all of the country's mineral riches and was, therefore, called *Ius regale montanorum* (Royal Mining Right). For the first time in history, this law set down the mining rights and prerogatives of a sovereign and ensured the right to free prospecting for precious-metal deposits and their exploitation—as long as all financial obligations with the crown were met. In addition to establishing principles for mining operations, management, and supervision, the law also guaranteed various social rights of mine workers. Promulgation of the mining law meant not only a definite transition from common law to written law but it was also the first attempt in Europe to create a uniform and generally valid legal system. It became a legal directive which regulated all Czech mining regions for more than three centuries and also became a model for a number of other European mining countries in formulating their mining legislation. In the mid-sixteenth century, it was even used in Spain's Latin-American colonies (Majer 1991).

By adopting the Roman and canon laws and adapting them to local needs, the Czech mining law of 1305—thanks to its completeness and realistic estimate of the further development of mining—became a general legal norm of broad scope. It made possible the transition from the hitherto simple forms of working ore deposits to really deep mining, to the use of the first animal-powered mining machines, and later to the era of water-powered machines as energy resources in mining engineer-

Figure 8.3 Medieval ore mine. Georgius Agricola: *De Re Metallica, libri XII*, Basileae 1556.

ing. It thus created suitable conditions for extracting silver ore from deposits of considerable depth, in some places reaching—by the end of the fourteenth century—400 meters (Majer 1975).

Guarantee of Silver Supply.   A major objective of the law was the uninterrupted shipment of silver to the royal mint. Nine extensive sections of the law were devoted to mining enterprising. The basis of the enterprising section were associations of mining operators (Latin *universitas colonorum*—colonizing associations) at the helm of which stood mine masters (Latin *magistri montium*), elected from their midst. The highest decision-making body was the assembly of mine operators, which met once a week. Several types of mining associations were codified. In addition to the so-called "primary mining associations," which gained the right to mining fields by a decree of the king's land registrar, there were also secondary mining associations which gained their mining rights by renting the fields from the primary mining associations. These, too, could lease a part of their mining field to other mining associations or to individual miners, but only for a time-limited period. Compensation for the temporary lease of a mining field was one-fifth to one-half of the extracted silver ore. With leases generally of only a few weeks, mine operators tried to extract as great a stock of ore as possible in the shortest possible time (Jangl and Bílek 1976–79).

High output was also encouraged by stipulating four six-hour work shifts so the mines could be operated on a nonstop basis. At the same time, the mining law sought to prevent plundering of the deposits, that is removing only the richest ore parts. To this end, it permitted the working of only small areas of mine fields, forcing the operators to extract silver veins as deeply as technically feasible. The lease mining area was stipulated at roughly 180×63 meters.

Social Guarantees.   In furtherance of its basic aim, ensuring uninterrupted and highly productive mining operations, the mining law of 1305 provided legal assurances of the social status of miners. These included a guarantee of regular weekly payment of wages in good silver coins in an amount guaranteeing a basic standard of living. A five-day work week was specified in the law, with Saturday counted as a day of rest and reserved for the payment of wages and the purchase of food and other necessities at fixed prices. The law also guaranteed payment for overtime and extra work during the days of rest. An unusual measure for its time was a partial or complete miner lien on a mine from which miners were unable—by arbitration or by legal action—to force payment of the wages due from the mine operator. Provision was also made for mines in which work had been interrupted for various reasons to be assigned forthwith to other parties interested in conducting mine operations. A number of directives required preventive measures to be taken against obstructions to uninterrupted mining, especially the construction of safety dams against possible ground water flooding, timbering of mine works, and so on. In addition to avoiding interruption of mining operations, these provisions also sought the social goal of ensuring labor safety in mines. These features rendered the Czech mining law beyond comparison with all other European legal codes at that time, establishing it as the predecessor of social legislation (Majer 1991).

Organization and Administration.   The mine law set up such a strong structure of mine administration and supervisory bodies that these underwent practically no changes up to the sixteenth century. Officers of the mining associations were responsible for proper working of the mines. The king's officers were responsible for ensuring adherence to legal measures, mainly in the financial sphere. Thus, the process of control took place simultaneously at the entrepreneurial and state levels, each from a different aspect.

The leading administrative and control functions were—as in the preceding period—held by the land registrar, the king's highest mining officer in the mine district. He was the head of the mine office and a justice of the mine court. In addition to the traditional duties in connection with leasing mining enterprises and supervising their proper operation, the registrar's duties included remedying any obstructions to operations that might arise so as to ensure uninterrupted mining operations. The land registrar also had the right to appoint and recall mine officers in case they failed to fulfill their duties. This jurisdiction soon became the subject of frequent disputes between the mine operators and the land registrars. Therefore, in 1329 mining companies were given the right to appoint their own mine masters, mine supervisors, and some personnel entrusted with lesser operating functions in the mines (Jangl and Bílek 1976–79).

Inspection activities in the mines were performed by the closest assistants of the land registrar, the *top climbers.* Their name was derived from their daily duty to climb down into each mine, supervise the proper performance of work, and preclude any possible cause of disputes between mine operators. Working with them was a staff of mine surveyors who assisted in solving more complicated disputes concerning property rights to underground ore veins. With the onset of ever deeper mine operations, their duties grew in importance.

Other officers involved in supervising mining operations included clerks of the land register, mine carpenters, and mine alderman. The clerks collected land taxes, checked the bookkeeping of the individual mines and checked the utilization of royal grants. Mine carpenters gave evidence in disputes on underground boundaries of mine fields and property rights in addition to their professional duties of putting up timbering in the mines. Mine aldermen were sworn in by the land registrar with duties, among others, of assisting in leasing the mine fields and cooperating in solving disputed problems in the sphere of property rights. In addition, they were responsible for providing miners with operating requisites and food (Jangl and Bílek 1976–79).

Mine masters, sworn in by the land registrar, were responsible for the ore extraction and processing. At least once a week they had to check the course of work carried on underground. In later times, their authority was increased and finally they stood at the helm of mine offices. They were assisted by mine scribes who were also employees of the mining company and who performed all the administrative tasks and did the accounting connected with the operation of the mine. While appointed by the mine operator, their naming was subject to approval by the land registrar or his clerks. The lowest echelon of the upper administrative force included the guards who—although employees of the mining company—were also sworn in by the land registrar. They were leaders of worker teams in mines and, therefore, had to fulfill a number of tasks as supervisors, inspectors, and record keepers (Jangl and Bílek 1976–79).

Thus, the law created a unique and highly detailed legal structure for ensuring uninterrupted mining operations and a corresponding control system. The purpose of the law was to achieve high labor productivity and to prevent losses. It is a paradox that this law left the actual process of producing the precious metal without governmental control. This was the case because the excavated ore was subject to free sale to metal traders who were independent entrepreneurs. They purchased the ore, smelted it in their own metallurgical plant and were obliged to deliver the refined silver or gold to the royal mint where they were paid according to the weight and purity of the precious metal. The criteria used for the purchase of the ore are not available from existing sources. However, it is possible to presume that some acceptance tests must have been carried out because acceptance of the precious metal by the royal mint and determination of the purchase price were carried out on the basis of an analysis by the mint's metal assayer (Majer 1991).

Quality Inspection and Warranties in Minting.   Similar to the situation with mining enterprises, more elaborate administrative and inspection systems were also introduced into Czech minting. After the abolition of 17 mints in the Czech lands and the opening of a single royal mint in Kutna Hora in 1300, minting of coins became a royal monopoly. Temporary leasing of the mint continued for a short period. For example, a short lease of the mint was granted in 1300 to Florentine entrepreneurs who were entrusted with launching the minting of the Prague groschen. However, this minting took place under the direct supervision and inspection of the monarch's officers. Shortly after the first groschen coins were minted, Czech minting was permanently organized according to the centralized French model. This move was instigated by close political ties between Czech monarchs and those of France.

A royal mint master managed the mint. Originally, the work involved administrative, legal, and inspection duties, but additional duties were rapidly added and soon an assistant—the mint clerk (Latin *procurator* or *notarius*)—appeared by his side as his deputy. The mint master's responsibilities included a currency exchange office headed by a superintendent and a deputy. As of 1300, it was obligatory for producers to deliver silver in exchange for cash payment in coins. In the fourteenth century, the duty of testing the purity of the silver offered for acceptance to the exchange office was assigned to a metal assayer who was very likely one of the royal minting officers. Another important person was the mint master's superintendent—the guardian (Latin *contrarotulator*)—who was named by the monarch and was directly responsible to him. His task was to act as the mint master's shadow, to take part in all managerial as well as checking operations, and to be fully informed of all events (Nohejlová-Prátová 1986).

Since the early Middle Ages, the minting process had not changed substantially. However, pressures for improving the production process had increased and in-process inspection became more strict. The minting process consisted of three main parts: preparatory work, minting work, and coining. Preparatory work involved refining impurities out of the precious metal and bringing it to a proper level of purity in preparation for alloying. Minting involved preparing the proper alloy with the desired level of precious metal content, forming the metal in bars or sheets in preparation for coining, cleaning the metal, and making the individual coin blanks. The coining step involved producing the coin itself and assuring that the design was properly impressed into the metal (Nohejlová-Prátová 1986).

The entire minting process was constantly supervised and checked not only by the mint officers but also by aldermen of specialized minting and coining associations. Negligence at work was punished by a deduction in pay, transfer to less-exacting work, or outright dismissal of the worker. Falsification of coins was subject to capital punishment by beheading and, in the sixteenth century, even by burning at the stake. The penalties were severe because counterfeiters committed a crime against the royal prerogatives of the monarch. To assure the quality of the coins, medieval coiners were provided with a hallmark of simple, generally geometrical shape (such as a triangle, circle, rectangle, or arch). These symbols can be found on even the oldest Czech coins—denars of the tenth century (Nohejlová-Prátová 1986).

An inseparable part of the inspection system was providing the new mintage with a mark of the origin of the coin and the person (Latin *monetarius*) under whose supervision the coin was minted. In Bohemia, marking of the coins was evidently introduced as a result of Italian influence, perhaps immediately upon launching the minting of the groschen in 1300. Mint marks were either written (first letters of the mint) or pictorial. The signatures of responsible mint workers (the mint master or guardian) were similar. Their range was thematically very broad—from emblems of tools or objects, illustrations of parts of the human body, animals, and celestial bodies to aristocratic emblems of the mint officials. Their hallmark was supposed to be a permanent personal warranty of the quality of the coin (Nohejlová-Prátová 1986).

Technology.   To speed up mining operations, use was made of the first auxiliary machines as early as the beginning of the fourteenth century. These were used for hauling ore and for pumping water. In

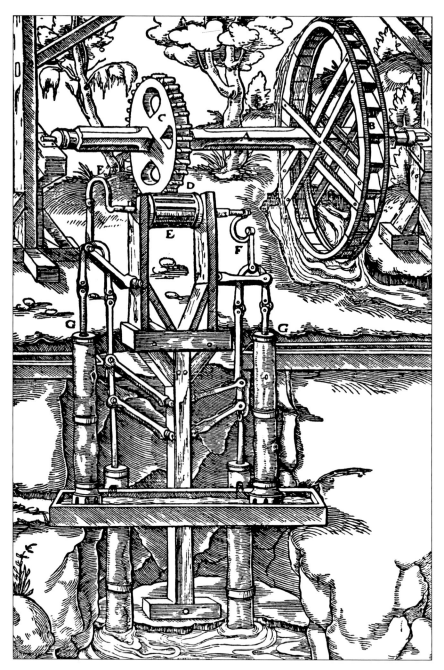

Figure 8.4 Mining pump, early sixteenth century. Georgius Agricola: *De Re Metallica, libri XII,* Basileae 1556.

Figure 8.5 Mining engine for ore extraction, early sixteenth century.
Georgius Agricola: *De Re Metallica, libri XII,* Basileae 1556.

smaller mines, the machines were hand winches, while in larger mines use was made of horse-powered capstans. Water wheels were used for powering mining mechanisms in Czech mines only in the second half of the fifthteenth century (Majer 1975).

The Tripartite Minting System—1469 Mining Reform

In the period between the thirteenth to fifteenth centuries the control and inspection of Czech coinage was a complicated process. Growth of the population and rapidly developing production and trade relations led to the need for many small silver coins to be used in daily commerce. However, during the fifteenth century, their weight and silver content dropped and a monetary crisis occurred in the early 1460s. The crisis arose mainly from the effects of inflation in the currencies of neighboring Austria, Bavaria, and Saxony and from a reduction in domestic silver mining. As a result, the minting of the Prague groschen was temporarily discontinued and only small coins were minted (Skalský 1937).

The situation improved only after the minting reform of 1469 was proclaimed by King George of Podebrady (1458–71). The reform introduced a tripartite minting system consisting of the Prague groschen, a *small coin* (Czech *peniz*), and the heller. The Prague groschen equalled seven small coins or 14 hellers. According to metrological determination, the newly minted groschen had an average mass of 2.70 to 2.80 grams and a purity of 56.4 percent to 58.0 percent. The small coin had a mass of 0.300 to 0.350 grams and a purity of 35.8 percent to 40.0 percent, while the heller weighed 0.179 grams and had a purity of 25.0 percent (Skalský 1937).

During the course of the second half of the fifteenth century, the raw material situation improved considerably. It is estimated that the Kutna Hora mines alone yielded about 4500 kilograms of silver annually so that during the reign of King Wladislaw of Jagellon (1471–1516) it was once more possible to mint Prague silver groschen of an average weight of 2.82 grams and a purity of 59.6 percent. The second half of the fifteenth century saw the renewal of the minting of the Czech golden ducats, which had first been minted in 1325. This new minting was made possible by intensive extraction of a gold ore vein in Jilove and in Knin, not far from Prague. The Czech ducat, coined roughly between 1471 and 1520, had a mass of about 3.5 grams and a purity of about 95.8 percent. However, the ducat did not attain the same importance as the silver groschen currency because by the beginning of the sixteenth century the Czech gold deposits had been almost exhausted (Skalský 1937).

During the first half of the sixteenth century, the groschen system ceased to fulfill the role of the principal exchange means in foreign and domestic markets. This was because in central Europe large, heavy coins minted from silver began to gain in importance. The value of these coins was to equal that of gold coins, to force them out of circulation or circulate as their equivalent—side by side with them. These coins were known as *thalers*.

Figure 8.6 Front of gold ducat of Charles IV, Emperor of Holy Roman Empire and King of Bohemia, coined 1346–78, Kutna Hora mint. Numismatic collections of National Museum, Prague.

The Thaler Period
(Sixteenth Through Eighteenth Centuries)

The first heavy silver coins of a greater nominal value were minted under Italian influence by the Tyrolian mint in Hall in the mid-1480s. These coins became the minting model for Saxon dukes who then began to mint similar coins with silver derived from newly discovered silver ore deposits on the slopes of the Ore Mountains. Geologically, these deposits were connected with silver deposits on the Bohemian side of this border mountain range separating Bohemia and Saxony. In 1516, the first of 150 silver veins were discovered on the Bohemian side of the Ore Mountains, most of them in a valley in which the town of Jachymov (Joachimsthal) was immediately founded. Its population soon reached the figure of 18,000 inhabitants, most of whom were engaged in mining. Silver-bearing ores found in the Ore Mountains and in other mountainous regions led to the development of hundreds of small silver mines during first half of the sixteenth century. The Jachymov mines alone produced around 9000 kilograms of silver annually. In the sixteenth century, this mining region produced some 330,000 kilograms of silver. During the sixteenth century, the yield also rose in other areas, particularly in the Kutna Hora region. Before the turn of the century, stocks of silver produced in the Czech lands over a 100-year period reached about 700,000 kilograms (Majer 1991).

The Thaler

In 1519 a new mint was established in Jachymov, the leading silver mining area. Minting of heavy silver coins began in 1520. From this location the coins obtained the name they bore for many centuries. Since it was a coin minted in the Jachymov valley, which is *thal* in German, they became known as *thalers* in German or *tolars* in Czech. The name then moved overseas where it took root in the United States of America, Canada, and Australia as the *dollar*.

The first coins of this type were 41 mm in diameter and had a mass of 29.37 grams. Their silver purity of 93.0 percent made them equal in value to one gold ducat. The two-thaler coin minted in the same year was 43 to 44 mm in diameter and weighed 58.42 grams. In 1529, when the thaler became the official currency in the Czech lands,

Figure 8.7 Front of Bohemian two-thaler, coined 1520–26, Jachymov/ Joachimsthal mint. Collections of National Museum, Prague.

its size and weight stabilized at a diameter of 41 mm and a weight of 29.095 grams. These coins were noted for their beautiful appearance. The coin design bore traces of the mastery of Italian and German renaissance medal makers. The obverse of the coin bore the portrait of King Ferdinand the First (1526–64), clad in a knight's armor and wearing the attributes of his power—the royal crown on his head, a scepter in his right hand, and a sword in the left hand. Depicted on the reverse side of the coin was a coat of arms with the emblems of the Czech and Hungarian kingdoms and in the middle a small coat of arms with the emblem of the Austro-Burgundian kingdom. Perched above the coat of arms was the royal crown (Nemeškal 1964).

The mint also coined half and quarter thalers and, later, multiples of thalers. Evidence of how quickly the new coin was incorporated into the economy of the Czech lands is the fact that in the 1520–28 period some 2.2 million thalers and their fractions worth about 4 million thalers were minted in Jachymov. At the same time, minting of groschen continued in Kutna Hora. The thaler was worth 30 of the so-called "white groschen" at 7 white small coins or 14 hellers to the groschen. In the mid-sixteenth century, the groschen weighed 2.85 grams and had a purity of 41.8 percent. These coins were predominantly used in domestic trade activities because they were accessible to the broad public. Thus, the thaler and the groschen coins complemented each other; the broad range of nominal values fully met the needs of both domestic and foreign trade (Nemeškal 1964).

The 1548 Jachymov Mining Code

Production of the vast amount of silver needed for minting the new coins was made possible by the new deposits with their higher silver content and by the qualitatively new approach used in managing mining and metallurgical activities. This approach was consistent with the more directive systems emerging from the centralization of state power in Europe. In the Czech lands, it was legally expressed in a new mining code promulgated for the first time in Jachymov in 1516. The Jachymov mining code was based on principles first formulated in the Saxon coal district of Annaberg in 1509 and was a proclamation of the directive system of management in mining. While it did not gain the character of a mining law in Bohemia, in 1548 Ferdinand the First, the first Hapsburg monarch on the Czech throne, succeeded in enforcing its validity, alongside the traditional Kutna Hora law, in the case of newly opened mines. Numerous attempts in the sixteenth century to formulate a uniform mining law in the Czech lands by unifying provisions of the Kutna Hora and the Jachymov mining codes met with the resistance of the Czech diet. Nevertheless, during the course of the eighteenth century the Jachymov code gradually predominated as a legal norm and was used up to the promulgation of a general mining law in 1854 (Majer 1968).

The Jachymov mining code of 1548, as it eventually became known, continued the emphasis of previous codes on ensuring uninterrupted mining and minting activities. Its application to mining and metallurgical practice led to a change in relations between suppliers and buyers. The system of mine enterprising, particularly its form of secondary leasing—permitted and legally ensured by the 1305 mining law—was replaced by the relationship of mine operator versus hired hand. It abandoned attempts to codify property-right relations in mining, diverting dispute resolution to civil-law procedures. To minimize interruptions in mining activities, one provision provided that mines not worked for three consecutive days for no serious reason should be taken away from the mine operators and the right to operate the mines granted to other interested parties. Circumstances which led the mining office to approve temporary interruption of mine work were carefully scrutinized and such interruption was permitted only for a period of three months (Majer 1968).

Mining Organization.   The directive system contained in the Jachymov mining code manifested itself mainly by strengthening the authority of the administrative and supervisory bodies. First, a strong administrative structure was set up for mining activities. At the top stood the Mining and Minting Department of the Czech Royal Chamber in Prague to which were subjected three Bohemian mining offices—in Kutna Hora, Jachymov, and Horni Slavkov—and two royal mints in Kutna Hora and Jachymov. Another mint was later added in Ceske Budejovice. At the head of each of the three mining offices was a mining controller who supervised subordinate mining offices in all mining districts. His duty was to remove all obstacles to uninterrupted mining activity and to supervise the work of all mining clerks. Each quarter of a year he or a clerk carried out an audit of the financial accounting of each mining enterprise and settled disputed operating matters not decided at a lower administrative level. The controllers also checked the cost of materials and equipment needed for conducting mining activities so as to preclude their excessive cost. Subordinate to the controller of the head mining office were mine masters heading up the individual mining offices, assisted by two sworn-in experienced miners and a mining clerk (Jangl and Bílek 1976–79).

The king's tax collector was entrusted with checking the volume of silver production and supervising proper payment of the compulsory 10 percent tax—the tithe—into the royal treasury, thus replacing the former function of the land registrar. He had the duty of checking the weight of the silver supplied by the smelting works as well as having its purity rechecked. The tithe collector also was responsible for ensuring that the mines accounted properly for all expenditures and receipts in order to preclude the mine's indebtedness. Because this officer was in constant contact with the mining enterprises and was subject to possible bribes, a supervisor—known as an inspection officer—was appointed to oversee him. The supervisor kept his own record of the silver levy accepted by the collection office and checked the accounting of the mining and metallurgical costs. He drew up quarterly inspection reports on the basis of balance sheets prepared regularly by all mines. If the financial balance in the report did not correspond to the balance sheet of the tithe collector, the reports were subjected to an audit. Serious discrepancies were followed by sanctions and, frequently, by the discharge of the tithe collector (Jangl and Bílek 1976–79).

To ensure the proper performance of mining operations, shift foremen and mine inspectors were appointed in addition to the royal officers. The shift foremen were responsible for the individual mines and were limited to six mines so they could manage and supervise mining operations properly. In each mine their subordinate was the mine inspector. Mine inspectors prepared written reports on the progress of work and a weekly accounting of operating costs. These were used by the shift master to prepare reports for the mining office (Jangl and Bílek 1976–79).

The regular weekly accounting routine was not only demanding but it was also subject to attempts at cheating on the part of the shift foreman. To reduce the likelihood of dishonesty, shift foremen had to deposit a financial security prior to assuming their posts and an inspection mining clerk was appointed to keep records concurrently with and independently of the shift foreman and to report the results to the mining office.

Despite this network of supervisory bodies for cross-checking all mining activities and performing the accounting work connected with it, the mining code of 1548 established two inspectors at the head mining office, responsible to the manager of this office. They constituted an emergency commission provided with broad powers and were sent on special inspections of mining enterprises. If necessary, they were empowered to take corrective measures on the spot. During these inspections, workers were permitted to draw the attention of the inspectors to shortcomings of any kind. In spite of these extensive administrative and inspection systems, it was sometimes impossible to preclude intentional harm to the interests of the mine operators and the royal offices (Jangl and Bílek 1976–79).

Smelting Organization.   An inspection system was concurrently introduced in the smelting works. It is mainly here that losses of the precious metal could take place, not only due to the use of an inappropriate smelting process but also due to various fraudulent machinations. Metallurgical clerks, assisted by the works' clerks, were responsible for determining whether appropriate production processes were employed, beginning with the preparation of the ore charge into the furnace up to tapping the melt and the final silver product. They could recommend firing unqualified workers and strict punishment for fraudulent actions. All the employees of the smelting works were obliged to abide by their orders and instructions. Smelting could not begin without their approval. As the highest inspection body of the smelting works, their duties also included keeping an exact record of the results of all smelting operations (Jangl and Bílek 1976–79).

Refining Organization.   The Jachymov mining code of 1548 entrusted an especially responsible function in this inspection scheme to the silver refiners—originally a specialized trade in minting works. As an intermediate element linking production of precious metals with their processing into coins, silver refiners were made responsible for achieving the prescribed purity of the minting metal. When they took over the silver from the smelting works they performed their own test analysis. Their main duty was to refine the silver in crucibles so as to achieve a purity of 98.5 percent, if admixtures of other metals in the silver did not preclude achieving this degree of purity. The amount of the refined silver was carefully weighed and the loss between the metal supplied by the smelting works and the final product was carefully recorded. The silver, together with a report on the weight and purity, was finally turned over to the tithe collector who computed the amount of the compulsory 10 percent levy to the royal treasury and turned over the remaining silver to the mint (Jangl and Bílek 1976–79).

Minting Organization.   While the Jachymov mining code of 1548 increased the responsibility of the mining and smelting administration for the proper operation of the mining and the smelting enterprises, little change was necessary in the administrative and inspection functions of the minting officers because these were well established in previous times. The minting officials remained the mint master, who had the highest responsibility for the proper operation of the mint, and the guardian who supervised the mint master's activities. The guardian kept his own records which he submitted to the superior authority—in the sixteenth century the royal Czech chamber—or directly to the monarch. Both of these leading mint officers—or at least one of them—had the duty to mark coins minted during their office with a special hallmark, which served as a warranty and personal guarantee of the prescribed purity of the coin. The coins were also marked with a hallmark of the location of the mint (Nohejlová-Prátová 1986).

Continued Centralization of Management and Control

The changes in organization from mining to minting indicate that the directive principle—a system of centralized state management and supervision of all phases of production by royal authorities—had gained a strong foothold in the sixteenth century. Increased pressure of the directive system from the beginning of the sixteenth century manifested itself in the extension of working hours from the original six hours at first to seven hours and later to eight hours per shift, setting a wage limit, mass introduction of piecework wages, and prohibition of any unauthorized gatherings. Efforts to change this trend were suppressed from the very beginning and usually severely punished. As a result, in the mid-sixteenth century attempts to resist these measures ceased completely (Majer 1991).

Technological Changes

The organizational changes incorporated in the mining code of 1548 were closely associated with the introduction of new technological approaches in mining and smelting that increased production and saved costs. In mining, this process is known as the era of early mechanization. Improvements first appeared in auxiliary operations. While the main work of extracting the ore by manually cutting ore veins with a high silver content continued without change, new types of machines were designed for hoisting loads, pumping ground water, ventilating the mine, and treating ore prior to smelting. A qualitatively new approach was the introduction of water wheels for providing power. For example, winches operated manually by one worker could hoist loads weighing up to several tens of kilograms from a depth of at most 30 meters and winches operated by two workers could lift the same load from a depth of 50 meters. In the middle of the sixteenth century, large extraction winches powered by a double water wheel 12 meters in diameter made it possible to hoist loads of 200 to 300 kilograms from depths of up to 200 meters. Single-pipe hand pumps achieved a pumping rate of 2000 liters per hour from a depth of 10 meters, while a bank of two parallel pumps with their pistons mounted on a common crankshaft powered by a water wheel delivered 16,000 to 20,000 liters of water per hour from depths of up to 380 meters. Similar increased capabilities occurred in ventilation, ore crushing, and other activities (Majer 1991).

The introduction of new machines and new production processes in mining practice of this period was described in detail and illustrated in the book *De re metallica, libri XII* by Georgius Agricola (1494–1555), published in Basel in 1556. Between 1527 and 1533, Agricola served as a town physician in Jachymov. He was the author of about 50 treatises on subjects in diverse fields of natural science. For more than two centuries this book was used as a basic textbook on mining and smelting by a number of European mining schools. In his book, Agricola also described new surveying methods which made it possible to extract ore deposits from depths of almost 500 meters. These methods were based on various new types of compasses and other measuring aids designed for measuring the direction and incline of ore veins. They also included various meters used in length measurement—both underground and on the surface.

During the sixteenth century, similar improvements occurred in smelting equipment and production processes. The aim was to achieve a greater yield from the ore when smelting precious metals, lower precious-metal losses, save fuel, and improve labor productivity. The basic production process did not change in principle, but changes in the design of smelting equipment did lead to alterations of some aspects of the production process. The beginning of the sixteenth century saw the end of smelting in low—about 150 centimeters high—shaft furnaces of a rectangular floor plan, from which the melt was occasionally tapped via a tap hole. With this method four to seven additional melts were necessary to separate as much silver from the slag as possible. By the middle of the sixteenth century, slag was being continuously drained through an open spout, saving fuel and time. The

Figure 8.8 Silver processing plant with condensation room, early sixteenth century. Georgius Agricola: *De Re Metallica, libri XII*, Basileae 1556.

raw material thus obtained—silver-containing lead—was then remelted in round cupel furnaces in which the silver foam was constantly raked from the surface by means of a wooden rake and the slag poured out through a special spout. In this way, silver of a purity of roughly 74.8 percent to 87.4 percent was obtained. This was followed by its refining in a small mobile furnace to obtain the prescribed purity of about 98.5 percent (Majer 1991).

During the first half of the sixteenth century, a new roasting method was developed for polymetallic ores which lowered fuel and lead costs and achieved a 3- to 4-fold greater output during smelting. Throughout the sixteenth century, numerous more or less successful attempts were made to improve ore yield and to make production more economical. One area of improvement involved replacing smelting methods by chemical means, such as distilling low-grade pyrites, amalgamating silver ores, and so on (Majer 1991).

Some of these manufacturing changes were described in Agricola's book. Methods for testing the quality of various ores and for their smelting were described in detail by one of Europe's leading experts on metallurgical processes and testing methods, Lazarus Ercker (1528–94) in his book *Beschreibung allerfurnemisten mineralischen Ertz und Bergwercksarten* (Description of All the Most Important Mineral Ores and Mining Methods), published in Prague in 1574. Ercker was Prague's minting master from 1583 to 1594 and from 1577 to 1590 held the post of the highest mining master of the Kingdom of Bohemia. His book became a classical metallurgical work and was used as a textbook in Europe until the eighteenth century. It was a priceless handbook of mining practice as well because it also contained a detailed description of methods used to prevent loss of metal during the production process, particularly detailed for minting metals.

The minting process also witnessed improvements in the preparation of the minting alloy, the casting of ingot bars, attempts to substitute cold rolling for manual hammering of the bars into sheets, improvements in shaping the coins ascribed to Leonardo da Vinci, and attempts to use a mechanized coining die (Nohejlová-Prátová 1986).

Mining Education

To improve knowledge of mining and metallurgy a state-subsidized mining school was established in Jachymov in 1716 for training mining officials. In 1733, the curriculum was expanded to a number of

Figure 8.9 Assaying laboratory, late sixteenth century. *Lazarus Ercker: Beschreibung allerfürnemisten Mineralischen Ertzt und Berckwerksarten, Prag 1574.* (Lazarus Ercker: Description of all the Most Important Mineral Ores and Mining Methods, Prague 1574.)

Figure 8.10 Portable assaying furnace, late sixteenth century. *Lazarus Ercker: Beschreibung allerfürnemisten Mineralischen Ertzt und Berckwerksarten, Prag 1574.* (Lazarus Ercker: Description of all the Most Important Mineral Ores and Mining Methods, Prague 1574.)

additional fields, including mining geology, mining engineering, civil engineering, assaying, metallurgy, mining law, and court procedures. In 1763 education in mining engineering began at the University of Prague in a newly established department of mining science. This was the first university-level training center of its kind in Europe. Studies continued at the mining science department of the University of Prague until 1772 when they were interrupted and transferred to the Mining Academy in Banska Stiavnica, Slovakia, which gradually acquired official recognition for all the lands of the Austrian monarchy. This ensured the necessary theoretical background for the mining and the metallurgical field in the monarchy (Majer 1991).

Crisis in the Thaler System

At the turn of the sixteenth to seventeenth century, the thaler system experienced a crisis caused by the political circumstances prior to the Thirty Years' War and by the depletion of deposits of precious metals at economically extractable depths. The countries of central Europe were being squeezed out of world trade by the discovery of the Americas, and their monopoly of precious metals was broken by silver and gold from Latin America. A collapse of the Czech currency and monetary inflation led to the declaration of bankruptcy in 1620 and an 89 percent reduction of the value of the currency. Although this crisis was followed by renewed minting of high-silver-content thalers and their parts, their value constantly dropped throughout the seventeenth century (Skalský 1937).

The Jachymov mint was dissolved in 1671, but minting of thalers continued in Prague until 1753. In the same year, a minting reform took place. Its purpose was to introduce Vienna marks weighing 280 grams instead of the traditional Prague mark weighing 253.14 grams. Thalers minted from the Viennese mark were 41 mm in diameter, weighed 28.06 grams and had a purity of 85.0 percent. These thalers were no longer limited to being only Czech legal tender but became a

Figure 8.11 Reverse of silver thaler of Empress Maria Theresia, coined 1758, Prague mint. Collections of National Museum, Prague.

component of the monetary system valid in all lands of the European Hapsburg dominion. Because Bavaria also acceded to this currency system, it got to be known as the conventional currency. Issuance of this new thaler concluded the history of independent Czech minting which, henceforth, received an all-Austrian character which expressed the growing absolutism and administrative centralization (Skalský 1937).

The First Banknotes

In the middle of the eighteenth century, the period when coins predominated as the principal means of exchange rapidly drew to a close. In the Czech lands, it had lasted a full thousand years. The succeeding era brought the predominance of a different means of payment—paper money—beginning with the issue of the first banknotes in 1762. It was only at the end of the eighteenth century that mining activities were gradually renewed in the Czech lands thanks to the gradual application of new findings in the natural as well as exact sciences and the use of new principles in designing mining and metallurgical equipment and evolving new metallurgical processes. However, it was then aimed more at deposits of utility-metal ores. At the same time, Jachymov moved once more to the forefront—first as a center of silver and lead mining and, beginning in the middle of the nineteenth century, mainly for the extraction and processing of the first radium ore and, later, uranium ore.

Conclusion

Coins minted over many hundreds of years in the Czech lands reached high levels of artistic achievement and maintained their value over long periods of time. In spite of the ongoing temptation for monarchs to add to their mining and minting profits by "debasing" the currency, and in spite of periodic depletion of precious metal mines, only four major silver coins, and their fractions, were required to provide a usable silver currency from the tenth century through the middle of the eighteenth.

In the process of providing these coins, the people of the Czech lands repeatedly solved a wide variety of quality management issues. Process technologies were developed and improved to reduce the loss of precious metals, to extract ever more difficult to reach ores, and to treat and smelt more-complicated and lower-grade ores. Administrative processes were developed to coordinate a complex, multiple-stage production process involving many different individuals and organizations. Innovative social actions were developed and implemented through legal codes which influenced future legislation in many European states. Two classic treatises in mining and metallurgy were written that were standard works in their fields for two centuries. An excellent system of mining education was developed.

During these eight and a half centuries, an elaborate governmental control system was developed. It was intended to assure efficiency and quality throughout the production system—from mining through coining. This extensive system of royal oversight arose from a number of needs and special aspects of the products and production system. The needs of successive kings made it critical that the productive process run smoothly and that many of the benefits of the process accrue to the kings. Precious metal mining and the minting process were of great economic importance to the monarchs, both as direct sources of royal income and because of their impact on the economic health of the kings' dominions. The nature of the products and processes provided many opportunities for fraud and theft. The high value of the gold and silver, its ease of portability in its various stages, and its ease of sale once stolen made it a particularly attractive item for theft. The many stages of the productive process, beginning with mining and ending with coining, combined with a variety of independent agents involved in the various stages to provide many opportunities for theft and fraud. The high value of the products also made inefficient production processes unusually costly in terms of wasted opportunities for revenues and profit at each of the stages of production.

To assure honest and efficient operations throughout the production process, successive kings developed progressively more elaborate control procedures for each step. The high value of the products stimulated the use of multiple layers of supervision—inspectors of inspectors were appointed. The value of the products also encouraged severe penalties for theft and fraud.

The fact that many of the control procedures were incorporated in public laws enabled the concepts and approaches to serve as models for other industries and countries. These laws went beyond simply penalizing and remedying errors in the various stages of the production processes. They included attempts to prevent problems from arising by establishing procedures for fair treatment of workers, assurance that mine operators and smelters would conduct their operations efficiently, and that disruptions in production would be acted upon promptly. They also supported associations of workers for mutual benefit, a means of encouraging an effective and healthy workforce.

Bibliography

Cach, F.: *Nejstarši české mince* (Oldest Bohemian Coins), Vols. I to III; Prague, 1970–74.

Filip, J.: *Keltové ve střední Evropě* (Celts in Central Europe); Prague, 1956.

Filip, J.: *Keltská civilizace a její dědictví* (Celtic Civilization and its Heritage); Prague, 1959.

Jangl, L., and Bílek, J.: *České horní právo* (Bohemian Mining Law), Vols. I to IV; Příbram, 1976–79.

Kořan, J.: *Přehledné dějiny československého hornictví* (Lucid History of Czechoslovak Mining), Vol. 1; Prague, 1955.

Majer, J.: "Těžba stříbrných rud v Jáchymově v 16. století" (Extraction of Silver Ores in Jáchymov in the 16th Century), *Acta Musei nationalis technici Pragae;* Prague, 1968, pp. 111–279.

Majer, J.: *Czechoslovak Mining Techniques throughout History;* Stockholm, Prague, 1975.

Majer, J.: *Po kovových stezkách dějin Československa* (Along the Metal Trails of the History of Czechoslovakia); Příbram, 1991.

Nemeškal, L.: *Jáchymovská mincovna v 1. polovině 16. století* (The Jáchymov Mint in the First Half of the 16th Century); Prague, 1964.

Nemeškal, L.: "Česká zlatá ražba a její surovinové zdroje" (Bohemian Gold Minting and its Raw-Material Resources), *Studies in the History of Mining,* Vol. 12; Prague, 1980, pp. 101–11.

Nemeškalová-Jiroudkova, Z.: "Keltské zlaté mince v našich zemích" (Celtic Gold Coins in Our Lands), *Studies in the History of Mining,* Vol. 12; Prague, 1980, pp. 93–100.

Nohejlová-Prátová, Em.: "Grossi pragenses" (The Prague Groschen), *Numismaticky sborník,* Vol. 12; Prague, 1973, pp. 91–115.

Nohejlová-Prátová, Em.: *Základy Numismatiky* (Foundations of Numismatics), 2nd Edition; Prague, 1986.

Skalský, G.: *Stručný přehled vývoje českého mincovnictví* (Brief Review of Bohemian Minting); Prague, 1937.

Turek, R.: *Čechy na úsvitu dějin* (Bohemia at the Dawn of History); Prague, 1963.

CHAPTER 9

The Arsenale of the Venetian Republic

Annalisa Conterio, Research Historian, Dipartimento di Studi Storici, Università di Venezia

Francesco Da Villa, Professor of Operation Management, Dipartimento di Innovazione Meccanica e Gestionale, Università di Padova

Introduction

Geography and history have conspired to make Venice unique. Her architecture and economic traditions have justly won her world fame as "a symbol of beauty, enlightened government and a capitalist system controlled by the community." This very uniqueness created "a tradition of noble liberty . . . and an economic system as unusual in its combination of freedom and controls as her architecture and network of canals."[1] The institutions that make the city unique grew up over hundreds of years.

From the sixth to the end of the eighteenth centuries, Venice was one of the most liberal cities in Italy. Until the eleventh century, the Venetians were a population of boatmen whose small craft sailed the lagoon and the rivers of northern Italy. Then, after the year 1000, Venice became a true seafaring nation. Not only did her trading empire stretch from the English Channel to the rivers of southern Russia, but she was willing, when necessary, to do battle to defend that empire and her position of supremacy in the southern Mediterranean.

Venetian shipping fell into two basic categories—the merchant ship and the longship, or galley. The former was a high vessel powered

Figure 9.1 Sails for a Venetian ship of the first rank, from G. M. Maffioletti, *Atlante velico 1785.* Used by permission of Civici Musei Veneziani d'Arte e Storia.

entirely by sail and used for transporting heavy goods, while the latter was low and narrow, equipped with oars, and primarily a warship. Some longships were classified as merchant galleys, and were used to transport valuable cargoes of up to 200–300 tons in weight.

Venice operated a system of regular shipping lines using these merchant galleys, on the basis of subcontracting to individual owners to make a convoy or *mude*. The contracts stipulated the number of voyages undertaken per year, the number of merchant galleys in each convoy, the number of crew, the ports to be visited, the type of cargo carried, and the markets in which it circulated.[2] By the fifteenth century, seven of these shipping lines were in operation: to "Romania" (Constantinople and the Black Sea as far as the Crimea); to "Barberia" (Libya, Tunisia, Algeria, Morocco); to Aigues Mortes in France; to Alexandria in Egypt; to Cyprus and Beirut; to "Trafego" (northwest Africa); and to Flanders and England.[3] The historian Luzzatto states that between 1440 and 1455 the number of galleys contracted annually for the *mude* varied from a minimum of nine to a maximum of 20—an average of 14—with an overall tonnage of 3000–3500 tons.[4]

The two different kinds of ships were manufactured by two different sectors of the shipbuilding industry. The merchant ships were built by the private shipyards, or *squeri,* and the galleys were built in the state shipyard, the *Arsenale di Stato* (also known as the *Arsenale di Castello,* from the name of the Castello district in the northeast of the city).

The main functions of the Arsenale di Stato during the twelfth and thirteenth centuries were warehousing, docking, and overhauling ships during the winter. Until at least the mid–fifteenth century, it seems that actual construction took place in the private shipyards.[5] As the republic increased in power and its shipping interests grew, however, the Arsenale gradually took the form of a state-controlled industry, responsible not only for construction but for everything to do with shipbuilding. It produced ships complete with rigging, weapons, and navigational equipment, even with the provisions needed during the voyage. It became the nexus of the Venetian economy.[6]

Historical Background

It is difficult to pinpoint exactly when the Arsenale was founded; it seems certain that it was in existence at the beginning of the thirteenth

Figure 9.2 The Arsenale in 1798, from A. Billanovich. Used by permission of Museo Storico Navale, Venezia.

century,[7] although its shipbuilding activities were not firmly established until the end of that century.[8] The shipyard was located on a small site near the castle—still known today as the *Arsenale Vecchio,* the old shipyard—and was a simple walled rectangular building.[9]

Over time, the facility was expanded. By 1330, its size had increased fourfold, and a new shipyard with covered berths had been added.[10] The expansion was on such a scale that by 1330 the Arsenale was the only shipyard building narrow galleys and warships.[11] In 1352, a rope factory called the *Tana* (with storage facilities for hemp) was added.[12] It served both private customers and the republic. No further additions were made for the next 150 years or so.

In the mid–fifteenth century, roof coverings were built over the berths. This meant that finished hulls could be kept under cover and that work could continue in adverse weather conditions. The Arsenale could now operate through the winter, readying the fleet for the following spring.[13]

Further expansion was undertaken in 1473, when the *Darsena Nuovissima*—the new wet dock—was built, providing moorings for ships awaiting repair or new ships waiting to sail.[14]

The Arsenale reached the height of its organizational and production facilities in the sixteenth century, with the construction of numerous warehouses and laboratories housing depots for timber, cloth, and pitch, as well as workshops for sails, oars, munitions, and equipment. Antonio da Ponte, the architect who designed the Rialto Bridge, undertook the redesign and enlargement of the Tana, which became an enormous building, more than 300 meters long.

At this time the Arsenale played a fundamental role in the city's defense.[15] Its covered shelter for vessels allowed Venice to maintain a defense fleet in constant readiness. The reserve fleet was originally 25 galleys, and this number finally peaked after more than 100 galleys were prepared for the Turkish–Venetian war of 1537–40. Twenty-five of these galleys were held fully armed and equipped in wet dock so that they could be manned and launched at a moment's notice. The rest of the fleet, complete with hulls and superstructures, was held in dry dock, ready to be launched after caulking.[16]

From 1570 until the fall of Venice in 1797, the shipyard covered an area of 263,000 square meters. The Darsena Nuovissima was equipped with 48 building yards and covered berths for 70 galleys.[17]

By 1600, the size and layout of the Arsenale were more or less complete, and no further major modifications were carried out under Venetian jurisdiction.

The scale and facilities of the Arsenale were such that it was considered "the best of its kind anywhere in the world."[18] Many different witnesses refer to it over the centuries, from Dante, Saint-Didier,[19] and the Belgian humanist Latomus[20] to the Venetian Gasparre Contarini,[21] Galileo Galilei, and the Venetian government itself, which in 1509 dubbed the Arsenale the "heart of the State."[22] In 1696, when Peter the Great of Russia decided to build a fleet, he appealed to Venice for a group of experienced shipbuilders—so, even at the end of the seventeenth century, the Arsenale still had an excellent reputation throughout the world.

Until the end of the war of Candia and the loss of Crete in 1669, the Arsenale had few organizational problems and managed to meet the republic's demand for ships. After this time, however, it began a slow decline, caused above all by the lack of innovation in terms of policy, management, and technology. At the technological level, for example, the Arsenale lagged increasingly behind the English and the Dutch shipbuilding industries—which were making great strides, particularly in improvements to the shape of the hull.[23] Skilled workers were increasingly hard to find and there was a shortage of raw materials such as timber.[24]

Both Venice and the Arsenale suffered with the Napoleonic occupation in 1797. Before handing Venice over to Austria, the occupying troops sacked the Arsenale. Venice returned to French rule for a brief period between 1806 and 1814. Between 1814 and 1848 Austria turned its attention somewhat halfheartedly to the Arsenale, but it was not until Venice was annexed by Italy in 1866 that an attempt was made to refit the shipyards to meet the new demands of naval war. The area of the Arsenale was increased to 318,000 square meters between 1873 and 1914.

General Features of the Arsenale

The Arsenale was a masterpiece of shipbuilding organization, whose function was to produce and maintain warships for defense and merchant ships for trade. It occupied an entire section of the city at the mouth of the port to the east of the Castello district, covering about

Figure 9.3 Shipyards at the Arsenale, from E. Dummer, 1685.
Used by permission of the British Library.

five percent of the city's total area as well as nine stretches of water. There was also an area given over to housing for the people who worked at the Arsenale—who were known as *arsenalotti*.[25]

The Arsenale was perhaps Europe's first great state industry. One of its outstanding features was its ability to function smoothly despite the strong fluctuations in the demand for warships and to guarantee operations even in times of crisis, such as outbreaks of war or plague. The network of canals that surrounded the Arsenale further guaranteed its security. Areas without this type of defense such as the Tana rope factory were patrolled by special guards. All roads leading to the Arsenale could be closed if necessary, and all access bridges were made of wood so that they could be quickly destroyed in times of danger. The entire area was patrolled during feast days to guard against the risk of fire.[26] During periods of plague, the republic maintained all the Arsenale's workers and their families inside the shipyard at its own expense. This guaranteed production levels and avoided contamination and a consequent drop in manpower.[27]

The many different sectors of the Arsenale—timberyard, construction berths, foundries, arms workshops, and the rope factory— were laid out to make the assembly of the ships as straightforward as possible.[28] The location of the various sectors, therefore, followed a logical sequence: the supervisors' offices and the administration were near the entrance, the berths and the building yards were linked by a network of canals and were surrounded by the supplementary workshops, the armories, and the storage depots.[29]

The work carried out by the Arsenale was continuous rather than cyclical or seasonal: its activities were regulated and monitored by the state[30] and the premises were carefully protected and guarded.

A tight watch was kept on wastage, and items of raw material such as wood shavings and scrap wood were carefully recycled. If a ship had to be dismantled, as much equipment and material as possible was salvaged from it. Wood items were given as payment to the workers or sold to bakers, while salvaged materials were taken to the *ufficiali al sal* (salt officials), who used them for canal repair work in the lagoon.[31]

The Arsenale successfully integrated all the different manufacturing phases.[32] Apart from shipbuilding, its huge range of activities included a rope factory, a cannon foundry, covered wet docks, dry docks, arms and ammunition depots, a test range for firearms, timber depots, oar factories and depots, and draughtsmen's offices. From

Figure 9.4 Weapons room in the Arsenale, from D. Gasperoni, *Artiglieria Veneta*. Used by permission of Biblioteca Querini Stampalia.

hemp[33] to timber, artillery to sails, the Arsenale was totally self-sufficient. The state also recruited the best craftsmen, procured materials, and supplied all the other shipyards within the republic's territories. Zante, Corfù, and Crete[34] depended on Venice for materials, equipment, and weapons. The Venetian shipbuilding industry was therefore a centralized organization.

One of the factors that made the Arsenale the leading shipyard of its day was the skill of its craftsmen.[35] In the first half of the seventeenth century, personnel at the Arsenale were divided into those responsible for running the shipyard (with political, technical, economic, and financial functions) and those responsible for building the hulls and equipping and arming the ships. Since each artisan was essentially self-supervising—he possessed all the necessary skills for construction and equipment operations—there was no distinction between management and execution of the work.

De Chambres remarks on the degree of specialization by type of work at the Arsenale: "some people work only on constructing galleys, others only on making oars, others make or repair sails, still more grind coal, sulphur or saltpetre, while others collect the powder."[36]

The Arsenale was also a model of industrial efficiency, as it proved when it had rapidly to prepare and equip as large a fleet as possible to meet a Turkish attack on Cyprus, a Venetian territory. In the spring of 1570, it produced 100 galleys in the space of two months. When Christian forces marshaled at Lepanto the following year, more than half the ships they used had been built in Venice.[37]

Another outstanding feature of the Arsenale's efficiency was the speed at which the hulls, always held ready in reserve, could be equipped. During a visit from King Henry III of France in 1573, a galley was completely prepared and launched in two hours.[38] Sources do not reveal exactly how this feat was performed in so short a time, but it obviously required the coordination of an enormous number of people and parts and is a noteworthy example of the expertise and organization of the Arsenale and its workers.

When Frederick IV of Denmark visited the Arsenale in 1708, he was astonished at its magnificence: "incredible huge warehouses, all full of masts, rudders, anchors, vast numbers of workshops where hundreds of workers did all kinds of different work. Before his very eyes an anchor was assembled. He then proceeded to an enormous chamber where hemp was processed and watched the manufacture of a huge cable . . . he was present when a galley hull was assembled and watched the launch of a 64-gun ship."[39]

Organization of the Arsenale

General Organization

The Arsenale was a state-owned manufacturing industry, subdivided internally into three different sections, referred to from now on as *divisions:* the artillery division, that is, the weapons factory, which was indispensable to both the navy and the merchant fleet; the shipbuilding division, which constructed the ships; and the rope division, which was vital for equipping the ships. The shipbuilding division assembled the ships one by one in a fixed location, while the other two divisions operated a system of batch production. Figure 9.5 corresponds approximately to the organizational structure of the Arsenale during the seventeenth century.

As can be seen in Figure 9.5, the Arsenale as a whole was presided over by a board of magistrates known as the *Savi agli Ordini.* After 1413 the five *savi* were required to visit the Arsenale and monitor the work in progress and report back to the Senate.[40]

The three *Provveditori all'Arsenal,* the directors at the top of the hierarchy, were responsible for the management of the Arsenale until the fall of the Venetian Republic in 1797. The directors were members of the nobility, appointed for a 16-month term.[41] The short-term nature of the appointment was typical of the Venetian administrative system, and was designed to minimize the risk of extortion, embezzlement, or the furthering of private interests. Initially there were two directors; then in 1583 a third was added.

The directors functioned as inspectors, reporting their findings to the Senate. They were responsible for organizing lines of supply, for setting the quality of the vessels built for the fleet and the defense of Venice in general, and for raising sufficient funds to increase production during wartime. From the last decade of the fifteenth century, the directors provided the link between the Senate and the workers in the Arsenale.[42]

Each division was responsible as far as possible for its own administration, and maintained a clear distinction between management and

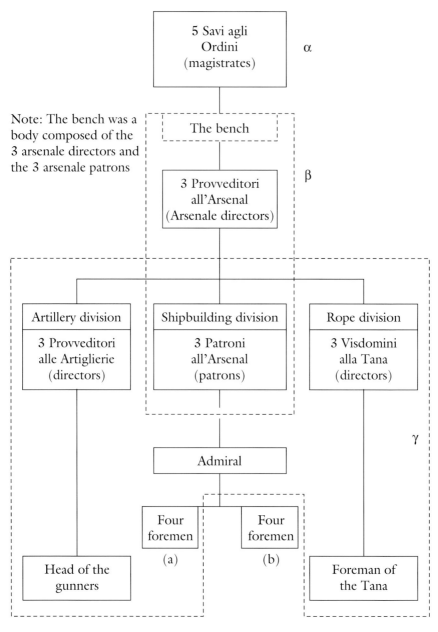

α: First level board (strictly political)
β: Second level board (political/technical)
γ: Third level board (strictly technical)

Figure 9.5 Organization of the Arsenale during the seventeenth century. Source: drawn by the authors.

labor. The three divisions represented three different units as far as the people who dealt with them were concerned, and the state regarded them as such for financing purposes. The remainder of this chapter addresses the shipbuilding division, perhaps the most important of the three divisions.

Organization of the Shipbuilding Division

Figure 9.6 is a diagram of the shipbuilding division, reconstructed from a wide variety of historical sources. It cannot be regarded as an absolute model, given that the organization of the Arsenale changed over the years and would have been modified periodically to meet different needs—such as wartime or peacetime requirements. The diagram does not show the structure that handled the Arsenale's other functions such as provision of materials and ship modifications or mooring.

In Figure 9.6, the organizational structure shown for the mast-maker foreman, subforeman, masters, and workmen applies to the other seven foremen in the figure.

From 1276, a board of three *Patroni all'Arsenal* (patrons)—aristocrats chosen from the members of the Great Council—were responsible for running the shipbuilding division. To ensure the best possible technical management, those chosen had to demonstrate an adequate knowledge of the naval disciplines and also had to have served in the armed forces. They held office for 32 months and stayed at the Arsenale in shifts of 15 days each to ensure continuous control day and night.[43]

The patrons were responsible for internal production. Their duties—both managerial and technical—covered the general coordination of activities, monitoring the supply of raw materials, and organizing the administration.[44] The Senate communicated its orders for shipbuilding, repairs, and equipment to the patrons, who in turn were expected to submit plans for new work to the Senate.

In February 1582, the Senate decided to allocate specific duties to each of the patrons. One patron was in charge of the carpenters (who built the hulls and keels) and caulkers (divided into two specialized groups) for a period of six months, after which he had to compile a report on his findings. The second investigated the production of rigging, artillery, and oars—in other words, the main equipment of a galley—and prepared a special report. The third supervised the entire shipbuilding process to ensure that it was being carried out as quickly

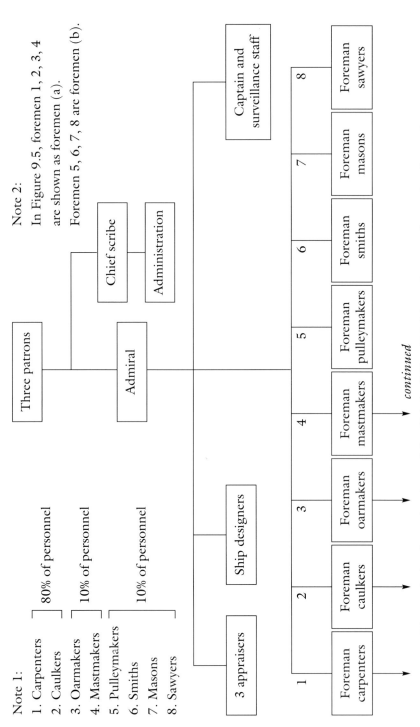

Note 1:
1. Carpenters
2. Caulkers
3. Oarmakers
4. Mastmakers
5. Pulleymakers
6. Smiths
7. Masons
8. Sawyers

80% of personnel
10% of personnel
10% of personnel

Note 2:
In Figure 9.5, foremen 1, 2, 3, 4 are shown as foremen (a).
Foremen 5, 6, 7, 8 are foremen (b).

Three patrons

Chief scribe

Administration

Admiral

Ship designers

3 appraisers

Captain and surveillance staff

1 Foreman carpenters

2 Foreman caulkers

3 Foreman oarmakers

4 Foreman mastmakers

5 Foreman pulleymakers

6 Foreman smiths

7 Foreman masons

8 Foreman sawyers

continued

Figure 9.6a Organization of the Shipbuilding Division. Source: drawn by the authors.

continued

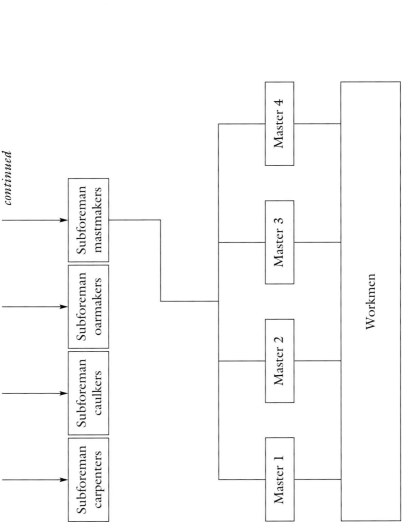

Figure 9.6b Organization of the Shipbuilding Division. Source: drawn by the authors.

as possible.[45] So the first two patrons were responsible for planning and control in their respective areas, while the third monitored work in progress and checked whether production schedules were being maintained.

As time went by, however, the patrons' duties were less directly involved in the production process. They became chiefly responsible for managing the financial side of the division, overseeing the purchase of raw materials and equipment, and liaising with the various institutions, such as the Collegio, the Senate, and the Council of Ten,[46] which were involved in the running of the Arsenale.

As the patrons' role became more managerial, their technical duties inside the Arsenale were taken over by the admiral and the four main foremen, responsible for the carpenters, caulkers, oarmakers, and mastmakers[47] (see Figure 9.6). The admiral reported directly to the patrons and was the equivalent of what today would be called a technical director. He had usually been promoted to admiral from the post of foreman for the carpenters,[48] and it was his job to ensure that the patrons' orders concerning production were carried out and to supervise the shipbuilding.[49] He also checked the requests for repairs, provisions, and modifications prepared by the ships' captains, and approved or modified them as required. The admiral also handled the cables and anchors, helped by several assistants.[50]

Immediately below the admiral were the four senior *proti* or foremen responsible for carpentry, caulking, oarmaking, and mastmaking. The oarmakers made the oars and the masts for the ships. The mastmakers cut wood suitable for making oars and masts.[51]

The most important of these was the foreman for the carpenters. Together with the admiral, he supervised the shipbuilding program, allocating work to the master carpenters and stipulating the number of workmen needed. He checked all the ships that entered the Arsenale and listed all the work that needed to be done on them. He was also responsible for checking and authorizing the dockets requesting materials from craftsmen in his section. Last but not least, he was responsible for the security and safety of all the ships in the Arsenale.[52]

The foreman for the caulkers was responsible for checking the work carried out by his craftsmen. He allocated shifts to the caulkers every Monday morning and changes to this schedule during the course of the week could be made only with his authorization.[53] The foremen for the oarmakers and the mastmakers not only supervised the production of oars and masts, but also the felling of trees for the purpose.[54]

The four main foremen were each helped by a subforeman, who also substituted for them in their absence.[55] The other four foremen (for pulleymakers, smiths, masons, and sawyers) worked alongside their craftsmen to supervise the quality of the work.[56]

Until 1569, the post of ship designer was usually held by either the foreman for the carpenters or the foreman for the caulkers, the only men with the necessary technical knowledge and expertise to design and transmit the measurements of the ships.[57] The designer worked from written documents, the equivalent of today's product specifications. These manuscripts, the earliest records we have of ship design, also contained information on the most appropriate shipbuilding techniques (manufacturing specifications in modern terminology).[58]

The information in these specifications was never printed, to protect the skills and construction methods of the shipyards. The system adopted by these codes did not require many explanatory drawings, and enabled a sketch of the hull to be drafted from brief instructions. The instructions were standardized and surprisingly exact, displaying a high level of technical knowledge: "The aim of the information listed in the Venetian texts was to describe a ship in such a way that it could be reproduced."[59] The foremen used these specifications to supervise the work carried out by the master craftsmen and their workmen.

In 1569, the Senate decided to divide the carpenters into 14 work groups, each supervised by a master craftsman or foreman capable of designing a galley and of constructing a hull.[60] The 14 master carpenters also took part in the design phase together with the two foremen, so that the original distinction between the foremen as engineers (or planners) and the master carpenters as workers (who executed the plans) was considerably narrowed.[61] The 1569 directive also simplified the work of the carpenters' foreman, who had formerly borne the sole responsibility for supervising hundreds of workers. Although no source actually documents the fact, it is also logical to assume that this subdivision of work was intended to enable each group to work on a separate ship.

Production estimates were worked out by three highly skilled *stimadori* or appraisers (see Figure 9.6). The appraisers were usually appointed from among the most competent master carpenters[62] and were under solemn oath to provide a fair estimate of the time necessary to perform each phase of the shipbuilding process, calculated in working days. All this information was recorded and given to the *nodaro* or chief scribe, who kept it in a secret place.[63] The appraisers also supervised the work of the sawyers, and noted all work completed in order to calculate the weekly wages. Together with the subforeman for the carpenters, they checked that all the timber supplied to the Arsenale corresponded to the written descriptions provided by the captain of the woods where it had been felled.[64] Finally, the appraisers checked the timber to be sent to the private shipbuilders to make sure that it corresponded to the sizes stipulated in their licenses.[65] They were also called upon to check for possible defects in new ships.[66]

Administration.   As the Arsenale developed and expanded, it was necessary to keep a detailed record of the enormous amounts of material and money involved. From the fifteenth century, two ledgers, the *quaderno* and the *zornal,* were in use, in which a note of every transaction was made. A single-entry system was originally used, but this was changed at the end of the fifteenth century to a double-entry system. One of the duties of the three patrons was "to check the quaderno against the zornal every month" and monitor cash.[67] Other ledgers were adopted later, such as a cash book, a personnel ledger, a materials ledger, and a weapons ledger.[68]

Various administration departments were set up in the Arsenale; the most important post was held by the *nodaro* or chief scribe, who was both secretary to the patrons and head of all administrative personnel. He wrote the letters to the public offices, the reports requested by the patrons, and the dockets for material leaving the Arsenale or used on the premises.[69]

The administration of the Arsenale involved a great number and variety of personnel. The accounts clerk recorded the Arsenale's payments and receipts. The materials clerk noted the value and amount of all material entering or leaving the premises. The personnel clerk kept the wages register, making a weekly list of everyone to be paid and the amount they were owed. The provisions clerk always had to be present to check the quality and quantity of goods brought in for the foremen by local tradesmen. He noted each consignment in a special book and stood to lose his post if he made any mistakes.[70] The rigging clerk took a note of all the rigging, cables, and ropes entering or leaving the premises. The general clerk recorded the amount of all lead, tallow, and fuses supplied and supervised their storage in special warehouses. When a withdrawal slip was presented by the workmen for this material, he deleted the corresponding amount from his register. He also made a note of day-to-day expenses. The auditor was a skilled accountant who checked all the Arsenale's ledgers and corrected any errors. The filing clerk kept all the registers and documents pertaining to the Arsenale. Four naval supplies clerks were responsible for keeping a register showing the quantity and value of all equipment and supplies on every ship that left the Arsenale. Whenever a ship returned, the clerks noted the equipment unloaded from it to calculate the amounts used during the voyage. They were also present at the weighing and measuring of all material leaving the Arsenale.[71]

Surveillance. There were five different categories within the group responsible for the important task of surveillance at the Arsenale: the captain, the work force overseer, four timekeepers, three overseers, and the doorkeepers. The captain patrolled the premises to ensure that the patrons' orders were always carried out, that no fires were lit, that none of the construction timber was damaged, and that no food was being sold on the premises. He immediately reported any offenders to the patrons.[72]

The very size of the Arsenale made it easy for workers to slip off, so the job of the workforce overseer was to ensure that no one disappeared during working hours. Anyone found shirking had to report to the timekeeper, who had a special list of all the workers who had come into the Arsenale. The offender's name was struck from the list and he was docked a day's wages.[73]

Two of the four timekeepers were for the carpenters, one for the caulkers, and one for the other workers. They noted the arrival of each man.[74] The three overseers—one for the carpenters, one for the caulkers, and one for the other workers—recorded the work actually carried out. They checked their records with those of the timekeepers at the end of each day, striking off the name of anyone who had entered the premises but had not worked, and docking the relevant amount of pay.[75] There were eight doorkeepers until 1562, when their number was increased to 24.[76] They kept watch on all the entrances to the Arsenale and prevented workers from entering or leaving the premises during working hours for reasons unconnected with work.

When the carpenters were divided into 14 work groups in the mid–sixteenth century, another change was made to ensure that everyone was at his appointed place of work.[77] The doorkeepers recorded the arrival of each carpenter, along with his relevant work group (*quartier*); the internal superintendents passed these records to the group's master carpenter, and he checked the names of anyone who was not at his workplace.[78]

Warehouses.   The timber, ironware, and other materials entering, leaving, and stored in the Arsenale's warehouses were managed by four classes of personnel. The delegate of the Arsenale Vecchio checked in all the timber arriving directly from the forests or from timber merchants. He then arranged for it to be stored and distributed to the workers on presentation of a withdrawal slip. Two ironware delegates checked in all iron supplies, arranged for their storage, and gave them out against presentation of a withdrawal slip. The pitch delegate ran the pitch warehouse. Finally, the cloth keeper received and stored all the cloth used to make the sails and distributed it to the sailmakers against a withdrawal slip.[79]

Masters and Workmen.   The industrial organization of the Arsenale should not be overestimated, however modern it may appear. All work was performed under an artisan system, by master craftsmen and their workmen who received their orders from the foremen and subforemen. The quality of the finished product depended essentially on the skill and ability of the workers who performed it.

The work of the Arsenale was organized according to the Byzantine system then in force in the building industry,[80] which was based on two key roles: the foreman, who was responsible for supervision because of his knowledge and experience, and the *maistro* or master craftsman, who was a specialist in his field.[81]

Originally, work was performed by individual masters from the city's private shipyards until the state decided that they should work for fixed periods to ensure continuity.[82] The Arsenale usually required its masters to have served as workmen for the full period specified by law. When qualified masters were in short supply, workmen who had not yet completed their apprenticeship were sometimes allowed to take the test to be admitted to the ranks of the masters. This was at the discretion of the patrons. In June 1589, the standard test for a workman to become a master carpenter was to "fit a 'maggier' and a 'baccalaro' to a galley in a suitable manner."[83] (*Madiere* is the central part of the framework of the hull, which is in direct contact with the keel. *Baccalara* are pieces of wood caulked and nailed to the poop deck.[84]) In other words, he had to demonstrate that he was capable of assembling the parts. It was also stipulated that only workmen between the ages of 16 and 18 who had completed a two-year apprenticeship could, with the consent of the patrons, take this test.[85]

When there was a serious shortage of masters, people were sometimes recruited from outside the Arsenale. Finally, every year three or four men, usually former sailors who had demonstrated their loyalty to Venice,[86] were given the opportunity of entering the Arsenale as masters. The workmen were divided into two groups: *minuti,* who were periodically enrolled in the Arsenale's registers, and *grossi,* who were called in emergencies. The only stipulation for the latter was that they be between 16 and 20 years of age. Workmen were apprenticed to a single master only in a nominal sense, as in fact they tended to work for more than one master.

Quantitative Estimates

A series of quantitative estimates can be made concerning the number of workers employed at the Arsenale, the time it took to produce a ship, and the number of ships produced within a certain period.

A total of 4000–5000 people were employed at the Arsenale at the time of Lepanto in 1571. Definite statistics also exist, taken from reports by two savi agli ordini—Giovanni Battista Contarini (1602) and Paolo Contarini (1643). The former notes that 1500 people worked at the Arsenale on a weekly basis. The latter records the following employees: 512 master carpenters; 439 carpenters' workmen; 549 master caulkers and 316 workmen; 233 master oarmakers and workmen; 37 master mastmakers; 153 *facchini* or laborers; a total of 100 smiths, sawyers, and women sailmakers—giving an overall total of 2339.[87] These figures show that the master craftsmen, whatever their field, did not always have a workman at their disposal, and also explains why the workmen were supervised by more than one master craftsman.[88]

It is not possible to estimate the exact strength of the fixed workforce at the Arsenale, for two reasons: a lack of statistics and the fact that no systematic research into the most important groups has ever been undertaken. It is known, however, that the carpenters and caulkers together made up the bulk of the workforce—about eight-tenths of the whole, divided into two more or less equal groups. Oarmakers and mastmakers together represented about one-tenth, while the remaining one-tenth was made up of pulleymakers, sawyers, smiths, sailmakers, and laborers.[89] Some contemporary documents contain exact figures for the workforce. The data available are summarized in Table 9.1.[90]

The number of working days necessary to complete a ship varied according to the period and the kind of ship being built. In the eighteenth century, the time necessary to build a frigate was calculated to be 85,000 working days, as shown in Table 9.2.

It has been calculated that the typical employee at the Arsenale worked an average of 270 days per year.[91] According to these statistics, the above ship required 315 man-years. A last quantitative estimate may be made concerning the number of ships produced by the Arsenale during a particular period. A manuscript at the Venice State Archive gives exact details of the ships produced between 1680 and 1793, including the types of model, the names of the designer and the director of operations, and even the number of years the ship spent in service.[92] 107 ships were launched, an average of about one per year. This figure may seem to conflict with the figures given earlier, but the manuscript concerned covers the last years of the Arsenale, when the

Table 9.1. Workforce at the Arsenale.

Year	Number of employees at the Arsenale	Population of Venice
1553	630	130,000
1602	1,500	87,000
1643	2,339	106,492
1645	2,343	107,000
1683	1,600	124,000
1696	1,393	124,000
1766	1,442	132,288
1780	1,751	132,143
1791	1,711	128,662

Table 9.2. Working days necessary for the
construction of a frigate in 1724.

Nature of work	Number of days
Carpentry	40,000
Caulking	15,000
Labor of the *facchini*[93]	30,000
Total	**85,000**

Source: VSA, Storia, reg. 588, c.88v, 1724.

production of new ships gradually decreased; presumably, the need
for maintenance work on existing shipping had increased.

Quality

Raw Materials

Two factors explain the Arsenale's superiority to other shipyards: the
skill of its craftsmen[94] and the quality of the raw materials they used.
Toward the end of the fifteenth century, the Republic of Venice tried
to raise the production capacity of the Arsenale by tightening up its
administrative procedures and by acquiring direct control over the
production of the main raw materials. Indeed, the state began to organize its territories in line with the Arsenale's requirements. Between
1457 and 1476, significant changes were made to the agricultural
land around Treviso, Ravenna, Montagnana, and Cologna with the
introduction of hemp for use in the Tana. During the same period,
forestry reserves were set up and timber regulations established, particularly with respect to oak production. Finally, the output of the
mines in the Belluno area was stepped up.[95]

Hemp. Toward the end of the thirteenth century, Venice decided to
centralize the production of raw materials. As hemp was vital for making
rope and cables, the state assumed direct control of its production.[96] Its
rope factories adopted the name of *Tana* and centralized their production
facilities. The Tana employed one of the largest workforces in Venice,
and standards and inspection methods were gradually adopted with a

view to rationalizing production. For example, all hemp from Bologna was spun in one workshop, while inferior-quality hemp from Venetian lands to the west of Padua (Cologna and Montagnana) was spun in another.[97] Each spool bore a special mark so that the inspectors could immediately identify spinners whose work did not conform to the standard weight set.[98] The best ropes were marked with a white ticket; those of inferior quality were given black, green, or yellow tickets[99]—thus making a distinction between first- and second-class products.

Until the state decided to grow hemp in its own lands near Montagnana and Cologna, all the hemp used by the Arsenale came from Bologna. The first decree concerning hemp production was issued by the Collegio on 25 January 1457[100] and was extremely precise and detailed. It stipulated that all farmers in the Montagnana and Cologna areas should plant all their fields with hemp within a year of the date of the decree, and that failure to do so would result in the destruction of any other crops. A local official known as a *deputà* carried out a census of all the fields in the area that were to be planted with hemp; the resulting register was lodged in the local land agent's office. At regular intervals, the *deputà* would ensure that the local farmers were complying with the regulations and that they were tending the crops in the prescribed manner. The fields were to be ploughed at least once a year, preferably in October, and were to be hoed regularly. Anyone who neglected to cut the hemp, or to keep it under cover once it had been cut, was subject to a fine of five lire per field. These stringent regulations were designed to produce the largest possible quantity of good-quality hemp for the Arsenale.

A superintendent was appointed by the Senate to organize the purchase of the Montagnana hemp crop. He visited the area with the foreman of the Tana to examine the hemp and only the best quality was bought. In spite of all its efforts, however, Venice was never able to do without the superior-quality hemp from Bologna, and even requested that a certain quantity should be put aside for the Arsenale.[101]

Timber. "Experience has taught us that the forests are not merely useful for our city—they are vital." This is the preface to one of the first and most important pieces of legislation concerning forests and timber. Issued in 1476, it stressed the necessity of conserving and defending the forestry reserves which were so essential to the survival of Venice.[102]

Apart from satisfying everyday needs, the forests provided timber for the hulls and masts of the ships which were the core of Venice's economic and military empire. The state legislation was designed to protect Venice's self-sufficiency in timber for supplying its shipyards, and the Arsenale in particular.[103]

Timber supply was a complex affair. Quality had to be strictly controlled and volume requirements had to be set well in advance to ensure that there was always a sufficient stock in hand to meet any unexpected contingency.

Inspection procedures and growth and shaping regulations were particularly important in safeguarding quality. Annual inspections were performed to check the rate of growth of the trees and to establish exactly how many could be used by the Arsenale. In addition, the trees were shaped, or trained, while they were growing so that they could eventually be used for specific purposes;[104] for example, for the skeleton of the hull, the supports, or the figureheads. Although Venice possessed forests rich in larch and fir, it lacked large quantities of other kinds of timber such as elm, beech, and oak. Its most important need was for oak—either straight or bent—for constructing the framework of the ships. All oak resources, therefore, were to be made available for the Arsenale to avoid the need for imported supplies.

Different kinds of forests were subject to different kinds of regulations, depending on the eventual use of their timber. The Montona forest near Istria and the Montello forest near Treviso, for example, provided oak for hulls, while Cansiglio forest near Belluno and the Altopiano of the seven communes of Asiago near Vicenza[105] provided beech for oars.

Forestry patrol was the responsibility of the *Casa dell'Arsenale*. The *Casa* operated as the technical branch of the Forests Administration Committee, which was charged with safeguarding the forestry reserves. In addition, at the end of their term of office, one of the patrons inspected the forests to make sure that they were being efficiently run. Regulations for the care of oak trees were particularly strict: the trees were felled only for the use of the Arsenale and severe penalties were imposed during wartime for illegal tree felling. Abuse of the regulations did exist, however, and in the eighteenth century an investigator was appointed to examine the work of the forest superintendents.[106] Overall responsibility for the administration of the forests was divided between the Council of Ten and the Senate. On a local basis, care and control was in the hands of the land agents, except in cases where special appointments were made, such as the superintendent of Montello or the captain of Raspo for the forests around Istria.

Assuring the supply and quality of oak: Because of its particular importance in shipbuilding and the difficulty of assuring adequate supplies, many regulations and procedures focused on the supply of oak. The first general laws originated in the second half of the fifteenth century. The *provisio quercuum* of July 1470, for example, decreed that all the oak grown in any part of the Venetian territories was to be reserved exclusively for the use of the Arsenale. Not only was all oak, without exception, declared to be the property of the state, but the land on which it was grown was to be used permanently for this purpose.[107]

The first case of a forest being taken over for the use of the Arsenale[108] occurred in 1471, and concerned Montello in Treviso—a mixed forest with a preponderance of oak. The reforestation program undertaken in this area, with sowing, planting, and felling, reflects the degree of rationalization adopted by Venice, which enabled the Arsenale to be supplied with timber for three centuries. The Montello was a man-made rather than a natural forest, and the tasks of sowing, planting, and felling were the price to be paid for interfering with nature. Frequent surveys were carried out as a means of controlling the forest reserves: the quality and quantity of the trees was recorded and the condition of the forest as a whole was appraised.[109]

In January 1476, the Collegio, under orders from the Senate, implemented one of the most detailed pieces of legislation concerning the forestry reserves.[110] It stated that timber production should be destined for the use of the Arsenale and that trees could not be felled to clear new land. A 10-year rotation period for felling firewood was to be strictly observed, and young oaks reserved for the Arsenale were on no account to be felled.

In July 1479 the Senate further decreed that no oaks—not even those on private land—could be felled without a license from the patrons. In addition, oak was sold to third parties only if it was of an inferior quality rejected by the *Casa dell'Arsenale*.[111]

Further laws were issued in 1488 establishing the state's prerogative.[112] All the oak trees in the forestry reserves, and even isolated trees, were stamped with the seal of San Marco[113] and recorded in a register kept by the patrons. Each village had to plant not less than

200 new oaks per field, surrounding the plantations with a ditch for protection and security.

When timber was scarce, it was collected from other areas of the republic, such as Friuli, Istria, and Dalmatia. In 1488, a Senate decree stipulated that when the republic's timber resources proved insufficient, the shortfall should be imported from abroad. Timber was even brought in from Albania and Germany.

In 1578 the Collegio ordered one of the patrons, Nicolo Surian, to carry out a census of all the oaks on the Venetian mainland. The orders indicate how the inspection was performed.[114] The patron had administrative and legal powers and was accompanied by a secretary, a surveyor, and six carpenters from the Arsenale. He was required to visit "diligently all the woods and other places where oaks might be found" and compile a detailed register of the plantations, leaving a space for making a record of future felling. The patron had to indicate the quantity and quality of the oaks, the condition of the land, the ease of transporting the felled timber to Venice, and the cost involved. The woods were measured to check for abuse of regulations and new oaks were numbered and stamped with the seal of San Marco. The bark was also marked in such a way that subsequent growth could be recorded.[115]

As time went on, however, abuse of forestry regulations became so widespread that in 1584 a patron, accompanied by several experts, visited all the forests under Venetian jurisdiction. They were equipped with two new and separate seals, and took a record of all the oaks, marking the bark in two separate places at a specific distance from each other, so that even if subsequent growth changed the shape of the seal marks, the double mark would remain, indicating that the trees were reserved for the use of the Arsenale.[116] In 1601 it was decreed that the marks on the trees should be renewed, and a new forestry superintendent was appointed to compile new surveys.[117]

Tree felling: Land agents in the Belluno area between the second half of the sixteenth and the first half of the seventeenth centuries highlighted the problem of incorrect felling. In their reports to the Senate at the end of their term of office, they noted on several occasions that tree felling was being performed without due respect for the resources of the forest. Felling was frequently performed by unskilled woodcutters, trees with a diameter inferior to the established standard were being felled, and there was a tendency to work only in easily accessible areas. Large areas of the forests were therefore being neglected. To solve this problem, and to facilitate control and use of the forests, the land agents advised dividing them into different sections.[118]

Alpago was a forest that produced timber for the Arsenale's galley oars; the deterioration caused by incorrect felling was a frequent cause for concern. In 1564, the mayor and captain of Belluno, Girolamo Foscarini, stated that oar timber should not be felled in areas that had been cut the previous year, and that the woodcutters should take care to saw the branches from the top of the tree first, then descend gradually toward the roots. He also suggested that the full moon of August was the best time for felling trees.[119]

In 1638, after an inspection of the forest of Cansiglio, Zorzi de Christofolo, a foreman for the oarmakers, established further important regulations concerning tree felling.[120] He advised that, to avoid waste, timber should be cut at the right time and in such a way as to ensure a minimum of damage to the rest of the forest. He even suggested how to use inferior-quality timber without compromising the quality of the finished product. He recommended that the trees should be felled sector by sector, following the divisions of the forest, from the highest part to the lowest to avoid damaging the felled trunks or the saplings. Christofolo also made sketches of three kinds of tree: "old trees," which would make good galley oars, even if the holes in the wood would require skilful cutting, and a second and third kind of "not good trees" which, with care, could be used to make galley oars. He suggested leaving trunks whose diameter was insufficient for at least six oars. In his report, Christofolo noted exactly the number of trees and the potential number of oars that could be manufactured from them. He also recorded the time necessary for the saplings to reach the point at which they could be felled. His inspection was obviously extremely detailed and complete.

Transportation and seasoning: Strict regulations were also in force regarding the transport of the timber. Special roads—*menadori*—were used to bring the timber down from the mountains to collection sites, from where it was shipped to Venice via the rivers under Venetian jurisdiction—the Brenta and the Piave.[121] The market for the supply of raw materials was also open to private individuals and the nobility, even from outside Venice.[122]

The timber sent to Venice was accompanied by dockets certifying its quality when despatched. Measured, stamped, recorded, and registered, the trunks were then immersed in the sea off the Lido of Venice, where they remained for 10 years. This procedure drained them of sap and rendered them impervious to rot—a vital requirement for a long-lasting hull.[123] As a point of comparison, Turkish galleys were less resilient than those produced in Venice because the timber did not undergo this seasoning process.[124]

The state policy and associated regulations concerning timber supplies have certain modern-day characteristics: they recognized that the forest reserves were not inexhaustible and that it was necessary to use them in a rational manner and renew them regularly. The regulations were also elaborated over time as new problems and circumstances arose.

Supply of Other Materials.   Apart from timber, the shipbuilding industry required other raw materials, such as iron, pitch, tallow, and tow. The Arsenale usually bought grey iron from the Austrian mines in Villach.[125] The smiths then turned it into nails, as well as other fasteners and fittings. Two kinds of pitch were used to tar the ships: soft pitch from Kotor in Yugoslavia and hard pitch from Vallona. Tallow was brought in from "the west" and the tow used for caulking usually came from Bologna. The semifinished products mainly consisted of equipment for the ships, such as various kinds of cloth from Viadana near Mantua and canvas from Vercelli, for making the sails. In short, the Arsenale relied totally on external sources of supply for iron, pitch, tallow, and tow, while most of its cloth requirements were met by the republic.

Recruitment and Craftsmanship

Basically a center of production, the Arsenale faced the problem of reconciling two schools of thought. On one hand were those who argued the necessity of reducing shipbuilding to a science based on demonstrable principles. On the other hand were those who upheld the empirical and autonomous nature of the craftsman's work, based on evolving traditions handed down from one generation to the next.[126]

Employment at the Arsenale was considered highly desirable: not only did it guarantee social prestige, because only the best craftsmen were admitted, but the economic rewards, too, were significant. The Arsenale used criteria based on efficiency to recruit its craftsmen, knowing full well that the arsenalotti, even if not excessively well paid, were regarded as a special group, a kind of workers' aristocracy.[127]

The minimum age of enrollment on the Arsenale's registers was 10, and the mandatory period of apprenticeship was eight years. When this period had been completed, it was possible to take the test to become a master craftsman.

The state decreed in 1601 that only the sons or relatives of master craftsmen could be accepted by the Arsenale. The object of this was to ensure that the workmen were carefully trained in their trade. In 1629 a *libro d'oro*—a golden register—was created, in which the sons of masters could be registered at birth and then employed and paid from the age of 10. They were the only workers accorded such a privilege,[128] and thus the masters were given a guarantee of employment for their offspring. The state also encouraged the masters to educate their sons in the ways of the Arsenale from their earliest years, so that by the time they reached the legal age to become workmen, they would have already acquired a basic knowledge of their craft.

The arsenalotti enjoyed a series of privileges. Dismissal was unlikely. They kept their jobs even in times of crisis, such as plague, calamity, surplus manpower, or periods of economic difficulty. They had the right to any discarded materials not used in the production process and also to a free ration of wine. They had so-called institutional privileges, such as the right to guard Palazzo Ducale when the Great Council was in session,[129] or to man the treasury. Finally, they received a pension. The Arsenale was, therefore, regarded as a large "family."

The masters were workers who had learned their craft by tradition, education, and practical experience. The work inside the Arsenale was governed by the principles of the artisan system; that is, it relied on the craftsman's skill in using the tools of his trade to find the best technical solution to each problem as it arose. It was, however, essential to keep written notes of mistakes to be avoided during the construction process. Work was carried out by masters helped by their workmen, under the orders of the foremen and subforemen, who maintained links with the managers.

The designers (foremen or master craftsmen) were capable of drawing up and modifying plans for constructing or improving the

Figure 9.7 Caulking of a Venetian ship of the first rank. Source:
J. Grevembroch, *Abiti de'Veneziani*. Venice, Museo Civico Correr.
Used by permission of Civici Musei Veneziani d'Arte e Storia.

hull. They had inherited the traditional secrets of their trade and consolidated their skills through long years of practice. They added their own touches, gained with experience, before handing their knowledge on to their successors.

Like all other European shipbuilding enterprises of the time, the Arsenale did not pay much heed to the actual science of shipbuilding. Over the years many new ship designs were proposed, but few were taken up. A case in point is the experience of Fausto Venanzio, an important sixteenth-century humanist and theorist. In 1532 he suggested transforming the four-oar quadrireme galley into a five-oar cinquereme, but the times were not ripe for such a change: only a vague description remains of his famous cinquereme galley (illustrated in Figure 9.8). Venanzio also proposed elevating technical knowledge to the level of a science, which would have meant separating the role of the engineer from that of the craftsman, another idea to which the shipbuilding industry was not receptive.

The Arsenale preferred to refine the tried and tested formulae of its individual master craftsmen, while the development of the ideal ship through a formal base of knowledge remained at best a theoretical possibility. With this emphasis on the skills of master craftsmen, the Senate and the Arsenale were always careful to recruit the services of the best masters, paying them high wages if necessary to discourage them from moving to a competitor and to maintain the rivalry among them.[130] The shortage of good masters was always a problem despite the efforts made by the Arsenale to keep its employees. In 1365, for example, carpenters and caulkers were prohibited from moving outside Venice and the surrounding area: three years later, similar restrictions were imposed on oarmakers and sawyers.[131]

In Venice, the family was the best school, and this was reflected in the life of the Arsenale, where the post of foreman for the carpenters was traditionally held by members of the same family. Nicolo Surian replaced his uncle Teodoro Baxon in 1407, and his son Giorgio il Greco would later become a leading expert on merchant galleys. When he died, the Bressan dynasty took over and dominated the Arsenale for almost a century.[132] So tradition dominated construction techniques in the shipbuilding industry. This emphasis on tradition helps to explain why, despite all the efforts made during the sixteenth century, Venice's shipbuilders remained craftsmen and never became naval engineers.

The actual quality of the finished ship depended largely on the skill of the men who built it. The shape and dimensions of the ships originated in the minds of the carpenters and caulkers, who passed on their skills from generation to generation, sometimes recording their

Figure 9.8 Cinquereme galley, with five men per oar, from J. Furtenbach, *Architectura Navalis*, Ulm 1629.

knowledge in written form.[133] There was no school to teach these men their trade—all their knowledge was acquired through years of experience and practice.

In short, the entire shipbuilding industry was based on the eye and experience of the master craftsman.[134] While this approach encouraged the passing on of skills, it meant that any standardization of work practices was impossible. Each ship was different from the rest, due to the simple fact that it had been built by different hands. Within these limitations, some attempt to achieve uniformity was made: measurements and specifications were set for the proportions of the principal parts of the ship and empirical rules were formulated to set the degree of curve of the framework. These efforts imposed some limitations on the builders, but it should be noted that the rivalry among the builders was responsible for a whole series of improvements, particularly as regards the construction details affecting the speed of the ships.[135]

To ensure the continuity of technical skills and the transmission of empirical knowledge, the state required that a retired master should be present to pass on all that he had learned during his working life to his younger colleagues.[136] The state's primary concern was that each craftsman should do his best to teach his workmen how to build a ship with their own hands as quickly as possible. This was encouraged by increasing the master carpenters' wages so that they had an incentive to instruct their workmen well.[137]

Ship Designing in the Eighteenth Century

In the eighteenth century, Venice realized that the Arsenale's working life was drawing to a close, as it had lost its former supremacy in shipbuilding. This was why, at the end of the seventeenth century, the state tried to standardize the criteria for ship designing and production. To improve designing, enormous efforts were made to standardize measurements and create an ideal model that would be suitable for repeated production and guarantee long and efficient service at sea.[138]

In 1716, Francesco da Ponte, a master carpenter, built a ship called the *Leone Trionfante*. After the ship had completed four years of naval campaigns, the Senate agreed that it was one of the best models the Arsenale had ever produced, and decreed that all future ships should be built along the same lines.

In 1732 the Senate met to discuss whether production of this model should continue or whether any improvements should be made. It was decided that the viability of the design "should not only be confirmed by the 16 years of good service of the *Leone,* but . . . this principle should hold good for all future naval construction." So the *Leone Trionfante* was used as a model until at least 1739. In that year, Marco Nobili, another master at the Arsenale, drew up "a design for adjusting the model," which the Senate submitted for examination by a panel of experts. The experts ruled that new designs should not be adopted because it was "not advisable to discard a tried and tested model in favor of trying out new experiments."[139] The only recommendation was that the measurements of the *Leone Trionfante* should be checked to make sure that they were correct. A double check was performed, by a group of foremen and the admiral on one hand and by Marco Nobili on the other. The findings conflicted, so it was decided that the two sides should each construct a model according to the measurements they had taken. These models were then examined by four ship's captains, and Nobili's model was finally judged the better of the two. A ship called the *San Carlo* was developed based on Nobili's design, "which . . . was adopted as the fixed model for future constructions."[140]

In 1779 some foremen and master carpenters were commissioned to build a new and improved prototype, "bearing in mind those ships which have given the best service at sea." They carefully prepared drawings and a model, which were accepted by a commission of generals and ship's captains, with some minor changes to give the ship a more streamlined appearance. Andrea Paresi, a master, was ordered to build a ship based on this model, and the project was followed and finished by the architects Andrea Chiribiri and Andrea Spadon.

When the new model had been approved, it had to undergo tests at sea to see whether further modifications were necessary. In fact, some years earlier, in 1768, the *San Carlo* had sunk in the Yugoslavian Gulf of Quarnaro, due to defects in the ship itself rather than to the bad weather conditions. The admiral and a group of naval architects were ordered to modify the defective part in the other five ships which had been built from the *San Carlo* design. These adjustments were carried out in 1788 by Andrea Chiribiri.

The examples briefly described here show how growing bureaucracy, the limitation imposed by respect for traditional practices and the creation of privileged positions combined to reduce the Arsenale's willingness and ability to innovate, which in turn contributed to the decline of its competitiveness.

Standardization and Modularity

Although the tradition-based production techniques made mass production of identical ships impossible, some progress was made in standardization. Two areas in which varying amounts of progress were made involve the timber used in shipbuilding and the many pieces of equipment used on the ships.

The procedure of shaping growing trees described earlier eventually reached a point of sufficient uniformity to encourage the cutting of the trunks into pieces intended for use as the different parts of the skeleton of the ship. These parts were stored in warehouses where they were subdivided according to type.[141] When they arrived at the shipyard where the ship was to be assembled, however, they bore only a faint resemblance to the part needed by the carpenters to build the hull. The master carpenters took the first two pieces of timber for the hull and adjusted them until they matched perfectly. Then they shaped the third piece, and so on until the entire hull, composed of hundreds of pieces of timber, was finished—an assembly process that produced what would today be called a "permanent dimensional deformity." When a group of carpenters completed a hull, it was therefore possible that it would differ significantly in size from the hull in the next berth built from the same plan.

The Arsenale made much greater progress in standardizing interchangeable pieces of equipment:[142] oars, sails, topsails, benches, masts, arquebuses, muskets, artillery, and other items were gradually standardized, so that they could be easily transferred from one ship to another. For example, rudder standardization meant that by 1516 it was possible to fit one type of sternpost to all the light galleys.[143] It was easier to standardize equipment such as ironware or pulleys that was manufactured inside the Arsenale instead of being purchased from external craftsmen. This was a good reason for bringing production of all material under the control of the Arsenale. Vertical integration reached a level where the master carpenters were sent to the forestry reserves not only to select timber but also to supervise the felling of the trees to be used in the production of oars and gaffs.[144]

Summary

The Venetian Arsenale evolved in about the twelfth century to provide services for merchant ships—warehousing, docking, overhaul. Over the centuries it expanded its functions and size to include a very large state-owned and fully-integrated shipyard which built warships for private customers as well as for the Republic of Venice.

When fully developed, the physical facilities of the Arsenale included numerous shipyards as well as covered docks. There was a large rope factory as well as warehouse facilities for timber, sail cloth, pitch, ironware, and so on. There was a cannon foundry and a firing test range, along with depots for arms and ammunition. All this was on a scale unmatched anywhere in the Western world.

At its peak the Arsenale was world-renowned for the scale of its facilities, its efficient organization, the volume of its production and the quality of its warships. Heads of state, including Peter the Great of Russia, visited the Arsenale, were impressed by its capabilities, and sought its counsel.

At the Arsenale, planning for quality was thoroughly integrated with planning of the entire enterprise. Provision for quality extended into the organization structure, the procurement and management of materials, the training and supervision of the workforce, and the system of checks and balances.

The organization of the Arsenale featured a chain of command running from the political leadership of the Republic of Venice down to the workforce, and extending to the suppliers of materials. The production hierarchy was headed by an admiral to whom reported the foremen of the various trades—carpenters, caulkers, oar makers, rope makers, sail makers, and so on. Below the foremen were the master craftsmen and their apprentices. The organization structure also included various offices for planning and control: preparation of specifications; cost estimating and cost control; controls over hours worked and payrolls; materials control over timber, hemp, sailcloth, ironware, and so on; and inspection for defects.

The Arsenale became fully integrated through its control of essential supplies and through its extensive array of processing facilities. The state took control of the oak forests and the land on which the oak required for ship construction was grown. Conservation practices assured self-sufficiency. Quality was assured through inspection and selection. Trees were even deliberately shaped during growth. After felling they were seasoned for 10 years. In like manner the state directed farmers to grow hemp needed for rope making and established a parallel system of quality controls.

A major force for quality was the skill of craftsmen: carpenters, caulkers, oar makers, rope makers, ironworkers, and so on. Craftsmen's families were the source of new apprentices. Apprentices were at least 10 years old and served an eight-year apprenticeship before they were eligible to take the qualifying test for master craftsman. While there were no formal schools for training apprentices, the family served as an informal school.

Under a paternalistic approach to employee relations, craftsmen received the security of lifelong employment. They were well-paid and enjoyed a high status in the community. Nevertheless, workers in critical trades were forbidden to leave Venice for work elsewhere.

Quality was aided additionally by adoption of concepts such as standardization and progressive assembly. Standardization extended to ships' equipment such as masts, rudders, oars, sails, artillery, muskets, and so on. However, standardization did not extend to hull construction. Variations in methods used by craftsmen created corresponding variations in hull dimension and construction. In effect, no two hulls were fully alike.

By the eighteenth century the Arsenale had lost its supremacy to competitors. This decline was largely traceable to the static nature of practices handed down from generation to generation through the apprentice system. Respect for tradition stood in the way of innovation. There was little attention given to the science of shipbuilding and to the need for separating ship design from ship construction.

Notes

1. Lane, 1978:3.
2. Thiriet, 1962:495–522, in particular p. 496.
3. Lane, 1978:158.
4. Luzzatto, 1954:53; also Lane, 1983:33–35, table 2.
5. Luzzatto, 1954:37–51.
6. Lane, 1983:3.

7. For a long time, historians held that the Arsenale was founded in 1104 (see Casoni, 1829:14, 16; Martini, 1877:121–38; Mocenigo, 1938: 20; Veludo, 1868). In fact, this date cannot be accepted as valid, as no evidence of it appears in the wealth of Venetian documentation (see Concina, 1984:9). The Arsenale was probably founded in the first half of the twelfth century at more or less the same time as the rationalization of the ports of Genoa and Pisa (see Concina, 1984:12).

8. Lane, 1965 and Pavan, 1987.

9. Venice, Biblioteca Nazionale Marciana.

10. Concina, 1984:30.

11. Lane, 1965:126.

12. Gorlato, 1984:200–217.

13. Aymard, 1980:295.

14. Mocenigo, 1938:26.

15. Concina, 1984:95.

16. Lane, 1978:417–18.

17. Bellavitis, 1983:91.

18. Mocenigo, 1935:8.

19. Yriarte:240.

20. Latomus, 1951:45–47.

21. Contarini, 1628:23–24.

22. *Venezia e le sue lagune,* 1847:136, 165.

23. Aymard, 1980:310–11.

24. Mocenigo, 1938:78.

25. Scarabello and Morachiello, 1987:210.

26. Mocenigo, 1938:37.

27. Mocenigo, 1938:61.

28. Lane, 1978:419 and Crovato, 1883:50.

29. Lane, 1965:161.

30. Concina, 1987:11–32.

31. Concina, 1984:36.

32. Luzzatto, 1954:383.

33. Lane, 1932:830–47.

34. Scarabello and Morachiello, 1987:210.

35. Romano, 1954:39–67.

36. Crovato, 1883:50 and Romano, 1954:41.

37. Lane, 1978:421.

38. Cacciavillani, 1984: 95.

39. Orlandini, 1900:12–13.

40. Mocenigo, 1938:26.

41. Venice State Archive (VSA) P., C., reg. 12:12 June 1583.

42. Concina, 1985:74.

43. Mocenigo, 1938:52–53.

44. Aymard, 1980:297.

45. VSA, P., C., reg. 12:9 February 1582.

46. Lane, 1965:143.

47. Forsellini, 1930:58, 62.

48. Forsellini, 1930:61.

49. Lane, 1965:152.

50. Forsellini, 1930:61.

51. Forsellini, 1930:61.

52. Forsellini, 1930:60.

53. Forsellini, 1930:60.

54. Forsellini, 1930:60.

55. Forsellini, 1930:62.

56. Forsellini, 1930:61–62.

57. Lane, 1965:51, 191–92.

58. Examples of this type of manuscript include: Florence, Biblioteca Nazionale Centrale, *Fabrica di galere,* ms. Magliabecchiano XIX. 7 (1410); Vienna, Oesterreichische Nationalbibliothek, *Arte de far vasselli,* ms. 6391; London, British Library, *Libro* by Zorzi Trombetta da Modon (known as Timbotta), Cotton ms. Titus A. XXVI; Venice, Biblioteca Nazionale Marciana, Pre' Teodoro de Nicolò, *Instructione sul modo di fabricare galere,* ms. ital. IV 26 (= 5131); VSA, Archivio proprio Contarini, b. 25, Baldassarre Drachio, *Visione;* VSA, Secreta, Archivio proprio Pinelli, b. 2, Carte di ragione of G. V. Pinelli. See also *Ragioni antique spettanti all'arte del mare et fabriche de vasselli. Manoscritto nautico del secolo XV,* edited by G. Bonfiglio Dosio, Venice 1987. On these treatises see F. C. Lane, "L'architettura navale

intorno al 1550," in *Le navi di Venezia fra i secoli XIII e XVI,* Turin 1983, pp. 284–307, particularly pp. 284–85.

59. Chiggiato, 1987:LVIII–LIX.

60. Lane, 1965:198 and VSA, P., C., reg. 11:31 March 1569.

61. Lane, 1965:198.

62. Lane, 1965:150.

63. VSA, P., C., reg. 11:31 March 1569.

64. Lane, 1965:194–95 and VSA, P., C., reg. 12:14 October 1588.

65. Forsellini, 1930:65.

66. VSA, P., C., reg. 12:14 August 1582.

67. Forsellini, 1930:58.

68. Forsellini, 1930:58.

69. Forsellini, 1930:67.

70. VSA, P., C., reg. 12:14 October 1588.

71. Forsellini, 1930:67–68.

72. Forsellini, 1930:63.

73. Forsellini, 1930:63.

74. Lane, 1965:157.

75. Forsellini, 1930:63.

76. VSA, P., C., reg. 11:2 December 1562.

77. VSA, P., C., reg. 11:31 March 1569.

78. VSA, P., C., reg. 11:31 March 1569.

79. Forsellini, 1930:69–70.

80. Walter, 1966:143–44.

81. Concina, 1984:17.

82. Forsellini, 1930:71.

83. VSA, P., C., reg. 12:8 June, 1580.

84. *Dizionario,* 1937.

85. VSA, P., C., reg. 12:29 December 1580.

86. Forsellini, 1930:75.

87. Forsellini, 1930:81–82.

88. Forsellini, 1930:79.

89. Forsellini, 1930:82.

90. Beltrami, 1954:212 and Fanfani, 1959:111–12.

91. Forsellini, 1930:89.

92. VSA, Catalogo, reg. 588.

93. The *facchini* were the equivalent of today's unskilled laborers; Forsellini, 1930:91–95.

94. Cacciavillani, 1984:91.

95. Scarabello and Morachiello, 1987:34.

96. Lane, 1932:830–47.

97. Lane, 1978:367.

98. Lane, 1978:367.

99. Lane, 1978:367–68.

100. VSA, Pien.

101. Forsellini, 1930:108–13.

102. Moreschi and Zolli, 1988:11.

103. Di Berenger, 1862; Lane, 1934:217–33; Braudel, 1949:109; and Braunstein, 1988:761–99.

104. Cacciavillani, 1984:95.

105. Cacciavillani, 1984:94–95 and VSA, Ambiente, 1989:13.

106. Mocenigo, 1938:63–64.

107. Lane, 1965:150–51.

108. Cacciavillani, 1984:90.

109. Cacciavillani, 1984:90.

110. VSA, Luogotenente, b. 272.

111. VSA, P., C., reg. 16:22 July 1679.

112. VSA, Luogotenente, b. 273.

113. VSA, Ambiente, 1989:13.

114. VSA, P., C., reg. 12:14 May 1578.

115. VSA, P., C., reg. 11:16 May 1565.

116. VSA, P., C., reg. 12:12 May 1584.

117. VSA, Compilazione.

118. Moreschi and Zolli, 1988:70–73.

119. VSA, P., C., reg.11:21 June 1564.

120. VSA, Provveditori.
121. Cacciavillani, 1984:97.
122. Concina, 1984:74.
123. VSA, Scritture.
124. Tenenti, 1962:138.
125. Braunstein, 1966:267–302.
126. Aymard, 1980:302.
127. Crovato, 1883:49.
128. Crovato, 1883:49–59.
129. Crovato, 1883:49.
130. Aymard, 1980:303–305.
131. Concina, 1984:47.
132. Lane, 1965:53–55.
133. Lane, 1934:89.
134. Lane, 1965:52.
135. Aymard, 1980:296.
136. Concina, 1984:46.
137. VSA, P., C., reg. 12:15 March 1577.
138. VSA, Storia, 1793.
139. VSA, Storia, 1793:2V.
140. VSA, Storia, 1793:3r.
141. Cacciavillani, 1984:95.
142. Crovato, 1883:50.
143. Lane, 1965:197.
144. Lane, 1978:420.

Bibliography

Alighieri, D. *Divina commedia, Inferno, XXI,* verses 7–15.

Aymard, M. "L'Arsenale e le conoscenze tecnico-marinaresche. Le arti" (translated by G. Arnaldi), in *Storia della cultura veneta, vol. 3/II, Dal primo Quattrocento al concilio di Trento.* Vicenza, 1980.

Bellavitis, G. *L'Arsenale di Venezia. Storia di una grande struttura urbana.* Venice, 1983.

Beltrami, D. *Storia della popolazione di Venezia dalla fine del sec. XVI alla caduta della Repubblica.* Padua, 1954.

Braudel, F. *La Méditerranée et le monde méditerranéen à l'époche de Philippe II.* Paris, 1949.

Braunstein, P. "De la montagne à Venise: les réseaux du bois au XVe siècle," an extract from *Mélanges de l'école française de Rome,* 2, 1988:761–99.

Braunstein, P. "Le commerce du fer à Venise au XVe siècle," *Studi veneziani,* VIII, 1966:267–302.

Cacciavillani, I. *Le leggi veneziane sul territorio 1471–1789. Boschi, fiumi, bonifiche e irrigazioni.* Introduction by A. Zorzi. Limena-Padua 1984, p. 95.

Casoni, G. *Guida per l'Arsenale di Venezia.* Venice: Antonelli, 1829.

Chiggiato, A. "Le 'ragioni antique' dell'architettura navale," in *Ragioni antique. . . ,* cit., pp. LVIII–LIX.

Concina, E. *L'Arsenale della Repubblica di Venezia.* Milan, 1984.

Concina, E. "Venezia: arsenale, spazio urbano, spazio marittimo. L'età del primato e l'età del confronto," in *Arsenali e città nell'Occidente Europeo,* edited by E. Concina. Rome, 1987:11–32.

Contarini, Casparis. *De Republica Venetorum,* libri quinque, lugduni Batavorum, 1628.

Crovato, M. "Arsenale e arsenalotti," in *L'Arsenale dei Veneziani.* Venice, 1883:49–59.

Di Berenger, A. *Saggio storico della legislazione veneta forestale dal secolo VII al XIX.* Venice, 1862.

Dizionario di marina medievale e moderno. Rome, 1937.

Dummer, E. *A Voyage into the Mediterranean Seas* (1685). London, British Library, King's mss. 40, fol. 50r.

Fanfani, A. *Storia del lavoro in Italia dalla fine del sec.XV agli inizi del XVIII.* Milan, 1959.

Forsellini, M. "L'organizzazione economica dell'Arsenale di Venezia nella prima metà del Seicento," *Archivio Veneto* serie V, VII (1930), pp. 54–117.

Gorlato, L. "Arsenali e 'squeri' nella Venezia ducale," *L'Universo,* LXIV/2, 1984:200–217.

Lane, F. C. *Navires et constructeurs à Venise pendant la Renaissance.* Paris: S.E.V.P.E.N., 1965:94–108.

Lane, F. C. *Storia di Venezia.* Turin, 1978.

Lane, F. C. "La marina mercantile," in *Le navi di Venezia fra i secoli XIII e XVI.* Turin, 1983.

Lane, F. C. "The Rope Factory and hemp trade in the fifteenth and sixteenth centuries," *Journal of Economic and Business History,* IV, 1932, pp. 830–47, republished in F. C. Lane, *Venice and History.* Baltimore, 1966.

Lane, F. C. *Venetian ships and shipbuilders of the Renaissance.* Baltimore, 1934.

Latomus, *Deux discours inauguraux,* edited by L. Bakelandis. Brussels, 1951.

Luzzatto, G. "Navigazione di linea," in *Studi di Storia economica veneziana.* Padua, 1954.

Luzzatto, G. "Per la storia delle costruzioni navali a Venezia nei secoli XV e XVI," in *Studi di Storia economica.* . . . 37–51.

Maffioletti, G. M. *Atlante velico.* Venice: Museo Civico Correr, 1785.

Martini, F. "Sunto storico e descrittivo dell'Arsenale fino al 1866," appendix to *Progetti e lavori per riordinamento ed ingrandimento dell'Arsenale marittimo di Venezia, vol. I.* Venice, 1877:121–38.

Mocenigo, M. Nani. *L'Arsenale di Venezia.* Ministero della Marina-Ufficio del Gabinetto, 1938.

Mocenigo, M. Nani. *Storia della marina veneziana da Lepanto alla caduta della Repubblica.* Venice, 1935.

Moreschi, E. Casti, and E. Zolli. "Boschi della Serenissima," *Storia di un rapporto uomo-ambiente.* Venice, 1988.

Orlandini, G. *Visita fatta all'Arsenale di Venezia da Federico IV di Danimarca.* Venice, 1900.

Pavan, E. Crouzet. "Le port de Venise à la fin du moyen âge entre la lagune et la ville un 'effet' portuaire?" extract from *I porti come impresa economica* (Atti della XIX Settimana di studio, Prato 2/6 May 1987):625–52.

Romano, R. "Aspetti economici degli armamenti navali veneziani nel secolo XVI," *Rivista storica italiana,* 1954:39–67.

Scarabello, G., and P. Morachiello. *Guida alla civiltà di Venezia.* Milan, 1987.

Tenenti, A. *Cristoforo da Canal. La Marine Vénitienne avant Lépant.* Paris, 1962.

Thiriet, F. "Quelques observations sur le trafic des galées vénitiennes d'apress les chiffres des incanti (XIe–XVe siècles)," in *Studi in onore di Amintore Fanfani, vol III.* Milan, 1962:495–522.

Veludo, C. *Cenni storici dell'Arsenale di Venezia.* Venice: Mutinelli, 1868.

Venice, Biblioteca Nazionale Marciana. *Chronologia magna* (fourteenth century) ms. lat. Z 2399 (=1610).

VSA (Venice State Archive), *Ambiente e risorse nella politica veneziana,* Catalogue edited by M. F. Tiepolo, Venice 1989. (VSA, Ambiente)

VSA, *Compilazione Leggi,* b. 43, c. 25. (VSA, Compilazione)

VSA, *Luogotenente nella Patria del Friuli,* b. 272, Ducali, reg. G, cc. 34–36. (VSA, Luogotenente, b. 272) (VSA, Luogotenente)

VSA, *Luogotenente nella Patria del Friuli,* b. 273, Ducali, reg. 1, cc. 109v–110r. (VSA, Luogotenente, b. 273)

VSA, *Patroni e provveditori all'Arsenal,* "Capitolare delle parti," reg. 11, cc. c. 6v, 2 December 1562. (VSA, P., C., reg. 11:2 December 1562). (VSA, Capitolare)

VSA, ibid., reg. 11, cc. 15r–16r, 21 June 1564. (VSA, P., C., reg. 11:21 June 1564)

VSA, ibid., reg. 11, cc. 26v–27r, 16 May 1565. (VSA, P., C., reg. 11:16 May 1565)

VSA, ibid., reg. 11, cc. 56r–57r, 31 March 1569. (VSA, P., C., reg. 11:31 March 1569).

VSA, ibid., reg. 11, cc. 92v–97r, 8 July 1571. (VSA, P., C., reg. 11:8 July 1571)

VSA, ibid., reg. 12, c. 12v, 15 March 1577. (VSA, P., C., reg. 12:15 March 1577)

VSA, ibid., reg. 12, cc. 27v–28, 14 May 1578. (VSA, P., C., reg. 12:14 May 1578)

VSA, ibid., reg. 12, c. 52r, 8 June 1580. (VSA, P., C., reg. 12:8 June 1580)

VSA, ibid., reg. 12, c. 59v, 29 December 1580. (VSA, P., C., reg. 12:29 December 1580)

VSA, ibid., reg. 12, cc. 68v–69r, 9 February 1582. (VSA, P., C., reg. 12:9 February 1582)

VSA, ibid., reg. 12, c. 75r, 14 August 1582. (VSA, P., C., reg. 12:14 August 1582)

VSA, ibid., reg. 12, c. 84v, 12 June 1583 (VSA, P., C., reg. 12:12 June 1583)

VSA, ibid., reg. 12, cc. 100r–101r, 29 May 1584. (VSA, P., C., reg. 12:29 May 1584)

VSA, ibid., reg. 12, cc. 150v, 14 October 1588. (VSA, P., C., reg. 12:14 October 1588)

VSA, ibid., reg. 16, c. 7v, 22 July 1679. (VSA, P., C., reg. 16:22 July 1679)

VSA, *Patroni e provveditori all'Arsenal,* "Catalogo di tutte le navi costruite dal 1680 al 1793," reg. 588. (VSA, Catalogo)

VSA, *Patroni e provveditori all'Arsenal,* "Scritture sulle costruzioni navali, pareri tecnici ed eruditi dal 1500 al 1797," reg. 533, cc. 2v–3r. (VSA, Scritture)

VSA, *Patroni e provveditori all'Arsenal,* "Storia delle venete navi ovvero del modo con cui furono costruite e della qualità e misure dei materiali adoperati," reg. 588, c. 88v. (VSA, Storia)

VSA, ibid., reg. 588, cc. 2r–4v, 1 March 1793.

VSA, *Pien Collegio, Notatorio,* reg. 9 (1453–60), c. 97, 25 January 1457. (VSA, Pien)

VSA, *Provveditori sopra boschi,* reg. 150 bis, cc. 17a–b. (VSA Provveditori)

Venezia e le sue lagune, vol. I, part 2, Venice, 1847.

Walter, G. *La vie quotidienne à Byzance au siècle des Comnènes (1081–1180).* Paris, 1966.

Yriarte, Ch. *La vie d'un patricien de Venise au XVIe siècle.* II ed., Paris (undated).

CHAPTER 10

The Story of the Quality of Clocks

Dr. Cornelis Spaans, Mechanical Engineer
Advisor on Technical and Transport Museums

Introduction

During the long history of clockmaking there has been continuing growth in precision of timekeeping. This growth, initially slow, later faster and faster, is the result of numerous improvements derived from multiple sources: a few great inventions; discovery of the underlying laws of stress and strain; a steady increase in craftsmanship; and incremental improvement in construction processes. Collectively these and other improvements have increased the precision of timekeeping by over ten orders of magnitude during the current millennium.

The chief quality feature of clocks is precision—precision of timekeeping. There are also other quality features. Clocks may serve as a public spectacle and a source of pride to the community. They may serve as a piece of jewelry which incidentally is able to keep time. In our journey through the history of managing the quality of clocks, we will focus on the chief quality feature—the precision of timekeeping.

The Sundial and the Clepsydra

The sundial, still popular in our time as a garden ornament, is one of the oldest known time indicators. It existed in primitive form in Egypt from at least the fifteenth century B.C.[1] Herodotus, the Father of History (fifth century B.C.), states "the polos and the gnomon and the twelve divisions of the day, came to Hellas not from Egypt but from Babylonia."[2] Polos and gnomon might not have been sundials in the form we know now.

The earliest specimen of a device indicating time by means of a shadow cast on a fixed scale was found in Greece and dates from the third century B.C.[3] In Greece the sundial was studied mathematically, which led to a considerable increase of the accuracy. The sundial, in its advanced form, remained in use until the nineteenth century, not only to measure the hours, but also for the purpose of setting and checking clepsydras (water clocks) and, later, mechanical clocks. This lasted until the invention and application of the telegraph and standard time (Universal time in 1884) made the sundial superfluous as a reference source.

The sundial indicates time only when the sun shines, and therefore the water clock was a good answer to the gap in the quality of clocks, defined as *fitness for use*. In its original form, a clepsydra consisted of a vessel with a hole in the bottom through which the water trickled out. Greek and Roman writings seem to indicate that it was used for limiting the length of speeches, which resembles the use of the still well-known sand glass. Clepsydras are very old—in Egypt and Babylon they were in use from at least the sixteenth century B.C. The earliest surviving Egyptian one dates from circa 1400 B.C.

A simple diagram of a clepsydra with a dial is given in Figure 10.1. Such clocks, indicating the hour and running 24 hours, appeared in the fourth century B.C. In the course of the ages the clepsydra developed into a quite complicated clock. Ctesibios of Alexandria (c. 300–270 B.C.) is known for his work on advanced and complicated clepsydras.[4] He used the feedback principle to obtain a constant water flow rate, and he might have been the inventor of the rack and pinion driving the hour hand.[5] Vitruvius, technical publicist in the first century A.D., writing about Ctesibios, mentions toothed racks and drums causing various motions which in turn move figures, cause balls to fall, trumpets to sound, and so on.[6]

Archimedes designed a water clock[7] which indicated time in three ways: a metal ball dropped every hour from a bird's beak onto a bell, the irises of the eyes of a "human" face changed color every hour, and rings were continuously moved along pillars with hour divisions on

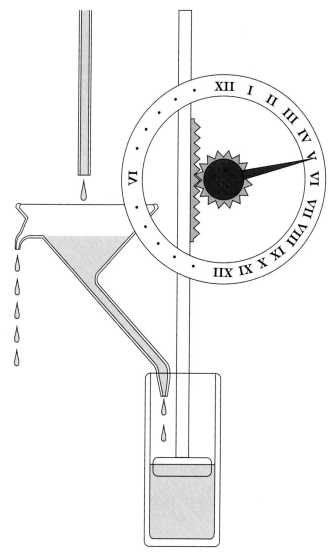

Figure 10.1 Inflow clepsydra. Source: Dr. Cornelius Spaans.

them. Furthermore, he applied a worm and worm-wheel and a "hypoid transmission" in his clock, and he introduced a means of regulating the speed of the constant rate of flow of the water.[8]

The clepsydra given by Haroun el Raschid, king of Persia, to Charlemagne in 807 A.D. is well known.[9] Every hour another little door opened and let through a number of balls, which dropped on a bell in order to strike the hour. At twelve o'clock twelve miniature horsemen appeared and closed the twelve doors.

The timekeeping accuracy of clepsydras was rather low, one of the causes being that the viscosity of water changes considerably with the temperature. But there was no need for high accuracy in those times. The length of the hour differed with the daily duration of light and dark, and the clepsydras were constructed and adjusted to indicate such differing hours.

A great step forward was the invention of the mechanical, weight-driven (later spring-driven) clock, so successful that in medieval Europe it pushed the clepsydra aside. It could now indicate equal hours throughout the year, thus marking the beginning of our present notion of time.[10]

The Mechanical Clock with Foliot Balance

Julien le Roy (1686–1759) describes a mechanical clock built in the middle of the fourteenth century by Henri de Vick.[11] It was located at the royal palace in Paris and made by order of King Charles V of France. Clock speed is controlled by a foliot balance, a beam swinging in a horizontal plane, and provided with weights at its ends as shown in Figure 10.2. Its vertical axis is provided with two pallets. The escape wheel, formerly called a *crown wheel* because of its resemblance to a crown, catches both pallets alternately, thereby causing the foliot balance to swing. By manipulating the position of the weights, the swinging time can be set. The time was indicated by only one hand as was the case with all clocks of that time. The error in timekeeping—roughly estimated in the order of between 15 minutes and half an hour per day—made a minute hand useless. The hand was moved by a gearwheel geared to the pinion on the escape wheel arbor of the foliot balance. The clock was driven by a weight of 500 pounds hanging on a rope wound on a drum, driving the escape wheel via a train of gearwheels.

Figure 10.3 shows a small turret clock movement from early in the sixteenth century.[12] The inventor of the foliot and the verge escapement is unknown. His great invention made possible the construction of mechanical clocks, pushing aside the water clock. Clepsydras can freeze in the wintertime and, therefore, the quality of clocks (the fitness for use) made an important step forward by the introduction of the mechanical clock.

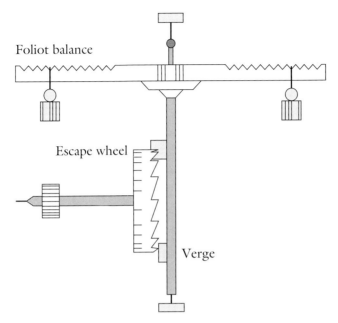

Figure 10.2 Verge escapement. Source: Dr. Cornelius Spaans.

Up to around 1650 the basic mechanism of clocks did not change. Numerous immense clocks were built to be placed in the towers of churches, cathedrals, and public buildings. Some were simple clocks like de Vick's; others were most complicated, indicating Christian festivals or planetary positions, supplemented by automata, and so on. Much attention was paid to the decoration of the clocks, but with respect to the accuracy of timekeeping the mechanism did not allow for better quality. But the way in which people dealt with time in those days differed so fundamentally from ours that the poor quality of timekeeping was nevertheless acceptable for medieval people.

Smaller clocks for domestic purposes also existed in the fourteenth century, but came into general use only from about 1550 onward. A reference to such clocks is found in the famous French poem "Le Roman de la Rose" by Guillaume de Lorris and Jean Chopinel de Meung, written between 1230 and 1305. It says, in translation,

He then made his clocks chime
In his halls and chambers
With (gear) wheels well contrived
And moving continuously

Figure 10.3 Turret clock movement (early sixteenth century), with foliot balance. Source: Zaans Uurwerk Museum, Zaandam, the Netherlands.

In the middle of the seventeenth century, clocks with mechanisms resembling that of De Vick's clock (Figure 10.4) were found in many households. Weights as power source remained popular even after the invention of the mainspring. Brackets made it possible for the weights to hang down. Beautifully decorated carved brackets, like those in Figure 10.5, were found on many such clocks.

A great improvement of the fitness for use is the invention in the first half of the fifteenth century of the mainspring and of the so-called "fusee." Their application to domestic clocks made possible the

Figure 10.4 Lantern clock, traditional English table clock, circa 1690, Museum of the History of Science, Oxford.

construction of table clocks. As the spring uncoils, the force it exerts decreases, thus causing the clock to slow down. This effect is counter-balanced by the increasing diameter of the fusee, so that the fusee arbor exerts a constant driving moment on the clock mechanism (see Figure 10.6). An early sketch of a fusee, by Leonardo da Vinci (four-

Figure 10.5 Friese Stoelklok (Frisian stool clock),
1736, Zaans Uurwerk Museum, Zaandam.

teenth century), is shown in Figure 10.7. Figure 10.8 shows an early spring-driven clock.

By the end of the fifteenth century clocks were usually made by skilled blacksmiths (Figure 10.9) belonging to a blacksmiths' or locksmiths' guild.[13] Guilds of clockmakers did not exist until, in 1544, King Francis I gave the statute of incorporation to the Paris Guild of Clockmakers.[14] Its members were subjected to severe regulations leading, among other things, to increased control of the quality of

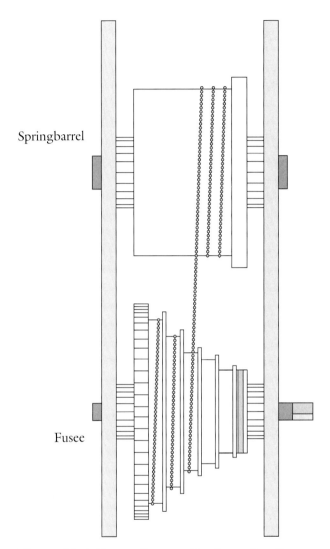

Figure 10.6 Fusee. Source: Dr. Cornelius Spaans.

manufacturing. It was only in 1631 that in London the Master, Warden and Fellowship of the Arts and Mystery of Clockmaking of the City of London came into being. This guild could impose laws on all persons involved in making or selling clocks, and had the right of tracing insufficient quality in all its forms. But the quality of timekeeping remained rather low and had to wait for a breakthrough in order to make the next step forward.

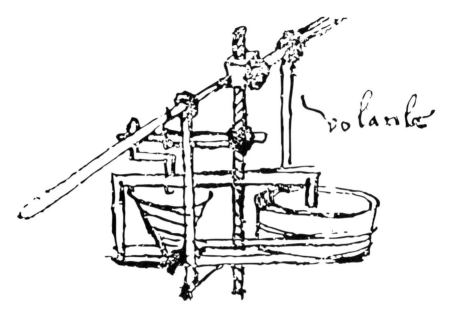

Figure 10.7 Sketch of a fusee by Leonardo da Vinci.

The Pendulum Clock

The breakthrough leading to a sudden increase of the accuracy of timekeeping came in 1656, when Christiaan Huygens, born in 1629 in Zuilichem in the Netherlands, applied the pendulum—with its constant swinging time—to a clock. Before him, the idea of a pendulum clock was also born in the minds of Galileo and his son Vincenzio (1641), and a few models of pendulum clocks were actually built in Italy before 1656,[15] but this did not lead to a general breakthrough. The improvement due to Huygens's independent invention was so apparent that his pendulum was fitted to all new clocks. Existing clocks very often were rebuilt to become pendulum clocks. The mean daily error ranged from 10 to 15 seconds—an enormous improvement with respect to clocks with a foliot balance.

Huygens still used the verge escapement (Figure 10.10). This escapement has two disadvantages. There is much interference of the escape wheel with the free motion of the pendulum, and the arc of swing of the pendulum must be large, thereby restricting the length of the pendulum. Huygens developed cycloidal cheeks to force the pendulum into a cycloidal motion and proved his theory of the

Figure 10.8 Spring driven German Tower Clock, circa 1570.
Museum of the History of Science, Oxford.

HOROLOGIA FERREA.
Rota æqua ferrea ætherifꝗ voluitur, *Recludit æquè et hæc et illa tempora.*

Figure 10.9 Sixteenth century clock factory. Engraving by Johannes Stradanus. Burndy Library of the Dibner Institute, Cambridge, Massachusetts, USA.

isochronism (that is, swinging time independent of the arc of swing) of the cycloid in his treatise "Horologium oscillatorium" in 1673.[16]

A further improvement of the quality of timekeeping was reached some 10 years later in England by the invention of the anchor escapement[17] (see Figure 10.11). Joseph Knibb built the earliest surviving clock fitted with this device around 1668. Sir Christopher Wren may have advised him.[18]

This escapement made it possible to produce clocks with a small arc of swing of the pendulum, so that the length of the pendulum can be longer than in the case of the verge escapement. This in turn made possible the introduction of a long standard pendulum beating one second. The interference of the escape mechanism with the freedom of the pendulum movement is reduced, thus promoting precision of timekeeping. As visible sign of the improvements, the minute hand and even the second hand became common. Beautiful clocks with a long pendulum, like the ones shown in Figures 10.12 and 10.13, were built.

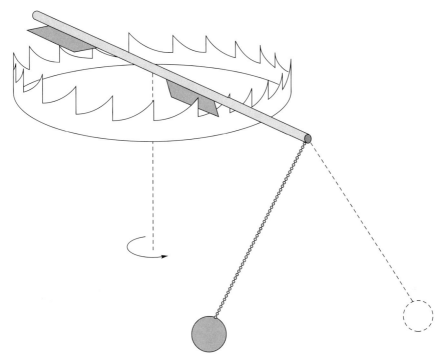

Figure 10.10 Pendulum with verge escapement.
Source: Dr. Cornelius Spaans.

Figure 10.12 shows a highly important one-second-long pendulum verge watch clock, circa 1670–75, made by Olaf Roemer, Copenhagen, Denmark (1644–1710). (He was an eminent scientist and one of only two non-French members of the Académie Royale des Sciences, with his friend Christiaan Huygens. Roemer recommended the use of the epicycloid for spur gears and the cycloid for crown wheels.) The clock is now owned by Mr. Wijnen of Paris.

The anchor escapement makes the escape wheel recoil at the end of each swing. Further progress in the accuracy of timekeeping was reached by the improvement of the escapement around 1700 by George Graham, who eliminated the recoil by a modification of the shape of the teeth of the escape wheel.

The quality of timekeeping of the clocks had by now increased so much that inaccuracies due to changes in the length of the pendulum caused by temperature changes were noted. Various compensating devices were invented. The first was George Graham's 1721 mercury compensation pendulum. A vessel of mercury replaces the pendulum

Figure 10.11 Anchor escapement. Source: Dr. Cornelius Spaans.

Figure 10.12 Clock with long pendulum, circa 1670, courtesy of the
owner Mr. Wijnen of Paris.

Figure 10.13 English Longcase Clock, circa 1710/20.
Museum Boerhaave, Leiden.

bob. By making the quantity of mercury just right, it is possible to off-set the expansion or contraction of the rod by that of the mercury. The so-called "gridiron pendulum," made by John and James Harrison in 1726, is the most practical. It consists of several bars of two different metals (steel and brass) designed so that expansion and contraction of the pendulum as a whole is eliminated (see Figure 10.14). The best

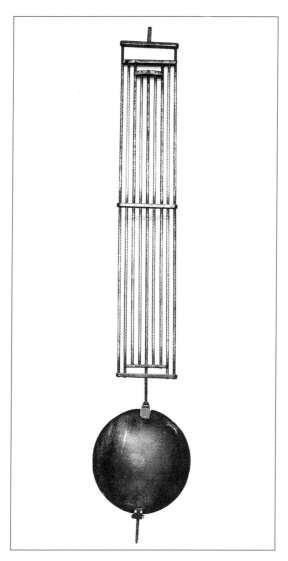

Figure 10.14 Gridiron pendulum. Source: Dr. Cornelius Spaans.

clocks on the market were fitted with compensated pendulums, while cheap clocks had simple metal rods. In this way buyers' wishes with respect to price (and quality) were fulfilled. The application for the buyer's market of wooden rods, a simple and effective solution for avoiding aberrations in timekeeping due to changes in temperature, was initially overlooked.

Accurate clocks made according to high design and production standards, fitted with high-quality escapements and temperature compensation, are called *regulators*. In the times of the mechanical clocks the highest quality of timekeeping was reached by the special regulators that were used in astronomical observatories, watch factories, and test sites for precision clocks. They were distinguished by airtight cases, a compensated pendulum, and a high-quality escapement, and they were placed in a so-called "clock vault." This is a brick room in a deep basement in which the temperature is kept constant and vibrations are eliminated by piers going deep into the ground.

Shortt's free pendulum (1921) was off by only one second per three months, which is a remarkable achievement for a mechanical clock and a monument of human ability in the field of quality of timekeeping. Shortt and Hope-Jones, with whom he collaborated, developed a system in which a free-swinging master pendulum synchronizes a slave pendulum, which drives auxiliary equipment, by coupling them electrically in an ingenious way.[19] Time signals derived from such accurate clocks were disseminated by telegraph and, since 1905, also by radiotelegraphy, in order to synchronize other, less-accurate clocks or to supply slave clocks with periodic impulses.

Watches and Chronometers

Because it would carry us too far to go deeply into the history of the quality of chronometers and watches, only a few remarks will be made.

John Harrison (1693–1776), who invented the formerly mentioned gridiron pendulum in 1726, developed an accurate chronometer for purposes of determining longitude at sea.[20] The accurate clocks relying on a pendulum were useless in ships, although Huygens did his best to construct one. The English parliament offered a £20,000 reward in 1714 for the construction of a more accurate timekeeper at sea. Harrison's chronometer won the reward after a 61 day sea trip.[21] At the end of the trip, the chronometer was out by only one minute and five seconds, which gives an error of 18 miles in longitude.[22] In today's money, £20,000 would amount to about one and one-quarter million pounds—the enormous sum demonstrates the gravity of the problem.

A successful construction for watches and chronometers is the lever escapement with pallet and balance. An example of this, in its final state of development, is shown in Figure 10.15.

In the course of the eighteenth century, the demand for watches in English styles and of English make had grown, and Swiss (and some Dutch) manufacturers were undercutting the British by supplying watches with English makers' names on them. In 1776 Fréderic Japy started a watch manufacture which produced on the basis of standard rough machined parts. Japy is a pioneer in the field of standardized production.

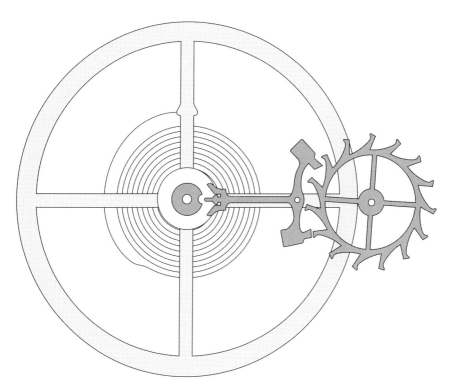

Figure 10.15 Lever escapement. Source: Omega en het geheim van de Tyjdmeting.

The Swiss were especially able watch manufacturers.[23] Their mass production of interchangeable miniature parts with high precision was famous. Their mechanical watches increased in quality and declined in price, conquering all competition and dominating the world market.

The development of chronometers and mechanical watches led to mass-produced watches of high quality in other countries as well. Manufacturers in the United States developed their own watch industry and were pioneers in the field of machine-made watches.[24]

The introduction of electronics in clocks and watches started the decline of the mechanical watch.

Electric Clocks

Once electricity was available as a common power source for households, it was applied to domestic clocks. Initially it was used for powered winding of the mainspring or lifting the weights of conventional clocks with pendulum and anchor escapement. Various ingenious solutions were tried to replace the latter with the aid of electricity, but most early attempts were based on conventional clock conceptions.[25]

A real breakthrough came in 1918 in the United States, when H. E. Warren developed the first clock driven by a synchronous motor. The clock itself is a perfect impulse counter, but its timekeeping depends on the stability of the frequency of the current supplied by the power plants (50 Hz in Europe, 60 Hz in the United States), which in general is sufficient for households. System frequency, in fact, is only guaranteed to ±2 percent. When such clocks were in general use, the power system controllers used to adjust the system frequency to correct clock errors. Now a simple and relatively cheap electric clock was available with the right quality, defined as fitness for use for domestic purposes. The new clock featured no winding, hardly any maintenance, good enough timekeeping, low price, simple construction, few defects, and small dimensions.

In the field of high-precision timekeeping the next breakthrough came in 1928 when Joseph W. Horton and Warren A. Marrison devised the first quartz clock. Its error amounts to one second in about three years. Quartz clocks started to play a role in the early 1940s as heavy, expensive devices. With the development of microelectronics, the size of the quartz clock could be reduced to such an extent that it can now be used in domestic clocks and watches. Being low priced and having high precision, no or few moving parts, no maintenance, and small dimensions, it drove out the synchronous motor clock.

Still higher precision is reached by the so-called "atomic clock." The first was built in 1948 by Harold Lyons, while the present caesium beam frequency standard dates from 1955.[26] An atomic clock is in fact a quartz clock synchronized by using the frequency of the energy (light or radio waves) emitted when atoms change their state of energy.[27] This frequency is independent of physical quantities such as pressure, temperature, humidity, and so on. In 1967, in the SI system of units, the second was redefined as 9192631770 periods of the caesium energy transition radiation. This is a physical definition. It makes an important change in the attitude toward time, as up until then all definitions were on an astronomical basis.

The results of the atomic synchronization of the quartz clock are spectacular. International atomic time (TAI) is now out by only one second in about 300,000 years. And it is exciting that this high precision is not only available in laboratories, but also directly to the average person. This is realized in commercial domestic quartz clocks and watches that are fitted with a built-in miniature radio receiver receiving transmitted radio signals generated on the basis of TAI for the purpose of periodic synchronization: an example of very high quality available at an acceptable price level.

Conclusion

In conclusion, a graphical representation of the remarkable increase of the quality of timekeeping in the past 800 years is represented in Figure 10.16. It shows that the history of managing for quality in the field of measurement of time is a story of success—a monument of human inventiveness, craftsmanship, and scientific progress. The steady increase in quality plus the steady decrease in costs made continuous, reliable, and precise indication of time available to everybody. This technical and scientific achievement led to a revolutionary change in our human culture, not only with respect to the notion of time itself, but to our whole life, both privately and socially. The precise measurement of time has become indispensable to industrial societies.

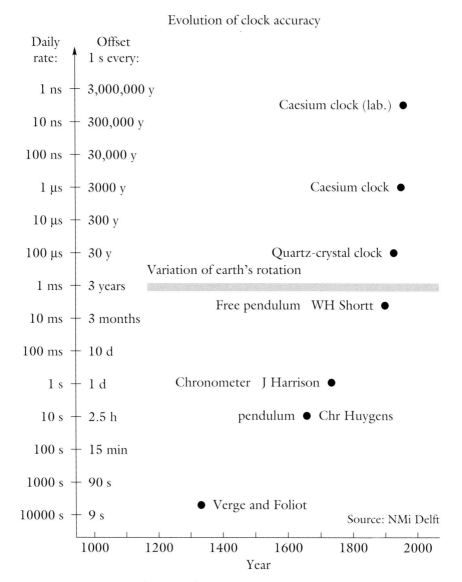

Figure 10.16 Evolution of Clock Accuracy. Source: Van Swinden Laboratory of the Netherlands Measuring Institute, Delft.

Notes

1. Ludvig Borchardt, *Die alte Ägyptische Zeitmessung* (Die Geschichte der Zeitmessung, ed. E. V. Bassermann-Jordan, Bd I.1g.B), Berlin & Leipzig, 1920.

2. Histories II, 109.3. tr. A. D. Godley.

3. Sharon L. Gibbs, *Greek and Roman Sun-dials,* New Haven, London, 1933.

4. A. G. Drachmann, "Ktesibios, Philon and Heron," *Acta Historica Scientiarum Naturalium et Medicinalium* IV (1948).

5. A. Wegener Sleeswijk, *De waterklok van Archimedes,* Histechnicon, jrg 16, Sept. 1990, 5–15.

6. ———, "Vitruvius' Waywiser," *Archives Internationales d'Histoire des Sciences* 29 (1979); and Plinius (Pliny) Historia Naturalis VII.

7. D. R. Hill, *On the construction of waterclocks, Kitâb Arshimîdas fi'amal al-binkamt,* London (1976); and B. Carra de Vaux, Notice sur deux manuscrits arabes," *Journal Asiatique* 8, série 17 (1891).

8. Sleeswijk, *De waterklok.*

9. Willis I. Milham, *Time and Timekeepers,* New York (1947).

10. M. T. Clanchy, *From Memory to Written Record, England, 1066–1307,* Oxford, 1979.

11. E. J. van der Molen, *Klokken: Zaans Uurwerkmuseum,* Zaandam, 1976.

12. Ibid.

13. Hans Sachsen, *Eygentliche Beschreibung Aller Stände auff Erden usw.,* Franckfurt am Mayn, 1568.

14. Milham, *Time und Timekeepers.*

15. J. Drummond Robertson, *The Evolution of Clockwork,* London, 1931.

16. Christiaan Huygens, *Horologium oscillatorium sive de motu pendulorum ad horologia Aptato Demonstrationes Geometricae,* Paris, 1673.

17. C. F. C. Beeson, T. O. Robinson, and F. A. B. Ward, "The Invention of the Anchor Escapement," *Antiquarian Horology,* VII, 3 (1971).

18. A. J. Turner, "Christopher Wren and the Wadham Clock," *Antiquarian Horology,* VII, 3 (1971).

19. F. Hope Jones, *Electrical Timekeeping*, 2nd ed., London, 1949.

20. G. H. Baillie, *Watchmakers and Clockmakers of the World*, 2nd ed., London, 1947.

21. *The Principles of Mr Harrison's Time-keeper, with plates of the same,* published by order of the Commissioners of Longitude, London, 1767.

22. Milham, *Time and Timekeepers.*

23. E. Jacquet and A. Chapuis, *Technique and History of the Swiss Watch,* 2nd ed., London, 1970.

24. Milham, *Time and Timekeepers.*

25. W. P. Hoogeveen, *Electrische Uurwerken*, De Bilt, 1938.

26. P. Kartaschoff, *Frequency and Time*, London & New York, 1978.

27. J. Vanier and C. Audoin, *The Quantum Physics of Atomic Frequency Standards*, vols. 1 & 2, Adam Hilger, Bristol and Philadelphia, 1989; and Wayne M. Itano and Norman F. Ramsey, "Accurate Measure of Time," *Scientific American*, July 1933, 56–65.

CHAPTER 11

Examples of Quality Management in the History of Russia

Dr. Ludmila A. Konareva, Senior Researcher
Institute of the USA and Canada
Russian Academy of Sciences

Introduction

Russian history offers many examples of high-quality products. Lack of documentary evidence prevents a complete description of the evolution of all elements of what is now called a total quality management system, but many examples of specific high-quality products and parts of a quality management system can be described. This chapter starts with a review of some of the elements of a quality management system occurring in early Russian history. It then presents examples of high-quality products and aspects of quality management systems occurring in three areas: the production of artistic articles made from gold and silver and with enameling techniques; the development of quality prizes and the success of a number of manufacturers in winning such prizes; and the building of weapons and the Russian navy.

Early Elements of a Quality Management System

Artisan Quality Standards

Quality of finished goods results from a combination of many factors: quality of raw materials, manufacturing techniques, process control, motivation of workers, level of individual craftsmanship, commitment of top management, and so on. The earliest and most vital element of quality assurance was high individual craftsmanship and the master's commitment to quality. This craftsmanship and commitment to quality can be seen in a number of household goods which have survived from ancient times: jewelry, leather products, ironware, and wooden items.

Peasants in old Russia produced by hand clothes and utensils that looked plain but were remarkably durable. Each finished product was crafted by one person from beginning to end, and that person looked after its quality. In the absence of any written standards, craftsmen depended on specimens to ensure quality. In most cases, no written records exist of production procedures. They must have been handed down from one generation to the next. Children were trained in various crafts at home, and quality resulted from a caring attitude to work and pride of workmanship. This tendency seems to have continued until the start of mass production.

Documenting Production Processes

The first written procedures for manufacturing individual items seem to date from the eleventh to twelfth centuries. During the diggings on the sites of old Novgorod, Smolensk, and Pskov, birch bark manuscripts (beresty) were found (Figure 11.1). Beresty were used as personal letters and written instructions for doing something. Some of them give, for example, ideas for making beresty themselves. According to these instructions, pieces of birch bark were boiled in water to soften the skin, after which the coarser layers were removed.

With the start of printing in Russia, descriptions of recipes and manufacturing procedures were recorded. Such instructions first appear in *The Domostroi,* a veritable encyclopedia of household management. Its first edition was compiled in Novgorod in the late fifteenth and the early sixteenth centuries. *The Domostroi* has three parts—one

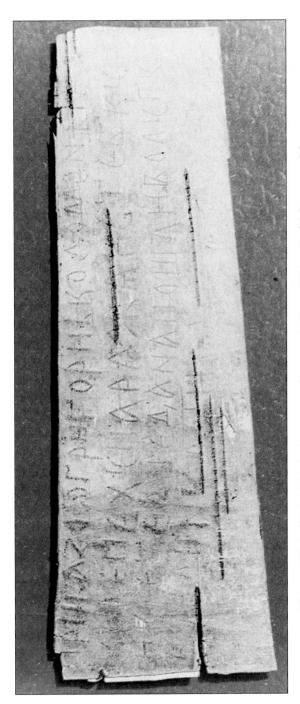

Figure 11.1 A birchbark document (beresty). State Historical Museum, Moscow.

containing religious instructions, the second treating relations between family members, and the third devoted to proper household management. The last part has such sections as "How to build a courtyard and a rural home nice to live in and fit for cultivating all sorts of fruits;" "How to dig wells, look for spring wells and to assess the quality of water;" and "On choosing cornfields."

Organizing for Quality

Early elements of organizing for quality arose in the eleventh and twelfth centuries when wealthy boyars started networks of artisan workshops, particularly in Novgorod. The excavations in old Novgorod have uncovered about 140 artisan workshops specializing in the manufacture of such items as locks, leather products, jewelry, shoes, and metal castings. Breweries, bakeries and dyeing, weaving and glass shops have also been found. The items from all those shops reveal a standard of workmanship and degree of specialization on a par with those of the most celebrated medieval centers of Western Europe and the Middle East.

The boyar who owned the workshop was its main customer, of course, and he obviously determined the specifications for quality. The quality of manufacture was controlled by the craftsman or a team of craftsmen.

In the Middle Ages, some principalities in old Russia had trading links between themselves and with other countries. From the excavations it is apparent that Novgorod's imports consisted mainly of raw materials unavailable in the city. Nonferrous metals (gold, silver, copper, lead, and tin) came from England, Sweden, Poland, and Hungary; semiprecious stones came from the Urals and (via the Volga waterway) from Iran. Most of the many hair combs unearthed are of box-tree wood from the Caspian Sea region. Amber from the Baltic was the favorite material for beads and rings.

As output increased, more imported raw materials and more exports to pay for them were required. The exports tended to be furs, wax, honey, flax, and valuable varieties of fish. One can suppose that there existed trading rules and a system of mutual inspection of supplies.

Since there was no well-documented and organized inspection system, one can suppose that craftsmen were internally motivated to keep up good quality of their products and tried to make even better and more beautiful things to feel satisfaction of workmanship.

Mass Production and Quality

As mass production grew, the temptation to reduce quality may have grown. One early example occurred in the manufacture of knives in Novgorod in the eleventh and twelfth centuries. In the eleventh century, Novgorod artisans fashioned knives by the *packet technique,* in which plates of softer iron were welded to both sides of a steel blade. The knife became a self-sharpening instrument: gradual wear of the outer plates revealed more and more of the steel blade, which could be used until it was totally abraded. By the first quarter of the twelfth century the packet technique had been replaced by a simpler construction: a narrow strip of steel was welded to an iron base to form a thin cutting edge. Such simplification of manufacturing technique to meet broader market demand enabled the artisan to manufacture more articles faster, but of course the articles became less durable—a situation with which we are familiar today.

Despite the temptations just noted, mass production did not bring universal deterioration of goods quality. On the contrary, many Russian workshops and factories manufactured high-quality products. Many articles surviving in the museums of Russia are strikingly exquisite and beautiful. These include many jewelry items made of gold and silver.

Gold and Silver Articles

Searches for silver ore began in Russia back in the fifteenth century, but it was only in the early eighteenth century that silver became available in large quantities. By the 1730s, Russian jewelers were working with domestically produced silver. Until that time, they had obtained this metal by remelting foreign silver coins and old silverware or by burning embroideries made with silver and gold threads. Despite the scarcity of precious metals, gold and silver masters had worked in many parts of Russia using different manufacturing techniques and producing high-quality goods.

The national distinctiveness of Russian silverware arises from the repetition of the rational, tranquil rounded shapes of wooden and ceramic utensils, dictated by centuries-old folk traditions. Early Russian craftsmen knew how to work the metal and show its beauty to advantage. Lengthy and thorough forging lent silver a slightly uneven, soft glimmer while its color excellently matched the pale gilding used. Old Russian silver drinking vessels such as dippers, bratinas (an almost spherical vessel served for drinking in the round), mugs, goblets, and charkas (wine cups) are steady and convenient, and their shapes perfectly suit the purpose.

The silver dippers are of special interest. Objects of this kind, with their outlines reminding one of a swimming bird, are a unique Russian feature not to be found in any other country in the West or the East (Figure 11.2).

Wooden dippers were produced in what is now referred to as Russia for many centuries before the Christian era. In the fourteenth century,

Figure 11.2 Silver bratina, engraved and chased. Seventeenth century. Silver dipper, cast figures and chased ornament, made by Ilya Kuchkin, Moscow, 1755. State Historical Museum, Moscow.

Novgorodian craftsmen first reproduced the shape of the wooden dipper in gold and silver. In ancient Rus, Russians drank the very popular drink mead from dippers. Silver dippers were also presented as awards for services to the nation, such as profitable trade and martial feats.

Niello

Interesting metal specimens made in the niello technique have come down to us from the time of Kievan Russia. In Russia, niello has always been practiced more widely than in any other country. Niello is a special alloy of silver, lead, copper, and sulphur taken in definite proportions. It is powdered, moistened with a solution of borax, and laid into a design deeply engraved on the object's surface. The object is then placed in a furnace to be fired. The niello powder melts and fuses with the silver. In this way, a dark design is brought out on a metal surface, or an engraved design is set off by a dark nielloed ground. Niello is highly distinctive in each particular locality and period. In Russia this technique achieved its peak in the second half of the sixteenth century when Moscow had become Russia's cultural center.

Niello designs vie in finesse and elegance with the paintings of that period. Later on the art of niello flourished also in the Russian north, notably in the towns of Veliky Ustyug, Vyatka, and Vologda, and also in Tobolsk and Tomsk in Siberia (Figure 11.3).

Figure 11.3 Nielloed silver snuff box. Veliky Ustyug, 1779. State Historical Museum, Moscow.

Filigree

Gold and silver are very soft and can be drawn into very fine wire. This remarkable property of the precious metals was noted long ago and gave rise to a decorative technique known as filigree. Filigree ornament, as openwork or attached to a metal ground, was made from plain wire of varying thicknesses, ribbonlike flattened wire, and plaits of two or three metal strands. Their combination enhanced the decorative effect of the filigree ornament, which was often enriched with silver or gold grains.

Filigree was well known in Russia back in the tenth century. Different objects of this type are found practically everywhere on excavation sites of ancient Russian cities and interments. The range of filigree articles is very wide—trays and caskets; airy openwork bowls; boxes of all kinds; baskets and salt-cellars; chains, buckles, and belts; buttons of different sizes; bracelets, rings, earrings, brooches, and necklaces; mountings for icons and church books; and so on (Figures 11.4 and 11.5). Composed of an airy lacelike ornament or embellished with such an ornament, they were both decorative and useful.

Filigree work does not require sophisticated equipment or numerous tools. The techniques of drawing wire by hand with forceps

Figure 11.4 Filigree silver box. Veliky Ustyug, late eighteenth century. State Historical Museum, Moscow.

Figure 11.5 Filigree silver biscuit basket. Moscow, 1841.
State Historical Museum, Moscow.

though a series of holes in a steel plate (drawing plate) and winding a
wire from one reel onto another after passing through the drawing
plate to make it finer were in use up to the twentieth century even at
large jewelry enterprises. Masters had to repeat thousands of very accurate operations making metal ground or openwork filigree ornaments and arranging fine grains. Early Russian craftsmen knew the
secret of neat soldering. One can barely notice traces of solder in antique filigree articles with grains; it seems as if some kind of invisible
glue holds the individual elements together. The secret of this very
skillful soldering was lost for many years until Prof. F. Mishukov, a Soviet researcher, proved experimentally that the old masters had used a
special kind of amalgam of gold, silver, and mercury instead of solder.

It is quite evident that strict maintenance of manufacturing techniques and thoroughness of master work were absolutely necessary to
assure quality. The manufacture of filigree wares requires exceptional
attention, patience, refined taste, clarity of conception, and precision
of performance. Once again we can see that good quality was the result of high craftsmanship.

The most significant centers of the filigree craft in Russia were Novgorod, Moscow, and northern Russian towns. Each had its specific features of ornament. Filigree was widely used in the fourteenth, fifteenth, and sixteenth centuries. In Moscow filigree art was at its height in the fifteenth and sixteenth centuries, but many outstanding works were also produced much later in the eighteenth, nineteenth, and twentieth centuries.

Enameling

The desire to embellish a metal surface arose at an early stage of jeweler's art, leading to the appearance of enamel, a glass alloy differently colored by metal oxides. Firing turns it into a hard shining mass of durable bright colors. Throughout the long history of the enamel art, the techniques of enamel application to a metal surface changed, and new designs, colors, and color combinations appeared. These varied by regions and localities. Starting from the sixteenth century, filigree enamel was especially widespread in Russia. The design, usually of floral motifs, circles, and so on, was worked in fine wire soldered to a metal base. The cells formed by the wire were filled with enamel of various colors.

At the end of the seventeenth century, enamel painting over a white enamel ground was first practiced in Russia at the Stroganov workshops in the town of Solvychegorsk. In the eighteenth century, diverse articles of domestic and religious use were decorated with enamel painted designs (Figure 11.6).

The technique made considerable headway in the second half of the nineteenth century with P. Ovchinnikov's firm, the largest in Moscow, taking the lead. Most of its works were filigree enamels. Masters of P. Ovchinnikov's firm were the first in Russia to use very fragile translucent enamel. Enamels of this kind resemble stained glass panels and are therefore termed *window enamels*. Translucent colored varnishes were also widely used. Applied to thickly gilded surfaces, they reduced production costs while lending the object a remarkably decorative effect.

Enamel was extensively used, of course, by the world-renowned Fabergé firm in St. Petersburg.

Figure 11.6 Pectoralia, part of icon mounting. Silver filigree enamelwork. Veliky Ustyug, seventeenth century. State Historical Museum, Moscow.

Rostov Enamel

Rostov the Great is an old Russian town which occupies a very special place in art history. It is the only place in the world where painted enameling, as practiced in the ancient Rus, still flourishes.

Archeological finds prove that artistic enamel—the creation of patterns and pictures by means of ground silica fused with metal oxides—was known in the days of the Kievan Rus. The craftsmen of those days were adept not only in the simpler champlevé style but also in the highly sophisticated methods of cloisonné enamelling. This technique was lately reproduced by P. Ovchinnikov's firm in the second half of the nineteenth century.

The colored glazes are unique in a number of ways: they have a relatively low melting point, are very hard when cooled, and their colors will remain workshop-fresh for centuries. This explains why enamels have been used to decorate weapons, religious artifacts, ceremonial tableware, chests and caskets, various types of personal adornment, medals and other decorations, the covers of particularly valued books, and so forth down the ages.

The art of Russian enamelwork was revived at the turn of the fourteenth century, in the northwest. A hundred years or so later, it was being extensively practiced in Moscow too. Enamel miniatures first became popular under Peter the Great, and for the next two hundred years craftsmen diligently perfected this branch of decorative enameling.

Although Rostov the Great did not come to the fore in this sphere until the mid–eighteenth century, there is every reason to believe that painted enamel was already well-established there by then. Rostov was traditionally a town of painters. So the art of painted enamel burgeoned and followed its own line of development in Rostov. It displayed certain artistic hallmarks—such as a particularly expressive line, vivid hues, and exuberant color combinations—in which one may trace the influence of the strong local fresco-painting tradition (Figure 11.7).

Records state that the majority of the Rostov enamel painters were humble townsmen or peasants from the neighboring villages. With full justification they did not consider themselves mere craftsmen, doing something that anyone could learn, but as artists in their own right.

Figure 11.7 Examples of Rostov enamel. Left, earrings. Right, two warriors. Alexander Khaunov. Raduga Publishing House, Moscow.

Rostov painted enamel reached such a degree of perfection that it virtually monopolized the domestic market. In the second half of the nineteenth century, however, it began to decline—ruined, in one sense, by its own success. By the 1870s, the demand for enamelware had grown enormously. The turnover reached two and one-half million rubles a year. Not surprisingly, this boom led to changes in manufacturing processes. The work, which to this point had been an individual or family undertaking, was heartlessly split into meaningless "specializations" simply to speed mass production.

First a whitener would cut a slightly convex copper circle or oval, spread iron oxide on both sides and fire it several times. These plain, white shapes were sold to a wholesale jobber. In the painter's hands, the mechanical work continued. The brush—made of marten or squirrel hair—flew across the shapes, dozens at a time, painting the background. After the first firing came the smoothing, then another firing. Hundreds of little icons came baked from the furnace every day. The framers finished the job off, putting the shape into a plain die-out or filigree frame which depended on customer and current demand.

On occasion, an important single order would be filled with care, using the time-honored methods.

In 1911 Konstantin Furtov, a renowned craftsman, wrote a book, *The Manufacture of Painted Enamel.* He remarked: "Instead of isolated craftsmen there should be well-appointed studios made to accommodate several persons, with all the latest appliances and placed under the supervision of a master craftsman." Furtov's dream did not come true until 1918, when a group of enamel painters came together into a cooperative workshop. The detail system was abandoned and a new approach was formulated. Later on a school of enamel painting was opened. Miniature painting on enamel reached its apogee before the war in 1940.

Today the art of enamel painting is in a new stage of development. The pioneering work done by the postrevolutionary cooperative is now being continued by a factory which was opened in 1960. Now it is a technologically advanced facility with electric ovens and custom-designed appliances. The Rostov school of enamel painting has benefited greatly from its cooperation with the artists and scholars at the Craft Industries Research Center. An old art of painted enamel is safe.

Prizes and Awards for Quality

In the nineteenth century, Russia introduced a system of awards for quality given out as prizes at domestic and international industrial fairs and exhibitions. The best Russian companies repeatedly won prizes and medals at international and all-Russia commercial and art exhibitions, providing recognition of the high quality of their products. The enamel and filigree articles made by P. Ovchinnikov's firm and the enameled objects with a variety of interesting shapes and colors produced by I. Khlebnikov's and O. Kurliukov's companies were frequent winners. The Baranovs' factory in the village of Karabanovo, Vladimir Gubernia, produced kerchiefs that won honorary prizes not only at national but at practically all international exhibitions. The Baranovs, one of the most famous manufacturers of kerchiefs, was known for its floral design printed in bright yellow, green, and blue over a red background.

At the fifteenth All-Russia Industrial and Art Fair that opened in Moscow on May 20, 1882, there were 4000 participants, factories, and trading houses. More than 2000 awards were given out, ranging from diplomas and citations to the top award—the right to put the state coat of arms on the product. Figure 11.8 shows the detail of a Cashmere-type shawl bearing, in the bottom-right corner, the woven initials of the factory owner, Nadezhda Merlina, and a double-headed eagle, Russia's state emblem, woven above the initials. The eagle signified that the manufacturer had received the highest awards and thereby won the right to show the state emblem on her goods.

The Kasli Works

One of the most remarkable prize winners was the famous Urals factory, Kasli. In 1747, merchant Ya. Korobov from Tula founded an iron-smelter and iron-making works in the south Urals, between the lakes Irtyash and Kasli. In 1752, these works passed into the hands of N. Demidov, one of the largest metallurgy magnates in the Urals. Under the Demidovs, the Kasli works produced iron and cast-iron articles (cannons, cannonballs, and weights) with the world-known trademark, "two sables." The manufacture of castings for household and architectural purposes was started by the end of the eighteenth century.

Figure 11.8 Detail of Cashmere-type woolen shawl with woven initials denoting "Nadezhda Merlina" and state emblem. Manufactory of Nadezhda Merlina, village of Scorodumovka, Lukanovsky Uuezd, Nizhni-Novgorod Gubernia, 1830s–40s. State Historical Museum, Moscow.

By the second quarter of the nineteenth century, art castings produced by the Kasli masters enjoyed great renown and popularity. The articles from the Kasli works were noted for the high mastery of their manufacture and artistic value. The high quality of cast iron produced with the use of charcoal, the finest sands used for the casting molds, and the joint creative work of the talented sculptors, molders, etchers, and masters of painting art castings all contributed to the high quality of the finished products.

An important role in the development of the Kasli art castings belongs to the sculptor Mikhail Kanayev (1820–83), a graduate of the St. Petersburg Academy of Arts. When he came to live in Kasli, he organized a school for the workmen where they were taught the art of drawing and modeling and the ways and methods of molding and etching iron articles. This instruction of workmen in modeling and drawing was continued by the young, talented graduate of the same academy, sculptor Nikolai Bakh (1853–85). The numerous vases, candlesticks, and ashtrays made from the models of Bakh have high artistic value.

The Kasli works participated in many all-Russian and international exhibitions, and its products were awarded honorary diplomas and medals at the world exhibitions in Paris, Vienna, Philadelphia, Copenhagen, and Stockholm.

The summit of the Kasli art castings is the famous Kasli iron pavilion made for the world exhibition in Paris in 1900. It was cast in 1898–99 by the best Kasli masters after the design by Russian architect Yevgeny Baumgarten. The decor of the pavilion employs the art motifs of ancient Russia, Byzantium, and the East. The Kasli iron pavilion (Figure 11.9), exhibited in the mining and metallurgy section, produced an unusually strong impression on the spectators and won the highest prizes—the Grand Prix Crystal Globe and the Big Gold medal. The pavilion is the only architectural construction from cast iron registered in the World Catalogue of Museums, a unique artifact of world value. The pavilion is now one of the most significant exhibits of the Ekaterinburg Arts Museum.

Weapons and Shipbuilding

The rise of industrialization in Russia was attended by processes that affected the quality of product and work both favorably and unfavor-

Figure 11.9 Kasli iron pavilion, 1899.
Museum of Fine Arts, Ekaterinaburg.

ably. On the one hand, quality standards and product development standards became more strict. Higher requirements were placed on production technology and technical control. A system of government quality assurance and special bodies of control emerged, introducing measures for strict responsibility for inferior quality. All these steps were instrumental in raising standards of quality.

On the other hand, an economy based mainly on serf labor did little to motivate the workers to be interested in higher quality. Quality breakthroughs in one field or another depended on the role of specific individuals in high administrative positions. A good example is the manufacture of weapons and shipbuilding in Russia.

Peter the Great

Industrial production started in Russia with the coming of rule by Peter the Great (1689–1725). He was indeed great. A man of strong personality, he had an amazing capacity for work—constantly learning new trades and sciences. He was a courageous and, at the same time, cruel person.

The young tsar quickly set out to increase Russia's military might, to expand its territory and "to cut through a window onto Europe." For these reasons, Peter the Great paid particular attention to the manufacture of arms and to building the navy.

Weapons Manufacturing

Peter the Great introduced a number of government measures of quality control in the manufacture of weapons. His decree of January 2, 1723 (Figure 11.10) says,

> *I command that the owner of the Tula factory Kornila Beloglazov be flogged and banished to hard labor in the monasteries. He the scoundrel, dared to sell to the Realm's army defective handguns and muskets.*
>
> *Foreman alderman, Frol Fuks should be flogged and banished to Azov, this will teach him otherwise than to put trademarks on faulty muskets.*
>
> *I thereby decree that the armory office be transferred from Petersburg to Tula in order to watch over good repair of muskets day and night.*
>
> *Let secretaries and scriveners keep an eye on how aldermen [foremen] put trademarks on. Should they have any doubts, let them examine the gun and check it by firing it. Let them fire from two guns during one month continuously until they break down.*
>
> *If a stoppage occurs among the troops during combat due to oversight by the secretaries and scriveners, the latter should be flogged on their naked parts without mercy. The master gets 25 whips and a fine of 10 rubles per one faulty gun. The foreman should be flogged until he loses consciousness. The elder secretary should be enlisted as a warrant officer.*
>
> *The secretary of the rank should be stripped to become a copier. The scrivener should be denied his Sunday glass of vodka for one year.*

УКАЗЪ ЕГО ВЕЛИЧЕСТВА

ИМПЕРАТОРА И САМОДЕРЖЦА ВСЕРОССИЙСКОГО

Повелеваю. хозяина Тульской оружейной фабрики Белоглаза бить кнутомъ и сослать въ монастырь на работу. понеже онъ подлецъ. дерзнулъ войску государеву продавать плохие пистолеты и фузеи. Старшего ольдермана Фому Миневу бить кнутомъ и сослать въ Азовъ. пусть он не ставитъ клейма на плохо сделанное оружие. Приказываю оружейной канцелярии изъ Питербурга переехать въ Тулу и денно и нощно блюсти исправность ружей. Пусть дьяки и подьячие смотрятъ какъ ольдерманы клеймо ставятъ. Будь сомнения возьмутъ за душу - самимъ проверять и смотреть. а два ружья каждый месяцъ стрелять пока неиспортятся и смекать, что делать надобно. Будъ заминка въ войне приключится. особливо при баталияхъ. по нерадению дьяковъ и подьячихъ бить оныхъ кнутами нещадно по оголенному месту ! Хозяина - 25 кнутовъ и пени по червонцу за каждое ружье. Старшего ольдермана - бить до безчувствия. Старшего дьякона отдать въ унтер-офицеры : дьяка отдать въ писаря : подьячего отлучить отъ воскресной чарки на одинъ годъ. Новому хозяину оружейной фабрики Демидову повелеваю срубить дьяку и подьячему избы. дабы не хуже хозяйской были . Буде хуже получиться пусть Демидовъ не обижается - повелю живота лишить.

Генваря 11 дня 1723 году

петрЪ

Figure 11.10 Peter the Great's decree of January 11, 1723. Russian State Chancery of Ancient Acts, Moscow.

I command that the new master of the gun factory Demidov build for his clerks and scriveners cottages to be in no way inferior to his own. Should the cottages be inferior, let Demidov take no offence, I'll command to deprive him of life.

Peter I

Although the decree places the entire responsibility for quality on the manufacturer (the factory's owner), government quality inspection in the form of the armory office also existed. Specially empowered persons did the inspection and stamped the products to certify good quality of the gun. Putting the mark of conformance on a faulty gun entailed severe punishment.

There existed a system of state acceptance by quality assurance representatives who checked up on the work of inspectors. There also existed reliability tests of finished products (two guns were to be fired continuously for one month or until there was a breakup).

Owners of factories were obliged to ensure decent conditions of life for the testers of guns, which positively motivated their work. At the same time the decree relies on cruel physical punishments, graded depending on the rank of those involved, to ensure high quality of finished products.

Threat-based methods such as the ones in this decree were widely used in the period of serfdom in Russia and they were one of the causes for gradual decline of craftsmanship as mass production was introduced. They may explain the existence in the Russian language of the saying that good quality can be expected from someone who works honestly, not under the pain of punishment.

Shipbuilding and the Russian Navy

The greatest ambition of Peter the Great was the building of the navy. As a young lad he went to Holland to study shipbuilding and to have firsthand experience as a shipyard worker. Back in Russia he supervised the building of ships and built up a substantial Russian navy. That navy then went through several development stages, rising and falling in extent and effectiveness.

The Russian navy fell into complete decay under Peter the Great's immediate successors, but Catherine I (1762–96) restored much of its strength. Becoming empress after a court coup, Catherine vigorously forged links with Europe and pushed across the Black Sea for an exit for Russia to the south seas. By the end of the eighteenth century, Russia's navy was behind only England and France in number of ships.

The navy lost its priority under Alexander I (1801–25). Under the state military doctrine he established, the navy was assigned an auxiliary, defensive role with the army posing as the main force. In this subordinate role, the navy started to degrade as a combat force despite the creation of the naval ministry in 1802, the appointment of a committee whose task it was to bring the navy up to date, and the taking of a number of other useful steps.

The decline was also due to the continued existence of serfdom and feudal relations in Russia's economy. The production capacity of the state-run and the few private capitalist enterprises was inadequate to provide the navy with better ships and the necessary military hardware. Russia had to import machinery, lathes, and tools and had to buy some of the finest models of military equipment and naval weapons. The army, navy, and even shipbuilding depended on recruitment of personnel under conditions that did not encourage production efficiency at government-run factories and shipyards. For example, laborers were recruited under the same status as sailors—they were on military service and like sailors had to serve for 25 years.

All these factors weakened the navy and supported the decline of its role in the armed forces. It lagged behind the navies of Europe's most important sea powers. Russia's technological and economic backwardness accounted for the fact that early in the nineteenth century, the Russian navy still had no steamships, which were taking firm positions in the navies of England and France. According to the naval historian E. I. Arens, the Russian navy was in the state of "shabbiness and decay."

Aleksei Samuilovich Greig

The Black Sea Fleet was precisely in this position when Vice Admiral Aleksei Samuilovich Greig[1] was appointed its commander in chief and commander of its ports in 1816. At the same time, Greig was military governor of the cities of Nikolaev and Sevastopol. He remained in these positions for nearly 18 years until 1833.

Greig's name is associated with a qualitatively new stage of development of the Black Sea Fleet. More than that, he is a glowing example of the great importance of an individual in leadership for quality management. A Russian admiral and *honoris causa* member of the Russian Academy of Sciences, Greig amazed his contemporaries by his wide-ranging knowledge of naval and other sciences. In addition to his interest in navigation, shipbuilding, and artillery, he was proficient in mathematics, physics, astronomy, medicine, law, economics, and chemistry. Greig's hobbies included music, drawing, teaching, botany, and history. His contemporaries described him as a person of encyclopedic knowledge who put the interests of the state first.

Right after his appointment to the Black Sea Fleet in 1816, he immediately became aware of the low quality of the ships and their short useful life. He wrote in his report to the naval minister on June 29, 1817, "Almost no ship is known to have served 15 years till this day, and after 10 years most of them, even if refitted, prove no longer seaworthy and should only be broken up." In yet another report he stresses once again: "Most of today's ships become decrepit 6 to 8 years after their launching. . . ." One of Greig's first ordinances pointed out, "Ships composing the Black Sea fleet are generally badly built . . . the subject being important, I consider it necessary to take measures and make improvements in the building of ships."

Right from the start, Greig worked to enhance the quality of shipbuilding and make the ships last longer. In the years he commanded the Black Sea Fleet, Greig carried through a set of measures that considerably improved the quality of design and longevity of ships. His efforts led to new scientific methods to improve the specification of quality standards, to mechanize some shipbuilding procedures, to set up new relations between the customer and the contractor, and to set up quality control of supplies and construction.

Improvements in Ship Design. The first major improvement Greig introduced was the new method of framing using riders, invented by R. Sepings. Without increasing costs, the new framing served to give added strength to the body and to reduce chances of fracture during launching. It also reduced the loosening of members in rough seas, thus prolonging the ship's useful life. Seping's system was introduced everywhere on the Black Sea in 1817.[2] Greig issued special directions (No. 186 of January 12, 1818, and No. 4156 of June 22, 1824) which gave a detailed description of the new method of framing.

Greig revived on the Black Sea the lining of the submarine part of vessels with sheet copper to prevent sea weeds and clams from attaching themselves and to protect the body from borers. Greig introduced iron knees, improved the design of cross pieces, established the use of cross bulkheads with diagonal props, improved caulking, introduced a new way of joining parts of ships' ribs, suggested the use of special felt lining under the outer shells, simplified the attachment of planking to the frame, introduced rounded sterns instead of the flat ones, and made other improvements. The result was stronger, more watertight and durable vessels. Whereas, the official useful life of a man-of-war was 10 years, ships built under Greig's supervision lasted 11–13 years. Refitted ships served as long as 17 years. The average useful life of ships of all classes built during Greig's time was about 14 years.

Greig directed the replacement of rock-and-sand ballast with that of pig iron. That change improved the ships' stability which also made it possible to increase the calibers of cannon. The 24-pounders on the main gun deck were replaced by 36-pounders, increasing their fire power.

Improved Quality Specifications.   Greig is also credited with the development and introduction of a number of scientific methods of calculations in designing of ships and the drafting rules guiding the drawing up of technical documents. He supervised the drafting and authorized the use (Ordinance No. 272 of November 1827) of the rules for deciding on the size of components of a ship's framing. Having studied the statistics of many vessels (there are plenty of calculations and graphs in the archives supporting this), Greig came up with a formula to calculate standard carrying capacity for vessels of all classes. This made it much easier to figure out their projected cost. This served to simplify calculations of carrying capacities and those relating to finance and management. The new method was decreed for official use by Greig in March 1828.

Seeking greater stability of ships, Greig paid attention to their masts, yards, and spread of canvas. The sizes of the latter had been selected more or less at random. Greig introduced standard rules for calculating the sizes (Instruction No. 4766 of March 22, 1824) and the thickness of ropes (No. 537 of February 4, 1826) depending on the vessel's class and dimensions. He introduced rules to calculate the thickness of anchor ropes and chains, weight of anchors, and the number of ship complements. He also introduced rules for making drawings of vessels showing tactical and technical specifications of their elements. Instruction No. 1753 of June 22, 1822, ruled that to preserve the drawings of the finest vessels, they should be duplicated on copper sheets.

Improvements in Production Processes. At Greig's request, the admiralty in Nikolaev switched to mechanical means for the first time: a steam engine was used to operate shears, presses, bending rolls, sharpening benches, lathes, and drilling machines. It built a steam-driven sawmill. Its workshops switched to burning coal instead of firewood to cut the cost of ironworks by 80 percent.

The Bogoyavlensk cloth factory started to use fulling, ginning, spinning, and other machines. The city opened a canvas factory man-ufacturing high-quality canvas for sails. In the past there was canvas of only two grades. Now the number was four, to suit vessels of different classes. Greig designed procedures for making sails: cutting, straight-ening of seams, facing of the bolt-ropes, and so on. He designed a new method of sampling hemp used in making canvas. In 1828 he de-signed and introduced procedures to raise efficiency in different workshops.

The framing components had been done manually with axes. In 1829 they began to be manufactured at the sawmill with the use of patterns.

Greig was also the first to set up special commissions to watch over the quality of shipbuilding.

Changed Relations with Contractors. During the years Greig was in charge of the Black Sea Fleet, he widely relied on the system of contracts in building ships. He used private contractors because they were more efficient than the government-run shipbuilding industry. Although one ton of a ship built by private contractors cost more (431 ruble 95.5 kopeks) than the same built by a government shipyard (308 rubles 68.75 kopeks), private contractors did the job much faster.

Greig framed a set of rules for suppliers and contractors building ships for the Black Sea Fleet. The measure helped to prevent malprac-tice. Of great use was the rule whereby contractors were selected from their bids submitted in sealed envelopes. Greig calculated that this de-vice saved the government more than 650,000 rubles between 1823 and 1825. Thanks to this bidding method, one ton of a ship built for the Black Sea cost less than one for the Baltic Sea, where the cost was 494 rubles 69 kopeks.

Admiral Mikhail Lazarev later thought that the rules designed by Greig were "useful and handy." He finally got them endorsed by the government for general use.

Supplier Quality Control. The cost of wood comprised between 60 percent and 80 percent of that of a ship or a frigate. For this reason, Greig paid special attention to the quality and storing of timber supplied for the fleet.

A big drawback in Russian shipbuilding at that time was the use of unseasoned timber, which considerably reduced a ship's useful life. Especially hard conditions prevailed in the Nikolaev Admiralty situated far from suppliers of timber. Timber came to Nikolaev from Kiev, Smolensk, and Poland. It had to be rafted down the long waterways. Greig found that Polish timber was not strong enough. He insisted that tracts of forests be appropriated in Podolia for the needs of the Black Sea Fleet. Timber of better quality grew there, and it could be rafted by shorter routes. Commissions to inspect forests and timber supplied for shipbuilding were also established.

Injunctions on the protection of Crimean forests producing timber suitable for shipbuilding came into force in 1820. Greig conducted experiments with pickling ship components to extend ships' service life.

Better Ways of Ship Conservation. Admiral Greig drafted a set of special measures to preserve ships. One of the measures was to remove part of the aft and stern cannon in time of peace to prevent possible fractures in ships. The use of pig iron ballast instead of sand and rocks decreased rot in the ship's frame and dampness in crew quarters, creating more creature comfort.

All improvements made by Admiral Greig in Russian shipbuilding serve to show an exemplary commitment to quality management on the part of a top executive. In addition to everything else, the control over the quality of shipbuilding materials reduced the time needed for building and made it less labor-consuming. In the $17\frac{1}{2}$ years Greig remained in charge, 125 men-of-war (not counting port ships) were launched in Nikolaev alone. This number is six times the number of vessels built in Nikolaev over the 23 preceding years.

Spreading the Black Sea Fleet Improvements to the Entire Russian Navy. In 1830 Admiral Greig was appointed chairman of the committee of the Main Naval Headquarters whose job was to improve the navy. The committee examined many proposals from naval specialists (M. P. Iazarev, A. I. Kazarsky, A. S. Greig, I. F. Kruzenstern, I. P. Avinov, K. P. Tornson, among others) aimed at better ways of building ships. Greig was in charge of the committee from October 24, 1830, to May 23, 1831, staying most of the time in Petersburg while remaining the commander in chief of the Black Sea navy. The committee examined 356 questions during its 53 sessions. Thanks to the committee's support, nearly all proposals were accepted and recommended for use in the Russian navy. Many of these recommendations for use in the Russian navy were improvements designed and developed under Greig at the Black Sea Fleet. The experience of that fleet received a special citation from the committee.

Summary

Many elements of a quality management system and examples of high-quality products are identifiable in early Russian history. The earliest and most important vital factor in establishing quality standards arose from the commitment of individual craftsmen. High levels of craftsmanship and a commitment to quality are demonstrated in a number of household products surviving from ancient times. These include jewelry, leather products, ironware, and wooden items. Documentation of production methods can be traced back to eleventh to twelfth century beresty (birch bark manuscripts). *The Domostroi*, first published in the late fifteenth to early sixteenth century, contained instructions for a wide variety of household management tasks. Early elements of organizing for quality arose in the eleventh to twelfth centuries when wealthy boyars started networks of artisan workshops, particularly in Novgorod. Items from these workshops demonstrate a level of workmanship on a par with the most celebrated medieval centers in Western Europe and the Middle East. Although the movement toward mass production did not yield a universal deterioration in product quality, examples of sacrificing quality for greater output can be identified. One example is the reduction in the durability of knives produced in Novgorod in the eleventh and twelfth centuries.

The design of Russian silverware captures the rounded shapes of wooden and ceramic utensils used for centuries, giving a national distinctiveness to the Russian products. Three decorative techniques—niello, filigree, and enameling—were developed to an especially high level of expertise and sophistication in Russian silver and gold products. Both niello and artistic enamel are traceable back to the time of the Kievan Rus, and filigree was well known in Russia in the tenth century. Niello reached its peak in the second half of the sixteenth century and its designs vie in finesse and elegance with the paintings of that period. Filigree reached its peak in the fifteenth and sixteenth centuries although many outstanding works were produced in the eighteenth, nineteenth, and twentieth centuries. Enameling techniques evolved through a number of stages. Russian enamel work achieved many successes: the world-renowned work of the Fabergé firm in St. Petersburg; the many products of the town of Rostov the Great, which occupies a special place in art history; and currently the factory established in Rostov in 1960 that carries on the ancient art with modern equipment and techniques.

Prizes and awards for quality were established in Russia in the nineteenth century. Russian and foreign products won awards at local fairs and exhibitions, and Russian products were exhibited abroad. These prizes encouraged continuing improvements in design and production quality and provided valuable recognition for successful firms. The highest form of recognition at the Russian exhibitions was permission to use the state coat of arms on products. One of the outstanding international successes of Russian design and workmanship was achieved by the Kasli iron pavilion, which won the grand prize at the world exhibition in Paris in 1900.

The development of weapons and the building of the Russian navy illustrate the key roles of leadership for quality played by two individuals, Tsar Peter the Great and the brilliant and dedicated naval officer, A. S. Greig. Peter the Great provided strong leadership for quality in both areas although his approach was authoritarian and often harsh. His decree of January 11, 1723, placed responsibility for quality of weapons manufacture firmly on the factory owners and their agents. Inspectors were empowered to stamp certifications of good quality on guns and state officials checked the work of the manufacturers' inspectors. Procedures for tests of samples of finished products were specified. Severe penalties for violations of required procedures were established. Quality work was also encouraged by requirements that sought to ensure decent living conditions for at least some of the workers.

After Peter the Great's early successes in building the Russian navy, periods of decay and progress alternated until Vice Admiral Aleksei Samuilovich Greig started his work with the Black Sea Fleet in 1816. Greig improved ship design; developed and improved quality specifications; improved production processes; reduced costs and improved quality by letting contracts to private builders under competitive bidding procedures; improved the quality of the most important raw material—timber, which accounted for 60 percent to 80 percent of ship costs; and improved methods for preserving ships. Later, a committee headed by Greig led to many of these improvements being adopted by the entire Russian navy.

Acknowledgment

The author thanks Dr. Yu. P. Adler for assistance in collecting materials for this chapter.

Notes

1. Aleksei Greig's father was the son of a Scot, a volunteer in the Royal Navy, who came to live in Russia where he was made a Russian naval officer.

2. R. Seping's book appeared in Russian translation about 1819. It was published by A. Pomorsky.

Bibliography

Arens, E. I. *Conspect of Russian Military Naval History*. Nikolaev. Naval Academy, 1910, p. 194.

Domostroi. "Soviet Russia." Publishing House, M., 1990, pp. 214–24.

"Improvement in Shipbuilding." *Directives made by Admiral Greig at different times*. Nikolaev, 1830, 32 pp.

Kryuchkov, U. S. *Aleksei S. Greig*. "Nauka" Publishing House, M., 1984.

"Main actions by Vice-Admiral Greig concerning the Black Sea Admiralty, navy and ports." Central State Archives of the Navy, v. 81, p.1, s. 34, 65 pp.

Melentev, Yuri. *The Old, the New, the Eternal.* Raduga Publishers, Moscow, 1984.

Yanin, Valentin L. "The Archeology of Novgorod." *Scientific American.* Feb. 1990, p. 86.

CHAPTER 12

Guilds and Cathedral Building

Michel Deleforge, Naval Officer and Engineer, retired
Member, French Movement for Quality

It has long been commonplace to sing the glory of French Gothic cathedrals. Yet their incomparable beauty hardly needs proving, and their renown is universally ensured for ages to come. Even today, these places of worship excite the curiosity, and indeed, the fascination of people from all walks of life. Why?

Because they inspire man at his deepest—at his very soul. At their root are two timeless qualities which make the world go round even today: beauty and virtue.

We use the word *quality* here in its root meaning—*way of being* (*qualitas*). And what is the way of being of cathedrals? Excellence.

- Excellence in beauty: Our pleasure and admiration respond directly to the harmonious shapes, balanced proportions, and the magical play of light.

- Excellence in virtue: Thanks to rigorous design, and impeccable workmanship of stone and glass, these structures have endured for centuries, veritable hymns to God in time.

- Beyond industrial or commercial standards of quality, beyond consumer satisfaction or optimization of output, beyond goods and services, the quality of these cathedrals is the way they elevate the soul.

But why are there cathedrals? Who knew how to build them? How were these huge projects financed? Where did the skills come from to achieve such mastery of mind over matter?

The questions as to the how and the why of these masterpieces are many, as are the answers. A large part of them lie in the history of those who built them with their own hands and know-how, and the unique way in which, as a group, these craftsmen plied their trade.

How have the guilds fared through the ages?

Origins

As it has been said, "the origins of guilds are lost in those of humanity itself" (Bernard de Castéra). The lack of formal documents expresses the very nature of guilds: they came about quite naturally, as artisans *of the same craft* spontaneously grouped together.

Companions—for so guild members called themselves (the French term comes via Old French from the Latin *cum*—with—and *panis*—bread) means people who share the same bread. "The absence of any formal document bears witness to the absence of any intellectual or doctrinal spirit behind these truly popular organizations."[1]

That guilds are old, there is no doubt: corporations of blacksmiths and dye makers (the first alchemists) flourished under the pharaohs of the Twelfth Dynasty. In eighth-century-B.C. Rome, there were closely-knit guilds of artisans whose craft *required specific training:* carpenters, smiths, potters, leather workers, and goldsmiths.

When the Roman Empire collapsed a thousand years later, the guilds saw that the best way to ensure their survival was to associate themselves with the monasteries. "Manual labor was held in high regard by St. Benoît [the father of the Western monastic orders] and this contributed to a fruitful dialogue between the *spirituality* of those who literally opened up Europe with their own hands, and the *wisdom* the artisans acquired through constant thinking about their craft. The various types of craftsmen's guilds, far from being the result of a planned ideology subsequently applied to the real world, or of any *a priori* approach, form an architecture of tradition, which takes root in the very soil of our history: the people."[2]

Legends

"Undertaking the study of an institution means first of all drawing the line between legend and historical fact—between, on the one hand, the varied and sundry accounts born of the popular imagination, and on the other, reliable data whence one can deduce, if not absolute certainties, at least reasonable hypotheses."[3]

- Three legends: King Solomon, Maître Jacques, Father Soubise
- Three companion rites:
  1. The Children of Solomon: "Companions of the duty of freedom" or "Companions of Hiram"
  2. The Children of Maître Jacques: "The Companions of Duty"
  3. The Children of Father Soubise: "The Companions of Duty"

These three legends and the rites that stemmed from them probably originated from a single source, that was carried down through oral tradition.

According to the Bible, during the construction of the Temple of Jerusalem, King Solomon laid down an elaborate code of artisanship.

A famous master artisan, Hiram, subsequently left his name to an ordered system of architecture.

Maître Jacques and Father Soubise, after learning new techniques in the East, traveled all over France; their influence was wide and lasting, and resulted in an intermingling of technical know-how and esoteric knowledge. Each trade—stonecutting, carpentry, glassmaking, cathedral-building—interpreted in its own way this mix of ancient precepts and myth.

Historical Evidence—The Cathedrals

It seems unlikely that guilds came into being long before the birth of Christ, because there is no written mention of them, aside from pure myth, until the sixteenth century. And yet, Martin Saint Léon writes,

> *We think that the first guilds were formed from the beginning of the 12th century to the end of the 13th, during the apogee*

of Gothic art. Artisans gravitated to cities where cathedrals were being built. It was a time, after six hundred years of Carolingian barbarism, of renewed hope for feudal society as a whole. Serfhood, tyranny and strife were finally coming to an end; worship became a joyous thanksgiving to God."[4]

Whatever the case may be, this intense activity produced the *ogival* cathedrals, monuments of incomparable grace and majesty. The oldest Gothic cathedral is at Noyon, and was built in 1190. The Chartres cathedral was begun in 1145; Notre Dame in 1160.

The new churches were the fruit of a wide collaboration of *maîtres ès oeuvres*. Architects such as Robert de Luzarches, Hugues Libeuge, and Ervin de Steimbach were nearly all laymen. Does this mean that there was no link between them, other than that of a common trade and a common religion? On the contrary: numerous associations and guilds existed, from which current-day guilds sprang.

Biblical legends captured peoples' imaginations; the Crusades brought back fabulous stories about the Holy Lands; all Christendom saw itself in Jerusalem as in a mirror. As for cathedral builders, they were naturally compared to the Hebrews, raising a temple to the Eternal. The popular imagination transposed these stories for its own use, and one or two centuries later, the myth had become a reality.

The first companions, Hiram, Maître Jacques, and Soubise, originators of the aforementioned rites, certainly did exist, even if they existed under different names; they were quite simply the *maîtres ès oeuvres*, cathedral builders of the twelfth and thirteenth centuries. Popular myth dated them back to Solomon—understandably, given the contemporary obsession for biblical times! The legends are many; the only clear historical truths are the cathedrals themselves.

The *Franc-Mestiers* of Builders—A Guild Apart

The only attested manuscripts on guilds dating from before 1500 is an English text written in 1390. It seems to be the oldest equivalent of a charter codifying guilds of builders. In poem form, the Regius text gives a good idea of the rules governing the trades involved in cathedral building. It is hardly surprising that this document comes from England: the Age of Faith left many cathedrals there, too (London, Canterbury, Salisbury, York . . .).

The Regius text has a religious character; it was clearly written by a cleric, who must have been initiated into the traditions of the maîtres d'oeuvre. As he says himself (art. 4.2.), "As masons, we are all Catholics, and Catholics only." The word Catholic (from the Greek *katholikon*) means *universal*—in other words, that of believers in a monotheistic religion as opposed to pagans. This is important, for the Regius text seems to have had

> *several goals, among which are:*
>
> - *to unify professions which, while scattered over a wide area, were nevertheless steeped in the Gallo-Roman tradition, and to codify their activity;*
>
> - *to exert influence on the artisans' religious leanings, with the aim of instilling the Catholic code of morality;*
>
> - *to lay down a code of relations between master artisans and the feudal lords, and between them and their own apprentices; and also to define proper workmanship;*
>
> - *to ensure the prestigious reputation of stonecutters and carpenters especially, through a mix of knowledge, legend, and esoteric tradition; to belong to the caste of apprentice masons was to assume a quasi-aristocratic stature. (René Dez, French translator of the Regius text)*

This text is a fundamental one in the history of quality in Europe, and even though the word *quality* itself is not used a single time, it is an absolutely central issue. The following extracts will enable the reader to judge for himself.

Article I

Master mason, here is thy rule: be always honest in thine actions, and rigorous, so that no one should find cause for disappointment in them.

Article XII

Another's work shalt not condemn, be he or not a brother of thy lodge. Give it rather frank and honest praise, and to preserve thine honor, strive to better thine own talent.

Second Point

Spare no effort: good work is its own reward and brings its author happiness.

Eleventh Point

Show him the proper way to proceed, be charitable in thine advice, and, by God, if he understandeth thee, deliver unto him the secrets of thine art.

There follows, as a kind of justification for such a dearth of professional ethics, a bold foray into legend. The author lays pragmatism aside, and launches into a fantastic series of mythical constructs, from Euclid, Master of Geometry, to the builders of the Tower of Babel, to God, glorified as the Master Builder himself.

It is hard to get a clear picture of the intellectual evolution of our builder ancestors of the twelfth through sixteenth centuries. What were the exact relationships between their thinking, idealized dreams, religious fervor, and their work and daily lives?

At any rate, their *chefs d'oeuvre*, testimony to a highly developed conception of quality, doubtless gave them access to a kind of nirvana ("the possession of truth"), to beauty, good—in short, to a tradition of excellence. And God was not far!

Let us now return to more detailed considerations on guilds.

Rites and Customs of the *Tour de France*

An elaborate system of rites of admission was adopted, which has survived to this day. Apprentices were generally recruited from the poorest segments of society, and this may explain in part the peculiarly symbolic nature of these rites. After all, ideas and concepts would have had little meaning for uneducated young recruits; but it sufficed to give these concepts color, to transform them into evocative images, for them to capture the young recruits' imaginations. All guilds' rites are at bottom simply an elaborate sign language in which the basic ideas, obvious to the initiated, are translated into a colorful shorthand made of a few key images, objects, and words.

Although each of the three main guilds (Solomon, Maître Jacques, and Father Soubise) and each trade (carpenters, stonecutters, locksmiths, and so on) has its own customs and rites, a common system of symbols overarches them all.

1. During his ceremony of adoption, the *aspirant* (apprentice) receives the coat of arms, with the colors of his trade, but also emblazoned with two symbols: the Labyrinth and the Tower of Babel. The age-old signs of a spiritual path, they stand for the apprentice's spiritual faith as well as an homage to religious tradition.

The Labyrinth symbolizes the long and tortuous path of the apprentice, full of obstacles and dead ends, which the apprentice must surmount in order to reach the spiritual maturity of the initiate. This path is at once spiritual and material, for the apprentice must also commit himself to knowledge, understanding, and serving the general good.

Once raw materials and the laws of nature have been mastered through diligent participation in the building of a temple or cathedral, the apprentice is said to have reached the center of the labyrinth.

Originally Greek, the labyrinth symbol was also known to megalithic civilizations (in Dublin especially); it can be found drawn on the floors of several cathedrals. The Chartres cathedral labyrinth is 18 meters wide; in its center are inscribed the names of the principal architects.

Figure 12.1 The labyrinth drawn on the floor
of the Chartres cathedral. Photo by Mr. R. Fièvet.

The Tower of Babel, contrary to the Labyrinth (symbol of modesty and hardship), is not only an image of success but also one of vanity; the Tower's fall is proof that perfection is an unattainable goal. It is also a caution to beware that the best things can become the worst, and that inordinate love for one's trade can become idolatry.

2. When the companion is initiated, he is given new colors, and new symbols too, in the following order: the pyramid, the temple, the tomb, and the cathedral. These symbols are all borrowed from religious architecture; as a parallel to striving for excellence and the supreme good in one's trade, this source of metaphor is understandably a privileged one. Also, the building *métiers,* among the oldest trades, naturally furnished symbols for all the other trades.

The pyramid's geometrical purity, and its solitary, desert situation, symbolize hardship surmounted and resistance to the ravages of time. Relic of a great civilization, it also stands for initiation to knowledge and manual skill, both of these receiving equal prestige.

The temple is the home of God in the land of men, and refers also to the Hebrews and the knowledge they gained from their time in Egypt. The slave of the pyramids has progressed to the status of a volunteer in a labor to God, whose work is an act of worship.

The tomb, last stage in human life, reminds us that even a man's last home is the handiwork of man, and that to accomplish a work of quality, we must be open to our essential nature.

Lastly, the cathedral, as the sixth stage in this initiation, symbolizes the value of sacrifice. In biblical tradition, the number six stands for perfection; it was on the sixth day that man was created!

The main elements of guild initiation symbolism are reflected in the Tour de France tradition, itself a living parallel to the abstract progress of the initiate's knowledge and skill.

3. Until recent times the Tour de France was the only way an apprentice artisan could acquire experience and skill: techniques and methods varied widely from one region to another. The tour was a highly elaborate system, with networks of artisans in the main towns and cities. Every apprentice on tour had a kind of passport, a letter of recommendation, a guarantee to contacts of the apprentice's reliability, honesty, and skill.

Upon arriving in a new town, the apprentice traditionally reported to a "mother"; this term referred at once to the inn to which he owed a roof and food, and usually to the innkeeper herself. He was then taken to the "first artisan" (*Premier en ville*) of the town, a kind of dean of the town's artisans. There, once his credentials had been seen, material arrangements were made for his stay in the town, and he was formally recognized in a secret ceremony, called the "Admission to the Chamber." These proceedings were crucial as they guaranteed the apprentice credit on room and board during the time necessary to establish himself with one of the town's master artisans.

During this time, the apprentice remained under the protection of a *rouleur*, or guide, who helped him in many ways; the *rouleur* was his formal link with the people of the town, and served as arbitrator between the new artisan and his prospective employer.

It is clear that in spite of the numerous aspects of these ceremonies which seem to us rather picturesque (insignia, symbols, and so on), the guild system was a highly efficient, pragmatically oriented one. It ensured that traveling artisans would receive material stability, quality training, and free medical care; in other words, what we would call today personalized follow-up.

Organization and Rules—Duty, Chef d'Oeuvre, Full Companion

I build for men, I build with men, and, what is less visible as I do this, I build men. (Emile Le Normand, Locksmith of the Order of Duty)

The guild system also based itself in a whole conception of the human personality, in which the general good was inseparable from each individual's spiritual quest, and both were held to be equally as important as technical skill. The code of ethics that resulted was based on the notion of duty.

- The apprentice was held to acquire perseverance and a thirst for perfection;
- The companion, discipline and mastery;
- The full companion, maturity, consciousness, and benevolence toward juniors.

Of course, guilds would not have had such a wide impact, nor have survived so long, if their organization and technical teachings had not been equal to their spiritual pretensions. This teaching had the merit of being immediately applicable, and dispensed in a nontheoretical way. An ideal in itself, this teaching was embodied in the notion of the artist's touch, *l'art du trait.* The exact opposite of a geometrically perfect but impersonal product, l'art du trait is the accomplishment of a practiced eye and a love for the materials the artisan worked in.

The Charter of the Guild of Duty (*Les compagnons du Devoir*) stipulated,

> *Diligence in one's trade leads a companion to consciousness of his humanity, and from this, to proper conduct in society. The* chef d'oeuvre *[an artisan's masterpiece] represents the artisan's elite status, in his trade, but also as he is bound to uphold a civic order.*

Duty to one's trade meant perfecting not only one's skill, but one's conduct as part of a larger order. As Jean Bernard said, "even today, duty is the most important part of our tradition."

In terms of ideology, the concept of duty sets the guild tradition apart from other traditions in labor. But while evidently setting itself apart from the larger masses of unskilled workers, the guilds' elite culture remained of a profoundly conciliatory nature. Duty also meant duty to social harmony, and the self-disciplined guilds aimed to promote the general good in its widest sense; the guilds upheld not a popular wisdom, but an ideal of wisdom more universal in character. The religious part of the guilds' tradition, whether expressed or implied, effectively deterred its members from undue pecuniary—or political—ambitions. In short, the guilds aimed to serve, and their honor lay in the quality of their workmanship.

The chef d'oeuvre, as a carriage-builder companion defines it, is exactly that—a masterpiece. Its necessary qualities: "perfect design and execution; beauty, harmony of form and of the various components in themselves."

This "exceptionally perfect piece of work" was also a necessary accomplishment for every guild member. Two chefs d'oeuvre were required of the future companion: one to graduate from the novice state, or *aspirant,* to that of *companion,* and the other to receive *full companion* status.

The chef d'oeuvre gave the candidate the opportunity to demonstrate not only the technical skills acquired, but also to express to the utmost his personality and maturity—his progress on the spiritual path.

This tradition is deeply anchored in French tradition and remains alive to this day. Every year there is a "First Artisan of France" competition, and many other "Best Worker" contests as well. At Troyes, artisan culture has its own museum, called the Maison de l'outil et de la pensée ouvrière (The House of Workers' Tools and Thoughts). And one must not forget that the Statue of Liberty's torch was restored by artisans from the Companions of Duty—after a call for tender to which 24 companies submitted.

The full companion has reached full maturity in his work, but in his social behavior, too.

> *The true goal of our work is to render service to our fellow men. This service is of several kinds:*
>
> - *serving a client (with all that implies concerning ethics, relationships of subservience and conflict of interests);*
> - *teaching young apprentices;*
> - *loyalty to oneself, and constant personal striving.*
>
> *The artisan's work is like a focal point, a magnet to which men are drawn, and in which a civilization that honors fine workmanship recognizes its own social ideal.*[5]

Conclusion

Work is a culture. From the earliest times, this culture is embodied in the unity of hand and mind, of skill and thought. It has produced countless masterpieces. From the Egyptian pyramids, Greek temples, the Temple of Jerusalem, and the Roman roads, to the medieval Renaissance and the cathedral builders, down to the present day, artisans have sought to transmit not only skill, but wisdom, and an authentic culture of work; not an ideology in the sense that implies conflict, but a contribution to mankind.

This contribution cannot be found in books, for it consists of acts, and concrete accomplishments meant for practical use. Those who turned their work into an art form and a way of life, founded a school for mankind.

The guilds' culture is that of experience, and the overarching ideal of all artisans is the *quality of the work* and *the quality of the man.*

To know how to do, know how to be. Each is the expression and the culmination of the other, and an accomplished culture is the harmony of the two.

Notes

1. *Le Compagnonnage,* Bernard de Castéra (Que Sais-je, #1203).

2. Ibid.

3. *Le Compagnonnage,* E. Martin de St. Léon (Librairie du Compagnon-nage, 1983).

4. Ibid.

5. Le Compagnonnage, Bernard de Castéra.

Bibliography

Ambelain, R., *Jésus ou le Mortel secret des Templiers* (Laffont, 1970).

Association ouvrière des Compagnons du Devoir, Brochure from the Maison de l'Outil et de la pensée ouvrière at Troyes.

Fremantle, A., *The Age of Faith* (Time-Life, 1972).

The Regius manuscript of 1390, anon.

CHAPTER 13

How the French Arms Industry Mastered Quality

A Historical Review

Michel Dunaud
Ancien Chargé de Mission Qualité Délégation Générale
pour l'Armement,
Ministère de la Défense France

Introduction

Today the notions of *quality, quality control, quality assurance,* and so on, seem natural to anyone involved in industry. Yet in the last 10 or 20 years we have seen a growing number of publicity campaigns focalizing around the word *quality.* This, occurring at a time when the media industry exaggerates everything, could lead the public to believe that quality is a brand new concept!

It is interesting for an engineer, just as it is for the "man in the street," to look back over time and see how the components that make up the concept *quality* have appeared gradually down through the centuries.

For this the weapons industry provides an unbroken chain of events, as it has existed from the dawn of time. All individuals and countries know that their very existence depends on the superiority of their weapons over those of their rivals. Thus, they make every effort to have a constant lead in this domain over their adversaries.

Since prehistoric times there has been a continuous effort to perfect weapons. As we moved from the Stone Age to the Bronze Age into the Iron Age, weapons remained mainly handmade and personal. The individual's control over his own workmanship ensured the level of quality as the weapons produced were still simple. With the passage of time, people began to settle down in one place, form tribes, create cities, and finally constitute nations. This evolution brought with it the creation of armies that had to be armed with weapons that could be used collectively—throwing devices, arms for sieges, combat ships, and so on. Man was constantly improving his construction techniques and building ever more effective weapons.

At the beginning of the nineteenth century, the industrial age began. Machine tools evolved, and more and more sophisticated technologies finally came into being. Since 1940, techniques have evolved even more rapidly; weapons have become highly complex, requiring more and more know-how, involving larger numbers of individuals in more and more diverse industries. It is not possible to give a complete picture of this evolution in such a short discussion. We shall endeavor, however, to outline the principal lines of evolution in the following order.

- First attempts
- Final product control
- The choice of suppliers
- Standards and rationalization
- Rationalizing conception and management methods
- Setting up a management structure

Naturally we shall deal only with the subject "how men worked to improve quality over time" and not "how quality was improved," as that would require an in-depth study of technological evolution and, consequently, a detailed history of the arms industry, which is not within the scope of this document.

First Attempts

The art of building and using weapons and weapons systems required knowledge and experience in various crafts, and from the start it was entrusted to men who were competent but who did not occupy a high place in society. Members of aristocracy were not inclined to do the work of a blacksmith, a carpenter, or a ropemaker. Their specific level of ethics, however, allowed them to carry out certain unpleasant tasks, such as imposing taxes or paying ransoms, just as long as one could "maintain his rank"; maintaining rank was paramount.

The weapons craftsmen of the time employed techniques which were not always well developed. Early cannons were made from a metal blade which was rolled lengthwise by hammer around a mandrel, with the two edges welded together parallel to the cannon. During construction the iron had to be heated several times in the forge. Defects due mainly to the heterogeneity of the metal around the welded zone could cause the cannon to explode during a trial firing, called *proof firing*, or eventually even when in use.

Quenching was all the more difficult and of uncertain results because the scientific basis of heat treatment technology was totally unknown. It was believed that the metal was modified by the intrinsic properties of the water in the area of manufacture. A given river, such as the Furan at Saint Etienne, was considered to be the main element in the quality of that which was produced in the region.

Given the resources available, professionalism required a long and difficult apprenticeship. The quality and finish of a product were the fruit of experience and a practiced eye.

In the course of time the specialist gradually improved on the methods he employed. For example the "Damas forge" produced better-quality but more-costly cannons. The tube was produced by heating and reheating a metal blade made of several basic "ribbons" of braided metal, which were fused together with a hammer and rolled in a spiral. Given the higher cost of this product, it was necessary to find a compromise between performance and cost. It is easy to understand that manufacturers at that time tried to increase their earnings by supplying their customers with products that were near the breaking point.

In the fifteenth century there were two famous French arms manufacturers, Jean Bureau (died 1463) who was grand artillery master under Charles VII, and his brother Gaspard (died 1469). They worked in all the areas of their specialty, from perfecting the manufacture of cannons, reducing their weight, arranging gun carriages, and redistributing calibers, to creating a vertical control system and introducing the bomb. The brothers even organized "technical conferences" which were attended by all the principal engineering and industrial specialists of the arms industry. Such conferences today have become a major industry in their own right—they are today held throughout the world.

The need to establish a technical verification of the weaponry being manufactured, or on those furnished to the state establishments, appeared quite early on in the history of arms manufacturing. We find the first really clear mention of the existence of a military quality control over the master blacksmiths in a "Decree to the State Council by the King," dated 1648, but this would appear to have originated even earlier, under Louis XI (1423–83).

Final Product Control and the Supervision of the Manufacturing Process

The famous Colbert (1619–83), who was Finance Minister (1661), Controller General (1665), Director of Buildings, Arts, and Manufacturing (1664), and Secretary of the King's House and to the Navy, was highly interested in the Navy. Because France, unlike England, had land frontiers to defend, it obviously gave priority to its land forces. Colbert however realized the importance of trade and the seas when it came to ensuring the supremacy of a country. King Louis XIV (1638–1715) was determined to affirm his power and glory, and he used diplomacy and the armies to accomplish his ambition. The Army was where he concentrated all his energy but he nevertheless supported Colbert's efforts to build up a Navy worthy of him.

In order to be effective on the seas, it is necessary to take quality into consideration. Colbert was worried about the quality of the production, as is shown in the multiple surveys he ordered concerning defects, "the good and bad qualities of the naval ships." Thus it is possible to read in one of his reports that the *Superbe* was "beautiful and seaworthy except for two stress points which resulted in its keel becoming arched" or that the *Triomphant* was made of "poor quality wood and was tilted forward."

The notion of overseeing construction was first introduced in the Navy by Colbert's eldest son, the Marquis de Seignelay (1651–90). This was not a coincidence as Seignelay was merely continuing his father's work. The contemporary historian Alain Guillerm wrote on the subject of these two men that "From 1660 to 1690 they almost made Louis XIV's kingdom the foremost maritime power in the world."

Louis XIV's decree concerning the Navy and the naval arsenals, dated Versailles, 15 April 1689, detailed the attributions and obligations for the supervision of the manufacturing process of the General Commissioner for Naval artillery and the provincial Naval Commissioners responsible for the receipt of wood for construction. Figure 13.1 shows an extract from this decree, which hopefully will lighten the overall austerity of this text and provide the reader with an insight into the kind of supervision in question.

The final control was effectively carried out for the purpose of verifying that the product corresponded to that which had been ordered. This is evident from Article 8 of the decree shown in Figure 13.1 concerning the responsibilities of the General Commissioner for Artillery.

The General Commissioner's role was not limited to that of a simple verification at the end of the manufacturing process. His role was more global. As Article 7 in Figure 13.1 shows, he supervised the whole production process, providing assistance rather than merely providing a mandatory point of control.

On 25 March 1765 Louis XV signed a decree that completed that of his predecessor. From then on the engineers of the ports of Brest, Toulon, and Rochefort were sent to the other ports where, working for the arsenal in question, they supervised the activity of the port.

This trend toward the supervision of the manufacturing process applied also to weapons used by the Army. In 1765, Gribeauval, who shall be mentioned later in the context of the army reform, appointed to each factory an artillery officer whose job it was to supervise the manufacture of war material from the very start of the manufacturing process. The officer did not depend on the arsenal because he reported directly to the Director General of Forges.

Choosing Suppliers

The major reference in this area is a famous letter that Vauban (1633–1707), fortifications commissioner, addressed in 1685 to his minister, Mr. Louvois. This eight-page letter concerning public markets underlined the importance of the choice of suppliers in order to obtain a quality construction. As a military architect, Vauban insisted particularly on the fact that cheapness should not be the sole selection criteria, as such a selection process in the long run ended up by being more expensive.

The General Naval Artillery Commissioner

Article 4

The cannons having been cast, he shall always be present when the mould is opened, and shall examine the pieces to see that they have been correctly cast and should they show any defects which the Master Caster could hide by pouring metal into them, he shall mark them by having one of the handles broken. . . .

Article 6

He shall take care that the non-defective pieces be completed properly; and when they have been weighed before him by the storehouse officers, he shall have the weight of each engraved upon it, and shall have them carried to their proper places and arranged according to caliber.

Article 7

He shall visit the forges in his department which mould iron cannons and bombs. He shall verify if the metal being used is clean, of good quality and has been correctly purged, and whether the specified proportions are followed; he shall notify the Foundry Master of any defects he has noticed in order that he may correct them. . . .

Article 8

He shall visit the factories that make arms, and verify that the cannons are of the correct weight and proportions, whether they are made of good iron, well-heated and bored, and whether all the pieces and shafts are in good condition . . . and when they arrive at the arsenal, he shall inspect them and carry out the necessary tests as exactly as possible.

Concerning the Visit and Conservation of Forests and Woods

Article 3

His Majesty wishes that all the naval commissioners in the provinces visit the forests located in their departments with a Master Carpenter, in order to mark the trees which are appropriate for the construction and refitting of his Majesty's ships. . . .

Article 4

As soon as the merchants in charge of providing wood have been through a forest, the Commissioner in which the forest is located shall go there with one of the Master Carpenters of the Port, to verify the wood suitable for the navy, so that it may be separated out, in order to prevent the merchant from cheating on this material in any way, whilst pretending to work for the King supplying it instead to individuals.

Figure 13.1 Excerpts from Louis XIV's decree concerning the navy and the naval arsenals, dated 15 April 1689, Versailles.

There still remains a number of buildings of previous years which are not yet terminated, and which shall never be, if we are to believe the builders. All this is due, Monseigneur, to the confusion caused by the frequent reductions in price which are attributed in your construction contracts. It is a fact that all the broken contracts, agreements not kept, and renewal of adjudications only attract the people who know nothing about the business, rogues and ignoramuses as contractors, while those who know what they are doing do not even attempt to sign such contracts. I say that in addition they increase the price and delay the construction of the buildings which is thereby much worse. . . .[1]

The last sentence of this text already mentions the three parameters that should be taken into account to make a quality product.

- Delay
- Cost
- Performance

The end of Vauban's letter is clear: "This should suffice, Monseigneur, for you to see the inconveniences of this way of doing business; stop now, and in the name of God reestablish the notion of 'good faith'; pay the correct price for a construction and do not deny an honest salary to an entrepreneur who is doing his work correctly. It will always in the long run be the cheapest deal you could make."

The Army was interested not only in having dependable suppliers, but also in the raw materials it bought from them, as can be seen from Article 3 of Louis XIV's decree shown in Figure 13.1, which specifies the task of the Naval Commissioners in charge of receiving the wood for naval construction.

Standardization and Rationalization

In 1765, the Navy and the Army were reorganized. Some of the measures taken during this period had as objective the creation of a continuous supervision of the manufacturing process. It is interesting to underline the introduction of two important aspects, that of the introduction of a methodology, and the desire to address in a rational manner the manufacturing process globally.

The Army and the Navy were under the responsibility of the same person, Minister of War Choiseul (1719–85), who was known as a reformist. Some of the regulations enacted were intended to set up the ongoing supervision of the manufacturing process.

Under Louis XV (1710–74) France was increasingly confronted with threats from other nations. Austria was becoming increasingly powerful, England was becoming an ever more ambitious economic and colonial power, and it was at that time that Prussia became a military power. All these factors meant that the King was often at war.

The Seven Years' War (1756–63) between England and France was to act on the King as an alarm signal. While military successes and failures on the continent averaged out, there was much at stake on the seas. Taking advantage of the conflicts raging on the continent, England began to overrun France's colonies. Faced with its enemy's naval superiority, France had to accept defeat. With the signing of the Treaty of Paris of 1763, which marked the end of the Seven Years' War, France had to cede Canada, the Indies, Senegal, and some of the Antilles islands.

France had thought it could conquer faraway lands without the need for a sufficiently powerful navy to keep them. All his life, Louis XV was against the creation of a powerful navy. However, following the Seven Years' War, and under the influence of Minister Choiseul, on 25 March 1765, he decreed the renovation of his vessels. This document contained three important points.

- It proposed a construction plan.
- It identified the number of seamen necessary.
- It organized a corps of construction engineers.

This was the end for the master carpenters who worked in an empirical personal manner. "From now on, shipbuilding, at least for naval vessels, with 74, 80 or 110 cannons, was rationalized so that any part could be used on a vessel, no matter in which arsenal it was built—Brest, Rochefort, Toulon."[2] The improvement was rapid and enabled the French navy to win the battles led by Suffren in the Indies, and De Grasse during the American War of Independence.

Sea power was crucial for France, but given its long borders, which were under constant menace (Paris is over 200 km from the north-eastern border), a strong army was also a top priority. Statistics show that during the eighteenth century, up until the Revolution, sieges outnumbered face-to-face encounters. Investment and the siege had become typical military operations which determined the outcome of a conflict. A war was not envisageable without the use of technically sophisticated matériel. Consequently there was need for people capable of designing, constructing, and using such matériel. It should also be noted that this was the Age of Enlightenment. Anyone who was considered cultivated attempted to make use of the sciences and technological innovations.

In spite of the fact that the notion of *model* appeared reasonably early in weapon manufacture, up to the eighteenth century, craftsmen worked in an anarchic fashion, with each weapons maker following his own inspiration and specific customer requirements despite many attempts at standardization. The French Army had to content itself for a long time with what it found, in France or abroad.

Jean-Baptiste Wacquette de Gribeauval (1715–89) first introduced the concept of interchangeability once other concepts, such as weapon type and official (réglementaire) model demanding a long experience in use, had been assimilated.

Gribeauval was an engineering genius; his innovations in artillery manufacturing, known as the "Gribeauval system," made possible the series of successful military campaigns in Europe during the Revolution and Empire periods. He was the first to institute two distinct types of artillery: light-mobile artillery, and heavy artillery. In general, he sought to lighten all existing weapons, including the mechanisms and machines used to transport them—what we would today call logistics. Gribeauval's improvements touched upon all aspects of weaponry; for example, wooden axles were replaced by iron ones, which were stronger and lighter.

The French artillery was the first to feel the need for the interchangeability of parts coming from different origins. From 1767 onward, under Gribeauval's urging, the matériel was completely specified in the smallest detail. Not only were the nominal dimensions specified but also the tolerance limits, the conditions of reception and even the instruments to be used for operational verifications. The basis of manufacture was also published for all to follow.

> *Thanks to Gribeauval, conditions in construction improved to the point where one could be sure that a nut from Metz or Douai would fit a corresponding bolt produced in Valence. The norm behind this new conformity was the standard "King's foot," of fixed length. This became the standard unit of measure for any manufacturing process which required a precise mathematical measure. It was used by experienced workmen under the supervision of officers who were well trained in the subject. (le Chevalier de Passac's biography of Gribeauval, early nineteenth century)*

Gribeauval can be considered as being the father of the methodology and measurement capabilities that were used in the metal industry. With him began a new era which brought with it the rational definition of matériel and the control and technical supervision by competent technically minded officers. Manufacturers found themselves being required to work to a new set of rules.

As for obstacles encountered and surmounted, cannon axles, and axles of arms vehicles in general (ammunition wagons, and so on), are a case in point. Having decided that they were to be made of iron, the problem was to ensure a source of high-quality raw materials in order to avoid fragile products.

> *We must be very vigilant, upon delivery, for we have had dismaying surprises with Mr. Dayange's iron which, while having been vaunted as "tested and ready for use," turned out to be full of impurities in many places. At other times, we have had an excellent iron from the same source. His work is decidedly lacking in constancy. It is imperative to have dependable axles, as any accident can render a weapon useless. Is not a weapon either totally useful or totally useless? Mr. Martiz may have secured a trustworthy forge in the Franche-Comté, with better iron and better smiths as well.[3]*

Gribeauval's test for axles was to hang a given weight on them, which would bend them to a given degree, beyond which the axle would be deemed too weak. But since the axles all had to be straightened out afterwards, tests were done one to a batch of twenty or thirty. An official decree took this into account "In the event of a failed test, the King shall confiscate ten axles." Tests were to be held "publicly, on the buyer's premises."

During the Revolution, efforts were stepped up to rationalize weapons manufacture. Wars confronted the advances of different countries' weapons systems, and brought about several improvements in design and production methods.

On 30 June 1794 (12 Messidor an II in the revolutionary calender), Claude Antoine Prieur Duvernois (1763–1827), better known as "Prieur de la Côte d'Or," passed a law in the Comité de Salut Public to establish a "precision workshop" which subsequently became the Central Arms Laboratory (LCA). This later became the Central Technical Laboratory for Arms (ETCA). Its purpose was to manufacture those instruments necessary to effect the many and varied checks on weapons and weapons components, "engines of war and missiles as well as firearms." On the 1st of August 1794 a temporary location was assigned to the precision workshop until a permanent location could be found. On the 23rd of November 1797 the workshop was permanently established in St. Thomas of Aquinas' Convent, the former Dominican convent of the Faubourg St. Germain.

Rationalization of Design and Management Methods

Manufacturing techniques evolved rather slowly until 1900. At that period weapons made use of a limited number of basic techniques and processes. They were frequently produced in a single factory containing everything necessary for their manufacture—the design teams, prototype workshops, manufacturing plant, and so on. Consequently the technical innovations were relatively basic and it was easy to protect them from industrial spying. The hydraulic recoil brake on the 1897 model 75 mm cannon remained unknown to foreign powers for several years, giving the French Army a notable advantage on the ground.

After 1935 and especially after 1945, the development of a weapons system brought increasingly into play specialized and different disciplines such as electronics, pyrotechnics, ballistics, and nuclear science. This led to a dispersion, in geographical terms, of the production centers. Former practices no longer sufficed, for three reasons:

- The ever more dangerous consequences of a weapon failure
- The sophistication of materials
- The importance and complexity of arms programs

The increasing seriousness of the consequences of a weapon failure made preventive actions more and more necessary and economically viable, even in the case of preventing a single failure.

The sophistication of the matériel made inaccuracy in any stage of the manufacturing process fatal for the weapon, especially as the most heavily stressed components (those called upon to deliver the power) became even more stressed to the limit than before.

Program complexity was an incentive to rationally organize the various stages of production so as to devote more attention to the critical phases, and less to the secondary ones. This in turn implied a highly sensitive organizational network, with explicit procedures and methods, and efficient communication.

As a consequence, the quality life cycle of a new product now depends on how all the stages of production are run, from initial conception through to manufacture, testing, and use. It ends only when the product is taken out of use. Planners must follow to the letter certain management principles, among which are

- The contractual, precise formulation of the requirements statement
- Judicious use of available tools to enable planning, cost control, and manufacturing efficiency of a product
- Organization of the process through the development of quality, reliability, and maintainability plans which ensure that the product development schedule is met

To obtain quality weapons systems today necessitates the application of elaborate methods of program management, themselves the result of the work of specialized teams. In 1982, a new structure was created within the General Delegation on Arms (DGA—Delegation Générale pour l'Armement) in order to ensure the coherence of the methods employed by the different weapons system development teams. This structure is made up of

- A Council for Quality Management (CGQ) presided over by the Director of the DGA,
- A Quality Assurance Mission (MAQ), and
- A group of quality control specialists.

In 1987, a Logistics Support and Maintenance Commission (SLM—Support Logistique et Maintenance) was created, with the specific purpose of applying Integrated Logistics Support methods (ILS). This group in 1990 was made responsible for the development and implementation of the French CALS (Computer-Aided Acquisition and Logistic Support, recently renamed Continuous Acquisition and Lifecycle Support) program. There are CALS/SLI correspondents in each branch of the DGA and of the Armed Forces. The objective is to rationalize the products employed, their associated data, and the organization necessary for their development. Current advances in the technologies behind the concepts employed permit such a rationalization to take place.

The Gradual Emergence of a Quality Management Structure

"Discovering a weakness" led to the dedication of resources to remedy the weakness. It very quickly became necessary to structure the resources dedicated to this task. Three major stages can be distinguished in this evolution.

- Initially, each army had its own procedures and methods of manufacture control.
- From 1964 these different procedures and methods were unified.
- Finally, the resources were all centralized in order to ensure a total quality control.

We will briefly discuss these three phases.

Each Force Looks After Its Own Resources

In the Navy, different agents supervised the selection of wood and the conduct of the manufacturing process. In 1874 a specific supervision unit was created. It included the Forestry Service, the on-site wood reception Service, and the Naval Surveillance Service which supervised the work carried out by private manufacturers. However, the

Navy Artillery maintained its own inspection service. This service remained separate until 1940. The centralized service for the supervision of naval construction in 1961 had 10 distinct branches. The Army's surveillance service never needed to be brought together as it had already been unified by Gribeauval's reforms under the title of the Forge Service. The service was replaced in 1939 by the Industrial Production Service. In 1961, it had five regional subsidiaries.

The Air Force, which hasn't been mentioned earlier due to its historically recent creation, closely regimented the production of its material from the start. The infancy of aeronautics was plagued with a great many accidents, and engineers were driven to constantly improve the methods for testing and quality control.

From 1910, two organizations concurrently provided technical supervision services for the air force, the Chalais-Meudon Laboratory (for research and testing) and the Vincennes Military Aviation Division (for artillery). After the First World War, these two organizations were known as the Technical Aeronautics Service and the Fabrication Service. The fabrication service was disbanded after the 1939/45 war.

After the Liberation, the six control divisions established in 1928 (when the Air Ministry was created), were reduced to four regional aeronautical centers.

At the start of the 1960s, each Technical Directorate of the French armed forces had its own control structure.

- Fabrication surveillance service for the Army (DEFA)
- Fabrication and Construction Surveillance Service for naval shipbuilding (DCCAN)
- The regional aeronautical centers for the Air Force (DTIA)

The Unification of Fabrication Control Structures

The Service for Weapons Industry Surveillance (SIAR—Service de la Surveillance Industrielle de l'Armement) merged these structures together in 1965. The project was under study from 1961, ever since the creation of a single interarmy organization now known as the DGA. The SIAR is the interarmy direction in the area of surveillance. This organization allowed the simplification and unification of the approach of the armed forces toward its suppliers. There were some complaints about the lack of harmony in the methods employed and the negative effect on productivity. Effectively up to that point each army had its specific work methods due to the fact that they came into being at different periods and they held on to their own traditional ways of doing things: "The accelerated pace of evolution towards quality control in every domain justified the search for more homogeneous methods that a new organization could more easily put into place. . . ."[4]

The SIAR has five regional directorates and a central headquarters. From its creation in 1964, it was given the double mission of supervising the execution of contracts made with industry, and promoting improvements in product quality.

In order to ensure that materials conform to their specifications and quality standards, the SIAR exercises on-site supervisory controls during the course of manufacture and over finished products. It may also confer official powers to inspection units, in which case it just verifies the results of the controls.

The promotion of quality is fundamental for the SIAR as it is the guarantor of the quality of the finished product. In the event of a mishap, the SIAR is just as liable as the supplier. Engineer-General Maurice de Lorris, the first Director of the SIAR, defined the role of its representative as follows. "The factory inspectors are conscious of the importance of their role, and their directives are binding. Factory directors are to use all the means at their disposal to implement the directives, and are held to maintain the highest standards of workmanship, in order to ensure that the end result is of the highest possible quality."[5]

As the inheritor of a long tradition of supervision of manufacturing processes for the army, the SIAR marked a decisive step in quality control. Its centralized nature enables it to carry a larger action, and to have a stronger influence with the industrial firms.

Creation of a Centralized Service in Order to Master Quality

We have previously seen that a quality assurance mission and a CALS France office had been set up in this respect.

Conclusion: The Way to Quality Assurance

Finally, the main points that this look back into history has brought to light can be summarized as follows.

- Rivalry between nations has obliged the weapons industry to unceasing improvement.

- The weapons industry has played a major role, not only in technological advancement, but also in the control of quality, especially since the eighteenth century.

- Quality has been taken into consideration in weapons manufacture in a significant manner down through the centuries. As in other areas in which products are intended for a market, albeit in simpler contexts than that of weaponry, the general trend has been from an empirical approach to a more rationalized one. This trend can be summarized in four phases.

    1. *The age of trial and error,* in which experience and luck played an important part. The manufacturer was the master, and buyers had to get by with whatever merchandise was delivered.

    Product design relied heavily on intuition. The design of the product was finalized by on-the-spot redesigns as faults were discovered. Blueprints were often vague and incomplete.

    In the same way, manufacturing procedures were rarely formalized, and tended to be transmitted orally and in an isolated fashion, varying greatly from region to region.

    Quality control was confined to verification that the goods delivered corresponded to their definition, supplemented by occasional operational tests. Goods were verified before leaving the factory and were either accepted, adjusted to satisfy a new control, or simply rejected, which entailed the complete loss of the material and effort used in the rejected product.

    2. *The age of inspection* (or of manufacturing supervision) saw a new and concerted attempt to correct faults through an analysis of manufacturing procedures (this prior to the finished product but after product definition).

    But action was still taken on a random basis, and it took time for a single method to take hold in the weapons industry. Certain more- or less-rigorous procedures were used. These procedures were particularily implemented for the management of modifications which is a prerequisite for interchangeability. Sizeable areas of the industry however still functioned in a pseudoanarchic way: the know-how of experience, the plodding gait of improvisation. The control was still a control of the policing type.

3. *The age of prevention*—detecting anomalies before they occur, and organizing the manufacturing process with the clear aim of preventing them. Product conception, design, and even marketing ended up coming under scrutiny and were recognized as integral stages in the production process.

Specific research and follow-up controls were put into place in order to ensure that products are designed, manufactured, and used correctly.

Criteria such as intense competition and ever-higher stakes have widely replaced state surveillance. Controls exist, but industry is now given the benefit of the doubt.

4. *The age of managing for quality.* At this point in time the objective is not simply to certify or verify quality. The objective now includes organizing industry in ways that will build quality into the product in the first place, at every phase of progression, from concept through usage. The question is no longer to certify *a posteriori* but to ensure it *ab initio*.

The reasons behind this evolution from quality control to quality assurance have been summarized in this chapter. One cannot overemphasize the importance of national and international competition, which as they intensified have made the weapons industry one in which quality control is an absolute necessity.

Notes

1. Letter from Vauban to Louvois, dated 1 September 1685.

2. Alain Guillerme, *La pierre et le vent (The Stone and the Wind)*, page 181.

3. Rapport de Gribeauval au Ministre, 1765—cité par *Pierre Nardin Gribeauval, lieutenant général des armées du roi (1715–1789)*, page 136.

4. Maurice de Lorris, Revue Armement, October 1973, "Le SIAR aura bientôt 10 ans."

5. Ibid.

CHAPTER 14

The History of Managing for Quality in the United Kingdom

David Hutchins, Chairman
David Hutchins International, Ltd.

Introduction

When researching the history of managing for quality in the United Kingdom, it soon becomes apparent that there is no single thread that connects the present with the past. Rather, there are multiple parallel threads, some of which are relatively recent developments, while others have their roots in antiquity. For this reason, each of these threads is considered separately in this chapter. At the end an attempt is made to summarize all of this and to bring all of the strands together into a common whole.

The chapter begins with a look at the roots of quality in medieval Britain before going on to the Industrial Revolution as a way of setting the scene for the more recent developments. The text then progresses through the history of measurements, and the development of industrial standards and consumer protection before considering the "people aspects of quality." Finally, the more modern developments relating to quality in the present day are considered before giving a summary of all of these elements together.

Background

The Norman Conquest of Britain in 1066, was the last successful invasion of these islands. Prior to that time, it is almost certain that any history related to managing for quality was introduced through the influence of the many Nordic, Saxon, Roman, Gaelic, and other invaders who had controlled all or part of England, Scotland, Ireland, and Wales from time to time. The further development of many of the features introduced by these peoples ceased or even disappeared with the retreat of these invaders. Others remained but were developed no further. Such was the case with road-building methods introduced by the ancient Romans. Today, there is much evidence of their industrious past. Many of the roads used in England today follow the course of roads built in those times. The Fosse Way which crosses the heartland of English England, Watling Street which marked the border of the lands living under English law and those under Danish law, and the Icknield Way are just three examples. Even today, archaeologists argue as to how the Romans built their roads so straight and with such precision. The most popular theory is that they "benchmarked" the highest points within sight and then lit three fires along the path of the road under construction. As each section of road was completed, a further fire was lit in the distance in perfect alignment with the previous three and so on along the route. Until the arrival of motorways in the 1950s these Roman roads could always be distinguished from almost all others by their straightness.

An interesting quality-related technique of medieval times (also to be found in northern France) was the method used in the construction of timber-framed houses. These beautiful buildings which are so much a part of the character of rural Britain can be found in great numbers along the borders between England and Wales and in many of the older towns throughout the country. Visitors seeking to discover for themselves this fascinating part of British heritage obtain much satisfaction from doing the "Black and White" tour in Herefordshire in the heart of Elgar country. The name is due to the custom of painting the wooden frames of these buildings black and the plaster infill white. Such was the strength and endurance of the oak structure of these buildings that many which survive to this day date back to the eleventh and twelfth centuries.

These early examples were usually fashioned from the product of a single oak tree. The master woodsman would determine, while the tree was still whole, which of its branches should form the various structural elements. The tree would then be dismembered by the woodsman's gang. Following this, they would construct the frame of the building in the forest. On completion of the basic structure, the rectangular holes between the elements of structure were filled with a mixture of lime, earth coloring, mutton fat, and cow dung. Due to the nature of the method of construction, the buildings could if necessary be disassembled. In fact, the Butcher Row Cottage in Ledbury, a town north of Hereford, is known to have been in two, possibly three, different locations at various times in its history. The first of these moves was for an interesting reason—quality of life—as set out in a letter from the town clerk.

Figure 14.1 The Butcher Row House. This sixteenth-century house was demolished in about 1830, re-erected, and then moved in 1979 to its present site. Photo by David Hutchins.

Ledbury November 2nd 1820

Sir,

I am directed, by the Trustees for improving the Town of Ledbury, to inform you, that they have resolved to apply the funds in their hands towards taking down the Butcher Row, in this Town. . . .

The advantage of removing this obstruction will be very great, not only in widening the street, which is the principal thoroughfare, but, also, in getting rid of the disgusting custom of slaughtering animals in the public street, when the gutters are, literally, running with blood; and the noisome smell from so many privies and slaughtering rooms, in the center of the town, is also, very disgusting and unwholesome.

The Trustees, therefore, earnestly solicit your aid upon this occasion. . . .

I am, Sir, your most obedient humble Servant,

Thomas Bibbs, Clerk to the Trustees

From around the fourteenth century, these buildings were prefabricated in the woodman's yard or *framing ground* from the produce of a number of different trees selected for their appropriate characteristics. Westminster Hall roof, for instance, was prefabricated at Farnham in Surrey and the enormous timbers were then taken by cart and barge to Westminster. Because of this the various pieces had to be identified in some way, and modified Roman numerals were nearly always used, scribed or chiseled on the upper face of the timber.

The buildings from around the fourteenth century can usually be distinguished from their earlier counterparts by the use of visibly straighter beams, more carved shapes, and ornamentation. On close inspection, the marks to ensure correct assembly can still be seen. It is still disputed as to whether the term *half timber* which is often used to describe these buildings refers to the fact that they are half wood and half plaster, or whether it refers to the practice of halving trees in the earlier times.

Quality, the Roots of a Civilized Society

While it is possible to identify specific quality-related examples such as the work of the woodsmen in the foregoing, it is impossible to be precise as to the origins of managing for quality in the United Kingdom as we know it today. As with so many things of historical interest, precise origins are lost in the mists of time. However, the earliest documented quality-related material available relates to statutes of the thirteenth and fourteenth centuries. H. E. Drew writes,

> *In Britain the reign of Edward III marked the great dawn of the fine arts and of commerce and was herald to an entire reconstitution of our trading and manufacturing fraternities. By charter the Guilds, Crafts and Mistery's (a* mystery *is a company) came to be called Livery Companies, which in the wording of the acts including legislation for the control of quality. Wardens of the Crafts were appointed to ensure ". . . that it may be seen that the work be good and right and to reform what defects they shall find therein, and thereupon inflict due punishment upon the offenders. . . ." Typically, the ordinances of the Grocers Company enjoin their wardens "to go and assayen weight, powders, confections, plasters, oyntments, and all other thynges belonging to the same crafte."[I]*

The authority invested in the guilds was a powerful ally of quality, many of the regulations being aimed at the maintenance of value and conformance to standards. The wardens of the Goldsmiths Company were empowered "utterly to condemn and seize and break all defective work and to force good work to be stamped with the Company's mark." In addition to the owners' and sayers' marks, products of gold and silver had to be stamped with the leopard's head. Work stamped with the Hall mark was said to "bear the touch" from the testing of gold with a polished stone. If this, the "touchstone" of quality, was satisfactory, the result was said to be "as true as touch."

The Hallmarking Concept

The concept of hallmarking as it is known today was introduced by act of Parliament in the year 1300 in the reign of Edward I. To this day, the British hallmark is still an important form of consumer protection and is accepted as a symbol of integrity all over the world.

Under the hallmarking concept, the measure of purity for gold articles is the carat. A gold carat is not a weight; it is a proportion equal to $\frac{1}{24}$. For example, 22 carat gold means 22 portions of gold to 2 portions of base metal.

When hallmarking began, gold articles were required to be of 19 carat quality. This standard has fluctuated over the years until today there are four standard levels of gold content: 22 carat, 18 carat, 14 carat, and 9 carat. In the case of silverware there are two standards: Britannia, which is 95.8 percent silver; and Sterling, which is 92.5 percent silver.

For gold and silver articles a complete hallmark consists of four symbols or marks. These show

- The maker of the product
- The standard
- The assay office
- The date of the assay

Figure 14.2 illustrates hallmarks. They are reproduced by kind permission of the Assay Office, Newall Street, Birmingham, United Kingdom.

The Dawn of Innovation and Modern Product Quality

The Industrial Revolution was cradled in Britain, beginning around 1750. There followed a period of such explosive growth that the future of every man, woman and child could be said to have been forged in the glowing furnaces and steelworks that lit the night skies in the heartlands of Britain. The roots of modern managing for quality were also forged at that time; with rare exceptions there was a lack of agreed standards as we know them today. The standards that did exist were mainly concerned with the sale of goods and not so much with the means for production. This is relevant, because, despite many punitive laws, medieval traders frequently attempted to defraud their customers with poor-quality products, and with deliberately giving false measures.

To this day, historians do not agree on the precise circumstances that brought about the Industrial Revolution, and why it originated in Britain rather than elsewhere. Some of these reasons have a direct bearing on the development of modern quality, others are of more passing interest. Among the suspected factors is the political climate which tended to encourage private enterprise and competition among

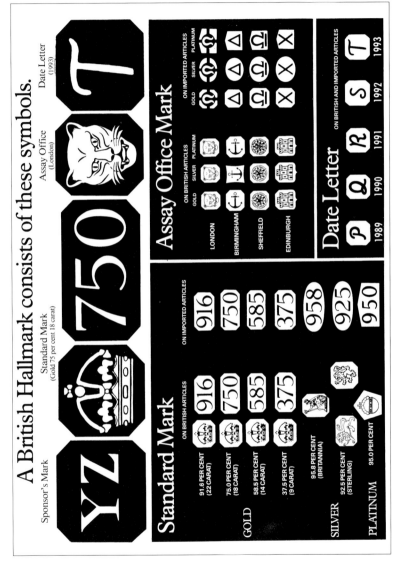

Figure 14.2 Examples of the British Hallmark. Permission of the Assay Office, Birmingham.

manufacturers and merchants. In such a climate markets could expand beyond the narrow range seen in some countries where the chief sources of affluence consisted of the nobility, the bureaucracy, and the clergy. In turn, expanding markets stimulated entrepreneurship, which could also avail itself of patent protection.

In *Dynasty of Ironfounders* by Arthur Raisterick,[2] there is a charming account of the experimental work done by the famous innovator Abraham Darby and one of his apprentices to find a method for successfully casting pots. The pot was the three-legged cauldron, the typical bellied pot with the largest diameter in the middle. One problem was to mold such a shape in a way that would enable the pattern for the pot to be freed from the mold without the mold's total destruction. It was also necessary to use a dry molding material which would not generate steam or other gases on contact with the hot metal, as the steam would either disrupt the mold or spoil the casting. Apparently, rivalry in the industry was so severe that even the keyhole was blocked during the experiments to stop spying. (Who says that benchmarking is a 1980s invention?)

Patent number 380 (to run for 14 years) was issued to Darby on 18 April 1707, for

> *A new way of casting iron-bellied pots and other iron-bellied ware in sand only, without loam or clay, by which iron pots, and other ware may be cast fine and with more ease and expedition, and may be afforded cheaper than they can be by the way commonly used, and in regard to their cheapness may be of great advantage to the poor of this our kingdom, who for the most part use such ware, and in all probability will prevent the merchants of England going to foreign markets for such ware, from whence great quantities are imported, and likewise may in time supply foreign markets with that manufacture of our own dominions.*

This extract indicates that even some 50 years before the Industrial Revolution commenced, the entrepreneurial spirit was strong. From a quality point of view, it is striking that there was such keen awareness of the importance of balance of trade, the need to produce low-cost products to satisfy a large market of poor people, and the intensity of the efforts at process improvement. It also serves as an illustration of the spirit which seemed to infect all of the great pioneers of

Figure 14.3 A typical "bellied" pot. Photo by David Hutchins.

the Industrial Revolution when it came. These include Isambard Kingdom Brunel, the great railway and shipbuilding engineer; Josiah Wedgwood, who developed most of the principles of fine bone china creation and decoration which still form the basis of the industry even to this day; Newcomen and Watt, developers of the steam engine; McAdam with his roads; Hargreaves' Spinning Jenny; and many many more. The entrepreneurial drive of these pioneers has few parallels in history.

The dynamic growth during the British Industrial Revolution was so intense that in one single century, Great Britain dominated virtually every market in the world. Its naval might was awe-inspiring and its dominions stretched to all corners of the Earth.

Beyond any debatable reasons for the rise of the Industrial Revolution are some specific events that are known to have set into motion a train of consequences. Two of the most important are the great plague in 1625 and the fire of London in 1666. Both of these traumatic events were recognized to have their origins rooted in the filth and overcrowding which prevailed at that time. Consequently, there followed serious attempts to improve sanitation and to reduce the density of population in the center of cities. These changes together with the fact that Britain experienced a long period without any major wars resulted in a significant reduction in both infant and adult mortality which in turn resulted in a sustained increase in population and an ever increasing demand for food, shelter, clothing, and fuel. Improved efficiency of farming methods and related government legislation contributed to a drift of population from the farms to the towns. The increasing wealth of merchants resulting from the slave/sugar trade between West Africa, the West Indies, and the United Kingdom also provided the means by which industrialization could be financed.

These factors interacted with each other. The rapidly growing population and the drift to the towns simultaneously created both demand for products and a supply of available labor, albeit unskilled. The buoyancy of trading on the high seas demanded an ever larger supply of ships and these of course were built with wooden hulls. This effectively put strains on the supply of wood, which was also heavily used both as a fuel and for building houses. This in turn resulted in a shift to the use of coal which at that time could be found in abundance on the surface.

Steam Engines and Quality

Such was the situation around 1750. For the next 50 or so years, the demands on both wood and coal increased significantly. Wood became very scarce and expensive, leading to the need for alternative materials. Surface coal largely disappeared, resulting in the need for both open cast and ever deeper shaft mining. In turn this required development of ventilation systems and of means for pumping water out of mines. The development of such pumps, driven by steam engines, became a classic example of quality improvement driven by competition.

According to Singer[3] the chief basis for comparing steam engine performance was the *duty*. This was a unit of measure equal to one million foot-pounds of work per bushel (82 pounds) of coal. To encourage rivalry and so to promote efficiency, the mine owners began to

publish reports on steam engine performance. Over the years the following data were reported for reciprocating steam engines.

Date	Builder	Duty	Percentage thermal efficiency
1718	Newcomen	4.3	0.5
1767	Smeaton	7.4	0.8
1774	Smeaton	12.5	1.4
1775	Watt	24.0	2.7
1792	Watt	39.0	4.5
1816	Woolf compound engine	68	7.5
1828	Improved Cornish engine	104	12.0
1834	Improved Cornish engine	149	17.0
1878	Corliss compound engine	150	17.2
1906	Triple-expansion engine	203	23.0

The availability of the steam engine stimulated entrepreneurs to
extend its use to a wide variety of manufacturing processes: iron
works, forges, bellows in blast furnaces, rolling mills, potteries, breweries, flour mills, spinning mills, and so on. In addition, application
was extended to non-manufacturing industries.

One major extension was to create the steamboat for water transport. Rowing was hard work and sail was useless if there was no wind
or if the wind was blowing in the wrong direction. However, when
the first steamboat appeared on the river Thames many people did not
like it. "It is strange to hear and see it hissing and roaring, foaming
and spouting like an angry whale."

Another major extension of use of steam engines was for land
transport. Richard Trevithick's 1801 invention consisted of two ideas:
mounting a steam engine onto a carriage so as to use its power to pro-
pel that and other attached carriages, and propulsion of the carriages
along a track made of parallel lines. The initial trains were mainly used
for the transport of coal out of the mines and then to the factories. In
1814 George Stephenson built a train that could carry no fewer than
eight trucks containing 30 tons of coal along the level and even up
slight slopes at a speed of about nine miles an hour. The Liverpool
and Manchester railway, which opened in 1830, ran passenger trains
as well as goods trains. In 1831, over 256,000 people traveled by train
in six months, although the total length of the railways was only 69

miles. While technologically impressive, these early railways left much to be desired in terms of quality and comfort. There was much jolting and shaking. But in 1837, the diarist Charles Greville, when traveling from Birmingham to Liverpool in four and a half hours, found nothing disagreeable about it except the "whiffs of stinking air."

In a leaflet, *Rules for Railway Travelling,* some amusing advice is given: "If a second-class carriage, as sometimes happens, has no door, passengers should take care not to put out their legs. . . . Beware of yielding to the sudden impulse to spring from the carriage to recover your hat which has blown off, or to a parcel which has been dropped."

Almost all of the railway lines that have ever been built in the United Kingdom were built during the period 1833 to 1862. Most of these were either built or planned by George Stephenson, his son, or Isambard Kingdom Brunel.

Beyond their impact on the British economy, these steam engines affected the quality of life of the workers. Savery's "fire engine" was called the "miner's friend" because it drained the pit without the hard work of pumping by hand and baling with buckets. During winter, when water mills were frozen, the steam engines enabled factories to continue in operation and to provide employment to impoverished workers.

Iron Production and Quality

In the early days of the Industrial Revolution, the scale of the production of iron could justly be described as domestic. In the period immediately prior to the Industrial Revolution production even went down due to restrictions on the cutting down of trees for iron-making. In those days charcoal was used as fuel in the furnaces and had been since the start of the Iron Age.

At the start of the Industrial Revolution, demand for iron increased rapidly, and in those early days, the locations of the iron works were generally in the thick woodlands of the Welsh borders, the south Yorkshire and Derbyshire valleys, and the Furness peninsula in Cumbria. The need in all such cases was an abundant supply of charcoal within reasonable reach of reserves of iron ore and water power. All of these newly expanding areas had an ancient tradition of ironworking. Many of the bloomery sites of the sixteenth century became small furnace units in the seventeenth century. These in turn gave rise to a number of related industries such as lock and nail makers, smithies, and makers of small ironware.

The discovery as to how to use coke as an alternative to charcoal came in 1707 when Abraham Darby of Coalbrookdale in the West Midlands developed the means to produce iron using coke, a derivative of coal. The principal problem of using coal itself was the high sulphur content which would render any iron produced by this means totally useless. The method of producing coke effectively removed this and other undesirable chemicals from the fuel. However, the method could not be used until Darby's grandson of the same name took up the method in 1760 due to difficulties in the coking process.

Apart from the growing needs of industry, much of the production of the small but expanding ironworks was for domestic applications including pots and kettles, hearths and fireplaces, and a host of other uses. These products were often extremely ornate, and the exquisite designs produced by these early craftsmen and the perfection of the finished product would be a lesson for many today. Much of the work produced in this period can still be seen in the museums of Coalbrookdale in the West Midlands of England. Abraham Darby who built the Coalbrookdale ironworks was one of the great innovators and experimenters of that period. It is also claimed that as a result of Darby's development of the means to produce iron using coke, the Industrial Revolution actually started in Coalbrookdale. There can be no doubt that this innovation made possible the other great innovations that followed. For that we owe him a great deal.

Abraham Darby's discovery of the means to produce iron using coke had to wait until his grandson, also Abraham Darby, took the idea up again around 1760. The reason was the difficulty of producing a strong enough blast of air in the furnaces using engines driven by water power. However, the steam engines developed by James Watt were able to generate the necessary power. These and still other changes resulted in Britain being able to produce sufficient iron for its own needs and to provide a surplus for export. Previously it had been necessary to import pig iron from as far afield as the Urals. Between 1788 and 1830 the total output of pig iron, the raw material of the iron manufacturers, was multiplied tenfold. Later, when Henry Bessemer discovered a means to produce cheap steel using the converter process, the basic building blocks of the Industrial Revolution were complete. Bessemer's discovery made possible the production of steel

Figure 14.4 The Iron Bridge Across the Severn River. It was built between 1777 and 1781. All the components were cast at Abraham Darby's Coalbrookedale Ironworks. Photo by David Hutchins.

from relatively poor-quality iron ore provided that there was no phosphorous present. Such ore could only be found in Sweden, Spain, and Cumbria in the United Kingdom. Ironically, it was another Englishman, S. Gilchrist Thomas, a few years later, with the improbable profession of being a London police court clerk, who found a method of making steel from phosphoric iron ore. Paradoxically, this enabled Germany to then begin developing its huge rival industry from the phosphoric ores of Lorraine. In the late nineteenth century, assisted by this development, Germany replaced the United Kingdom as the worlds' largest producer of steel.

The Evolution of Units of Measure

Origins of the British Imperial System

The imperial system of weights and measures has some curious anomalies. These resulted from the series of invasions which were referred to at the beginning of this chapter. Each successive wave of invaders introduced their own units of measure, and crudely related them to the indigenous system.

The cumulative result of those invasions is an assortment of units of measure, many derived from ancient origins and bearing names from multiple languages. For example, the yard was the distance from the tip of the nose to the finger of Edgar, an Anglo-Saxon King of about 1000 years ago. An inch was the knuckle of the thumb. The cubit was the distance from the elbow to the tip of the middle finger, which apparently equalled six palms, a palm being the width of four fingers. The cubit has its roots in biblical times and is referred to in Egyptian hieroglyphics as the forearm. The foot was not a person's foot as widely believed, but four palms. Later, this was standardized as 36 barley corns taken from the middle of the ear. The mile at present used in the United Kingdom originated in the sixteenth century and is based on the old Roman mille or 1000 paces, two steps being a pace.

The development of currency has its roots in Mediterranean countries and from the time of King Offa of Mercia (757–796). The silver penny was called the *easterling* to denote its origins. Later this was abbreviated to *sterling* which has become the name of the entire British currency system. The ordinances of 1266, known as the Assize of Bread and Ale, stated that a penny sterling ought to weigh 32 wheat grains, that the ounce weighed 20 pennies and the "Tower" pound 12 ounces or 20 shillings sterling.

The proliferation of names is also evident from the many market measures used in the sixteenth century (B. W. Petley).[4] Ales and wines were measured in hogsheads, kilderkins, pipes, puncheons, tuns, and barrels. Barrels were also used to measure beer, butter, fish, gunpowder, and tar. Cartloads were the measure of faggots, hay, lime, and straw, and so on and on.

An obvious anomaly of the imperial system is the lack of any common basis for multiples and submultiples of the fundamental units. For example, the fundamental unit of length is the yard. Multiples include the chain (22 yards) and the mile (1780 yards, or 80 chains). Submultiples include the foot ($\frac{1}{3}$ yard) and the inch ($\frac{1}{36}$ yard). The unrelated sequence of multiples and submultiples, and the fact that the names of the units bear no relation to their magnitude or to their relation with other units, makes the imperial system cumbersome to use in conjunction with modern computing aids.

A second anomaly is that identical names do not necessarily mean identical quantities. For example, a stone of hay or straw may weigh 14 pounds in Ross shire, 23 pounds in Inverness, or 28 pounds in Caithness and Sutherlandshire. Similarly, the weight of a boll of grain varies according to district from 140 pounds to 240, 264, 280, or 320 pounds. In Berwick market, corn and wheat are sold in some instances per boll of six bushels while in Dunbar and Haddington a boll of wheat is four bushels.

A further anomaly of the imperial system is that the definitions of the units of measure do not necessarily result in precision and reproducibility of measurement. For example, an acre was the amount of land one yoke of oxen could plough in one day. There appears to be no record as to the length of a standard day, whether it was from sunrise to sunset or at what time in the year. It is not surprising therefore that all of these dimensions were given wide interpretation.

Alfred the Great, who reigned in England in the ninth century A.D., is accredited with the use of tallow candles to measure time at night. These burned at the rate of about three inches per hour, modern candles burn rather more slowly. Time as measured by burning candles was sometimes written into contracts, for example as part of the time allowed for servants to spend on off-duty socializing. King David of Scotland (1124–54 A.D.) defined a land rod as the combined length of the feet of 18 average-sized men and a building rod the feet of 20 men.

The above anomalies (and others) created problems for manufacturers, merchants, and consumers. These problems intensified as commerce expanded across district and national boundaries. By the dawn of the Industrial Revolution, units of measure and standards were in total disarray. Mistakes could be made with almost any unit of measure, and some quite spectacular catastrophes may have occurred. In fact, the literature abounds with accounts of such calamities. One of the most well-known of these stories concerned the manufacture of cannon balls for the navy. The cannon balls were made by one supplier and the cannons by another. When the two came together, it was discovered to the horror of the sailors who were about to use them, that the balls were too large for the bore of the cannons. The reason for the problem was the lack of any traceability in the units of measure. The two manufacturers were working to different expressions of the same base units.

The Moves Toward Standardization

The need for standardization had been recognized as far back as Saxon times. In 1340 a king's office, the clerk of the market, was appointed to each town to see that all weights and measures in trade use were "answerable" to the standards.

A parliamentary select committee was set up in Britain at the beginning of the nineteenth century in order to sort out the differences among the various standard measures. In its report of 1 July 1814 the committee, having examined the pendulum method of defining the length of the yard, reported that a pendulum having a period of one second in London would have a length of 39.13047 inches. Despite the considerable amount of careful work that went into the preparation of this report, there was still some doubt as to the exact length of the seconds pendulum and also of the relation between the yard and the meter.

Soon after this, a method of fixing and defining units of measure became a serious issue when the definitive parliamentary standard yard, the pound, and other standards were effectively destroyed during the Houses of Parliament fire on 16 October 1836. After several years of argument, the yard was reconstituted from the other standards that were available from around the country rather than using the pendulum method.

The length standard in the United Kingdom was a bar known as the imperial standard yard. Comparisons between its length and that of meter length standards during the twentieth century showed that it was shrinking in length relative to them at a rate of 1 ten-thousandth of an inch per century. The yard is now defined as 0.9144 meter, which makes the inch equal to exactly 25.4 mm.

In France the system of units of measure had been, if anything, in even greater disarray. Then, following the French Revolution (1789), France investigated its system and prepared a report (1790) offering a remedy "for the serious lack of uniformity in weights and measures." The French invited Britain to cooperate, but owing partly to the political relationship with France and also to the fact that Britain had just made some attempts to standardize its own system the offer was declined.

The resulting French system (now known as the metric system) undertook to choose units of measure based on naturally occurring quantities. In addition it featured a coherent decimal system and uniform terminology for defining multiples and submultiples of basic units of measure.

In the metric system, the basic unit of measure for distance is the meter. The French attempted to define the meter as one ten-millionth of the distance along a meridian of longitude from the equator to the Earth's pole. Unfortunately, the French were unable to measure this distance accurately and therefore the standard meter was defined as the distance between two marks on a designated metal bar. However, during the twentieth century, the standard was redefined in terms of a number of wavelengths of a particular radiation of light.

The Move Toward Metrication

The merits of the metric system stimulated efforts to adopt it in Britain, but these efforts faced cultural resistance. (It is reported that following the creation of the metric system in France, a proposal for this to be adopted in the United Kingdom was defeated by a majority of one in the British Parliament.)

The movement toward Britain's adoption of metric weights and measures began in 1864. In that year Parliament legalized the use of metric units in contracts. From that time onward, Britain has been bilingual in weights and measures, imperial and metric units appearing side-by-side in everyday contexts.

In 1871 a bill for the compulsory adoption of the metric system was defeated by five votes in the British Parliament. Following this, in 1873 the British Association for Advancement of Science selected the gram and centimeter as basic units for scientific and physical purposes. The second was adopted as the unit of time, and so developed the centimeter-gram-second system, (known as the cgs system) establishing a metric technical system of units for scientists and physicists.

The next "milestone" was a recommendation by the Hodgson committee of the Board of Trade in 1950 recommending that the imperial system of units should be replaced eventually by the metric system. However, nothing of real consequence happened for a further 15 years. In the meantime, in 1962, the International Organization for Standardization (ISO) and the International Electrotechnical Commission (IEC) endorsed and adopted the modern form of the metric system referred to as *systeme international de unites* or SI units, in its abbreviated form.

In May 1965 the British Board of Trade issued a policy statement which made it clear that the government was determined to implement the adoption of the metric system in its form as SI units. In 1966 a joint standing committee on "metrication" was formed to "encourage, assist and review the progressive adoption within British Industry of the Metric System of Weights and Measures."

Prior to the introduction of the metric system in the United Kingdom in 1968 and its subsequent replacement of the imperial system in schools, it was estimated that the increased complexity involved in calculations, plus the demands on the memory to hold all the appropriate multipliers in the head, meant that a child brought up on the imperial system would be effectively one year behind an equivalent French child at the age of 10 or 11 in terms of subject matter covered. Of course, advocates for the retention of the imperial system maintained that the arithmetical convolutions required to use the imperial system were "good for the brain."

The simplicity of the conversion 1 inch = 25.4 mm owes much to the necessity to change mechanical lathes from metric to imperial screw threads by a simple interchange of gear wheels. Even with the convenience of this factor, there are still many problems associated with screw cutting lathes when designed to imperial standards. The reason for this is that although these lathes are usually capable of producing the more commonly used metric threads as well, the reverse operation, that is the production of fine inch pitch threads on a machine with a metric lead screw is more difficult. This is because 1 inch being equal to 25.4 mm exactly means that the high prime number of 127 (5×25.4) must be used. This in turn makes the necessity of inserting a 127-toothed wheel in the gear train in order to obtain an accurate conversion from one system to the other. Such a gear is large and occupies much space when it is fitted, as it usually is either in the change wheel assembly or in the threading box. Where accuracy is not considered important however, it is customary to use a 63-tooth gear in place of the 127-tooth and accept that the inch pitch threads will have a slightly inaccurate pitch.

The Growth of Industrial Standards

Prior to the year 1900 there had been no coordinated attempts to speak of to establish any form of a national standards organization. However, following the success by John Wolfe Barry to reduce the number of different sizes of tram rails from over 150 to just 72, the advantages of variety reduction and standardization became apparent. Consequently, in 1901 an Engineering Standards Committee was set up by the Institution of Civil Engineers and other professional bodies. This later became the British Engineering Standards Association. A royal charter was granted in 1929 and a supplemental charter in 1931 when the present name, British Standards Institution (BSI), was adopted. In its publication PD 4845; 1977 it says,

> *The British Standards Institution is an independent body and its objectives are set out in the Royal Charter as follows:*
>
> *(a) to co-ordinate the efforts of producers and users for the improvement, standardization and simplification of engineering and industrial materials so as to simplify production and distribution, and to eliminate the national waste of time and material involved in the production of unnecessary variety of patterns and sizes of articles for one and the same purpose.*
>
> *(b) to set up standards of quality and dimensions, and prepare and promote the general adoption of British standard specifications and schedules in connection therewith and from time to time to revise, alter and amend such*

specifications and schedules as experience and circumstances may require.

(c) to register, in the name of the Institution, marks of all descriptions, and to prove and affix or license the affixing of such marks or other proof, letter, name, description or device.

(d) to take such action as may appear desirable or necessary to protect the objects or interests of the Institution.

Subject to the ultimate sanction of the subscribing members, the executive board, which brings together a broad range of national interests, is responsible for overall BSI policy. Under the board are six divisional councils and the quality assurance council. Some 80 standards committees are responsible to the divisional councils for authorizing the initiation of standards projects, deciding the broad program, and priorities for work in their fields.

Standards are prepared by some 1000 active technical committees, which report to the standards committees and are required by the bylaws to represent the main interests concerned in the work referred to them. Under the Quality Assurance Council, responsible for BSI's certification activities, a similarly representative management committee structure exists.

In recent years, the BSI has pursued a policy of continually bringing its standards into line with international standards as agreed with the International Standards Organization. In the Department of Trade publication "Quality Count" issued October 1986 it states that some 70 percent of British standards projects are now in some way related to international standards work, and of a total of over 10,000 British standards, 25 percent are identical with international standards, and are dual numbered to be readily identifiable.

Consumer Protection

During the early centuries of village life, consumer protection against poor quality was largely based on the principle of *caveat emptor*—let the buyer beware. In those days producer and consumer met face-to-face in the village marketplace. The goods on display consisted mostly of natural products, or products that had been produced from natural materials. Consumers had long familiarity with such goods.

To a considerable degree, quality could be judged by the unaided human senses. Under the circumstances, the principle of *caveat emptor* was a sensible element of consumer protection. It demanded that consumers learn to protect themselves through vigilance and self-reliance.

Nevertheless, there were added forms of consumer protection available in some towns. The guilds tended to exercise control over their members, and this control was especially strict with respect to quality. In addition, the town authorities tended to deal severely with flagant abuses by tradesmen.

> *In 1365 . . . John Russell, a Poulterer was charged with exposing 37 pigeons for sale, putrid, rotten, stinking and abominable to the human race; to the scandal, contempt, and disgrace of the city. He was sentenced to the pillory and the said pigeons were burned under him.*[5]

With the growth of industrialization and commerce, along with the rise of towns and cities, producer and consumer no longer met face-to-face. The flow of goods now passed through intermediate processors and merchants. Many critical qualities could no longer be judged by the unaided human senses. In the towns and cities the village marketplace became largely obsolete, and with it the doctrine of *caveat emptor*. In its place there emerged laws to help protect the consumer against poor quality, and to reduce the widespread practice of cheating.

Most of the regulations related to weights and measures were for the protection of consumers and to assist in the regulation of trade. Any aid to industry in the achievement of traceability of measure was probably largely coincidental.

To understand the development of consumer protection in England, it is first necessary to understand the basis of English laws. Laws relating to consumer protection and associated litigation have their roots in the developments following the signing of Magna Carta in the time of King John in 1215. At that time there emerged two primary branches of law and the same is still true today.

The first branch is the body of law as established by acts of Parliament and is referred to as *statute law*. A proven breach of statute law is regarded as a criminal offense and is therefore also known as *criminal law*.

The second branch concerns the relationships between individuals rather than the relationship between the individual and the state. It is known as *common law* and also as *civil law.*

Both of these forms of law are governed by what is known as *the rule of precedent.* Under this rule, any dispute under common law must take into account the decisions of judges on previous disputes which have similar aspects. These cases are written up and therefore are referred to by lawyers on both sides of the dispute. Over the passage of time, volumes of such decisions are recorded, and these are known collectively as *the law of torts.* In the case of criminal law, the concept of judicial precedent still applies, only this time, to the interpretation of the written law. The judges give interpretation to such laws on a case-by-case basis. Collectively these interpretations then become the law under the principle of precedent.

Prior to 1893, most statute law enacted for consumer protection related to weights and measures. Then, under the Sale of Goods Act (1893), a contract of sale in the course of business normally implies that "goods are of merchantable quality," that is, that they are reasonably fit for the purpose for which goods of that kind are usually bought. The effect is to impose strict liability. However, there are two limitations imposed by the principle of privity of contract. Under this principle,

1. The remedy is available only to the purchaser.
2. The remedy is available only against the seller.

Under these limitations, if a third party suffers any loss in any way, he cannot use the Sale of Goods Act as the basis of his argument. His remedy would have to come through common law based on tort. However, under tort the plaintiff must prove that the defendant was negligent in some way and that this negligence led directly to the loss which the plaintiff argues that he has suffered. To do so the plaintiff must prove that

1. The product was defective.
2. The product caused the injury or loss.
3. The defendant failed in his duty of care because the injury or loss was a foreseeable consequence of the defect.

Despite the seeming protection, this was not the case, and prior to 1936 there had been no successful actions based on negligence. The reason was the extreme difficulty of proving negligence due to a lack of expert knowledge of the processes involved in the manufacture of the product in dispute, and to lack of access to the production process or any records pertaining thereto. This difficulty was well dramatized by the first successful action, namely the case of *Donoghue v. Stephenson* [1932] AC 562, 1932 SC (HL) 31. This became an important reference in subsequent developments in laws relating to consumer protection. In this case a woman was injured as the result of drinking a bottled beverage. The injury was clearly traceable to the manufacturer—the bottler of the beverage. The woman was unable to secure redress under the Sale of Goods Act due to lack of privity. (A friend of hers had been the purchaser.) Then, despite the lack of precedent, she sued the manufacturer. The judge ruled in her favor, and the case was appealed all the way to the House of Lords, which upheld the judge's ruling by a majority of three to two.

Lord Atkin, one of the majority, wrote,

> *The liability for negligence whether you style it such or treat it as in any other systems as a species of* culpa, *is no doubt based upon a general public sentiment of moral wrongdoing for which the offender must pay. But acts or omissions which any moral code would censure cannot in a practical world be treated so as to give a right to every person injured by them to demand relief. In this way rules of law arise which limit the range of complainants and the extent of their remedy. The rule that you are to love your neighbor becomes in law, you must not injure your neighbor; and the lawyer's question, who is my neighbor? receives a restricted reply. You must take reasonable care to avoid acts or omissions which you can reasonably foresee would be likely to injure your neighbor. Who, then in law is my neighbor? The answer seems to be—persons who are closely and directly affected by my act that I ought reasonably to have them in contemplation as being so affected when I am directing my mind to the acts or omissions which are called in question.*

The problem of providing adequate protection to the users of products was not unique to the United Kingdom. This is well illustrated in the comprehensive report by the Royal Commission on Civil

Liability and Compensation for Personal Injury, under the chairmanship of Lord Pearson, and presented to Parliament in March 1978. In
this comprehensive three-volume report, the situation in other countries around the world is described in detail. The question of product
liability, as it became known, was also a major topic of debate
throughout Europe at around that time. The Committee of Ministers
of the Council of Europe published a text adopted in January 1977
usually referred to as the "Strasbourg Convention," and the European Economic Community document referred to as the "Draft Directive on Product Liability" was presented to the Council on 9
September 1976.

The English Law Commission recommended a change in the burden of proof; that is, that rather than the plaintiff having to prove
negligence, it would be the responsibility of the defendant to prove
that he was not. This would of course make it considerably easier to
obtain a remedy in common law situations, but it violates the principle that someone is innocent until proven guilty.

The EEC (now EU) Draft Directive embodied proposals for a different kind of strict liability. The directive states that the producer of
an article shall be liable for damage caused by a defect in the article,
whether or not he could have known of the defect. The producer shall
be liable even if the article could not have been regarded as defective
in the light of the scientific and technological development at the time
when the article was put into circulation. This contemplates a system
of liability not referable to failure on the part of a manufacturer to
take reasonable care. Liability is to be channeled to the final producer
subject to a right of indemnity against those responsible for the fault.

The Strasbourg Convention, on the other hand, contemplates yet
another system of channeling liability, thereby giving rise to yet another set of problems and proposals for solutions.

As can easily be imagined, these various recommendations stirred
up considerable controversy and this was exacerbated by a number of
horror stories on the subject emanating from developments on similar
lines in the United States. Under the Treaty of Rome, when a directive has been ratified and signed by the ministers of the various countries, it is necessary for the respective countries to bring relevant laws
into alignment within one year. The main concern in Europe regarding differences in product-related legislation is the effect on competitive advantage. Clearly a country with the most lax laws in this respect
has lower manufacturing costs due to lower insurance premiums, less

litigation, and the ability to get away with fewer controls on the manufacturing process. Of course, those who understand Total Quality know that this does not have to be the case, but that was the prevailing opinion of the day. In the end, the directive with some modifications was signed by the British government.

Other Legislation

In addition to the effect of product liability legislation, there was other relevant legislation in the case of products used at the place of work. This was covered by Section 6 of the Health and Safety at Work Act 1974 (HASAWA). There are 10 subsections to this section, of which only the first is quoted below. It is evident that the provisions are highly relevant to the development of quality as it is perceived today.

> *(1) It shall be the duty of any person who designs, manufactures, imports, or supplies any article for use at work:*
>
> *(a) to ensure as far as is reasonably practicable, that the article is so designed and constructed as to be safe and without risks to health when properly used;*
>
> *(b) to carry out or arrange for the carrying out of such testing and examination as may be necessary for the performance of the duty imposed on him by the preceding paragraph;*
>
> *(c) to take such steps as are necessary to secure that there will be available in connection with the use of the article at work adequate information about the use for which it is designed and has been tested, and about any conditions necessary to ensure that, when put to that use, it will be safe and without risks to health.*

The British government issued a white paper "The Safety of Goods" in July 1984 which put forward a number of measures for strengthening consumer safety legislation. It proposed the introduction of a "general safety requirement," under which suppliers would have to ensure that consumer goods were safe in accordance with "sound, modern standards of safety." This brings consumer goods into line with the requirements of the Health and Safety at Work Act 1974.

Other relevant legislation includes Consumer Protection Act, 1961; Supply of Goods (Implied Terms) Act, 1973; Consumer Credit Act, 1974; Unfair Contract Terms Act, 1977; Consumer Safety Act, 1978.

Development of the Quality of Workmanship

The carpenters who crafted and assembled the timber-framed buildings served long apprenticeships to learn the skills of their craft. Craft-based apprenticeship was an important precursor to the Industrial Revolution and to the development of the industrial world as we know it today. Apprenticeships were the only route to becoming recognized as a craftsman. For a person of lowly parentage, to become a craftsman was the only sure way of having any prospects for a reasonable standard of living and security for the family. Apprenticeships for one's children were therefore highly sought after and often had to be purchased at high cost to the family of the child. Wages during the term of the apprenticeship were minimal, and conditions were often severe. While such conditions improved gradually though a series of acts of Parliament, and in recent times through pressure from trades unions, the accusation that apprenticeships were a form of cheap, almost slave labor lasted even until the middle of the twentieth century.

While the conditions under which these early craftsmen learned their trade were often severe, the fact that they survived the process and were then accepted by their peers as being fully trained was a major source of pride. For many, these early experiences resulted in a lifetime quest to continuously improve their craft skills. The quality of life today owes much to the results achieved through the development of the craftsmanship concept. A craftsman, by definition, is responsible for the quality of his or her own work, and the origins of modern quality have their roots in the work of the early craftsmen such as the carpenter engaged in the construction of the timber-framed buildings, the shipbuilder, cooper, tanner, blacksmith, iron smelter, potter, and so on.

There are many people today who would argue for a return to some more modern form of the craftsmanship concept. For craftsmanship in itself carries some of the more precious of human values: pride, self-respect, the respect of others, recognition of one's work, a role in society, the opportunity for continuous self-development, mutual dependency, and the ownership of the task. These values are fundamental to the health both of an individual and of a society. Many people believe that these values were paramount during the period of the British Industrial Revolution, and to a great extent this was true. Yet while the craftsmanship concept was being perfected, the concept of the division of labor was also developing rapidly, and not only in Britain but also in France and probably elsewhere.

This development is graphically portrayed by Adam Smith in his classical work *Wealth of Nations,* first published in 1776.[6] Yet even this work was preceded, as pointed out in the 1937 edition of Smith's book, with the following quotation of a passage from Mandeville, *Fable of the Bees.*[7]

> . . . "Cleo. *Man, as I have hinted before, naturally loves to imitate what he sees others do, which is the reason that savage people all do the same thing: this hinders them from meliorating their condition, though they are always wishing for it: but if one will wholly apply himself to the making of bows and arrows, whilst another provides food, a third builds huts, a fourth makes garments, and a fifth utensils, they not only become useful to one another, but the callings and employments themselves will, in the same number of years, receive much greater improvements, than if all had been promiscuously followed by every one of the five."*

In the first chapter of Adam Smith's book entitled *The Division of Labor,* the concept is further elaborated through the graphic example of a factory making pins. Pin-making had been a distinct trade, though consisting of 18 separate tasks. In one factory cited by Smith, these 18 tasks were divided among 10 workmen who collectively produced 48,000 pins per day, or a per person equivalent of 4800 pins per day. This rate of production was orders of magnitude greater than would be achieved if each worker were to produce pins by performing all 18 tasks.

Adam Smith's example of pin-making suggests that the craftsmanship concept, as then practiced, could not possibly compete with the productive capability of the division of labor method. However, the social consequences of this approach to work were to a large extent ignored. At the height of the Industrial Revolution, these consequences were vividly described in the works of Karl Marx. In a series of newspaper articles published in 1849, he contends that,

> *The increasing division of labor has several effects.*
>
> *First, it enables one worker to do the work of ten, and so increases the competition among workers for jobs, thus driving wages down.*
>
> *Second, it simplifies labor, eliminates the special skills of the worker and transforms him into "a simple, monotonous productive force."*
>
> *Thirdly, it puts more small-scale capitalists out of business. They can do nothing but join the working class.*

Thus, says Marx, "the forest of uplifted arms demanding work becomes ever thicker, whilst the arms themselves become ever thinner."

Later, in his famous work *Das Kapital*, Marx develops the idea that ". . . human beings are in a state of alienation, a state in which their own creations appear to them as alien, hostile forces and in which instead of controlling their creations, they are controlled by them." Marx therefore postulated that labor must always be in a state of struggle with the forces of capitalism in order to be able to satisfy its needs.

In the United Kingdom, these postulations of Karl Marx appeared ever more relevant as the Industrial Revolution passed and the twentieth century began. Following World War I when the soldiers returned to "a land fit for heroes" according to Prime Minister David Lloyd George, it very soon became evident that there were more people than jobs. Unemployment was severe. In the absence of modern forms of social security, poverty was rife. During this period the Labor Party developed and the trades unions increased their membership, power, and influence.

The landslide Labor victory following World War II enabled the trades unions to consolidate their power with a membership of some 9,500,000 people. In the 20 years that followed, Britain went through a period of unprecedented boom. During this time, businesses could sell everything they could make. Unfortunately, when that happens for a sustained period, quality lacks high priority. Most managers are concerned with shipping more product at less and less cost regardless of quality. In fact in many cases, including the motor industry, and the manufacture of white goods (refrigerators, washing machines, and so on) and brown goods (television and radio sets), there developed a perverse attitude toward quality. In these cases, rather than attempt to improve the reliability of products, many managers took the view that emphasis on volume kept manufacturing costs down, which in turn made the product available to a wider market. The fact that the product was cheap meant that even if the product did fail, it could be replaced at low cost. Attempts were made to make this practice appear acceptable by introducing the notion of a "throwaway society."

The effect on the workforce of these explosive changes in division of labor was twofold. Firstly, the need for high-volume manufacture at low cost increased pressure on manufacturers to develop further the division of labor concept so abhorred by Karl Marx. Secondly, the low price of these products enabled the workers themselves to purchase the products of their own labor. This led to an unprecedented period of affluence which was underlined perfectly by the then Prime Minister, Harold McMillan in the general election campaign of 1958, "You never had it so good."

The affluence created during this period and the need for ever more rapid expansion meant that business managers sought ever more effective ways to reduce the work content in tasks. This trend was accelerated by the wholesale introduction of very refined work study methods from the United States. These methods, based on concepts evolved and advocated by the American engineer, Frederick W. Taylor, led to the virtual elimination of the craftsmanship concept. Taylor, as had Adam Smith more than a century earlier, not only advocated this approach, but together with contemporaries such as Frank and Lillian Gilbreth, developed means by which tasks could be broken down even further into their smallest possible elements. Added to this was the concept of separation of planning from execution, so that all decision making became the exclusive province of the managers and engineers. Managers generally recognized that these methods were socially demoralizing but believed that the material benefits to the workers outweighed the social consequences. Probably for this reason, managers wrongly assumed that the only problem was that of boredom resulting from highly repetitive tasks. This belief assumes that the worker is interested only in money and ignores the other basic needs of a human being. For this reason, managers failed to understand the reasons for the growing symptoms of alienation by workers, and reacted by trying to solve the problem through such means as pay incentives, improved sanitation in the work place, provision of social facilities, and so on. Acceptable though these provisions were they failed to address the heart of the matter, with the consequence that in the late 1970s after almost a decade of ever worsening industrial relations, Britain went through what has become known as the "winter of discontent."

It was around this time that there emerged a new challenge to "Taylorism," this time from within the quality profession. By now, both the high quality of Japanese goods and the highly effective production methods they use were being studied by British management scientists. During the 1970s Japanese pressure on a growing number of British industries had become severe. The automotive industry was in trouble, not only with the worst industrial relations in its history but with an appalling reputation for quality. In contrast, their Japanese counterparts were believed to have both excellent industrial relations and vastly superior product quality. In many other industries, particularly in the field of consumer electronics, famous names were disappearing at an ever increasing rate. For example, in 1973, there were many British television manufacturers. A walk along any main shopping street would confront the passerby with such names as McMichael, Sobell, Bush, Ultra, HMV, Decca, Pye, Ferguson, Philips, and so on. In the space of just a few years, all of them had disappeared with the exception of Philips and Ferguson. In their place were names hitherto unknown to the British public: JVC, Panasonic, Hitachi, Toshiba, and so on.

Having identified that Taylorism was at the root of the problem, however, did not imply an immediate solution. Clearly it was not possible to turn back the clock and return to a craft-based regime. There followed a period of experimentation which included test applications of Japanese-style quality circles. These circles comprise small groups of workers who perform similar tasks in the same workshop. On a voluntary basis they are trained in the use of problem-solving tools, and are allocated time, usually one hour or so per week, to study problems in their work and to present solutions to their manager. The foreman or supervisor is normally the leader of the group. In the early 1980s the concept was very popular. However, the circles soon began to disappear and it was realized that the social problems of the workplace could not be solved simply by introducing a different concept of work organization; it was necessary to reexamine the nature of the whole work environment. In most cases this would involve a major change in the thinking and attitudes of the managers themselves.

Decades of Taylor-style thinking meant that the majority of managers had no other experience, and this affected their whole attitude, not only toward the workers but to their peer group as well. Such attitudes could not be changed simply by training the workers; it was first necessary to change the thinking and style of the managers. This is proving to be a more difficult task than many of the behavioral scientists would have believed. After all, many managers owe their own personal status to their ability to operate in a Taylor-style environment, whatever its disadvantages to others. So they are unlikely to change unless they can be convinced that they will either personally be amongst the beneficiaries or alternatively amongst the survivors. Many organizations which are now changing their approach to work practices are doing so because they know that they will simply be put out of business if they do not. As Dr. Johnson is reputed to have said "Nothing concentrates the mind more than the threat of impending death."

Looking to the future, it is likely that the concept of self-directing work teams will replace Taylorism in Britain. This concept has the advantage of allowing the benefits of the division of labor so well illustrated by Adam Smith while at the same time bringing craftsmanship back to the work groups. Although Karl Marx advocated eternal conflict between worker and management as the remedy for the division of labor, the concept of self-directing work teams means that while the individual may not own the whole task, a group can be formed to do so. In the early to mid-1990s the continuing pressure for improvements in British quality and productivity has led many companies to make a fresh appraisal of the merits of this concept and there are now several examples where this approach is beginning to produce results.

Twentieth-Century Trends in Managing for Quality

Early in the twentieth century the main quality-related activity in most manufacturing organizations was inspection; either self-inspection by craftsmen or post-operation inspection. The latter was more prevalent in high-volume production. The most formally organized was in defense procurement, aircraft manufacture, or other industries where high levels of safety were demanded. This emphasis on inspection is also evident in the name chosen in 1922 by a professional body then incorporated for the promotion of quality—The Institution of Engineering Inspection. (The name was changed in 1972 to The Institute of Quality Assurance in order to reflect the then-modern thinking.)

The twentieth century also witnessed the evolution of new developments in managing for quality, both in the private sector and in military procurement. These developments followed separate but parallel paths until they converged in the 1980s. In what follows we will first look at the trend of events in military procurement, after which we will look at the evolution in the private sector.

Trends in Military Procurement

Early in the century the military method for approving a supplier's quality was the *Approved Firms Inspection system*. This was developed in 1920 by the Aeronautical Quality Assurance Directorate (AQD), which was previously known as Aeronautical Inspection Department (AID). Under this scheme, there were basically two possibilities for approval.

The first was the approval by AQD of the supplier's chief inspector, and was known as *6/49 Conditions of Contract*. For this it was necessary for the prospective supplier to provide sufficient evidence to satisfy AQD that the chief inspector was both suitably trained and capable to carry out the management of the relevant inspection activities. Furthermore, he must have an appropriate record system, the means to segregate inspected from noninspected materials, quarantine facilities, bonded stores where appropriate, and inspection stamps to identify the inspector who carried out the inspection. It was also the responsibility of the chief inspector to ensure that the inspectors had been properly trained. (The changes that took place in 1974 did not abandon these principles, they were merely absorbed into the more elaborate system which followed.)

Contracts under 6/49 Conditions of Contract would be placed with those organizations whose inspection arrangements had been approved by the Assistant Master General of the Ordnance (AMGO) on behalf of the War Office, and the Director General of Inspection

(DGI) on behalf of the Ministry of Aviation. Supervision of the contractors was carried by one or more of the following five inspectorates: Inspectorate of Armaments (I Arm); Inspectorate of Fighting Vehicles and Mechanical Equipment (IFVME) and the Chemical Inspectorate (CI), who were responsible to AMGO; and the Aeronautical Inspection Directorate (AID) and the Electrical Inspection Directorate (EID), who were responsible to DGI.

Failure to satisfy the relevant inspectorate that these requirements could be met did not by itself preclude the would-be supplier from a possible contract. He would usually be given the opportunity to make the requisite changes to achieve compliance. If he was reluctant or unable to do this he could still be awarded a contract provided he made suitable facilities available for the inspectorate to conduct these activities itself. This type of approval was known as *6/48 Conditions of Contract*. This involved the provision of an office and filing facilities as a minimum. At the time when this system was replaced in 1973 the Ministry of Defence employed some 15,000 personnel in this field.

The termination of the Approved Firms System of Inspection came with the adoption of a revolutionary system based on a series of North Atlantic Treaty Organization (NATO) standards produced in 1968. The intention of these standards was to reduce the need for inspection through the use of preventive measures. The theory was that if an organization had a good system of well-documented procedures based on a clearly defined quality policy signed by the chief executive, then provided that the system followed certain prescribed principles, there would be no reason for producing defects. This is a gross oversimplification, but in essence this was the basis of the concept. The development of the systematic preventive approach came partly from central government and partly from the Ministry of Defence, and most of the development work originated in the 1960s.

In 1968 an independent committee of enquiry was set up under the chairmanship of Colonel G. W. Raby, a leading national industrialist. The work of this committee had a major effect on the direction and pace of development of quality assurance in both the public and private sectors.

According to Mr. Harry Drew (referred to earlier in this chapter, and who became the Director General of Quality Assurance, Ministry of Defence), the mission of the Raby committee was

> *to examine the organisation and methods of the equipment inspectorates of the Ministry of Defence and the then Ministry of Technology. The Committee had to consider the relevance, effectiveness*

and economy of the inspectorates and how they could be improved. After wide ranging discussions with industry, the Armed Forces, trade associations and Government Departments the Committee reported in July, 1969.

The Committee's report was accepted by the Government and the process of implementing the recommendations was begun in 1970. The Committee considered that the fundamental problem was how to ensure the quality of a product. They defined a good quality product as one which meets the requirements of the service adequately, is available at the right time and will be economical and reliable through its whole life. The committee did not consider that "inspection" by an outside body can itself ensure the quality required. They said that what was needed is a comprehensive approach to quality assurance in which the customer, the designer, and the producer all play their part. The Committee emphasised that the customer must define his requirements in terms of performance, environment, reliability, maintainability, and similar criteria with the maximum precision. The supplier must use such systems and procedures both in overall management and design and production methods, as well as quality assurance, as give confidence that the end product will meet, in all respects, the defined requirement of the customer. This basic philosophy underlines the whole of the report, three important recommendations of which are:

(a) that overall responsibility for design, development, production and quality assurance of an independent item of equipment should be brought together at the lowest effective managerial level, inspection being combined with the other activities of equipment procurement;

(b) the setting up of a Defence Quality Assurance Board (DQAB);

(c) that the Chief Executive of the DQAB should be assisted by an Industrial Advisory Committee.

The report emphasised the need for placing an increasing measure of responsibility for quality assurance on industry and for reducing direct Government inspection.[8]

Following this development, in July 1973 the Ministry of Defence introduced what were referred to as the *Defence Standards for*

Quality Assurance. These standards were based on a series of NATO standards entitled *Allied Quality Assurance Publications* (AQAPs) and included the following:

AQAP 1. Quality control system requirements for industry.

AQAP 2. Guide for the evaluation of a contractor's quality control system for compliance with AQAP 1.

AQAP 3. NATO sampling schemes.

AQAP 4. Inspection system requirements for industry.

AQAP 5. Guide to the evaluation of a contractor's inspection system for compliance with AQAP 4.

AQAP 6. Measurement and calibration system requirements for industry.

AQAP 7. Guide for the evaluation of a contractor's calibration system for compliance with AQAP 6.

AQAP 9. Basic inspection requirements for industry.

The content of these publications was modified but with minimal change in order to meet the specific requirements of the Ministry of Defence. The publications were also renumbered by placing the numbers 05-2 in front of the existing numbers. For example, the replacement for AQAP 1 became Defence Standard 05-21, AQAP 2 was replaced with Defence Standard 05-22, and so forth. These standards became the basis for contracts with the Ministry of Defence from April 1973 onward. At the time that the standards were introduced, it was claimed that approximately 10 percent of all manufactured product was for use in defense-related contracts. It can be seen therefore that the Ministry of Defence was a major influence on the development of quality practices in the United Kingdom.

One principle of great importance included in the standards, which had a major effect on the development of quality in subsequent years, was the requirement that prime contractors must conduct audits of their own suppliers in line with these standards. The object of this from the point of view of the Ministry of Defence was to reduce the number of contractor assessors required on its own payroll. Unfortunately, this quickly led to a serious problem. Many organizations that supplied the prime contractors were also suppliers to other prime contractors and even to each other. The defense standards required that every supplier conduct audits of each of its suppliers irrespective of the possibility that its suppliers may have already been audited satisfactorily by someone else to the same requirements. For example, in one case known to the author of this chapter, a company that supplied pipe fittings claimed to have been audited by no fewer than 80 audit teams in the first six months of 1978. This became known as the problem of multiple assessment and became so severe that an inquiry was set up.

Trends in the Private Sector

At this point we turn to the events that took place in the private sector. Following that, we will return to the problem of multiple assessment, which involved both the public and private sectors.

The first serious postwar national attempt to raise awareness of the importance of quality as being part of a business competitive strategy was an initiative in 1967 entitled *National Quality and Reliability Year*. This initiative, supported by the Labour government, was part of Prime Minister Harold Wilson's plan for "white hot technological revolution." The quality program was organized jointly by the British Productivity Council (BPC) and the National Council for Quality and Reliability (NCQR), the latter having been set up in 1962 as a part of BPC. NCQR did an important job in its short life in raising industry awareness of a wide range of productivity-raising concepts. Nevertheless, in the early 1970s, despite protests from many quarters, the Conservative government under Edward Heath disbanded the BPC and, with it, NCQR.

Q. and R. year, as it was known, was the first serious attempt to alert industry to the importance of the prevention of defects in manufacture rather than simply to continue postactivity sorting. As one regretfully unrecorded advocate of this revolutionary approach commented, "it doesn't matter how much you inspect a bad product, it doesn't make it any better, all inspection does is to separate good from bad and it is not very reliable at that. All inspection does to a good product is to add cost. Better to attempt to prevent the defects in the first place." In those days, the state of the art in terms of quality improvement tools was the Shewhart chart. The national quality and reliability campaign gave a useful boost to quality, but unfortunately the momentum was not maintained. At that time the quality improvement "breakthrough" process as developed by Dr. Juran was not known in the United Kingdom. Unfortunately, despite the efforts of several people, including the author of this chapter, the application of the statistical method was slow to catch on, the concept badly taught, and, consequently, most initiatives quickly faded and disappeared. However, the concept of prevention rather than segregation of good from bad had caught on even though the means to achieve this were not clear.

In June 1968 a committee chaired by Sir Eric Mensforth was appointed by the then minister of technology "to consider and make proposals for the voluntary coordination and extension of national arrangements for the surveillance of quality control, inspection, testing and certification of engineering products and materials to declared standards of performance, safety and reliability; and to ensure that the proposals made will be directed at improving industrial efficiency and take particular account of the needs of the export market."

The committee sought the views of some 800 trade associations, industrial firms, government departments, professional institutions, and research organizations. It reviewed quality assurance arrangements for statutory purposes and in relation to UK exports. The committee also commented on quality costs, on the need for education and publicity about quality, and on the specialized needs for certification in a number of fields. The report of the committee was published in 1970.

Multiple Assessment and National Accreditation

Returning now to multiple assessment, the severity of the problem resulted in setting up an inquiry. This led to recommendation G in the report under the name of Sir Frederick Warner on *Standards and Specifications in the Engineering Industries* (published by the National Economic Development Organisation [NEDO] in 1977) which says,

> *I also recommend that the Secretaries of State for Industry and Prices and Consumer Protection should consult all concerned on the steps necessary to build a rational structure of quality assurance bodies with mutual acceptance of approvals to avoid multiple assessment.*

While there was widespread agreement on the need for mutual acceptance of assessment approvals, the difficulty was to agree on the basis of the approvals. During the time that the defense standards had been in operation, a large number of other major procurement bodies had developed their own criteria. Some of these had been in existence far longer than the Ministry of Defence requirements. All of the motor manufacturers, the Central Electricity Generating Board, and many others had developed schemes, some of which were similar to the MOD standards, while others were not. The scheme operated by the Ford Motor Company for example was very different. Most of these bodies were naturally reluctant to subordinate their own arrangements in favor of some other plan. Eventually however, there was a breakthrough when the Ministry of Defence decided to adopt a new British standard (BS 5750) for all levels of assessment other than those requiring Defence Standard 05-21. (In this case, the MOD agreed to conduct assessments in accordance with AQAP 1.) This was an easy step for the Ministry of Defence because BS 5750 as originally created was nothing more than the Defence Standards in a BSI cover. While not all of industry accepted BS 5750 at first, and some still do not, the idea of passing responsibility for assessment to a third party proved an irresistible temptation to many organizations and BS 5750 gathered momentum.

In the United Kingdom there are now over 25 accreditation bodies which are approved by the National Accreditation Board to carry out official certification audits of applicant organizations. When successfully audited in this way, the organization is listed on the *Register of Quality Assessed United Kingdom Companies.* In 1984 this register, published by the Department of Trade, had some 6000 company entries. By 1986 the figure had risen to over 9000.

In 1983 the Department of Trade launched a national quality campaign as being part of an overall effort to increase the competitiveness of British industry. Under this scheme, a National Accreditation Council for Certification Bodies (NACCB) was formed in 1985. The National Measurement Accreditation Service (NAMAS) was formed by the amalgamation of the British Calibration Service (BCS) and the National Testing Laboratory Accreditation Service (NATLAS), also in 1985.

While this program undoubtedly helped raise the level of awareness of the importance of quality in British industry, the campaign was almost entirely focused around the systems elements of quality with

virtually no attention given to the participative aspects. This was unfortunate, because if this approach was correct then the positive outcomes would have been very evident during the period of the defense
standards in the 1970s. It seems that rather than discover why the approach did not provide a remedy for a worsening of Britain's competitive position with regard to the Far East, the advocates were saying
that all that was necessary was the same medicine but with a larger
spoon. In the opinion of the author of this chapter, what appeared to
be happening was consistent with the proverb To a man who only has
a hammer, every problem looks like a nail.

Fortunately, toward the end of the 1980s, some industrialists and
some institution members did become aware that a much broader
approach was necessary, and they began to experiment with total
quality as it is practiced in both the United States and Japan. This
trend has been further influenced by the success of the National
Quality Award in the United States and the more recent European
Quality Award. In 1992 the Department of Trade published a consultative document on the feasibility of a new British Quality Award
to supersede the existing award which had been based on rather subjective criteria. By 1994 it has been agreed that the award should be
based on the European Quality Award. The requirements for this
award go far beyond the requirements of British Standard 5750 as it
was amended in 1987 to bring it into line with the newly published
ISO 9000 standards.

Summary

It is clear that managing for quality is an ever changing concept.
Looking back over this brief history, it is evident that quality as a science today is very much more sophisticated than in previous generations and is likely to become even more so in the future. What we are
witnessing now is the fusing together of all of the strands referred to
in this text, together with other concepts not covered due to the con-
straints of the work, into one composite whole. Basically, there appear
to be four principal elements to modern managing for quality.

1. *The quality of systems,* planning, and organization as can readily
   be seen in the development of such concepts as BS 5750 (ISO
   9000) assessment systems, and so on.

2. *The quality of processes* as seen in the development of the means to produce, the growth of standardization on best practices, and the recent development of process reengineering not covered in this work.

3. *The quality of management* both in terms of management style as applied to people management, and also management in terms of the strategic development of the organization. Although Dr. Juran has been advocating this for years, it is the most recent development in managing for quality in the United Kingdom and is likely to be the main source of quality-related innovation in the future.

4. *The management of people,* while theoretically part of the role of management, is such a broad and deep subject in its own right that it deserves a place of its own. In the future, there is likely to be a profound change in attitudes toward human beings at the place of work. Self-directing work teams will probably become the norm because those organizations that resist the current trends in this direction will simply not be able to compete with those that do.

Finally, what we are witnessing today is a revolution through the convergence of all of these separately developed concepts. It is a revolution brought on by the fact that for the first time in history, in the industrialized world at least, we are confronted with a situation where supply exceeds demand in almost every conceivable product or service. In the past, when demand exceeded supply, when a producer could sell everything he could make, quality did not have top priority. In the current situation, where supply grossly exceeds demand, only the best will survive. Quality has therefore become a boardroom issue not only in the United Kingdom but throughout the world. This situation is not likely to change very much for a number of decades, and very soon those organizations that do not respond to this challenge will only be found in the history books of the future.

Notes

1. Drew, H. E., Quality—Its Origin and Progress in Defence Procurement, *The Quality Engineer,* January 1972, pp. 7–8.

2. Raisterick, Arthur, *Dynasty of Ironfounders,* published by Sessions Book Trust in association with Ironbridge Gorge Museum Trust, ISBN 1-85072-058-4, first published 1953.

3. Singer, Charles, *et al.*, *A History of Technology; Volume IV, The Industrial Revolution, 1750–1850,* Oxford Univeristy Press, New York and London, 1958.

4. Petley, B. W., *Measurement from the Pyramids to the Twenty First Century,* Royal Institute Proceedings 1988 60, pp. 45–71.

5. *The Livery of the City of London,* printed by the Corporation of London in conjunction with the Livery Committee and the Livery Consultative Committee, 1986.

6. Smith, Adam, *The Wealth of Nations,* 1776; Random House edition published in 1937.

7. Mandeville, *Fable of the Bees,* pt. 11 1729, dial. vi., p. 335; referenced in Adam Smith, *op. cit.,* p. 3.

8. Drew, H. E., *op. cit.,* p. 16.

CHAPTER 15

Quality Management in Nineteenth-Century Czech Beer and Sugar Production

Dr. Ludmila Cuřínová, Head of Sanitary Museum, Prague
Dr. František Dudek, Private Scientist and Entrepreneur

I. Quality Management in Nineteenth-Century Czech Beer Production

Introduction

Part I of this chapter examines the development of managing for quality of Czech beer production during the nineteenth century. That century witnessed an acceleration of the historical trends away from the numerous small local breweries which served local markets and relied on tradition, empiricism, and trade secrets to manage for quality. The trend during the nineteenth century was toward large breweries which could serve broad domestic and international markets. For these large breweries, the trend in managing for quality focused mainly on quality improvement by replacing empiricism with science. The resulting improvements in input materials, in the brewing process, and in measurement of quality all contributed importantly to the ability of Czech beer to compete in international markets.

Early Beer Brewing

Brewing malt wort with hops is one of the most important processes in brewing beer. (Malt is germinated grain, usually barley. Wort is an unfermented or fermenting infusion of malt, which becomes beer after fermentation.) Transfer to the brew of valuable substances contained in the hops gives the beer its typically bitter taste and simultaneously provides a preserving effect. The quality of the final product depends strongly on the quality of the hops. No suitable substitute for hops has ever been found.

The exact date of the first use of hops for brewing beer is not known. In the Czech lands there are reports about beer brewing dating back to the eighth and ninth centuries. In the eleventh and twelfth centuries a lively trade in beer already existed. Czech hops were exported, along the Labe (Elbe River) to Hamburg. There, they were sold on the so-called "hop market" where specialists assessed the quality of the hops. The very existence of this profession testifies to the fact that dependence of the quality of beer on the quality of the hops was already well known at that time.

In the fourteenth century, traditional small-scale beer brewing on an artisan basis first developed in the Czech lands in royal towns as a privilege of free citizens. Later, from the sixteenth century onward, beer brewing became a privilege on estates of the nobility.[1] Up to the end of the eighteenth century, the privileged beer brewers were able to compel their subjects to purchase their beer, thus ensuring themselves of a stable market without having to pay heed to the quality of brewing. Because of these local monopolies and because of the eating habits of the farm population, primitive, limited, and irregular production of unripe white beer made of wheat malt predominated. The beer was insufficiently hopped and, therefore, was also less durable. This slightly sour cloudy alcoholic beverage was used up to the beginning of the nineteenth century.

During the Napoleonic wars, potatoes began to be widely introduced in small-scale agricultural production as the basic food component of country people, particularly the poorer classes. These potatoes were used to produce white beers which were the basic raw material for the preparation of a variety of soups. Their poor taste could be improved by the addition of various condiments and preserving agents.

Figure 15.1 Work in a brewery in the 18th century. Source: Institute of History, Czech Academy of Science.

Evolution of Industry

The development of manufactories at the end of the seventeenth century was associated with a general acceleration of the growth of the population and with a broader demand for basic foodstuffs. At the same time, interest in a broader assortment of goods and in better quality increased.

This increased demand for improved quality included basic beverages to which beer traditionally belonged. During this period, brewing by the nonagricultural population also expanded. At the end of the eighteenth century, annual beer consumption exceeded 100 liters per capita. The estimate is derived from data on the average daily consumption of one liter of beer by the economically active population. During the Napoleonic wars, the quick rise in the price of cereals, especially wheat, and the spread of potato growing brought an end to the production of low-grade white wheat beers. Consumer pressure also encouraged production of better, sufficiently hopped, light beers made of barley malt. From the end of the eighteenth century, increased demand and the removal of noneconomic obstacles to competition led to economic pressure for gradual modernization of traditional, empirical production processes.

Reforms introduced by Emperor Joseph the Second toward the end of the eighteenth century removed the duty of subjects to buy beer from gentry breweries, the tie-in purchase of beer in inns, and the prohibition of beer imports from the countryside to royal towns. At the same time, it was forbidden to brew and sell beer in dwelling houses of townsmen, a measure aimed at encouraging entrepreneurial cooperation and the establishment of municipal breweries. Although these reforms increased competition in the brewing industry to some extent, the feudal brewing monopoly remained. The brewing of beer and production of alcoholic beverages continued to be the privilege of the landowning aristocracy and free citizens until 1869. While beer brewing continued to be performed and managed by experienced and guild-organized brewers, in most instances they could only act as employees or lessees of privileged owners.[2]

Early Quality Standards

The question of beer quality was an important state interest because the extensive brewing industry brought considerable financial returns to the crown. An emperor's patent of 1805—supplementing provisions of a beer tax—contained strict prohibition of the production of inferior beer from decocted (spent) malt. At the same time, it reminded breweries of their duty to keep a continuous record of the individual production batches.

Selection and Improvement of Hops

Czech hops have established a reputation as outstanding raw materials for beer brewing. The high quality of Czech hops is the result of natural growing conditions and improvements in plant species over time. The natural growing conditions are a blending of many factors that match the needs of the hop plant. These conditions include the particular atmospheric conditions, the geomorphology of the surrounding countryside, composition of the soil, protection against northerly winds, as well as some other factors. The relation between the quality of the hops and its place of origin were already clear in the sixteenth century when numerous new breweries and hop fields were founded. The sixteenth century was also the time that the origin of hops began to be certified by town seals showing where the hops were cultivated. Special regulations were prepared for hop growers (for instance by officials of the town of Rakovník in central Bohemia in the early sixteenth century). The regulations included numerous recommendations on how to cultivate the hop plants in order to ensure a high yield of satisfactory quality.

Basic requirements placed on hops for use by beer breweries were defined in the sixteenth and seventeenth centuries. Expanding trade contacts led to increasing attempts to falsify high-grade hops. Inferior hops were frequently falsified by the addition of pinecone blossoms which were sprinkled with sweet beer, thoroughly mixed, and baled.[3] Interest of the state in the quality and origin of hops is evidenced by patents issued by the Austrian Empress Maria Theresa on July 13, 1758, and August 14, 1769. These patents prohibited any mixing of Bohemian and foreign hops. Equally strict measures were taken for prohibiting the export of seedlings to other countries. The central administration's efforts to prevent falsification of the hops and the exports of seedlings were not, however, sufficient. Therefore, a Hops Association was founded in 1833 in Žatec, central Bohemia, for the purpose of certifying the genuineness of Žatec hops. For the same purpose, Žatec established a Hops Certification Station in 1884, the Hop Union in 1891, and the Bohemian Hops Association in 1894. It was only in 1921 that the compulsory marking of all hops according to the place of origin was ordered to be carried out in the producer community. Hops shipments had to include documentation on the country, year, producer region, and producer community.

Quality Criteria for Hop Selection and Improvement

Attempts to guarantee and communicate the quality of hops for brewing and to provide means for quality improvement led to a series of criteria for defining and measuring quality. The initial criteria focused on the place of origin. Subjective sensory measures based on characteristics believed to be important for brewing followed. These measures were elaborated into explicit and detailed scales to measure the anticipated commercial value of the hops. Later, improvements in chemical analysis techniques provided additional means of assessing the potential value of hops for brewing purposes.

The first criteria in assessing the quality of hops were their origin and variety. Evaluation of hops prior to their use for the brewing of beer was difficult because the factors influencing the relationship between raw material and brewed beer were not well understood. As a result, up to the last quarter of the nineteenth century, evaluation of quality was based mainly on a subjective sensory assessment of the external features and properties of the hops. This subjective assessment method gave brewers and tradesmen a basic idea of the quality of the hops, expressed at first sight on four dimensions: the color, uniformity, ripeness, and size of the catkins.

Nineteenth-century changes in the process of beer brewing led to efforts to acquire a thorough knowledge of the raw materials used and their proper evaluation from the point of view of the quality of the beer. This attention to raw materials focused primarily on hops and barley. Diverse point evaluation systems—in which each quality indicator was assigned a given number of points—were gradually introduced for the purpose of a numerical expression of expert opinions on the quality of the hops. In time, these systems were perfected, but they were not unified on a European scale until the twentieth century.

In the second half of the nineteenth century, the point evaluation systems generally consisted of two parts. One was a commercial evaluation and the other a mechanical analysis of the catkins, the methodology of which was thoroughly worked out in Bohemia at the end of the nineteenth century by F. Chodounský.

Commercial Evaluation.   The commercial assessment usually consisted of 10 points which evaluated the following properties of the hops.

1. Picking of the hops—Cleanliness of the hops, occurrence of catkin clusters, bracts, leaves, and so on.

2. Color—Intensity of the hop color and the frequency of spot occurrence. Until the beginning of the nineteenth century, dark hops were given preference. A change toward lighter colors took place in connection with the increasing popularity of light beer and changes in hop drying techniques. The color scale has practically not changed since that time and remains in the following sequence: green, golden green, yellow, grayish yellow, yellowish brown, rusty, mottled, light red, brick red, red, reddish violet, and reddish brown.

3. Luster—Ripeness and degree of care devoted to the hops during harvesting, drying, and storage.

4. Size of catkins—The optimum diameter is deemed to be about 2.5 centimeters.

5. Uniformity—A uniform size of the catkins is required.

6. Structure and shape of the catkins—In the 1890s, the dependence of the brewing value of the hops on the structure of the floral axis of the catkins, that is the axis of the hops catkin, was determined. The structure of the catkin was evaluated according to the regularity of the structure of the floral axis; another guide was the difference between the average length of the catkin and that of the floral axis. The greater the difference, the greater the brewing value of the hops.

7. Shape of the catkins—Shape differs depending on the variety and origin of the plant.

8. Amount of powder, the lupuline, in the hops catkin—An indicator of the amount of bitter substances in the hops catkin.

9. Color of the lupuline—Properly ripened hops contain light to golden yellow lupuline.

10. Odor of the hops catkins—Indicates the presence of essential oils. The Bohemian hops are known for their characteristic aroma.

Mechanical Analysis.   Mechanical analysis served as an aid in determining the refinement of the hops. In time, it concentrated on four important indicators.

1. The weight of 100 dry catkins (the optimum being 15 to 16.5 grams)
2. The weight of the floral axis—in the case of fine hops 8 percent to 10 percent; of coarser hops 10 percent to 12 percent; of coarsest hops 14 percent to 15 percent; and of wild hops 17 percent
3. The mean floral axis length
4. The average number of floral axis elements

Chemical Analysis

In the second half of the nineteenth century and, in particular, during its last 20 years, advances in the chemical sciences made it possible to analyze hops chemically. These analyses were aimed at components important from the point of view of brewing beer, that is, those components that contribute to the body and bitterness of the produced beer. As long as the quality of hops was evaluated on the basis of their aroma and color, foreign-grown hops could not make headway as local brewing inputs. Evaluation of hops quality on the basis of chemical analysis opened an opportunity for using imported hops. However, as chemical analysis began to be used, it became evident that quality is not only a question of the bitter substances contained in the hops. Of no less importance is the proportional presence of other components. In the case of the Bohemian hops, the presence and proportion of other components ensured smoothness and quality of the hops despite the lower content of some bitter resins.

Because the catkin contained the most important components of the hop plant, it naturally became the center of interest. The content of the most important brewing components in the hop catkin depend on the ripeness of the plant. Therefore, it is of utmost importance to fix the correct time of the hop ripeness. From the chemical point of view, the catkin contains bitter hop substances, tannin, and essential oils. The basis of the bitter hop substances is the alpha-bitter acid (humulone) and the beta-bitter acid (lupulone). The aim of beer hopping is the transfer of these valuable brewing substances into the solution.

Both of the bitter acids are insoluble in cold malt wort. In the last century, it was learned that the solubility of these acids is temperature-dependent and that brewing causes gradual oxidation and polymerization which convert the alpha and beta acids into hard and soft resins, respectively. A part of these resins is transferred into the beer.

The first one to point out these changes was Hayduck (1888). Shortly afterward, Neumann worked out a method for determining the amount of bitter substances in hopped wort and beer by ether extraction. This method was later made more precise by Wiegmann who employed benzene for leaching these substances. However, all of these methods were subject to considerable inaccuracies which were finally explained by Wöllmer. Wöllmer studied conditions for the solubility of humulone and lupulone in the malt wort and found that the acidity of the environment in which the bitter substances are dissolved is of decisive importance. Their solubility depends, in addition to temperature, on the concentration of hydrogen ions, with humulone being the more soluble of the two. The dependence of the solubility of the alpha- and beta-bitter acids on the pH value thus explained why their occurrence is quite different in hopped wort and beer than in the hops.

The Wöllmer method for determining the amount of bitter substances in the hops made it possible to determine five characteristics of the hops: all resins, all soft resins, all hard (insoluble) resins, the alpha-bitter acid, and the beta fraction. The resultant brewing value of the hops—according to Wöllmer—is understood to be the sum of the percent content of the alpha-bitter acid and one-ninth of the content of the beta-bitter acid. The optimum value of bitter substances on the Wöllmer scale was 5.5 to 6.5.

The Wöllmer method became widespread in the twentieth century. In addition to this method, a number of polarimetric, colorometric, spectrophotometric, and conductometric methods were worked out for determining a variety of other properties, such as the isomers of bitter acids.

Wöllmer's work confirmed what the majority of chemical engineers had already presumed at the end of the past century, namely, that it is not possible to determine the quality of hops from only its chemical analysis and that the mere content of bitter acids cannot be the only criterion of hops quality. Smoothness and refinement of the hops depends on the mutual relation between the bitter acids as well as on the amount of tannins, essential oils, and other hop components.

The following table illustrates the mechanical analysis of hops of diverse origin.

Hop variety (origin)	Weight of 100 catkins		Number of catkins contained in a 100-gram sample
	Original (g)	Waterless (g)	
Bohemian	13.2	11.9	769.1
Moravian	12.7	11.6	797.6
Yugoslav	14.3	13.1	718.4
Polish	11.9	10.8	852.2
Belgian	14.2	13.1	723.4
English	17.2	15.8	582.5
American	19.3	17.8	520.6

The table indicates the largest catkins were those of the American and English varieties. A chemical analysis of these hops showed their resin content to be 15 percent to 17 percent. Despite this, American hops are not well suited to the manufacture of fine beers. The best Bohemian hops contain 7 percent to 9 percent of resins, of which alpha-bitter acids make up 35 percent to 45 percent, and tannins around 4 percent. It is exactly the harmonious proportion between the individual hop resins and hop tannin which ranks Bohemian, particularly Žatec, hops in first place in the world.

Thus, at the end of the nineteenth century, commercial assessment and mechanical and chemical analyses rendered a good idea of the quality and suitability of hops for beer brewing. These assessments were augmented by brewing and tasting tests because it is the latter that complete the final assessment of a given variety of hops.

Raw Material Improvements

In general, Bohemian hop varieties are divided into "reds" and "greens," differing in the amount of pigment in the anthocyanin which affect the coloring of the hop vines and catkins. The reds variety was always better quality and finer than the greens variety. The Žatec reds were the best. In the nineteenth century, efforts to achieve a better grade of hops by improving this plant were directed at methods of both mass and individual selection. In 1856, Kryštof Semš of Vrbice—by selection from a population of the Stáry Uštěk red hops—

succeeded in developing a better variety noted for its yield. It became known as the Semš variety. In England, this method was used for producing the well-known Golding variety.

In addition to its origin, the quality of the hops also depended on the plant variety. The nineteenth century brought about new findings which contributed to improving the varieties of hops and selection methods. At the end of the century, attention centered on hybridization methods. Cultivation of hops by hybridization is more tedious in view of the fact that, in general, no cultures of male plants are available.

In the nineteenth century, many new findings were made in agricultural production processes and nutrition and in fertilizing, drying, and storing hops. All this new knowledge contributed to increasing the yield of the hop fields and the quality of the harvested hops. In the seventeenth century the hop yield (with considerable fluctuation due to pests and plant diseases) averaged 200 to 300 kilograms of dried hops per hectare. By the end of the century, the average yield had already risen to 550 kilograms per hectare.[4]

Quality of Bavarian Hops

The following table presents an index of world hop prices in relation to Žatec hops during the second half of the nineteenth century. It testifies to the primacy of Bohemian hops in world markets.

Hops variety	Percent ratio	Hops variety	Percent ratio
Bohemian	100	Alsatian	55
Bavarian	60	Poznan	48
Wurtenberg	84	Styrian	77
Baden	75	Kent	70

Improvements in the Brewing Process

In view of traditional consumer habits, the quality of beer was for a long time judged mainly by human senses according to color, foaminess, transparency, taste, and aroma. As the market range of the breweries increased, another important requirement was added—that of durability. From practical experience, it was found that durability depended not only on the degree of hopping but also on the amount of alcohol in the beer. In the absence of measuring instruments, the alcohol content was estimated on the basis of the density and viscosity of the beer. This estimation process led to the use of some curious inspection methods by the breweries. One of these was the Bavarian method in which an inspector dressed in buck-leather trousers sat on a wooden bench coated with beer. The quality of the beer was supposed to have been proven if after one hour he could not get unstuck from the bench.

Up to the end of the eighteenth century, traditional empirical brewing processes were kept secret and were affected by many superstitions. According to these, conjuring and singing of religious songs were more important than carrying out production inspections. The production inspections consisted of random temperature and density checks and completely subjective checks by the human senses.

Improvements in Scientific Knowledge

At the end of the eighteenth century, information began to seep out from neighboring Bavaria into Bohemia about the modernization of the brewing trade in England and in what is today Belgium. Newly introduced brewing by bottom fermentation was resulting in better quality and more durable light and dark beers. In the Bohemian brewing trade, this modern process was not quickly adopted, being introduced only much later under market pressure and after a change in consumer habits.

As large-scale brewing expanded in the nineteenth century, the need for the introduction of scientific inspection methods grew and modern preserving processes and agents were gradually introduced. However, new techniques still had to take into consideration traditional production processes in accord with the taste of the consumer. Application of modern innovations was also inhibited by conflicting theories of fermentation processes and their insufficient contribution to practical production.

The theoretical vagueness of scientific opinions on the mechanism and essence of fermentation supported the long-term survival of traditional empirical methods in controlling and inspecting fermentation processes. Until the introduction of Pasteur's findings of the end of the 1850s, fermentation was deemed to be a purely inorganic chemical process, independent of biological processes. Scientific knowledge was completely separated from production practice and brewers were convinced that they could influence fermentation only to a small degree, and mainly by influencing the temperature of the brewing process.

The initiation of systematic research into the mechanism of fermentation at the end of the nineteenth century, and the introduction of modern biochemistry, led to increased changes in the brewing process. A single major change in the nineteenth century, the introduction of bottom fermentation according to Bavarian examples during the 1840s to 1860s, did, however, lead to other important changes.[5]

From the point of view of monitoring the quality of beer brewed in the Czech lands, the entire nineteenth-century period represents an important intermediate breakthrough in the transition from empirical sensory quality control to the purposeful use of modern scientific findings. The use of precise inspection instruments and the gradual practical utilization of knowledge gained in unifying scientific theories played an important role during this transition period. At the same time, many traditional empirical findings were gradually confirmed and corrected. At the beginning of these efforts at the turn of the eighteenth and nineteenth centuries, the endeavors of the brewer Poupě to reform the outmoded Bohemian brewing trade were particularly noteworthy. Poupě was an example of an empirical brewer who followed up new possibilities for utilizing and controlling traditional brewing processes. In this period of increasing industrialization, efforts to understand and master chemical and natural processes in the brewing industry were similar in significance to the introduction of working and driving machines in manufacturing processes.

F. A. Poupě and *The Art of Beer Brewing*

The main contribution made by the self-taught practitioner Poupě was his summarizing, checking, and supplementing an extensive set of practical brewing knowledge; clearing it of superstition and prejudices; and publishing it in an accessible form in German in 1794 and in Czech in 1801. At the same time, he promoted objective forms of production management and inspection.[6]

In his two volume work *Die Kunst des Bierbrauens* (*The Art of Beer Brewing*), Poupě stressed the importance of monitoring the quality of the basic raw materials and devoted great attention to the preparation of high-grade barley malt. He improved substantially the traditional methods of drying malt by flue gases by recommending the use of metal trays and a thermometer. He also urged removal of the malt roots, the so-called "flower," because he had confirmed their negative effect on the taste and color of the beer. He recommended a water test of the quality of malt. According to this method, a fistful of dry malt was tossed into a water-filled dish and if only 1 percent to 2 percent of the grains submerged, the malt was deemed to be of good quality. If more than a tenth of the grains submerged, the malt was deemed to be of poor quality. At the same time, the grains were not supposed to lie on the surface of the water but were to stand up in the water either diagonally or vertically. Malt earmarked for brewing light beer was not permitted to be burnt or roasted.

Developing Measuring Instruments

The use of thermometers with a Reaumur scale and variously modified densimeters was an important improvement in brewing practice. Bohemian primacy in this field again goes to the brewer Poupě, who began to use a thermometer in 1788 and, on the basis of his own experience and the study of available literature, designed a brass densimeter, the so-called "beer gauge," for measuring the specific weight of brewing liquids. His beer gauge is illustrated in Figure 15.2. The figure shows the stem (*a*) with a scale calibrated at 10°R; float (*b*); and weights (*c* and *d*). From readings of the density scale Poupě estimated the strength of the beer; however, he was aware of the fact that the specific weight does not determine the amount of alcohol in the beer or its strength.[7]

This lack of direct relationship between specific weight and alcohol content was proven by the pharmacist Erxleben who adapted the densimeter for measuring the amount of sugar and malt extracts in weight percentages at the beginning of the nineteenth century. Figure 15.3 shows the Erxleben densimeter. (*A* is a modification with a scale graduated from 0 to 60 and calibrated at 14°R; *B* and *C* are modifications with a scale graduated from 55 to 113; *a* and *b* are weights; *c* the float; and *d* the stem with scale.) Even after Erxleben's work, the beer strength had to be determined by complicated conversion of the specific weight of the distillation product. In the 1840s, a professor of chemical engineering at the Prague Polytechnical Institute—Professor Balling—replaced this impractical method by designing a new practical saccharimeter. He arrived at this design by improving a densimeter developed by Baumé. The apparatus read saccharimeter weight degrees or the percentage of sugar in solution. A contributing factor to its rapid adoption by breweries was the legal assessment of taxes not only according to the volume of beer but, as of 1852, also according to its sugar strength. Wide-scale use of the saccharimeter for precise

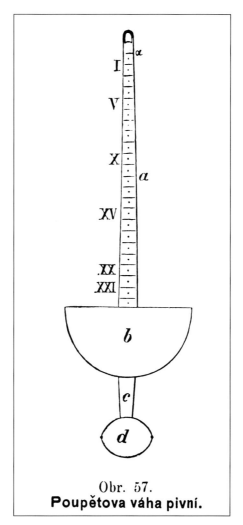

Obr. 57.
Poupětova váha pivní.

Figure 15.2 Poupě brass densimeter (the so-called beer scales) of 1788, used in Bohemia up to the beginning of the nineteenth century. Source: Institute of History, Czech Academy of Science.

continuous monitoring of the whole production process in the fermenting industry was made possible when Balling's proposed reduction of the density of the fermenting solution was formulated in a lucid table. This table made possible quick determinations of the degree of fermentation of the sugar solution and the amount of alcohol in the fermenting solution.[8]

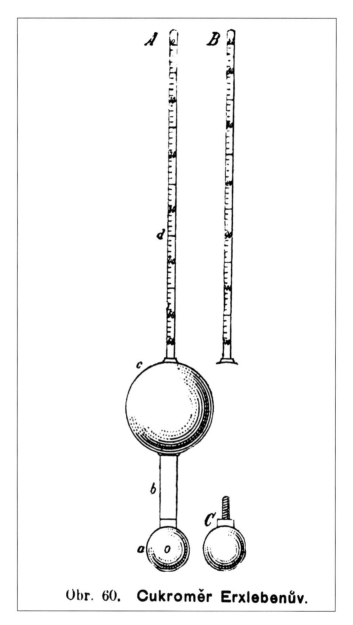

Obr. 60. **Cukroměr Erxlebenův.**

Figure 15.3 Erxleben densimeter used in Bohemia at the beginning of the nineteenth century to determine the amount of sugar in beer. Source: Institute of History, Czech Academy of Science.

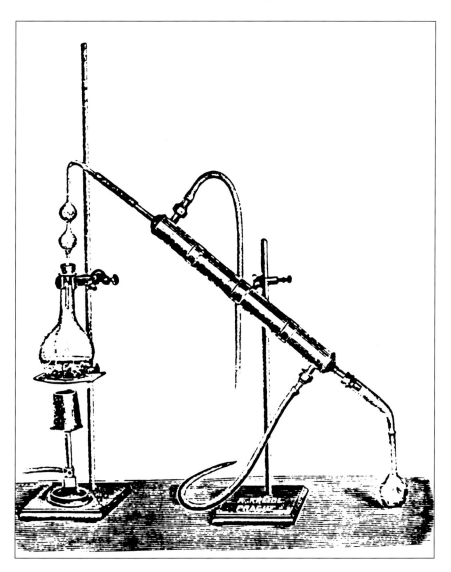

Figure 15.4 Instrument for measuring the alcohol content in a solution, used in the late nineteenth century. Source: Institute of History, Czech Academy of Science.

Change in the Brewing Process As a
Stimulus to Improvement

For a long time, these fundamental innovations ran up against the traditional conservatism of brewers. Perhaps a twentieth of them appreciated the advantages brought about by the use of a thermometer and densimeter. Throughout all of the first half of the nineteenth century the majority of brewers, and many up to the end of the century, persisted in using the traditional sensory testing. One barrier to the adoption of the new measuring instruments was the variability in their readings—these inspection instruments showed a difference of as much as five degrees of the saccharimetric scale up to the end of the nineteenth century. A second barrier was the decentralization of production in a dense network of small rural breweries which obstructed introduction of the new methods of quality inspection and control. Only a tenth of the brewers had a satisfactory knowledge of modern production processes. Finally, in brewing beer empirical use of sensory testing of the foaminess, color, clarity, flavor, and aroma remained practically irreplaceable.

Decisive changes in introducing precision control began only in connection with the transition from the traditional empirical process of surface fermentation to regulated bottom fermentation. In Bohemian breweries, this transition followed Bavarian models and took place in the 1840s to 1860s. The biologically and hygienically harmless, highly hopped light beer was fermented at a temperature of 7°C to 10°C and finish-fermented in barrels in cellars for a period of four to 16 weeks. It proved itself dramatically for the first time during the Prague cholera epidemic in 1853.[9] The new beer brewing processes spread widely during the 1860s under the pressure of changed marketing conditions and consumer requirements. These conditions offered brewers new opportunities in an integrated domestic market interconnected by the railways—at that time under completion—and linking up other countries as well. These changes were closely connected with industrial development and the accompanying urbanization.

The newly introduced bottom fermenting process and longer after-fermentation at a lower temperature not only necessitated modernization of the breweries and the development of cooling systems but also the observation of technological discipline and better knowledge of fermenting chemistry. Whereas the hitherto employed surface fermentation took place spontaneously, bottom fermentation required active expert supervision and continuous monitoring. Connected with these requirements was the need for scientifically confirming and making more precise the traditional empirical findings. From the 1840s onward these and other theoretical findings on fermentation—including use of Balling's saccharimeter and teachings on reducing the density of the fermenting solution—were widely put into practice in a number of fields other than the production of malt and brewing of beer. These other areas included the production of yeast, spirits, wine, and vinegar.

In addition to the use of a thermometer, bottom fermentation in vats was inspected visually. The foam on the surface was supposed to be in a uniform layer resembling a sheep fleece and the amount of carbon dioxide generated was supposed to be sufficient to extinguish a burning torch, at first only at the surface and later also above the vat. The clarity of young beer and the amount of yeast used was determined visually in deciding when it was ready to be poured into lager barrels. As of the 1860s, the increasing requirements placed on the purity and clarity of beer brought about the introduction of filtering the dregs and the use of preserving agents such as salicylic acid when transporting barrels over longer distances. Pasteurization began to be used at the end of the nineteenth century when the sale of bottled beer expanded.

The popularity of light lager beer, headed by the Pilsner Urquell (founded in 1842) spread quickly through the intermediary of the World's Fair held in Vienna in 1873. After bottom fermentation became dominant during the 1860s and abolition of the feudal beer brewing privileges in 1869, beer brewing began to be concentrated in large joint-stock enterprises built in places advantageous for marketing opportunities. These modern municipal breweries, having annual capacities over one million liters of beer, differed substantially from small village breweries. These two groups of breweries employed different standards both of equipment and processes. After the 1880s, large breweries took advantage of discoveries made in the field of microbiology. They used pure yeast cultures, laboratory analyses, and specially trained employees, and introduced indirect steam brewing, artificial machine cooling, effective filtration, and more complete mechanization. The majority of the small rural breweries—even after introducing bottom fermenting—remained at the level of empirical small-scale production (generally as a supplement of agricultural production). They hung on until the beginning of the twentieth century only thanks to the conservative taste of a limited circle of permanent customers.[10] Thus, modern innovation and scientific ways of monitoring quality were used almost exclusively by the large-capacity breweries.

Formal Training and Research

On the initiative of the large breweries, a private brewing and malting school was established in 1869 at the Prague brewery Na Slovanech. The school offered six-month specialized courses. However, it gained in importance only after its reorganization in 1881. The continued suspicion on the part of brewers toward innovations began to be broken by the publication of a number of specialized journals in the malting and brewing field starting in the 1870s. The effort to use scientific theory to make the traditional empirical practice more accurate culminated in the founding of the Brewery Research Institute in Prague in 1887. The institute specialized in chemical analyses, cultivating pure yeast cultures, and holding courses for brewers.

The slow pace of innovation in the brewing sector of that period is indicated by the facts that in 1892 only 10 of the existing 750 Bohemian breweries purchased pure yeast from the institute and that the number of laboratory analyses made at the institute for breweries remained very limited up to the beginning of the twentieth century. It was only later that large breweries began to build their own works laboratories. At the same time, under the pressure of stiff competition, they began to devote attention to the question of biological purity of fermentation and after-fermentation as the main condition for the quality of beer, especially its durability.

The Bohemian brewing industry thus moved toward an optimal symbiosis between the important sensory evaluation and exact measurement and laboratory analysis of production specimens. This integration of empirical experience and science then led to increased uniformity of production and stricter technological discipline. Deserved attention also began to be devoted to checking the harmlessness and quality of water, one of the basic raw materials, next in importance to malt and hops. Systematic research into the mechanism of fermentation finally confirmed existing experience associated with maintaining optimum temperatures, degrees of dilution, sugar content of the ferment solution, and the amount of yeast.

Later Standardization Steps

The original 1805 legal efforts to ensure beer quality and to maintain traditional customs were echoed in legally binding standard specifications of beer quality in the three-volume Austrian Alimentation Code (Codex alimentarius austriacus), published from 1911 to 1917. This state standard specification strictly prohibited the production of beer from substitutes of barley malt; that is, from potato starch, sugar, and rice. It also prohibited the sale of beverages made of substitutes for hops or their extracts. It prohibited improving bad beer and its mixing with good beer. Although these strict norms were violated during the First World War, they were taken over by the new state of Czechoslovakia established in 1918. Again their validity was somewhat alleviated. It was only after the Second World War that a Czechoslovak standard specification on the quality of standard types of malt was adopted. Thus, the Czechoslovak standard specification CSN 56 6605 distinguishes between the Bohemian (Pilsen), Viennese, and Bavarian (Munich) types; contains a binding production process; and defines the mechanical and chemical quality characteristics of the malt. A separate standard specification concerns special grades of malt for the production of dark beers. The standard specification CSN 56 6635 concerns the manufactured types and varieties of beer. It stipulates chemical, physical, and biological stability requirements and common requirements of foaminess, clarity, taste, fragrance, and consumption containerization. It also stipulates, for the purpose of laboratory analysis, the amount of alcohol in the beer, the saccharimetric degrees of the beer, its pH value, color, saturation with carbon dioxide, and biological durability.

Summary

The Czech beer production industry evolved from a long history of local breweries which served local markets. These breweries managed for quality through tradition, empiricism, and trade secrets handed down from generation to generation. The brewery owners were generally comfortable with their results and exhibited strong conservatism when faced with potential change in the industry.

The nineteenth century broadened the boundaries of trade, both domestic and international, and stimulated the emergence of large breweries. The resulting threats and opportunities then intensified competition, including competition in improving quality. The resulting improvements extended to all phases of producing beer.

Improvements in Materials

The most critical input materials in beer production are agricultural products, hops being an example. The properties of hops vary significantly from region to region. Efforts to minimize the variability of hops had included mandating use of locally grown hops rather than using lower-priced imports. During the nineteenth century, much progress was made in identifying those properties of hops that influence the quality of the product. In addition, systems of measurement and sensory evaluation were evolved for grading various crops according to their possession of desired properties. Such grading systems provided brewers with increased flexibility in choice of materials (local and imported) as well as in regulation of the brewing process. In addition, these grading systems were helpful in efforts to improve the selection, growing, and cultivation of hops and other materials.

Improvements in the Brewing Process

Improvements in the brewing process arose from advances and applications of scientific knowledge. One such application was an increased use of measuring instruments, including development of new instruments. The instruments used included thermometers, densimeters, and saccharimeters.

Additional improvements resulted from advances in scientific knowledge. These advances provided an increased understanding of the fermentation process and of the techniques of chemical analysis.

The advances in scientific knowledge also stimulated new contributions to the literature on the subject. Dissemination through publication and training then extended the availability of the new knowledge.

II. Quality Management in Nineteenth-Century Czech Sugar Beet Refining

---

Introduction

Part II of this chapter describes managing for quality in a second nineteenth-century Czech industry—beet sugar production. In contrast to the evolution of the traditional beer brewing industry described in the preceding part, beet sugar refining represented an important non-traditional industry. Both production equipment and process innovations were newly developed for the industry in the nineteenth century, starting in many European countries during the Napoleonic wars and, particularly, during the 1830s. The complicated chemical aspect of this production process required—even in the first primitively equipped pilot plants—at least the use of a thermometer, possibly litmus paper and a densimeter as well as a relatively high degree of empirical know-how. Only specialists—trained in the first French or German sugar refineries and having a fairly high knowledge of chemistry—were able to control the exacting manufacture of beet sugar. These experts generally required university-level education.

Sugar beets are one of the two main sources of commercial refined sugar (sucrose). The other, of course, is sugar cane. Refined beet and cane sugars are indistinguishable in their final form and the conversion processes from raw material to finished product are similar. One difference in the production processes for the two raw materials involves the conversion of raw sugar into refined sugar. In the cane sugar industry, raw sugar is produced in a tropical or semitropical area and then shipped to more developed areas for refining. One major cause of the division of the process in this manner is the difference in technological sophistication of the two stages of the manufacturing process. Obtaining raw sugar from cane is a relatively simple process, while converting raw sugar into refined sugar is much more complicated. This separation of the manufacturing process was also encouraged by the shortage of inexpensive fuel and abundant pure water in tropical areas where cane is grown.

In the case of beet sugar refining, the process of extracting raw sugar from the beets has been a sophisticated process from the very beginning of the industry, and both raw sugar extraction and refining are normally performed in the same factory rather than in different locations. The process involves extracting sugar juice from the beet, purifying the juice, extracting the liquids and solids used for purification, thickening, and finally crystallizing the thickened juice. During the early stages of the beet sugar industry, when consumers were less demanding in terms of final products and refining techniques were less developed, a separation between raw beet sugar production and refining was more common than it was by the end of the nineteenth century.

Evolution of the Industry

Sugar in the beet root was discovered in 1747 by the Berlin pharmacist Andreas Sigmund Marggraf. He produced crystal sugar from the dried roots by means of alcohol maceration. At that time, the sugar beet contained about 5 percent sugar. In 1802, Francois Charles Achard built the first beet sugar refinery in the world in Silesia. He succeeded in gaining sugar yields of 2 percent to 3 percent from the beet. In the Czech lands the expansion of beet sugar refining occurred first during the Napoleonic wars when the import of cane sugar was stopped. Additional expansions occurred in the 1830s and then in the second half of the nineteenth century as steam-driven equipment, new scientific knowledge, new instruments, and improvements in raw material and production processes enabled large output increases to occur. The sugar yield was gradually increased by achieving higher sugar content in the incoming raw material and by perfecting the production processes employed. By the end of the nineteenth century, refined beet sugar was a major export of the Czech lands.

Consumer Tastes and Types of Sugar Products

During the first half of the nineteenth century, the first sugar factories sold beet sugar syrup and raw sugar to consumers, gingerbread bakers, and sweets manufacturers. Syrup was also cooked in small quantities for self-consumption by farming households. In the 1850s, when sugar became an article of mass consumption, the sugar factories had to establish a refining department or sell ground and dried raw sugar to large sugar factories equipped with refineries. In the 1880s, independent sugar refineries were also established for processing raw sugar. Some of the raw sugar factories produced sugar mainly for export by centrifuging and steam whitening fine-grained crystal or crushed consumption sugar. In place of the original lengthy process of spontaneous crystallization, the pressing and centrifuging of loaves was introduced in the 1880s.

The production of refined sugar loaves predominated throughout the nineteenth century. These loaves weighed 12 to 13 kilograms. Later, from the beginning of the twentieth century, small loaves weighing 5 kilograms were produced, and even smaller loaves of about 2 kilograms were also made for export to the Orient. In addition, the sugar factories produced small amounts of lump sugar by pressing and casting, and granulated sugar in the form of coarse or fine crystals, "sand," and powder sugar.

For export the sugar factories produced special types of sugar such as pile (an irregular coarse-grained sugar), fine powder icing sugar, and rock candy (large white to brown sugar crystals used as candy or for sweetening beverages). Polarization, the use of light rays traveling in different directions to reveal different properties of a substance, was used to determine the quality of the sugar. Sugar quality was also judged by the uniformity of size and grain and by the luster, color, purity, hardness, solubility, brightness, and transparency of the crystals. A substantial part of these visually assessed quality properties was subject to the tastes of the region and of the period. Since the end of the nineteenth century, the Czech sugar industry has ranked among the world's main exporters of sugar, adapting quality, finish, and price to purchaser requirements.

Quality Control and Sugar Refining Research

The direct dependence of profitability on quality was apparent when the first sugar refineries were founded in the early nineteenth century. Therefore, quality control developed hand-in-hand with the development of sugar refining. Quality control and improvement focused not only on all stages of the production process but also on the incoming raw material. The sugar beet and the whole process of cultivating and growing this plant received attention. Because the value of the beet for sugar refining is based on the amount of sugar contained in the root, methods for determining the sugar content took on paramount importance.

Sugar refining research had a tradition of longer standing and a broader base in the Czech lands than was true in other branches of the fermenting industry. This research started with the first experiments performed by local pharmacists and business clerks working for the nobility with the aim of gaining sugar from local plants—primarily sugar beet and maple trees—during the Napoleonic wars. These early experiments were followed by numerous experiments made after the 1830s in introducing new methods of purifying and leaching sugar juice. As a result, many early refineries had the character of experimental and pilot plants.

Trained Experts and Research Laboratories

The position of the privileged empirical experts began to be threatened in the 1850s by the appearance of highly qualified graduates of the Prague Polytechnical Institute, where they received theoretical training in the field of chemical technology under the guidance of Professor Balling. A lower level of education was considered inadequate for the sugar industry so that—unlike the situation in the brewing and malting industries—secondary-level training centers were not established in the sugar refining field.

The first chemical laboratories were set up in large sugar refineries as far back as the 1850s and the chemists who led them were called the "conscience of the factory."[11] Up to the 1880s, specialized graduates of the Prague Polytechnical Institute found employment mainly in the laboratories of about 200 domestic sugar refineries and later on also in breweries. In 1888—after the introduction of a consumer tax on sugar—they could also hold the post of technical and financial inspectors. However, utilization of their knowledge for the systematic introduction of scientific process control remained limited—even in large-capacity sugar refineries—by the restricted degree of production concentration and technological modernization.

In 1859 the Bohemian Sugar Industry Association established a Sugar Testing Laboratory at a sugar factory in Zbraslav near Prague. Here, the Association's chemical engineers perfected the sensory as well as the more accurate instrument test methods, and investigated the effect of soil conditions on the sugar content of the beet. During the first half of the 1860s, the Sugar Testing Laboratory significantly contributed to perfecting and disseminating findings on the new diffusion and saturation method. Agrochemical research gave impetus to the development of sugar beet growing and to an increase in the sugar content of the beet of up to 12 percent.

Applied specialized research remained limited to better-equipped laboratories of a few large refineries and depended mainly on the personal initiative of the individual chemical engineers and directors of the sugar refineries. It was only in 1896 that the Bohemian Sugar Industry Association set up a small research laboratory in two rooms in Prague. The rooms and equipment were rented from the Chemical Department of the Czech Technical University. However, the advanced Czech sugar industry had to wait until 1923 for the construction of a modern research institute of its own.[12]

Figure 15.5 Laboratory of a beet-sugar refinery at Dolni Bousov in Bohemia (1915). Source: Institute of History, Czech Academy of Science.

Measuring Instruments

The development of measuring instruments played a key role in improving the industry. The saccharometer evolved by Professor Balling found wide application.[13] The specific weight of the sugar solution was generally given either in degrees of the Balling or Baumé saccharometer and precise tables were used for conversion of the two. Herles invented a densimeter for rapid checks when selecting beet for seed and was also the inventor of the hot water digestion method for beet juice (1887).

Whereas at the beginning of the 1850s the basic instrument used in production analyses was the Balling saccharometer, by the end of the century it had become the polarimeter. In 1862, newly evolved optical measurement by means of polarimeters facilitated and made possible a more accurate quantitative analysis of the sugar juice. As against density meters, which read the total amount of the sugar and the nonsugar components, the optical instruments measured only the amount of sugar contained in the juice. Its design and ready use were based on the finding that the proportion of pure saccharose in the product can be determined from the deflection of light passing through the polarimeter. The first polarimeters were available by the 1840s, but their practical mass use did not take place until the 1870s, in connection with the standardization of commercial and consumer habits. In the 1870s, demands for higher quality came from the increasingly export-oriented character of Czech sugar refining and from consumers. These demands speeded up the equipping of sugar refineries with inspection instruments and the establishing of works' laboratories.

When processing the sugar juice, refiners tried to introduce simple inspection aids that could be easily used in production even by untrained seasonal workers whose employment traditionally predominated in sugar refineries. Generally, there was no time for complicated calculations, and results of subsequent theoretical research could be applied in practice only in the form of lucid tables. This, for example, was the case in the late 1890s with improved precision testing of vacuum thickening. As a result, sensory evaluation continued to exist for a long time. In addition to conventional thermometers, density meters, and saccharometers, broader application was made of (1) phenolphthalein indicator paper for determining the alkalinity of the sugar juice and (2) titration instruments evolved by the Czech sugar refiner Hodek and used since 1872 for checking saturation.

Raw Material

The wild predecessor of the sugar beet gradually spread from its original domicile (probably Caucasia and the surroundings of the Caspian Sea) to Europe. Originally, the sugar beet was used as fodder, even though the sweetness of the root of some varieties was known as early as the sixteenth century. Marggraf's 1747 discovery of sugar in the beet was later put to practical use by the German chemist of French descent Achard, the first real sugar beet cultivator. In addition to building the first Silesian sugar beet refinery, he was the author of many practical hints and pieces of advice for his followers. On the basis of long-term comparative experiments, he reached the conclusion that the white Silesian sugar beet was best suited to the production of sugar.

Improving Sugar Beets for Use in Refining

France was the cradle of sugar beet improvement. One of the representatives of the famous French family of cultivators and improvers—Vilmorin—devoted himself systematically to raising the sugar content in the beet root. He achieved good results. Around 1850 he began to improve the sugar content by the method of mass selection in both the positive and negative sense. Because he realized that the sugar content of individual beets differed considerably, he determined their sugar content according to the advice of the chemist Boussingault. He immersed a small cylinder cut out of the beet into saline solutions of diverse concentration. From the specific weight of the solution he determined the sugar content and selected seedlings, the progeny of which he then tested again. By this method he soon succeeded in cultivating sugar beets with a substantially higher sugar content, achieving a sugar content of between 8 percent and 9 percent.

Similar improvements occurred elsewhere. In Germany, for example, specialists at an improvement farm in Wanzleben advanced sugar beet propagation by the method of individual selection, by the seedling method, and by the method of dividing select varieties of beet. They also developed some new methods of quality control in the refining process. In 1862 they evolved a method for polarizing juice; in 1879 they developed a method for checking the juice by alcohol extraction; and in 1886 digestion of the beet slurry was introduced.

Seed developmental work went on hand-in-hand with the growing requirements placed on seed quality. Experimental work began in the 1870s to find the relation between properties of the seed and the quality of the beet. Since no significant dependence was found on the color, size, or scent of the seeds, the sowing of control fields remained the most important method of quality control of the seed.

The first seed inspection station was established in 1880 in Opava. Founding the Society for Propagating Beet Seed and establishing its seed station in Semčice in 1894 were of decisive importance. Legal approval of the seed quality was not instituted, however, until the passing of the required law in 1921.

Balancing Growing and Refining Requirements

Sugar beet improvement in the 1850s and 1860s was directed chiefly at the sugar content. The successes in doing so carried disadvantages with them. While the new types of beet had a high sugar content, the size and weight of the root diminished. These changes led to disagreements between the beet growers and the sugar refiners. In the beginning, sugar refiners stipulated payment for the purchased beet according to the sugar content. The unwillingness of farmers to adapt to that requirement led to a situation in which the sugar refineries stipulated that the beet be grown from seed supplied to the farmers by the sugar refineries. However, sugar beet seed improved exclusively for a high sugar content led to small yields.

These problems were solved by changing the goal of improvement efforts to aim for maximum production of sugar per unit area. Improvers thus had to take into consideration a number of other factors for determining the quality of the plants. Included in their new evaluations was the hitherto overlooked leaf of the plant—the size of its assimilation area; the color of the leaf; its luster, surface, border, shape, and position. The weight and shape of the root and the number of secondary roots were also found to be of great importance. The root was to be conical in shape with a thin white skin and a dense crisp pulp. The improvement farms also searched for the most suitable method of cultivation and fertilization.[14]

The rapid development of chemistry made it possible to concentrate attention on the composition of the beet. This knowledge made it possible to improve both the production and inspection processes. One of the important control indicators introduced by the 1860s was a coefficient of purity which expressed the purity of the sugar juice. This was necessary because the sugar juice in addition to sugar and water also contains other substances. These include nitrogenous and nonnitrogenous organic compounds and inorganic minerals. These convert the juice into molasses.[15]

Increase in Beet Sugar Content

The increase in the sugar content of the beet—the most important characteristic of its quality—is documented during the course of the nineteenth century by a number of authors whose data differ somewhat. From the average data of different sources and from the polarization records of various sugar refineries the following improvements appeared to have occurred.

	Mid–nineteenth century	End of nineteenth century
Sugar content	9% to 10%	12% to 16%
Purity coefficient	about 70%	88% to 90%
Root solids	18% to 20%	25% to 27%

The Refining Process

For the Czech sugar industry, the first half of the nineteenth century was a period of gaining empirical experience, unifying and demystifying practical experience, and beginning to verify and improve production processes using scientific theories and experiments. Despite progress in introducing exact measuring instruments, early sensory evaluation methods continued to be used. For many years, the latter proved irreplaceable, especially in the final production stages.

Production of beet sugar consisted of relatively complicated, lengthy, and energy-consuming phases. The process started with extraction of sugar juice from the beet. The next stages involved purifying the juice, extracting the liquids and solids used for purification, and then thickening. The final stage consisted of crystallizing the thickened juice.

For a long time, the successful completion of this exacting production process depended on the production control knowledge of experts. In the beginning, the basic condition for successful production

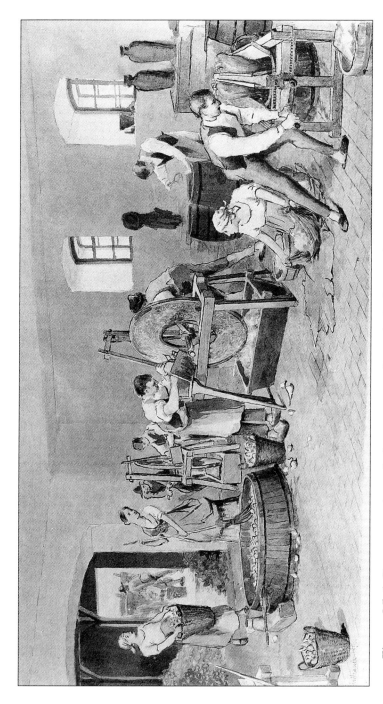

Figure 15.6 Reconstruction of a beet-sugar refinery in Bohemia during the 1811 to 1814 period; preparatory work, including washing and grating sugar beet, packing beet pulp into filter cloths, pressing, and the first stage of sugar juice refining. Source: Institute of History, Czech Academy of Science.

did not necessarily depend on gaining high-grade sugar beet but mainly on engaging experienced refiners who kept their know-how in deep secrecy. Thus, until the middle of the nineteenth century, these circumstances prevented cooperation and the exchange of experience in production and slowed down the application of scientific findings and production control.

Improving the Refining Process

One of the earliest process improvements occurred in the mid-1830s, when two German experts in the Czech lands—Weinrich and Kodweiss—modified the process for juice purification. Even under the continuing primitive technical conditions of small-scale sugar refining occurring at that time, they emphasized the necessity of more thorough production control. This improvement largely involved better sensory evaluation of the optimum amount of lime in the sugar juice by successive testing of juice specimens on a test spoon. The purification process was monitored on the basis of sludge separation and a sufficient supply of lime was determined according to the formation of a calcium carbonate layer on the surface of the specimen.[16]

Steam-Powered Equipment, Greater Knowledge, and New Instruments

In the early years of production, a great amount of human labor was required for operating beet-root slicers and presses to produce sugar juice. A significant breakthrough took place during the 1850s when—even though the inefficient method of pressing and purification of the juice continued—the sugar refineries made full use of steam power for driving sets of production machines and for heating complicated process equipment. At the same time the position of privileged empirical experts was being breached by the increasing availability of trained chemists and the mass introduction of basic measuring instruments. These, in addition to the existing thermometer and densimeter now included the new Balling saccharometer.

By the 1870s, introduction of steam-driven machinery and new processes involving diffusion and saturation had reduced the human labor required considerably. However, considerable room for improving yields remained. Even with 100 percent thinning of the beet slurry, at best only 90 percent of juice was gained from it. While thinning of the slurry lowered this loss, power costs for evaporation and thickening increased.

Improvements in Extracting Sugar Juice

The broader use of scientific control and inspection methods in Czech sugar factories took place only after the introduction of large-scale production methods. Large-scale production became possible with the discovery and introduction of domestic technological innovations on a wide scale, which replaced the original methods of pressing and purifying the juice. In 1864 the university-trained Robert, who headed a family-owned sugar refinery in Moravia, determined the optimum temperature for leaching beet slices. By taking advantage of his knowledge of osmosis, he was able to complete his father's earlier experiments and those of numerous other production specialists. Their experiments had failed in the 1830s because of the mistaken principle of killing the beet cells by high temperatures. Robert worked with equipment enabling accurate temperature measurement and control. After many experiments he arrived at the principle of gradually leaching the beet slices by preheated sugar juice of various densities. By determining the optimum temperature he ensured an adequate leaching effect and applied the principle of gradual leaching by arranging diffusion vessels into a staircase-arranged interconnected bank.

In 1870, the German sugar refiner Schulz replaced the danger of overheating the beet slices by admitting hot sugar juice on the already partly leached beet slices and the necessity of their tedious mixing by admitting the sugar juice under pressure into the bottom of a diffusion vessel. This new leaching process quickly replaced pressing both at home and abroad. Diffusion contributed to a rise in labor productivity, increased the sugar yield from the beets, brought about power savings, and opened the way to mass production.

Purifying the Sugar Juice

The costly juice extracting phase was followed by an exacting chemical phase of purifying the sugar juice. The Czech sugar refineries initially adopted and modified the German Achard process with use being made of sulfuric acid and lime. It was found empirically that inorganic acids speed up the hydrolysis of the polysaccharides into monosaccharides incapable of crystallization and that basic substances restrain this process. Therefore, after 1830 use was made of lime milk and sulfuric acid as the principal purifying agents.

The complicated chemical part of the production process was continuously monitored only in those phases that depended mostly on empirical experience, the failure of which could lead to considerable production losses. After the purification phase the next major area of concern was the subsequent boiling of the sugar juice. Here, for a long time, use was made of sensory evaluation in addition to precise temperature and density measurements. The purity of the sugar juice was assessed before the evaporation and thickening of the sugar juice according to color and taste. A higher degree of chemical control by means of a litmus paper was used for removing excess lime by means of sulfuric acid. Next, the sugar juice was thickened to 45° Baumé by evaporation. This was followed by the final thickening to a supersaturated sugar juice which had to be capable of spontaneous crystallization during gradual cooling and stirring.[17]

Simultaneously with the evolution of the diffusion process in the Czech lands, another decisive production process was developed which modernized existing methods of purifying the sugar juice. It was based on improved temperature control and a previous finding, associated with the thorough separation of lime mud after reaction of the juice with lime. For removing the excess lime, it was desirable to replace sulfuric acid with other acids which had a lesser effect on sugar inversion. Until the early 1860s, however, greater use of phosphoric and carbonic acid had run up against an insufficient and unproven temperature control. Inability to use these alternative acids had made it necessary to perform expensive and lengthy filtration with bone charcoal.

A second decisive shift in this sphere took place thanks to the Czech engineer Jelínek—a pupil of Professor Balling. Jelínek linked the old method (purifying the sugar juice with lime) with saturation of this solution with carbon dioxide (generated during the burning of lime in kilns on the courtyards of sugar refineries). In addition, Jelínek elaborated and introduced exact temperature control which significantly affected sugar losses. The course of saturation was controlled visually according to specimens taken by means of a test spoon. The end of the process was determined according to the distinct separation of

Figure 15.7 Reconstruction of a beet-sugar refinery in Bohemia
during the 1811 to 1814 period; chemical end of the process,
including refining of the sugar juice, filtration, and evaporation.
Source: Institute of History, Czech Academy of Science.

pure sugar juice from the mud and disappearance of the calcium carbonate film from the surface of the specimen. After further improvement during the 1860s, the new method substantially simplified and
speeded up production. This suitable supplement to diffusion became
the basis for additional technological improvements, such as the process of triple saturation introduced in the middle of the 1880s.

Thickening

Determining the right degree of thickening was one of the supreme
empirical arts of sugar refiners until Claassen elaborated theoretical
principles of sugar refining and devised practical temperature and pressure tables in Germany in 1898. Although vacuum thickening equipment—heated by steam and equipped with a built-in thermometer

and pressure gage—was gradually being introduced in Czech sugar refineries by the 1830s, sensory evaluation methods continued until the end of the century. The optimum degree of thickening was determined according to the sound and movement of the heavy juice, observed through a view glass, in addition to sensory test of an extracted sample. In the so-called "bubble test," a perforated scoop was immersed into the syrup and the density was judged according to the size, luster, and longevity of the blown-out bubbles. In the so-called "fiber test," an experienced sugar refiner held a drop of syrup between his fingers and by spreading it determined the density according to the length and thickness of the fibers. The reason for the long survival of the sensory tests was that a practical inspection instrument—the brasmoscope, operating on the principle of a mercury pressure gage—was not evolved until 1893 by the Czech technician Cuřín.

Figure 15.8 Reconstruction of a beet-sugar refinery in Bohemia during the 1811 to 1814 period; final part of the production, including thickening of the syrup and crystallization.
Source: Institute of History, Czech Academy of Science.

Increase in Sugar Yields from Beets

The following review of sugar yield from sugar beets and the required amount of beets per sugar unit clearly reveals the great improvements starting in the mid–nineteenth century and continuing into the 1890s.[18] During this period, a significant breakthrough took place in Czech beet sugar refining reflected in the introduction of modern production processes and equipment, the use of precision inspection instruments and methods as well as the results of theoretical and applied research, and the influence of the manufacturers on the quality of the basic raw material.

Year	Sugar yield (%)	Tons of sugar beet per 100 kg of sugar
1841	5.5	1.8
1851	6.5	1.5
1861	7.5	1.3
1871	8.2	1.2
1881	9.5	1.0
1891	11.8	0.8
1901	15.7	0.6
1911	15.7	0.6
1921	17.5	0.5

State Taxation Policies and Sugar Quality

The state taxation policy—as in the case of brewing—had a favorable effect on the attention given to the quality of sugar. By the early 1830s the state was facilitating the development of domestic sugar production by tax exemptions and by imposing duty on imports. It was also stipulating the compulsory marking of sugar loaves with a legible stamp of an assigned factory mark.[19] Beginning in 1880, measurement of the percentage share of pure sugar by polarimeters for meeting commercial standards was also used for assigning a tax restitution during export. In such an event, sugar manufacturers received a tax refund of different rates for two groups of raw sugar with a polarization of 88 percent to 92 percent and 92 percent to 99.5 percent and for refined sugar of a minimum polarization of 99.5 percent. The need for exact measurement led to the development of excellent instruments. High-grade polarimeters of Czech origin even penetrated the exacting American market. In 1910, the specialized Prague firm of Josef a Jan Frič—which in 1887 evolved a polarimeter of its own—received an order for these instruments from the United States Bureau of Standards for checking imported sugar.

Uniform Quality Control Standards

By the end of the nineteenth century, chemical analytical methods were quite precise. Building on this progress, the Bohemian Sugar Industry Association was among the first in Europe to introduce a uniform procedure for implementing quality control in sugar refineries. In 1896 this Association issued a Manual for Performing Chemical Analyses in Sugar Refineries According to Uniform Methods. The Manual contained an exact description of the quality control process, beginning with taking specimens directly from the field, from the carts that transported the sugar beet to the sugar refinery, and from the beet slicer to the analysis of all individual production processes in the sugar refinery. In 1911, the Manual was revised by the Sugar Refining Research Station in Prague so as to take into account newly developed instruments and newly evolved analytical methods.

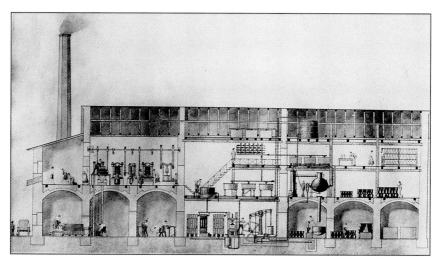

Figure 15.9 Model of the Bilina sugar refinery in Bohemia according to the state in 1855—example of a factory-type steam operation prior to introduction of new diffusion and saturation processes.
Source: Institute of History, Czech Academy of Science.

Summary

While the discovery of sugar in sugar beets dates back to 1747, the impetus for large-scale production came from the Napoleonic wars which cut off the import of cane sugar.

At the outset, beet sugar yields were low due to use of low-yielding beets and to empirical methods of extraction and refining. Then multiple actions were taken to improve quality and increase productivity.

• The government took steps to help a potentially profitable industry. From 1831 to 1849 the government exempted the industry from taxes and protected it against import of cane sugar by a high customs tariff. The industry then withstood the tax burden imposed in the 1850s, and in sharp competition with cane sugar managed to displace it completely in the 1860s.

• A wide array of technology was adopted to design sophisticated processes for sugar extraction and refining.

• The factories increasingly appointed university-educated mechanical and chemical engineers to managerial posts.

• Instrumentation and laboratories were evolved for precise measurement of process conditions and product quality.

• Quality control systems were adopted to assure stability of the manufacturing processes.

• Quality control was extended to beet growing by mandating use of high-yield seed provided by the factories, and by auditing the quality control practices of the beet growers.

Between the 1850s and 1870s, Czech beet sugar refining reached a relatively modern large-scale production level. Domestic production innovations opened up new markets and made sugar available as a mass-consumption commodity rather than a luxury delicacy. With the assistance of the state, domestic beet sugar production began to assert itself in foreign markets. In the 1880s the industry already exported two-thirds of its total production.

The industry continued to progress in the final third of the nineteenth century. New measuring instruments helped to support continued improvement of production processes. Agricultural experiments continued the increase in sugar content of sugar beets. The availability of university-trained chemists and mechanical engineers encouraged the expansion of laboratories in the plants and improvements in production processes. The Bohemian Sugar Industry Association published a uniform procedure for implementing quality control for all related processes, from the beet fields through the steps in the refineries. In the final three decades of the nineteenth century plus the first decade of the twentieth century, the sugar yield from a kilogram of beets doubled.

Notes

1. Janáček, J. *Pivovarnictví v českých královských městech v 16. století* (Beer Brewing in the Bohemian Royal Towns in the Sixteenth Century); Prague 1959.

2. Vilikovský, V. *Dějiny zemědělského průmyslu v Československu* (History of the Agricultural Industry in Czechoslovakia); Prague 1936.

3. Olbricht, F. *Böhmens Hopfenbau und Handel* (Bohemian Hop Growing and Trade); Prague 1835.

4. Mohl, A. *Chmelařství* (Hop Growing), Vol. 2; Prague 1924.

5. Štrbáňová, S. "Počátky biochemických přístupů v kvasné chemii v Čechách" (Beginnings of a Biochemical Approach to Fermenting Chemistry in Bohemia), *Dějiny věd a techniky*, Vol. 9; 1976.

6. Poupě, F. A. *Die Kunst des Bierbrauens* I–II (The Art of Beer Brewing, Vols. 1 and 2); Prague 1794.

7. Ibid.

8. Balling, C. J. N. *Die Gärungschemie wissenschaftlich begründet* I–IV (Scientific Explanation of Fermenting Chemistry, Vols. 1 to 4); Prague 1845 to 1847.

9. Daněk, J. *Popis pivovarnictví na spodni kvaseni* (Description of Beer Brewing by Bottom Fermentation); Prague 1852.

10. Brettschneider, A. *Nástin vývoje techniky československeho pivovarnictví od konce 18. stoleti do roku 1945* (Outline of the Development of the Czechoslovak Beer Brewing Industry from the End of the Eighteenth Century up to 1945), *Sborník pro dějiny přodních věd a techniky*, Vol. 10; Prague 1965.

11. Kopecký, R. "Stručný přehled technického vývoje českého cukrovarnictví" (Brief review of the Technological Development of the Czech Sugar Refining Industry), *Sborník pro dějiny věd a techniky*, Vol. 10; Prague 1965, pp. 195–252.

12. Dudek, F. *Monopolizace cukrovarnictví v českých zemích do roku 1938* (Monopolization of the Sugar Refining Industry in the Czech Lands up to 1938); Prague 1985.

13. Balling, *Die Gärungschemie wissenschaftlich begründet.*

14. Proskowetz, P. *Pokroky v pěstění a šlechtění řepy cukrové* (Advances in Cultivating and Improving Sugar Beet); Prague 1934.

15. Diviš, J. V. *Rukověť rotborů cukrovarnických* (Handbook of Sugar Refining Analyses); Prague 1873.

16. Diviš, J. V. *Příspěvky k dějinám průmyslu cukrovarnického v Čechách. Období 1830–1860* (Contribution to the History of the Sugar Refining Industry in Bohemia. 1830 to 1860 Period); Prague 1891.

17. Dudek, F. *Vývoj cukrovarnického průmyslu v českých zemích do roku 1872* (Development of the Sugar Refining Industry in the Czech Lands up to 1872); Prague 1979.

18. Vilikovský, *Dějiny zemědělského průmyslu v Československu.*

19. Říha, O. *Počátky českého cukrovarnictví* (Beginnings of Czech Sugar Refining); Prague 1976.

CHAPTER 16

The Recent History of Managing for Quality in Japan

Izumi Nonaka, Associate Professor
Josai University, Faculty of Economics

Introduction

Japan has a long history of involvement with quality. Over the centuries its craftsmen achieved high levels of quality in products such as paper, silks, lacquer-ware, swords, etc. However, the policy of isolation during the Tokogawa Shogunate (1603–1867) contributed to a lag in technology.

The Meiji Restoration (1867) brought an end to isolation and to the feudal system. The country swiftly adopted technology and industrialization. In the military area, the resulting weaponry proved to be quite competitive in quality during the early stages of World War II (WWII). In contrast, civilian goods produced for export were often of such poor quality that Japan acquired a reputation as a producer of shoddy goods.

The defeat during WWII was a severe shock to all aspects of Japanese life, and it took years for the nation to recover. The major companies, that had been suppliers to the military, suddenly lost their chief customer. They were faced with converting to civilian products, deciding what products to make, designing such products (or copying the designs of others), learning how to make them, and then trying to sell them despite Japan's poor quality reputation. The chief obstacle to completing such a changeover was Japan's poor quality reputation. The challenge was to change that reputation by learning how to achieve high quality.

The Japanese met that challenge. They revolutionized their quality and thereby became recognized as the world leaders in quality. This achievement, which took place within four decades after World War II, is without precedent in industrial history. For this reason, this chapter focuses on the principal events and contributions which led to that revolution. Three major contributions came from American sources: the training courses organized by the Civil Communications Section of the American occupation forces; Dr. W. Edwards Deming's lectures on statistical quality control; and Dr. J. M. Juran's lectures on managing for quality. Additional contributions came from Japanese institutions such as the Japanese Union of Scientists and Engineers, through training seminars, conferences, publications, and so on. Further contributions came from the Japanese companies as they applied the concepts and methods provided by this dissemination.

The Era of Statistical Quality Control

Pre–World War II Developments

In Japan, as in most countries, the first phase in the evolution of modern methods of managing for quality was the adoption of statistical tools to improve the control of quality. Prior to WWII it was rare for Japanese companies to be using what we today call *statistical quality control* (SQC). Yet there were a number of researchers working on their own. At a seminar on industrial efficiency held in Osaka in 1924, for example, Kinnosuke Ogura reported his thought of application of statistics to industry.[1] Kanzo Kiribuchi also devoted a scant but significant three pages to the introduction of quality control in chapter 5 of *Kogyo kanri yoko* (*An Outline of Industrial Management*), published in 1934.[2] It is not clear, however, how these individuals obtained their knowledge of quality control. It is said that there were also others who applied statistical quality control during the prewar era, but we will describe one notable example, Yoshida Ishida.

Yasushi Ishida of the former Tokyo Shibaura Electric Company (now the Toshiba Corporation) expended great effort on behalf of quality control in the prewar period, introducing control charts there. He also later worked with Dr. Toshio Kitagawa to translate E. S. Pearson's *The Application of Statistical Methods to Industrial Standardization and Quality Control* into Japanese. Let us examine how Yasushi Ishida, who was awarded the Deming Prize in 1956, arrived at his understanding of quality control.

According to Ishida,

> When I was close to graduating from the Tokyo Higher Technical School (which later evolved into the Tokyo Institute of Technology), I had to decide what company I was going to work for. At that time, the company that had sought to bring in American management methods earliest was Tokyo Electric Company, Ltd. [predecessor of today's Toshiba]. Tokyo Electric had a tie-up with General Electric of the U.S., and was introducing scientific management. I had studied the Taylor system at the university . . . and, as a part-time job while still a student, translated an English paper on scientific management for a magazine known as Efficiency. I wanted to put my knowledge to work after graduation, and consequently chose Tokyo Electric.[3]

Ishida joined Tokyo Electric Co., Ltd. in 1920 and, in 1923, was assigned to work on research and manufacturing of lightbulbs, one of the company's main products at the time. He quickly realized that statistical methods were necessary to make longer lasting bulbs, but there was no one in the company capable of guiding him. He thus had no choice other than to carry out his own studies of modern statistics. He wrote directly to Karl Pearson, the famous British statistician, after coming across his name in publications, and Dr. Pearson replied encouragingly that:

> I too am very interested in lengthening the life of lightbulbs and in the application of statistics to production. However, my age prevents me from proceeding with these investigations and I would like to recommend this sort of study to my son, Egon S. Pearson.[4]

Shortly thereafter, Ishida found out about the results achieved by Dr. Walter A. Shewhart of the United States in his application of statistics to quality control in mass production. It is unclear when

Ishida came to know of Dr. Shewhart's control charts, but in the period from 1931 to 1933 he was already producing his own *makimono* (scrolls of control charts) which became known as Ishida-type control charts for improving the quality of lightbulbs.[5]

Often referred to as the "phantom control charts," they were destroyed by the bombing accompanying WWII, meaning that almost no one alive today claims to have seen them, although they are reported to have been written vertically like Japanese scrolls. Also, because they tended to be quite long, they were rolled up for storage, leading to the affectionate appellation, "the scrolls." When the manufacture of lightbulbs at the Tokyo Electric was interrupted because of some breakdown, those in charge of production would come to Ishida and ask to see "the scrolls" in order to take action.[6] However, rigid controls on technical information around the year 1930 meant that very few people within Tokyo Electric knew of the top secret control charts, and absolutely no mention of their existence was made outside the company.

Even after the war, there was very little awareness of control charts or quality control within the company, as revealed by an episode involving Dr. Eizaburo Nishibori. The occasion was a visit to Toshiba by Frank A. Polkinghorn of the Occupation Forces' General Headquarters' Civil Communications Section (CCS) to place an order for transmission-type vacuum tubes. Dr. Nishibori, known later both for his role as a pioneer in quality control and as the chief of the first Japanese Antarctic Expedition, was then working for Toshiba. He later reminisced that, "I had never heard the words *quality control* until queried by Mr. Polkinghorn, who asked, 'Do you do quality control?'" Nishibori responded in a confident manner, "We place great emphasis on quality, so you need not worry," but was stymied when Mr. Polkinghorn asked to be shown the company's control charts. It was literally the first time that Nishibori had heard of them. When he showed charts detailing the fraction defective, Mr. Polkinghorn exclaimed, "Those aren't control charts! Your company doesn't seem to know much about methods of quality control."[7]

While there existed scattered knowledge of SQC in the prewar era, there is no evidence that the three pioneers—Ogura, Kiribuchi, and Ishida—had any contact with each other. Each appears to have been working alone on SQC research without knowledge of the others' activities. Yasushi Ishida, however, was acquainted with the statistician Dr. Jiro Yamanouchi and with Dr. Toshio Kitagawa, and the three of them attempted to introduce statistical methods to military production during the war. When Ishida was working on lightbulbs, he had the opportunity to work with Yamanouchi, then a researcher with the prewar Ministry of Communications. Around 1937 or 1938, the two men were often discussing the standardization of lightbulbs, with Ishida strongly pressing his case for the introduction of Pearson statistics to Japanese industry. Through his contact with Yamanouchi, Ishida was introduced to Toshio Kitagawa, then a professor at Kyushu University in Fukuoka, leading to their joint translation of the afore-mentioned book by E. S. Pearson,[8] published in Japanese in 1942.

Developments During World War II

The Ishida/Kitagawa translation of Pearson's book was published together with a translation of an important American article, "Report of the War Preparedness Committee of the Institute of Mathematical Statistics." As a result, Kitagawa, Ishida, and several others were instructed by the military to provide guidance to factories producing war-related goods.

In an example of the contemporary state of affairs, when Dr. Motosaburo Masuyama (the first winner of the Deming Prize in 1951) visited a dry cell battery factory that had been specially identified for its excellence, he found a huge pile of rejects; this was because the testing was so rigorous as to certify the entire output as defective.[9]

In a second example, Ryoichiro Sato was dispatched to the Itabashi Arsenal in Tokyo to check on the capabilities of an automatic inspection machine that was being used to determine whether or not cartridges were of standard length. He found that, of cartridges that had been identified as being too short, 20 percent were actually of standard length; of those cartridges certified as having passed, 20 percent were actually substandard. When he called the problem to the attention of the officer in charge of cartridge production at the arsenal, the officer merely called in the shop supervisor and passed on Sato's observation that something ought to be done. The shop supervisor responded that the arsenal had been using the inspection machine since 1896 and had never had a problem, and that he did not understand what all the fuss was about. At this point, Sato reportedly gave up in exasperation.[10]

In a third example, when Motosaburo Masuyama, Toshio Kitagawa, Ryoichiro Sato, Yasushi Ishida, and Tatuo Kawada all went together to visit another military production site, they found that plans called for a 5.2 mm hole in a certain location of a certain part. The subcontractor in charge of the part, however, was not reliably producing holes of 5.2 mm, leading to subsequent production problems. The factory's solution was merely to widen all the holes with a 6 mm drill. The five men quickly realized that there were more fundamental problems that would have to be addressed prior to the application of statistical methods. To men working at places like the Yokosuka Naval Arsenal, the statisticians' talk of probability density functions and other complicated mathematical concepts seemed completely otherworldly and unrelated to the problems at hand. Ishida's and Sato's comments were reported by the workers to be somewhat more practical, as Ishida had actual experience at Tokyo Electric and Sato had studied in England under the practically minded Pearson.[11]

Records of these activities were virtually all destroyed as military secrets, making historical access impossible, but the visitors' subsequent reports are of being surprised at the sloppiness and haphazardness that they found at the factories. Factory workers, on the other hand, were simply doing their best to increase output, and the advice of the statisticians seemed too remote, couched as it was in difficult terminology. In fact, one of the major bottlenecks in the prewar and wartime application of SQC was the difficulty of the language used to describe the concepts, preventing the spread of knowledge to the shop floors.

Still, the statisticians and Ishida sought to introduce statistical thinking to production in the prewar and wartime periods. They worked hard to collect what little academic material was available on SQC, with Ishida himself making twice-monthly journeys to libraries in order to photograph the latest English articles, returning home to type them up and file them.[12] However, the wartime restrictions on the spread of technical information and the traditional production methods being used at military factories served to prevent discoveries concerning SQC from being widely disseminated, although there is evidence of the partial introduction of SQC by the prewar pioneers.

Kinnosuke Ogura did not live to see the end of the war, and after the war Kanzo Kiribuchi became a professor at Asia University in Tokyo. Yasushi Ishida continued the quiet pursuit of his pioneering efforts with the Japan Standards Association (JSA), serving as a historical link to the prewar period. Other statisticians, although endeavoring to teach SQC immediately following the war, did not remain in the mainstream of the field's subsequent development. The driving force behind the spread of SQC shifted away from the prewar statistical researchers and toward a new generation who learned about American methods of quality control, as will be discussed. However, the biggest difference between the prewar and postwar periods was the postwar emergence of organizations—such as the Union of Japanese Scientists and Engineers (JUSE) and JSA—dedicated to the promotion of quality control on a national scale, and the consequent development of a core of quality control engineers. It was concurrent with the founding of these national organizations, and the educational framework that they provided, that the American know-how arrived on the scene.

The Occupation Era in Japan (1945–1951)

In August 1945 Japan accepted the Potsdam Declaration, thereby bringing World War II to a close. Defeat came as a blow to many Japanese. For the first time in its history Japan was occupied by a foreign power, represented by the General Headquarters (GHQ) of the Supreme Commander for the Allied Powers (SCAP). Inflation was chronic, food was in short supply, and production ground to a halt at many factories.

GHQ consisted of nine sections, one of which was the Civil Communications Section (CCS) in charge of all communications, including telegraph, telephone, domestic and international radio, and broadcasting. CCS sought to demilitarize communications and restructure broadcasting along democratic lines.

Telephone Communication Difficulties

One of GHQ's first surprises upon setting up in Japan was the high frequency of breakdowns in the telephone system, causing frequent interruptions in important GHQ communications. At first, the situation was thought to be the result of anti-American sabotage, and a thorough check of the telephone network was undertaken. It was found that 5 percent to 10 percent of long distance circuits and about 25 percent of the switching stations had been destroyed during the war,[13] and that the communications problem was affecting the whole country. Some Japanese also appealed to General MacArthur to remedy the situation. According to a postcard addressed to MacArthur from a resident of Shibuya in Tokyo, telephone service in Shibuya was unavailable for 50 days during the year of 1948.[14] Repair of the system was a high priority, both for the daily work of GHQ and for the Japanese citizenry. Following an investigation, the most significant cause of breakdowns was identified as the poor quality of vacuum tubes used in repeater stations along long distance lines.

In response, MacArthur requested Secretary of War Patterson to contact the president of AT&T asking for civilian personnel skilled in telephone communication and equipment manufacture to be sent to Japan to assist in rebuilding the telephone network. As a result, about half of the CCS staff were actually AT&T employees. Most of these came to Japan for two to four years and then returned to their posts at AT&T and its subsidiaries (the regional Bell Telephone Companies, Western Electric Company, or Bell Telephone Laboratories).

The CCS staff members who were closely associated with the events of this chapter included

- Wilbur S. Magill, who was CCS Wire Equipment Supervisor, Industry Division. He returned to Western Electric Company in December 1946.

- Homer M. Sarasohn of Raytheon Manufacturing Company. He came to Japan in 1946 to replace Magill. He returned to the United States in 1950. (Sarasohn was astonished when he received a telegram from the War Department informing him that GHQ in Japan had requested his services.[15])

- Charles W. Protzman, also of Western Electric Company. He was resident in Japan from November 1948 to May 1950.

- Frank A. Polkinghorn, of Bell Telephone Laboratories. He was resident in Japan from August 1948 to May 1950, and was the supervisor of Protzman and Sarasohn.

Prior to Sarasohn's arrival, CCS had already undertaken its survey of telephone malfunctions, requested the dispatch of engineers from AT&T and other U.S. companies, and had sent observers to Japanese telephone and vacuum tube factories. The aim was to eliminate telephone outages at the manufacturing level. From 1946 through 1950, CCS staff (including Magill, Protzman, Polkinghorn, and others) visited the factories of a large number of manufacturers all over the country, from representative large electrical equipment makers to small companies with as few as six employees. In reports of their observations, they pointed out serious deficiencies in cleanliness, process layout, and safety measures.

> *It should not be necessary to restate that, in the communications equipment industry, products must be manufactured in a clean factory. If vacuum tube parts are contaminated with grease or dust, good vacuum tubes cannot be produced, and if connections in telephone relays are dirty, good relays cannot be produced. The majority of rejected products in the communications equipment industry are caused by dust, which is the result of a poorly maintained factory.*[16]

Not all of the Japanese electrical equipment makers were in such bad shape; some were well organized, as evidenced by Furukawa Electric's Nikko Works being cited as "well laid out" and "well equipped."[17] Another report on Furukawa noted that, "In general, it appeared well managed and there was not an accumulation of junk copper and other materials as has been observed in some other factories."[18] Thus, while there were counterexamples, defects in communications equipment were common and the manufacturers were not generally well organized.

This led Sarasohn and others in CCS to recommend that training in business administration, quality control, and cost control be provided to Japan's makers of telephone equipment, communications equipment, and vacuum tubes. This recommendation was challenged by others in GHQ who favored a long occupation over training Japanese managers to work on their own. The matter was debated during a session with General MacArthur. According to Sarasohn, "MacArthur just listened silently to the debate until he said to the CCS side, 'OK, do the seminar.' And that was how it got started."[19]

The CCS Management Seminars

Before organizing the training, six of the companies that had been visited were selected for yet closer examination.[20] Meanwhile Sarasohn had identified nine points that he felt Japanese companies needed to address. Two of these were closely related to quality control.

1. Company presidents often seemed not to believe that quality improvement and employee training were the jobs of management.

2. There was not enough research and/or implementation of control methods such as quality control, cost control, and technical control.[21]

In order to address these nine issues, it was decided to hold a management seminar for the highest ranking executives of the communications equipment makers. First, a kind of preseminar was held for three days at the Daiichi Seimei (Life Insurance) Building, the seat of GHQ.[22] Then, the CCS management seminar was held from September 26 to November 18, 1949, in Tokyo, and from November 21, 1949, to January 20, 1950, in Osaka.[23] The seminar was officially recorded by the American Federal Record Center as the Management Indoctrination Course for the Telecommunications Manufacturing Industry.

The seminar was conducted from 1 to 5 P.M. every weekday, in English, by Homer M. Sarasohn (presenting on policy, organization, control, and operations) and by Charles W. Protzman (presenting on organization, control, and operations).[24] In Tokyo, the seminar was attended by representatives of NEC Corp., Toshiba Corp., Fujitsu Ltd., Oki Electric Industry Co., Ltd., Mitsubishi Electric Corp., Hitachi, Ltd., and so on, and a total of 19 presidents and executive directors were present.[25] In Osaka, participants came from Matsushita Electric Industrial Co., Ltd., Hayakawa Electric Industry (now Sharp Corp.), Toshiba Corp., Sumitomo Electric Industries, Ltd., and others, with 25 presidents and executive directors present.

The content of the seminar was published as *CCS keiei koza* (*CCS Management Seminar*),[26] made up of four chapters: "Policy," "Organization," "Control," and "Operations," with quality control taken up in part of the third chapter ("Control"). The Japanese version of the text came to 488 pages, of which just over 60 pages were devoted to quality control. However, according to a participant, Dr. Masao Kogure, "Almost no one knew very much about statistical quality control, and it attracted everyone's attention."[27]

The portion devoted to quality control was subdivided into eight sections: (1) quality of products, (2) inspection, (3) types of inspection, (4) statistical quality control, (5) practical application of SQC, (6) benefits of SQC, (7) quality surveys, and (8) checking on complaints about quality. Instructor Sarasohn recommended that in addition to normal testing in the factory, there should be a separate quality control department that would perform check testing and statistical analysis. Then, when the defect level came down, the normal testing department and the check testing would be merged, leaving the quality department to do only statistical analysis. Sarasohn taught that the responsibilities of the quality control department were sampling inspection, the creation of control charts, quality surveys, and checking on complaints about quality.

Participants at the CCS management seminars included some university professors and some staff members of the Federation of Japanese Electric Communications Industries. These attended as observers. The seminars proceeded in an informal, roundtable manner, and was taught on a question-and-answer basis. This was to help alleviate the nervousness of the Japanese concerning comprehension and taking notes in English, although some interpretation was provided.[28] Participants would be asked questions about Japanese companies and organization, with participants then asking the instructors about the situation in America. Through this process, the two American engineers were able to find out more about Japanese companies, and the Japanese participants were able to learn about the modern American approach to business and about the democratic way of life.

Impressions of the Japanese Participants

Some of the Japanese participants recorded their impressions of the CCS management seminar. Three of these impressions are set out here.

According to Mr. Takeshi Kayano (then of Nippon Telegraph and Telephone), the staff would distribute the typed text (in English) to the participants at each session. Attendance policy was quite strict, with the CCS staff telling participants that they should not be absent for any reason, and calling their companies when absences did occur. Kayano was impressed by the overall scientific approach and organization of the seminar, and with the volunteer zeal and sincerity of the instructors.[29]

Mr. Hiroshi Toyoda (then of Hitachi, Ltd.) recalls that, although he did not hear very much that was new, he was impressed with the ability of the Americans to put the information together in such a structured manner.

When we put what was taught at the CCS Management Seminar into practice at our company, the results were quite

effective. For example, prior to that time, we did not have re-
sponsibilities and authority written down on paper. But when we
did introduce written guidelines, we found that we had to take
the responsibility outlined. The scientific approach was also valu-
able. First, establish clear goals; then collect relevant data; then
plan, take action, and evaluate. It was not that we were not
doing any of these things before, but it was good to get it all into
a structured form.[30]

Mr. Toshio Takahashi (then senior director of Kikuna Electric
Co.) indicates that, although he had many opportunities to hear
about quality control after the war, and had read information about it,
he did not have a clear idea of how to go about implementing it before the seminar.

We had been working hard through first half of the previous
year to improve quality, mainly by undertaking more rigorous
testing in selecting materials, improving processes and toler-
ances, and introducing new machinery. But when we applied
what we had learned at the seminar, we realized that what we
had been doing was all wrong, and we were able to make dra-
matic progress. That is, when quality control methods are ap-
plied, it is not necessary to increase the number of testing points
as we had been doing. This was an important result.[31]

What was learned at the CCS management seminar was not generally brand new and epoch-making theoretical material. Rather, the
content is highly reminiscent of coursework in a university faculty of
business administration. In fact, the author happened to find a copy of
the venerated seminar among the books of one of her university professors, who commented that he had been urged by the renowned
professor of management Dr. Eiichi Furukawa to study the text.

The most important thing about the seminar for the participants,
then, was probably not the actual content of the seminar, but rather,
for the presidents and executive directors who attended, the opportunity to spend 160 hours with Sarasohn and Protzman, discussing
democratic management methods, the scientific approach to business,
and SQC. The Japanese who attended were virtually ordered to participate by GHQ, and were probably not very enthusiastic at first, but

for Japanese at that time GHQ orders were not to be disputed. Still, the participants were gradually attracted by Sarasohn and Protzman, becoming more and more enthusiastic, even such that they began to look forward to the next day's session. They were impressed with the instructors' dedication, and by the end of the seminar they had made a commitment to introduce what they had learned back at their companies.[32] In short, the seminar was helpful in encouraging the top-level managers to get down to the business of rebuilding their companies in the aftermath of the war.

Another item of significance was the early introduction of SQC to the telecommunications manufacturing industry. However, the overall effect in this sense was limited by the low number of participants, all from a single industry. In terms of numbers of participating companies and individuals, the lectures delivered by Dr. W. Edwards Deming and Dr. J. M. Juran, to be discussed later, were far more extensive than the CCS management seminar.

Establishment of Promotional Organizations for Quality Control

In 1946, three Japanese promotional organizations began to offer educational programs in quality control. These organizations were

- Japan Management Association (JMA), established in 1942;
- Japan Standards Association (JSA), established in 1945; and
- The Union of Japanese Scientists and Engineers (JUSE), established in 1946.

In May 1949, Dr. Eizaburo Nishibori became an advisor to JMA, and began to provide SQC guidance. The organization transmitted information about SQC to factories of such companies as Daido Ltd.; Honshu Paper Co., Ltd.; Toray Industries, Inc.; Daihatsu Motor Co., Ltd.; and Tonen Corp.[33] Dr. Nishibori and other quality control consultants made great contributions to the field in the early 1950s.

Reminiscing about Dr. Nishibori, Tokai University professor Dr. Hajime Karatsu recalled that,

> *Professor Nishibori was always very easy to understand, and if he stayed two or three days at a factory, the quality there almost*

always improved. He was almost like a god. Once, the Nobeoka plant of Asahi Chemical Industry Co., Ltd. was having a problem with occasional hard defective strands appearing in the Bemberg rayon they were making. Professor Nishibori had them to draw up the control charts and told them to check the resulting curve. After a lot of discussion, they realized that the defects appeared at the same time as typhoons. The fraction defective was perfectly matched with the water level in the dam above the factory site. Professor Nishibori, who was a chemistry specialist, suggested that something must be dissolved in the river water feeding the dam to cause the problem. When they checked the content of the water, the found that a certain level of silicon ions seemed to prevent the defective production; a lower level silicon ions resulted in a higher fraction defective. Then Professor Nishibori asked what would happen if there was even more silicon, and when they added more silicon ions they found that they got an extremely soft variety of Bemberg rayon. Previously, the company had purchased the manufacturing technology from Germany, but now they were able to patent the new variety and export it.

In another example, there was a problem with automatic knitting machines at a lace factory near Kyoto, which would sometimes produce defective patterns in the lace output. Since the output could not be conveniently undone, about 30 women using knitting needles were needed to correct the defective lace by hand. Professor Nishibori, after touring the factory, told the management, "You have to pay 30 women to fix your lace by hand; if you would listen to what I have to say, you wouldn't need any of them any more." They all thought he was crazy, but three days later the problem was completely fixed. Sometimes the machines would knit smoothly, and sometimes they would make the defective patterns. As soon as he noticed the defects starting, Professor Nishibori changed the needle and other parts of the machine. He and the plant engineers then changed another part which turned out to be the cause of the problem. He ordered a bunch of those parts and had the engineers change them on all the machines in turn as they would go defective, until by the evening of the third day the problem was completely eliminated.

Professor Nishibori always thought about what was going on the shop floor, and he was very good at motivating the people in the factories to strive for quality.[34]

JSA was formed in 1942 as the combination of two other groups. JSA is dedicated to the promotion of standardization and quality control, particularly the spread of standards for industrial products. It also publishes books on standards and standardization, and conducts a wide range of activities (including quality control activities) aimed at industrial standardization in both large corporations and small businesses. In June of 1949, the association sponsored a series of lectures on quality control, three months before the CCS management seminar. The instructors were Yasushi Ishida and Toshio Kitagawa, previously mentioned; on the first day Dickson Reck of GHQ's Economic and Scientific Section was invited to speak as well. The lectures were held to commemorate the implementation of the Industrial Standardization Law of 1949, resulting in the creation of the Japan Industrial Standards system and the JIS mark. Later, in 1953, the Excellent Factories in Implementation of Industrial Standardization awards were initiated.

JUSE was started on May 1, 1946, but predecessor organizations can be traced back to 1918. It offered its SQC seminar (now known as "the basic course") over the yearlong period from September 1949 to August 1950. The course was subsequently offered for the second time over a six-month period. Chemical and steel companies provided many of the participants for the first offerings, although they were joined by other participants such as Furukawa Electric Co., Ltd. and Toshiba Corp. The SQC seminar was based on material written by E. S. Pearson, Shewhart, H. F. Dodge, and H. G. Romig, in addition to translations of Z1-1 and Z1-2 (American War Standards). The first such JUSE seminar took place in the form of lectures based on translated foreign texts on SQC.

The Japanese soon realized that this kind of direct study of foreign material was unlikely to become widespread in Japan; revision and adaptation were needed. The problem, however, was just what to change and adapt and how to go about it. The answer was not clear in the late 1940s as the instructors of the first basic course spent time together rewriting the text. This was the first step toward a Japanese style or way of quality control, although it would be some time before the actual development of "Japanese" modifications and techniques such as QC circles and company-wide quality control.

The instructors of the basic course were generally university professors who, while also carrying out their full-time teaching duties, regularly visited the factories of basic course participants to see for themselves just what and how the content was being implemented. The aforementioned Nishibori and the basic course instructors became pioneers among Japanese quality control consultants.

The Lectures of Dr. W. Edwards Deming

Dr. W. Edwards Deming (1900–1993) began his career as an instructor in physics (1921–27), and as a mathematical physicist for the U.S. Department of Agriculture (1927–39). Along the way he became increasingly interested in statistics, including a close association with Dr. W. A. Shewhart, a pioneer in application of statistical methods to control of quality. Deming became an advisor in sampling at the U.S. Bureau of the Census (1939–46), after which he became a consultant while serving as professor of statistics at New York University's Graduate School of Business Administration. For decades his consulting business card read "Consultant in Statistical Surveys." Deming's name was already familiar to the instructors of JUSE's basic course— he had been coauthor of some of the publications that JUSE had translated into Japanese. In addition Deming had been one of the architects of the eight-day courses on SQC so widely conducted during WWII by the American War Production Board.

When Mr. Ken-ichi Koyanagi, managing director of JUSE, learned that Deming would be visiting Japan in May 1950 in his capacity as advisor on sampling to GHQ, he asked Deming to deliver lectures on SQC during his stay. The resulting series of lectures was given for eight days, starting on July 10, 1950, and was attended by 230 engineers from 96 companies.[35] In the summer of 1951, introductory and advanced courses in quality control, as well as a course in market surveying, were also given by Dr. Deming. These courses provided the Japanese with a sense of direction and purpose, and their wide-ranging effects deserve special consideration. Dr. Shigeru Mizuno, a JUSE instructor and Deming lecture participant, recalls that,

> The JUSE [basic course] instructors were, up until that time, merely self-taught concerning [the fundamental ideas of] quality control but, through Dr. Deming's lectures, they were able to approach for the first time the true essence of quality control. The lectures had a great historical significance for the history of quality control in Japan.[36]

According to Dr. Deming,

> *The stage was perfectly set. Had it been even a year or two earlier, things would probably not have gone so well, but in 1950 Japan was ready for a fresh start. During my 1947 visit, I had made friends with statisticians and economists. Through these friends the invitation came to lecture on statistical techniques and to do the series of presentations in 1949. The lectures were sponsored by JUSE.*[37]

The Japanese learned from Deming's 1950 lectures how to use SQC as an aid to making the cheapest, most consistent, and best quality products. Days one through six were spent on how to draw control charts. Days seven and eight were spent on acceptance sampling, including single sampling and double sampling plans. This eight-day lecture series consisted of the very same lectures which Deming had given in the United States during World War II.

During the lectures, sampling was demonstrated with the aid of a box of beads. White beads represented acceptable products, and red beads represented defectives. Participants also practiced drawing up control charts. They then continued to practice, using data from their own factories. Deming explained the significance of control charts, saying,

> *The control chart is a tool for obtaining the most economical manufacturing methods. Look for the trouble and its explanation and try to remove the cause every time a point goes out of control.*[38]

Deming also encouraged the Japanese, saying that statistical methods were resources for a poor nation without natural resources to use in pursuit of international markets, and that guaranteed quality was the road that postwar Japan should take. This statement provided a sense of direction, and continues even now to serve as a guiding beacon to Japanese engineers in turbulent economic times. The lectures in 1950 gave the Japanese the impetus and the tools to begin implementing SQC. Coincidentally, that same year marked the beginning of the Korean War and "special procurement" for many industries, giving the Japanese economy a much needed boost.

The notes from the eight-day lecture series were published and sold as a booklet titled *Dr. Deming's Lectures on Statistical Control of Quality,* the royalties from which were donated by Dr. Deming to Mr. Koyanagi of JUSE. Koyanagi was so impressed with this act of generosity that he recommended to the other JUSE directors that a foundation be established using the royalties and interest revenues in order to fund prizes for advances in the field of quality control. In 1951, JUSE established two prizes: the Deming Prize, for individual contributions in the areas of education and service to the field of quality control; and the Deming Application Prize, for the outstanding implementation and application of statistical quality control by companies/factories.

The range of prizes has since been gradually increased. In 1958, the Deming Application Prize for Small Enterprise was established, followed by the Deming Application Prize for a [company] Division in 1966, the Japan Quality Control Medal in 1970, and the Quality Control Award for a Factory in 1973. The Deming Prizes are currently financed by the JUSE operating budget.

The Deming Application Prize became one of the major goals for postwar Japanese companies—a standard against which to measure a company's progress in quality relative to others. Thus, when one company in an industry won the Prize, its competitors also made efforts to win the Prize, thereby stimulating the entire industry to improve quality. For example, in 1951 the Deming Application Prize was won by Tanabe Seiyaku Co., Ltd., a major pharmaceutical company. A year later, the Prize was won by Shionogie Co., Ltd. and Takeda Chemical Industries, Ltd., both major pharmaceutical manufacturers.

Relative to prizes, it should be noted that by the 1950s, the United States and others had created quality awards for individuals or for product designs, but only Japan had such a prize for entire companies. Thus, while American instruction was fundamental, the process of its absorption differed in the two countries.

It should also be noted that while the Japanese were strongly motivated, this in itself did not lead to success. As demonstrated by the example of Tanabe Seiyaku, there was resistance at first on the factory floor, as was probably the case in other countries. Some Japanese companies succeeded in overcoming this resistance and were honored for their achievements in the area of quality; others were not as successful.

In 1947 there were over three million tuberculosis (TB) patients in Japan, and TB was the leading cause of death.[39] An antituberculosis medicine—para amino salicylic acid (PAS)—had been originally developed overseas, but was difficult to manufacture because of its instability. In spite of this, Tanabe Seiyaku set itself the goal of marketing its version of PAS by 1950.

Masashi Asao, then working for the company, recalls,

> *The process used to make salicylic acid at the company's Onoda plant was similar to the PAS process, so it was decided to use the Onoda plant for PAS as well. The conditions for the process were completely different, however. . . . since I had studied statistical quality control, I was called in. . . . my boss had come to understand that statistical quality control required mathematics and he had me assigned to the project. . . . I was able to apply statistical methods at Onoda to analyze seven factors in the PAS process such as temperature, pressure, and reaction time.*[40]

During the development of SQC in Japan, the leading promoters expended intense efforts in support of their cause. Yet they sometimes ran into resistance in the factories. In the case of Tanabe Seiyaku, for example, experienced factory workers had their own ways of doing things; attempts to standardize the processes encountered much resistance. The workers complained that they were already doing their best every day to make quality products, and that there was no need for newfangled standardization. The quality control promoters then adopted the approach of asking the workers to write brief memos on what they were doing. In the process of rewriting the memos to make them more legible, the promoters would go back to the workers and ask for clarification. For instance, if a certain process was said to require a reaction time of 3 hours at a temperature of 95 degrees, promoters might ask what would happen at 96 or even 100 degrees. If there was disagreement about would happen, experimental design was undertaken to arrive at an operation standard.

It was quite difficult to introduce the new SQC methods to processes that had already been used for long periods of time. However, as new or revised products were introduced, the new methods were introduced with them. It turned out to be easier to convince people that they were doing something new than to alter existing methods.

Tanabe Seiyaku succeeded in producing PAS in 1949, and it was marketed domestically from 1950. The company received the Deming Application Prize in 1951, which was indicative of its early efforts to achieve process quality.

Features of Japan's Quality Control in the Occupation Era

The years from 1945 to the early 1950s, coinciding with the occupation of Japan by the allied forces, can be designated as the era of full-scale introduction of SQC, as opposed to the partial introduction that was taking place in the prewar and wartime periods. Of the changes that took place during the occupation period, three deserve special attention: the formation of QC educational organizations; the establishment of competitive prizes such as the Deming Application Prize; and the construction of the legal framework represented by the Industrial Standardization Law.

Until the mid-1950s, quality control in Japan was statistical quality control, consisting of the creation of control charts, the accumulation of records, and the improvement of quality through the use of the resulting analysis. The main industries in which SQC was introduced were electric communications, and process industries such as pharmaceuticals, chemicals, and steel. According to an article published in 1955 in *JIS* magazine entitled "The State of Quality Control in Our Country's Industry," only 13 percent of factories overall, 34 percent of factories in the electrical machinery industry, and 25 percent of factories in the chemical industry had implemented SQC.[41]

Prior to receiving instruction from CCS and Deming, the foundation for quality control in Japan had already been laid, as is demonstrated by the preparation and training conducted by the quality control educational organizations. The seeds had already been planted. However, when the Americans came to Japan it became overwhelmingly clear that the American approach was more advanced. It is not difficult to imagine the motivation to improve quality that was presented to Japanese engineers and top management by Japan's utter defeat in World War II. Thanks to CCS, Deming, and the others, the Japanese began to apply themselves to the task at hand, supported in their endeavors by the educational organizations.

Many Japanese companies struggling to introduce quality control sent employees to seminars offered by the educational organizations.

On returning to their companies, these participants became quality control instructors. It is important to note that these companies did not try to recruit outside quality consultants. According to Junji Noguchi, executive director of JUSE, "Japanese companies preferred to train their own engineers who are working in the company, rather than employing special engineers of quality or reliability from the beginning stage [sic]."[42]

Japanese consultants differ from their American counterparts. Japanese quality control consultants are typically university professors in departments of science and engineering. Most of them maintain their full-time academic obligations and it is rare that they start up independent consulting companies. An exception can be found in the multifaceted career of Eizaburo Nishibori who, after completing the course in radio science at Kyoto University, worked for a time in a private company, subsequently became a consultant with Japan Management Association, returned to Kyoto University as a professor for two years, led the first Japanese Antarctic expedition, and served as a director of a nuclear research agency. (There are, however, a few instances of engineers starting consultancies upon retirement from their companies.)

Japan During the Period of Rapid Growth

The period from the mid-1950s through the 1960s was one of rapid growth, both in the effectiveness of Japan's quality control and in the Japanese economy. During this same period Dr. J. M. Juran made the first three of his many visits to Japan. These visits were influential in changing Japan's direction from emphasis on SQC to emphasis on managing for quality and on company-wide quality control.

The Lectures of Dr. J. M. Juran

Juran had joined Western Electric Company (the manufacturing arm of the Bell System) in 1924. He was assigned to the inspection branch of the huge Hawthorne Works, where he rose to become quality manager in 1934. During the United States' involvement in World War II, he was an official in the federal government. At the end of the war, he became a freelance consultant, specializing in managing for quality.

Juran's third book, *Quality Control Handbook,* was published in 1951. It came to the attention of Ken-ichi Koyanagi, managing director of JUSE, who took steps to translate the book into Japanese. Koyanagi also met with Juran in 1952 at an American Society for Quality Control (ASQC) convention in Syracuse, New York, and invited him to Japan.[43] (Deming participated in arranging this meeting.)

At the time, one of the biggest worries for the Japanese consultants was that, although quality control could not be implemented without the understanding of top and middle management, these executives did not seem to show much interest or concern. To be sure, the CCS management seminar had been held for the top management of electrical equipment firms, but the participants represented only a minute fraction of the companies in Japan. According to Ichiro Ishikawa, then chairman of JUSE (also chairman of the Federation of Economic Organizations, and the father of Kaoru Ishikawa), Deming had briefly explained to the top executives of a small number of Japanese firms the importance of quality control. But the understanding of such executives and of middle management was far from sufficient. To quote Dr. Masumasa Imaizumi, "In those days the top management people . . . didn't tell us to put priority on quality, . . . because they were [mainly] concerned about increasing the market share, how to gain more profit . . . and so they didn't tell us about [quality] and talk to us about quality."[44]

Juran accepted JUSE's invitation, and made plans to visit Japan during the summer of 1954. At that time Japan had not yet fully recovered from the war. This is made clear by a comparison of trade statistics with the prewar period. In 1954, the volume of imports was 77 percent of the level recorded during the period from 1934–36, and exports were only 46 percent.[45]

Juran recalls that,

> The year 1954 was only nine years removed from the Second World War. Japan had suffered much damage and there still remained a sizable residue of this in the form of antiquated plants, equipment, roads, buildings, and other essential facilities. . . . Road transport was mainly on overloaded bicycles and three-wheeled mini-trucks.[46]

In planning for his 1954 visit, Juran prepared written lectures which he sent to JUSE for translation. He asked that the participants read the translated lectures in advance. The planning also included arrangements for visiting factories. In the Tokyo area he visited factories making chemicals, steel, electrical equipment, and cameras. He noted that Nihon Kogaku K.K. (making Nikon cameras) was "at the same level as America," and that the Toshiba factory was on par with "the highest American standards." He also pointed out in his preface to *Total Quality Control* (the Japanese edition of *Quality Control Handbook*) that "... there has been some over-emphasis of the importance of the statistical tools, as though they alone are sufficient to solve our quality problems. Such over-emphasis is a mistake. The statistical tools are sometimes necessary, and often useful. But they are never sufficient."[47]

Following the factory visits, he conducted a two-day seminar in Hakone for company senior executives, and a 10-day seminar in Tokyo for division and section chiefs. The same process was then repeated in Osaka, starting with factory visits, making for an intense schedule from Juran's arrival on July 4 to his departure on August 17.

The lectures for company senior executives were attended by 140 chairmen, presidents, and other top managers representing firms in the textile, pulp, paper, steel, chemical, glass, pharmaceutical, electrical equipment, and other industries, while the 10-day seminars were attended by 300 division and section chiefs. Juran was surprised by the high level audiences, saying that,

> *I had never before encountered so high a degree of participation on the part of upper management.[48] When I gave such lectures in the United States, the audiences consisted of engineers and quality control managers. Never before my 1954 trip to Japan, and never since, has the industrial leadership of a major power given me so much of its attention.[49]*

The special lectures for company executives focused on their responsibilities in the quality function: (1) responsibility for high policy or doctrine, (2) responsibility for choice of quality design, (3) responsibility for the plan of organization of the company with respect to quality, (4) responsibility for setting up measurement of what is actually taking place with respect to quality, and (5) responsibility for reviewing results against goals, and for taking action on significant variation.[50] The lectures also stressed the relationships among production, technology, testing, quality control, accounting, sales, materials management, personnel, and so on in the process of deciding on quality of design.

The course for division and section chiefs was held for three hours each morning and afternoon for 10 days at Waseda University in Tokyo and at the Chamber of Commerce in Osaka. The participants used Juran's prepared text materials as a basis for creating "focus groups" to discuss various topics such as vendor inspection, process inspection, and final inspection, and for consideration of staff quality functions, quality assurance, diagnosis, and still other areas. Juran presented numerous actual examples of company practice, especially with respect to quality improvement. These examples were presented with the aid of an overhead projector which he had sent to Japan in advance. It evidently was the first such projector to have come to Japan. During the breaks, crowds of participants would come up for a closer look at the "lecturing machine." When Juran announced that he would donate the machine to JUSE on completion of the lectures, he received a long round of applause.

Some of the contents of Juran's lectures were not new to the Japanese. However some were "new," whether in concept or in exposition. These included the distinction between quality of design and quality of conformance, a systematic approach to diagnosis for improvement, the Pareto principle of the "vital few and the useful many," and so on. Probably the most important point of the lectures was to encourage quality improvement through use of the managerial tools for quality. After his initial factory visits, Juran noted the overemphasis on statistical tools and the underemphasis on the use of managerial tools. He stressed that control charts, while necessary, were far from sufficient, and that use needed to be made of the managerial tools, requiring the understanding and cooperation of top and middle management. In fact, Juran stated during his lectures that, "To me, the very nature of the invitation by JUSE was expressive of a desire to help achieve, in Japan, the necessary balance in use of all tools for quality control."

It is important to emphasize that the content of Juran's lectures differed from that of the lectures given by Deming. In particular, it should be remembered that while Deming's field was statistics, Juran's field was management. This distinction was emphasized by the late, renowned Japanese expert Dr. Kaoru Ishikawa, who contrasted the contributions of Deming and Juran:

In 1950, JUSE invited Dr. W. E. Deming from the U.S. to conduct a QC seminar for top management, department and section managers, and engineers. This seminar was extremely enlightening....

Initially, however, Japanese quality control also suffered from various problems. The first was that statistical methods were overemphasized.... The third problem was that top management and department and section managers did not develop much enthusiasm for quality control....

To help solve these problems, Dr. J. M. Juran was invited to Japan in 1954 to give a seminar for executives and department and section managers. Quality control at last started to be used as a management tool. This marked the beginning of a gradual transition from statistical quality control to total quality control, and in turn led to the promotion of quality control in which all departments and all employees participated—in other words, total or companywide quality control....[51]

Juran's and Ishikawa's comments hit the nail on the head. Control charts were being drawn up in companies in the machinery, steel, nonferrous metals, chemical, and electrical equipment industries, but some important matters were lacking.[52] Juran's lectures sparked the realization in many that quality control should be pursued on a broader level than mere emphasis on statistical methods. (Subsequently, there was a swing away from statistical methods and, still later, a reconfirmation of their importance.) However, there was no single, all-embracing leap forward in the integration of quality control efforts at the top, middle, and factory management levels, nor in the interconnection of efforts from design, to manufacturing, to sales.

Japan in the Late 1950s

After Juran's 1954 visit, JUSE followed up with a middle-management course starting in 1955 and a top-management course starting in 1957. These courses continue to this day, with 1488 middle managers and 285 top managers taking part in 1990.[53]

Additionally, in 1956, quality control training for shop supervisors and factory workers was started via the medium of radio. By 1962, a total of over 17 courses on quality control and standardization had been sent over the airwaves,[54] addressing the important issue of how to tackle the training of this important group. While middle and top management could be assembled for training activities, the question of how to go about the instruction of the massive number of production workers remained. Even if a standard-type course were prepared for them, only a small number of the total were likely to have a chance to participate. The idea was then hit upon to try radio broadcasts, which could be heard by everybody, everywhere. The first seminar featured consultants Kaoru Ishikawa and Shigeru Mizuno, along with JUSE managing director Koyanagi, and was broadcast for a three-month period, Monday through Saturday, for 15 minutes starting at 4:15 P.M.

While most factories wanted their supervisors and workers to hear the programs, they found that the 4:15 time slot interfered with work. In response, many factories resorted to taping the program and having workers listen during the lunch hour or in one long session on the weekend. In some cases supplemental comments were added by those in charge of quality control. The following year when NHK (the public broadcasting organization) broadcast the course as *New Management and Quality Control,* 85,000 copies of the accompanying text were sold, surpassing English conversation to make it the most popular course offered, and laying the groundwork for the formation of quality circles a few years later.

By 1955 Japan had again reached prewar levels of consumption and, after a brief recession, experienced the Jinmu Boom in 1956 and the Iwato Boom from 1959 to 1960. As economic recovery began in earnest and production began to expand, a shift in Japan's industrial structure also began to be seen. Traditional mainstays such as textiles, for example, began to be overtaken by machinery. By 1960, cameras, sewing machines, and transistor radios were obvious success stories.[55] The image of Japanese products as being cheap and shoddy was already being swept away in certain industries.

In 1958, a 10-member quality control specialist study team, led by Mr. Noboru Yamaguchi of Toshiba Corp. as team leader and Kaoru Ishikawa as deputy team leader, was dispatched to the United States by the Japan Productivity Center. For 45 days the team traveled through the United States, starting at San Francisco and winding up in Washington D.C., where members were able to meet and confer with Juran and Deming. Of the companies that the team visited, Western Electric, United Airlines, and the Bell Telephone Laboratories were found to have especially good statistical quality control, research, development, and results. However, the team found that, with regard to the general state of the implementation of quality control in the United States, there was quite a divergence, with some companies exerting great efforts and some hardly at all. The team concluded that there was not a great deal to learn from the generality of cases and, if Japan continued to implement quality control as was already being done, that Japanese quality would eventually become superior. In fact, a member of ASQC stated that same year that, "In terms of the design of experiments and other aspects, the Japanese seem to be doing better; perhaps it is America that should send a study team to Japan."[56]

Still, the Japanese did find some things in the United States that they did not have in Japan. The first was a professional society such as ASQC. The team recommended that a counterpart to ASQC be established in Japan. In due course, the Japanese Society for Quality Control was founded in 1971. Another finding in the United States was the concept of quality control for services (as contrasted with quality control for goods), which was being implemented by United Airlines and the Bank of America. Japanese companies in service industries became eligible for the Deming Application Prize starting in 1970.

A note about the then-current American quality teams (QC teams) should be inserted at this point, because it is sometimes claimed that the origin of Japanese quality circles (or QC circles) can be found in the QC teams observed at Western Electric, General Electric, and other American companies. This impression is mistaken, as the American QC team was typically a three-member task force consisting of a QC manager, a shop supervisor, and a product manager. At first the team would meet once every two or three days, but would be disbanded when the number of defects was seen to go down. Although it is true that the visiting study team of Japanese specialists did observe QC teams, they are fundamentally different from quality circles and did not provide the historical basis thereof. In the study team's judgment, Japan had only to continue on the path that was already being taken in order to catch up with and surpass the world in terms of quality.

The Liberalization Policy of the Early 1960s

During Juran's second visit to Japan, from November to December 1960, he repeated the courses for top executives and for division and section chiefs as in both Tokyo and Osaka in 1954, speaking to some

700 participants on the theme of "Technological Innovation and New Management." This time he demonstrated his enthusiasm by hiring a tutor in the United States to help him study the Japanese language before his visit.

As an American viewing the rapid changes from 1954 to 1960, Juran stated that,

> *The country was undergoing an immense construction and modernization boom. New building construction, offices, apartments, factories, etc., was rising to unprecedented heights. The factories were exhibiting new and exciting machines, tools, and instruments, many made in Japan. . . . Productivity and salaries were rising sharply and the atmosphere of industrial progress was all pervasive.*[57]

Japan was welcoming rapid growth, expanding supply and demand, and actively investing in new plant and equipment.

Facing pressure from overseas to open its economy, the Japanese government had announced only five days before Juran's visit the basics of a plan to liberalize trade and foreign exchange. Liberalization, which was reckoned to be 44 percent complete in 1960, was to expand to 62 percent by 1962 and further to 92 percent by 1964.[58] As a result, restrictions on imports were to be allowed only on 122 items, the level of protection then generally enjoyed by the advanced Western nations. Liberalization, and the accompanying fear of being overwhelmed by foreign companies coming in, led to the development and introduction of what became known as company-wide quality control at textile producers, followed by makers of automobiles, auto parts, and heavy construction equipment.

Total Quality Control, a journal published by JUSE, popularized the slogan, "Ride out liberalization with quality control." Trade liberalization (capital liberalization was instituted later) was the key word of the early 1960s, and Japanese companies embraced company-wide quality control as a way to develop the level of quality necessary to compete against the feared inflow of foreign goods. In the case of automobiles, for example, carmakers rushed to build new plants and offer new models. For Japan, where motorization occurred much later than in the United States, the 1960s represented a shift from trucks to passenger cars and from commercial to personal demand. As sales increased, claims against new models were collected by the sales forces, evaluated, and fed back to the design departments, establishing as early as the 1960s direct quality control links from design through to manufacturing and sales, and back again. Here, the consultants took an active role in spreading the phrase, "Quality designed in."

Let us briefly go back to Juran's 1954 lectures, in which he referred to a research study on 39 U.S. companies that had attempted to introduce quality control after World War II. Of the 39, five were reported to have succeeded, 13 to have been making progress, 14 to have stalled, and seven to have failed.[59] That is, half of the companies were succeeding and half had stalled or failed. Juran concluded that the primary factors separating successes from the failures were not adequacy of budget or technical competence of the engineers, but rather clarity of program definition, adherence to objective, managerial competence of the program leaders, and the level of shop participation. Returning to Japan in the 1960s, we find that, while many companies were successful in introducing quality control, others in fact failed, although the latter cases did not receive much publicity. Further, it is possible to find Juran's four factors at work in the success stories.

Liberalization threatened Japanese companies with the possibility of losing large sections of their domestic markets, or even bankruptcy, as a result of inflowing foreign goods, unless quality was brought up to the same level or higher. A crisis atmosphere virtually pervaded the country, meaning that the program definition was to produce products that would not be inferior to imported items, and that if adherence was not maintained entire markets might be lost. Furthermore, the significance of the crisis was recognized by both management and workers. In short, it can be said that clarity of program definition, adherence to objective, managerial competence of the program leaders, and the level of shop participation, all applied to Japan in the 1960s.

Concerning Juran's fourth point, the level of shop participation, let us consider why and when quality circles were established by supervisors and shop participants.[60] Many of the supervisors who had been listening to the radio seminars expressed the desire for a version of the JUSE journal *Total Quality Control* that was easier to read and understand. This led to the creation by JUSE of a new journal, *Quality Control for the Foreman,* which began publication in 1962. In its first issue it put forth the idea of quality circles stating that quality was not something to be accomplished individually, but which required complete worker participation in "quality circles" centered on supervisors. Such groups were not only to read and discuss *Quality Control for the Foreman,* but also to consider quality issues on the shop floor. A message on the back cover of the first issue asked groups to meet at least once a month, discuss quality-related problems, and to send in to the editors actual examples of the solutions that were achieved.[61] The activities that formed the basis for quality circles are to be found in unofficial work groups formed to improve quality on shop floors from the late 1950s. The editors of *Quality Control for the Foreman* named them "quality circles" and made them official. Subsequently, the quality circles proved to be helpful in relieving the tedious specialization brought about by the conveyor system of production.

In April 1966, Juran visited Japan for the third time, offering his lectures to both top executives and to section and division chiefs as before, this time on the theme of his book *Managerial Breakthrough.*[62] On this visit he acquired an in-depth understanding of the nature, scope, and achievements of the QC circle movement. This inspired him to inscribe a *Q* banner with the message "The QC circle is on the road to world quality leadership."

Two months later, Juran was in Stockholm to address the annual conference of the European Organization for Quality Control. In his address he included a summary of what he had learned about the Japanese QC circle movement. It aroused great interest, but also much doubt that the concept could be applied in Europe.

In addition, Juran ventured a prediction:

> *The Japanese are headed for world quality leadership and will attain it in the next two decades because nobody else is moving there at the same pace.*[63]

That warning went unheeded, after which the prediction was fulfilled, well ahead of schedule.

Summary

Japan's industrial revolution began in the mid-nineteenth century, using technology purchased from the West. This revolution advanced rapidly, along with a shift to self-developed technology. By the early twentieth century, industrialization had taken firm root, along with a trend toward self-sufficiency.

In contrast, the concept of an organized approach to quality control was still in its infancy. A few pioneers were exploring such an approach, including the application of statistical methods. However, these pioneers worked mostly in isolation at their respective companies or universities. During World War II these efforts intensified, but collaboration among the pioneers was limited by the atmosphere of military secrecy.

Following World War II, special organizations (the Japanese Union of Scientists and Engineers, Japan Management Association, and Japan Standards Association) were created to provide education and other services to industry, including education in quality control. These organizations became centers for setting up committees of experts to develop modern approaches to quality control. The committees made progress through their own researches as well as through translation of foreign publications.

During the postwar occupation, progress was accelerated by the CCS management seminar and especially by Deming's lectures on statistical quality control. However, this was followed by an overemphasis on SQC and an underemphasis on the managerial processes for quality control.

In the postoccupation period the emphasis shifted to the managerial processes. The shock of losing the war contributed to a willingness of managers to accept change. There emerged an awareness that for Japan's economy to recover, the quality problem must be solved, especially as the liberalizing policy became effective. Juran's lectures provided a structured approach to managing for quality and to quality improvement.

As progress continued, the Japanese added new inventions which led to a revolutionary rate of improvement. Japan not only became self-sufficient as to managing for quality; it emerged as the world quality leader. Education in quality began to flow from Japan outward instead of the reverse.

Japanese concepts, such as company-wide quality control and quality circles, are now well known. Following their crystallization in the 1960s, other ideas and concepts, including affiliated-company-wide quality management, the seven management tools for QC, and management by policy (*hoshin kanri*), continued to be developed and adopted.

In recent writings Juran has stated, "Had Deming and I stayed home, the Japanese would have achieved world quality leadership all the same."[64] This is simply a case of being overmodest. Had they not come to Japan, Japan's quality control could not have developed so soon, or to the same extent. It is also pertinent to ask, as Deming and Juran delivered their lectures in both Japan and the United States, why was the reception so different, and why did the Japanese become their star pupils?

The first reason is the early understanding of the necessity of quality control by top Japanese executives. For postwar Japan, quality improvement became a number one priority, and top executives gave their attention to changing the image of Japanese goods as being cheap and shoddy. In this connection Juran has stated: ". . . the unsung heroes of the Japanese quality revolution were the Japanese managers."[65]

Additionally, Mr. Takeshi Kayano has suggested that the shock of the defeat during World War II caused many Japanese top executives to reexamine their prewar premises.[66]

A second reason is the role played by educational organizations such as JUSE, JSA, and so on. These were the organizations that invited Deming and Juran, provided the audiences of top and middle managers beforehand, and followed up with appropriate courses afterward. It was their wide-ranging activities that made possible consistent quality control education. The Japanese study team that visited the United States in 1958 concluded that while there were some U.S. companies with excellent quality control programs, others were not even trying. However, there was not such a large gap among companies in Japan. The main reason for this Japanese consistency can be found in the Japanese educational organizations.

Whether executives in charge of quality control were formerly specialists or not can be seen as a further difference between the two countries. It is rare for a quality control manager to become president of an American company. In Japan of the 1960s, however, a number of central figures in the struggle to upgrade quality later became the top executives of their companies. These include Shoichiro Toyoda of Toyota, Yutaka Kume of Nissan, and Shoji Nogawa of Komatsu.

Finally, the Japanese supervisors and shop workers who listened avidly to radio seminars on quality control and who later formed quality circles deserve credit. It was the idea of the Japanese to have radio seminars, but if such seminars had been available in the United States, would the result have been the same?

Why was Deming's name relatively unknown in the United States until NBC's broadcast of the program, "If Japan Can . . . Why Can't We?" Why, when both American and Japanese companies had access to the teachings of Deming and Juran, were the results so different? These are questions that deserve consideration in the United States.

Notes

1. Suguru Fujita, "Development of Japanese Quality Control," *Standardization,* vol. 13, no. 11, p. 13.

2. Kanzo Kiribuchi, *Kogyo kanri yoko,* Yoshida Komusho Shuppanbu, 1934, pp. 84–86.

3. Yasushi Ishida, "Efficiency and Statistics in Mass Production Systems," *Kikai no kenkyu,* vol. 1, no. 3, Yokendo, 1949, pp. 7–10; Suguru Fujita, "A Pioneer of Quality Control: Memories of Yasushi Ishida," *Standardization and Quality Control,* vol. 28, no. 10, 1957, pp. 55–57.

4. "Taidan, hinshitsu hito-suji no 40 nen," *Standardization,* vol. 14, no. 11, 1961, pp. 8–13.

5. In an interview with Suguru Fujita, Ishida indicated that it was about 1931, but Fujita thought that 1933 or 1934 would have been more likely.

6. "Nihon no hinshitsu Kanri no ayumi wo kaeri-mite," *Total Quality Control,* vol. 9, no. 6, 1958, p. 35.

7. At Toshiba, SQC had been conducted only in the lightbulb section. The vacuum tube section, where Dr. Nishibori was then posted, had not yet been introduced to the concepts. "Nihon no hinshitsu Kanri," p. 37; and Eizaburo Nishibori, *Hyaku no ron yori hitotsu no shoko,* JSA, Tokyo, 1985, pp. 220–23.

8. E. S. Pearson, *The Application of Statistical Methods to Industrial Standardization and Quality Control,* British Standard 600, London, 1935; and "Report of the War Preparedness Committee of the Institute of Mathematical Statistics," *Annals of Mathematical Statistics,* vol. XI, no. 4, 1940.

9. Fujita, "Development of Japanese Quality Control," p. 16.

10. "Development of Statistics in Japan," *Tokei-Suri Kenkyujo,* no. 1, 1980, pp. 66–67, and no. 48, 1982, p. 11.

11. Fujita, "Development of Japanese Quality Control," p. 16.

12. "Taidan, hinshitsu hito-suji no 40 nen," p. 10.

13. Letter from G. I. Back to C. F. Craig dated May 28, 1948. Washington Records Center, Record Group 331 (Allied Operational and Occupation Headquarters, World War II) Civil Communications Section, Box No. 3170, File ATT.

14 Ibid., Box No. 3197, File: Telephone Reports.

15. Letters from Mr. Sarasohn to the author, dated January 19 and February 19, 1989.

16. Homer Sarasohn, "Criticism of Japanese Manufacturing Industries," *Keieisha,* vol. 4, no. 4, 1950, p. 8. (Retranslated from the Japanese.)

17. Washington Records Center, Magill's Report in October 1946. Box No. 3158, Memoranda for Record, #2C.

18. Ibid., Mr. Baker's Report on Furukawa Electric's Yokohama Plant, October 1946, Box No. 3158, Memoranda for Record.

19. Eizo Watanabe, "Sarasohn-shi wa kataru, watashi wa, Nihon ni konna kangae de hinshitsu kanri wo uetsuketa," *Engineers,* JUSE, September 1984, p. 17. (Retranslated from the Japanese.)

20. "CCS keiei koza to wa," *Keieisha,* vol. 4, no. 4, 1950, p. 1.

21. Hiroshi Takimoto, "CCS keiei koza sono go no hatten," *Management,* vol. 11, no. 12, 1952, p. 2.

22. Masao Kogure, *Nihon no TQC,* JUSE, Tokyo, 1988, pp. 18, 495.

23. Washington Records Center, Management Indoctrination Course for the Telecommunications Manufacturing Industry, Record Group 331, Box No. 3162, File: Memoranda for Record Book #1. In this record, dated January 23, 1950, 24 top mangers and four professors took part in the seminar in Tokyo, and 26 top managers and two professors took part in Osaka.

24. Mr. Sarasohn states that he and Mr. Protzman delivered the lectures for the seminar.

25. "CCS keiei koza to wa," p. 9.

26. *CCS keiei koza,* Daiyamondo-sha, 1958. In English, Kenneth Hopper has written about the CCS management course; see "Quality, Japan and the US: The First Chapter," *Quality Progress,* September 1985, pp. 34–41.

27. Interview with Dr. Masao Kogure.

28. "Zadankai: America no kagakuteki kanri gijutsu ni manabu," *Keieisha,* vol. 4, no. 4, 1950, pp. 24–35.

29. Interview with Mr. Takeshi Kayano.

30. "Kowa made keiei kanri no shushifu wo utsu," *Management,* vol. 11, no. 12, 1952, p. 12.

31. "Zadankai," p. 30.

32. Ibid., p. 24.

33. *10 Nenkan no sokuseki,* JMA, 1952, p. 1.

34. Izumi Nonaka, "The Origin of Quality Control in Japan: Introduction of SQC (2)," *Total Quality Control,* vol. 41, no. 3, 1990, p. 56; and interview by the author with Dr. Hajime Karatsu.

35. Ken-ichi Koyanagi, ed., *Dr. Deming's Lectures on Statistical Control of Quality,* JUSE, Tokyo, 1950. The revised second edition of this book was *Elementary Principles of the Statistical Control of Quality: A Series of Lectures,* JUSE, Tokyo, 1952.

36. Shigeru Mizuno, *Zensha sogo hinshitsu kanri,* JUSE, Tokyo, 1984, p. 351. The book is translated into English as *Company-Wide Total Quality Control,* Asian Productivity Organization, Tokyo, 1984.

37. W. E. Deming, "Hinshitsu kanri omoide no ki," *Total Quality Control,* vol. 26, no. 3, 1975, p. 9. [Retranslated from the Japanese.]

38. Koyanagi, *Dr. Deming's Lectures,* p. 40.

39. Tanabe Seiyaku Co. Ltd., *305 Years History of Tanabe Seiyaku,* Tanabe Seiyaku Co. Ltd., 1983, p. 192.

40. Nonaka, "Origin of Quality Control," pp. 61–62.

41. Kaoru Ishikawa, ed., "Quality Control in Japan (2)," *Total Quality Control,* vol. 9, no. 9, 1958, p. 94.

42. Junji Noguchi, "National Quality Promotion in Japan" (30th EOQC Conference, Stockholm, 1986), *Societás Quálitátis,* vol. 6, no. 3, p. 91.

43. According to Juran, "In 1951, the first edition of *Quality Control Handbook* was published. It was actually my third book but it became the flagship. It generated numerous invitations for lecturing and consulting. The original invitation to visit Japan was a direct result of the publication of *Quality Control Handbook.*" J. M. Juran, "A Tale of the Twentieth Century," *Juran Report,* Juran Institute, Inc., No. 10, Autumn 1989, p. 11.

44. Interview with Dr. Masumasa Imaizumi, March 16, 1992, for the documentary video *An Immigrant's Gift,* WoodsEnd Productions.

45. Takemaro Mori et al., *Current Japanese Economic History (Gendai Nihon keieishi),* Yuhikaku, 1993, p. 115.

46. J. M. Juran, "Development of Quality Control in Japan 1954–1974" (in Japanese), *Total Quality Control,* vol. 26, no. 3, 1975, p. 5. This article was published in English in J. M. Juran, "Then and Now in Quality Control," *Quality Progress,* 1975, pp. 183–84.

47. "Dr. Juran 4 kaisha, koujou e iku," *Total Quality Control,* vol. 5, no. 8, 1954, pp. 12–17.

48. Juran, "Then and Now in Quality Control," p. 183.

49. J. M. Juran, "Made in the USA: A Renaissance in Quality," *Harvard Business Review,* July–August 1993, p. 43.

50. J. M. Juran, *Planning and Practices in Quality Control: Lectures on Quality Control,* trans. by Ken-ichi Koyanagi, JUSE, 1954, p. 2.

51. Kaoru Ishikawa, *Introduction to Quality Control,* 3A Corporation, Tokyo, 1990, p. 10

52. Ishikawa, "Quality Control in Japan (2)," p. 89.

53. "Participants Allocation of JUSE Courses on Quality Control and the Related," *Societás Quálitátis,* JUSE, vol. 5, no. 5, 1991.

54. Seminars included "Production Management," "Production and Standardization," "Use of Statistics," "JIS Mark," "Keys to Management," "A Study of JIS," and so on. The courses were broadcast in succession from 1957 to 1962.

55. Nobuo Kawabe, "Made in Japan: The Changing Image, 1945–1975," in James H. Soltow, ed., *Essays in Economic and Business History,* Michigan State University, 1979, p. 33.

56. Japan Productivity Center, *American Quality Control (Productivity Report 65),* 1959, pp. 33–34.

57. Juran, "Then and Now in Quality Control in Japan 1954–1974," p. 184.

58. Takemoro Mori et al., *Current Japanese Economic History,* p. 149.

59. Juran, *Planning and Practices in Quality Control: Lectures on Quality Control,* 1954, Lecture 6, pp. 23–24. For the original research report, see J. M. Juran, "Insure Success for Your Quality Control Program," *Factory Management and Maintenance,* October 1950, pp. 106–9.

60. See, Izumi Nonaka, "Origin of Quality Control in Japan (8): Birth of the QC Circle in Japan," *Total Quality Control,* vol. 41, no. 9, 1990.

61. *Genba to QC [Quality Control for the Foreman],* no. 1, April 1962, back cover (no number).

62. J. M. Juran, *Managerial Breakthrough,* McGraw-Hill, New York, 1964.

63. J. M. Juran, "Made in the USA," p. 44.

64. Ibid., p. 42.

65. Ibid., p. 44.

66. Conversation, Takeshi Kayano with J. M. Juran and Dr. A. Blanton Godfrey, Tokyo, 1990.

CHAPTER 17

A History of Managing for Quality in the United States of America

J. M. Juran
Chairman Emeritus, Juran Institute, Inc.

The Origins of the United States of America

Until the voyage of discovery by Christopher Columbus in 1492, the North American continent was populated by numerous native Indian tribes. Some had evolved advanced civilizations, including sophistication in astronomy, but most were lacking in technology and even a system of writing. These lived off the land as food gatherers, farmers, fishermen, hunters, and so on. Nevertheless some of their handicrafts reached high levels of quality as evidenced by artifacts that are preserved in museums.

What is now the United States was colonized mainly by Great Britain, Spain, and France. These European countries subdued the natives through superior weaponry, and took possession of the continent. In due course the colonists revolted against foreign rule, declared their independence in 1776, and formed the United States of America (USA).

Following independence the USA became a haven for large numbers of immigrants, at first mainly from Great Britain and northern Europe, and later from southern and eastern Europe. It also expanded its territory, by purchase and conquest, to reach its present boundaries.

Early Systems of Managing for Quality

The origins of managing for quality in the USA are to be found in Europe rather than in North America. Other chapters in this book deal extensively with those European origins. (See, for example, chapter 7.) In view of this, the author has chosen to focus chiefly on the events that resulted in departures from European practice.

At first the principal industries in the colonies were agriculture plus production for self-use. The British government favored retaining for the British Isles the roles of manufacture and sale of finished goods while using the colonies as a source of materials and as a captive market for manufactured goods. The colonists resisted these restricted roles, and sought to create their own manufacturing capabilities.

The early colonists and immigrants also faced the problems and opportunities associated with exploiting the immense natural resources of their new world. An innovative spirit emerged and became a driving force when the new nation undertook to industrialize. Self-reliance and risk taking became major and respected traditions. These traditions in turn raised individualism and entrepreneurship to a state of respect.

Craftsmanship

In their approach to manufacture, the colonists and immigrants tended to follow the craftsmanship concept prevailing in their respective European countries of origin. A boy learned a skilled trade as an apprentice to a master. The master trained the apprentice in how to produce the product. The master also maintained a form of quality control by inspecting the goods before sale.

Once the apprentice had learned his trade he became self-employed or employed by the master of a small shop. Quality under craftsmanship was usually in good hands—the hands of the craftsmen. Achievement of quality was one of the essential skills learned by the apprentice. Most goods were sold locally, so the craftsman had a large personal stake in meeting his customers' needs for quality.

The Industrial Revolution

The Industrial Revolution, which originated in Europe, created the factory system. The factory system usually subdivided former trades into multiple specialized tasks. It soon outproduced the craftsmen and the small independent shops, and made them largely obsolete. It forced many craftsmen to become factory workers, and many shop owners to become production supervisors. (The factories employed many semiskilled and unskilled workers as well.)

Managing for quality remained a production function. Large production departments employed full-time inspectors who reported to the respective production supervisors. Quality was assured through the skills of the workers supplemented by supervisory audit or by departmental inspectors. When the Industrial Revolution was exported from Europe to North America, the USA again followed European practice, with further damage to craftsmanship.

The Taylor System and Its Impact

Late in the nineteenth century the USA broke sharply with European tradition by adopting Frederick W. Taylor's system of scientific management (Juran 1973). Taylor's goal was to increase production and productivity without increasing the number of skilled craftsmen. His concept was to separate planning from execution. In those days, planning of factory work was done largely by factory supervisors and workers who, in Taylor's view, lacked the necessary technological literacy. Taylor's solution was to assign the planning to engineers, and to limit the supervisors and workers to executing the plans. This approach became the basis for a remarkable rise in productivity. In the judgment of the author, the Taylor system was a major contributor to making the USA the world leader in productivity.

The Emergence of Independent Inspection Departments

The Taylor system also had negative consequences. It damaged human relations by further crippling of the craftsmanship concept. In addition, the new emphasis on productivity had a negative effect on quality. To restore the balance, factory managers created central inspection departments, headed by a chief inspector. The various departmental inspectors were then transferred to the new inspection departments. This was done over the bitter opposition of the production supervisors.

The major job of the new inspection departments was to keep defective products from reaching the customers. This was done by inspection in various forms. Raw materials and goods in process were commonly sampled. The results of the sampling determined the disposition of the lot. Finished goods were usually detail inspected to separate the good from the bad.

In many companies the assignment of responsibility for quality took a curious turn. If defective goods did get out to clients, it was common for the upper managers to ask the chief inspector, "Why did you let this get out?" It was less common to ask the production manager, "Why did you make it this way?" In due course there evolved a widely held belief that quality was the responsibility of the inspection department.

The First Wave of Statistical Quality Control

The middle 1920s witnessed the first significant wave of so-called "Statistical Quality Control" (SQC). It had its origin in the Bell System. It was initiated in 1926 when a team from the Bell Telephone Laboratories proposed that the Hawthorne Works of Western Electric Company (the manufacturing arm of the Bell System) apply certain tools of statistical methodology to the control of quality of manufactured telephone products. Those tools consisted of

- The new Shewhart control chart
- Use of probability theory to put sampling inspection on a scientific basis and
- A demerits plan for evaluating outgoing quality of telephone products.

That initiative resulted in creation of a Joint Committee on Inspection Statistics and Economy. The most fruitful activity of the committee was the development of sampling tables. The Hawthorne Works made extensive use of sampling inspection, but in empirical ways. The committee produced many innovations: the identification and terminology of sampling risks; sampling plans—single, multiple, and continuous; the average outgoing quality limit (AOQL) concept;

the process average concept, which was an early version of the process capability concept; and so on. Derivatives of the sampling plans were published as MIL-STD-105; the Dodge–Romig tables (Dodge and Romig 1959); and others.

In contrast, the control chart concept did not arouse much interest at the Hawthorne Works, whose major quality problems required remedies of a far more fundamental sort:

- The physical layout of that huge plant was on a colony basis—each production department housed a single species of process machinery. This arrangement resulted in long production intervals, huge process inventories, gridlocked transportation, and chaotic paperwork.

- Manufacturing planning was done empirically. The planners had no grasp of the concept of quantifying process variability.

- Measuring instruments were mostly of the go–no go type, to facilitate sorting of good products from bad.

- The priorities assigned to the production departments were to meet the schedules, achieve high productivity, and maintain piecework earnings. Quality was left to the inspection department.

During the 1920s and 1930s, the committee activities did impact Bell System practices, notably with respect to sampling inspection. However, there was hardly any impact on American practice as a whole. That had to await the events of World War II. During that war the work done by the committee became the basis for the wartime training courses in statistical quality control, and for various published sampling tables. (For elaboration on the role of the Bell System, see AT&T, 1989.)

Quality During World War II

The American involvement in World War II began as a supplier to the Allies during the late 1930s. The Japanese attack on Pearl Harbor in December 1941 then brought the United States into the war as a combatant. Legislation was enacted to put the country on a war footing. A War Production Board was created to gear the civilian economy to the war machine, and to produce enormous quantities of military products, many of which used new, sophisticated technology.

Regulations were established to give the war effort priority in allocation of facilities, materials, skilled personnel, and services of all sorts. Production of a wide range of civilian products came to a halt. These included automobiles, household appliances, entertainment products, and many others. A massive shortage of civilian goods developed while defense factory employees were working overtime and building up a great hoard of purchasing power.

The Effect on Quality of Military Products

The traditional approach had been to award military contracts based on competitive bidding, the contract usually going to the lowest bidder. Upon delivery, the products were inspected and tested for conformance to specifications. Often this involved inspecting and testing every single unit of product.

This same basic approach was retained during World War II. It required a huge expansion of the inspection forces, with massive problems in recruitment, training, employee turnover, and so on. The armed forces tried to reduce these problems by greater use of sampling inspection. In doing so, they decided to replace their empirical ways of sampling with methods based on the laws of probability. With the aid of industry consultants, especially from the Bell Telephone Laboratories, they adapted the sampling tables which had earlier been devised by the Bell System. The resulting tables were published as MIL-STD-105, and were incorporated into the contracts by reference. In turn, many contractors referenced these same tables in the contracts they made with their suppliers.

Despite this progress in improving the inspection process, the top priority was on meeting the delivery schedules. This was underscored by the system of awarding the coveted Army–Navy "E" to government contractors. The award was for meeting delivery schedules.

The Effect on Quality of Civilian Products

World War II ended in 1945, but meanwhile a massive shortage of goods had built up. It then took the rest of that decade to refill the pipelines and for supply to catch up with demand. During those years the quality of products declined severely. (Quality always goes down during shortages.) The traditional, experienced manufacturers gave top priority to volume of production in order to secure maximum share of market. The shortages also attracted new competitors, and their inexperience contributed further to the decline in quality.

The most subtle effect of the shortages was to create a habit of giving top priority to meeting schedules. As the years went on this priority found its way into company policies and procedures. The resulting habit patterns then developed vested interests which resisted change. So the habit of giving top priority to delivery dates persisted long after the shortages were gone.

The Second Wave of Statistical Quality Control

During World War II, there reemerged a surge of interest in statistical quality control. The War Production Board, in its effort to help contractors to improve their quality, sponsored numerous training courses in the statistical techniques evolved by the Bell System during the 1920s. (Working 1945; Grant 1953). Some of this training stimulated quality improvement in specific companies. However, most wartime applications of SQC were tool-oriented rather than results-oriented. As long as government contracts paid for everything, the companies could not lose. In due course the government contracts came to an end, and the SQC programs were reexamined from the standpoint of cost-effectiveness. Most of them failed the test, resulting in wholesale cutbacks.

Creation of ASQC

One aspect of the training courses appealed to all attendees. They relished the opportunity to meet for eight days with people who faced the problems of quality control in other companies. For many attendees, this opportunity for sharing experiences was unprecedented. Some proceeded to create local societies to enable such sharing to continue. These local societies then merged to form the American Society for Quality Control (ASQC).

(For some recollections of quality-related events during World War II, see AT&T, 1989. See also Grant, 1991; Juran 1991; Wareham and Stratton, 1991.)

Quality Control Engineering

A residual effect of the War Production Board training courses was the creation of quality specialists who were assigned to make use of the new tools. Many of these specialists prepared texts and conducted in-house training courses within their own companies. Some went further: they established data systems, investigated abnormal conditions, initiated quality planning, prepared manuals of procedure, conducted quality audits, published quality reports, and so on. The conduct of such activities created a demand for a new job category for quality specialists. The companies responded positively, and the term *quality control engineer* emerged as the most popular title.

There also arose the question Where shall we put the quality control engineers on the organization chart? Large companies tended to create new departments called *statistical quality control* or *quality control engineering* for the new specialists. Such departments were not made subordinate to the chief inspectors. Instead, a new office was created—the quality control department, headed by a quality control manager. This new department then presided over the inspection department and the new quality control engineering department. The quality control manager was usually assigned to report to the plant manager.

The Quality Control Department

The new quality control department now occupied a higher place in the company hierarchy than any previous quality-oriented organization unit. Yet this situation soon changed as a result of the postwar decline of product quality due to shortages.

During the years of shortages the merchants tended to avoid complaining about quality. They were fearful that their suppliers might reduce their allocations. Then, as the pipelines did fill up, the complaints about quality intensified. The unqualified suppliers soon disappeared, but poor quality also threatened the market share of the survivors. That threat then attracted the attention of the marketers and upper managers. The solution usually took two major forms. One was to create a function of reliability engineering. The other was to raise the stature of the quality control department.

Reliability engineering was a response to the growing problem of field failures of durable goods. Conventional quality control had focused on time zero—performance when tested prior to shipment. This focus did not assure that the products would perform reliably during long use in the field. Reliability engineering evolved to develop tools and procedures that would contribute to reducing field failures. Many companies recognized this need, and created a new job category of reliability engineer. Some went further, and established a department of reliability engineering. In such cases the new department became a part of the quality control department.

The name of the quality control department was also changed, as well as its status. It now housed the functions of inspection and test, quality control engineering, reliability engineering, and quality audit. In addition there was a need to give it added status to help it deal with the entrenched habit of giving top priority to meeting schedules. To provide this new status the department name was changed (typically) to quality department. The chief was given (typically) the title of quality manager, and (typically) reported to the vice president for manufacture. Considering that early in the century the organization charts were devoid of anything oriented to quality, this was a high status indeed.

Managing for Quality at Mid–Twentieth Century

By the middle of the twentieth century, managing for quality in the USA was carried out largely as follows:

Each functional department in the company carried out its assigned function and then handed off the result to the next function in the sequence. This was often called *throwing it over the wall*.

At the end of the sequence the quality department separated the good products from the bad.

For defective products that escaped to the customer, redress was to be provided through customer service based on warranties.

This approach contained numerous deficiencies, such as

• Training in how to manage for quality was limited to members of the quality department.

- Quality had top priority in the quality department, but not in other departments.

- The over-the-wall concept permitted departments unilaterally to create quality problems for their customers, internal and external.

- The reliance on inspection and test fostered the belief that quality was the responsibility of the quality department. The extreme dimensions of this strategy can be seen from the situation prevailing in the Hawthorne Works of Western Electric Company during the late 1920s. Hawthorne was at that time virtually the only factory in the Bell System. At the peak (about 1928) it employed over 40,000 people, of whom 5200 were in the quality department.

- The upper managers were detached from the quality function. In their mind they had delegated quality to the quality managers.

- There was no organized approach for quality improvement— for improving the processes so as to reduce the incidence of defects and field failures. The responsibility for prevention was vague.

By the standards of later decades these deficiencies seem formidable. Yet they were no handicap to companies whose competitors employed the same concepts, and such was usually the case. Despite the deficiencies inherent in the concept of detection, many USA goods came to be well regarded as to quality. In some product lines American companies became the quality leaders.

In addition, the American economy grew to superpower size. The domestic economy was unified by the laws governing movement of goods in interstate commerce; these laws avoided the obstacles inherent in the national boundaries then prevailing in Western Europe. The American belief in a market-based economy and the spirit of entrepreneurship stimulated investment to bring new and improved products to market. Additionally, managers were willing to invest in facilities to improve productivity. Some of those investments (for example, in machines, tools, instruments) improved quality as well.

The Emerging Forces

During the second half of the twentieth century some massive forces emerged to challenge the adequacy of quality in the USA. The chief forces included

- The growth of consumerism
- The growth of litigation over quality
- The growth of government regulation of quality
- The Japanese quality revolution

In due course American managers evolved responses to those massive forces, but not before much damage had been done to the economy.

The Growth of Consumerism

(The text for this topic includes some extracts and paraphrases of material from Juran 1988, pages 34.2 to 34.13.)

Consumerism is a popular name for the movement to help consumers solve their problems through collective action. Applied to quality, consumerism addresses such problems as

- Ignorance, before purchase, of the relative merits of competing products
- Misleading advertising or labeling
- Products that fail during use
- Poor after-sale service
- Inadequate redress following complaints

For elaboration, see Sentry 1976.

No one knows whether the *rate* of consumer grievances has grown over the centuries. However we know very well that the *volume* of grievances has grown to enormous numbers due to the growth in volume of goods and services. By the mid–twentieth century, consumer frustrations had reached levels that stimulated attacks on industrial companies for their alleged responsibility for consumers' problems. Lacking the credible data needed for a successful defense, the companies lost the initiative for action. The resulting vacuum attracted numerous contenders for leadership of the consumerism movement: government agencies, politicians, social reformers, consumer advocates ("consumerists"), consumer associations, standardization organizations, independent test laboratories, and still others.

A serious risk arose that a bargaining agent would intervene between industrial companies and their customers.

Product Information Before Purchase

Consumers would be helped in their buying decisions if they had access to information relative to competitive product quality, after-sale service, and so on. Many industrial companies possess such information but regard it as proprietary. In the field of finance, companies that are publicly owned do publish independently audited statements disclosing their financial status. This practice does not extend to disclosure of information about the quality of their products. As a result, other forms of quality information have emerged to fill the vacuum.

Consumer Test Services. Test laboratories have emerged that are independent of the companies producing and selling the products. (*Independence* depends largely on whether the financing comes from unbiased sources.) These laboratories evaluate the quality of competing goods and services, and then make the resulting information available to consumers. The most widely known is Consumers Union, which publishes its findings in the journal *Consumer Reports*. It derives its income from selling the journal and related publications.

Certification Testing. In this form, the test laboratory derives its income from manufacturers who want a certificate (mark, seal, label) attesting to certain features of their products. These test services vary widely in their purpose and especially in their objectivity.

An example of such a laboratory is Underwriters' Laboratories, Inc. (UL). It was originally created by the National Board of Fire Underwriters to aid in fire prevention, but has since been made independent. UL is mainly involved in matters of safety—fire protection, burglary protection, hazardous chemicals, and so on. Its activities include

- Developing and publishing standards for materials, products, and systems.

- Testing manufacturers' products for compliance with these standards (or with other recognized standards).

- Awarding the UL mark to products that comply. This is known as *listing* the products.

Numerous other laboratories are similarly involved in safety matters; for example, steam boilers, marine safety.

In some of these product categories it is now unlawful to market the products without the certificate of the testing service. In other cases it is lawful, but the testing is done for economic reasons—the insurance companies will demand extremely high premiums or will not provide insurance at all.

Government Certification.   In the United States, federal law requires that certain health-related products must be government-approved before they may be sold to the public. The trend to such legislation began early in the twentieth century. It now extends to such products as pharmaceuticals as well as foods and food additives.

Data Banks on Business Practices.   Many consumer complaints are traceable to company business practices such as failure to meet the provisions of guarantees. Experience has shown that a small percent of the companies create the bulk of such consumer complaints. As a result, a data bank on companies' business practices can help to identify those companies that have the worst records, and so aid in removing their influence.

The organizations known as Better Business Bureaus (BBB) have been active in creating such data banks. When citizens call the BBB, they are able to learn whether the company under inquiry has a significant record of complaints lodged against it. (The BBB also receives consumer complaints on unethical business practices, and tries as an ombudsman to get these practices changed. See later discussion.)

Remedies After the Fact

Consumers who encounter product quality problems during the warranty period are faced with a choice of alternatives. They may be able to resolve the problem unaided—they study the product information and then apply their skills and ingenuity. Alternatively they may decide to complain, in which case they have a range of choice. By a wide margin, consumers complain to the merchant (store, dealer) rather than to the manufacturer. A third choice is to complain to the Better Business Bureau. (Sentry 1976, 15). There are other choices as well.

The Ombudsman. Ombudsman is a Swedish name for an official whose job is to receive citizens' complaints and to help them secure remedial action. The ombudsman has no authority to compel action, but has the power to publicize failures to act.

The concept of the ombudsman has been applied to problems in product quality. Some companies have created an in-house ombudsman and have publicized the name and telephone number. Consumers can phone (free of charge) to air grievances and to secure information. In the United States a more usual title for the ombudsman is manager of consumer relations. Such managers often carry additional responsibilities such as stimulating changes to improve relations with consumers generally.

Another form is the industry ombudsman. An example is the Major Appliance Consumer Action Panel (a group of independent consumer experts) created by the Association of Home Appliance Manufacturers to receive complaints from consumers who have not been able to secure satisfaction locally.

The concept of the ombudsman is fundamentally sound. It is widely supported by consumers and regulators, as well as by a strong minority of business managers (Sentry 1976, 77). Some newspapers now provide an ombudsman service as part of their department of "Letters to the Editor."

Mediation. Under this concept, a third party—the mediator—helps the contesting parties to work out a settlement. The mediation process tends to open up the channels of communication and thereby to clear up misunderstandings. In addition, an experienced mediator exerts a moderating influence which encourages a search for a solution. The mediator lacks the power of enforcement—there is no binding agreement to abide by the opinion of the mediator. Nevertheless mediation stimulates settlements. Best (1981) reported that the New York City Department of Human Affairs achieved a 60 percent settlement rate during 1977 and 1978.

Arbitration. Under this concept the parties agree to be bound by the decision of a third party. Arbitration is an attractive form of resolving differences because it avoids the high costs and long delays inherent in most lawsuits. In the great majority of consumer claims the cost of a lawsuit is far greater than the amount of the claim. Nevertheless there are obstacles to use of the arbitration process. Both parties must agree to binding arbitration. There is need to establish local, low-cost arbitration centers and to secure the services of volunteer arbitrators at nominal fees or no fees. These obstacles have limited the growth of use of arbitration for consumer complaints.

No Remedy.   Under the system of free enterprise prevailing in the United States, many valid consumer complaints result in no satisfaction to the consumer. This is a defect in the free-enterprise system, but in the experience of the author, every other system is worse. Nevertheless the system includes some built-in long-range corrections. Companies that fail to provide satisfaction to consumers also fail to attract repeat business. In due course they mend their ways or lose out to competitors who have a better record of providing satisfaction.

Consumer Organizations

Consumer organizations exist in a wide variety of forms. Some are closely focused; for example, product testing, automotive safety, truth in lending. Others are adjuncts of broader organizations such as labor unions or farm cooperatives. Still others set out to deal broadly with consumer problems in general. In addition, there are efforts to strengthen the consumerism movement through umbrella organizations which try to unify the collective force of all consumer groups.

The consumerism movement is extensively supported by government agencies at all levels—national, state, and local. Some agencies try to help complaining consumers, either in an ombudsman role or by threat of legal action. Some have the legal power to investigate malpractice and to punish the guilty companies. Others are active in consumer education—they publish information to aid consumers in making purchase decisions and in handling grievances. (See, for example, *Consumer's Source Handbook* 1980.) Still other agencies conduct research on consumer problems. Their reports become the basis for proposing new legislation or issuing new administrative regulations.

It should be noted that consumer organizations exhibit strong biases. They are quite emphatic when discussing the failings of industrial companies but they have little to say about the failings of consumers.

Yet many consumer grievances are based on consumer neglect or deceit—the instruction manual had been discarded; the product failed because it was misused. In addition, many consumers exhibit unwise behavior. They spend money on drugs, alcohol, or tobacco; kill themselves (and others) by driving in a drunken state; eat junk food; gamble their money away. Unbiased observers may well conclude that consumers who are gullible or stupid will learn only from their mistakes. However, consumer organizations never characterize consumers (their clientele) as being gullible or stupid.

Of course, industrial companies exhibit corresponding biases. In fact, the early business indifference to the very real problems of consumers was part of the reason for the rise of the consumerism movement in the first place. In those days the economic forces were tilted in favor of the industrial companies. The consumerism movement has helped to balance those forces, with an assist from the fact that politically the consumers greatly outnumber the industrial managers.

Government Regulation of Quality

(The text for this topic includes some extracts and paraphrases of material from Juran 1988, pages 34.13 to 34.19.)

From time immemorial, governments have established and enforced standards of quality. Some of these governments have been political—national, provincial, local. Others have been nonpolitical—guilds, trade associations, standardization bodies, and so on. Whether through delegation of political power or through long custom, these governing bodies attained a status that enabled them to carry out programs of regulation.

Safety, Health, and the Environment

The earliest applications of government regulation were chiefly concerned with the safety and health of the state and its citizens. Since then, and especially in industrialized countries, government regulation has widened in scope, The United States had generally followed this trend, but the second half of the twentieth century witnessed considerable proliferation.

A major segment of such proliferation has related to safety and health of the citizenry. New laws were enacted to deal with major areas such as highway traffic safety, consumer product safety, occupational safety and health, environmental protection, and so on. Each such major area has involved establishing new statutes along with new government agencies to administer them.

Economics of the Consumer

An extensive body of the new legislation falls within the scope of the Federal Trade Commission, which exercises a degree of oversight relative to "unfair or deceptive practices in commerce." That scope has led to specific legislation or administrative action relative to product warranties; packaging and labeling; truth in lending; and so on. In its oversight the Federal Trade Commission stresses two major requirements.

1. The advertising, labeling, and other product information must be clear and unequivocal as to what is meant by the seller's representation.

2. The product must comply with the representation.

Such government regulation is a sharp break from the ancient rule of *caveat emptor* (let the buyer beware). That rule was (and still is) quite sensible as applied to conditions in the village marketplaces of developing countries. However it is no longer appropriate to the conditions prevailing in industrialized, developed countries. (For elaboration, see Juran 1970.)

In the United States there is much resistance to the idea of applying government regulation to the area of consumer economics. Some of the resistance is on ideological grounds—the competitive marketplace is asserted to be more efficient in meeting consumer needs than government regulation. Other resistance is based on the widespread belief that government operation is inherently much less efficient than private industry. Nevertheless, the growth of the consumerism movement has stimulated an associated growth of government in the area of consumer economics.

Powers of the Regulatory Agencies

The statutes give the regulatory agencies wide powers such as the right to

- Investigate product failures and user complaints
- Inspect the companies' processes and systems of controls
- Test products in all stages of distribution
- Recall products already sold to users
- Revoke the companies' right to sell, or to apply the mark
- Inform users of deficiencies
- Issue cease-and-desist orders

Nevertheless, the companies retain the right to challenge agency decisions by appeal to the courts.

The Effectiveness of Regulation

Regulators face the difficult problem of balance—how to protect consumer interests without adding burdens to the economy—burdens which in the end are damaging to consumer interests. Political expediency can be an obstacle to striking the proper balance. An example is seen in the regulation of highway traffic safety.

Political Expediency. In 1966 the National Highway Traffic Safety Administration (NHTSA) was created to administer two new laws:

1. The National Traffic and Motor Vehicle Safety Act, directed primarily at the vehicle, and
2. The Highway Safety Act, directed primarily at the motorist and the driving environment.

As of 1966 the USA traffic fatality rate was in fact the lowest among all industrialized countries. This was largely due to cumulative improvements in safety made by the designers of vehicles, roads, traffic signals, and so on. In addition it was known, from overwhelming arrays of data, that the limiting factor in traffic safety was the motorist.

- Alcohol was involved in about half of all fatal accidents.

- Young drivers (under age 24) constituted 22 percent of the driver population but were involved in 39 percent of the accidents.

- Excessive speed and other forms of "improper" driving were reported as factors in about 75 percent of the accidents. (During the subsequent oil crisis of 1974 the mandated reduction of highway speeds resulted in a 15 percent reduction in traffic fatalities, without any change in vehicles.)

- Most motorists did not buy safety belts when they were optional, most did not wear them when they were provided as standard equipment, and many do not wear them even when their use is mandated by law.

In the face of this overwhelming evidence NHTSA paid little attention to the main problem—improving the performance of the motorists. Instead, it concentrated on setting numerous standards for vehicle design. These standards did provide some gains in safety. However these gains were minor, while the added costs ran to billions of dollars—to be paid for by consumers.

In effect, the policy of NHTSA was one of dealing strictly with a highly visible political target—the vehicle makers—while avoiding any confrontation with a large body of voters—the motorists. The policy was safe politically but it did little for safety. (For elaboration, see Juran 1977.)

Design Standards or Performance Standards.   Regulation often involves setting standards. A major question is whether to establish design standards or performance standards.

Design standards admit of precise definition, but they have serious disadvantages. Their nature and numbers are such that they often lack flexibility, are difficult to understand, become very numerous, and are difficult to keep up-to-date.

Performance standards are generally free from these disadvantages. However, they place on the employer the burden of determining how to meet the performance standard; that is, the burden of creating or acquiring a design. Performance standards also demand a level of compliance officers who have the education, experience, and training needed to make the subjective judgments of whether the standard has been met.

When this question was faced by the Occupational Safety and Health Administration (OSHA) it opted for design standards, and encountered all the associated problems. Later a presidential task force was assigned to review the question. The task force recommended going to a performance/hazard concept. Under that concept employers are free to determine the most appropriate manner in which to guard against any hazard, but compliance is objectively measurable by determining whether or not an employee is exposed to the hazard. (For elaboration, see *OSHA Safety Regulation* 1977.)

Focus on the Vital Few.   A common deficiency in the regulatory process is failure to concentrate on the vital few problems that are responsibe for the bulk of the adverse effects—injuries, malpractices, and so on. Regulatory agencies receive a barrage of alerts: consumer complaints, reports of injuries, accusations directed at specific products, and the like. Collectively the numbers are overwhelming. There is no possibility of dealing thoroughly with each and every case. Agencies which try to do so become hopelessly bogged down. The resulting paralysis then becomes a target for critics, with associated threats to the tenure of the administrator, or even to the continued existence of the agency.

OSHA faced just such a threat in the mid-1970s. In response it undertook to establish a classification for its cases based on the seriousness of the threats to safety and health. It also recalled about 1000 safety regulations which were under attack for adding much to industry costs and little to worker safety.

With experience, the agencies tend to adopt the Pareto principle of vital few and useful many. This helps them to concentrate their resources on the opportunities to provide the public with maximum benefits.

What to Do About the Useful Many.   Focus on the vital few is a valid policy, yet it provides no solution for a prickly problem—what to do about those consumer complaints, employee injuries, and so on, each of which is of a minor nature—the so-called "useful many." These cases are numerous, but their collective impact is far less than that of the vital few. It is rare for a regulatory agency to have the resources to deal with every one of these cases, individually.

One solution involves forthrightly making clear that a federal agency is in no position to resolve such problems on an individual basis. What the agency can do is to provide the public with information and educational material of a self-help nature: where to apply for assistance; how to apply for assistance; what are the rights of the individual; what to do and not to do. (See, for example, *Consumer's Source Handbook* 1980.)

Some agencies have failed to face up to their inability to deal individually with the useful many. The typical end result has been a huge backlog of cases, a frustrated public, and a badly damaged public image. (For elaboration, see Sentry 1976, 70.)

Costs and Benefits of Regulation

The costs of regulation consist largely of two major components.

1. The costs of running the regulatory agencies. These costs can be determined with precision. They are paid for by the public in the form of taxes.

2. The costs of complying with the regulations. These are not known with precision, but are reliably estimated to be many times the costs of running the regulatory agencies. While these costs are in the first instance paid by the industrial companies, they are ultimately paid by the public in the form of higher prices.

(For an example of a study of industry costs, see The Business Roundtable 1978.)

The benefit from all this regulation is difficult to estimate. (There is no agreement on the value of a human life.) Safety, health, and a clean environment are widely believed to be enormously valuable. Providing consumers with honest information and prompt redress is likewise regarded as enormously valuable. Ideally, each instance should be examined as to its cost–benefit relationship. Yet the statutes have generally been vague on setting guidelines to be followed when making cost–benefit analyses and on requiring the regulators to make such analyses. In addition, the regulators have generally not been eager to get into cost–benefit analyses.

In contrast, the industrial companies have supported cost–benefit analyses. For example, a study of mandated vehicle safety systems found that,

> . . . *states which employ mandatory periodic inspection programs do not have lower accident rates than those states without such requirements.*

> . . . *only a relatively small portion of highway accidents— some 2 to 6 percent—are conclusively attributable to mechanical (vehicle) defects.*

> . . . *human factors (such as excess speeds) are far more important causes of highway accidents than vehicle condition.*

(For elaboration see Crain 1980.)

Any indifference of regulators to costs inevitably creates regulations and rigid enforcements so absurd that in due course they become the means for securing a change in policy. The companies call such absurdities to the attention of the media, who relish publicizing them. The resulting publicity then puts the regulators on the defensive while stimulating the legislators to hold hearings. During such hearings (and depending on the political climate) the way is open to securing a better cost–benefit balance.

The political climate is an important variable in securing attention to cost–benefit considerations. During the 1960s and 1970s the political climate in the United States was generally favorable to regulatory legislation. Then, during the 1980s the climate changed, and with it a trend toward requiring cost justifications.

Product Safety and Product Liability

(The text for this topic includes some extracts and paraphrases of material from Juran 1988, pages 34.19 to 34.22.)

Growth of the Problem

Until the early twentieth century, lawsuits based on injuries from use of manufactured products were rarely filed. When filed, they were often unsuccessful. Even if successful, the damages awarded were modest in size.

Since then the number of such lawsuits has risen remarkably, as has the success rate and the size of the damages awarded. Collectively these changes have done much damage to the USA economy, and continue to do so.

As a by-product, insurance rates for product liability have also risen remarkably, and have become major factors in cost of operations. For elaboration, see *Interagency Task Force on Product Liability: Final Report* (ca. 1978), chapter III. See also Kolb and Ross (1980), pages 287–327.

In some fields the costs of product liability have forced companies to abandon specific product lines or go out of business altogether. Grant (1994) notes, "Twenty years ago, 20 companies manufactured football helmets in the United States. Since that time, 18 of these companies have discontinued making this product because of high product liability costs." Similarly, prohibitive insurance rates have forced many surgeons into early retirement.

Several developments have converged to bring about this growth of the product liability problem.

1. *The "population explosion" of products.* The industrial society has placed huge numbers of manufactured products into the hands of amateurs. Some of these products are inherently dangerous. Others are misused. The injury *rate* (injuries per million hours of usage) has been declining, but the total *number* of injuries has been rising. Each such injury becomes the basis for a potential lawsuit.

2. *Erosion of manufacturers' defenses.* During the twentieth century the law courts eroded some long-standing legal defenses available to manufacturers. Formerly, a plaintiff's lawsuit rested on one of two main grounds:

A *contract* for purchase of the product, with an actual or implied warranty of freedom from hazards. In such cases the plaintiff had to establish *privity*, that is, that he/she was a party to the contract. The courts have in effect abolished the need for privity on the theory that the warranty (of freedom from hazards) follows the product around, irrespective of who is the user.

Negligence by the manufacturer. In such cases the burden of proof was formerly on the plaintiff to show that the manufacturer was negligent. The courts have to a high degree adopted the principle of strict liability on the ground that the cost of injuries resulting from hazardous products should be borne "by the manufacturers that put such products on the market rather than by the injured persons who are powerless to protect themselves." (Sometimes the injured persons are not powerless; they cause or contribute to their own injuries. However, juries are notoriously sympathetic to injured plaintiffs.)

Avoiding Lawsuits

The best defense against lawsuits is to eliminate the conditions that generate lawsuits in the first place. To this end, many companies have adopted strategies that involve contributions from all company functions and from all levels in the hierarchy. To illustrate,

Top management can evolve policies and goals relative to product liability, and institute measures and audits to assure that the policies are followed and the goals are met.

Product design can adopt product safety as a design parameter; adopt a fail-safe philosophy of design; organize formal design reviews; follow the established codes; secure listings from the established laboratories; utilize modern tools of design technique.

Manufacture can establish a sound system of quality control; provide procedures for errorproofing matters of product safety; train supervisors and workers in how the product is used (and misused); open up suggestion plans to ideas on product safety; set up means for providing traceability; and so on.

And so for other functions: legal, marketing, advertising, customer service. (For elaboration, see Juran 1988, 34.20, 34.21.)

Additional activities require contributions from multiple functions. For example, the growth of safety legislation and of product liability has enormously increased the need for documentation. A great deal of this documentation is mandated by legislation, along with retention periods. (For a compilation, see Kolb and Ross 1980, 547–84.)

Defense Against Lawsuits

The growth of the product liability problem has also led to reexamination of how best to defend against lawsuits once they are filed. Experience has shown the need for special preparation for such defense, including reconstruction of the events that led up to the injury; study of the relevant documents—specifications, manuals, procedures, correspondence, reports; analysis of internal performance records for the products and associated processes; analysis of field performance information; physical examinations of the pertinent facilities; study of the failed hardware. All this should be done promptly, by qualified experts, and with early notification to the insurance company. For elaboration, see Gray *et al.* (1975), pages 67–93; also Kolb and Ross (1980), pages 275–86.

Whether and how to go to trial involves a great deal of special knowledge and experience. See generally, Gray *et al.* (1975); also Kolb and Ross (1980), pages 275–86.

Prognosis

As of the mid-1990s there remained some formidable unsolved problems in the area of product liability. To many observers the American legal system for dealing with product liability lawsuits contained some serious deficiencies.

- Lay juries lack the technological literacy needed to determine liability on technological matters. In most other developed countries, judges make such decisions.

- Lay juries are too easily swayed emotionally to determine the proper size of awards.

- In the United States, punitive damages may be awarded along with compensatory damages and damages for pain and suffering. Punitive damages sometimes run into many millions of dollars.

- In the United States, lawyers are permitted to work on a contingency fee basis—an arrangement which greatly stimulates lawsuits. This arrangement is illegal in most countries.

- Only a minority of the award money goes to the injured parties. The majority goes to lawyers and to pay administrative expenses.

The legal system which endures these deficiencies is deeply rooted in the American culture. It is therefore speculative whether the system will soon be changed. The main resistance has come from the lawyers, who have strong vested interests in the present system. In addition, they are very influential in the legislative process—many legislators are lawyers.

In most developed countries the legal system for dealing with product liability is generally free from the deficiencies mentioned. Those same countries are also free from the extensive damage that product liability is doing to the American economy.

(For some incisive comments on the deficiencies in the USA legal system, see Grant 1994.)

Life Behind the Quality Dikes

During the twentieth century there emerged a growth of public suspicions and fears relative to the negative by-products of industrial progress. These fears are evident in multiple trends, all quality-related:

- Fear of major disasters and near disasters resulting from quality failures

- Growing concern about damage to the environment

- Action by the courts to impose strict liability

- Public annoyance with the numerous minor quality failures

- Growth of consumer organizations and an associated demand for better quality and more responsive customer service. (Juran 1970).

These trends are traceable to society's adoption of technology and industrialization. Technology confers wonderful benefits on society, but it also makes society dependent on the continuing performance and good behavior of technological goods and services. This is "life behind the quality dikes"—a form of securing benefits but living dangerously (Juran 1969). Like the Dutch who have reclaimed much land from the sea, we secure benefits from technology. However we need good dikes—good quality—to protect us against the numerous service interruptions and occasional disasters. These same trends have also led to legislation which at the outset was bitterly opposed by our industrial companies. Since then it has become clear that the public is serious about its concerns, and is willing to pay for good dikes.

The response of progressive companies to "life behind the quality dikes" has consisted mainly of

- Creation of high-level committees to establish policies and goals with respect to product safety, environmental damage, and consumer complaints.
- Establishment of specific action plans to be carried out by the various company functions.
- Audits to assure that the action plans are carried out.

In addition, the ingenuity of companies has begun to find ways to reduce the costs of providing solutions.

The Japanese Quality Revolution and Its Impact

Following World War II Japan embarked on a course of reaching national goals by trade rather than by military means. The major manufacturers, who had been extensively involved in military production, converted to civilian products. They then found that a major obstacle to selling these products in international markets was Japan's reputation as an exporter of shoddy goods.

This major obstacle convinced the Japanese of the need to improve their quality reputation. The shock of losing the war made them willing to explore new ways of thinking about quality, including learning from other countries. Through Keidanren (the Japanese Federation of Economic Organizations) and JUSE (the Japanese Union of Scientists and Engineers) the Japanese companies acted collectively.

- They sent teams abroad to visit foreign companies and study their approaches to managing for quality.
- They translated selected foreign literature into Japanese.
- They invited foreign lecturers to come to Japan and conduct training courses. These lecturers, W. Edwards Deming on statistical methods and J. M. Juran on managing for quality, provided seed courses which became influential inputs to the quality revolution that followed.

Building on these and other inputs, the Japanese adopted some unprecedented strategies for creating their revolution in quality:

- The upper managers personally took charge of leading the revolution.
- The companies trained their engineers and the workforce in how to use statistical methods as an aid to control of quality. The seed courses were Deming's 1950 lectures.
- They trained the entire managerial hierarchy in how to manage for quality. The seed courses for this training were Juran's 1954 lectures.
- They undertook quality improvement at a revolutionary rate, year after year.
- They evolved the QC circle concept to enable the workforce to participate in quality improvement.
- They enlarged their business plans to include quality goals.

During the 1960s and 1970s many Japanese manufacturers greatly increased their share of the American market. A major reason was superior quality. Numerous industries were impacted: consumer electronics, automobiles, steel, machine tools, and so on. Some researchers quantified the quality differences. See Juran 1979 (color television sets); also Garvin 1983 (room air conditioners).

The impact of the Japanese exports on the USA was considerable. Consumers benefited greatly by access to goods of superior quality at competitive and even lower prices. However, great damage was done to other areas of the USA economy.

- The impacted manufacturing companies were damaged by the resulting loss of market share.
- The workforce and the unions were damaged by the resulting export of jobs.
- The national economy was damaged by the resulting unfavorable trade balances.

Collectively these impacts called for responsive action.

Interestingly, some people believe that had the two Americans (Deming and Juran) not given their lectures, the Japanese quality revolution would not have happened. In the view of the author, this belief has no relation to reality. Had the Americans never gone there, the Japanese quality revolution would have taken place without them. Each of the Americans did bring to Japan a structured training package which the Japanese had not yet evolved. In that sense each gave the Japanese a degree of jump start. But the same Americans also gave their lectures in other countries, none of whom succeeded in building such a revolution. That is why the author has told his audiences that "The unsung heroes of the Japanese quality revolution are the Japanese managers."

(For a Japanese view of postwar events in Japan, see Ishikawa 1989, pages 9–13. See also, chapter 16 in the present book.)

Responses to the Japanese Quality Revolution

Price Competition

In the early postwar period the impacted American companies logically considered Japanese competition to be in price rather than in quality. (Japanese wages were far below those in the United States.) So one major response was to move the production of labor-intensive products to low-wage areas, often off-shore.

Block the Imports

Some of the impacted companies tried to solve their problem by blocking the imports. They urged legislation that would establish restrictive import quotas and tariffs. They urged criminal prosecutions on the grounds of violation of laws against "dumping" (selling below cost, or at less than fair value). They filed civil lawsuits on the grounds of unfair trade practices. They appealed to the public to "Buy American."

These efforts yielded a modicum of relief, but did nothing to improve American competitiveness in quality. In addition, restriction of imports generated serious side effects: domestic users lost access to better values; trade restrictions invited retaliatory restrictions; the impacted companies had no incentive to become more competitive. In some cases, import restrictions have damaged the very industries they were intended to protect (Levinson 1987).

Lack of Early Warning

As the years unfolded, price competition declined while quality competition increased (Juran 1979).

Figure 17.1 is the author's estimate of Western and Japanese automotive product quality during the period 1950 to 1990. At the

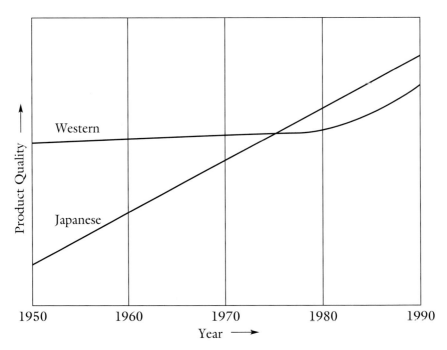

Figure 17.1 Trends in quality of automobiles. Source: J. M. Juran.

outset, Western companies were clearly the quality leaders. Moreover, they continually improved their products, but at a gradual, *evolutionary* rate.

In contrast, Japanese automotive quality was at the outset well below that of the West. However the Japanese undertook to improve their quality at a *revolutionary* rate, enabling them to overtake the West during the mid-1970s.

The American upper managers were generally unaware of these trends. The reports available to them consisted mainly of financial information. In those days the executive instrument panels lacked information on customer satisfaction, competitive quality, cost of poor quality, and the like. So the managers continued to believe that Japanese competition was primarily price competition rather than quality competition.

In June 1966, at the conference of the European Organization for Quality Control (in Stockholm), the author sounded a warning:

> *The Japanese are headed for world quality leadership and will attain it in the next two decades because no one else is moving there at the same pace. (Juran 1967)*

That warning went unheeded. To the West it was unthinkable that Japan, of all countries, could become the world quality leader.

Efforts to Become Competitive in Quality

During the 1960s and 1970s a growing quality crisis became evident, and company managers became increasingly concerned. Some upper managers recognized that the soundest response to a competitive challenge was to become more competitive. Not being trained or experienced in managing for quality, these same upper managers sought advice from the experts, internal and external. As it turned out, most experts were specialists in tools and techniques, and tended to assume that what they had to sell coincided with what the companies needed. As a result there emerged a long list of potential strategies, including

- Exhortation of the workforce
- Organization and training of quality circles
- Statistical process control

- Awareness training for managers and supervisors
- Computation of the cost of poor quality
- Project-by-project quality improvement
- Preparation of complete manuals of procedure
- Revision of organization structure
- Incentives for quality
- Automated inspection and test
- Automation and robotics

Every one of those (and other) strategies had some degree of merit under proper conditions. However the companies needed a plan of action that addressed their major quality problems. Yet in most cases the major quality problems had not been identified. In companies where the design of the action plan was by a functional manager, there was a risk that the plan would be biased toward the goals of that function. Where the design was by the upper managers, the risk was that they lacked the necessary training and experience. They were experienced managers, but not in managing for quality. Generally they opted for "action now," that is, do something plausible promptly rather than endure delay. The results were predictably unsatisfactory.

The Major Initiatives of the 1980s

By the end of the 1970s the American quality crisis had reached major proportions. It attracted the attention of the national legislators and administrators. It was featured prominently in the media—it was regularly on the front page. It increasingly forced the company chief executive officers (CEOs) to provide personal leadership in managing for quality.

During the 1980s a great many American companies undertook initiatives to deal with the quality crisis. These initiatives were largely focused on three strategies: exhortation, project-by-project quality improvement, and statistical process control.

Exhortation

Some consultants proposed a sweeping solution by exhorting the workforce to make no mistakes—"Do it right the first time." This simplistic approach was persuasive to those managers who, at the time, believed that the primary cause of their company's quality problems was the carelessness and indifference of the workforce. The facts were that the bulk of the quality problems had their origin in the managerial and technological processes. In due course this approach was abandoned, but not before a lot of divisiveness had been generated.

Quality Improvement, Project By Project

One of the consulting companies, Juran Institute Inc., created and published a series of videocassettes titled *Juran on Quality Improvement* (Juran 1980). These were tested by many companies. Some achieved notable quality improvements; others did not. The decisive variable was the extent of personal leadership provided by the upper managers. By the end of the 1980s, the improvement process described in those videocassettes had become the basic model for the process of continuous quality improvement adopted by most companies.

The Third Wave of Statistical Quality Control

The 1980s also witnessed a broad movement to train company personnel in application of statistical methods to quality problems. The stimulus came from a widely viewed videocassette titled *If Japan Can, Why Can't We?* It implied strongly that Japanese success in quality had resulted solely from use of statistical methods. The videotape was influential in persuading many companies to train numerous employees in basic statistical methods. The term *statistical process control* (SPC) became the popular label for this third wave.

Such training had merit—it provided trainees with a useful set of tools. Yet it was premature. It was done before the companies had defined their quality goals and the strategies needed to reach those goals. In a sense the personnel were trained in remedies when the diseases were not yet known.

Eastman Chemical Company, when relating its approach to managing for quality (it became a 1993 winner of the Malcolm Baldrige National Quality Award) stated that it had trained 10,000 of its personnel in SPC. However, many trainees lacked the opportunity to apply the training, so much was forgotten (Eastman Chemical Co. 1994).

This third wave of statistical quality control (now SPC) is destined to become a permanent addition to the tools of managing for quality.

However, during the 1980s many companies limited their quality initiative to SPC, assuming it to be the panacea claimed by its advocates. Those companies lost precious years before learning that quality leadership comes from a mixture of strategies, no one of which is a panacea.

Results of the Initiatives of the 1980s

In retrospect, the results of the quality initiatives of the 1980s were deeply disappointing. Most of the initiatives fell well short of their goals. Some achieved negative results—the companies lost several years of potential progress. The disappointing results were due mainly to poor choice of strategies and to poor execution of valid strategies. In turn these were largely traceable to the limitations of leadership by upper managers who lacked training and experience in managing for quality. In the minds of some observers, the lessons learned during the 1980s were chiefly lessons in what *not* to do.

The Role Models

During that same disappointing decade a relative few company initiatives achieved stunning results. Such companies attained quality leadership—"world-class quality"—and thereby became the role models for the rest of the American economy.

The role models were few in number. They included the winners of the National Quality Award plus other companies that had achieved similar results. Together they made up only a tiny part of the American economy. Yet there were enough of these companies to prove that world-class quality is attainable within the American culture.

The successes achieved by the role model companies stimulated great interest among upper managers and others who sought to learn how such stunning results had been achieved. The role models were quite willing to share information about the strategies they had used to achieve those results. In addition, steps were taken to share the lessons learned through company visits, conferences, publications, and so on.

Lessons Learned

Each role model is different. In groping for ways to attain world-class quality each serves as a laboratory, testing out various strategies, adopting some, modifying others, rejecting still others. Moreover, each company houses resourceful people whose ingenuity knows no bounds. So the role models have contributed invention of new strategies as well as stunning results. In this way, each role model came up with its own unique collection of strategies adopted.

Nevertheless, analysis of these collections shows that they include extensive commonality. There is *a core list of strategies* which achieved adoption by most of the role model companies. These core strategies deserve careful study. They are the central body of lessons learned—a list of the key strategies which produced those stunning results. As such they become an essential input to future quality planning.

Customer Focus

All role models adopted the concept that the customer has the last word on quality. Adoption of this concept then led to intensified action to identify: who are the customers, internal as well as external; what are the needs of customers; what product features are required to meet those needs; how do customers decide which of the competing products to buy; and so on.

To illustrate, it is now widely recognized that many quality problems of the past were traceable to failure to meet the needs of *internal* customers. (A widespread example has been product designs that designers "threw over the wall" to be made by the manufacturing department.) The concept of customer focus led to broader acceptance of the concept of participation—internal customers should participate in those planning activities that will impact their operations.

Upper Managers in Charge

One element present in all successes, and absent in most failures, was the personal involvement of the upper managers. In effect, the upper managers took charge of quality by accepting responsibility for certain roles, including

- Serve on the Quality Council.
- Establish the quality goals.
- Provide the needed resources.
- Provide quality-oriented training.
- Stimulate quality improvement.

- Review progress.
- Give recognition.
- Revise the reward system.

Many upper managers resisted such additions to their own workload. Their preference was to establish broad goals and then to urge their subordinates to meet the goals. However, the lessons learned from the role models are that *the above roles are not delegable*—they must be carried out by the upper managers, personally.

Strategic Quality Planning

The role models recognized that the new priority given to quality requires enlarging the business plan to include quality-related goals. These goals are then deployed to identify the needed actions and resources, to establish responsibility for taking the actions, and so on. The resulting plans parallel those long used to meet goals for sales and profit. A common name for this concept is *Strategic Quality Planning*.

The Concept of "Big Q"

The role models grasped the concept that managing for quality should not be limited to manufacturing companies and manufacturing processes. It should also include service companies and business processes. This concept broadens the area under the quality umbrella. It bears the name "Big Q," to distinguish it from the traditional "little Q." (For elaboration, see Figure 18.7 in chapter 18.)

Quality Improvement

Without exception the role models went extensively into quality improvement—most of the stunning results came from projects to improve quality, These projects extended to all activities under the Big Q umbrella. They reduced costs, raised productivity, shortened cycle times, improved customer service, and so on.

Quality improvement required special organization. The vital few projects were carried out by multifunctional teams of managers and specialists. The useful many projects were carried out at lower levels, including members of the workforce.

The role models also adopted the concept that quality improvement must go on year after year—it must be woven into the company culture. To this end they mandated that goals for quality improvement be included in the annual business plans. They also redesigned the systems of recognition and reward to give added weight to performance on quality improvement.

Business Process Quality Management
(Also Reengineering)

A major extension of quality improvement was to the area of business processes. This extension resulted from fresh thinking relative to the multifunctional processes prevalent in functional organizations.

Figure 17.2 depicts the interrelation between the typical vertical functional organization and the horizontal macroprocesses through which things get done.

Each horizontal macroprocess consists of numerous steps or microprocesses which thread their way through multiple functions. Every microprocess has an owner, but there is no clear ownership of the macroprocess.

The role models concluded that each key macroprocess should have an owner, and they took action to create such owners (individuals or teams). They also defined the responsibilities of an owner, including responsibility for improving the macroprocess. An important part of the stunning results achieved by the role models came from improvements made in the business processes.

Training in Managing for Quality

The earliest formal training courses in quality-related matters were the wartime courses in statistical quality control sponsored by the federal government during World War II. Following the end of the war these courses were offered by some colleges (as extension courses), by societies such as American Management Association (AMA) and ASQC, and by consultants. Then, as the company quality departments broadened their scope, there emerged courses oriented to the functional needs of those departments: inspection and test; quality engineering; reliability enginering; advanced courses in statistical methodology, such as design of experiments and analysis of variance.

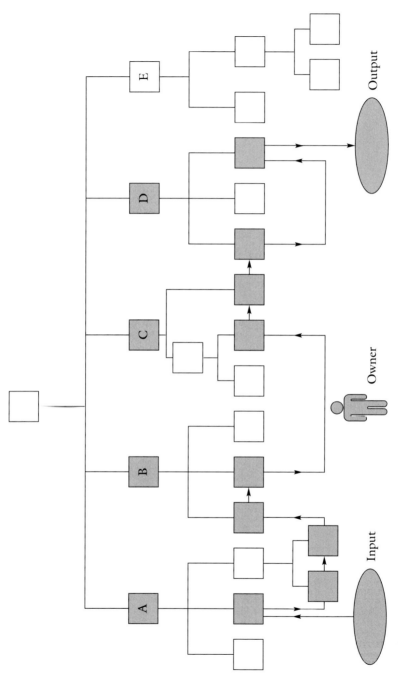

Figure 17.2 Interrelation between "vertical" functions and "horizontal" processes.
Source: Juran Institute, Inc.

During the 1970s there emerged the quality crisis resulting from the Japanese quality revolution. As companies tried to respond, it became clear that training should not be limited to the quality department—it should be extended to all functions, and to all levels of the hierarchy. Such extension required creating an expanded variety of courses to meet the various special needs of the multiple functions and levels.

It also became clear that training should not be limited to exhortation and statistics—it should be expanded to include managing for quality. At the time, training courses in managing for quality were still in the early stages of evolution. Many designs of training courses emerged, and companies selected those that seemed to fit the strategies they had chosen.

By the 1990s numerous designs had become available for training in managing for quality. No consensus had been reached, but some designs were in wide use. One was based on the criteria for the Malcolm Baldrige National Quality Award (discussed later in this chapter). Another was based on Deming's lectures—statistical quality control plus his 14 points (Deming 1986). A third was based on the Juran Trilogy,* which organizes the subject matter into three fundamental processes: quality planning, quality control, and quality improvement (Juran 1986).

A further development has been a growing feeling among industrial companies that while quality has risen greatly in importance, the educational system has not kept up with this trend. As a result, school graduates lack knowledge of the subject, forcing the companies to fill the gap through training. Schools at all levels have begun to address this problem. In addition, some companies have set up alliances with selected schools to help redesign the curricula, provide training materials, train faculty members and otherwise support the alliance.

Measurement of Quality

Measurement of quality at the technological level has been used for many centuries. What is new is the need for measuring quality at the business level—measures of customer satisfaction, competitors' quality, performance of key business processes, and so on. To meet such needs often requires invention of new measures as well as creation of

---

*The Juran Trilogy is a registered trademark of Juran Institute, Inc.

related methods of analysis and presentation. The need for measurement may also require development of a National Quality Index to parallel the indexes already in use, such as those for consumer prices, unemployment, and productivity.

Benchmarking

The concept of benchmarking grew out of the need to establish quality goals based on factual analysis rather than empirical judgment. For example, in one company the warehouse takes an average of five working days to fill customers' orders. The leading competitor takes an average of four days. A company in a totally different industry takes only three days. The benchmarked goal becomes three days. There may well be a reaction "It can't be done," and this may be valid as applied to the present process. However, the fact is that the goal is already being met. So the problem is then to create (or re-create) a process that can meet the benchmark.

The concept of benchmarking has been widely accepted in the USA. Progress is being made to developing data banks on what are the best-known performances, and on the methods used to achieve them.

Human Resources and Quality: Empowerment

As of the early 1990s many American companies still retained the separation of planning from execution inherent in the Taylor system of Scientific Management. As a result, those companies were failing to make use of a huge underemployed asset—the education, experience, and creativity of the workforce. It is generally agreed that the Taylor system is obsolete and should be replaced, but there is no consensus on what should replace it.

Replacing the Taylor system requires transfer of tasks from specialists and supervisors to nonsupervisory workers. The word *empowerment* has become a label for such transfer. Empowerment takes various forms, all of which have been undergoing test. The more usual forms of empowerment have included the following.

1. *Establish worker self-control.* This requires providing workers with all the essentials for doing good work: means of knowing what are the quality goals; means of knowing what is the actual process

performance; and means for adjusting the process in the event that quality does not conform to goals.

A state of self-control makes it possible to empower workers to make decisions on the *process*—decisions such as Is the process in conformance? and Should the process continue to run or should it stop? Ideally such decisions should be made by the workforce. There is no shorter feedback loop.

2. *Establish worker self-inspection.* This empowers workers to make decisions on whether the *product* conforms to the quality goals. Such empowerment shortens the feedback loop, confers a greater sense of job ownership, and removes the police atmosphere created by use of inspectors.

3. *Enlarge workers' jobs.* The enlargement may be horizontal—assigning a greater assortment of tasks within the same function to reduce the monotony of short-cycle work. It may also be vertical—assigning multiple functions around the core task. A widespread example has been the training and empowerment of workers who answer telephones, to enable them to provide "one-stop shopping" to customers who call in.

4. *Establish self-directing teams of workers.* Under this concept a team of workers is trained and empowered to conduct operations which consist of multiple functions as well as multiple tasks. The empowerment may include process planning, establishing work schedules, deciding who is to perform which tasks, recruiting new team members, maintaining discipline, and still other responsibilities formerly carried out by specialists and supervisors.

The concept of self-directing teams has been widely tested. The published results indicate that quality and productivity improve significantly. The ratio of workers to managers rises sharply. Jobs cross functional lines and become team jobs. Workers become team members. All this requires extensive training.

Because empowerment involves extensive transfer of work from supervisors and specialists to the workforce, it is meeting much cultural resistance. There is also some resistance from labor unions. They sense that empowerment establishes a new communication link between management and the workforce which may weaken the linkage between workers and the union.

In the view of the author, replacing the Taylor system is an idea whose time has come. It is also his view that all of the above options will grow, and that the major successor to the Taylor system will be self-directing teams of workers.

Motivation: Recognition; Reward

To meet the new competition in quality has required company personnel to adapt to numerous changes, such as

- Quality is to receive top priority.
- Personnel are to accept training in various quality-related disciplines.
- A new responsibility—quality improvement—is added to the traditional list of responsibilities.
- The use of teams requires the personnel to learn how to behave as team members.

Generally, American companies have recognized that for such changes to be accepted it is necessary to make revisions with respect to motivation. The companies reponded by increasing the use of recognition and, to a lesser degree, by revising the reward systems.

Recognition is public acknowledgment of superior performance. The companies expanded their use of prizes, placques, ceremonial dinners, publicity, and so on. Generally they did this with skill and in good taste.

While recognition relates to voluntary action, the reward system relates to the mandated actions that define the job description. Here the company responses were less sure-footed—there was no precedent on how to make the needed changes. Mostly the companies expanded the list of parameters used annually to judge employee performance by adding a new parameter such as "performance on quality improvement." (Some companies even failed to realize that there was need for changing the reward system.)

The Malcolm Baldrige National Quality Award

In 1987 the United States government established the Malcolm Baldrige National Quality Award as a stimulus to improving quality. During its first few years the Award greatly increased national awareness of the subject, and did provide the intended stimulus. The annual number of applicants for the Award has been low—usually under 100. However, a great many companies have used the Award criteria as a basis for self-audits to evaluate their strengths and weaknesses.

Establishment of the National Quality Award has stimulated the growth of state awards. As of late 1994, over two-thirds of the 50 states had created such awards. There has also been a growth of regional awards, as well as awards within companies. (Numerous European and Latin-American countries have created quality awards, as has the European Foundation for Quality Management.) This proliferation of awards is strong proof of the growing recognition that quality has risen greatly in importance.

The ISO 9000 Series of Standards

During the 1980s the countries of Western Europe began to use the International Standards Organization's ISO 9000 series of standards as the basis for judging the adequacy of the quality control systems of companies.

Compliance with ISO 9000 is voluntary. There is no legal requirement that companies must be certified as complying with the ISO criteria before they are allowed to sell their products in Europe. However, any company which lacks a certificate of compliance may be at a significant marketing disadvantage if its competitors do have such certificates. Such is the belief of most heads of companies, including those in the United States. As a result there has been a rush to become certified.

The ISO standards have a degree of merit. The criteria define a comprehensive quality control system. The certification process may well get rid of the plague of multiple assessments which have burdened suppliers in the past. However, the criteria fail to include some of the essentials needed to attain world-class quality, such as personal leadership by the upper managers; training the hierarchy in managing for quality; quality goals in the business plan; maintaining a revolutionary rate of quality improvement; participation and empowerment of the workforce.

All in all, there is a risk that European companies are in for a massive let down. They are getting certified to ISO 9000, but this alone will not enable them to attain quality leadership.

Total Quality Management

As the quality crisis deepened during the last half of the twentieth century, more and more prerequisites were identified as essential to achieving world-class quality. A need then arose for a short label for this list of prerequisites. As of the 1990s, the most popular label was the term *total quality management,* or TQM.

Although TQM became a popular label, there was no agreement on what were the essential elements of TQM. One widely available, comprehensive list was the criteria used by the National Institute of Standards and Technology to evaluate applications for the Malcolm Baldrige National Quality Award. As of the early 1990s, that list became, in the opinion of the author, the most complete available definition of TQM.

Prognosis for the Twenty-First Century

Until the 1980s the prognosis for the United States was gloomy. Japanese companies had successfully invaded the American market with products that offered superior quality and value. The resulting public perception then became a force in its own right, continuing to damage those American companies that had been slow to respond.

During the 1980s the quality crisis deepened despite initiatives taken by many companies. However a small number of companies distinguished themselves by raising their quality to world-class levels. The results they achieved have been publicized. The methods they used to get those results have also been publicized. The fact that such results were achieved proved that world-class quality is achievable within the American culture. (If those companies did it, it is doable.) The job ahead then became one of scaling up.

By the early 1990s some powerful forces had converged to stimulate scaling up. The growing quality crisis had raised awareness of the subject, as did the growth of awards for quality, notably the Malcolm Baldrige National Quality Award. Self-assessment against the Baldrige criteria helped many companies to identify their strengths and weaknesses. The publicized results achieved by the role model companies stimulated a desire to secure similar results. The publicized lessons learned showed the way to get such results. The successful companies began to shrink their supplier base, and a major criterion for supplier survival was to attain world-class quality.

An additional powerful force is waiting to emerge—the urge to "buy American." Most Americans do prefer to buy American, all other things being equal. During the 1960s and 1970s other things were not equal, so the urge to buy American was overcome by the superior quality and value of Japanese products.

More recently, some American companies have narrowed or eliminated the gap between Japanese and American quality. That action enabled those companies to regain some of the market share they had lost. We can expect the quality gap to continue to narrow in the coming century. That will translate into growth in market share for American companies once customer perception catches up with the facts. Some of this has happened already.

Of course quality is a moving target, and competitors do not stand still. But the trend remains clear. The revolution in quality will persist into the next century. The twentieth century has been the Century of Productivity, but the twenty-first century will be the Century of Quality.

In the view of the author, the United States is now well-poised to become a world leader in quality during the next century.

Summary

Managing for quality in the United States originated in the systems prevailing in Europe at the time the North American continent was colonized. Those systems were rooted in craftsmanship and in the associated regulations by the monopolistic guilds and political authorities.

The Industrial Revolution and the factory system originated in Europe and were then exported to the United States. Reliance on craftsmanship was reduced, while reliance on inspection and test was increased.

The Taylor system of separating planning from execution resulted in giving top priority to productivity, but at the expense of quality. The managers tried to minimize the damage to quality by giving the inspection function an organization status that was not subordinate to production. An unintended by-product was emergence of a belief that quality was now the responsibility of the inspection department. A further by-product was that the upper managers became detached from the quality function and thereby became progressively less and less informed on how to manage for quality.

The United States became deeply involved in World War II, first as a supplier to the Allies and then as a combatant. The approach to quality relied heavily on inspection and test. Final product quality was less than satisfactory, while the costs of poor quality were shockingly high. These problems carried over into the postwar period when shortages of civilian goods resulted in a severe decline in quality.

During the twentieth century Americans enthusiastically accepted the benefits of technology. The volume of technological products rose enormously, bringing with it some uninvited guests. Consumers lacked the technological literacy needed to make informed decisions on what to buy, how to deal with product failures, and so on. Quality of life became increasingly dependent on the continuing performance of technological goods and services. With greater volume of products came more product failures and more dissatisfied consumers. More product failures also resulted in greater damage to human health and safety. The threat to the environment reached dangerous levels.

Collectively these impacts stimulated some powerful reactions. Consumerism emerged in unprecedented force. Extensive new legislation and government regulation emerged relative to consumer protection, product safety, the environment, and still other matters. The law courts eroded the traditional defenses of producers to a point approaching strict liability.

These problems all seem to be different, but the fundamental remedy for all of them is identical—better quality. The importance of those problems suggests that the pressure on producers to improve quality will never let up so long as the Americans insist on accepting the benefits of technology. There is no indication that many Americans prefer to return to life in primitive villages.

Following World War II, the Japanese became the world quality leaders by focusing on quality improvement and defect prevention rather than on inspection. Japanese goods benefited American consumers but damaged other parts of the economy. Responses by American companies were for several decades ineffective, largely due to lack of upper managers' leadership as well as to upper managers' ignorance of how to manage for quality.

Then, during the 1980s, a relative few American companies did attain world-class quality, and thereby became the role models for the rest of the economy. As of the 1990s the results achieved by the role models were being widely disseminated, along with the methods they used to attain those results. In addition, some powerful forces emerged to stimulate additional companies to use those same methods to attain world-class quality. There are now strong indications that the United States will become a world leader in quality during the twenty-first century.

Bibliography

AT&T (1989). *A History of Quality Control and Assurance at AT&T, 1920–1970.* This series of 14 videocassettes contains interviews with Ralph Wareham, W. Edwards Deming, J. M. Juran, and others who played significant roles in quality control during the 50-year span 1920–1970. Available from AT&T Customer Information Center, phone 1-800-432-6600, select code 500-721.

Best, Arthur (1981). *When Consumers Complain.* New York, Columbia University Press.

The Business Roundtable (1978). *Cost of Government Regulation Study for the Business Roundtable.* This is a study of the direct incremental costs incurred by 48 companies in complying with the regulations of six federal agencies during 1977. The Business Roundtable, New York.

Consumer's Source Handbook (1980). A publication of the US Office of Consumer Affairs. Includes: a "complaint handling primer"; where to go for assistance; functions, services, and information available from federal offices; directories of federal, state, and local offices. Available from Consumer Information Center, Dept. 532G, Pueblo, CO 81009.

Crain, W. Mark (1980). *Vehicle Safety Inspection Systems. How Effective?* American Enterprise Institute for Public Policy Research, Washington, D.C.

Deming, W. Edwards (1986). *Out of the Crisis.* Massachusetts Institute of Technology, Center for Applied Engineering Study, Cambridge, MA.

Dodge, Harold F., and Romig, H. G. (1959). *Sampling Inspection Tables,* Second Edition. John Wiley & Sons.

Eastman Chemical Co. (1994). Papers presented at 1994 Quest for Excellence Conference. National Institute for Standards and Technology, Washington, D.C.

Garvin, David A. (1983). Quality on the Line. *Harvard Business Review,* September–October, pages 64–75.

Grant, E. L. (1994). Why Product Liability and Medical Malpractice Lawsuits Are So Numerous in the United States. *Quality Progress,* December, pages 63–65.

Grant, E. L. (1991). Statistical Quality Control in the World War II Years. *Quality Progress,* December, pages 31–36.

Grant, E. L. (1953). Shewhart Medal address, *Industrial Quality Control,* July.

Gray, I., Bases, A. L., Martin, C. H., and Stemberg, A. (1975). *Product Liability: A Management Response.* (Emphasis is on defense against product liability suits.) New York, American Management Association.

Interagency Task Force on Product Liability; Final Report (undated; about 1978). (A comprehensive study on product liability, including the impact, the legal implications, the insurance problems, and, especially, the merits of various proposals for remedy.) Distributed by National Technical Information Service, Springfield, VA 22161.

Ishikawa, Kaoru (1989). How to Apply Companywide Quality Control in Foreign Countries. *Quality Progress,* September, pages 70–74.

Juran, J. M. (1991). World War II and the Quality Movement. *Quality Progress,* December, pages 19–24.

Juran, J. M. (1988). *Juran's Quality Control Handbook, Fourth Edition.* McGraw-Hill, Inc., New York.

Juran, J. M. (1986). The Quality Trilogy; A Universal Approach to Managing for Quality. *Quality Progress,* August, pages 19–24.

Juran, J. M. (1980). *Juran on Quality Improvement.* A series of 16 videocassettes plus associated manuals. Published by Juran Institute, Inc., Wilton, CT 06897-0811.

Juran, J. M. (1979). Japanese and Western Quality—A Contrast. *Quality,* January, pages 8–12; and February, pages 12–15. Also published under the same title, in *Proceedings of the International Conference on Quality Control,* Tokyo, 1978, pages A3-11 to A3-25.

Juran, J. M. (1977). Auto Safety, A Decade Later. *Quality,* October, pages 26–32; November, pages 54–60; December, pages 18–21. Originally presented at the 1976 European Organization for Quality Conference (Copenhagen).

Juran, J. M. (1973). The Taylor System and Quality Control. A series of articles in *Quality Progress,* May through December (listed under "Management Interface").

Juran, J. M. (1970). Consumerism and Product Quality. *Quality Progress,* July, pages 18–27.

Juran, J. M. (1969). Mobilizing for the 1970s. *Quality Progress,* August, pages 8–17.

Juran, J. M. (1967). The QC Circle Phenomenon. *Industrial Quality Control,* January, pages 329–36.

Kolb, John, and Ross, Steven S. (1980). *Product Safety and Liability—A Desk Reference.* (A comprehensive reference treatise: attaining safety throughout the product life cycle; defenses against lawsuits; insurance; reference tables.) New York, McGraw-Hill, Inc.

Levinson, Marc (1987). Asking for Protection Is Asking for Trouble. *Harvard Business Review,* July–August, pages 42–47.

OSHA Safety Regulation (1977). This is the report of a presidential task force assigned to review the safety regulatory practices of the Occupational Safety and Health Administration. American Enterprise Institute for Public Policy Research, Washington, D.C.

Sentry Insurance Co. (1976). *Consumerism at the Crossroads.* Sentry Insurance Co., Stevens Point, WI. Results of a national opinion research survey on the subject.

Wareham, Ralph E., and Stratton, Brad (1991). Standards, Sampling and Schooling. *Quality Progress,* December, pages 38–42.

Working, Holbrook (1945). Statistical Quality Control in War Production. *Journal of the American Statistical Association,* December, pages 425–47.

CHAPTER 18

Summary, Trends, and Prognosis

J. M. Juran
Chairman Emeritus, Juran Institute, Inc.

This chapter traces the evolution of the principal concepts of managing for quality—their approximate chronological sequence and the likely reasons behind the emergence of each concept. The chapter also examines the broad trends of the chronological sequence and offers a prognosis of what will emerge during the twenty-first century.

Managing for Quality in Primitive Societies

Quality is a timeless concept, so the origins of the human approach to managing for quality are hidden in the mists of the ancient past. Yet, we can be sure that humans have always faced problems of quality. Primitive food-gatherers had to discover which fruits were edible and which were poisonous. Primitive hunters had to learn which types of trees supplied the best wood for making bows or arrows. The resulting know-how was then passed down from generation to generation.

The nuclear human organization unit was the family. Isolated families were forced to create self-sufficiency—to meet their own needs for food, clothing, and shelter. There was division of work among family members. Production was for self-use, so the design, production, and use of the product were all carried out by the same persons. While the technology was primitive, the coordination was superb. The same human beings received all inputs and took all remedial action.

603

The limiting factor for achieving quality was the primitive state of the technology.

The Village: Division of Labor

Villages were created to serve other essential human requirements such as mutual defense and social needs. The creation of the village opened the way to further division of labor and to development of specialized skills. There emerged farmers, hunters, fishermen, and craftsmen of all sorts—weavers, potters, shoemakers, and so on. By going through the same work cycle over and over again, the craftsmen became intimately familiar with the materials used, the tools, the steps in the process, and, of course, the finished product. The cycle also included selling the product to users and receiving their feedback of product performance. The experience derived from this intimate familiarity then enabled human ingenuity to take the first steps toward the evolution of technology.

The Village Marketplace; Caveat Emptor

As villages grew they needed multiple craftsmen who then competed with each other. Much of this competition took place in the village marketplace, where craftsmen and buyers met on scheduled market days. In that setting producer and user met face-to-face with the goods between them. The goods were typically natural products or were made from natural materials. The suppliers and purchasers had long familiarity with the products, and the quality of the products could, to a high degree, be judged by the unaided human senses.

Under such a state of facts, the village magistrates tended to avoid being drawn into quality disputes between buyer and seller. This forced buyers to be vigilant so as to protect themselves against poor quality. In effect, the seller was responsible for supplying the goods but the buyer became responsible for supplying the "quality assurance." This arrangement came to be known as the doctrine of *caveat emptor*—let the buyer beware. So, buyers learned to beware—they used product inspection and test. They looked closely at the cloth, smelled the fish, thumped the melon, tasted a grape. Their failure to beware was at their own peril. Under the circumstances, caveat emptor was quite a sensible doctrine. It is widely applied to this day in village markets all over the world.

Note that within the village both producer and buyer engaged in inspection of the goods. The producer did so during the production process and upon completion of the final product. If the product was defective, producers preferred to discover this themselves rather than to have it discovered by a customer in the marketplace or later during use. A vigilant buyer would also inspect the product prior to purchase, as added assurance against receiving defective goods. We shall see later that the growth of commerce expanded the use of inspection to involve numerous other parties—suppliers, merchants, the guilds, the city authorities, and others.

A further force in the village marketplace was the fact of common residence. Producer and buyer both lived in the same village. Each was subject to scrutiny and character evaluation by the villagers. Each was also subject to village discipline. For the craftsman the stakes were high. His status and livelihood (and those of his family) were closely tied to his reputation as a competent and honest craftsman. In this way, the concept of craftsmanship became a quiet, yet powerful, stimulus to maintaining a high level of quality.

Effects of the Growth of Commerce

In due course, villages expanded into towns and cities, while improved transport opened the way to trade among regions.

> *A famous example of organized multi-regional trade was the Hanseatic League which was centered among the cities of northern Europe from about the 1200's to the 1600's. Its influence extended into Scandinavia and Russia as well as to the Mediterranean and Black seas. (von der Porten 1994)*

Under trade among regions, producer and user could no longer meet face-to-face in the marketplace. Products were now made by chains of suppliers and processors. Marketing was now done by chains of marketers. The buyers' direct point of contact was now with some merchant rather than with the producer. All this reduced the quality protections inherent in the village marketplace to a point requiring invention of new forms of quality assurance. One such invention was the quality warranty.

Quality Warranties

Early quality warranties were no doubt in oral form. Such warranties were inherently difficult to enforce. Memories differed as to what was said and meant. The duration of the warranty might extend beyond the life of the parties. So, the written warranty was invented.

> *An early example of a written quality warranty is on a clay tablet found amid the ruins of Nippur in ancient Babylon. The transaction involved a gold ring set with an emerald. The seller guaranteed that for twenty years the emerald would not fall out of the gold ring. If it did fall out of the gold ring before the end of twenty years, the seller agreed to pay to the buyer an indemnity of ten* mana *of silver. The date is the equivalent of 429* B.C. *(Bursk, Clark, and Hidy 1962, vol. I, 71)*

The complexities of commerce gave rise to multiple forms of quality warranties. Some warranties were implied by law from the behavior of the parties. If the seller made claims as to the features and/or the performance of the product, the law would imply a warranty to that effect. If the seller knew how the buyer would be using the product, the law would imply a warranty that the product was fit for that purpose.

Quality assurance (not necessarily warranties) could also come from third parties. Many medieval guilds maintained a form of quality control over their members, and used seals to identify products that had been inspected by the guild and approved for quality. Those seals served to provide added quality assurance to the buyers of such products.

Quality warranties are now widely used in all forms of trade and commerce. They are intended to provide buyers with quality assurance prior to purchase and with redress in the event of quality failures. They stimulate producers to give priority to quality, and stimulate sellers to seek out reliable sources of supply. They are an indispensable element of modern commerce. So great is their importance that recent legislation has imposed standards to assure that the wording of warranties does not mislead the buyers.

Quality Specifications

Sellers need to be able to communicate to buyers the nature of what they have to sell. Buyers need to be able to communicate to sellers the nature of what they want to buy. In the village marketplace, oral communication could take place directly between producer and user. With the growth of commerce, communication expanded to include multiple producers and merchants who were often widely separated. New forms of communications were needed, and a major invention was the written quality specification. Now quality information could be communicated directly between designer and producer, or between buyer and seller, no matter how great the distance between them and how complex the nature of the product.

Like warranties, written specifications are of ancient origin. Examples have been found in Egyptian papyrus scrolls over 3500 years old (Durant 1954). Early specifications focused on defining products and the processes for producing them. In due course, the concept was extended to defining the materials from which the products were made. Then, as conflicts arose because buyers and sellers used different methods of test, it became necessary to establish inspection and test specifications as well.

The emergence of inspection and test led to evolution of measuring instruments. Instruments for measuring length, volume, and time evolved thousands of years ago. Instruments have continued to proliferate, with ever-increasing precision. (Chapter 10, on clocks, shows that in recent centuries the precision of measurement of time has increased by over 10 orders of magnitude.)

The Rise of Craftsmanship

Among the benefits of division of work was the development of the skills needed to produce specific products. Such production typically required performance of a sequence of tasks, each demanding acquisition of the associated skills. Collectively, such skills became the basis of crafts or trades. Those who practiced such trades were generally known as craftsmen, tradesmen, or artisans, and each acquired a descriptive title—stonemason, shoemaker, and so on.

The ability of a craftsman to produce high-quality products was principally the result of

- The training received during apprenticeship,
- The experience acquired through many cycles of producing products, and
- The fact that while performing that sequence of tasks, the tradesman was his own customer, over and over again.

That last point deserves some elaboration. The best way for producers to learn of quality problems is to use the product—to be their own customer. Consider a production process involving a sequence of 30 tasks. If the same person performs all 30 tasks, that person will discover that doing task number 11 creates a quality problem at task number 24. That discovery will help to bring that problem to attention and get it solved. In contrast, if those 30 tasks are performed by 30 different persons, the problem is more likely to go on and on.

Possession of the skills of a trade was a source of income and status as well as self-respect and respect from the community. To perpetuate these benefits, tradesmen tried to secure monopolies on practicing their trades and on use of their titles. To this end there evolved a formal process for training apprentices, a hierarchy of titles, and the organization of guilds for creating and administering monopolies.

The Guilds

Guilds were monopolistic craft and trade organizations that flourished during the Middle Ages until the Industrial Revolution reduced their influence. They derived their powers from charters granted (for a fee) by the prevailing authorities, whether the nobility, the church, or the wealthy. They used their monopolistic powers chiefly to provide a livelihood and security for their members. They established rules governing apprenticeship as well as qualifying tests for advancement to the grade of master. Only qualified masters were permitted to practice the trade. (For numerous examples of guild practices, see chapters 7, 9, and 12.)

The guilds also provided extensive social services to their members. In addition, they were heavily involved in political matters of all kinds. For elaboration, see Bursk, Clark, and Hidy 1962, vol. III, 1656–78).

Apprenticeship

In many societies the recruits for future craftsmen were young boys who were indentured for the purpose of learning a trade. The indenture was a formal contract that bound the apprentice to serve the master for a specified period of years. In turn, the tradesman became responsible for teaching the trade to the apprentice.

The treatment bestowed on apprentices varied widely. The master might treat the boy as a member of his own family. At the other extreme, brutal cruelty prevailed. Several chapters of the book describe in detail the workings of the apprenticeship concept. Those chapters make clear that while the purpose of apprenticeship was common to many societies, the associated human relations differed remarkably.

The Craftsman Hierarchy

Each trade maintained a hierarchy of (usually) three categories of workers: the apprentice, the journeyman, and the master. Considerable formality surrounded the entry into each category.

At the bottom was the apprentice or novice whose entry was through the indenture contract. To be promoted to the middle category he was obliged to serve out the full term of apprenticeship. In addition, he was required to pass an examination by a committee of masters. Beyond the oral part of the examination, the apprentice was required to produce a perfect piece of work—a masterpiece—which was then inspected by the examination committee. Success in the examination led to a ceremonial admission to the status of journeyman.

The journeyman's right to practice the trade was limited. He could become an employee of a master, usually by the day. He could also *journey* to other towns, seeking employment in his trade. Only after admission to the rank of master could he set up shop on his own.

Admission to the rank of master required first that there be an opening. Guilds imposed limits on the numbers of masters in their areas. Upon the death or retirement of an active master, the guild would decide whether to fill that opening. If so, a journeyman would be selected and admitted, again through a formal ceremony.

For elaboration, see chapters 7 and 12.

Guilds and Quality Planning

Guilds played an active role in managing for quality. In the case of quality planning, the guilds established detailed specifications for input materials, manufacturing processes, and finished products, as well as for methods of inspection and test.

Guilds and Quality Control

Guild involvement in quality control was extensive. Guilds maintained inspections and audits to assure that craftsmen followed the quality specifications. Control of quality included establishing means of traceability to identify the producer. In addition, the guilds applied their mark to finished products as added assurance to consumers that quality met guild standards. (See "The Mark or Seal" later in this chapter.)

Control by the guilds also extended to control of sales. The sale of poor-quality goods was forbidden, and offenders suffered a range of punishments—all the way from fines to expulsion from membership. The guilds established prices and terms of sale, and enforced them. No member was allowed to compete with other members by offering to sell his products on terms that differed from those mandated by the guild.

Guilds and Quality Improvement

An overriding guild policy was solidarity—to maintain equality of opportunity among members. To this end, internal competition among members was limited to honest competition. No member was permitted to take advantage of other members. For example, if a member bought a supply of materials at a bargain price, he had to share this good fortune with other members.

Quality *improvement* through product or process innovation was *not* considered to be honest competition. This limitation on quality improvement did indeed help to maintain equality among members, but it also made the guild increasingly vulnerable to competition from other cities that did create superior products and processes.

Guilds and External Forces

The guilds were able to control internal competition, but external competition was something else. Some external competition came in the form of jurisdictional disputes with other guilds, which consumed endless hours of negotiation. More ominous was competition from other cities, which could be in price and value as well as in quality.

The policy of solidarity stifled quality improvement and thereby became a handicap to remaining competitive. So the guilds urged the authorities to restrict imports of foreign goods. They also imposed strict rules to prevent their trade secrets from falling into the hands of foreign competitors. (The Venetian glass industry threatened capital punishment to those who betrayed such secrets.)

The Rise of Inspection and Inspectors

The concepts of inspection and inspectors are of ancient origin. Wall paintings and reliefs in Egyptian tombs show the inspections used during stone construction projects. The measuring instruments included the square, level, and plumb bob for alignment control. Surface flatness of stones was checked by boning rods and by threads stretched across the faces of the stone blocks. (Singer, Holmyard, and Hall 1934). Figure 18.1 shows an Egyptian stonemason dressing a stone block, while an inspector checks the block for flatness, using a thread (Davies 1943).

In the days of the guilds, craftsmen might employ other craftsmen. Some of this was short-term in order to meet temporary overloads. In other cases a craftsman might attract enough customers to enable him to create a shop employing multiple craftsmen full-time. Figure 18.2 shows an early printing shop. The inspector came to be called the *proofreader*. (See also the clock-making shop in chapter 10.)

As the seller of the finished product, the employing craftsman was responsible for the quality of all products leaving his shop, including those produced by employees. The chief way of meeting this responsibility was through inspection of the work done by the employees. The amount of inspection would depend on the performance record of the employee.

For shops employing many workers, the amount of needed inspection could grow to a point such that the employer lacked the time to do it. In such cases, the solution was to appoint craftsmen to do the

Figure 18.1 An ancient example of inspection. From an Egyptian tomb painting, Thebes, C. 1450 B.C. The workman at the left is dressing the stone block while the inspector at the right checks the quality of the work with a piece of string. Source: Norman de G. Davies. "The Tomb of Rekh-mi-rē at Thebes," Vol. 2, Pl. LXII. New York, Metropolitan Museum of Art, 1943.

inspection, part-time or full-time. So, the function of inspection gave rise to a new job category of inspector. In due course, inspectors multiplied in numbers to become the basis of inspection departments, which in turn gave birth to modern quality departments.

Government Involvement in Managing for Quality

Governments have long involved themselves in managing for quality. Their purposes have included protecting the safety and health of citizens, defending and improving the economics of the state, and protecting consumers against fraud. Each of these purposes includes some aspect of managing for quality.

Figure 18.2 This early printing shop, engraved by Johannes Stradanus, includes an inspector in the form of a proofreader. Source: Burndy Library of the Dibner Institute, Cambridge, Massachusetts, USA.

Safety and Health of the Citizens

Early forms of protection of safety and health were after-the-fact measures. The Code of Hammurabi (c. 2000 B.C.) prescribed the death penalty for any builder of a house that later collapsed and killed the owner. In medieval times, the same fate awaited the baker who inadvertently mixed rat poison with the flour.

Economics of the State

The growth of commerce created competition among states, including competition in quality. While the guilds tended to stifle quality improvement, the state governments favored improving the quality of domestic goods in order to reduce imports and increase exports. For example, in the late sixteenth century James VI of Scotland imported craftsmen from the Low Countries to set up a textile factory and to teach their trade secrets to Scottish workers (Bursk, Clark, and Hidy vol. IV, 2283–85).

With the growth of interstate commerce, the quality reputation of a state could be an asset or a liability. Many states took steps to protect their reputation by imposing quality controls on exported goods. These controls typically consisted of appointing independent inspectors to inspect the finished products and affix a mark or seal to certify as to its quality. This concept of independent inspection was especially prevalent in the case of high-volume goods such as textiles.

The famous Rembrandt painting *Dutch Masters* shows a group of textile inspectors employed by the city of Amsterdam. The Dutch name was *Staalmeesters,* meaning masters of the steel (stamps) used to attach the seals to the bolts of cloth.

Many states also imposed trade barriers to protect domestic industries from imports. See under "Responses and Prognosis" "Competition in Quality" later in this chapter.

Consumer Protection

Many states recognized that as to some domestic trade practices, the rule of *caveat emptor* did not apply. One such practice related to measurement. The states designed official standard tools for measuring length, weight, volume, and so on. Use of these tools was then mandated, and inspectors were appointed to assure compliance (see, for example, chapter 1). During times of shortage, states tended to fix the prices of essentials such as bread, and to commandeer the supplies of the input materials.

The twentieth century witnessed a considerable expansion in consumer protection legislation. For elaboration, see chapter 17.

The Mark or Seal

A mark or seal applied to products has, over the centuries, been made to serve multiple purposes. Marks may be used to

- *Identify the producer,* whether craftsman, factory, town, merchant, packager, or still others. Such identification may serve to fix responsibility, protect the innocent against unwarranted blame, enable buyers to choose from among multiple makers, advertise the name of the maker, and so on.
- *Provide traceability.* In mass production, use of lot numbers helps to maintain uniformity of product in subsequent processing, designate expiration dates, make selective product recalls, and so on.
- *Provide product information* such as type and quantities of ingredients used, date when made, expiration dates, model number, ratings (for example, voltage, current), and so on.
- *Provide quality assurance.* Quality assurance was the major purpose served by the marks of the guilds and towns. It was their way of telling buyers, "This product has been independently inspected, and has good quality."

An aura of romance surrounds the use of seals. The seals of some medieval cities are masterpieces of artistic design. Seals of some guilds, factories, and towns have become world-renowned. An example is the British hallmark seen in chapter 14. A modern counterpart to the early seals is the corporate trademark (the logotype or logo).

The Quality Control Process

The quality control process is an essential aid to reaching quality goals and to maintaining stability of operating processes—business processes as well as manufacturing processes. The quality control process consists of a series of steps as follows:

- Evaluate actual quality being produced.
- Compare actual quality to the quality goal.
- Take corrective action if actual quality does not conform to the goal.

The first step—evaluation of actual quality—is usually called *inspection* if done by human beings. It is usually called *test* if done by technological instruments. Many chapters of this book provide examples of the various ways in which inspection is employed during quality control.

Quality Control in Biological Organisms

The oldest approaches to quality control are those evolved by biological organisms. Biological species have existed for hundreds of millions of years. Their design includes mechanisms for *prevention* of change. Each organism contains built-in processes for maintaining body temperature, blood count, and so on. These processes are autonomic—they go about their business without taking up the time and attention of the central nervous system. Other autonomic processes exist to digest food, eliminate waste, and so on. These processes, likewise, do their work without disturbing the central nervous system, which is thereby free to concentrate on survival—hunt for food, guard against predators, and so on.

The most amazing achievement in quality control also takes place during a biological process—during the growth of the fertilized egg into an animal organism. In human beings the genetic instructions that program this growth consist of a sequence of about three billion "letters." This sequence—the human genome—is contained in two strands of DNA (the double helix) that "unzip" and replicate about a million billion times during the growth process from fertilized egg to birth of the human being.

Given such huge numbers, the opportunities for error are enormous. (Some errors are harmless; others are damaging and even lethal.) Yet, the actual error rate is of the order of about one in 10 billion. This precision is achieved through a feedback loop involving three subprocesses.

- A high-fidelity selection process for choosing and attaching the right "letters."
- A proofreading process for reading the most recent letter, and removing it if incorrect.
- A corrective action process to rectify the errors that are detected (Radman and Wagner 1988).

The evolution of that astonishing process is as yet unknown to us. However, there is much to be learned by studying the processes through which biological organisms carry out quality control.

The Feedback Loop

All quality control takes place through the operation of the "feedback loop." Figure 18.3 is a generic model for process control. A sensor is plugged into the operating process to evaluate actual performance. An umpire then determines whether actual performance conforms to the goal. If not, an actuator is energized to restore conformance.

Figure 18.3 is the universal model. What varies is the responsibility—who is to be made responsible for setting goals, sensing, and

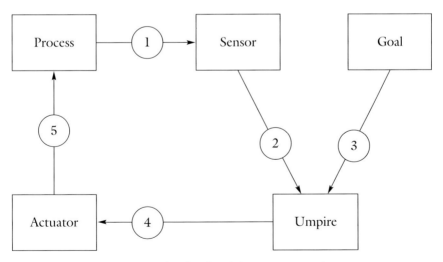

Figure 18.3 The feedback loop in generic terms.
Source: J. M. Juran.

umpiring. Such responsibility may be assigned to technological instruments, to data systems, or to human beings.

Control through the feedback loop is the oldest process used in managing for quality. All biological organisms are equipped with internal goals, sensory organs, and umpires to enable them to respond to the numerous variables that affect their well-being—their intakes, the environment, threats, and so on. Many chapters of this book provide examples of the many and varied ways in which the feedback loop is employed during control of quality.

Self-Control

Figure 18.4 shows the usual pattern of responsibility for process control as applied to the sequence of tasks performed by the craftsman. For each of these tasks, the craftsman has virtually complete responsibility for every activity within the feedback loop. The name given to this pattern of responsibility is *self-control,* because the craftsman acts out every step of the feedback loop. Workers are said to be in a state of self-control when they are provided with the means for

- Knowing what is the quality goal,
- Knowing what is the actual quality being produced, and

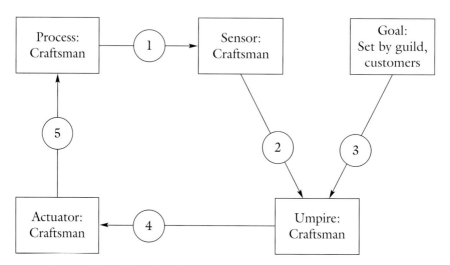

Figure 18.4 The feedback loop as applied to the craftsman.
Source: J. M. Juran.

- Readjusting the process in the event of nonconformance to the quality goal.

This state of self-control is further enforced by the fact that during his performance of the sequence of tasks the craftsman is his own customer, over and over again.

Self-Inspection

When the product reaches its finished state, the craftsman is no longer his own customer—someone else is the customer. The question then arises: Who should make the final decision on whether the finished product meets the quality goal? Note that now we are talking about *product* control rather than *process* control.

In the primitive village marketplace, the craftsman was the decision maker. However his decision was subject to check (and veto) by the buyer, in an atmosphere of *caveat emptor.* Then, as craftsman and buyer became increasingly separated by middlemen, new decision makers evolved. An early form was the inspector.

With the growth of commerce, there emerged new stakeholders with an interest in quality reputations: employers, merchants, guilds, cities, and others. In many cases these stakeholders were unwilling to rely solely on craftsmen to make sound decisions on quality of finished products. To provide added assurance to themselves and their customers they invaded the self-inspection monopoly of the craftsmen by giving independent inspectors the last word on finished product quality. Figure 18.5 shows the resulting feedback loop.

The growth of commerce also opened the way for cities to export their manufactured goods. Export benefited many sectors of the population—craftsmen, guilds, merchants, the political authorities, and so on. A major aid to export was the quality reputation of the city's goods.

For specialty goods it was possible for one or a few cities to dominate the market. For example, the city of Lüneberg secured a large share of the market for cutlery. For high-volume goods, such as textiles, there was intense competition among many cities. Success in the export market required the employment of large numbers of craftsmen in the associated trades. No wonder that the governments intervened to create and support a reputation for high quality.

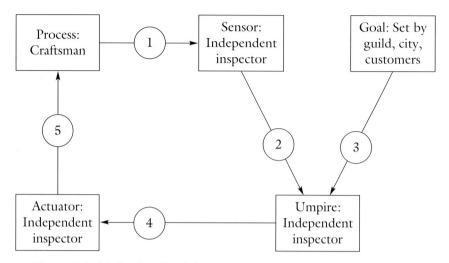

Figure 18.5 The feedback loop as applied to use of independent inspectors. Source: J. M. Juran.

The Industrial Revolution

The Industrial Revolution was cradled in Europe at about the mid–eighteenth century. It was made possible by the simultaneous development of power-driven machinery and sources of mechanical power. The resulting factories soon outperformed the small independent shops and made them largely obsolete.

The Factory System

The major goals of the factories included increasing productivity and reducing costs. The dominant reason for low productivity was the absence of technology. The dominant reason for high costs was the wages of skilled craftsmen. (In those days, the chief cost of production was direct labor.)

To achieve high productivity and the associated mass production, the factories reengineered the manufacturing processes. Under the craft system, a craftsman performed every one of the many tasks needed to produce pins, shoes, barrels, wagon wheels, and so on. His inputs were basic materials (steel wire, leather, lumber) and simple tools, plus his years of apprenticeship and experience. Under mass production the crafts were broken up. The tasks within a craft were divided up among several or many factory workers. Special tools were designed to simplify each task down to a short time cycle. A worker then could, in a few hours, carry out enough cycles of his or her task to reach high productivity.

Destruction of Crafts

Adam Smith, in his book *The Wealth of Nations,* was one of the first to publish an explanation of the striking difference between manufacture under the craft system versus the task system. He noted out that pin-making had been a distinct craft, consisting of 18 separate tasks. When these tasks were divided among 10 factory workers, production rose to a per worker equivalent of 4800 pins a day, which was orders of magnitude higher than would be achieved if each worker were to produce pins by performing all 18 tasks (Smith 1776). For other types of processes, such as spinning or weaving, power-driven machinery could outproduce hand-craftsmen, while employing semiskilled or unskilled workers to reduce labor costs.

All this reengineering took place over the bitter opposition of the craftsmen whose livelihoods were being destroyed. In Britain, the Luddites took to destroying the machinery or to threatening the factory workers who had replaced craftsmen. It was to no avail. For elaboration on the social effects, see chapter 14, under "The Development of the Quality of Workmanship."

Economic Effects

Mass production at low costs made the resulting products more affordable. Demand increased, requiring a revolution in the systems of distribution. At first the factories concentrated their production on basic consumer products—food, textiles, clothing. Availability of these products at affordable prices contributed greatly to economic growth in the industrialized countries. Then, with growth in affluence and technology, came the demand for better housing, household appliances, vehicles, and luxury goods. The factories helped to make all these things possible, as well as the associated rise of a large middle class.

Mass production and distribution required not only reengineering of the respective processes; it also required a wide array of supporting equipment to generate power, produce steel, provide efficient transport, and so on. Inventors and entrepreneurs were drawn into this vacuum, and they responded with enthusiasm. However, to bring their inventions to market demanded greater and greater depth of technology as well as increased levels of precision with accompanying specifications, tests, instruments, and inspections.

Figure 18.6 shows some of the leading figures whose inventions contributed greatly to the Industrial Revolution.

Quality Control Under the Factory System

The factory system required associated changes in the system of quality control. When craft tasks were divided among many workers, those workers were no longer their own customers, over and over again. The responsibility of workers was no longer to provide satisfaction to the buyer (also customer, user). Few factory workers had contact with buyers. Instead, the responsibility became one of "make it like the sample" (or specification).

Destruction of crafts led to destruction of self-control. Workers employed at one or few tasks were limited in their ability to complete the feedback loop. They were seldom provided with measuring instruments, and they were no longer their own customers. In the main, the feedback loop could be completed only for the finished product.

Mass production also brought new quality problems. Products that consisted of assemblies of bits and pieces demanded that those bits and pieces be interchangeable. Then, with the growth of technology and of interstate commerce, there emerged the need for standardization as well. All this required greater precision throughout—machinery, tools, measurement. (Under the craft system the craftsmen fitted and adjusted the pieces as needed.)

In theory the new factory quality problems could be avoided during the original planning of the manufacturing processes. Here the limitation rested with the planners. During the early stages of the Industrial Revolution, manufacturing planning was done largely by master mechanics and shop supervisors. They had extensive practical experience but their ways were empirical, being rooted in craft practices handed down through the generations. They had little understanding of the nature of process variation and the resulting product variation. They were unschooled in how to collect and analyze data to assure that their designs had process capability—that their process would enable the production workers to meet the specifications. Use of such new concepts would have to await the coming of the twentieth century.

Figure 18.6 Inventors from many countries contributed greatly to the spread of the Industrial Revolution. Among American inventors were nineteen shown in this portrait by Christian Schussele. From left to right, they are: William Morton, dental practice; James Bogardus, iron buildings; Samuel Colt, the revolver; Cyrus McCormick, the reaper; Joseph Saxon, metrology; Charles Goodyear, vulcanized rubber; Peter Cooper, iron works; Jordan Mott, iron stoves; Joseph Henry, the physicist; Eliphalet Nott, steam engines; John Ericsson, ironclad ships; Frederick Sickels, steam engine controls; Samuel Morse, the telegraph; Henry Burden, production machinery; Richard Hoe, the cylinder printing press; Erastus Bigelow, looms; Isaiah Jennings, production machinery; Thomas Blanchard, lathes; Elias Howe, the sewing machine. Source: The National Portrait Gallery, Washington, DC, USA. For elaboration, see Petroski, 1994.

Given the limitations of quality planning, what emerged was an expansion of inspection by departmental supervisors supplemented by inspectors. If inspectors were used, they were made responsible to the respective departmental production supervisors. The concept of a special department to coordinate quality activities broadly had not yet emerged. Such coordination as was needed took place on a crisis-by-crisis basis.

Quality Improvement

Before discussing quality improvement, it is necessary to distinguish between two kinds of improvement.

1. Improvements aimed at increasing customer *satisfaction* include product innovation to provide new and improved product features to customers. They also include process innovation to make it possible to produce new and improved product features. If successful, such improvements result in products that are more competitive, provide greater customer satisfaction, and increase the income of the producing company.

2. Improvements aimed at reducing customer *dissatisfaction* consist of reducing chronic waste in such forms as field failures, factory scrap and rework, inspection and test, and so on. Under the recent broadening of the scope of the word *quality* to *Big Q,* such improvements extend to reducing rework in business processes as well as in factory processes. If successful, improvements of this type result in cost reduction and increased productivity. Note that customer satisfaction and customer dissatisfaction are not opposites.

The line between these two types of quality improvement is blurred. Some forms of dissatisfaction, such as field failures, are not only costly; they also reduce income by discouraging repeat sales.

The Industrial Revolution provided a climate favorable for continuous quality improvement through product and process development. For example, chapter 14 shows that progressive improvements in the design of steam engines increased their thermal efficiency from 0.5 percent in 1718 to 23.0 percent in 1906. Inventors and entrepreneurs emerged to lead many countries into the new world of

Topic	Content of Little Q	Content of Big Q
Products	Manufactured goods	All products, goods, and services, whether for sale or not
Processes	Processes directly related to manufacture of goods	All processes; manufacturing support; business, etc.
Industries	Manufacturing	All industries; manufacturing; service; government, etc., whether for profit or not
Quality is viewed as:	A technological problem	A business problem
Customer	Clients who buy the products	All who are impacted, external and internal
How to think about quality	Based on culture of functional departments	Based on the universal Trilogy
Quality goals are included:	Among factory goals	In company business plan
Cost of poor quality	Costs associated with deficient manufactured goods	All costs which would disappear if everything were perfect
Improvement is directed at:	Departmental performance	Company performance
Evaluation of quality is based mainly on:	Conformance to factory specifications, procedures, standards	Responsiveness to customer needs
Training in managing for quality is:	Concentrated in the Quality Department	Companywide
Coordination is by:	The quality manager	A quality council of upper managers

Figure 18.7 Contrast, Little Q and Big Q. Source: *Juran on Quality by Design.* The Free Press, New York, NY, 1992.

technology and industrialization. In due course, some companies created internal sources of inventors—research laboratories to carry out product and process development. Some created market research departments to carry out the functions of entrepreneurship.

In contrast, the concept of continuous quality improvement to reduce chronic waste made little headway. The reasons for this are not fully clear. One likely reason is that most industrial managers give higher priority to increasing income than to reducing chronic waste. The guilds' policy of solidarity, which stifled quality improvement, may also have been a factor. In any event, the concept of quality improvement to reduce chronic waste did not find full application until the Japanese quality revolution of the twentieth century.

The Taylor System of Scientific Management

A further blow to the craft system came from F. W. Taylor's system of "Scientific Management." This originated in the late nineteenth century when Taylor, an American manager, wanted to increase production and productivity without resorting to training additional craftsmen. His solution was to separate planning from execution. He brought in engineers to do the planning, leaving the shop supervisors and the workforce with the narrow responsibility of carrying out the plans.

Taylor's system was stunningly successful in raising productivity. It was widely adopted in the United States, but not so widely adopted elsewhere. It had negative side effects in human relations, which most American managers chose to ignore. It also had negative effects on quality. The American managers responded by taking the inspectors out of the production departments and placing them in newly created inspection departments. In due course these departments took on added functions to become the broad-based quality departments of today.

(For elaboration, see chapter 17, under "The Taylor System and Its Impact." See also, Juran 1973.)

The Rise of Quality Assurance

The anatomy of quality assurance is very similar to that of quality control. Each employs the feedback loop. Each evaluates actual quality performance. Each compares actual performance to the quality goal. Each stimulates corrective action as needed. What differs is the prime purpose to be served.

The Purpose of Quality Assurance

Under quality control the prime purpose is to serve those who are directly responsible for conducting operations—to help them regulate current operations. Under quality assurance the prime purpose is to serve people who are not directly responsible for conducting operations, but who have a need to know—to be informed as to the state of affairs, and hopefully, to be assured that all is well.

In this sense, quality assurance has a similarity to insurance. Each spends a small sum to secure protection against a large loss. In the case of quality assurance the protection consists of early warning which may avoid the large loss. In the case of insurance the protection consists of compensation after the loss.

Quality Assurance in the Village Marketplace

In its simplest form, quality assurance was practiced in the village marketplace. Buyers wanted to be *assured* that what they bought would provide quality satisfaction. The nature of the products enabled the buyers themselves to provide much of this assurance through use of their senses and vigilance. So, in effect, the sellers provided the product while the buyers provided the quality assurance, and this was enforced by the doctrine of *caveat emptor.*

Effect of Growth and Complexity

The growth of commerce introduced chains of suppliers and merchants to separate consumers from the producers. In addition, the growth of technology made consumers' senses and vigilance largely academic for providing quality assurance. Quality warranties could be helpful, but new forms of assurance were needed as well.

In the cities, the guilds created a form of quality assurance by establishing product and process standards and then auditing to assure compliance by the craftsmen. For examples, see chapters 7, 12, and 14. In some cities and even countries, the political authorities established independent product inspections to protect their quality reputations as exporters, and for other reasons as well. For examples, see chapters 1, 7, and 14.

Audit of Suppliers' Quality Control Systems

In purchases by large industrial companies, the early forms of quality assurance were mainly through final product inspection and test. During the twentieth century there emerged a growing concept under which customers defined and mandated *quality control systems.* These systems were to be instituted and followed by suppliers as a condition for becoming and remaining suppliers. The concept was then enforced by audits, both before and during the life of the supply contracts.

At first this concept created severe problems for suppliers. Each buying company had its own idea of what was a proper quality control system, so that each supplier was faced with designing its system to satisfy multiple customers. In addition, each supplier was subject to being audited by each customer. There was no provision for pooling the results of audits into some data bank, and customers were generally unwilling to accept the findings of audits conducted by personnel other than their own. The resulting multiple audits were especially burdensome to small suppliers.

In theory, it is feasible to design a quality control system that is universally acceptable. There is much commonality among company systems, but many companies will not accept standards set by others. "Our business is different." Nevertheless, steps to standardize were taken by professional societies, by national standardization bodies, and, most recently, by the International Organization for Standardization (ISO). ISO's 9000 series of standards for quality control systems is now widely accepted among European companies. There is no legal requirement for compliance; but, as a marketing matter, companies are reluctant to be in a position in which their competitors are certified as complying but they themselves are not.

There remains the problem of multiple audits (also assessments). Here again it is feasible in theory for one audit to provide information that would be acceptable to all buyers. This is already the case in quality audits conducted by Underwriters' Laboratories and in financial audits conducted by Dun & Bradstreet. Single audits may in the future also turn out to be feasible under the emerging process for certification to the ISO 9000 series of standards for quality control systems.

Extension to Military Procurement

The need for quality assurance also extends to military procurement. Most governments supply their military needs from contractors as well as from government arsenals and shipyards. In earlier centuries, defense department officials secured their quality assurance through inspection, test, and use of the products. During the twentieth century there was a notable shift to developing standards for quality control systems and mandating their use by suppliers. An example is the United States Defense Department's standard MIL-Q-9858. Such standards are mandated by including them in the purchase contracts and then auditing to assure compliance. An application on a grand scale is the AQAP standards used by the North Atlantic Treaty Organization (NATO). These are largely based on the provisions of the United States' MIL-Q-9858.

Resistance to Mandated Quality Control Systems

At the outset, suppliers resisted the mandated quality control systems imposed by their customers. The long-standing plea had been, "Tell us what you need, but don't tell us how to make it. We are the experts in how to make such products." Some pointed to their established record for good quality as proof that their system was already adequate. Hence, they argued, the mandated systems are an unnecessary and added cost.

In addition, there was cultural resistance. The mandated systems were an invasion of the long-standing suppliers' right to manage their business, an intrusion into suppliers' private matters, and even an insult to their reputation. The mandated standards also disturbed the status system within the suppliers' hierarchy.

None of this could stop the movement to quality assurance. The economic power of the buyers was decisive. Then, as suppliers gained experience with the new approach, they realized that many of its provisions were simply good business practice. So, the concept of mandated quality control systems seems destined to become a permanent feature of managing for quality.

Shift of Responsibility

It should be noted that the concept of mandating quality control systems involves a major change of responsibility for quality assurance. In the village marketplace the producer supplies the product, but the buyer is responsible for supplying the quality assurance. Under mandated quality control systems, the producer becomes responsible for supplying both the product and the quality assurance. The producer supplies the quality assurance by

- Adopting the mandated system for controlling quality, and
- Submitting the data that prove that the system is being followed.

The buyers' audits then consist of seeing to it that the mandated system is in place and that the system is indeed being followed.

For examples and additional discussion, see chapters 9, 13, 14, and 17. See also Juran 1977.

The Twentieth Century and Quality

The twentieth century witnessed the emergence of some massive new forces that required responsive action. One of the needed responses was a revolution in managing for quality. However, it was not easy for companies to recognize the need for such a revolution—they lacked the necessary alarm signals. Technological measures of quality did exist on the shop floors, but managerial measures of quality did not exist in the boardrooms. So, except in Japan, the needed quality revolution did not start until very late in the twentieth century. To make that revolution effective throughout the world economies will require many decades—the entire twenty-first century. So, while the twentieth century has been the Century of Productivity, the twenty-first century will be known as the Century of Quality.

Before going on to examine the nature of the needed quality revolution, it is useful to look at the major forces that have demanded such a revolution. They include the following:

- Greater complexity and precision of products
- Threats to human safety and health, and to the environment
- Government regulation of quality
- The rise of the consumerism movement
- Intensified international competition in quality

Greater Complexity and Precision of Products

One of the massive forces that emerged during the twentieth century was an explosive growth in science and technology. This expansion made possible an outpouring of great benefits to human societies: longer life spans, superior communication and transport, household appliances, new forms of education and entertainment, and so on. Huge new industries emerged to translate the new technology into those benefits. Nations that accepted industrialization found it possible to improve their economies and the well-being of their citizenry.

The new technologies required complex designs and precise execution. The empirical ways of earlier centuries were unable to provide appropriate product and process designs, so process yields were low and field failures were high. Companies tried to deal with low yields by adding inspections to separate the good from the bad. They tried to deal with field failures through warranties and customer service. These solutions were costly, and they created dissatisfactions among customers. The need was to prevent defects and field failures from happening in the first place.

Threats to Safety, Health, and the Environment

With the benefits from technology came uninvited guests. Acceptance of the benefits created a dependence on them. Product failures produced interruptions in continuity of service. Most of these were minor, but some were serious and even frightening—threats to human safety and health, as well as to the environment.

There also emerged a gathering awareness that continuity of the benefits depended on the quality of the products—goods and services—that provided the benefits. The number and severity of the interruptions likewise depended on the continued performance and good behavior of the products of technology. This dependence came to be known as "life behind the quality dikes." For elaboration, see Juran 1970.

Government Regulation of Quality

Government regulation of quality is of ancient origin. At the outset it focused mainly on human safety and was conducted after the fact—

laws provided for punishing those whose poor quality caused death or injury. Over the centuries there emerged a trend to regulation before the fact—to become preventive in nature.

This trend was intensified during the twentieth century. In the field of human health, laws were enacted to assure the quality of food, food additives, pharmaceuticals, and medical devices. Licensing of practitioners was expanded. Other laws were enacted relating to product safety, highway safety, occupational safety, consumer protection, and so on. For elaboration, see Juran 1988, pages 34.13 to 34.21. See also, in the present book, chapter 17, under "Government Regulation of Quality."

Growth of government regulation was a response to twentieth-century forces as well as a force in its own right. The rise of technology placed complex and dangerous products in the hands of amateurs— the public. Government regulation then demanded product designs that avoided these dangers. To the companies, this intervention then became a force to be reckoned with.

The Rise of Consumerism

In countries that adopted industrialization, the twentieth century greatly improved the economics of consumers. They welcomed the features offered by the new products, but not the associated new quality problems. The new products were unfamiliar—most consumers lacked expertise in technology. Their senses were unable to judge which of the competing products to buy, so the concept of *caveat emptor* was no longer valid.

When products failed in service, consumers could be frustrated by vague warranties, confused responsibilities, and poor service. Many became victims of the inability of "the system" to provide recourse when things failed. While consumers individually were unable to fight the system, collectively they were numerous, and potentially powerful, economically and politically. During the twentieth century the consumerism movement emerged to make this potential a reality and to help consumers deal more effectively with those problems. This same movement was also successful in stimulating new government legislation for consumer protection. For elaboration, see Juran 1988, pages 34.2 to 34.13. See also chapter 17, under "The Rise of Consumerism."

Intensified Competition in Quality

While the guilds tried to stifle internal competition in quality, competition among cities and countries has been on a growth curve for centuries. The Industrial Revolution accelerated this growth to a point that demanded the attention of leaders at the highest levels of government and industry.

> *For example, in 1769, Nicholas Demarest of the French Bureau of Commerce, visited Dutch and French paper mills to discover why Dutch paper was superior in quality. One result was creation of a model French paper mill, using the most efficient processes, to serve as a training ground for French paper makers. (Gillispie 1983)*

In effect, this was carrying out an earlier policy of Jean-Baptiste Colbert, King Louis XIV's finance minister, whose 1664 report to the king included the observation, "If our factories, through careful work, assure the quality of our products, it will be to the foreigners' interest to get supplies from us, and their money will flow into the kingdom" (Gogue 1988).

The oldest form of international competition in quality has probably been in military weaponry. Examples of efforts to improve the quality of such weapons can be seen in chapters 9 and 11 (naval vessels), and in chapter 13 (artillery). This competition intensified during the twentieth century under the pressures of the two world wars. It led to the development of new and terrible weapons of mass destruction.

A further stimulus to competition in quality came from the rise of multinational companies. Large companies had found that foreign trade barriers were obstacles to growth through export. To get around these barriers, many set up foreign subsidiaries which then became their bases for competition in foreign markets, including competition in quality.

The most spectacular demonstration of the power of competition in quality came from the Japanese. Like their Western competitors, Japanese boardrooms lacked measures of quality to provide alarm signals. However, following World War II, Japanese companies discovered that the West was unwilling to buy their products—Japan had acquired a reputation for making and selling shoddy goods.

The inability to sell their postwar products became an alarm signal and a stimulus for launching the Japanese quality revolution during the 1950s. Within a few decades that revolution propelled Japan to a position of world leadership in quality. This quality leadership in turn enabled Japan to become an economic superpower. It was a phenomenon without precedent in industrial history.

Responses and Prognosis

While the subject of quality has a lengthy history, most of it took place in relative obscurity. A massive change then took place late in the twentieth century—quality moved to center stage, and became a major parameter in human affairs.

Humans are usually slow to respond to massive changes, and they tend to delay action until events approach crisis proportions. In a crisis atmosphere their actions tend to be hasty and ill-advised. The resulting chaos makes it difficult to detect trends and predict outcomes. What we will do is to look at some of the principal responses and try to judge their likely direction. Our prognosis will be aided by looking back at the usual scenario of earlier human responses to massive changes.

A Common Scenario

When any parameter moves to center stage it has a notable impact on society. Many people may be benefited; many may be damaged. There is confusion on how to deal with the damage. The impact demands the attention of national leaders—industrial managers, government officials, media heads, and so on. Numerous experiments get under way. (In a sense, each company is a potential test laboratory.) The experimental results provide lessons learned—what works and what does not.

The results achieved and the lessons learned are then disseminated through word of mouth, conferences, journals, and so on. The successful companies—the role models—receive special attention. They are invited to tell and retell their stories. They are asked to accept visits from companies eager to witness the miracles. Other companies try to use the lessons learned to achieve similar results. Scaling up gets under way.

Meanwhile, steps are taken to organize a coherent body of knowledge for the parameter, and to create a source of expertise. Consultants and specialists are attracted to a potential growth activity. In due course, the education system opens up to absorb the new body of knowledge. New educational courses are created. These may expand into entire new curricula, degrees, and even new colleges. A new category of teachers arises to teach the courses, to conduct research, and to expand the body of knowledge.

The above scenario has been followed for many earlier cases of parameters that have moved to center stage. It is now being followed with respect to quality, so it helps us to judge the emerging trends and their likely effects.

Top Priority on Quality

Producers have always been faced with meeting numerous types of goals: financial, schedule, cost, productivity, and so on, including quality. What has varied has been the order of priority. When trade expanded beyond village boundaries, the guilds tended to set static quality goals through specifications and long-standing craft practice.

The Industrial Revolution gave top priority to raising productivity. Much of its focus was on reducing direct labor, which was the chief component of production costs. (Until the twentieth century, laborers outnumbered machines. Now it is the reverse.) The Taylor system intensified the focus on reducing direct labor. It studied the human being as a machine for work and tried to establish piecework rates on a scientific basis. (Piecework—wage payment by the piece— once had a long and durable history in the Western world.)

The twentieth-century Japanese quality revolution soon showed that competition in quality had become a powerful force. As Japanese goods invaded the United States, many U.S. industries suffered severe losses in share of market.

During the 1960s there were over 20 American-owned companies making and selling color television sets in the United States. Now there is only one. News of such disasters stimulated a shift in company priorities from reducing costs to preserving income. In turn, this shifted top priority from improving productivity to improving quality. It became clear that quality goals could no longer be regarded as static specifications. Quality now had to be regarded as a moving target, requiring continuous improvement.

Along with the trend to raise the priority on quality there came a trend to enlarge the scope of what is covered by the quality umbrella. The name given to this enlarged scope was *Big Q* to distinguish it from the traditional *little Q*. For elaboration, see Figure 18.7.

During the 1980s many companies adopted policies to the effect that quality has top priority. This was a natural reaction to quality having moved to center stage. As it turned out, making this policy effective demands extensive cultural and procedural changes, plus added work for all, including the upper managers. So progress has been slow, and much remains to be done. However, we can expect progress to continue, as quality is destined to remain on center stage for the foreseeable future.

This same shift in priorities will, in due course, begin to influence national economic policies. The pace will be slow because economists, legislators, and administrators have been slow to grasp the fact and effect of quality having moved to center stage. One evidence of progress has been the proliferation, during the 1980s, of national quality awards. In contrast, many countries have evolved national indexes of productivity, but none have as yet evolved national indexes of quality. It can be expected that action at the national level will continue to lag behind action at regional, industry, and company levels.

Customer Focus

The concept of meeting customer needs is ancient, but *customer focus* is a recent term. The new emphasis (or reemphasis) is traceable to the increased competition in quality. In addition, there have been some major changes in the meaning of the word *customer*.

It would seem obvious that managers should give top priority to customer needs. Yet other matters often get in the way. To the guilds, the top priorities were to protect their monopolies and the well-being of their members. In large organizations, priorities include meeting functional goals, which can conflict with customer focus. Customer preferences for imported products often run into resistance from domestic producers and their political allies.

The Big Q concept broadens the scope of the word *customer*. In the village, the customer was generally the buyer/user of the product. Then, as producer and buyer/user became separated by intervening chains of suppliers and merchants, *customer* became a whole cast of characters. This has required redesign of the systems for transmitting information on customer needs to all who are faced with meeting those needs.

Under Big Q, the scope of *customer* extends to many who are not directly involved in producing or using the product, but who nevertheless have a legitimate concern—legislators, regulators, consumer organizations, and so on. Also included are internal customers. (Most products are delivered to internal customers.) In addition, the public is an important category of customer. This has been emphasized by the growing concern over safety, health, the environment, and consumer protection.

The term *customer focus* has been widely accepted by managers as a key guiding principle. However, in many companies there is only a dim awareness that the scope of *customer* has widened, so there is no longer a consensus on who is the customer. The need is to face this problem head-on. Special meetings should be convened to address the question, Who is the customer? For elaboration, see Juran 1992, pages 44–67.

The term *customer needs* also should be reexamined, especially for long-life products. For such products, quality is required not only at the time of purchase, but during the entire product life cycle. For a thoughtful analysis as applied to automobiles, see Sakai 1994.

Competition in Quality

The merits of competition are by no means universally accepted. The guilds did not tolerate competition among their members. When competition spread beyond city and national boundaries, there were efforts to block imports, and this persists to the present, with negative effects on domestic buyers. Destructive competition has generated antitrust legislation. However the trend has clearly been toward free trade, so we can expect the economic power of customers to continue to be decisive. Again, the priority is on customer focus.

Early in the twentieth century the Soviet Union launched a planned society on a huge scale. The anticipated benefits included elimination of internal competition, as well as the "anarchy of the marketplace." In the 1990s the system collapsed, having failed to provide adequately for its citizenry. The failure extended to the area of quality.

There were exceptions. Equipments for the military and the space program were competitive with that of the West. However, for the bulk of the economy—goods for export, domestic products, and domestic services—quality was shockingly poor.

The collapse of the Soviet Union is widely believed to confirm the claims of the advocates of competition. Their views are likely to dominate economic thinking for a long time.

The Processes of Managing for Quality

One of the twentieth-century findings was that all company functions have an influence on the company's quality performance and its quality image. Yet, each of those functions was being managed for quality in empirical ways. Many companies concluded that empiricism should give way to a more structured approach.

There are many ways to organize the subject of managing for quality into a structured approach, so numerous designs have emerged and are now in use. As of the 1990s none has become dominant. One design that has attained some popularity is the author's "Juran Trilogy™." It defines three managerial processes, each of which consists of a sequence of steps that is applicable universally.

- *Quality planning* makes use of the "quality planning road map." For extensive elaboration, see Juran 1992 (the entire book is devoted to the quality planning process).

- *Quality control* is based on the feedback loop, and is discussed in this chapter under "The Feedback Loop."

- *Quality improvement* is based on the author's book *Managerial Breakthrough,* which was originally published in 1964 (see Juran 1994).

For elaboration on the Quality Trilogy®, see Juran 1986.

Quality Improvement

Within the trilogy, the quality improvement concept deserves special attention. Historically, many companies have used this concept to increase income through new product and process development. This was done formally. Goals for such development became a part of the company business plan. Special full-time departments were funded to provide the needed technology. The upper managers participated actively during the business planning and through progress reviews.

While the improvement concept was well accepted as to product and process development, there was need to improve the execution. By the late 1980s, progress was being made through concurrent engineering, reduction of cycle time, and use of robust designs (Godfrey 1993).

In contrast, few companies had used the improvement concept to reduce the chronic waste due to internal and external quality failures. Their business plans included no goals for this purpose. The functional organizations provided no structure for making such improvements.

Then, starting in the 1950s the Japanese made quality improvement a part of their quality revolution. Their improvement goals included reduction of chronic waste. Their methodology included the approach presented in the author's 1954 lectures (Juran 1956), along with Japanese inventions such as the quality circle concept. Within several decades, the leading Japanese companies were each making many thousands of quality improvements annually.

Despite the mounting quality crisis, Western companies were slow to accept the need for continuous improvement to reduce internal and external quality failures. Then, in the 1980s, numerous companies launched initiatives to deal with the quality crisis. Of the many strategies tested, three dominated.

- Exhortation to urge the workforce to "do it right the first time."
- Training in statistical tools as an aid to process control.
- Training in the quality improvement process based on the author's videocassette series *Juran on Quality Improvement* (Juran 1981).

By the end of the 1980s some Western companies had emerged as the role models—they had attained rates of quality improvement that paralleled those of the leading Japanese companies. However, most Western companies are still lagging. Much of this is due to poor execution. In addition, there is lack of awareness of the need to revise the reward system to stimulate company personnel to accept quality improvement as a new and permanent part of their responsibilities. An added complication is that reduction of chronic waste threatens to eliminate jobs, and hence becomes a source of employee apprehension. Most Western managers have failed to face up to this apprehension, and this has contributed to the lag in making improvements.

Quality improvement has turned out to be essential for quality leadership. The targets for improvement must include business processes as well as factory processes. The quality leader's rate of improvement must be at least as high as that of the most aggressive competitor. In addition, quality improvement must be institutionalized—it must go on, year after year, forever. This is done by enlarging the annual business plan to include goals for improvement, by expanding the use of recognition, and by revising the reward system so that it recognizes the new responsibilities involved.

The results achieved by the role model companies do provide a stimulus for others, and scaling up has gotten under way. American companies, having endured the chief impact of Japanese competition, are now scaling up at a pace faster than that of their European counterparts, who have become preoccupied with getting certified as meeting the criteria of the ISO 9000 series of standards. The European lag in improvement is likely to continue through the 1990s.

Collaboration for Quality; Partnering

The increasing separation of producers from ultimate customers has resulted in much suboptimizing. Within a single company, managers pursuing functional goals can readily damage overall results. Between companies, an adversarial relationship can do damage to both, and to their customers as well.

The classic needs for collaboration among companies included standardization and interchangeability. In early mass production, parts made by one supplier were not interchangeable with those made by competing suppliers. This created inventory problems for merchants, as well as service problems for ultimate customers.

A great fire which destroyed much of the city of Baltimore provided dramatic evidence of the need for standardization. The neighboring cities sent their equipment to help put out the fire, but then were unable to help. The threads of their fire hose couplings did not fit the threads of the Baltimore fire hydrants!

The rise of national and international standardization bodies has meanwhile made it possible to simplify life for entire industries—producers and customers alike.

The recent emphasis has been on *partnering,* meaning (usually) collaboration between supplier and customer.

> *A pioneering example involved a photographic plate. Aluminum Company of America (Alcoa) supplied the aluminum base and Kodak supplied the coating. Quality problems persisted in an atmosphere of mutual blame. A joint Alcoa–Kodak team was then created and assigned to solve the problems. The results were a stunning benefit to both companies and to the ultimate customers as well. (See Kegarise and Miller in IMPRO 1985)*

Partnering provides a win–win result, and is a welcome change from the adversary relationship that has been the rule in supplier–customer transactions. Despite cultural resistance, partnering is gaining, and should gradually replace much of the adversary relationship.

Partnering is also being applied to other situations involving multiple companies: producer–merchant, project management, and so on. A major project may involve product and process design being divided up among several countries. Production may be similarly divided. Installation and use may take place all over. Such projects face formidable obstacles due to differences in language, standards, and culture. It becomes necessary to provide participants with special training to help them deal with such obstacles.

For some partnering projects, the joint team needs access to information classified as secret. Traditionally such secrets have been protected through special language in the contracts. However, some recent cases (such as Alcoa–Kodak) have substituted mutual trust for contract language. This may signal a new trend.

Research in Managing for Quality

In recent centuries the trend in managing for quality has been to replace tradition and empiricism with methods based on science and technology. This trend accelerated during the twentieth century, but the application has been slow, and some is still undergoing test. There remains much need for research in how to manage for quality.

Some of this research is feasible through analysis of how some companies have achieved stunning results by revising their systems of managing for quality. As to these role models there is a vague awareness of the relationships between cause and effect, but this has not been researched in the depth needed to inspire confidence in the lessons learned. Even for companies that have failed to get stunning results there is value in similar researches, in order to provide lessons learned in what *not* to do.

Dr. A. Blanton Godfrey has identified ten areas that need research in managing for quality (Godfrey 1993).

- Achieving revolutionary rates of improvement, including use of cloning and technology transfer.
- Expansion of managing for quality to all functions and industries.
- Improving product and process development, especially through concurrent engineering, reduction of cycle time, and use of robust designs.
- Improving training through analysis of results achieved by alternative approaches.
- Improving information systems through closing the loops and through discarding unused loops.
- Learning to make use of self-directing teams.
- Extending partnering between suppliers and customers.
- Applying self-assessment and benchmarking.
- Making customer focus effective throughout the entire company.
- Applying strategic quality planning and the associated deployment of quality goals.

Godfrey's paper, which includes numerous pertinent case examples, will repay careful study.

There are also some long-standing problems for which the conceptual research is well advanced; the solutions are known, but many applications are blocked by cultural resistance. For such cases, the needed research lies in how to deal with the cultural resistance.

A case in point is *life cycle costing*—purchasing based on the cost of usage. For many products the purchase price is a minor part of the cost of using the product over its lifetime—the major costs are energy, maintenance, wear out, and so on. Some progress has been made by writing purchase contracts based on the cost of using the product. For example, automotive fleets do not "buy" tires; they buy kilometers traveled. Airlines also do not buy tires; they buy number of landings (which is when the bulk of the wear takes place). (For elaboration on life cycle costing, see Juran 1988, pages 3.20 to 3.27.)

While the need for research in managing for quality is extensive, the sources of funding remain to be identified and convinced. A role model is the research funded by the John A. Hartford Foundation to examine the applicability of the quality improvement concept to hospitals. The end result was the book *Curing Health Care*. It describes numerous successful applications, and has been influential in stimulating many hospitals to adopt quality improvement as a strategy (see Berwick, Godfrey, and Roessner 1990).

Measurement of Quality

Many chapters of this book give examples of measuring quality in early civilizations. Those were measurements of technological features of goods. During the twentieth century there emerged a need to measure quality at the managerial level—measures of customer satisfaction, competitive quality, and so on. Such measures are new, so they must be invented, field tested, and then refined.

That will be a lengthy process. Ideally, the end result will include a core list of measures much as has evolved in finance—the balance sheet, profit statement, and so on. Development of the core financial measures took centuries, and such may be the case with respect to core measures of quality. It is also desirable to evolve broad national quality indexes to parallel those already in use, such as for consumer prices and for productivity.

These and other future measurement problems will require corresponding revisions in information systems. Modern data processing and networking is available to measure and report quality to upper management levels with minimal need for human relay stations.

Another problem for the future is secrecy of company information on quality. Here it is useful to look at the scenario as played out in the field of finance. Centuries ago, company finances were closely guarded secrets. Today, in many countries, publicly owned companies must make public disclosure of such information, including review by independent auditors.

A similar scenario may be evolving relative to quality. Some consumer organizations contend that company information on product tests should be made public in order to help consumers make informed decisions on which products to buy.

An example of mandated disclosure is that of product recalls. In some countries, safety-related product recalls must be publicized in order to alert merchants and consumers, and to expedite locating and disposing of the product under recall.

Benchmarking

Related to measurement is benchmarking, a most useful tool which gained broad acceptance during the 1980s. The concept is to set quality goals based on realities rather than on empirical judgment. To apply the concept requires discovery of what is the best performance being achieved, whether in-house, by a competitor, or by someone in a totally different industry.

Early in the twentieth century, some German generals visited the Barnum and Bailey circus to study the world-renowned methods it used to transport equipment, animals, personnel, and so on from city to city.

Benchmarking requires availability of data banks to identify which are the best performances, and how they have been achieved. Such data banks are now being evolved.

Human Relations and Quality

By the beginning of the twentieth century the approach to managing for quality had already changed radically from the days of crafts and guilds. The Industrial Revolution had dealt a severe blow to the craft system by dividing crafts into tasks that could be performed by machines. The Taylor system went further by separating planning from execution and limiting the workforce to executing short-cycle, repetitive tasks.

The basic premise of Taylorism was that the workforce lacked the literacy needed to plan how to do work. This premise was largely valid at the turn of the century. Since then, the rise in education levels has made Taylor's premise obsolete, and with it Taylorism itself. One result was the growth of a huge underemployed asset—the education, experience, and creativity of the workforce.

By the 1980s it was clear that Taylorism was obsolete and should be replaced. It was also clear that means should be found for employing that huge underemployed asset. The key to solving those two interrelated problems was the concept of *empowerment*—a transfer to the workforce of selected decisions and actions previously assigned to managers and to professional specialists. An added stimulus to adoption of empowerment was the belief that it would contribute to the quality of work life.

As companies experimented in order to learn which decisions and actions should be assigned to the workforce, it turned out that there were multiple options, including

- *Self-control*—This involves creating the conditions needed to enable workers to fully regulate production processes.

- *Self-inspection*—The self-inspection option assigns to workers the decision of whether their products conform to the quality goals.

- *Job enlargement*—Job enlargement broadens the range of tasks assigned to workers. A widespread example has been in customer service departments. Workers who are contacted by customers (whether by telephone or at the service window) are armed with the means to provide "one-stop shopping"—to give answers and take action then and there, rather than "handing off" the customer to others.

- *Self-directing work teams.* Under this concept, teams of workers are trained and empowered to conduct operations involving a wide array of functions and tasks. These functions may include some or all of process planning, scheduling, materials management, production, work assignment, equipment maintenance, personnel recruitment, maintaining discipline, process improvement, and so on.

- *Quality improvement.* This concept is new as applied to the workforce. It began in 1962 when the Japanese invented QC Circles as a means of enabling workers to make improvements (in quality and otherwise) within their own departments. Such circles spend about an hour a week working on improvements rather than on production. These circles have been stunningly successful in Japan, and have since been widely copied in many other countries.

Of these (and other) options, self-directing teams have been the most impressive to managers. Tests of the concept have shown significant improvements in quality and productivity. These improvements have been accompanied by a sharp drop in the ratio of supervisors to workers. On the negative side, there is cultural resistance from several sources. Supervisors and professional specialists see threats to their jobs and status. Unions see threats to their communication link with the workforce. Despite this resistance, the author believes that self-directing work teams are the most likely major successor to the Taylor system.

Motivation for Quality

In the early stages of the twentieth-century quality crisis, many managers were persuaded to solve their quality problems in a melodramatic way: motivate and exhort the workforce through speeches, banners, and slogans. The universal failures of this simplistic approach not only confirmed that the prime problem was the system rather than the workforce; it also showed how limited was upper management's understanding of the problems of managing for quality.

While no one is *against* quality, there are some real obstacles which interfere with being *for* quality: conflicts in priorities; the need to meet functional goals; apprehensions about the side effects of proposals for change; cultural resistance. The least understood of such obstacles have been the apprehensions and cultural resistance relative to reducing chronic waste. To managers, reducing chronic waste is an obvious benefit to company competitiveness. To the workforce it is a threat to job security. To supervisors it is a threat to status, if not to job security.

Some managers have faced employee apprehensions head-on. They have quantified the rate at which jobs will be created through attrition and in other ways. They have also estimated the rate at which jobs will be eliminated through reduction in chronic waste. The resulting comparison has helped them determine whether they are able to give assurances that can ease apprehensions. In contrast, most managers have failed to deal forthrightly with apprehensions, thereby inviting rumors to fill the vacuum in communication.

A further problem in motivation has been the need to stimulate employees to accept the changes needed to become competitive in quality, and hopefully to attain quality leadership. These changes include revising the priority assigned to quality; becoming trained in managing for quality; accepting participation in quality improvement as a new responsibility; learning to work as a team member.

Most companies have made good use of recognition to provide some of the needed stimulus. Recognition is public acknowledgment of superior performance. Because superior performance is voluntary, it deserves public acknowledgment. Most companies have provided such acknowledgment effectively and in good taste.

In contrast, the reward system relates to the work mandated by the employment contract through the job description. Here the companies have been less effective. In many it is not clear whether responsibility to participate in quality improvement is voluntary or mandatory. Many companies have made no revision in their reward system to reflect the changes that employees are asked to accept. Failure to make such revisions has contributed to the failure of many quality initiatives.

Training for Quality

Formal training for achieving quality probably began centuries ago within the apprenticeships of the craft and guild systems. The advent of departments for inspection and test stimulated training in metrology. During World War II, the United States government offered training courses in statistical quality control based on tools evolved by the Bell System during the 1920s (see Working 1945; Grant 1953; AT&T 1989; Juran 1991; Wareham and Stratton 1991; Grant 1991). In Japan, the training courses by W. Edwards Deming on statistical quality control and by J. M. Juran on managing for quality were important inputs to the Japanese quality revolution (see Deming 1950; Juran, 1956).

Following World War II, inspection departments expanded to become broad-based quality departments. This expansion included creation of quality specialists who require training in such topics as quality engineering, reliability engineering, and advanced statistical methodology (for example, design of experiments and analysis of variance).

Increasing competition stimulated a need to design products and processes based on science and technology rather than on tradition and empiricism. The engineers assigned to produce these designs were well trained in their respective engineering disciplines, but not in such tools as reliability modeling or process capability analysis. Yet, competitive pressures demanded that the designs meet the parameters of reliability and process capability. Two solutions emerged to deal with this problem of "quality planning by amateurs." In the West, in-house consultants (quality engineers, reliability engineers) were assigned to assure that the designs did make use of the quality disciplines. In Japan, the solution was to "train the amateurs to be professionals," a solution preferred by the author.

The emerging quality crisis of the 1970s required that quality-related training be expanded to include managers in all functions and at all levels of the hierarchy. For these categories of personnel the subject matter had to go beyond statistics and tools; it had to include the concepts and methodology of *managing for quality*. All this was without precedent. Previously, only quality managers had received training in managing for quality.

As it turned out, training courses for managers exhibited much commonality as well as variety. The core training courses included topics such as quality concepts, policies, and goals; the processes of managing for quality—planning, control, and improvement; strategic quality planning and deployment of goals; measurement of quality; motivation. Specialized courses were also evolved to focus on functions such as product development, supplier relations, human relations, and so on.

Training for upper managers was certainly without precedent. Most upper managers had to be convinced that they needed such training. Traditionally, upper managers had delegated managing for quality to subordinates. This concept was now obsolete. Instead, certain roles were now nondelegable—they must be carried out by the upper managers, personally (see "Upper Managers in Charge," later in this chapter).

Strategic Quality Planning

Once upper managers accepted the need to raise the priority of quality, they faced the question of how to make the new priority effective. Most upper managers decided to avoid making managing for quality yet another semiautonomous function. Instead, they opted to make managing for quality a part of managing the business. The emerging method for doing this is often called *strategic quality planning* (SQP). The Japanese term is *jishu kanri*.

The concept of SQP follows closely the approach long used in managing for finance. The application to quality involves the following:

- The business plan is enlarged to include goals for quality.
- These goals are "deployed" to lower levels in order to determine the resources needed, agree on the actions to be taken, and fix responsibility for taking the actions.
- Measures are developed to permit evaluation of progress against the goals.
- Managers, including upper managers, review progress regularly.
- The reward system is revised to give appropriate weight to meeting the quality goals.

Application of SQP in the West is quite new—it did not emerge noticeably until the 1980s. The parallel to managing for finance has appealed to upper managers. The likelihood is that SQP will emerge as the dominant approach toward making managing for quality a part of managing the business.

Total Quality Management

By the 1980s it was becoming clear to upper managers that quality leadership could not be achieved by pecking away—by bringing in this or that tool or technique. Instead, it was necessary to apply the entire array of quality know-how (the "quality disciplines") throughout the entire company—to all functions and all levels—and to do so in a coordinated way. One shorthand expression for this comprehensive approach is the term *total quality management,* or *TQM.* (The usual Japanese term is company-wide quality control.)

At the outset there was no agreed standard definition for TQM, so communication became confused—among company departments, in their training courses, and in the general literature. This confusion has since been reduced by the publication of the criteria used by the American National Institute for Standards and Technology (NIST) to judge the applications for the United States' Malcolm Baldrige National Quality Award (Baldrige Award). For elaboration, contact NIST.

Those criteria have been widely disseminated—NIST has filled over a million requests for application forms. While there have been relatively few applications for the award, many companies have conducted self-audits against the criteria. In addition, as national quality awards have proliferated, many have used the Baldrige Award criteria as inputs to their own list of criteria. By the early 1990s, this wide exposure had made the Baldrige Award criteria the most widely accepted definition of what is included in TQM.

Upper Managers in Charge

Historically, upper managers in large companies have avoided direct involvement in the managing for quality. Instead, they delegated it, often vaguely, to some subordinate manager. With the creation of inspection departments in the twentieth century, it became convenient to "delegate quality" to the chief inspector, and, later, to the quality manager.

It has now become evident that attaining quality leadership requires that upper managers personally take charge of the quality initiative. Such has been the conclusion from study of what happened in those companies that did attain such leadership. In every case the upper managers took charge. They did not just make the speeches and then delegate all else to subordinates. Instead, they personally carried out certain nondelegable roles, as set out in chapter 17:

- Serve on the quality council.
- Establish the quality goals.
- Provide the needed resources.
- Provide quality-oriented training.
- Stimulate quality improvement.
- Review progress.
- Give recognition.
- Revise the reward system.

It should be emphasized that these roles are *nondelegable*—they must be carried out by the upper managers, personally. For elaboration, see Juran 1993.

Managing for Quality—A Long Look Ahead

Throughout this chapter the author has ventured to look ahead and offer bits of prognosis—estimates of where the emerging trends are leading us. Our final bit of prognosis goes beyond the near future—it examines what managing for quality will look like well into the next century, beyond the year 2050.

For such prognosis, it is helpful to look at scenarios that were followed by other disciplines—those that moved to center stage centuries ago. Such disciplines have reached a greater state of maturity than managing for quality—they have been at it for centuries rather than decades. Good examples are finance and, especially, one of its subdisciplines—accounting.

Accounting has been under study for centuries. These studies have yielded a consensus on numerous aspects of that field.

- The subject is organized into distinct processes such as general accounting, cost accounting, auditing.

- Numerous concepts have been invented to permit translation of actions into money—concepts such as depreciation, accruals, amortization.

- Standardized reports have been evolved: balance sheet, profit statement, cash flow statement. Anyone trained to read these reports can acquire a reasonable understanding of the financial condition of the associated company.

- Key words and terms have been precisely defined, and these definitions have largely been standardized.

- Tools have been invented and standardized: charts of accounts, double-entry bookkeeping, spreadsheets.

- Standing committees continue to explore the field. Their findings often get embodied into legislation.

- The industry has been professionalized through degree-granting schools of accounting, and through examinations to qualify for title of Certified Public Accountant (CPA). (In the United States, anyone may practice accounting, but only those who have passed the examinations may use the title of CPA.)

Study of recent developments in managing for quality shows much commonality with the above scenario. We can expect such commonality to continue. We can also speculate on what will take place during the twenty-first century as these developments impact the national economies.

• Awareness of the new importance of quality will spread to national policy makers: legislators, administrators, economists. (Some of this has already happened at local and regional levels.)

• Correlations will be established between performance on quality versus financial results.

• Standardized reports will evolve to provide a summary of the quality achievement record of companies as well as their current status.

• Financial analysts will use achievements in quality as inputs for rating creditworthiness as well as for judging the financial potential of companies.

• National, industry, and other quality indexes will be evolved, paralleling those already available on productivity, prices, and so on.

• Degree-granting colleges oriented to quality will proliferate among universities, business schools, and engineering schools. (This movement became evident during the 1980s.)

• The K–12 schools (kindergarten through 12th grade) will evolve courses relating to managing for quality. (Here again, a trend was already evident during the early 1990s.)

• With the emergence of college faculties oriented to quality, research will intensify. This will produce standardized terminology, a consensus on how to divide up the subject, and so on.

• Professionalism among quality specialists will grow. This has already happened at the technical level (quality engineers, reliability engineers) but not at the business level. There will be national examinations for the right to use the resulting broad professional title whose name has yet to be invented. Comparable titles in other fields include Professional Engineer, CPA, and so on. A corresponding title in the quality field might be "Professional Qualitist" or "Certified Public Qualitist." (We need to find or coin a new generic term to describe someone active in the quality field, paralleling generic terms such as accountant, engineer, economist.)

- It is conceivable that future laws will extend the use of licensing in the quality field, on the ground of protecting the public interest. Licensing is already widely required for technician jobs that involve risks to human safety and health or to the environment. Examples include laboratory technicians in hospitals or welders in the aircraft and nuclear industries.

References

AT&T, *A History of Quality Control and Assurance at AT&T, 1920–1970.* This series of 14 videocassettes, published in 1989, contains interviews with Ralph Wareham, W. Edwards Deming, J. M. Juran, and others who played significant roles in quality control during the 50-year span 1920–1970. Available from AT&T Customer Information Center, phone 1-800-432-6600, select code 500-721.

Berwick, Donald M., A. Blanton Godfrey, and Jane Roessner, *Curing Health Care.* Jossey-Bass, 1990. The research report which showed that quality improvement is fully applicable to health care.

Bursk, Edward C., Donald T. Clark, and Ralph W. Hidy, *The World of Business.* Simon and Schuster, New York, 1962.

Davies, Norman De G., *The Tomb of Rekh-mi-re at Thebes,* Vol. 2, Pl. LXII. Metropolitan Museum of Art, New York, 1943.

Deming, W. Edwards, *Elementary Principles of the Statistical Control of Quality.* Japanese Union of Scientists and Engineers, Tokyo, 1950.

Durant, Will, *The Story of Civilization, Part I, Our Oriental Heritage,* pages 182–83. Simon and Schuster, New York, 1954.

Gillispie, Charles Coulston, *The Montgolfier Brothers and the Invention of Aviation,* pages 17–19, 127. Princeton University Press, 1983.

Godfrey, A. Blanton, Ten Areas for Future Research in Total Quality Management. *Quality Management Journal,* Oct. 1993, pages 47–70.

Gogue, Jean-Marie, in *Juran's Quality Control Handbook,* Fourth Edition, pages 35C.1 and 35C.2. McGraw-Hill Book Co., New York, 1988.

Grant, E. L., Statistical Quality Control in the World War II Years. *Quality Progress,* December 1991, pages 31–36.

Grant, E. L., Shewhart Medal address, *Industrial Quality Control,* July, 1953.

IMPRO®. Proceedings of Juran Institute's Annual Conference on Quality Management. Published annually by Juran Institute, Inc., Wilton, CT 06897-0811.

Juran, J. M., *Managerial Breakthrough,* Second Edition. McGraw-Hill Book Company, New York, 1994.

Juran, J. M., Made in USA, a Renaissance in Quality. *Harvard Business Review,* July–August, 1993.

Juran, J. M., *Juran on Quality by Design.* The Free Press, A Division of Macmillan, Inc., New York, 1992.

Juran, J. M., World War II and the Quality Movement. *Quality Progress,* December 1991, pages 19–24.

Juran, J. M., *Juran's Quality Control Handbook,* Fourth Edition. McGraw-Hill Book Co., New York, 1988.

Juran, J. M., The Quality Trilogy; A Universal Approach to Managing for Quality. *Quality Progress,* August 1986, pages 19–24.

Juran, J. M., *Juran on Quality Improvement.* A series of 16 videocassettes plus associated manuals. Juran Institute, Inc., 1981.

Juran, J. M., *Quality and Its Assurance—An Overview.* Second NATO Symposium on Quality and Its Assurance, London, 1977.

Juran, J. M., The Taylor System and Quality Control. A series of articles in *Quality Progress,* May 1973 through December 1973 (listed under "Management Interface").

Juran, J. M., Consumerism and Product Quality. *Quality Progress,* July 1970, pages 18–27.

Juran, J. M., *Lectures on Quality Control,* (in Japanese). Japanese Union of Scientists and Engineers, Tokyo, 1956.

Kegarise, Ronald J., and George D. Miller, *An Alcoa–Kodak Joint Team.* 1985 Juran IMPRO Conference.

NIST, National Institute of Standards and Technology. (It manages the United States' Malcolm Baldrige National Quality Award.) Gaithersburg, Maryland 20899.

Petroski, Henry, "Men and Women of Progress." *American Scientist,* May–June 1994, pages 216–19.

Radman, Miroslav, and Robert Wagner, The High Fidelity of DNA Duplication. *Scientific American,* August 1988, pages 40–46.

Sakai, Shinji, *Rediscovering Quality—The Toyota Way.* IMPRO 94, Juran Institute's Annual Conference on Managing for Quality, 1994.

Singer, Charles, E. J. Holmyard, and A. R. Hall, editors, *A History of Technology,* Volume I, page 481, fig. 313. Oxford University Press, 1954.

Smith, Adam, *The Wealth of Nations,* 1776. Random House edition published 1937.

von der Porten, Edward, The Hanseatic League, Europe's First Common Market. *National Geographic,* October 1994, pages 56–79.

Wareham, Ralph E., and Brad Stratton, Standards, Sampling, and Schooling. *Quality Progress,* December 1991, pages 38–42.

Working, Holbrook, Statistical Quality Control in War Production. *Journal of the American Statistical Association,* December 1945, pages 425–47.

Index

architrave, 204
aribiter, 203
ark, Noah's, 35–36
Ark of the Covenant, 37
arms industries. *See also* weapons
  in China, 27
  competition in, 633
  in France, 415–31
  inspection in, 390, 392, 420,
    427–28, 521–22
  in Japan, 521–23
  quality assurance in, 430–31,
    467–68
  quality planning in, 426–29
  testing in, 424
  in United States, 558
army, French, 423, 428
Arsenale di Stato, 303–38, 339
  accounting, 318–19
  administration, 311–13, 318–19
  efficiency, 310
  master craftsmen, 320–21,
    329–31
  materials, 308, 320, 323–29
  organization, 306–21
  standardization in, 317
  surveillance in, 319–20
  weapons factory, 311
  workforce, 321–23, 329–31
Arsenal of Philon, 70–71
Arthashastra of Kautilya, 106–14
Asao, Masashi, 535
ASQC. *See* American Society for
    Quality Control
assembly lines, 248
AT&T, personnel in Japan, 524
Athens
  Acropolis, 64, 71, 78–80
  temple of Athena Nike, 66
  Theater of Dionysos, 80–81
atomic clocks, 369
Austrian Alimentation Code, 495
automation, 248

automobile industry
  in Britain, 463
  in Japan, 544–45, 582–83
  quality in, 582–83
  regulation of, 570–71
  in United States, 570–71, 582–83
awards. *See* prizes
axles, testing, 424
Ayalon, E., 54

Babylon
  Code of Hammurabi, 614
  warranties in, 606
Bakh, Nikolai, 388
Baldrige, Malcolm. *See* Malcolm
    Baldrige National Quality
    Award
Balling, C. J. N., 488, 500, 502
Baltimore, 640
Bank of America, 543
banknotes, in Czech lands, 297
Baranovs, factory of, 386
Barnum and Bailey circus, as bench-
    mark, 644
Baumgarten, Yevgeny, 388
Beckel, August, 251
Becker, A., 252
Becker, Karl, 251
beer. *See also* brewing industry
  quality improvements, 478
  raw materials, 476, 479–85
  standards, 478–79, 485–86, 495
  testing, 492
beer gauges, 488, 489, 490
beer scales. *See* densimeters
beet sugar. *See* sugar beet refining
Belgium, Roman roads in, 177, 178
bells, Chinese, 14–16, 18
benchmarking, 592, 644
beneficentia, 204
beresty, 374, 375
Bessemer, Henry, 445–47
Better Business Bureaus (BBB), 565